K.S. INGLIS

THE STUART CASE

Black Inc.

Published by Black Inc.
An imprint of Schwartz Publishing
Level 5, 289 Flinders Lane
Melbourne Victoria 3000
Australia
email: enquiries@blackincbooks.com

First published 1961 by Melbourne University Press

National Library of Australia Cataloguing-in-Publication entry

Inglis, K. S. (Kenneth Stanley), 1929- .
The Stuart case.

New ed.
ISBN 1 86395 243 8.

1. Stuart, Rupert Maxwell - Trials, litigation, etc. 2.
Hattam, Mary Olive. 3. Aborigines, Australian - Crime. 4.
Trials (Murder) - Australia - South Australia. I. Title.

345.942302523

In memory of Judy Inglis
born Judy Betheras
1930–1962

CONTENTS

A Note on Sources ix

A Note on the Text [2002] ix

1 TRACKS TO CEDUNA 1

2 A CASE TO ANSWER 16

3 THE JURY DECIDES 29

4 ENTER FATHER DIXON 41

5 A RACE WITH DEATH 51

6 A VISIT TO FUNLAND 64

7 AN UNDERTAKING TO PARLIAMENT 82

8 THE COMMISSION SITS 96

9 ALIBI 106

10 A RATHER STARTLING REMARK 117

11 EXIT MR. SHAND 134

12 A MOTION OF CENSURE 149

13 A STATEMENT FROM GAOL 169

14 A CLOUD OF WITNESSES 182

15 ENTER AND EXIT MR. TRAVERS 192

16 LIFE FOR STUART 202

17 THE PRISONER SPEAKS 213

18 POLICEMEN IN THE BOX 231

19 LAST WORDS FROM COUNCIL 252

20 A VERDICT CONFIRMED 270

21 AN EDITOR ON TRIAL 279

22 GUILTY OR NOT GUILTY? 293

23 LESSONS FROM STUART 310

EPILOGUE, 1959–2002

24 ADELAIDE 325

25 YATALA 340

26 ALICE SPRINGS 357

27 A NEW MAN? 372

Epilogue Sources and Acknowledgements 400

Chronology, 1958–2002 401

A NOTE ON SOURCES

In Chapter 1, events at Ceduna and Thevenard have been reconstructed from the depositions of witnesses at later judicial proceedings and from the transcript of the Royal Commission; whenever varying accounts of an event were offered, the differences are made clear in the text. The account of how the Rev. Father Thomas Dixon became interested in Stuart's case has been drawn partly from his evidence to the Royal Commission and partly from interviews by the writer; the meeting with Giesemans's party in Queensland is described wholly from the former source. Mr. T.G.H. Strehlow's account of his visit to Stuart in gaol and to the solicitors' office is taken from the letter which he gave to the Attorney-General of South Australia on July 1, 1959. In a very few cases, stenographers' errors in official reports of judicial proceedings and of the Royal Commission have been corrected, but nowhere is the change substantial.

The writer is grateful to the Attorney-General of the Commonwealth of Australia for permission to quote extracts from proceedings in the High Court; to News Ltd. for permission to reproduce the cartoon on p. 85; and to Australian Consolidated Press Ltd. for permission to reproduce the cartoon on p. 208.

The passage about race relations on p. 5 is from an article by a research student, Mrs. Fay Gale, in *On Dit* (organ of the University of Adelaide Students' Representative Council), September 18, 1959. The anthropologist cited on p. 6 is Mr. Jeremy Beckett, writing in *Quadrant*, Spring 1958, p. 42. The quotation on p. 7 is from Mr. T. G. H. Strehlow's book *Aranda Traditions* (Melbourne University Press, 1947), p. 6. Remarks by Mr. A. P. Rowe are from his book *If the Gown Fits* (Melbourne University Press, 1960).

A NOTE ON THE TEXT [2002]

The text of the original book has not been altered. Some usages generally accepted in 1961 may now distract or jar, such as "aborigine" and "aboriginal" rather than "Aborigine" and "Aboriginal". The Aranda are now commonly known as the Arrernte, and that form is used in the epilogue.

Page numbers in brackets in the epilogue refer to passages in the original text.

1

TRACKS TO CEDUNA

In the main street of Ceduna, one sign points 1,250 miles to Perth and another 516 miles to Adelaide, the capital of South Australia. The street is wide and dusty, and bordered by low buildings with roofs of corrugated iron and verandas to keep the sun back. Some nine hundred people live in Ceduna, and another five hundred in Thevenard, two miles along a neck of land jutting into the Great Australian Bight, where ocean-going ships are loaded with grain. At Ceduna farmers and their wives come to shop, the Murat Bay District Council meets, and pictures are shown twice a week in the Memorial Hall. At Thevenard people lump wheat, catch and pack fish, and make gypsum plaster. Each town has a hotel and a police station. Both depend for medical services on the Bush Church Aid Society's flying doctor base on the edge of Ceduna. There is no rail connexion with Adelaide; supplies come by road or sea. The weekly *West Coast Sentinel*—published nearby at Streaky Bay—prints the name of everybody who arrives in Ceduna by bus or aeroplane.

Until the end of 1958 the name of Thevenard was unknown to most people in Australia. The name of Ceduna rarely appeared in the press, except when cars in a round-Australia reliability trial passed through or there was trouble involving some of the local aborigines. Group-Captain Peter Townsend once made the town newsworthy by driving through; "sunny far-off Ceduna" he called it in his book, "so remote from the scene of strife . . ." Ceduna and Thevenard were suddenly thrown on to the front page of every newspaper in Australia by the death of a nine-year-old child, Mary Olive Hattam, and the effort to discover for certain who was her murderer.

The ensuing controversy, which involved the police, the judiciary, the government and the press, was of a character unusual in South Australia or in any other part of the nation. Most chapters in any history of Adelaide and its hinterland would be happier than this one. The reader can decide for himself whether another such affair is conceivable, in South Australia or in any similar society.

* * *

Mr. Glen Hattam took his wife and children, Peter and Mary, to the west coast of South Australia late in 1957. His wife's sister was married to a butcher in Ceduna, and Hattam went to work in the shop. The family moved into a small, corrugated-iron house, standing halfway between Ceduna and Thevenard, next to the stacks of the Australian Wheat Board, not far from the state school which the two children attended, and close to the beach, where they liked to play.

On Saturday, December 20, 1958, it was not as hot as Ceduna can be in midsummer, but it was warm enough. When Mary and Peter Hattam and the boy next door, Peter Jacobsen, went to the beach about 2.30 that afternoon, they were dressed lightly. Mary wore only sandals, bathers and a blouse. They played on the sand and the rocks, and in the shallows they floated Peter Hattam's toy boat. Leaving Mary on the beach, the two boys went to get a tin tub which they remembered seeing behind the school, and which they decided to float. Mary was not in sight when they returned. Between 5 and 5.30, the usual time, Peter Hattam went home for tea. His father, who had been home all afternoon digging the foundations of a new house, walked to the beach to call the girl. After looking there and elsewhere, Hattam got someone to tell the police that she was missing.

The message was received at the police station by Sergeant H. L. Walker, who had come to Ceduna earlier in the year. He lit a storm lantern and Constables Howard Herde and Leonard Green and a number of citizens joined him for the search. No trace of the child had been discovered as late as 11 o'clock, when picturegoers filed out of the Memorial Hall after seeing "Dial M for Murder". Many of them helped to look for the girl. By midnight forty men were out. The body was found about half an hour later by a group of men searching along the beach. It was lying in a cave not far from the Hattams' house. Nearby were the child's bathers; close to the head was a bloodstained stone. There was blood on the body, and on the sand beside and under it. The police had a photographer come to the scene, called for a doctor from the Bush Church Aid Society's base, and sent a message to police headquarters in Adelaide.

Dr. Kathleen Thompson was there within ten minutes. She had been working at the base for a few months, having graduated at the University of Melbourne three years earlier. At the request of the police she estimated how long the girl had been dead. Next day, in the mortuary of the Murat Bay private hospital, Dr. Thompson performed a postmortem examination. She reported multiple abrasions on the back, chest, and right thigh, torn tissues consistent with violent sexual intercourse, multiple lacerations to the face and head, and a shattered skull. In each of the child's hands she found some hair.

Three men from the Criminal Investigation Branch reached Ceduna early on Sunday in a chartered aircraft which left Adelaide just after 5 a.m. The senior officer was Detective-Sergeant Paul Turner, a man with twenty-five years in the force and enough popularity among his colleagues to be elected president of the Police Association. With him flew Constable Richard Jones and Sergeant William Low, who was a fingerprint expert and photographer. More than one person who saw

Low's photographs of Mary Hattam's body found them impossible to forget. At Ceduna these three met the local men and two others, Senior Constable Frank Whitrod and Constable John Fairweather, who had driven 250 miles from Port Lincoln.

Footprints were noticed near the cave. About 10.30 a.m. on Sunday, Constable Green took to the beach an aborigine about fifty years old who had once before helped the police to identify tracks. Like many aborigines on the fringe of European society he answered to a nick-name conferred by whites: his was Sonny Jim. From time to time he worked for farmers, making fences and digging stumps. Once, briefly, he became a film actor, for an English company making "Robbery Under Arms". Sonny Jim now followed a variety of footprints back and forward along the beach. These, he said, were the girl's; these belonged to one of the boys; these were made by an adult in sandshoes. The tracks that interested him most were prints of bare feet, going from the cave to a pool and back again. Later, supported by the testimony of two policemen, Sonny Jim said he had deduced on this Sunday morning that these were the tracks of an educated aborigine. Another aborigine named Harry Scott, who lived with Sonny Jim and was related to him, came to the beach with the policemen next day. Scott, aged 65, had spent his life out at Koonibba, the Lutheran mission beyond Ceduna, until 1957, when he took a job on the Thevenard wharf. After inspecting the barefoot tracks between cave and pool, Scott said that the man who made them had walked slowly each way and then to the road that leads to Ceduna.

Throughout Sunday and Monday the policemen followed up clues and interviewed suspects, two of whom they took to the beach where Sonny Jim decided that neither man had made any of the tracks that he could see. One white man whose footprints did appear to correspond with certain tracks on the beach was taken to the police station, and was released after saying how he had spent Saturday afternoon. A pair of trousers, dark blue with red stripes, was found on the beach between the cave and Ceduna, examined for bloodstains, and put aside when it was concluded that they must have been lying there for weeks. Several people were questioned at the Thevenard Hotel. Others were interviewed either because they had police records or because they were newcomers with unknown characters.

Ceduna's position as a frontier town had often troubled its permanent residents. According to Mr. John May, clerk to the Murat Bay District Council: "We're bothered by drifters. They come with the seat out of their trousers, trying to make an easy penny—and not too careful how they do it—before they move off again." Some three weeks before the murder a correspondent in the *West Coast Sentinel* wrote: "Our quiet town has suddenly developed into a staging camp for dead-beats. Citizens are wondering why they have to keep everything under lock and key every night. Perhaps if the gendarmes kept these itinerants moving . . ." But no dead-beat, black or white, and nobody else interviewed by the police, seemed to have difficulty in accounting for himself—until on Monday evening a party of policemen went to the premises of the Australian Wheat Board at Thevenard and asked a slightly built dark-skinned man to come with them to the station. The man had come to Ceduna on Friday with a travelling fun-fair. His name was Rupert Max Stuart.

* * *

It was not the first time that Stuart had been inside the Ceduna police station. Only two nights before, on Saturday, Constables Green and Herde arrested him on the instruction of Sergeant Walker, took him to the station, searched him, and locked him up. According to the policemen this happened about 9.30 p.m., not long after they were told that Mary Hattam had disappeared. Herbie Sumner, another aborigine who spent Saturday night in the cells, after drinking with Stuart and others, had been arrested for drunkenness. In Herde's judgment, Stuart was not drunk; but it was clear that he had been drinking, and that was an offence under the licensing laws of South Australia. As the prose of the Aborigines' Protection Board puts it: "aborigines enjoy the usual privileges of citizenship, with the exception of partaking of intoxicants". The state's law defined as an aborigine anyone with an aboriginal ingredient in his ancestry. No such person could drink unless he carried a certificate of exemption from the provisions of the Aborigines Act—known to some dark people as a "dog licence". The prohibition was not always enforced strictly. If the police in a town like Ceduna were to lock up every legally-defined aborigine who had taken a drop, there would never be room for a white man in the cells. But during 1958 efforts more strenuous than usual were being made in Ceduna to stop aborigines from drinking. There had been high anxiety about what people called "the native problem" and a widespread conviction that alcohol was a large part of it.

In January the District Council had discussed with alarm conditions at a place about two miles out, where two hundred aborigines were camped in hovels made of bark and bags while the men among them worked on the wharf at Thevenard and at the nearby wheat stacks. Councillors feared that disease would sweep the area. They were also alarmed at how much liquor was being consumed by natives in the district. Late in January this report appeared in the *West Coast Sentinel*: "The clerk of the District Council (Mr. John May) said last night that in the past ten weeks there had been 33 local native convictions for liquor offences, and ten white men had been convicted for 'supplying'. Gaol sentences of from six to eighteen months had been imposed. There had also been cases of an aborigine assaulting a white woman, and a white man having carnal knowledge of an aboriginal woman. Unless the conditions of the natives are improved and they are helped to attain a decent standard of living, it is generally believed that the record of lawlessness will worsen to a dangerous degree". The report went on to deplore the part played by white men in supplying liquor, often at exorbitant prices. The Murat Bay district hospital, it was said, recently admitted an aboriginal child who was starving because the father, though making good money, was spending most of it on liquor supplied by whites.

The mixture of attitudes expressed here—disapproval and solicitude, sexual apprehension and paternalism—is not uncommon among the small minority of white Australians who live near a community of aborigines. Attitudes to dark people are understandably vague in the cities, which hold most of Australia's ten million whites, hardly any of her 40,000 or so full-blood aborigines, and about ten per cent of her 30,000 mixed bloods. There is a vague sense of guilt, sometimes of a sentimental sort; there is, perhaps less often, vague contempt. In Ceduna and Thevenard, where some 1,500 whites live near a few hundred dark people, opinions are sharper. Intimacy between individual black and white is not a normal thing there. At the pictures, aborigines sit in a part of the hall known informally as "the native section". When a fun-fair, of the kind that brought Rupert Max Stuart, comes to town, it is patronised by many aborigines and few whites. Whites do not sit in the street in the sun. Aborigines do not work at jobs requiring much skill. When a fisherman was asked a question about aborigines in the Ceduna area, he replied: "I wouldn't know whether they are of different types . . . they all look the same to me."

In some people such a remark goes with overt hostility to the aborigines, in others not. Even the most vigorous exponent of racialism in Australia is less authoritarian and dogmatic, more capricious in theory and practice, than his fellows in South Africa, or even in the United States. It is the lifelong plight of an aborigine who moves among white Australians that he cannot be sure whether the next one he meets—taxi-driver, shop assistant, farmer or labourer—will or will not make him aware of his colour. The bitterness of aborigines in this situation is apt to be furtive. "Ask many a part-aborigine whether he thinks the white community is prejudiced," said a student of South Australian race relations in 1959. "If his tongue has been loosened by 'metho' he may say, 'You think we are a lot of dirty niggers,' or he may say, 'I'm as good as you whites any day,' or 'I'm crooked on you whites; you just came and took everything from us'."

The aborigines squatting near Ceduna early in 1958 were mostly from the Lutheran mission at Koonibba, twenty-five miles away. Like other missions and government stations, Koonibba offered its residents a roof and some rations, but little work. Jobs could be had at Thevenard, but twenty-five miles would be a long way even if the transport were more adequate. So men and their families moved in to camp as near as possible to the job. When white people protested to the council, and to the government in Adelaide, the authorities agreed to close the camp and send the squatters back to Koonibba. Workless and in many cases faithless, their children attending school irregularly, the aborigines at Koonibba ate food paid for by the government and handed out by the Lutherans. Drinking was an important occupation for them, as it was for de-tribalised aborigines elsewhere in the country, and they drank what they could smuggle from Ceduna. "Drinking," observed an anthropologist studying aborigines in 1958, "is not just a matter of taking alcoholic refreshment . . . There is all the excitement of getting the liquor, running the police blockade, risking gaol and sneaking out into the bush to consume it with a great deal of noise and flourish." Drinking sprees were celebrated, the student found, in such ballads as this:

> The people in town just run us down,
> They say we live on wine and beer.
> But if they'd stop and think, if we didn't drink,
> There'd be no fun around here.

Fighting and drinking were reported at Koonibba mission during 1958 by the superintendent, a Lutheran pastor. "The majority are fairly well behaved," he said, "but there are some who have persistently misbehaved. The chief offences are drunkenness and insolence." Aborigines were to come from Koonibba to say where they had seen and not seen Stuart when, on December 20, 1958, they went to Ceduna to wander around the town and into the fun-fair.

Towards the end of 1958 local students of the native problem in Ceduna were happier. A welfare officer, Mr. A. R. A. Kleinig, appointed by the Aborigines Department after persistent requests, was keeping an eye on the aborigines in a manner that pleased white citizens; and action by police had reduced the supply of liquor to the aborigines. But a dark man could still get liquor if he was determined, prepared to pay high prices, and not unduly worried by the threat of a short term in prison. On the morning of December 20, Stuart and a companion swilled wine from a flagon offered by an aborigine they met on the beach. Later in the morning Stuart bought some wine from a drunken white near the Ceduna Community Hotel. Later again he took a taxi down to the hotel at Thevenard, where somebody supplied him with more wine. Back at the fair Stuart offered twenty-five shillings to the owner's wife and asked her to get him a bottle of wine and a bottle of beer. "No," she said, "I am not going to buy you any beer to get six months in gaol." A young mixed-blood woman went to Ceduna for him and brought back some liquor. Early in the evening Stuart set off again with a companion towards Ceduna, and met some dark men on the beach; they let him have some wine. Conflicting accounts of Stuart's movements that day agree on one thing: he managed to get plenty to drink.

* * *

There are white Australians who are one-eighth aboriginal, but nobody describes them as "part-European". Stuart's father was a full-blood, and his mother had only one white grandparent; yet newspapers in 1959 were calling Stuart "part-aboriginal". Outposts of European civilisation had been visible to him since childhood; but the first language he knew was an aboriginal one, and his body bore the marks of a tribal initiation. To older men, he and his generation seemed sadly ignorant of the traditions and ceremonies by which the spirit of the indigenous society used to pass down the centuries. The non-European past was nevertheless closer to him than to most of the aborigines, varying in colour from black to a shade lighter than Mediterranean, whom he met in Ceduna; an initiated person was a rarity there.

Stuart's one white ancestor was a man who headed inland with animals from the settled southern areas after the first explorers in the 1860's had found land that looked suitable for pasture. Through the hot and arid territory of the Aranda people the cattle men scattered, expecting some black men to work for them, some black women to sleep with them, and the rest of the native inhabitants to stay well out of the way. Often without knowing what they were doing, the Europeans blocked off the Aranda people's sources of water and food, disturbed their camping sites and violated their sacred places. The first Christian mission, run by hardy German Lutherans, reached the Aranda with the first generation of settlers and began to offer unfamiliar spiritual and material food. The material food was accepted at once.

The invaded society was not a robust one. Aranda people were not the free spirits described in romantic European accounts of primitive man. "The thoroughness of their forefathers," wrote Mr. T. G. H. Strehlow, the man who came to know the Aranda best, "has left to them not a single unoccupied scene which they could fill with creatures of their own imagination. Tradition and the tyranny of the old men in the religious and cultural sphere have effectually stifled all creative impulse; and no external stimulus ever reached Central Australia which could have freed the natives from these insidious bonds. It is almost certain that native myths had ceased to be invented many centuries ago. The chants, the legends, and the ceremonies which we record today mark the consummation of the creative efforts of a distant, long-past age. The present-day natives are on the whole merely the painstaking, uninspired preservers of a great and interesting inheritance. They live almost entirely on the traditions of their forefathers. They are, in many ways, not so much a primitive as a decadent race."

In pictorial art, as in other fields of expression, creativity was stifled. Paintings on cave or rock were few and crude. When Albert Namatjira and several other Aranda men took to water-colour painting under the influence of a white artist, many Australians lamented that their work appeared so European in technique and vision. Professor A. P. Elkin retorted that Namatjira and his friends "deserted nothing, for there was almost nothing in their own art tradition which could be developed." Some ceremonies and chants died with old men unwilling to pass them on to the unfit. "I am a member of the younger generation," said an Aranda man. "I was always working for white men. I was not judged worthy to be entrusted with the verses. I am wholly ignorant, just like a white man."

With each generation, the culture communicated to the young became more dilute. One of Stuart's grandfathers went through every stage of tribal initiation and became the leader of a totemic clan. Stuart's father also participated both in the youthful rites that made an Aranda a man and in the later ceremonies which gave him the full stamp of citizenship. But the father, Paddy Stuart, learned a repertoire of chants and dances less rich than was known in the old days. He spent much of his life working on white men's stations, and he seems to have been the first of his family to assume an English surname. His only son, who was born on a pastoral station near Alice Springs, became a man according to Aranda standards, but like most males who grew to adolescence after World War II he penetrated no further into the old mysteries. At an age when, in earlier days, the old men would have been letting him share more and more of the sacred things, Stuart was wandering as a casual labourer thousands of miles from tribal land.

Although Aranda tradition held a declining authority for Stuart's generation, the initiation to which he and his peers submitted at puberty was a serious affair to them as well as to the elders who administered it. At the ground set aside for the ceremony, youths, old men and initiated spectators assembled. Women and children were banned on pain of death. Every morning the young fellows rose to the sound of bull-roarers, hunted food all day, and returned to the edge of the camp; then, when the bull-roarers sounded again, they laid what they had caught before the old men and danced. The old men cooked and everybody ate. Singing, dancing and jesting went on until nearly dawn. The novices were allowed to see for the first time some of the ceremonies of their clan, and hear for the first time some of its secret chants. After sleeping briefly, with a sacred mound of earth for a pillow, the young men were up again and off for more game. The physical strain of this life, which lasted for months, was intense. The bodily rites of circumcision and sub-incision, performed near the end of the period, were painful—though not so painful as the scalp-splitting and head-biting which went on in the old days. "None of the young men of the present generation could endure such pain," an old man explained to Strehlow. "We have had to dismiss them with a lighter payment." When it was all over, boys and men returned to the profane company of women. For a long time afterwards the initiation ground was forbidden territory.

Had he wished, Stuart could also have been initiated into the rudimentary mysteries of European civilisation by going to the Lutheran school at Hermannsburg. But he refused to go. His only sister, younger than he, attended the school, and it was she who taught him to write the only words his hand ever formed: RUPERT (sometimes ROPERT) MAX STUART. He told people later that Albert Namatjira taught him to paint.

Before leaving Aranda territory Stuart had a vague acquaintance with the white man's religion. The Western Aranda people to which most of his family, including his mother and her father, belonged, were familiar with the services conducted by Lutherans at Hermannsburg and on the government settlement at Jay Creek, near Alice Springs, where Stuart lived as a child. Other relatives were based at Santa Teresa, a Catholic mission some fifty miles south of Alice Springs run by a Sacred Heart priest, nuns, and lay brothers. Some drifted between different forms of Christian worship, and if asked to name their religious preference they could honestly have identified themselves as Catholic or Protestant or neither. Stuart was an initiated Aranda and not a baptised Christian; but in his wanderings after he left the Aranda community he was an occasional visitor to more than one sort of Christian church.

Like most Aranda men in this century Stuart went to work as a stockman, having his first job when he was about eleven. Later he worked in and around Alice Springs—clearing a backyard, serving petrol, cutting wood. In 1953 a new Federal Ordinance gave full citizenship in the Northern Territory to him and all other "people of mixed blood living after the manner of Europeans". In practical terms, this meant that the law permitted him alcohol—though he could be, and was, punished for supplying it to full-bloods who were still defined as wards of the government. He wandered farther than most Aranda, and got into more trouble. As a member of Jimmy Sharman's boxing troupe he travelled as far as Thursday Island, off Australia's northern tip. One of a number of gaol sentences was given to him in Cloncurry, Queensland, some five hundred miles north-east of the place where he had been initiated. In September 1958 he was five hundred miles north-west of home, at Hall's Creek in Western Australia, after droving cattle from Victoria River Downs to the meat works at Wyndham. It was here that he joined Mr. Norman Gieseman's fun-fair, half as hitch-hiker and half as employee. The journey with Gieseman was expected to end at Port Augusta, two hundred miles north of Adelaide, where Stuart said he hoped to find work with a team of cattle going north; instead it finished at Ceduna.

* * *

Gieseman called his outfit Funland Carnival. He and a diminishing number of men like him work the backblocks of the continent, places reached rarely or never by the public pleasures devised for city dwellers. They set up at agricultural shows, and out of the show season look for towns where the picture shows are least frequent. Norman Gieseman, who was thirty-five when Stuart joined him, went into the business straight from school in Burpengarry, Queensland. After war service in the army he married a light-skinned mixed-blood girl from north Queensland, and except for a short spell when he drove a truck the couple had been on the road ever since with their modest stock of amusements—a few games, a little magic, some wooden horses for thrills. No skill was needed for the business except Gieseman's ability to keep an engine running and his wife's capacity for watching the pennies. Edna Gieseman handled the money and gave each employee ten per cent of what he had collected. Sobriety was essential; the show had to open smartly when customers were about, the tolerance of policemen and local officials had to be preserved, and the takings from one place had to be kept thriftily for food and petrol in case the next pitch turned out to be unprofitable. Gieseman liked an occasional beer in a pub, but was not in the habit of bringing liquor back to the show.

Two trucks and a caravan carried the show from Hall's Creek south into the more thickly settled part of Western Australia. In the middle of December they drove east across the Nullarbor Plains. The larger truck, a Commer, was driven in turns by Gieseman and Billy McNeish, a quiet young white man with few teeth and big muscles, who had been working with Gieseman, on and off, for eight years. Nobody else in the party had been with the show for more than a few months. Stuart rode in the Commer. So did Johnny Woods, a man of about thirty-five who had joined the show a few months earlier in Darwin and who left it early in 1959; he was said to be descended in part from aborigines and in part from the Afghans who came to central Australia with their camels two generations ago. Also in the big truck was Allan Moir, a short, sturdy youth of fifteen who had hung around Funland every day while it was in Norseman, in Western Australia, and who had been allowed, like Stuart, to come along as a way of getting to Port Augusta. He and Stuart spent a good deal of time with each other on the journey from the west. Some people at Ceduna were to call Moir "the white boy" to distinguish him from his companion; but he could easily have been taken for a mixed-blood. Like Stuart he could read nothing and write only his name; he had been expelled from a Catholic school and left a state primary school on his fourteenth birthday.

In the smaller truck, an Austin utility, Mrs. Gieseman drove with a mixed-blood girl, Betty Gadd, and an older white woman, Betty Hopes, who had been with Funland since it left Queensland earlier in the year. Each evening the party camped by the road, and sat by a fire listening to McNeish's portable wireless. The Giesemans then retired to the caravan and the others slept under the sky. On the morning of Friday, December 19, the trucks stopped at the South Australian Government's road block just outside Ceduna, where an official charged with eradicating fruit-fly told them that no fresh fruit or vegetables must be taken through. Mrs. Gieseman cooked twenty-eight pounds of potatoes on the spot rather than waste them.

Late that morning Funland reached Ceduna and was unpacked on the parklands (or, in a local phrase, cow pastures) about a mile from the centre of the town. Gieseman opened the stalls on Friday evening without expecting to do any business, for his arrival was so far unadvertised. Moir and Stuart went together to the pictures in the Memorial Hall. McNeish went by himself.

When the show opened on Saturday morning, Mrs. Gieseman drove through town in the Austin, inviting custom over a loudspeaker. After a quiet morning the women served a meal in the food tent. Business picked up in the afternoon, though not spectacularly; Gieseman estimated later that thirty to forty people had come to the show—most of them aborigines. McNeish worked the horse-o-plane, Funland's only motor-driven pleasure. Woods was in charge of the laughing clowns. Gieseman helped to keep the horses running and did some repairs to the Commer. Moir was on the knock-em stall, where for sixpence a ball people could win what they hit. Mrs. Gieseman took the money in another tent for the Girl in the Goldfish Bowl—Betty Gadd in a bikini, apparently reduced to the size of a dwarf by trick glass; the trade called it an illusion. The roll-em-down, or skittles (five for two shillings), and the darts (four for two shillings) occupied a single tent. Betty Hopes was on the roll-em-down. Stuart worked for a while during the afternoon. According to his companions he was on the darts.

Stuart and Moir had been away drinking in the morning, though Moir returned in good time for a meal that was eaten about one o'clock. In the evening when the show had to be dismantled, Stuart and Moir were both drinking on the beach. When Moir came back late at night after losing consciousness several times, Gieseman wanted to throw him out, but was persuaded by his wife to give the boy another chance. Stuart returned next morning. No charge had preceded or followed his night in the cell; the police said later that everyone at the station was too busy looking for the murderer of Mary Hattam to bother with a drinking aborigine. Gieseman told Stuart he should be ashamed of himself for getting young Moir drunk. Other words were exchanged. Stuart, according to Gieseman's later account, said that he had arranged a job with the Wheat Board at Thevenard.

The two trucks and the caravan headed east on Sunday morning for Whyalla, three hundred miles away on Spencer Gulf, where the show was to remain over Christmas. Camped by the road on Sunday night they heard on McNeish's wireless, for the first time, that a child had been murdered in Ceduna. On Monday evening in Whyalla a policeman, Detective-Sergeant Alexander Phin, asked Gieseman and Moir some questions about events in Ceduna. On Tuesday, Phin took a signed statement from Moir which contained a detailed description of Stuart's movements. The show was at Moonta, on the Adelaide side of Spencer Gulf, for the New Year holidays. Early in 1959 the Giesemans and their nomadic helpers—including Moir, who had decided not to stop at Port Augusta after all—drove towards the dust and heat of western New South Wales, taking the sixpences where they could find them and—if their later story of the journey is to be believed—hardly ever reading a newspaper.

Detective-Sergeant Phin's first visit to the fun-fair in Whyalla was a routine one, he said later; a normal thing when such a show came to town. When Gieseman told him where the party had come from, however, Phin began to examine him, and later Moir, closely. He gained from Moir a good deal of information about Stuart's movements on Friday and Saturday, and he began to suspect that Stuart might be the murderer.[1] A little before 9 o'clock on Monday evening Phin went to the police station and told his superior, Inspector Blyth, what he had learned. Blyth rang Ceduna. Phin spoke to Sergeant Walker and Detective-Sergeant Turner. As a result of this conversation the three C.I.B. men from Adelaide, the two men from Port Lincoln and one stationed locally drove to the Wheat Board's area in a police van. The first two tents they looked in were empty. In the third were two beds, one empty and the other occupied by Herbie Sumner, the aborigine who had spent Saturday night locked up with Stuart. A few minutes later the policemen found Stuart nearby. "Are you Max Stuart?" asked Turner. "Yes." "Why did you leave your tent and hide when we pulled up?" Stuart said he had been visiting the lavatory, not hiding. Turner asked him to show the policemen which lavatory he had used. He led them to the toilet block two hundred yards away from his tent and pointed to a pedestal. According to the police there was thick dust on the seat, which Stuart explained by saying that in the dark he had sat down before noticing that the seat was raised, and lowered it later. The police inspected Stuart's knees and noticed scratches. They asked him to come to the station.

It was a little after 10 p.m. when the van reached the station. At first Stuart denied any knowledge of the crime. Jones told him to undress. Stuart took off his jacket, shirt, trousers and elastic-sided boots. The police searched his body for lacerations. Turner said there

[1] According to a report in the *Whyalla Times* in 1960, after his retirement from the force, Phin was certain that the murderer was an aborigine as soon as he heard the crime described. As reported by the paper, Phin said that he had been born among aborigines and knew them well. "Most of them, I believe, have the mentality of an uneducated child . . . Like children they possess a great sense of fair play, and they appreciate any act of kindness, but like elephants they never forget a wrong or an injustice. I know some of their language or should I say gibberish; they have a different monkey gibberish for every tribe." A half-caste under the influence of wine was "an untamed animal". He had learned that "half castes and darkies generally . . . will always make for the head in an attack on close quarters. A stone in the hand is a favorite weapon with them in a fight. . . . When I was told . . . that a little child's body had been found foully murdered, and that the head had been battered in . . . , I did not for a moment consider that outrage as the work of a white man. I immediately thought it was the work of a darky."

were scratches on his legs, and asked him how they had got there. Stuart said he did not know. There were other scratches on his back, Turner said. Turner took some of Stuart's hair so that it could be compared with hairs found in the dead girl's hands. The policemen now began to question Stuart as he sat at the desk normally used by the sergeant. Turner sat across the desk from him, while Jones sat beside Stuart. Whitrod, Fairweather and Low were also in the room. Walker moved in and out during the interrogation to visit his wife, who was ill, in the station's private quarters. Herde and Green were out getting the trackers.

Not long before midnight Stuart printed his name at the bottom of a confession, typed by Whitrod, which read as follows:

> I, RUPERT MAX STUART, aged 27 years, labourer, of Alice Springs, having been warned by Detective-Sergeant Turner, that I need not make this statement do voluntarily without any fear, threat, reward or promise of any nature state the following:—
>
> I came to Ceduna, on Friday 19th December, 1958, at about 9 a.m. as an employee of Fun Land Carnival, a travelling show owned by Norman Keasman. There was a show on Friday Night and I slept in the show tent at Ceduna. At about 7.30 a.m. on Saturday, 20th December, 1958, I awoke and started work at the show. I had a drink of tea first but nothing to eat. I worked at the Show until 10 o'clock and then I left. The Show was situated at the Ceduna Oval. Me and Allan walked down to the Jetty. Then we were talking to one half caste bloke. He's the bloke that lives around the beach but I don't know his name. We walked down the beach near the Jetty and into a little cave. The three of us sat down and drank a flagon of wine. The three of us came up to the town here. Allan went back to the Show Ground. It was then about half past eleven I think. I got a flagon of wine off a white fellow I met near the Ceduna pub. He was drunk and I gave him eighteen shillings to get it. I went down to the same place. I stopped there by myself and drank the flagon. No I only drank half of it. I put the other half flagon in a sugar bag. I came into town carrying the bag. I left the bag with the flagon in it down behind the Picture show wall. I jumped in a taxi. Went down to the Thevenard pub. I got off there. I was sitting down outside the pub. I think I must have stopped there about an hour I think. Then I seen a fellow with a bottle of wine. He offered me a drink. He had a little bit. I said to him, "I think I will buy this off you." He said, "You can have it for nothing." I got it off him. Then I started walking back. It was one o'clock I think. Just after coming out of Thevenard town I stood and I finished that bottle. I walked back to the pub again. Could not see that bloke. Then I came back. I walked down to the beach. Then I saw this little girl. I was pretty full then. She was standing in a pool of water playing. I said to the

little girl, "There is some little birds over there" I pointed up towards the cave. She said, "I will go and have a look". She walked in the cave. No I am wrong I crawled in the cave first and she crawled after me. She said, "Where's the birds," I said, "They are gone now" I punched her on the side of the head. She went unconscious. I took her bathers off. Then I raped her. She was hard to —. I done her. Then I hit her with a stone. Before I raped her I took my clothes off. I was wearing a shirt and pants. I also took my boots off. I think I hit her six times with a stone. I left her. I think she was dead. I went and had a wash in the sea. I had no clothes on. I went back to near the cave where I had taken my clothes off and put them on. I started to walk back along the beach towards Ceduna town. I got on the road from the beach near the Church. I went around the back streets to where the caravan park is. Got a flagon of wine. That was the one I had left in a bag. I drank that. I then went back to the Show. I worked around there for about two hours. About sun down me and another fellow went down to the Jetty. We were looking for other fellows drinking. Then we saw two blokes sitting down drinking. When we went down there they put the bottle away. I had more wine that night with them. On Sunday morning 21.12.1958 I got the sack from the Show. A friend of mine named "Herby" helped me to get a job with the Wheat Board. I started work there on Monday, 22nd December, 1958, at 8 a.m. I slept at the Wheat Board with another native in a tent. We went to bed at about 7 o'clock tonight and I went to sleep and after a while I got up to go to the lavatory. When I went back I seen a car standing in front of the tent and you blokes then spoke to me and took me to the Police Station. I killed her because I did not want her to tell what I done. I cannot read English. I have heard this statement read to me and it is true and correct in every detail.

ROPERT MAX STUART

The trackers, Sonny Jim and Harry Scott, had been called. Stuart walked barefoot through sand from the beach which had been placed in the cemented yard of the police station. Turner asked the trackers whether these prints were the same as the ones they had seen on the beach, between the cave where Mary Hattam's body was found and the nearby pool and between the cave and the road to Ceduna. The trackers, according to the police, said they were the same; the police, according to the trackers, told them first that this man was the murderer. At this point, according to the police, Stuart was arrested and charged with murder. Next morning, Tuesday, Stuart was brought before Mr. John May, who was a Justice of the Peace as well as clerk of the District Council. May formally charged and remanded him. "Stuart showed little sign of remorse or emotion when he appeared in court," said the local paper.

All work stopped in Ceduna and Thevenard on Tuesday afternoon for one of the largest funerals ever seen in the district. The chairman of the District Council, Mr. P. S. Morrison, was a pall-bearer. Sergeant Walker and two other policemen saluted at the graveside. Meanwhile, on the ordinary civilian flight and in the custody of the policemen from headquarters, Stuart was on his way to Adelaide.

2

A CASE TO ANSWER

A MONTH AFTER Mary Hattam died, Stuart was back in a cell at the Ceduna police station, having been taken to attend the preliminary hearing of the case against him. On January 21 the Police Court sat in the Memorial Hall, where Stuart had seen pictures on his first evening in the town. More than a hundred people, white and dark, had come along to listen and watch. They saw a visiting magistrate, Mr. L. K. Gordon, presiding, and Inspector L. P. Hansberry, head of the police force on the west coast, appearing for the prosecution. Stuart himself was represented by a lawyer from Adelaide, Mr. J. D. O'Sullivan.

Since Stuart had only four shillings and sixpence halfpenny to his name when arrested, he could not afford fees for a lawyer. In the remand yard of the Adelaide Gaol was a notice advising prisoners how to apply for legal aid. To Stuart, who could not read, the procedure was explained by a warder, who then filled in a form setting out the prisoner's financial position and previous convictions, and requesting the services of a barrister and solicitor. (Lawyers perform both functions in South Australia.) The application was sent to the office of the Law Society, governing body of the legal profession, whose secretary put it before a Legal Assistance Committee. Like nearly all his three hundred or so colleagues in South Australia, Mr. J. D. O'Sullivan was prepared to take a case assigned to him by this Committee, and to take it if necessary without any fee. The scheme was available for civil as well as criminal cases. Stuart was one of some 1,500 applicants for the year, of whom more than a thousand were assigned a lawyer. O'Sullivan was chosen in this case as a practitioner who appeared often in criminal cases.

In some other states, Stuart's defence would have become the direct responsibility of a government servant known as the Public Solicitor. South Australia appointed such an official in 1925 but dispensed with him eight years later, when the council of the Law Society offered to take over all his work. The plan under which Stuart now asked for legal representation was inspired by the same mixture of generosity and prudence that moved doctors to work without fee in public hospitals; and like the honorary medical system it could sometimes seem an imposition on the profession as the state took over more and more responsibilities once left to voluntary philanthropy. "The scheme works efficiently and well," said the council of the Law Society in

1959, "but has become increasingly burdensome on members of the profession." It was not burdensome on the state government, which paid only the cost of administration (in 1959, £5,000).

In twelve years of practice O'Sullivan had taken many Law Society cases. It was not the only public activity he performed without payment. When he undertook to defend Stuart he was already well known in South Australia as a leading member in the nation's newest political organisation, the Democratic Labor Party. At the federal election late in 1958, O'Sullivan was the party's campaign director in South Australia and had his name at the top of its ticket for the Senate. His election was unlikely. But in his campaign speeches, carefully argued and passionately delivered, he did not sound like a man fighting a hopeless battle. It was in the month following the Federal election that O'Sullivan was assigned to Stuart. Before the Stuart case was through, barristers from Melbourne and Sydney were to be involved in it; but in the police court at Ceduna on January 21, O'Sullivan was on his own.

* * *

Before the case for the Crown opened, O'Sullivan applied for orders to remove all spectators from the court and to prohibit any publication of its proceedings, on the ground that prospective jurors might be prejudiced if they learned of the grim details. Hansberry opposed the application. For the time being the magistrate decided against O'Sullivan.

Hansberry, the prosecutor, outlined the case against Stuart. By subterfuge, he said, Stuart had enticed Mary Hattam under a shelf of rock, struck her violently on the head with a stone, criminally assaulted her, and murdered the child to prevent her telling what had happened. Stuart then walked to a pool of water and washed himself clean of blood. This walk, said Hansberry, led to Stuart's undoing; the police, with the aid of two black trackers, picked up his tracks and deduced that the person who made them was an educated aborigine. Hansberry sketched what each of the witnesses would say, and called them.

Dr. Kathleen Thompson was first, describing the condition of the body, offering an opinion about the cause of death, and estimating that the child had been dead at least three hours when she examined the body about 12.30 a.m. When O'Sullivan cross-examined her, the doctor put the probable time of death at approximately six hours before 12.30 a.m., and the earliest possible time of death at ten hours before her investigation. She agreed with O'Sullivan's suggestion that the death might have occurred at half past nine; she did not know that Stuart at that time was in custody. A little later O'Sullivan asked that publication of the medical evidence be forbidden. The application was not opposed by Hansberry, and was granted.

Peter Jacobsen, Mary Hattam's playmate, told the story of her disappearance. Constable Herde reported his discovery of the body, the clothes near it, and the bloodstained stone. He was questioned by O'Sullivan about his part in the search for the murderer and in locking up Stuart for drinking on the Saturday night. Next came Sonny Jim, the tracker, who gave his occupation as rabbit-trapper and who answered questions partly in pidgin and partly in his own aboriginal language through an interpreter (a local grazier who employed natives on his property and had learned their language as a child).

Sonny Jim was still in the box when the court adjourned for the day. He was told not to go walkabout, and turned up punctually next morning, in the uniform of a lance-corporal of the Royal Military College at Duntroon. Nobody seemed to know where he had got it. The court now moved to the beach, where Sonny Jim was asked about tracks which he said were still visible. A court reporter sitting on a rock took down his answers. Back in the Memorial Hall, O'Sullivan examined him for a long time about his identification of the tracks on the beach and of Stuart's footprints at the police station.

Herde returned, to be asked about entries in the station journal and about the interrogation of Stuart. Mr. John Oscar Jacobsen, a fisherman, was called to say that he had known the child and that he identified her body in the hospital mortuary. Cross-examined by O'Sullivan, Jacobsen said that he came ashore in a dinghy at a quarter to four on the Saturday afternoon near where Mary Hattam had been playing (as he learned afterwards), and he did not see her. There was one other local witness, Dennis Blackham, a youth employed as a labourer by the District Council, who sometimes drove his father's taxi. About 2 p.m. on the Saturday, he said, he picked up Stuart and another native in Ceduna, dropped the other man at the fun-fair, and drove Stuart to Thevenard; he heard Stuart say that at Thevenard he wanted to see a girl. To O'Sullivan, Blackham said he was quite certain both that Stuart had said nothing about wanting to get a drink at Thevenard, and that he *had* mentioned a girl.

The enquiry at Ceduna had now taken two days, the second unusually long; for to finish hearing local witnesses the court sat into the evening. Next day the magistrate, O'Sullivan, the Adelaide policemen and the prisoner flew back to Adelaide, where the hearing resumed on January 28.

In Ceduna the court-room had been crowded; here it was nearly empty. The witness heard at Adelaide, Constable Richard Jones, was the one with most to report. When the C.I.B. had returned from Ceduna on December 23 it was Jones who was made responsible for composing the official account of the search and interrogation. He was now given permission to refer to several pages of typewritten notes about these events, which he had dictated for about two hours while Sergeant Turner typed. O'Sullivan asked for the court to be cleared when Jones began to describe the appearance of the child's body. The magistrate turned down the application. It was renewed when Jones reached the conversation between Stuart and the police at the station on Monday night. This time the magistrate consented, and the three spectators and two reporters were ordered out. Jones reproduced in detail the circumstances in which Stuart was alleged to have confessed. "You say that the defendant dictated every word . . . ?" said O'Sullivan. "Yes." O'Sullivan put it to Jones that Stuart was assaulted before he signed the statement. Jones denied that there had been any violence or threat of violence. Jones was still giving evidence on the next and last day of the hearing, January 29, when O'Sullivan cross-examined him mainly about the trackers' evidence and the pursuit of other suspects.

After Hansberry had summed up the case for the prosecution, O'Sullivan said that his client did not wish to give or call evidence. Prompted by O'Sullivan, Stuart spoke for the first time in the four days of the hearing, to say: "I reserve my defence." The magistrate then committed him for trial in the Supreme Court of South Australia. Bail was not applied for.

The Crown witnesses had not included anybody from Gieseman's show. In cross-examination of Herde it had emerged that somebody in the show had helped to direct the attention of the police towards Stuart. From the station journal O'Sullivan read out these jottings: "Received telephone message from Det. Sgt. Phin of Whyalla and Inspector Blyth re questioning of man named Max Stuart, who could be likely suspect. Their informant was a fellow-worker of Stuart's from the show they were travelling with together at Ceduna. Stuart had received the sack for drinking on Sunday morning, and was believed to be employed by the Australian Wheat Board at Ceduna." Herde agreed that this was the first entry relating to Stuart in the journal. The name of the fellow-worker and the nature of his information were not mentioned.

Jones said that the call from Whyalla had come through about 9 p.m., or maybe a little later, and that he himself had received information in Ceduna about 6.30 p.m. "that Max Stuart who had been dismissed from a show there on the Saturday was now working at the Wheat Board and that he was a person who was violent towards women if he had any alcohol at all." Who in Ceduna told the police that, and how he could have known such a fact about a stranger, were never revealed.

* * *

The case was set down to be heard at the March criminal sessions of the Supreme Court, but was postponed until April 20. A jury panel was summoned from the roll of electors for the state's Legislative Council—a roll composed, broadly speaking, of those heads of households who chose to be on it. When Stuart's twelve jurors were selected the defence did not exercise the right to challenge any of them.

The sedate classical Supreme Court building faced Victoria Square, at the centre of the city which those radicals, Nonconformists and misfits who founded South Australia a century and a quarter before had planned as the capital of their middle-class paradise. The sons of the founders erected around this square the courts, a police station, a Congregational church, a post office and other government buildings. The next generation added a barn for trams, an emporium and some nondescript shops. A tall glass and steel container for insurance, set there more recently by architects from Melbourne, emphasised the archaic gentility of its neighbours. From a balcony outside the court-room where Stuart was to be tried—a vantage point occupied often by waiting witnesses—one could look down at the square's English trees and flowers, and at its statues. In the distance were the explorers Sturt and Stuart, who had struck north from early Adelaide in search of pastures. Nearer stood a politician, Charles Kingston, who campaigned at the turn of the century to spread downwards the benefits of middle-class civilisation and who earned South Australia its reputation, in those days, for social enlightenment. And at the centre was Queen Victoria, in the shape she had assumed by the last decade of her reign, surveying the community where her own values and tastes were shared as earnestly as anywhere in the whole empire.

When Victoria came to the throne, convicted criminals were being sent to eastern colonies; but none were ever sent to South Australia. In the year of the great Exhibition the discovery of gold brought a rush of people, many of them feckless, to Victoria and New South Wales; but not to South Australia. The less glittering metals found here tended to attract people who had been mining them already in Britain. Cornishmen came in thousands, and helped to make this the most Methodist part of the continent. At the time the Queen's statue was placed in Victoria Square her South Australian subjects believed, on good evidence, that they were more sober, thrifty, law-abiding and God-fearing than any of their neighbours (some of whom called Adelaide "the holy city"). These characteristics, though diluted, were still noticed in the reign of Elizabeth.

In the dock of Number 2 Criminal Court, Stuart sat behind cedar and spikes, with a warder from the gaol alongside him and the jury in two stalls opposite. Between the accused man and the jury, at the bar table, were four people in short wigs and gowns. Nearer the jury sat O'Sullivan and his partner, Miss Helen Devaney, who now entered the case as his junior. Along the table were Mr. R. R. St. C. Chamberlain, Q.C., and Mr. E. B. Scarfe. Chamberlain, a tall, lean man of 57, was South Australia's Crown Solicitor. It was his custom to appear in some of the most serious cases. In court he seemed to move with ease between legal textbooks and a seamy real world in which people were robbed and murdered. In cross-examining a hostile witness he might sound jocular, even gentle, working by coaxing irony rather than a direct attack; but in this trial there was to be no hostile witness.

Mr. Justice Reed, in wig and robes, presided over the court. Like all the lawyers in front of him, Sir Geoffrey Reed grew up in South

Australia and had his legal education at the University of Adelaide. He had been on the bench since 1943. He was now 67, and would therefore retire in three years. Temporarily, in 1949-50, he had been a federal public servant, when the Labor government appointed him Director-General of Security with the task of establishing a new Australian Security Intelligence Organisation. In court he was an alert listener, less prone than one or two of his brothers to question witnesses or direct counsel; his manner was quiet and considerate.

The clerk of arraigns stood, read out the indictment and asked Stuart how he pleaded. The prisoner said: "Not guilty." Before the Crown case opened, O'Sullivan asked the judge to prevent Chamberlain mentioning evidence which was to come from Constable Jones. (In the Police Court, Jones had described Stuart's interrogation and confession.) This evidence, O'Sullivan said, would be objected to, and should therefore not be put at this stage to the jury. The judge said that the danger of injustice was rather remote, and declined to make the order as requested. Chamberlain opened by declaring that this was probably the most shocking crime in the annals of the court. The defence, he said, would doubtless try to argue that Mary Hattam did not die until after Stuart was taken into custody for drinking on the Saturday evening; but the Crown would show that this was not so. Having set out why it was clear that Stuart killed the girl, Chamberlain proceeded to anticipate any defence on the ground of mitigating factors. The only excuse Stuart had offered, he said, was that he had been drinking. The jury must ask whether the child's injuries were or were not caused intentionally. It would be monstrous, Chamberlain said, to suggest that the intention was not there. He began to call witnesses, some of whom, but not all, had appeared at the Police Court enquiry.

The girl's father, her brother Peter and his playmate Peter Jacobsen were sworn and examined briefly about her disappearance. It seemed that the children went to the beach about 2.30 p.m. and that Mary was missing by 3.30. Peter Jacobsen's father said that he returned from fishing at about 3.45 within sight of where the children usually played, but saw nobody on the beach. The next witness sworn was Dr. Kathleen Thompson, who had left Ceduna since the Police Court hearing and was now practising in Victoria. When Chamberlain showed her two photographs of the victim O'Sullivan objected to their being tendered; a juryman appalled by the photographs might on that account, he suggested, be prejudiced against the man they saw accused of the crime. Mr. Justice Reed admitted the photographs. Examined by Chamberlain, the doctor explained that she had revised her estimate of the time of death. At the Police Court she had suggested that when she inspected the body, at about 12.30 a.m., the child had been dead at least three hours. She now believed that from four to eight hours would be a more accurate estimate. It was difficult to estimate exactly how long a time had elapsed between the time of injury and the time of death, but she put it at probably between half an hour and two hours. (On this estimate the child was probably assaulted between 2.30 p.m. and 8 p.m.) She described the position of the body in the cave, and the injuries discovered at the post-mortem. She told Chamberlain why she inferred that the child had been raped.

Before cross-examining the doctor, O'Sullivan observed that witnesses were present who had not given evidence at the lower court, and asked for an adjournment until the Crown gave him statements of what they intended to say. Stuart, his counsel said, would state that he had been severely manhandled by police at Ceduna. He did not know what the new witnesses might say. Chamberlain opposed the application. Since the defence had alleged violence, he said, the Crown would have to call the policemen to repudiate it. The Crown was not calling any new evidence, he said, or taking the defence by surprise. The judge ruled that O'Sullivan might be entitled to an adjournment at some stage, but not at present.

Dr. Thompson told O'Sullivan that her present estimate of the time of death had been made after talking with the police pathologist in Melbourne, Dr. Keith Bowden, and after consulting literature on the subject. Had she approached Dr. Bowden at the request of anybody in South Australia? No. Did she know that just three hours before she inspected the body, Stuart was in custody? Yes, she had heard that. Was it possible that death had occurred *within* three hours? It was possible, but improbable. To further questioning Dr. Thompson agreed that anybody having intercourse with the child would have been fairly widely covered with blood, and would have been likely, though not certain, to bear swellings and abrasions after the act. She had not heard it suggested that Stuart was so marked in any way. Re-examined by Chamberlain, the doctor said that she found nothing in the account of what happened to the girl in Stuart's confessional statement that was inconsistent with the post-mortem findings, except possibly on one point. When O'Sullivan took up this point, Dr. Thompson said that the child seemed to have been battered on the head first and then raped, although in the confession the order of these two events was reversed.

The Crown now called Dennis Blackham, the young taxi-driver, who said that about 2 p.m. on Saturday, December 20, he picked up Max Stuart and a shorter, lighter man whom he took to be Stuart's brother. While he was driving them from Ceduna to the fun-fair, Stuart said he wanted to go to Thevenard to see a girl. The other man said he wanted to go, too. Stuart replied: "You're not old enough. Stop at the fun-fair." Blackham then drove Stuart alone to the Thevenard Hotel. He smelt liquor on his passenger. Stuart asked him to call back in half an hour, but he did not. When he next saw Stuart, at 7 p.m. in Ceduna, he did not seem to be any different.

To O'Sullivan, Blackham said that he was first in touch with the police some three weeks after December 20, when they rang to ask if he had driven anyone to Thevenard that day. How had he been sure he drove Stuart? "By the look of him." Constable Herde, he added, said that the man charged with murder was the man he had driven to Thevenard that day. Blackham remembered, too, that the man in the taxi had said his name was Max and that the shopkeeper who rang to order the taxi had given the name Stuart. But when he read that Stuart had been arrested, he did not then know that this was the man he had taken to Thevenard. O'Sullivan asked about girls at the Thevenard Hotel. Blackham said he believed that coloured men from Ceduna visited two young girls there. Could aborigines get liquor at the Thevenard Hotel? He did not know. Probably they could get it more easily than at Ceduna. It was not uncommon to see an aborigine affected by liquor at Thevenard. Had he taken any other natives to Thevenard that day? Yes, three natives, about nine o'clock in the morning. While making other trips to Thevenard during the day, had he noticed a blue Holden car parked on the cliffs near the cave? No.

It was the morning of the second day, Tuesday, before Blackham left the box. He was replaced by the tracker, Sonny Jim. Mr. Justice Reed took him through a swearing-in ritual used for aborigines. Did he go to church? Did he believe in God? Did he know that if he swore to tell the truth he might be punished if he told lies? He did. "When you die you're dead and gone," he added. Sonny Jim told Chamberlain how he followed barefoot tracks between the cave and a nearby pool and then to the road. As the court reporter took it down, turning question and answer into a narrative, Sonny Jim said: "It was an aborigine track. I see he was not a wild aborigine. Between an aborigine barefoot track and a white man track there is a difference, a mark on the foot. The aborigine does not walk the same way as a white man in bare feet. White man don't use bare feet. These tracks along beach went straight along." In sand at the police station he saw tracks made by the same man.

O'Sullivan began by asking the witness how he felt about Stuart. The record says: "I am mad with him. I tell people at Ceduna that white men's court waste of time. I say he ought to hang and not waste time like that. I tell that to lot of people, yes. Bad thing for black people when black man does something wrong."

O'Sullivan's next questions were about the identification of tracks at the police station. Sonny Jim told this story: "Policeman say to me and Harry Scott 'Them same tracks.' When policeman say that I and Harry Scott say nothing for long time. I could not talk, I got cold. . . . Policeman say again 'Them same tracks.' When policeman say that again I still not talk for long time. I was bringing my throat around. Harry Scott did not have a cold. His throat was all right. . . . Then Harry Scott, he say 'Yes.' He say 'Yes' before I say 'Yes.' When Harry Scott say 'Yes' then I say 'Yes' too."

Did he tell the police on the Sunday that tracks near the cave were made by a native? Yes; Constable Herde pointed to the ground and said, as Sonny Jim recalled: "There tracks of man who killed girl." Herde walked with him to the pool and said the man must have washed his hands there. Why had Sonny Jim thought the tracks those of a native? Because they went over stones. "White man look for sand . . . put his foot where there no stones." He told Herde on Sunday that the tracks were those of an Aranda native. He did not know that the defendant was an Aranda. He told Herde that the man was a "wadi-chinner" or educated black man, and a stranger to Ceduna.

The older tracker, Harry Scott, was sworn. Like Sonny Jim (who was, he said, his nephew or uncle), he told Chamberlain he had been able to track since he was a boy. He described his visit to the beach on Monday, December 21, and later that day to the police station. To O'Sullivan he said that on the Sunday, before he saw any tracks, an aborigine in Ceduna had told him that Stuart was an Aranda man. On the Monday evening, he said, Constables Herde and Green called on him and Sonny Jim while they were having tea and told them that the man who killed the girl was at the police station. When Stuart made prints in the sand and the police asked whether they were the same as the tracks on the beach, Sonny Jim said "Yes" first, and he himself had agreed after about a minute. "Why did you wait that long?" asked O'Sullivan. "Can't bring the tongue," Scott replied. Finally O'Sullivan asked about the tides. Yes, the water came up on the beach every night, covering the pool; but the tracks were still not hard to see on the Monday. They were still there even now, in April, Scott said.

Constable Herde now gave evidence. He told O'Sullivan that he had noticed footprints on the beach on the Saturday night and Sunday. They were not photographed or sketched or cast in plaster, but he thought their length was measured. Herde was cross-examined by O'Sullivan on the other events at which he had been present. When he arrested Stuart for drinking on Saturday evening, did the man show anything like alarm? No. On the Sunday he heard Sonny Jim say the tracks were those of a native. But at the Police Court hearing, O'Sullivan reminded him, he had said he did not hear until the Tuesday that the tracks were said to be those of aborigine or half-caste. Would that be the true position? Yes, his memory would have been fresher then. On certain matters Herde's evidence differed from Sonny Jim's; he denied that the tracker had hesitated before identifying Stuart's tracks with those on the beach, and he said that on Sunday he had not accompanied Sonny Jim to the pool, and had not suggested to him that this was where the man washed.

Constable Jones was in the witness box nearly twice as long as anybody else. From notes made on December 23 he gave a detailed account of what occurred between the police and Stuart at Ceduna. When Stuart was taken to the police station Turner informed him that he was not obliged to answer any questions but that whatever he said would be taken down and given as evidence. Stuart said he understood that. He denied that he knew anything about the little girl. When the policeman examined him naked and asked about scratches on his body, he said: "I don't know how they got there." Turner said: "We have reason to believe that you were round at Thevenard on Saturday afternoon." "Yes," said Stuart; "I will tell you the truth. I did go round to the pub there, because I couldn't get any more wine at Ceduna, so I caught a taxi to the Thevenard pub." He had got the taxi about one o'clock, and walked back partly along the beach with his boots on. He had not seen any girl.

Turner now confronted Stuart, according to Jones' notes, with the fact that the murderer had left barefoot tracks. "We have had these tracks examined by the black trackers, Sonny Jim and Harry Scott. They told us if they saw tracks made by the same man, they would know him. Do you think that is right?" "Yes," said Stuart. "They would know them." Jones then reported the following conversation:

Turner. "We are going to let them have a look at some of your tracks. What do you think they will say?"
Stuart. "I will tell you the truth. I was there and I saw the little girl murdered, but I didn't do it."
Turner. "What did you see?"
Stuart. "I saw a white bloke kill the girl on the beach. He had a car at the top of the cliff. He pulled out a gun and made me pick up the little girl on the beach and carry her into the cave. He then told me that he would kill me if I ever tell anyone what he had done. That is why I never said anything about what I saw."
Turner. "What did you do then?"
Stuart. "I went down and washed the blood off myself in a pool."
Turner. "What did you do then?"
Stuart. "The bloke drove off in his car and I walked along the beach and went back to Ceduna."
Turner. "Your story is not true. The little girl was raped and murdered in that cave. We know that, because of the blood splashed up on the side of the cave and on the roof."
Stuart. "Well I must have done it but I don't remember doing it."
Turner. "You have remembered everything else clearly enough, I think you can remember what you did."
Stuart. "I might as well tell you what I did. I did do it. I was pretty full or I wouldn't have done it."
Turner. "What happened when you came down on to the beach?"
Stuart. "I will tell you the truth."

Jones said that Stuart then gave a detailed account of the crime. In reply to a question of Turner, Stuart said he wished to make a statement. Turner pointed out that he did not have to say anything unless he wished to. Stuart said he understood that. He then dictated his confession, had it read over to him, and signed it. The first few sentences, Jones said, were in reply to questions. After that, "the accused made his statement and when he would stop, which was about three times,

Det. Sgt. Turner would say: 'Did anything happen then?' and he would go on. Otherwise the statement is exactly as he said it." The jury now heard the confession for the first time. It was read by Jones and put in as an exhibit. Jones said that when Stuart had signed the confession Turner asked him: "Has any promise or threat or inducement been given or held out to you by any police officer connected with these enquiries to get you to make this statement and sign it?" "No," said Stuart. Next morning Jones and Turner went to the cells carrying a piece of rock and a pair of bathers. "Is this the stone that you killed the young girl with?" asked Turner. "It looks like it," Stuart replied. "Are these the bathers?" "They are the same colour. They look like it."

Jones' notes were passed on to O'Sullivan before he began his cross-examination. Did Jones, he asked, make any notes at Ceduna? No, nothing but the names of people questioned. Had Turner a notebook with him? Yes, but Jones did not see him making notes in it. Did Whitrod, who typed Stuart's statement, keep any notes which he later made available to Jones? No. When he made these notes back in Adelaide, had he first written a rough draft? No, he just sat down and dictated them off to Turner. Was it unusual for him not to take notes when questioning a defendant? No, it was not. Was the conversation in the police station recorded accurately? Yes, it contained everything that was important.

O'Sullivan then turned to the confession. Jones repeated his assurance that except for the beginning it was exactly as spoken by Stuart, with no more than two or three interruptions from Turner. Jones agreed that it contained nothing superfluous and left out nothing of importance. Had Stuart himself used the word "rape"? He had. The word "lavatory"? Yes. "The words used in the statement," Jones testified, "are what he said and are not altered to suit the occasion. They are exactly his words . . ." Where dates appeared, would they have been given by Stuart himself? "Turner would say 'Do you mean the 21st December?' and he would say 'Yes.' Any dates were clarified by Turner." Jones was still in the box when the second day of the trial ended.

On Wednesday morning O'Sullivan put questions implying violence by the police. Was a razor blade found in Stuart's possession? Not to Jones' knowledge. Did one officer threaten him with a razor blade? "Nothing happened like that at all. . . . There was no officer with a razor blade . . ." At O'Sullivan's request, Jones described exactly where Stuart and the policemen were sitting and standing during the interrogation. Were hairs pulled from Stuart's legs and head? No hair was taken from the legs, Jones replied; Turner cut some hairs from the head, but did not pull any. Jones denied suggestions by O'Sullivan that he punched Stuart over the right eye, on the right shoulder and in the ribs. He denied that Sergeant Walker pushed his thumbs into the man's throat. Jones did not say: "You had better tell us the bloody truth now . . ." or "If you don't tell us we will kill you."

Were the defendant's private parts examined, O'Sullivan asked, for bruising or swelling? The underneath part was red, Jones replied, and could have been called swollen; but he had recognised the redness as a consequence of a native initiation, so in fairness to the defendant he omitted the matter from his notes. Stuart was not examined by a doctor.

O'Sullivan turned next to the footprints. The police noticed no tracks, Jones said, until Sonny Jim pointed them out on Sunday. Herde never told Jones that he had noticed tracks the night before. Was Harry Scott sent along separately on the Monday to make his judgment about the tracks? No, he and Sonny Jim went together. Nor were the two men asked to give separate opinions about Stuart's tracks at the station. Was Sonny Jim's information that the tracks on the beach were by an educated northern black man recorded anywhere in writing? No. When Jones was asked about the blue Holden car, he said he had heard that it was seen near the cave between 4 and about 5 p.m.; he had been unable to ascertain the name of the driver, and the car was never found.

Re-examined by Chamberlain, Jones said that people often parked at the place where the blue Holden was supposed to have been seen, because it afforded a panoramic view of the harbour. He agreed that it was part of his training to remember accurately and to recall conversations like the one at the police station. "One of the main reasons why notebooks are not produced," he said, "is that when the person being spoken to sees a notebook, then he automatically doesn't say as much as what he would normally."

Detective-Sergeant Paul Turner, the officer in charge of the case, was the first of five police witnesses who had not appeared at the Police Court. He was not kept long by Chamberlain, for the main body of the police evidence had already been offered. He produced some hairs, which he said came from the child's hands and from Stuart's head. Turner agreed with O'Sullivan that in the notes made by Jones there was no reference to hairs. He said that at the time he had thought them of little value, but about a fortnight ago, at Chamberlain's request, he had sent them to the Institute of Medical and Veterinary Science. Were notes made of Sonny Jim's claim that the tracks on the beach were those of a northern or an educated native? No; but Sonny Jim explained at the time why he thought so. Turner had then thought the tracker was guessing; he had not worked with trackers before. Later, to Chamberlain, the detective said his faith in trackers had improved since this case. O'Sullivan asked whether any of the policemen said to Stuart that they knew he was on the beach because the trackers had told them. No, said Turner. The tracker did not see the accused. "I do not think I told him the trackers had seen where a man had washed himself at the pool. . . . He was only told that the tracks had been identified."

Why did the police go to interview Stuart on the Monday? "I went to the Wheat Board as a result of a message I received from Whyalla."

Was the defendant arrested at the wheat stacks? No, he was merely asked to come to the station. Turner said he did not believe Stuart's story, repeated in the confession, that he had left his tent to go to the lavatory when the police van pulled up. "If he was making a frank and free confession as to a murder and a rape," asked O'Sullivan, "can you think of any reason why he would finish his statement with a lie about going to the lavatory?" "I don't know," replied Turner, "other than that that is what he had already told us." When questioning Stuart, did Turner have in mind that the person in the blue Holden might have had something to do with the crime? Yes. Did he ask Stuart any questions about a white man? No. Like Jones, Turner said that no violence had been exercised or threatened. "Is not this the position," asked O'Sullivan: "that you kept accusing the defendant of committing the crime and that he at first denied it and then after some physical violence he started to say 'Yes, Yes,' to everything?" "No, that is not so. . . . Nothing remotely like that happened. . . . It was typed by Whitrod word for word as the defendant dictated it."

Senior Constable Whitrod, from Port Lincoln, confirmed this account when he appeared as next witness. He too told O'Sullivan how the policemen and Stuart were disposed about the room. So did Sergeant Walker, Sergeant Low and Constable Fairweather, who followed him in the box, and who, like him, had been called by the Crown to rebut the charge that the confession was extorted. All said that no violence was applied or threatened. Low, the photographer from headquarters, told Chamberlain that the scratches on Stuart's flesh were not photographed because the colour of his skin would have prevented a good reproduction.

The last witness was Mr. John May, J.P., district clerk at Ceduna, who said that when Stuart was brought before him on Tuesday, December 23, in daylight, he showed no sign of having suffered any injury and made no complaint of ill-treatment. To O'Sullivan, May said that Stuart was in the custody of the arresting officer, and that he himself had no reason to be looking for any signs of violence. He agreed that there was naturally a lot of feeling in Ceduna over the case.

The case for the Crown had taken three days to put before the jury. There were no witnesses for the defence. Neither side had called anybody from the fun-fair. Gieseman was merely named (as "Norman Keasman") in Stuart's confession. Allan Moir appeared in the document as "Allan", and in the evidence of the taxi-driver as Stuart's brother. Those were the only references to people in Gieseman's show.

3

THE JURY DECIDES

When the Crown case ended, Stuart could do one of three things. He could remain silent; he could go into the witness box and give evidence on oath in reply to questions; or he could make an unsworn statement from the dock. O'Sullivan chose the third course for his client.

If Stuart had gone into the witness box, Chamberlain would have cross-examined him. Once the defence alleged that the confession had been extorted, the Crown could presumably have made known to the jury his long list of convictions. The common law has always provided that the prosecution cannot bring against an accused person evidence of bad character—including previous convictions—which would merely prejudice a jury against him in general without helping to prove the particular charge before them. An exception to this principle has long been recognised: if an accused person calls witnesses to his good character, the evidence can be countered by evidence of his bad character. But in the late nineteenth century, legislation in South Australia as in other British communities went further; it provided that where the defence involved imputations on the character of a witness for the prosecution, prosecuting counsel was entitled to cross-examine a defendant-witness in an attempt to destroy *his* good character.

Australian lawyers and judges are especially familiar with one case in which the rule operated. In Victoria in 1945, a youth was charged with having had carnal knowledge of a child. When a confession was produced at the trial, the accused alleged that policemen had extorted it by threats and physical violence. The Crown prosecutor was then permitted to cross-examine the accused as to his character. The youth was convicted. The High Court ruled that the judge had been right to permit the cross-examination—a decision, in Chamberlain's words, "extremely welcome to people responsible for the conduct of prosecutions". Not every student of the criminal law thought the provision fair to accused persons. "There is hardly any rule of the law of evidence that is more in need of change," declared the English writer Glanville Williams in his book *The Proof of Guilt*; ". . . the question whether the defendant's character should be regarded as being in issue is totally distinct from the question whether the defence should be allowed to make imputations upon the character of a witness." Right or wrong, the rule was plain. If O'Sullivan wanted Stuart to communicate his version of the facts to the jury without allowing Chamberlain to disclose his criminal record, his only option was to have the accused make a statement from the dock that would not expose him to cross-examination.

But it seemed to O'Sullivan, so he said later, that Stuart was not articulate enough to make a statement orally. Had the defendant been literate, he could have read a statement. But as Stuart could not read, his counsel asked that a statement be read out for him. Late on Wednesday, the third day, the jurors were sent out of court while O'Sullivan asked the judge to let them hear a statement which had been typed out for Stuart and read over to him. "I want to have the document read to him first," said O'Sullivan, "and then he could say, 'That is right,' or else he could get up in the dock and say, 'This is my statement,' and Your Honour or the clerk could then read it." Chamberlain opposed the application, saying: "If my friend has instructions as to what this man's story is, then he could tell his client what he wants to say, and then my friend can say, 'What about so and so?' And if the defendant misses anything, then he could have a conference with his client and say to him: 'Would you mind telling us about this?' I am not prepared to have someone else make a statement." Mr. Justice Reed said he would consider the matter.

Next morning the jury was kept out while the lawyers and the judge argued about it. It seemed essential, the judge remarked, that the defendant should himself *say* something to the jury. "He can do that by telling the jury what he wishes to say," the judge suggested to O'Sullivan, "and you can prompt him if you like." O'Sullivan replied that this was undesirable except as a very last resort. The judge said: "I will do my best to see he gets out anything he wishes to say on these matters."

O'Sullivan asked for an adjournment to see the prisoner. "Perhaps I could spend half an hour or so with him and see what he might possibly be able to say on his own. I did not do so before, as I thought it would be done my way." "My friend had no right to think that," said Chamberlain. "I suggest that the simple matter is whether the prisoner is fit to be tried or not, and he is obviously fit to be tried, and if so, then he has the three courses open to him, and that must have been obvious a long time ago." The adjournment was granted. Three quarters of an hour later, in the presence of the jury, O'Sullivan said: "The defendant will say a few words, and he will formally ask that his statement be read. I ask that that be entered in the record. The defendant will make a statement. I do not know that I can assist him in any way with his statement." The judge made it clear that he was willing to let Stuart's counsel prompt and help him through the statement. "Now how do you wish the statement to be given?" he asked O'Sullivan. "I want him to stand up," O'Sullivan replied, "and say what he wishes to say. I am prepared to leave it at that. I do not think I want to do any more than that." "All right," said the judge; "we will do our best to get the statement down."

Stuart stood up behind the spikes in the dock, holding a typed statement, and said to the jury: "I cannot read or write. Never been to school. I did not see the little girl. I did not kill her. Police hit me. Choke me. Make me said these words. They say I kill her."[1] O'Sullivan spoke to him, and Stuart went on, indicating the typed statement: "That is what I want to say. Someone to read this out for me." Stuart had spoken so softly that Mr. Justice Reed had the reporter repeat his words to the jury. The judge said to Stuart: "Do you want to say anything about the evidence the police officers gave as to what happened at the police station?" "No," Stuart replied. "I do not ask for any further questions to be put to him," said O'Sullivan. "I prefer that Your Honour did not suggest anything further to him." "Very well," said the judge. "I cannot accede to the defendant's request for someone to read what he has out to the jury. It can be marked for identification." "I do not ask for that," said O'Sullivan, "unless it is to be read. I ask for nothing short of that. That is the case for the defence."

It was time for each counsel to address the jury. Chamberlain spoke first. The jury must not get the impression, he said, that Stuart had been denied opportunity to tell his story. He belonged to a race which, some people might think, had not had much of a deal. But the jury was concerned to uphold the criminal law, which could not be any respecter of persons. The duty of the police was to uphold the law and to bring offenders to punishment. Sometimes their reward was the suggestion, which had been made in this case, that they rounded up an inoffensive aborigine who as far as they knew was innocent, and brought him to court to put a rope around his neck. Examination of the evidence would show that the suggestion was impossible. The jury must not think that Stuart had suffered any injustice during the trial. He could give evidence from the witness box, and be asked questions, or he could make an unsworn statement; if he did that, he was the one who must make it. Chamberlain reviewed the facts at Thevenard as they appeared to the Crown and argued that at some time between 3 and 4 p.m. on Saturday, December 20, Stuart had committed a murder of which he should now be found guilty.

O'Sullivan said it was not suggested that any police officer would manufacture evidence against a man whom he believed to be innocent. But a conscientious officer believing that a man had committed an offence might supply some of the deficiencies of the evidence. In this case, O'Sullivan suggested, the police witnesses might have lied when

[1] As a reporter from the Adelaide *Advertiser* took down Stuart's words, they were a little farther away from normal English usage: "Can't read or write. Not go to school. I didn't see little girl. I didn't kill her. Police hit me, choke me, make me said those words, said that I killed her."

they described the circumstances of Stuart's confession and when they denied using violence against him. The purported confession contained many discrepancies which made it unacceptable. The time of death, a vital factor, had not been established. The evidence about footprints was unsatisfactory; there were conflicts between what the trackers and the police said about the methods of identification, which were on either account useless. O'Sullivan did not contest Blackham's evidence that it was after two o'clock when Stuart took the taxi for Thevenard.

The points made by each counsel were reviewed by Mr. Justice Reed when he spent a little over two hours summing up for the jury. He reminded the twelve men who had to decide Stuart's fate of a remark from the bench on the first day. "I said earlier, gentlemen, that I was sure you would not proceed on the assumption that, the more horrible this crime is, in all its ghastly details, the more likely it is that the defendant committed it." Their duty, he said, was to act only on the evidence given in this court, disregarding whatever they might have seen in newspapers or heard by way of conversation and rumour. Their primary task was to determine whether they were satisfied beyond reasonable doubt that the defendant murdered the little girl.

"Your attention has been drawn to the fact that the defendant is a native. . . . Like every other person who lives in this state it is his duty to obey the law. He is bound by the law of this country just as much as white men, and his being a native, of itself, is no excuse for any departure from the provisions, particularly of the criminal law. At the same time, gentlemen, when you are considering the probabilities of the case . . . you will be entitled to take into account the mentality and make-up of the defendant, so far as you have any evidence upon which you can consider this aspect."

Anything he put to the jury on the facts of the case, he said, was offered only to assist and should not be understood as an attempt to direct them. On questions of law it was his duty to rule and theirs to accept his ruling; but beyond that the decision was entirely theirs.

The Crown case, said the judge, was simple. The little girl was last seen on the beach during the afternoon, and her body was found raped and shockingly murdered. The defendant, as his counsel admitted, went to Thevenard about 2 p.m. or a little afterwards; he was there perhaps between a quarter and half past two. Tracks on the beach, identified as the defendant's, went from the cave where the body was found to a pool and back again, and along the beach. There were scratches on his knees and back. The confession was obtained properly, without violence or promise or inducement.

The defence case was a complete denial. The defendant had made an unsworn statement (which the judge now read to the jury), and it was his legal right to do so. The mere circumstance that he had made an unsworn statement only, rather than going into the witness box where he would have been subject to cross-examination by the Crown prosecutor, did not warrant any inference of guilt against him. "Of course, it is not sworn evidence, but it is what the defendant has said and you give it such weight as you consider it is entitled to." Mr. O'Sullivan had suggested that the defendant be permitted to hand in a written document. "It may be thought that it is an unfair thing that a man with practically no education and a man facing a very serious charge, and a man who perhaps may find some difficulty in expressing himself, should not be permitted to say, 'Well here is a document. That is what I want to say.'" But in the judge's view, what Mr. O'Sullivan wanted was something the law did not allow.

The defence, Mr. Justice Reed continued, was founded largely on the suggestion that the police had extracted the confession improperly. Mr. O'Sullivan had been critical of what the police had done and not done. "I do not know that we are here to criticise or enquire into the methods by which the police obtain information or conduct enquiries, except so far as it is alleged that they have made unfair use of their powers or have committed acts of violence or made threats. The police, whatever their lot may be, have not an easy task to perform, and they are men who go about their work with the best skill that they can summon up, and while it may be said that they could have told the defendant something else or that they could have followed up some other lead, as I reminded you, the question is, the issue in this case, the guilt or innocence of the defendant."

Having surveyed the two versions of the facts before them, the judge now proceeded to give his own review of the evidence. The jury might well find that the girl was last seen between 3 and 4 p.m., and possibly about half past three. O'Sullivan had mentioned the possibility that the girl was murdered much later; but there was no evidence that anybody saw her after her brother left her. On the defendant's movements there was, apart from the confession, the evidence of Blackham—which the jury would doubtless accept—that he got into a taxi about two o'clock and went to Thevenard. He was next seen about seven, and at 9.30 he was arrested for being an aborigine who had drunk liquor. On the Monday night about ten o'clock he was interviewed at the Wheat Board; there was some suggestion that he may have been hiding from the police, but the Crown did not regard that part of the evidence as very important. "No doubt, Mr. O'Sullivan would point out to you that the defendant had not left the town. It is possible he had no means of leaving it, I do not know, but there is evidence that he obtained a job . . ."

The doctor had given the opinion at the Police Court that the child died between three and ten hours before the body was found. She now thought the minimum was four hours and the maximum eight; and she said that having regard to the injuries, death would have occurred from half an hour to two hours later. The jury would no doubt remember criticism of the doctor's evidence. She did not claim to be a specialist in these matters, but she gave her opinion and the jury should give it as much weight as they thought fit.

The evidence about tracks had been criticised. It was suggested that if the police wanted a proper test, Sonny Jim and Harry Scott should have been taken to the beach individually and not together, and that instead of putting sand on the concrete outside the station at night, the police should have taken Stuart to the beach and made an impression there. There had been criticism on the ground that the trackers were told, when asked to look at the defendant's tracks at the police station, that these were from the man who killed the girl. It must be remembered that this statement, if made, was made after the defendant signed the confession.

A good deal of comment had been made on the reaction of the trackers when they saw the defendant's footprints at the station—the pause, the dry throats. The suggestion was that although doubtful, they were prepared to say what the police wanted in return for past and future favours. Perhaps the trackers answered slowly because they felt some revulsion at being called on to express an opinion to the defendant's face, "although that may not have been so with regard to the undoubted hostility which Sonny Jim, at any rate, bears toward the defendant." It was common knowledge in Australia that black trackers could pick up tracks and follow an animal or a man. The jury had to decide whether these people could not only see things white people would not notice, but also draw deductions from what they saw. "You will perhaps take into consideration the possibility that in view of the obvious hostility of Sonny Jim to the defendant, which is perhaps shared by the other witness, and possibly shared by a good many people in the Ceduna district, that the evidence may be somewhat unreliable because it is coloured or prejudiced by that feeling of hostility."

After an adjournment for lunch, Mr. Justice Reed spent most of the trial's last half hour reviewing the interrogation of Stuart. Six policemen had given evidence on oath that the defendant freely confessed. The defendant had alleged in his unsworn statement that he was hit and harassed into making a confession. Unless the jury were satisfied beyond doubt that the confession was obtained without the police taking unfair advantage of their position, then they would no doubt reject the confession and the answers which preceded it. Mr. O'Sullivan had invited the jury to assume that it was not impossible that police officers at times used violence or offered threats to suspected persons. "Well, human nature being what it is, we can start with the assumption I suppose that the allegations are not entirely impossible." On the other hand the jury would have some regard to the circumstances of this case. The suggestion really was that the police had got enough information to warrant almost a conviction in their minds that the defendant was guilty. "They had pursued their enquiries for some two days . . . they got some information from Whyalla—whatever that was we do not know—but by and large they had really made up their minds that they had got the guilty man. Their feelings were much aroused . . . and there is no doubt at all, gentlemen, that anybody associated with the investigation of this crime must have been horrified at the awful nature of it and been anxious to bring to justice, if possible, the man responsible. So it is put to you that . . . the police proceeded to help him along with his confession by some kind of violence, some kind of threat . . . which would destroy the voluntary nature of the confession." Mr. Chamberlain had suggested that this would be a very stupid course of conduct for police officers. Mr. O'Sullivan had replied that nobody was likely to see them, and that anybody who did would not take much notice of such treatment being given to an aborigine whom everybody in the district believed guilty. The fact that no notes were taken on the spot had been criticised, and it might appear a little strange to some people that others could write down an accurate account of a conversation or observations after a lapse of even twenty-four hours. On the other hand, police officers were trained to remember and record better than many other people what they saw and heard.

If the jury decided that the confession was voluntarily made, the next thing was to see whether it was safe to act on it as a real admission. "You may consider that there is no sort of violent change of direction anywhere in it. The suggestion of course from the defence is that it takes that course because it was that way that the police were directing it. . . . But then you test it against other facts which you find to be proved, and that would include the evidence about the tracks, the injuries to the girl, and the evidence about the place where she was found and so on, all these other matters, so long as you are satisfied they are accurate, and test the confession against that."

Except for the confession and the answers given by the defendant to the police, Mr. Justice Reed concluded, "it would be a very dangerous procedure to draw the inference that he was guilty of murder." At 2.20 p.m. on Friday, April 24, the jury retired, having been told, in effect, that the case against Stuart stood or fell on the evidence of the policemen about Stuart's oral and written confession.

The twelve men returned an hour and a quarter later. "Gentlemen of the jury," said the clerk of arraigns. "Are you agreed upon your verdict?" "We are," said the foreman. "Do you find the accused guilty or not guilty?" "Guilty."

The criminal law of South Australia gave Mr. Justice Reed no alternative other than to sentence Stuart to death. It would have been different if Stuart's trial had occurred in Queensland, where capital punishment was abolished in 1922, or in New South Wales, where it was abolished in 1955 for everything except treason and piracy. In Tasmania, whose Labor government was against hanging, the sentence of death would have been pronounced but commuted. But Stuart happened to be tried in a state where the politicians in power believed earnestly in the need for capital punishment. Stuart would be hanged at the Adelaide Gaol (by an executioner whose identity was secret) on the twenty-eighth day after his conviction, unless he appealed to a higher court or unless the government saw grounds for commutation. The condemned man was unable to eat the first meal offered to him after being sentenced to death. The prison doctor, called to the condemned cell, diagnosed shock and ordered him to bed for two or three days.

* * *

Ten days after the trial, Stuart signed an application, drawn up by his lawyers, for leave to appeal to the Full Court of the Supreme Court of South Australia against the conviction and sentence. Four grounds of appeal were set out: (1) The judge's decision not to allow someone to read the unsworn statement "was wrong in law and prevented the jury from hearing my version of the facts as I cannot make a speech for myself and can only answer simple questions when they have been fully explained to me". (2) The prosecutor committed a breach of the Evidence Act when he commented to the jury on Stuart's failure to give evidence. (3) The judge's decision to allow the prosecutor to describe in his opening address certain evidence, to which O'Sullivan said he would object, seriously embarrassed the course of the defence. (4) The verdict was against the weight of the evidence. A fifth ground, added later, was that photographs of the body should have been excluded.

The appeal was not a re-trial, though a re-trial was one of its possible consequences. In the British judicial tradition the jury is given such esteem that although judges will readily uphold an appeal if it seems to them that the judge has erred, they will rarely find that a jury has been mistaken. It is a commonplace among lawyers that an appellant has a far better chance if he takes up a technical point of procedure than if he tries to show that the jury was wrong. In Stuart's appeal the first, third and fifth ground attributed errors to the judge, the second criticised the prosecutor, and the fourth asserted that the jury itself was mistaken.

The Court of Criminal Appeal in South Australia, as in other states, is composed of judges of the Supreme Court sitting as a Full Court. The judges have power to set aside a conviction on the ground that the verdict was unreasonable, or that an error of law was made by the judge; they can vary the sentence; and they can direct that a new trial be held if, in their view, a miscarriage of justice has occurred.

Stuart's appeal was heard by three of the six members of the Supreme Court bench: Mr. Justice Mayo, Mr. Justice Abbott, and the Chief Justice, Sir Mellis Napier. Mr. Justice Abbott was 69, and would retire in a few months. Sir Herbert Mayo (73) and the Chief Justice (76) were on the bench already when legislation fixed the retiring age at seventy. Sir Mellis Napier was the only member of the Supreme Court bench not an Australian by birth, having come out from Scotland in 1896. He graduated in law at the University of Adelaide in 1902, took silk in 1922 and was made a judge in 1924. His adult environment was wholly South Australian. Since 1942 he had been both Chief Justice and Lieutenant-Governor, and since 1948 Chancellor of the University. In 1951 he had signed a "Call to the People of Australia"—an appeal for national unity in the face of "moral and intellectual apathy" and "the mortal enemies of mankind which sap the will and darken the understanding and breed evil dissensions . . ." Sir Mellis Napier's signature on the "Call" was no mere formality; not every Chief Justice in the country put his name to it, and his own sponsorship was heartfelt. His manner was slow, even ponderous; his mind was clear and alert. Whether presiding over a legal argument or deputising ceremonially for the monarch's representative, he always displayed courtesy and dignity.

His was the voice heard most often from the bench when O'Sullivan, accompanied by his partner Miss Helen Devaney, appeared before the Full Court on May 6. The Attorney-General was represented on this occasion by Chamberlain and Mr. J. R. Kearnan. The appeal was heard in Number 1 court-room, used for both criminal and civil cases. Stuart, escorted from the gaol, sat in a stall designed to serve as either a dock or a press-box.

O'Sullivan proceeded to put his case on the first ground—that Stuart should have been allowed to have his statement read by someone else. "There are people who can read and people who cannot," he said. "If the practice is to allow people to read statements without enquiry, it is an advantage to the man who can read and a handicap to the man who cannot." The Chief Justice asked why Stuart, directed by his counsel, could not have used his own language. O'Sullivan replied: "You can only extract evidence from this man by asking him 'Did you do this?' or 'Did you do that?' " During the argument on this point Mr. Justice Abbott said: "Because you have a man you regard as illiterate and incapable of understanding and expressing himself, you want a special system of justice built up for him which is not in existence. That seems to me to be a fallacy in your argument . . ." If the man could not make a coherent statement, said the Chief Justice, and could not even read a statement put into his hands, there was always the possibility of putting him into the box. "It may be a desperate remedy but if he has really any answer, if there is really any way of affecting the evidence for the prosecution, that may be your only course . . ." To this O'Sullivan replied: "The police can, with impunity, hit any man, knowing very well that he cannot go into the witness box and give evidence on it." "You can put all that to the jury," the Chief Justice said. "Not without showing that he has a record," said O'Sullivan. Chamberlain amplified this point later in the day when he said: "If it came out that he had been in many different gaols in Australia for crimes of violence, the jury may not have had much difficulty and may be able to assess the weight of what he said about half a dozen police officers; that is the reason I felt it my duty not to waive the law any further than it had been waived already."

On the second ground of appeal, O'Sullivan argued that Chamberlain had put it to the jury in effect that Stuart was avoiding cross-examination. Chamberlain said the comment arose on the spur of the moment when O'Sullivan was protesting that Stuart was not to be heard. But supposing—which he did not concede—that the comment was technically in the forbidden area, the judge had spoken similarly to the jury. Moreover, Chamberlain said: "Although there may be an irregularity in the trial, it does not follow that the conviction has to be disturbed unless the court sees some reason for thinking there has been a miscarriage of justice."

The third ground of appeal arose from O'Sullivan's objection to letting Chamberlain, in his opening address to the jury, foreshadow the evidence of Constable Jones about the confession. In considering this point the court discussed generally the allegation of violence by the police. The Chief Justice observed that Stuart's signature on the confession showed no obvious signs of distress. O'Sullivan said the suggestion was not that his arm was twisted to make him hold the pen, but that he was severely attacked and kept saying "Yes" afterwards. "You are saying," asked Mr. Justice Abbott, "that six police officers perjured themselves?" "Yes." "For no reason?" "For a very good reason—their jobs and careers would have been at stake." "Their jobs and careers would have been at stake if they had done it," said Mr. Justice Mayo. "And their liberty too I should think," said Chamberlain. "We all know it is done," said O'Sullivan. "I have heard it done with one or two," said Mr. Justice Abbott, "but not a group of policemen."

Events in the police station were discussed again when the court reached the fourth ground of appeal: that the verdict was unreasonable. O'Sullivan said that any jury ought to have regarded the confession with grave suspicion. The evidence from policemen was that an aborigine had dictated nearly two pages of a perfect statement, "with nothing superfluous, not a single thing, not one single omission, not a mistake or withdrawal or having to get the typist to cross it out and start again". "How would you suggest it was compiled?" asked Mr. Justice Mayo. "By the police asking questions," O'Sullivan replied, "getting answers, disregarding some, getting him back on to the track, more questions, more answers, stopping him as he rambled off on some other subject. They asked a lot of questions and after the assaults he said 'Yes' to anything because he thought he was going to be killed."

"That is utter rubbish," said the Chief Justice. For the time being nobody outside the court learned of this remark, but it was to be quoted in newspapers throughout Australia four months later. The Chief Justice observed that the jury saw the witnesses who said there was no such treatment, and there was the justice of the peace who saw the man the following morning. "No violence was alleged which left marks," said O'Sullivan. "Suppose we think that he was guided along his course?" asked the Chief Justice. "If you think that," said

O'Sullivan, "you must hold that Jones was committing perjury when he says nothing was done." "You throw these allegations about with reckless abandon," said the Chief Justice. "Coming from a member of the Bar—one ought to be careful of accusing people of perjury. Even quite capable people make mistakes, even quite capable people under stress of examination will sometimes say more or say less than they intend to say." Moreover, he said a little later, "our experience has not been that police officers as a class are unreliable. As a rule—I will say no more than that—they tell the truth to the best of their ability."

Discussion on the fifth ground—the admission of photographs—was brief, O'Sullivan suggesting that they were of a sort that must inflame the mind and the Chief Justice, like Mr. Justice Reed before him, arguing that they could inflame a jury only against a man they were convinced had done the act, and that they were relevant to a consideration of how the child died.

O'Sullivan finished off with what was, in effect, a criticism of the law rather than a contribution to his case. "I think more people would give evidence on oath where there are allegations of assault on the part of police officers were it not for the fact that it is an imputation on the character of the Crown's witnesses. . . ." Mr. Justice Abbott said he could never understand how a few blows from a policeman could force a confession of a serious nature out of anybody. "It all depends upon his mentality," said O'Sullivan; and the argument was over.

Without retiring to consider its decision, the court dismissed Stuart's appeal. In a written judgment of some 5,000 words issued later, the judges gave their reasons. First, Mr. Justice Reed had gone as far as he could properly go in helping the defence to put the prisoner's version of the facts to the jury. Second, "We agree with the trial judge that Mr. Chamberlain's comment came near to the borderline, but we do not think that it infringed the prohibition." Nor, in the court's view, could the comment have affected the result. On the third and fourth grounds, the judges held that the evidence had been properly admitted. To the assertion that the verdict was unreasonable, they replied that the appeal court could not make its own valuation of the evidence.

It was for the jury to say whether the evidence for the prosecution left room for doubt. It seemed to the appeal court, as to the trial judge, that apart from the confession there would be little more than suspicion attaching to the prisoner. The appeal judges made rather more, however, of certain other evidence: "the evidence of the footprints, and of the scratches . . . fortified the confession in two ways, first, by corroborating it, and, secondly, by the way in which it fitted into, and brought about the confession." The inference from Stuart's reaction when asked what he thought the trackers would say was really irresistible. "It is obvious that he knew, first, that black trackers can recognise footprints, and, secondly, that the prints in question were his own. We have not seen the witnesses, but we must assume that the jury, who did see them, were satisfied that this evidence was given in good faith, and, if that is so, it seems to us that the verdict was a necessary conclusion upon the evidence."

* * *

The Full Court had turned down Stuart's appeal instantly and without the slightest reservation. Unless there was a further appeal, to the federal High Court, or a commutation, Stuart would hang sixteen days later. His parents, Paddy and Jean Stuart, who were living at a natives' camp called Bungalow, near Alice Springs, were flown down by the authorities to visit the condemned man. The South Australian Aborigines Department, which until now had not been in touch with Stuart or his lawyers, looked after the couple while they were in Adelaide. Stuart was brought out of his cell and allowed to speak with his parents through bars. They talked in a mixture of English and Aranda. At first his mother wept, and a warder gave her a drink of water. Father and son were both composed. Next day they came again, bringing at Stuart's request a pile of illustrated magazines. A warder inspected them, removed some women's papers and passed on the rest. The parents were taken out to the airport and made their way to the Alice Springs plane through an excited crowd of people singing hymns as they waited for Billy Graham to land.

When they set out for Adelaide Paddy and Jean Stuart expected their son to die on May 22. But on the day they first saw him, his execution was put off for four weeks. On May 14 a Catholic priest not known to either of Stuart's solicitors called at their office to talk about the case. On May 20 Stuart gave notice of a motion to apply for special leave to appeal to the High Court. Four of the grounds were quite new.

4

ENTER FATHER DIXON

PRISON CHAPLAINS ARE APT to take a special interest in condemned men. Although Stuart put himself down as a Catholic when entering the gaol, he was visited by a Salvation Army officer and a Lutheran pastor as well as by the junior Catholic chaplain, the Rev. Father John O'Loughlin. O'Loughlin learned a little from Stuart about his background, but did not find the prisoner very communicative. The priest mentioned Stuart to the Rev. Father Thomas Dixon, who was living in a presbytery about a mile from the gaol, and who, as O'Loughlin knew, had worked for some years in the part of the Northern Territory from which Stuart came. Shortly after the Full Court had rejected Stuart's appeal, Dixon went to see him.

Dixon had spent most of his adult life as a missionary among dark people. He was born in Sydney in 1916, the fifteenth (and fourth from last) child of an Irish-English couple who had emigrated from Liverpool two years earlier. At the age of twelve, after attending a nuns' school and a Christian Brothers' College, he entered a seminary of the Sacred Heart Society (Missionarii Sacri Cordis, or M.S.C.) whose vows he subsequently took. The activities of this body in Australia are extensive and various; missionary, parochial and teaching work is undertaken in every state, and in the Northern Territory M.S.C. priests are the only representatives of their church among a scattered and heterogeneous population.

In November 1941 Dixon was appointed to Rabaul, in New Britain, but Pearl Harbour was bombed before he got there. Then he was asked to replace a sick priest for three months at a mission for aborigines on Palm Island, near the coast of north Queensland. He stayed more than seven years. In Toowoomba, Queensland, he taught English, French and algebra for a year to white Catholic children. Again he was posted to a mission, this time at Thursday Island, off the far north coast of Queensland. Here, and on nearby Hammond Island, he served four years among a population of whites, aborigines, Papuans, Samoans, Filipinos, Malays and even Sinhalese, as well as most of the possible combinations. On Hammond Island he designed, and he and a team of natives built, a mortarless stone church with windows whose amber glass had begun life as beer bottles. From these tropical islands Dixon was sent in 1954 to the parched centre, to the mission at Santa Teresa, near Alice Springs, which his society had founded among the Aranda people.

At Santa Teresa, nuns ran a school, nursed the sick and taught hygiene to mothers. Lay brothers worked as handymen. Dixon, the only priest, tried to communicate spiritual and material lessons to his aboriginal charges; the Mass and the cabbage became familiar to Aranda people. Aborigines came and went. Women and children were fairly permanent residents, though from time to time some of them drifted off with the men. Some men were employed on the mission, branding its cattle, tending a garden watered from bores, doing odd jobs; but most moved between the mission and the surrounding pastoral stations where, if they were lucky, they could get jobs as stockmen. Nearly all the children and some of the adults were baptised Catholics. Other adults had been baptised as Lutherans, or had at any rate been accustomed to attending Lutheran worship at Hermannsburg, a hundred miles away to the west.

Dixon learned to speak to the Aranda in their own language. As in the north, he found opportunities to act as a foreman stonemason. Many aborigines were living in lean-to hovels of corrugated iron. Directing them and working with them, Dixon enlisted a number of men to build houses for one another. Local stone was chipped by hand and carried on the mission's trucks; local gypsum was used for doorways. A man was given rations while he helped to build his own house, and money as well as rations when he worked on somebody else's. By the time Dixon left the mission in 1956, every resident lived in a trim stone house.

Sentimentality might move a Christian into missions for the heathen, but it would not keep his spirits up for long. Reviewing a book about another missionary (who also worked on Thursday Island), Dixon wrote: "One can become excited about raising their standards of living and hope, nay even know, that this scheme is the saving of the race, but the genius of the missionary is to put it over and get the people to stay with you, not merely during the initial stages of rosy promise, but to battle through the inevitable doldrums with patience and expectation. It takes years of sad experience even with the best of intentions to realise this . . ." Toughness of body and serenity of spirit; a rich sense of comedy; a wholly unromantic affection for the people among whom he is placed: these are qualities useful in a missionary, and they were all plain in Dixon.

When he called on Stuart the priest had been out of the mission field for three years, working as a curate in the parish of Hindmarsh, of which his society had charge with the permission of the Archbishop of Adelaide. He visited the gaol expecting to take on the task of preparing the prisoner for death.

The two men spoke in a mixture of English and Aranda. Stuart told Dixon, in Aranda, that he had not killed the little girl. The priest was not impressed. Nor, at the first interview, was he prepared to believe Stuart's story that he had relatives at Santa Teresa. Next day Dixon brought along photographs taken on the mission and asked Stuart to pick out and name people he recognised. He did so, accurately. It seemed possible to Dixon that Stuart's profession of Catholicism was intended somehow to exploit. Had he been baptised? No. Then why had he put himself down as a Catholic? He had been to a lot of churches, in different parts of Australia, Stuart said, and preferred Catholic worship. Again Stuart denied his guilt. The priest suggested it would be better to admit it. This conversation was repeated several times during the next week. Stuart never chose to discuss the matter unless Dixon raised it, never protested, and never budged from his statement that he did not commit the murder. Stuart's whole demeanour, as well as his unprotesting words, led Dixon to consider the possibility that he was telling the truth. Much later Dixon said: "I am sure he could not deceive me for so long. He would have to be a wizard to do that."

Since Stuart was not a baptised Catholic, no sacramental confession took place. If he had been a Catholic, and if Dixon had heard his sacramental confession, he could never have taken up the prisoner's case, whatever the man said. For the Catholic Church holds that the seal of the confessional is inviolable, and even to say after hearing a man confess that he was not guilty of murder would be, in the view of the church, to break the seal. Dixon's Irish forbears would have relished the remark made to friends once he became convinced of Stuart's innocence: "Thank God he's not a Catholic!"

The execution was eight days off when Dixon, on May 14, sought out Stuart's solicitors. Press reports of the trial and appeal had not caught his attention. Stuart had told him that he signed a confession after being assaulted by policemen. Now Dixon learned for the first time how crucial the confession had been. O'Sullivan showed him the document. He took it and a transcript of proceedings at the trial back to the presbytery. After studying the confession, Dixon doubted whether Stuart could have dictated it in the manner alleged.

* * *

Although Dixon had conversed with Stuart in Aranda and English, he was not a trained student of linguistics. Wondering how he might test his doubts about the language of the confession, he thought of Mr. T. G. H. Strehlow, whose book *Aranda Traditions,* a study of language and ceremony, had impressed him deeply.

Strehlow was himself the only white man ever brought up in Aranda society. His German father was pastor in charge of the Lutheran mission at Hermannsburg, where Strehlow was born and where he grew up among aborigines; Aranda, German and English were his childhood tongues. After graduating in English at the University of Adelaide he began an investigation of Central Australian dialects, myths and rituals which led him to write a grammar of the

Aranda language, *Aranda Traditions*, and other works. When the federal government in 1935 appointed a Board of Enquiry into charges that Northern Territory policemen were ill-treating natives, he was engaged to assist it. He prepared a memorandum on native evidence which the Board attached to its report, and which led the authorities to introduce certain safeguards for aboriginal defendants and witnesses. The chairman of the Board of Enquiry said that Strehlow had "a better knowledge of the native way of thinking than perhaps any other white man has ever attained to in Central Australia". The federal government appointed him as a patrol officer in 1936, and in 1939 as Deputy Director of Native Affairs. It was often his responsibility to appear on behalf of aborigines in the Police Court at Alice Springs and to give expert evidence to the Supreme Court of the Northern Territory. Since the war he had been at the University of Adelaide undertaking research in Australian linguistics, which took him four times on visits to the Territory.

During Stuart's trial and appeal, Strehlow was out of South Australia. He had been back only a week when Dixon called on him, and he would not have been there at all had he stuck to a plan of going straight from Sydney to the Territory. Dixon explained why he had come. Strehlow told the priest that he was well acquainted with Stuart's parents and that he had known Stuart himself from babyhood until a few years ago; he had last seen the young man at Alice Springs in 1955. At Dixon's request Strehlow agreed to go to the gaol, to hear Stuart talk, and to judge whether, in his view, the language of the confession rang true.

Two days later, on Monday, May 18, Strehlow, Dixon and O'Sullivan visited Stuart, who was brought from the condemned cell and sat at a table with the three white men. Strehlow asked him to describe the events at Ceduna and Thevenard. "He talked in Aranda," Strehlow wrote later, "the only language in which he possesses full fluency of expression and a reasonable range of vocabulary." There was no prompting from Strehlow, who wanted to find out whether Stuart could give a clear, coherent, chronologically exact account of his movements. "I had never seen this happening," wrote Strehlow, "during all my years of court experience in taking statements and extracting evidence from aboriginal or uneducated half-caste witnesses in the Northern Territory. Stuart proved to be no exception. His account was a perfectly plausible one, and so were his protestations of complete innocence. But Stuart introduced many fragments of conversations with white mates and drinking companions into his story, leapt over a number of time-sequences which were unimportant in his own eyes, omitted to give reasons for certain of his actions, and gave his story in accordance with the normal repetitive and rambling pattern that I had heard before on dozens of occasions when I was seeking information from persons of aboriginal blood who had not received a good white education." Strehlow asked Stuart to repeat his story, still in Aranda but more slowly, so that his words could be translated for O'Sullivan. Now, for the first time, the lawyer heard Stuart say that he paid £4 to an aboriginal girl at the Thevenard Hotel who consented to intimacy with him. It seemed to Strehlow that this would have been persuasive evidence in his favour if it had been available to O'Sullivan during the trial, since Stuart would have been unlikely, shortly after having intercourse, to molest a small, strange white girl. "After speaking to Stuart personally," wrote Strehlow, "I could find no real grounds for doubting his innocence."

Strehlow went from the gaol to O'Sullivan's office and read the confession. "I read it through slowly," he said, "and with growing amazement. In my ten years of varied experience of evidence given by aboriginals, part-aboriginals, police officers, and white residents in the Northern Territory, I had never seen a document even faintly resembling the one I was now looking at. Far from bearing any resemblance to any statement ever made by an aboriginal or illiterate part-aboriginal person within my own experience, this succinct and purposeful typescript, in point of its contents and the arrangement of its subject matter, began to reveal itself as a document which could have been composed only by some person who was well versed in legal procedure and in the practice of giving court evidence." At the gaol Strehlow had listened to Stuart speak English with O'Sullivan as well as Aranda with himself. "In plain Australian," Strehlow declared, "my immediate reaction upon reading the Police Confession was—'Rupert Stuart just does not talk like that'."

On May 20, Stuart applied for leave to appeal to the High Court against the decisions of the South Australian courts. A respite of four weeks was granted by Mr. Justice Reed, moving execution day to June 19. Four grounds of the first appeal (all but the admissibility of photographs) were repeated, with some amplification. To the assertion that the judge should have allowed Stuart to have an unsworn statement read for him, these words were now added: "His only fluent language is Arunta[1] and his knowledge of the English language is inadequate." There were four new grounds:

"5. At the time of the trial the appellant was unable to obtain the services of an interpreter in the Arunta aboriginal language.
6. Since the trial and appeal the appellant has obtained the services of Mr. Theodor George Henry Strehlow an Australian authority on the Arunta language who was absent from South Australia at the relevant time. Had Mr. Strehlow been then available the appellant could adequately have presented his defence in his native tongue.
7. The appellant has now ascertained that Mr. Strehlow had he been available at the time of the trial could have also given vital

[1] "Arunta" and "Aranda" are alternative renderings of the same aboriginal word.

evidence as to the composition vocabulary and idiom of the confession allegedly dictated to police officers by the appellant.
8. Since the said appeal the appellant has ascertained after conferring with Mr. Strehlow and his counsel that his original instructions to counsel were inadequate in some respects."

The High Court of Australia was designed to interpret the federal constitution, to deal with cases in fields within the jurisdiction of the federal government, and to be a court of appeal against decisions of courts in each state. In criminal matters a convicted prisoner may apply for special leave to appeal, which will be granted only if, in the words of one High Court judge, "it is shown that exceptional and special circumstances exist, and that substantial and grave injustice has been done." In an affidavit addressed to the High Court explaining Stuart's application Miss Devaney wrote: "matters of general interest and public importance arise for determination in this appeal . . ."

The application was heard in Melbourne. Chamberlain and Scarfe went over to oppose it on behalf of the Crown. O'Sullivan and Miss Devaney had their train fares paid by the South Australian government. Five of the seven federal judges were on the bench. None was a South Australian; for reasons about which people disagreed, no judge from that state had ever been appointed to the High Court. The Chief Justice, Sir Owen Dixon, came from Victoria, and so did Sir Wilfred Fullagar; Sir Alan Taylor, Sir Edward McTiernan and Sir Victor Windeyer were from New South Wales.

The judges showed keen interest in Stuart's English, a matter which was much more prominent in his application to them than in his application to the Full Court in Adelaide. Strehlow submitted an affidavit mainly about Stuart's understanding of English. "From my past knowledge of Stuart," he wrote, "and my conversation with him in pidgin English at the Adelaide Gaol I can say his knowledge of English is inadequate." Of the confession he declared: "In my opinion it could not have been dictated by a totally illiterate part-aboriginal who has never had any formal education of any kind. It includes many words, phrases and sentences which do not resemble any form of pidgin or broken English spoken in the Northern Territory. The style of the document is not in any way akin to the mode of expression found in the Arunta language which is the only tongue in which Stuart has any complete fluency of expression."

Mr. Justice Windeyer asked about the language of Stuart's interrogation at Ceduna. Was it in English? "According to the police," said O'Sullivan, "in the most perfect English all round." Did the accused speak English? "Very broken pidgin English," O'Sullivan replied. If it was so important for Stuart to have an interpreter, why had O'Sullivan not arranged for one at the trial? O'Sullivan said that had he known Stuart would not be allowed to have a statement read for him, he would have sought an interpreter. What Stuart did say from the dock, his lawyer explained, was recited parrot-like "after half an hour's coaching by me out in the cells at the back . . . but he broke down even in that." Mr. Justice Taylor pointed out that the trial judge offered to let O'Sullivan prompt Stuart. "I can only prompt him in English that he might or might not understand," said O'Sullivan. ". . . He can answer some questions but one never knows whether the complete understanding is there . . ."

Chamberlain had two replies to O'Sullivan's submissions about language. First, the evidence indicated that Stuart's command of English was not inadequate. "The prisoner, so far as all the police officers are concerned and the taxi-driver and one or two other people, could speak quite adequate English . . ." Second, the time to call for an interpreter, if one was wanted, was at the trial, not now; both as interpreter and as an authority on Stuart's linguistic capacity, Strehlow had come forward too late. He suggested that O'Sullivan had ample time before the trial to consult people with special knowledge of aborigines. The defence could have approached the Protector of Aborigines on Stuart's behalf; for as soon as Stuart came into South Australia he was under the guardianship of the Protector.

The Chief Justice, Sir Owen Dixon, quoted from Strehlow's affidavit an assertion that Aranda was the only tongue in which Stuart had any complete fluency of expression, and remarked: "It is that which has disturbed me a little, really, as to the understanding of the accused of what was going forward." Later, he said: "I express some concern . . . to be quite sure that this aboriginal was capable of really understanding the proceedings and expressing himself." On the language of the confession itself, Mr. Justice Windeyer drew Chamberlain's attention to a passage in the report of the trial where Constable Jones swore that the confession was "in the words exactly as the defendant spoke them". This matter, said the judge, "troubles me a lot. Do not think I am suggesting that he may not have said this; I find some difficulty about what is said as to *how* he said it."

Although the judges did refer to Strehlow's affidavit, Chamberlain argued that the court had no jurisdiction to look at it. More than one of the judges themselves observed that they were not permitted to entertain an appeal on the ground of new evidence. At one point Mr. Justice Taylor said to O'Sullivan: "Those things are all very good jury points, perhaps, but what part do they play in an application for special leave? We cannot re-try the case." Before one of his expressions of concern, the Chief Justice said: "I do not know that it is much business of the High Court . . ."

The argument lasted two days, and took in the four grounds repeated from the application to the South Australian appeal court as well as the four new ones. Chamberlain was questioned more closely than he had been in Adelaide both on his opposition to having Stuart's statement read and on his subsequent comment to the jury that Stuart had chosen not to enter the witness box. On the latter issue Chamberlain submitted that even if his remark had been one technically forbidden (which he denied), it could not have affected the result of the trial. It was an informal, wide-ranging discussion, in which a few sharp exchanges between counsel were cut short by mild interventions from the bench. Once, in reply to a question from the bench, O'Sullivan referred to the difficulty he had found in collecting evidence for his case. "You see, this is a man from Alice Springs; it was not somebody who lived around Adelaide where you could go down to his butcher or his baker or his local policeman or somebody like that." The travelling show, O'Sullivan said, had left Ceduna before he saw Stuart. "There was nobody in South Australia that I knew who knew him."

* * *

Unlike the Full Court in Adelaide, the High Court reserved its judgment. A week went by, and another. Stuart's respite, granted for this appeal, was due to run out on June 19. On June 18 a further respite until July 7 was granted by Mr. Justice Reed. It would appear from later events that if the High Court had issued a judgment against Stuart by June 17, he would have been hanged two days later. It was not until June 19, however, that the High Court announced its decision. The prisoner was refused leave to appeal.

"Certain features of this case have caused us some anxiety," the judgment began, "but we are of opinion that it would not be in accordance with the principles governing the exercise of our jurisdiction . . . to grant this application." Like the trial judge before them, the federal judges thought that the confessional statements formed the substance of the case against Stuart. "All that was added to connect him with the crime was an opinion expressed by the black trackers that the footprints on the beach were his. There was of course much evidence besides, and none of it was inconsistent with his guilt, but it was not evidence which implicated him as the author of the crime."

It had not been suggested at the trial that the prisoner needed an interpreter. "Counsel for the applicant did not think fit to raise any question of his understanding of English at the proper time, which was, of course, on the arraignment, and neither Mr. Strehlow's affidavit nor any evidence to a similar effect was put before the Court of Criminal Appeal. Generally speaking, this court is confined on appeal to the material which was before the court appealed from . . . But in any case it is entirely consistent with this affidavit that the applicant was fully capable of understanding and answering questions put to him and of describing intelligibly simple acts and events. It is to be observed that the objection to the police evidence appears to have been based throughout on alleged extortion by violence and threats rather than on any ability of the applicant to understand questions put to him. Having regard to all the circumstances, we do not think that a ground for granting special leave is disclosed by Mr. Strehlow's affidavit."

The submission that it was improper to let Chamberlain, in his opening address, refer to evidence about the confession, was rejected by the High Court quite as decisively as it had been by the Court of Criminal Appeal in South Australia. On Mr. Justice Reed's attitude to the reading of Stuart's unsworn statement, the federal judges said: "We agree with the Full Court that the applicant had no legal right to have his prepared statement read for him. At the same time, it could, of course, have been done with the consent of the Crown, and, in the special circumstances of this case, one might perhaps have expected consent to be given." It might well be thought that the course which the trial judge was prepared to allow his counsel to follow, and which he declined to follow, was more favourable to the applicant than that which his counsel wished to adopt. "It came very near to allowing him to examine the applicant in chief without having him sworn or cross-examined. The Court of Criminal Appeal has held that no miscarriage of justice occurred by reason of what took place, and we do not think that any ground which would justify the intervention of this court can be found therein."

The High Court disagreed with the Court of Criminal Appeal over Chamberlain's comment on the unsworn statement: "the jury was in effect told by counsel that the applicant had a right to give evidence on oath and subject to cross-examination." Any such statement was capable of being understood "as inviting the jury to take into account against the accused the fact that he is apparently unwilling to exercise that right . . . What was said by counsel for the Crown was in our opinion . . . such a comment as is forbidden by the statute. In this respect we are unable to agree with the judgment of the Court of Criminal Appeal." That court would nevertheless have been justified in dismissing the appeal "even if it had taken the view of counsel's observations which we think correct . . ." For in the first place, the observations by counsel for the Crown had been occasioned by the altogether exceptional circumstances attending the making of his statement by the applicant; the remarks were made mainly "by way of answer to any suggestion that the accused had not had a fair opportunity of putting his case". Secondly, "the learned trial judge covered the same ground and informed the jury of the courses which were open to the accused. His comment was clear and emphatic." In these circumstances, it would be unrealistic to treat the comment by counsel as a ground for granting special leave to appeal.

"As we have said," the judges concluded, "this case has caused us a good deal of anxiety, but, after full consideration, we are of opinion that no sufficient ground has been shown for granting special leave to appeal." Two final sentences referred to a document, said to bear on Stuart's capacity to understand English, which the prosecution had sent while the judgment was being prepared. "This communication we have entirely ignored and we do not think it ought to have been made." The document was a record of a case in which Stuart had been involved at Alice Springs; much was to be heard of it later.

The expressions of anxiety which began and ended the judgment of the High Court were to be quoted widely and interpreted variously. From a reading of the transcript it seems a reasonable guess that unless the judges felt on some matters a concern which they did not reveal during the argument, their uneasiness centred on one matter—whether Stuart was fluent enough in English to have understood the judicial proceedings or to have composed his confession as alleged.

* * *

The normal opportunities for appeal were exhausted. In theory, Stuart could ask the judicial committee of the Privy Council in London to set aside the three Australian judgments; but that had never been done by a convicted person in South Australia. The only appeal on Stuart's behalf which now seemed feasible was to public opinion. When a man is condemned to death in South Australia, as in other places, his solicitors always draw up a petition that the sentence be commuted to one of life imprisonment. In England such an appeal goes to the Home Secretary; in South Australia it goes to the Executive Council (in effect, the cabinet). According to an account of the procedure given by the premier, Sir Thomas Playford, in 1959, every member of the Executive Council is required to read the whole of the evidence and the judge's summing-up. The trial judge is summoned; the Crown Solicitor—at this time, Chamberlain—is also interrogated. The Executive Council then decides whether there are any extenuating circumstances, any defects in the trial, or any hint of an undisclosed fact which make it desirable to waive the death penalty. The decision whether to hang Stuart or commute his sentence thus lay with politicians. Already, before the approach to the High Court, Father Dixon had enlisted on behalf of Stuart South Australia's most distinguished student of aborigines. Now that his task was to persuade the elected representatives of the people, he approached the man best known in Adelaide as a campaigner for aboriginal rights.

5

A RACE WITH DEATH

On the evening of June 27, ten days before Stuart was due to be hanged, about fifty people gathered at the home of Dr. Charles Duguid in Magill, a suburb of Adelaide. From this meeting came a campaign to keep Stuart alive.

Duguid had come from Scotland to practise in South Australia. Unlike his fellow-Scot Sir Mellis Napier, he retained a rich Scottish accent. He retained, too, energy remarkable in a man of 75. Not only was he still in general medical practice; as president of the Aborigines' Advancement League, and as founder of Ernabella, a Presbyterian mission in the north of South Australia, he was devoting all his leisure to the problems of dark people.

Ernabella, begun in 1937, was an unusual place in a state where most missions to aborigines were conducted by a fundamentalist evangelical body which was uncompromisingly hostile to the whole primitive culture. When a missionary of this body urged in 1959 that governments should prohibit "heathen tribal customs", Duguid retorted that the man had "no understanding . . . of the aborigines and their spiritual beliefs". Swift conversion was not sought at Ernabella. Medical work and education were prominent in statements about its purpose. Visitors were more likely at Ernabella than at other missions in South Australia to see aborigines going around without trousers.

Duguid's other institution, the Aborigines' Advancement League, opposed much of the policy which the government implemented through its Aborigines' Protection Board, and challenged the very principle of "protection" as an attempt merely to smooth the dying pillow rather than to help aborigines cope positively with European civilisation. Duguid was once a member of the Aborigines' Protection Board, but disagreements over policy led him to resign. Through the Aborigines' Advancement League he campaigned for the extension of legal rights. On the initiative of the League, the South Australian parliament removed from the Police Offences Act a clause making it an offence to "consort" with aborigines. Led by Duguid, the League was pressing for amendments to the Aborigines Act, and in the long run for the recognition of aborigines as full citizens.

Dixon had visited Duguid on Monday, June 22, to discuss Stuart's situation. Next day Duguid talked with Strehlow and borrowed from Stuart's solicitors reports of the legal proceedings. "I was troubled by much that I read," Duguid said later. "My wife and I decided that Father Dixon and Mr. Strehlow should be given an opportunity to tell their story." The meeting at their house was held for this purpose. It was attended by members of the Aborigines' Advancement League, university teachers (including two from the Law School), clergymen, and representatives of the Howard League for Penal Reform.

Duguid, Strehlow and Dixon spoke, each saying that the confession appeared to have been crucial in convicting Stuart, that its language was implausible, and that according to Stuart it had been extorted from him. Duguid mentioned the statement which the illiterate man had not been allowed to have read for him. Dixon read extracts from the High Court judgment, including the passages in which anxiety was expressed. He had been astonished, Dixon said, to learn that no welfare officer attended Stuart's interrogation. In Queensland, he knew from experience, no confession by an aborigine was admissible in court unless strict safeguards had been observed. Strehlow described the special facilities for aboriginal defendants in the Northern Territory, and said that the Aborigines Department in South Australia should take some responsibility in a case like Stuart's. All three speakers agreed that no further legal action seemed possible, and that the government should be asked to commute the sentence. It was informally decided by the meeting that a petition for commutation would be circulated as widely as possible in the week that remained before Stuart was to be executed. Most people present agreed to take copies of the petition, which was to be drawn up by the Howard League for Penal Reform.

The Howard League, like the Aborigines' Advancement League, had at its head an upright septuagenarian, born in Britain, with conservative tastes and radical opinions. Mr. Eliott Thorp was a retired journalist, a leader in the Adelaide meeting of the Society of Friends, and an opponent of capital punishment. The committee of the Howard League met at his request and drew up a petition addressed to the Chief Secretary, noting that the High Court had expressed anxiety and praying that the sentence be commuted. Copies of this petition were distributed fast, for overlapping interests were no less common among people active in the philanthropic bodies of Adelaide than among those who directed her public companies. The Aborigines' Advancement League and the Howard League shared a number of members. One keen supporter of the latter body, Mrs. Winifred Green, was secretary of the Women's Christian Temperance Union, whose headquarters became a clearing house for petition forms. "Most of our members are opposed to capital punishment," she said, on behalf of the W.C.T.U., "but in this case we are opposed to the execution on the specific merits of the case."

An oblique report of Duguid's meeting appeared in the *News*, Adelaide's evening paper, on June 29, announcing that a campaign for commutation was under way but mentioning no names. It was accompanied by a statement from Mr. Frank Borland, warden of the students' union at the university, expressing concern that the Aborigines Department had not given Stuart any help and remarking on the precision of language used in the confession. "No one at any time," said Borland, "has seen Stuart's own free statement which he sought unsuccessfully to read in court. I hope that the Executive Council will decide to commute the death sentence to one of life imprisonment." Borland was a Presbyterian minister from Melbourne, of a generation which sought earnestly to discover and apply the social consequences of the gospel. As well as performing ordinary pastoral work, Borland had been a missionary in Korea and a chaplain in the army. In Adelaide he combined a good deal of preaching with his full-time job in charge of students' activities. He was to remain active in the campaign to keep Stuart alive. Adelaide's morning paper, the *Advertiser*, printed a letter from Borland on June 30: "I hope," he wrote, "that the 'anxiety' of the judges of the High Court will be sufficient to persuade the Executive Council to commute his sentence to life imprisonment." The same issue carried a letter from Mrs. Winifred Green, writing as general secretary of the Women's Christian Temperance Union and suggesting that even defenders of capital punishment must feel some uneasiness as to its application in Stuart's case. A letter from Duguid's wife appeared in next day's *Advertiser*; without a signed confession, she said, there would have been insufficient evidence against Stuart. "Is it really just that a man should be allowed to condemn himself to death before counsel is available to him?" The *News* on July 1 had a letter from a university lecturer urging commutation on the ground of doubt, and a story headed "Petitioners run a race with death."

On this same day, Dixon and Strehlow called on the Attorney-General—the minister formally responsible for justice—and tried to persuade him that the sentence should be commuted. With them was the dean of the university's Faculty of Law, Professor Norval Morris. It was less than a year since Morris, at 35, had come to the chair at Adelaide. He was unusual among Australian professors of law in having specialised in the study of crime; his book, *The Habitual Criminal*, was based on research undertaken in England after his graduation from the University of Melbourne. Back in Melbourne he had conducted a new university department of criminology. In Australia as elsewhere, some practising lawyers and many judges were suspicious about the effort, embodied in this discipline, to wed law and the social sciences. When Morris visited Adelaide in 1953 and read to a legal convention a paper setting out some criticisms of judges offered by criminologists, a member of the South Australian Supreme Court bench, Sir George Ligertwood, said he was irritated by the address, "and particularly the statement that judges came from people who had lived a sheltered life. That might be true in other states, but it was not true in South Australia where the busy life of a practitioner at the Bar was certainly not sheltered. . . . Another criticism was that judges did not know anything about prison life. He had been in Yatala prison only once but he had the services of the Sheriff who was in charge of all the prisons. The Sheriff had a wide experience and was able to tell the judges much about prison life." Morris, replying, said he did not agree that twenty years' experience at the Bar really gave an insight into the personalities of the criminals to be sentenced. "Judges . . . should not think that by their contact with criminals, perhaps with some of them in criminal practice, they gained any real insight into their characters and conditions. The stage when the criminal approached a lawyer in his office to discuss his problems was not the occasion when one could expect from him his most normal, ordinary behaviour; nor was prison a typical situation in which you could expect his typical behaviour." In asking Morris to take charge of its Law School, the university council was bringing to Adelaide a man who would ask judges, and politicians, searching questions about the behaviour, punishment and treatment of law-breakers. When Mary Hattam died, Morris was in Colombo as chairman of a Royal Commission on capital punishment. This enquiry confirmed, in Morris' view, the conclusion of the British Royal Commission under Sir Ernest Gowers that murders do not increase when capital punishment is abolished.

Morris had been unable to accept Duguid's invitation to hear Dixon and Strehlow. After the meeting two men from the Law School asked Dixon to call on their professor. At his house, about midnight, a solid cross-examination began. The three lawyers were convinced after two hours that the priest had a story worth investigating. For this reason Morris accompanied Dixon and Strehlow to see the Attorney-General, Mr. Colin Rowe, who was himself a lawyer. The meeting ended with agreement that for the time being nobody would mention that it had occurred. The Attorney-General was given a signed copy of the statement which Stuart had sought to have read for him at the trial.

Strehlow left with the minister a long letter setting out his qualifications, his experience with aborigines and the law, and his reasons for doubt about the confession. In his affidavit to the High Court he had expressed these doubts in general terms; now he went through the confession in detail. All Northern Territory aboriginals and part-aboriginals, he said, showed when giving evidence an "irritating vagueness about all dates and clock times . . ." The court evidence did not indicate whether Stuart had a watch, or whether he could interpret one accurately. "Yet in his alleged confession, the illiterate Stuart, who has never had any formal education of any sort, is depicted as a person with a perfect obsession for ascertaining clock times at short intervals and for thinking about days in times[1] of the calendar."

[1] "Terms" was perhaps intended here.

Strehlow suggested next that the confession was too lucid and well-organised to be plausible. "In his own Aranda story as related to me Stuart . . . continually interrupted his account by telling me, in a boring and rambling fashion, what he had said to some of the men whom he had met, and what they had said in their turn. Most of these quoted snatches of conversation were, of course, quite irrelevant from a legal viewpoint, and no court would have been interested in hearing about them. It is noteworthy that the Police Confession does not include any of these irrelevant actions or conversations. . . . For him to have composed a statement free of irrelevant ramblings and repetitions in what was for him a foreign language which he had never been formally taught, would have been a complete linguistic impossibility. Moreover, the alleged 'confession' is by no means a simple, straightforward essay or account. It is a completely damning document which sets out in their logical order only those facts and details which would be of use in a Court of Justice, and even here only to the police and to the prosecution. How Stuart could have composed, without any outside assistance and at his very first attempt, such a first-class legal document to ensure his own destruction, is beyond human understanding. For an illiterate person to achieve this feat would mean that he would have had to be born as a legal genius, and that his intelligence would have had to be of such a high order, that most white Australian children would have had to be re-classified as sub-human morons in comparison with him." And Stuart, he added, was a person of no more than medium intelligence, whose capacities had been hampered by an unsatisfactory cultural environment.

Finally, Strehlow turned to the actual language of the document. As a boy, he said, Stuart had learned pidgin English, "and later on he made some headway in the slightly-improved form of it which bears a closer resemblance to what may be termed 'Northern Territory English', i.e., the language spoken by most educated part-aboriginals." Northern Territory English, he explained, was in many ways like ordinary conversational Australian English; "but it is marked out, firstly, by an extraordinary lack of range in its vocabulary, and, secondly, by certain characteristic idioms of its own. Among the latter is the use of 'he' or 'she' after a noun. . . . Thus, in Northern Territory English, it is common to hear expressions like 'that woman *she* told me' (for 'that woman told me'), 'that man *he* wants to know' (for 'this man wants to know'), and so on. Another Northern Territory English idiom is the use of 'them' in place of 'those', as in '*them* two blokes came up today' (instead of '*those* two men arrived today') or 'I *seen them* two boys standin' on verandah of hotel' (for 'I *saw those* two boys standing on *the* verandah of *the* hotel)." Small divergences from normal Australian English, Strehlow suggested, could be seen even in the few words spoken by Stuart during his trial, "even after he had carefully discussed with his solicitor the statement he was going to make in the Court in his own defence. After these few sentences he apparently broke down, unable to remember what to say next." Yet the English of the confession owed nothing to Aranda, "and—with the exception of a few unimportant words and minor phrases—nothing even to pidgin English, or to Northern Territory English either".

Among particular words and phrases in the confession Strehlow singled out as implausible the word "awoke" ("how many white Australians, educated or otherwise, say '*I awoke*' instead of the common and normal '*I woke up*'?"), "such better-class elements of the English language as 'unconscious' and 'raped'," and the following sentences:

> "The Show *was situated* at the Ceduna Oval."
> "The *three of us* sat down and drank a flagon of wine."
> "I put *the half flagon* in a sugar bag."
> "I left the bag with the flagon in it down *behind the Picture Show wall.*"

These passages, said Strehlow, were "in complete opposition to all the stylistic and grammatical features of Northern Territory English". Strehlow cited the evidence of Constable Jones that the body of the confession represented "the words exactly as the defendant spoke them", and wrote: "In spite of Constable Jones' protestations, the voice that can be heard speaking in the Police Confession is not the voice of Rupert Stuart." Strehlow remarked that the act of raping small girls was, in his experience, exclusively a white man's crime. The letter closed with an appeal for commutation.

On the day the Attorney-General received Strehlow, Dixon and Morris, a petition against the death sentence prepared by O'Sullivan and signed by Stuart reached the office of the Chief Secretary. In this document Stuart said that he had no assistance in his own language (Arunta) at the trial, and was unable to present to the jury his version of the incidents of December 20. He wanted to tell the jury certain things, but did not know how to. "I am now told that if my trial had taken place in Queensland or the Northern Territory the document which I signed in the presence of the police would not have been admitted as evidence against me unless certain safeguards had been taken before I signed any document. I did, in fact, sign the alleged confession in the presence of six police officers, and without any Protector or other person being available to advise me. At the time I was confused, anxious, worried and frightened, and I would have signed anything to get out of the room." The petitioner also offered an account of the case at Alice Springs about which the Crown Law authorities had tried in vain to inform the High Court while the federal judges were preparing their judgment. "I was a defendant in a case at Alice Springs in 1956," he said, "when another aboriginal, one Sansbury who could read and write, assisted me by writing out a statement which I wished to present to the court and I did in fact present such statement to the court. I was also assisted in court on that occasion by the Native Welfare Officer."

More letters about Stuart were coming into the newspapers. At the High Court, the Crown Solicitor had observed that when Stuart entered South Australia he came under the guardianship of the state's Protector. In the *Advertiser*, Duguid now rebuked the Aborigines Department for not having its welfare officer present when Stuart was interrogated. "This welfare officer," Duguid wrote, "was stationed at Ceduna so that he would be on hand to assist aborigines on the West Coast when in trouble." There was no official comment on this criticism. In the *News*, Duguid suggested grounds for doubting Stuart's guilt and observed: "If Stuart was responsible it is the first time on record since white people came to Australia in 1788 that an aboriginal man has so acted." An Anglican clergyman associated with the Howard League, the Rev. Norman Crawford, wrote to the *Advertiser*, saying: "The whole moral standard of the community suffers when it inflicts the supreme penalty with little or dubious rationality." The president and secretary of the League of Women Voters of South Australia reproduced in the *Advertiser* a letter informing the Chief Secretary that their Society had reaffirmed its opposition to capital punishment and urging commutation in this case.

A few correspondents said that the hanging should take place. "The attack on the British judicial system by those opposing the death sentence on Rupert Max Stuart," said one writer in the *Advertiser*, "raises the interesting question as to what system of law they would prefer; perhaps that of the Communists (shades of Cardinal Mindzenty)?" An uncle of the murdered girl, Mr. H. H. Hattam, was provoked by Borland's statement in the *News* to ask: "Do you think in your own mind, Mr. Borland, that Stuart gave Mary Hattam any fairness? . . . Mary Hattam's father fought with the 2/27 Battalion in Syria and over the Owen Stanleys so that justice could be preserved in our country. I wonder, Mr. Borland, whether you would be seeking a reprieve for Stuart if a daughter of yours had been his victim?"

This was vehement controversy, which in some private places became quite violent. (At a meeting of a Protestant ladies' guild some sixty miles from Adelaide it was asserted that the crime had involved not only rape and murder, but cannibalism.) But the debate was still small news outside the correspondence columns of the Adelaide press. It reached the top of the front page in the *News* on Friday, July 3, when people travelling home from work read that Dr. H. V. Evatt, Leader of the Opposition at Canberra, had intervened.

In a long political and judicial career Evatt had made a number of unexpected and even imprudent gestures. To leave the Commonwealth parliament for the High Court was a fairly common step, but Evatt was the only man in federal history to move the other way; he left the High Court bench in 1940 to become a Labor member of the House of Representatives, and in 1960 he was to become the first former High Court judge appointed to a state court. During the Royal Commission into espionage which followed Vladimir Petrov's defection from the Russian Embassy at Canberra in 1954, Evatt the barrister had his leave to appear withdrawn and Evatt the politician delighted his enemies by announcing that after correspondence with Molotov he could assure parliament that a certain charge of Petrov's was false. To the people who formed the new Democratic Labor Party and fought elections against their old allies, nothing seemed more offensive about "Evatt Labor" than its leader. Now, after conferring on the telephone with O'Sullivan, the D.L.P. leader who was Stuart's counsel, Evatt sent a long telegram to the South Australian government.

The former High Court judge said that he was impressed with certain remarks by the High Court. "While the court refused to exercise its jurisdiction to give special leave to appeal from the Supreme Court of South Australia their openly declared anxiety about the circumstances is of supreme importance when the executive government concerned has to determine whether the death sentence should, in fact, be carried out, or whether it should be commuted to life imprisonment or some other sentence." Evatt cited the High Court's remarks on the irregularity of comment by Chamberlain about the unsworn statement and on his refusal to let the statement be read. He referred to the suggestion that Stuart could not have dictated the confession. The crime was dreadful, Evatt said. "This, however, makes it even more essential to see that the trial of an accused person is conducted with the greatest strictness, guaranteeing to the accused person all the rights that the law provides in a case where the penalty is capital punishment. The principle must be equally applied to our own Australian aborigines."

Evatt recommended more than commutation. "From a legal point of view the case is of great importance, and I submit it would be a just and proper thing if time were allowed for Stuart to test the High Court judgment before the Privy Council." O'Sullivan said later in the day that although Stuart wanted to appeal to the Privy Council, the expense would rule it out unless the government helped.

A statement quite as remarkable as Evatt's was printed alongside it in the *News*. The author was the secretary of the South Australian Police Association, Mr. L. B. Fenwick. The statement read:

> "We feel concerned at recent statements aimed at six reputable police officers. It has been suggested that Stuart was an illiterate aboriginal and his confession was couched in 'impeccable English'.[2] The facts are that Stuart was a resident of the Northern Territory and, according to law, is regarded as a white man. Stuart's convictions include supplying liquor to aborigines, consorting with a female aboriginal, being found within 300 chains of an aboriginal reserve. None of these offences can be committed by aborigines.

[2] The writer has been unable to find that anybody had used this phrase.

Stuart was also convicted of aggravated assault on a 10-year-old girl in Queensland. He admitted that on December 20 he lured an innocent child, happily playing on a deserted beach, into a cave 'to see the birdies', criminally assaulted her and, because he knew from personal experience in Queensland that to assault a child and allow her to live would result in her testifying against him, he calmly killed her with a rock in an attempt to escape the consequences of his deed.

"Stuart was ably and competently defended, yet it was not suggested until after his trial that his command of English was inadequate.

"It has now been established that some time ago he conducted his own defence at Darwin when he fluently cross-examined a number of witnesses in English and gave evidence on his own behalf, using some of the phrases contained in the confession which he made at Ceduna.

"Stuart had the right to enter the witness box and give evidence on his own behalf, yet he did not elect to do so.

"While we feel that statements following Stuart's sentencing have been actuated by the best of motives, we also feel that the public should be reminded of the real facts."

O'Sullivan described this statement as "false in almost every detail". His reply was printed by the *Advertiser* and the *News* on Saturday, July 4. The police record of Stuart's convictions, tendered at the trial and signed by Detective-Sergeant Paul Turner, O'Sullivan said, showed that he had been convicted seven times "for being an aborigine, did drink liquor"; on the night of the murder, in fact, he was arrested for this offence. "A survey of the penalties imposed on Stuart for all previous offences makes it obvious that none of them were particularly serious. In fact, with the exception of four charges of supplying liquor to aborigines, the longest term of imprisonment imposed was six months." At the trial neither Turner nor any other police witness suggested that Stuart had admitted being moved to kill by any memory of what had happened in Queensland. It *was* suggested at the trial, in cross-examination of the police, that Stuart was too illiterate to have dictated his alleged confession. "Furthermore, Stuart has never been involved in a court case at Darwin, nor has he ever fluently cross-examined a number of witnesses in English, either in Darwin or anywhere else, as alleged by the police." The assertion that Stuart had chosen not to go into the witness box was reprehensible. "A similar statement by the Crown Prosecutor during the trial was strongly criticised by the High Court. The fact is that Stuart's imperfect knowledge of English made it impossible to give evidence on his own behalf." The police statement, O'Sullivan said, "was carefully designed to be read as the disinterested opinion of police officers generally. What the public should know is that the association's president is

Detective-Sergeant Paul Turner, the senior of the 'six reputable police officers' who obtained the statement from Stuart."

Words almost as strong as O'Sullivan's came from a more unexpected source. Mr. J. L. Travers, Q.C., president of the Law Society of South Australia, said: "I was simply appalled to read a published statement attributed to the Police Association. If there were an appeal, as I see it, one possibility would be that a new trial would be ordered. It seems to me to entirely surpass the bounds of ordinary decency, to say nothing of the question of contempt of court, for the association to have made at this stage to every potential juryman a statement of the type which apparently the Police Association has seen fit to make."

Travers referred also to the possibility of an approach to the Privy Council. "To Mr. O'Sullivan, who has in obedience to our assignment fought the case through various courts, and without any fee at all, the community should feel extremely grateful. I have been made aware of the fact that the accused wishes to take the appeal further and that there appears to be a considerable body of public opinion to the same effect." There was nothing further that the Law Society could do. "We assign counsel who do their work without any fee, whereas in England in like circumstances a lawyer would be paid by the government 85 per cent of his ordinary fee. We are provided with no funds by the government either to pay lawyers in England to apply to the Privy Council for leave to appeal or to send anyone from South Australia to apply. . . . If the government agrees to provide funds for a further appeal to test the matter, the Law Society will gladly cooperate and consider the matter. If the government prefers to hang the man, that is entirely its concern." The Attorney-General was not available for comment on Travers' statement.

Suddenly the debate had caught fire. On a single day Evatt, the Police Association, O'Sullivan and Travers had all spoken out. In the long run the Police Association did even more than Evatt to throw the name of Stuart into the headlines and keep it there. The president of the Association helped to keep the headlines going over the weekend. On Saturday morning Detective-Sergeant Paul Turner said that the Police Association was concerned with the protection of its officers and not with the merits and demerits of the case or with red herrings. "Because I am one of the investigating officers," he added, "I do not feel in a position to comment further." He did so, however, later in the day. On Saturday evening Turner explained that the previous day's statement had been made before it was known that an appeal to the Privy Council was being suggested. "Copies of depositions have been received from the Northern Territory," he said, "of a case in which Stuart, conducting his own defence, cross-examined in English. I have also received a statement from the Alice Springs gaoler that Stuart, while an inmate, conducted English classes. All of Stuart's aborigine convictions, mentioned by Mr. O'Sullivan, were before 1953, when the Northern Territory law was altered giving all but full-blooded aborigines the rights of white men. This included Stuart. Mr. O'Sullivan's claim that Stuart was arrested on the night of the murder for being an aborigine found drinking liquor is false. Stuart was arrested that night charged with disorderly conduct. Stuart was sentenced twice in Queensland after he was convicted of aggravated assault on girls. In the Northern Territory he served six months after he was convicted of common assault against a female."

This statement and O'Sullivan's reply to it were the main news on the front page of the *Sunday Mail*, a joint product of the *Advertiser* and the *News*. "The two recent irresponsible and reckless outbursts of the officer who conducted the interrogation of Stuart," O'Sullivan now declared, "must cast grave doubts on the whole of his evidence against Stuart . . ." From the sworn evidence of two policemen at the trial, O'Sullivan quoted statements that Stuart had been arrested on the night of the murder for drinking and for nothing else. The claim that Stuart conducted English classes in gaol, he said, was fantastic. "It is amazing that the government is allowing its police officers to continue issuing these statements. One can be pardoned the suspicion that the government is determined to hang Stuart and is using the Police Association to do its propaganda work."

O'Sullivan said he had been denied access to any information about other cases in which it was alleged Stuart had been involved. "If the police are going to continue to bombard the public with allegations based on reports from other parts of Australia, they should at least be prepared to make them available to Stuart's counsel . . ." Turner's last outburst made it imperative, O'Sullivan said, that the government immediately set up a Royal Commission to enquire into the arrest and interrogation of Stuart. This was the first suggestion that a Royal Commission should investigate the Stuart case.

Turner spoke again, to the *Advertiser* on Sunday evening, offering evidence that Stuart's English was good, and speaking with emotion on behalf of himself and his subordinates. Stuart, he said, "can't read or write well—but that also applies to quite a few white Australians". He quoted a welfare officer of the Aborigines' Protection Board who visited Stuart in gaol and who said: "I am surprised to think that anyone could suggest that he couldn't understand a normal conversation in English." "What is suggested," said Turner, "is that we questioned a man in a language that he did not understand, typed out a confession that he could not have made because of his lack of knowledge of the language and got him to sign it—thereby convicting him of a murder of which he was innocent. That is a pretty unpleasant thing to say. It suggests that six officers got together to commit a crime worse than the one they were investigating."

Stuart's execution was due in less than 36 hours when his solicitors replied yet again. It was pointless, they said, engaging further in a newspaper controversy. The action of the police in launching it was without precedent. Their client's previous convictions had nothing to do with the question whether or not he should be hanged for murder. The police had shifted their ground in each successive statement. "As various allegations are refuted, they drop them and bring forward others to such an extent that it is difficult to know at any given point of time just what is being alleged against Stuart. A few days ago they referred to a trial in Darwin which apparently never took place. On Saturday they claimed that Stuart 'had conducted classes in English while in gaol at Alice Springs'. This was refuted. Yesterday Detective-Sergeant Turner made the grudging admission that Stuart 'cannot read or write well'. The fact is, of course, that Stuart cannot read or write at all, except to print his name in block capitals. If the government, in deciding whether or not to hang Stuart, is to be influenced by police allegations of this nature, it should in all fairness give Stuart's counsel an opportunity to consider the precise details of the allegations and to reply to them."

Sir Thomas Playford and his ministers had not yet sat as Executive Council to consider Stuart's petition for commutation. They were to meet some time on Monday. That morning the *Advertiser* devoted the whole of its correspondence columns to letters about Stuart. Three writers said that the sentence of death should be carried out, and nine said that it should not.

The petition circulated by the Howard League was delivered on Monday morning to the Attorney-General with several thousands of signatures attached. News of another petition, from Ceduna, reached the government before the Executive Council met. It was organised by Mr. P. S. Morrison, a man well known and respected in the town. He was the Shell agent and the Ford dealer, the travel agent and the exhibitor of films in the Memorial Hall. He was about to decline nomination for chairmanship of the Murat Bay District Council after holding the office for thirteen years. He got up the petition, he explained, to show how residents of the district were incensed "that people living away from the scene were interfering in the matter". It was offered for signatures on Saturday morning in his general store, in the afternoon at a football match attended by people from many miles around, and at his picture show in the evening. "Only one person approached refused to sign," said Morrison. "We were by no means unanimous about that document," one resident said later. "Thinking people would not sign it," remarked another. Many people, including active churchgoers, never saw it. None of the local clergymen was shown the petition or told that it was going around. It was posted on Sunday night, with 334 signatures.

Morrison telegrammed the text on Monday morning so that it would reach Adelaide in time for the meeting of the Executive Council. It read: "The petition of the people of Ceduna, Thevenard and surrounding districts sheweth that it is the unanimous desire that the course of the law should be allowed to prevail and proceed according to the judgment of the courts of this great Commonwealth of ours insofar as the death sentence has been passed on Rupert Max Stuart . . ."

The Executive Council met at 12.30 p.m. to consider the petition from Stuart. The meeting lasted twenty minutes, and produced this statement: "The prisoner is left for execution in the due course of the law. No recommendation is made for pardon or reprieve."

A warder gave Stuart a cigarette as he broke the news. There were preparations for the ceremony to be performed at 8 a.m. next day. That ceremony could not be postponed unless Stuart became the first convicted person in the history of South Australia to appeal to the Privy Council.

Dixon was asked to keep Stuart calm so that there would be no trouble.

"Are you afraid to die?" the priest asked.

Stuart replied that he would not be afraid if Dixon stayed with him through the night.

After a silence, Dixon asked Stuart what he was thinking. There was no answer. Dixon asked again.

"Some bloke lucky," said Stuart.

"What do you mean?"

"Bloke who done this."

Dixon was still at the gaol when news came that Mr. Justice Reed had granted a respite of fourteen days. During the afternoon Stuart's solicitors had decided to take the case to the Judicial Committee of the Privy Council.

6

A VISIT TO FUNLAND

O'Sullivan's resort to London was going to be expensive. The journey to make the application to appeal would require £1,000 or so; and if the application were allowed, a similar sum would be needed, months later, for the appeal itself. No word came from anybody in cabinet about the suggestion by the president of the Law Society that the government might help. Several offers of money reached the lawyers before they decided to approach the Privy Council, and informal fund-raising went on throughout July, especially among the people who had met at Duguid's house. The Law Society opened a trust account to which money for O'Sullivan's expenses could be sent. The *Sydney Morning Herald* published on July 11 a letter from the Rev. Frank Coaldrake, chairman of the Australian Board of Missions, saying that some readers would surely feel moved to contribute. By the end of the month just on £1,000 was in hand, most of it in small sums.

By no means everybody who gave money for the application believed that it had any chance of succeeding. Some saw it frankly as a means of keeping Stuart alive while new efforts were made to have the doubts of Dixon and Strehlow explored. A Sunday paper in Sydney, the *Sun-Herald*, reported prominently on July 12 a statement by Strehlow that a re-trial was necessary and that he was prepared to give evidence on Stuart's behalf. Next weekend, on July 18, the fortnightly review *Nation*, in Sydney, printed a survey of the controversy by the present writer, and in particular of the intervention by the Police Association. This account ended with a reference to the cases of Timothy Evans, hanged in England for a crime to which another man later confessed, and of Frederick McDermott, who was found guilty in 1947, in New South Wales, of a murder committed in 1936, and who was released in 1952 on the strength of new evidence.

In the latter case a reporter on the *Daily Telegraph* in Sydney, Mr. T. H. Farrell, found in 1951 that wheel-tracks near the scene of the crime could not have been made by the car at McDermott's disposal. A Royal Commission appointed at once by the New South Wales government heard this evidence, and heard the policeman who had worked on the case discomfited by one of the best cross-examiners at the Sydney bar, Mr. J. W. Shand. The Commissioner reported that McDermott's trial had clearly miscarried, and he was released. In 1959 Farrell was a senior reporter on the *Sydney Morning Herald*. He now decided that the Stuart affair was worth investigating, and was sent to Adelaide on Sunday, July 19.

In the office of the *News*, where Farrell had once been a copy-boy and cadet reporter, he was told on July 20 that only a few busy-bodies were troubled about Stuart's conviction. He called on Dixon at the presbytery in Hindmarsh. That evening the priest went to a meeting in the Friends' Centre in North Adelaide. The meeting was attended by a number of people who had met at Duguid's, and by others who had become interested in the case since then.

All agreed with Dixon that fresh evidence should be sought, and that the members of the fun-fair, wherever they were now, seemed the people most likely to know about Stuart's movements on the day of the murder. After the meeting Dixon met Farrell by accident in a coffee lounge. Farrell asked the priest if he would make a public statement. So far his name had not appeared in print: by inclination as well as by order of his superiors, Dixon was avoiding publicity. A lifetime in the seminary and in outback missions had not prepared him for the complexities of secular controversy. How to have the case of a convicted murderer re-opened was a problem very different from how to build a church without mortar or skilled labour; but to a man of Dixon's temperament neither problem seemed insoluble. He would have liked advice from the solicitors about whether to talk for publication, but O'Sullivan had left for London that day and his partner Miss Devaney was at an inquest fifty miles out of town. He agreed to talk.

Next morning the *Sydney Morning Herald* carried some five hundred words on its front page and another eight hundred inside, headed: "CONFLICT ON HANGING IN SOUTH AUSTRALIA. From a Special Reporter." The story ended with this "considered statement" by Dixon:

> "For the past eight weeks I have been in constant and intimate contact with Stuart, conversing with him in the Arunta language and in his simple conversational pidgin or Territorian English that was used at Alice Springs and at the Santa Teresa Mission near Alice Springs.
>
> "At no time have I been able to say that Stuart is the man who committed the crime. On the contrary my personal conviction is that he is not the man.
>
> "We have conversed in Arunta and in his own peculiar style of English, and on all occasions he has consistently and constantly denied all connection with the actual deed.
>
> "Knowing his tongue and his English, I can confidently say that the confession upon which we are assured legally he has been condemned could not have been dictated by him in the form it was presented. My personal conviction has only been strengthened by my thorough knowledge of the evidence advanced.

"I have been amazed at the absence of any official protection to assist either Stuart or his counsel, being used to conditions in the Northern Territory and Queensland, where all natives, either full blood or half-castes, receive informed protection on being charged.

"Stuart had been only a few days in South Australia when arrested and had no friends except those in the travelling show who left Ceduna a day and a half before his arrest. That show I believe is still travelling somewhere in Australia and in it I believe there are people who can supply Stuart with evidence that is badly needed.

"I cannot rest until I am certain that Stuart is the man who committed the crime. I exhort the authorities to delay his execution at least until that has been proved beyond all possible doubt."

Next day Melbourne's evening paper, the *Herald*, printed a rearranged version of Farrell's story across most of its second page. The headline was: "Could 'illiterate' have made vital statement? 'SPARE THIS MAN,' PRIEST PLEADS." In Adelaide that afternoon the *News* printed Dixon's statement in its late editions, under the heading: "IMPASSIONED PLEA FOR STUART. Priest's doubts." The Melbourne *Herald* followed up the controversy in its next issue on Thursday, July 23. Detective-Sergeant Paul Turner, it reported, said that affidavits would be placed before the Privy Council in London to show that Stuart was convicted for sexual assault on a girl in Queensland and conducted his own defence fluently in Darwin. The *Herald* went on: "Commenting on the statement made yesterday by the Rev. Father Thomas Dixon . . . that people in a travelling show could supply Stuart with badly needed evidence, Turner said; 'We interviewed people in this travelling circus and rodeo at Whyalla on December 22 last year. There was nothing in his favour in what they told us.' " On the following Monday, a day before the Privy Council hearing, Miss Devaney filed in Adelaide a motion for leave to issue a writ of attachment for contempt of court against Turner, on the ground that his statement published in the Melbourne *Herald* and sold in Adelaide was calculated to prejudice Stuart in the event of a new trial. Nearly three months later, Turner was to say that the *Herald* report was false.

Whether Dixon liked it or not he now had publicity in plenty. His photograph was printed all over Australia. In Sydney, films of Farrell interviewing both Dixon and Professor Norval Morris were shown on television. Morris said that the conviction depended too much on the confession and that many people had doubts about Stuart's guilt; Dixon appealed to viewers to help him find the travelling show. The Melbourne *Herald* sent its columnist Mr. E. W. Tipping over to Adelaide to write about the case. The one *comment* offered by a newspaper at this stage was hostile. It appeared in the Adelaide edition of *Truth*, a weekly newspaper which could strike English migrants as a sort of low-brow *News-of-the-World*, reporting such things as pyjama parties, royal romances, and the more stirring of the week's court cases. "STOP DEATH-CELL WRANGLING!" it exhorted; the whole thing was "unseemly".

Later in the week of Farrell's story it was reported that Dixon himself contemplated going in search of the fun-fair. It was after an executive of a Brisbane newspaper told him that the show was now in Queensland that Dixon first sought permission to go. His house superior in Adelaide rang the provincial superior in Sydney, who declined to give permission. Dixon asked if he himself could ring the provincial superior—the head of the Sacred Heart clergy in Australia. The house superior let him ring. After about ten minutes it was agreed that Dixon could go if the Archbishop of Adelaide consented. The Archbishop said it was a matter for the house superior, who then gave his permission. Dixon was assuming that the paper in Brisbane would pay his fares. When he rang Brisbane about midday on Friday, July 24, to say he was ready to leave, it was explained that the paper had not intended to meet the cost of his journey. An hour later he met for the first time the editor of the Adelaide *News*.

* * *

Rohan Deakin Rivett had been editor-in-chief of News Ltd. since 1951 after university education at Melbourne and Oxford, experience as a prisoner-of-war in Java, Burma and Siam, and newspaper work in Melbourne, London and China. About his wartime experience he wrote a moving and harrowing book, *Behind Bamboo*, which sold more than 100,000 copies. He was born into a tradition of imaginative liberalism. One grandfather was Alfred Deakin, the only prime minister of Australia whom cautious historians are tempted to call a great man. The other grandfather was one of a very few Protestant clergymen who, refusing to identify religion and patriotism, opposed military conscription for overseas service in World War I. His father, Sir David Rivett, a Fellow of the Royal Society, was for some years at the head of Australia's most popular government agency, the Council for Scientific and Industrial Research, and resigned after having opposed the conscription of scientific minds into Cold War service. In a country where few journalists are university graduates and where newspapers tend to have no coherent policy other than opposition to Labor, disapproval of taxation, and a conviction that it is wicked to pull down trees, Rivett was an unusual editor. Of all Australian papers, the *News* was the strongest critic of the Menzies government and the staunchest advocate of a friendly response towards Asian nationalism. Listeners to Rivett's voice on the radio, as well as readers of *News* editorials, were familiar with his hostility to the White Australia policy. On Cyprus the paper printed the disturbing dispatches of James Cameron to the London *News Chronicle* (which of all English papers was perhaps the closest in spirit to the *News*). The paper vehemently opposed the British and French landings in Egypt, and

Rivett wrote a news commentary for the Australian Broadcasting Commission which he was not allowed to broadcast (though when this fact became public the A.B.C. let him speak freely a few days later). When the editor of the *New Statesman* visited Australia in 1958, the *News* seemed to him "the one genuinely liberal daily in the continent". In stature and looks Rivett seemed to some people rather like Billy Graham. The resemblance was more than physical. Though their messages differed, each was a man of abnormal energy using the means of mass communications as instruments of persuasion. Rivett's sermons were no less fervent for being secular.

As editor Rivett travelled extensively overseas. When in London from time to time he spoke on the B.B.C. He appeared to have a degree of editorial freedom not common in Australia or anywhere else. In a *News* of, say, 52 tabloid pages, many bore no mark of the editor's mind; eight might be filled with sporting news and three with gossip for women, while on others a thin scrape of news from agencies was sandwiched between advertisements. The editorial personality of the paper was thus diluted to entertain readers and enrich shareholders; but not, as in many papers, to express views held by the proprietor rather than the editor. When Rivett came to the *News* it was part of the mighty newspaper empire built by a working journalist, Sir Keith Murdoch, and ruled from the grey palace of his *Herald* in Melbourne. Most of the empire held together after Murdoch's death in 1952, but the *News* passed as a separate kingdom to his son, Rupert, who was at the time an undergraduate at Oxford. Happily for Rivett, the new ruler shared his own radical liberal outlook. In a debate at Australia's most expensive school, Geelong Grammar, he had once put the case for socialism (against the son of the *Sydney Morning Herald's* proprietor), and at Oxford he was active in the Labour Club. With the blessing of the younger Murdoch, Rivett often rebuked the anti-Labor state government of Sir Thomas Playford for retaining power by an electoral system which gave two out of every three seats in the House of Assembly to the minority of voters who lived in country districts.

Rivett did not belong to the Adelaide Club—a plain three-storeyed building opposite Government House in North Terrace which could have been designed by one of the less ostentatious bankers in fifteenth-century Florence, and which had as members, according to Professor L. F. Crisp in *The Parliamentary Government of the Commonwealth of Australia*, "the key financial, commercial and landed men" of the state. In Crisp's view these men met as an unofficial, extra-parliamentary, anti-Labor caucus. Some members were grandsons, and a few even great-grandsons, of members, their families having come out very early, made good, and settled down to become an informal bourgeois aristocracy. Some representatives of the "old families" (as they were called) belonged also to the Pioneers' Association, a body which deplored the custom of celebrating January 26—the day in

1788 when convicts landed in New South Wales—as Australia Day. Mr. A. P. Rowe, an Englishman who spent ten years as vice-chancellor of the University of Adelaide, found in the city a "small section of the community which claimed leadership in local society, often for no other reason than the possession of money, or because their grandfathers, by the act of coming to Australia, created a spirit of ancestor worship worthy of China".

Rivett had an entertaining time in 1957, at the expense of "old families", when Dr. Douglas Pike, a university historian, published his *Paradise of Dissent: South Australia, 1829-1857.* On the front page of the *News* appeared a notice saying: "He Blasts Pretensions of our 'Founding Families'. S.A. Writer's Book Sensation. . . . In the *News* to-morrow will be published an exciting review of the most revealing, yet carefully documented, book . . . This will startle those who accept the beliefs carefully fostered by a handful of well-known Adelaide families. It sets down in gay, gamey and sometimes garish details the documented facts about S.A.'s foundation. MAKE SURE OF THE NEWS TOMORROW." Next day the posters said:

BOOK BLASTS
S.A. PIONEERS

The reviewer, Rivett himself, quoted the author's conclusion that the pioneers were often greedy and quarrelsome fellows overrated by pious antiquarians. Any reader of the *News* who had put down his fourpence in the hope or fear of learning that this family was founded by accident, or the fortune of that one built on embezzlement, was sent away with nothing more juicy than the words "red-blooded", "buccaneering", "intrigues", and—just once—"lusts". But no book costing seventy shillings had ever sold as briskly in Adelaide as *Paradise of Dissent* did for one day. In light and serious matters the *News* was not always respectful towards people who enjoyed power or prestige.

* * *

Rivett and Dixon met for lunch in the university by invitation of the Rev. Frank Borland, who had been wanting to bring the two men together since he first heard Dixon at Duguid's house. During the afternoon Rivett told Dixon the *News* would pay his fare to Queensland. An editorial five days later explained Rivett's decision.

> "On Friday the *News* talked with Father Dixon for most of three hours. Father Dixon established two things. First, that he, an utterly sincere man, unmoved that the real criminal should hang for this offence, was certain after seven or eight weeks of communication with Stuart in Stuart's cell that Rupert Max Stuart was not that man. Secondly that physical and psychological evidence pointed strongly to Stuart's innocence.

"Father Dixon said he wanted a chance to search Queensland to find people who might afford him the proofs of Stuart's innocence. The *News* thought it was a poor thing that a man should hang in the South Australia of 1959 just because no one would put up a few hundred pounds to investigate the possibility of his being innocent."

The *News* also thought, no doubt, that it was on to a good story. Dixon had agreed that he would be accompanied by a reporter from the paper who would have first access to any news.

Travelling as "Mr. Jones" and accompanied by the *News* police roundsman, Mr. Jack Clark, Dixon left Adelaide airport on Saturday, July 25. On Sunday night they reached Cairns, a thousand miles north of Brisbane (and in Queensland terms not far from Palm Island, Dixon's first station). Clark's first report appeared on Monday, July 27, at the top of the front page:

> "We make an odd pair—the Roman Catholic priest, Father Dixon, and the Protestant reporter—jet-propelled on a search for truth. We are not sure where we are going. We don't know what we will find when we get there. We have in common a zeal for justice in the matter of Rupert Max Stuart. The priest is deeply troubled with doubt that Stuart is guilty . . . He is chasing evidence he believes may have eluded the authorities so far. I, with full confidence in the police force, with which I have been privileged to work for so long and particularly the officers who handled the case, have been assigned a watching brief by my office."

On Monday morning Dixon set off by car with Clark and Mr. Kevin Kehoe, a justice of the peace from Cairns, to look for Gieseman and his show. In Brisbane he had been told that it might be at Cairns. In Cairns he learned that Gieseman had left heading south. Late on Monday morning the three men found him at the showground in Atherton.

Dixon said he had come from Stuart in Adelaide. At first Gieseman said: "I'm afraid, Father, I can't help you." (Dixon said later that a journalist from a Queensland paper had rung Gieseman already to ask if he would be willing to help the priest.) Dixon asked after people whose names he had heard from Stuart. Betty Gadd and Johnny Woods, it appeared, had left the show; Billy McNeish and Allan Moir were travelling on their own with another section of the outfit. Dixon asked if they could talk somewhere. Certainly, said Gieseman, and led the way to his caravan while Clark and Kehoe waited in the car. Here Dixon met Mrs. Gieseman. He told Gieseman in her presence that Stuart, convicted on the strength of a confession, seemed to know nothing at all about the murder. "I mentioned to him," Dixon recalled later, "how Stuart had only been one day in South Australia . . . there was nobody else who seemed to know him or stand up for him in any way, and I said: 'You people knew him and saw him some time during that time. I was wondering what times you saw him because he told me that you had seen him.' " It was a profound surprise to the priest, he said later, when Gieseman replied casually: "The only time we saw him was from two to four." "Are you sure?" he asked. Gieseman said he was sure. Would he sign an affidavit saying so? He would. Dixon asked him not to speak to any reporters, joined Clark and Kehoe in the car, and set off for the Catholic presbytery. They drove in silence as Dixon tried to remember exactly what had been said at the trial about the times within which the child must have been murdered. After a while he said: "I think I've cracked it. They are prepared to give me affidavits covering the times from two till four." "Are you sure they are talking about Saturday?" asked Clark. Had he misunderstood? "Perhaps they are talking about Friday," Dixon said. They drove straight back to the showground and Dixon went into the caravan. "Saturday, of course," said Gieseman.

This time the priest interviewed Betty Hopes as well as the Giesemans. He asked them all to remember as much as they could of events in Ceduna and to tell only the truth. In the afternoon Gieseman and his wife and Betty Hopes came to the presbytery to make their statements. Mrs. Gieseman and Miss Hopes waited on a veranda while, in a hot and stuffy room, Gieseman dictated, Clark typed slowly, Kehoe advised on the formalities, and Dixon insisted that only the truth should go down. Then each of the women in turn made a statement. The three statutory declarations were carried back to Cairns in Dixon's pocket and that night they were posted to Miss Devaney in Adelaide.

"I, Norman George Gieseman," the first of them began, "fun fair proprietor, of Burpengarry in the State of Queensland, do solemnly and sincerely declare and say as follows:—

"The man, Rupert Max Stuart, is well known to me. I gave him a lift from Hall's Creek to Ceduna and in return he sometimes helped in erecting and working a stall.

"We landed in Ceduna late on Friday, 19th December 1958, and erected the carnival on parklands there.

"About 10 a.m. on Saturday, 20th December, Stuart went out and came home late for lunch and had been drinking. Normally lunch time was about 12.30 p.m. but Stuart did not arrive back until between 1.30 and 2 p.m. The recognised peak carnival period is between 2 p.m. and 4 p.m.

"I told Stuart he might find some lunch in the camp if he was lucky and as we were just opening for the afternoon I told him that if he wanted to earn a few shillings, there was a stall for him to work. He took about £4 on the stall, of which his share would be 8/-.

"He was definitely at the stall after he had lunch until about 4 p.m. when people started to thin out and he said he was going up the street. I saw him leave at about 4 p.m. with Allen Muir,[1] who had been working getting things ready at the fair all day. Later, Allen Muir landed home pretty drunk about 11 p.m. and Max came in the next morning.

"I asked him where he had been and he said in gaol all night and was staying in Ceduna as on the Saturday morning he had got himself a job at the Wheat Board.

"My carnival left Ceduna about 9 a.m. on Sunday."

At Whyalla, Gieseman went on, he first heard of the murder and was asked by Detective Phin whether he knew anything about it. He replied that he did not, and that "none of the lads on the carnival had left it on the Saturday at all except Max who had left in the morning and then returned for lunch and went out again with Allen at 4 p.m. Detective Phin then talked to Allen. After Detective Phin talked to me I don't know what happened one way or the other."

Mrs. Gieseman declared that Stuart came back to the caravan about 1.45 p.m. "We had just finished dinner and the girls had just finished washing up and wiping the table. I told him he should be on time for meals and he said he was sorry." She told Betty Hopes to give him some bread and butter and vegetables, which he ate. He worked on a stall and took £4 before he left the park with Moir between 4 p.m. and 4.30 p.m. "On Saturday night I had searched for both Max and Allen as we wanted to pull down the show, but could not find them around town and I went along to the pictures and put an advert on the screen, but this did not bring them."

Betty Hopes declared: "I worked on the same stall as Max Stuart where he looked after the darts and I looked after the roll-em-downs at Ceduna on Saturday . . . We worked together in the stall from about 2 p.m. to 4 p.m. Max did not leave the stall all the time and he was in full view of me."

Nothing about these statements was to be made public until they reached the lawyers in Adelaide. Clark's story in the *News* on Tuesday mentioned the visit to the Giesemans and Miss Hopes but not what they had said. "Travel-worn, grim, but far from beaten," Clark wrote from Cairns, "Father Dixon returned here last night from another leg of his long journey for evidence to save Rupert Max Stuart from the gallows . . . Father Dixon is on the trail again today—destination unknown." He was now in search of young Allan Moir, who was with the other part of the show somewhere in Queensland.

* * *

Dixon's journey was being logged on the front pages of newspapers in every state. Everybody knew about it, except people who depended for news on the Adelaide *Advertiser,* in which the priest's name did

[1] Some people spelled and pronounced the lad's name this way; others made it MOIR. Spelling of his forename also varied.

not appear until after the Privy Council hearing. Until late July the *Advertiser* and the *News* had given the case fairly similar treatment. The approaches now diverged widely. When one of Adelaide's two papers had identified itself with Dixon's quest it was not to be expected, perhaps, that the other should display equal enthusiasm for it. As a song in an undergraduate revue later in the year put it:

> Nothing must go in the *'Tiser*,
> That's already been in the *News*.

For the *Advertiser*, in any case, it would have been out of character to encourage an unofficial investigation on behalf of a duly convicted person. A new building which was rising to house the *Advertiser* in 1959 was described in the paper as "modern, but dignified". The makers of the *Advertiser* itself would have been happy to hear it characterised in those words.

For more than a hundred years its broadsheet pages had appeared every morning except Sundays, and for nearly thirty years there had been no morning competitor. Most readers could remember when the front page was still covered with classified advertisements. Until 1929 it was owned by South Australians. Then it was sold to a new company in which Sir Keith Murdoch's Herald and Weekly Times Ltd., of Melbourne, had a large holding. Men prominent in Adelaide affairs still sat on its board. Solid conservative political opinion was expressed in its editorials. The cultural life of Adelaide was enriched here and there by its essays in goodwill; the *Advertiser* sound shell in Elder Park housed each year part of the *Advertiser* open-air exhibition, and from an *Advertiser* office was being planned, throughout 1959, Australia's first major festival of arts. It was not a paper that would ever launch a crusade, for to do so would suggest undue dissatisfaction with the way things were. The *Advertiser* was here representing a feeling widespread in the detached brick villas of Adelaide.

The *Advertiser* and the *News* had, nevertheless, a good deal in common, inevitably so when each was trying to sell itself to the whole of a single community (of whom roughly 180,000 bought the morning paper and 120,000 the evening one). The sports sections were broadly similar. Each printed columns about the middle-classes at weddings and parties. Each had a range of style and subject which by English standards was unusually wide: not far from a piece of close analysis by Mr. Walter Lippmann (in the *News*) or Mr. Denis Warner (in the *Advertiser*), either paper might print the latest rumour about Princess Margaret invented by the London *Daily Sketch*. In policy, too, there were resemblances which to a visitor from Moscow or Peking would seem more striking than the differences; though such a reader might notice that the *News* never said, as the *Advertiser* did, that "the only people who endanger peace are the aggressive Communists."

To South Australian eyes, however, the differences of taste and opinion between the broadsheet *Advertiser* and the tabloid *News* were plain. In the morning, the posters outside newsagents were printed in a thin black type; in the evening, they were thick and red. The *Advertiser* did not deplore the state's electoral system, and had no misgivings about the anti-Labor government which the system kept in power. It admired Mr. Menzies a good deal more than the *News* did, and the foreign policy of Mr. Nehru rather less. While the *News* was denouncing the landings in Egypt the *Advertiser* was expressing unwavering support for the Anglo-French enterprise, which it described at the time as an intervention between Arab and Jew but in retrospect as an "attempt to nip Nasserism in the bud". In the case of Professor S. S. Orr, dismissed from the chair of philosophy at Hobart, the *News* wanted a further enquiry and the *Advertiser* saw most of his supporters as self-deluded. On the death of Marie Stopes the *News* had an editorial tribute and the *Advertiser* did not. Some admirers of the morning paper might have defended this omission in words similar to those used by a member of Adelaide "society" (to Mr. A. P. Rowe) after a controversial lecture by Julian Huxley: "It is all right for him to say these things, but not in Adelaide." After Mr. J. B. Priestley had grumbled his way through Australia in 1959, the *News* wrote: "It is good for people to have their prejudices jolted. Those who live in isolated settlements, where the intercourse of ideas is lacking, are the most backward and ignorant. The stimulation of criticism is good mental medicine." South Australians would have been startled to read those words at breakfast.

* * *

The Judicial Committee of the Privy Council was to hear O'Sullivan on July 28. Stuart's respite—the fifth—was extended to August 4. If Australian politicians in 1900 had been a little more aggressive towards the motherland, the English judges could not have considered Stuart's petition at all; for some framers of the federal constitution wanted to allow no right of appeal to a court outside Australia. The Labor Party in the federal parliament was pledged to abolish the right of appeal to London, though Labor governments never got around to doing so. In the week of Stuart's approach to the Privy Council, Labor's deputy leader, Mr. Arthur Calwell, described the provision as "a major affront to Australian nationalism". Critics like Calwell had in mind civil and especially constitutional cases; for an appeal in a criminal matter was very rare. Yet on July 28 the Privy Council considered *two* petitions against decisions of the High Court of Australia in criminal cases, both of them from South Australia.

The subjects, both convicted of murder, were locked in adjoining cells at Adelaide Gaol. The second man was John Whelan Brown, who shot and killed his employer in November 1958. A jury rejected his plea of insanity, and Mr. Justice Abbott sentenced him to be hanged. The South Australian Full Court dismissed an appeal. The

High Court unanimously held that the judge had misdirected the jury and ordered a new trial. The crown solicitor, Mr. R. R. St. C. Chamberlain, Q.C., took the view that the High Court was mistaken, and was supported in his opinion by a retired judge of the Supreme Court. The Chief Justice, Sir Mellis Napier, sent a memorandum to the premier pointing out "the grave embarrassment to which the judges of the State Court are likely to be subjected . . . if appeals to the High Court in serious cases are to become common form and if the High Court acts on the lines that it has acted on in this case". The government sought leave to appeal to the Privy Council against the High Court's judgment. Professor Norval Morris remarked that in England, when the Crown appeals to the House of Lords in the case of a man charged with murder, it is announced that he will not be executed whatever the result; if, therefore, the South Australian government were interested in a point of law and not a man's life, Morris said, it should declare its intention not to hang Brown. To this suggestion the government made no reply.

A few days later Chamberlain flew to London with the task of persuading the Judicial Committee of the Privy Council that the High Court was right about Stuart but wrong about Brown. Among lawyers in Adelaide the latter case held the more professional interest. The Brown case, especially in the light of Sir Mellis Napier's comment, was widely regarded as a trial of strength between the South Australian and federal judges. In Stuart's case there had been differences merely of tone. But to the popular press in London, Stuart, as the first aboriginal petitioner to come from Australia, was more newsworthy than Brown. "The highest court in the British Commonwealth," wrote one paper, "will decide whether a Stone Age man 12,000 miles away on the other side of the world shall be given another chance to prove his innocence."

Their lordships were deciding only whether to grant leave to appeal; if they agreed to hear the appeal, it would be considered at a later date. It was very rare indeed for such leave to be granted. Just before O'Sullivan was due at Whitehall, a cable and a telephone call from Adelaide told him what the Giesemans and Miss Hopes had said. On Tuesday morning, July 28, he spoke for nearly two hours to the five Lords of Appeal. For the most part his argument was similar to the one he had put before the High Court in Melbourne. When he explained that for fifty years it had been the practice in South Australia to let a person make a statement prepared by his lawyers, Lord Tucker said that possibly as a result of this case the practice would end. Viscount Simonds said that the course proposed by the trial judge for getting Stuart's statement to the jury, was "most merciful", and that O'Sullivan's complaint on the matter was "wholly unjustified". Lord Tucker said that if Stuart's language was as O'Sullivan described, "it would have assisted him greatly . . . that the jury should have been able to hear his faltering effort to describe his movements and judge therefrom as to the value of any statement made to the police." "Had I prompted him phrase by phrase," replied O'Sullivan, "the jury would have heard no more than a parrot-like repetition . . ." O'Sullivan added that in the event of a re-trial, Stuart would give evidence in the Arunta language through an interpreter. "If he was able to convey to you what his defence was," asked Lord Tucker, "why could not he convey it to the court?"

O'Sullivan said that he had conducted long interviews with Stuart in very simple English, "disregarding answers to questions that made it obvious that the questions had not been understood, stopping him from long irrelevant unintelligible statements . . . ascertaining . . . what had happened and where the girl had been killed and all the geography and times and relevant dates from other sources and filling them in by asking him questions, and that occurred over a period of months." To a remark of O'Sullivan's about the methods of the police, Viscount Simonds said that he was not entitled to put before the Committee suggestions about the police contrary to what had been accepted by the jury and the Australian courts. When he referred to the conduct of the Police Association, Viscount Simonds observed that statements made now could not possibly have influenced the judgment of the High Court or of the Supreme Court. O'Sullivan said that the statements from members of the travelling show would appear to establish that, at highly relevant times, Stuart was in their company and that it was highly improbable that he could have committed the crime. Viscount Simonds asked why this evidence was not obtained before. It was a problem of distance, O'Sullivan replied, which must be somewhat difficult to understand in England. The show had moved two or three thousand miles since Stuart's arrest; and no money had been available for finding them. He asked for an adjournment of the hearing so that the fresh evidence could be examined. Viscount Simonds pointed out that O'Sullivan had come prepared to argue on material that was before the High Court. He had better proceed on that; anything else was a matter for the Executive Council.

When O'Sullivan had finished Viscount Simonds congratulated him on having put the case very fully and clearly. Without calling on Chamberlain, who was present, to speak for the South Australian Attorney-General, the judges cleared the chamber, consulted privately, and after a few minutes recalled O'Sullivan to tell him that the petition would be refused. Viscount Simonds said that he and his brothers saw no ground upon which, in accordance with the practice long established in regard to criminal appeals, they would be justified in interfering with the judgment of the High Court. "Counsel for the petitioner," he went on, "has urged that the hearing of this petition should be adjourned in order that certain further matters which have recently come to his notice may be examined; but it is clear that these matters could not affect their Lordships' decision . . . however relevant they may now be for consideration by the executive authority in

South Australia." "I still have not given up hope," O'Sullivan said to a reporter. "Viscount Simonds gave a pretty clear hint that there is a case for the South Australian Executive Council studying new evidence. . . . We could not gain another trial; but Parliament could set up a Commission as was done in New South Wales in the McDermott case, to look into the whole of the evidence."

The Privy Council decision was known in Australia late on Tuesday night and was the main story next morning in all the newspapers. They also carried news that the judges in London had granted the South Australian government leave to appeal in the case of John Whelan Brown, on the ground that it was a quite exceptional case raising a question of far-reaching importance (relating to the defence of insanity) not only to South Australia but to other states in Australia.

* * *

A warder informed Stuart on Wednesday morning that the last judicial resort had failed. On Wednesday afternoon Miss Devaney told him about the statements secured by Dixon, and got him to write his signature on another petition to the authorities, renewing the request for commutation on the ground of the new evidence. The statutory declarations posted by Dixon in Cairns on Monday night had reached the office of O'Sullivan and Devaney on Wednesday morning. Miss Devaney at once sought an interview with the Premier, Sir Thomas Playford; the Attorney-General, Mr. Colin Rowe, was ill, and the Premier had taken over the portfolio. She was asked instead to submit the documents to the Assistant Crown Solicitor, Mr. J. R. Kearnan. In a letter accompanying Stuart's petition, Miss Devaney wrote: "We respectfully suggest that the Attorney-General should have the matters raised in the statements investigated without delay. Prima facie they are of vital importance, covering as they do the time which the Crown Solicitor in his own address to the jury suggested was the time that the crime must have taken place." A stay of one month was suggested to enable the appropriate authorities to test the authenticity of the declarations.

During Wednesday a number of appeals reached the Playford government from outside the state. Unionists in Melbourne, Sydney and Canberra sent telegrams urging a stay of execution for further investigation. More than five hundred students in Sydney called for a general meeting to consider asking the Queen to intervene. The Aboriginal-Australian Fellowship in Sydney drew up a petition for a full investigation and got signatures from professors, an Anglican bishop, representatives of twenty-one unions, and a number of other people.

Within South Australia 15,000 copies were distributed of a pamphlet called: *Why not Hang Rupert Stuart? Some Questions about a Murder*. The pamphlet was prepared by a number of the people who had met at the Friends' Centre on July 20, and who invited the present writer to help draft it. The authors said that the case had disturbed "a large and growing number of citizens, Protestant and Catholic, Labor voters and Liberal, lawyers and laymen, opponents of capital punishment and defenders of it—people who share a concern for justice, but who often differ widely about how it is best achieved. . . . It would be inhuman not to be appalled by the crime, and not to have the utmost sympathy for the child's family. But many people think it has not been shown beyond doubt that it was Stuart who killed the girl." Grounds for doubting his guilt were suggested. The intervention of the Police Association was criticised. To the assertion by police that Stuart had conducted his own defence fluently in Darwin, the pamphlet replied that he had never been tried in Darwin, and that once, in Alice Springs, he recited a statement in court after all-night briefing by a half-caste. On another matter mentioned by the police, a conviction for aggravated assault against a child in Queensland, the pamphlet said: " 'aggravated assault' . . . does not necessarily involve physical violence . . . Stuart did not touch the girl." The pamphlet ended with references to Dixon's plea for a delay of execution and Viscount Simonds' comment on the evidence from Queensland.

On Wednesday and Thursday copies of the pamphlet were posted to members of parliament and distributed by scores of people in city streets, in suburban letter boxes and at factory gates. A number were sent to Ceduna; according to a newspaper report they were burned. An almost complete version reached a million purchasers of the *News* in Adelaide and the *Herald* and *Sun* in Melbourne.

The *News* on Wednesday had nearly four pages on Stuart. A story from Clark in Cairns appeared on the front page under the heading: "PRIEST: 'STUART HAS PERFECT ALIBI'. Murder case bombshell." Next to this report was a large photograph of Stuart with the caption: "Will he die?" Also on the front page (instead of the normal inside page) was an editorial headed: "DELAY THIS HANGING", which quoted from Viscount Simonds and from the High Court's judgment, declared that the *News* had no sympathy with the Howard League and no brief for keeping alive whoever committed the dastardly crime at Thevenard, and demanded a new investigation into whether Stuart was the man. "Rupert Max Stuart should not hang next Tuesday," the editorial ended. "It is the bounden duty of the government sitting as Executive Council to delay execution of that sentence until all matters relevant are brought into the full light of day."

In the state parliament that afternoon two members asked questions about Stuart. Mr. T. C. Stott, one of two Independents in the House of Assembly, said: "As the eminent Privy Council judges have made their decision and stated in rejecting the petition that the matter of new evidence was now one for the Executive authorities, will the Premier state whether the government is prepared to consider the new evidence?" The speaker ruled that the question related to the prerogative of mercy; and such a question, he said (quoting from Erskine May in the House of Commons, whose procedure and practice the parliament of South Australia followed), in connexion with persons sentenced to capital punishment, was not in order. The next question was about the danger of electricity seeping from underground cables to water pipes. The Premier, Sir Thomas Playford, answered it, as he had answered perhaps half the questions asked in the House for the past twenty years. Then Mr. G. B. Bockelberg, a government supporter whose electorate included Ceduna and Thevenard, was on his feet enquiring, indirectly enough to get past the speaker's ruling, whether the government would now go ahead and hang Stuart. "Where appeals in court cases are dismissed by superior courts," he asked, "can the Premier say whether it is the policy of the Executive Council to permit the law to follow its course if a verdict of 'guilty' has already been reached?" Playford replied: "The general procedure is that the Executive Council examines all aspects of the crime, and we invariably do so. It would obviously be wrong if some new factor arose not known to the Executive Council at the time it made its decision. A decision might then be made on wrong premises. On the other hand, the Executive Council would have to satisfy itself that the new premises were real premises, warranting examination."

The press next morning took Playford's answer as a hint that the government would re-examine the case. The *Sydney Morning Herald*, the Brisbane *Courier-Mail*, the Melbourne *Age* and the Hobart *Mercury* treated Stuart's situation as the main story of the day. In the *Advertiser* it ran second to an announcement by Playford that an area of suburban swamp was to become a garden suburb. But the *Advertiser* gave first place in its correspondence columns to a plea for investigation of the new evidence, followed by two letters from people who wanted the death sentence to be carried out.

A statement by Allan Moir appeared in Thursday morning's papers. He and the smaller section of Gieseman's show had been traced to the stark township of Collinsville, in north Queensland. Dixon made his way there by aircraft and car. Farrell also headed for the town, by car. But when Moir made his statement neither Dixon nor Farrell had yet reached him. The youth spoke on the telephone to the Brisbane *Courier-Mail* (an affiliate of the *Advertiser*), by arrangement of the newsagent who was its local representative. "The *Courier-Mail*," announced the paper, "found him last night in 'Sideshow Alley' at Collinsville Showgrounds."

In this interview, which the *Advertiser* among other papers printed, Moir said that he did not know Father Dixon had flown from Adelaide to find him and others in an attempt to save Stuart's life. (Nor, until that moment, did readers of the *Advertiser*, unless they happened also to see the *News*.) According to Moir's account of the Saturday in Ceduna, Stuart returned to the show from the beach "about five or six o'clock in the afternoon—it could have been an hour earlier". When the *Courier-Mail* reporter read to Moir the declarations by the Giesemans and Miss Hopes, and asked him further about times, he said Stuart might have returned to the show an hour or more earlier than he had first estimated. "I am not too sure of the time he came back," Moir said. As the *Courier-Mail* summed up the conversation, Moir "differed greatly, but with a lack of certainty", from the other three.

Next day Moir gave statements to Farrell, to the Sydney *Daily Mirror* by telephone, to at least one other newspaperman, and to Dixon. One reporter described him as "very slow of thought and speech. He would not make an impressive witness. He frequently appears doubtful when making a statement, and changes in mid-speech . . . he hung his head when asked how a youth of his age came to be travelling around Australia with a sideshow and drinking rum with coloured people." When Dixon reached him on Thursday afternoon Moir readily went with the priest, Clark of the *News*, and a justice of the peace from Bowen, to a room in the local Catholic school, where he dictated a statement. Before doing so he said: "What happens if Stuart gets off? Do they look for another bloke?"

According to Moir's statement to the *Courier-Mail* he seemed not to have seen Stuart between some time in the morning and late in the afternoon. He told Dixon, however, that he saw Stuart about 1.30 p.m., and added: "I saw him working the darts during the afternoon and I went down to the beach with him about 4 p.m." After describing a drinking session with Stuart and others on the beach later in the day, and a walk to the town in the evening, Moir said (as reported by Clark): "There is one thing, and that is that when I was down the beach Max Stuart said to me 'There is blood on my chest.' He opened his overalls. I could not see any blood. I think Max said he had 'knocked off' Lennie and went out in a boat and dumped it." The statement was read over to Moir (who could not read) and signed by him.

The poster for the early edition of Thursday's *News*, which appeared at midday, said:

ADELAIDE LEADERS
DEMAND DELAY

Among churchmen who had been asked to express an opinion, investigation of the new evidence was recommended by the Anglican bishop, the president of the Methodist conference, the president of the Churches of Christ, the president-general of the Evangelical Lutheran Church and the Rabbi. The Catholic auxiliary bishop was noncommittal. The president of the Seventh Day Adventists said that his church had every confidence in the state's authorities and that fresh evidence often proved to be just a hoax.

More comments reached the government and the newspapers from other states. To the Premier himself, some time on Thursday, came a message from Sir John Latham, former Chief Justice of the High Court and now president of the Australian Association for Cultural Freedom, saying: "Fresh evidence has now come to light which if believed shows that Stuart could not have committed the crime as alleged. It is urged that this evidence should be carefully examined and that the government should postpone execution of the sentence of death until this has been done." Another ten thousand copies of the pamphlet *Why not Hang Rupert Stuart?* were printed on Thursday morning; to the sub-title "Some Questions about a Murder" was now added: "If the answers disturb you, get in touch with your M.P." They were distributed quickly—though not so quickly as suggested by next morning's *Advertiser*, which said that copies were dropped on the city from an aeroplane.

When the House of Assembly met at 2 p.m. on Thursday the Leader of the Opposition, Mr. M. R. O'Halloran, moved that the standing orders and practices of the House be so far suspended as to enable him to move a motion concerning a capital sentence which was pending. With the Speaker's permission O'Halloran read the motion: "That in the opinion of this House the government should ensure that the sentence of death on Rupert Max Stuart should not be carried out until there has been full opportunity for investigation of all aspects of this case." Labor leaders were confident that the two Independents would vote for the suspension of standing orders. A member of the Liberal and Country League executive said later that two government members intended also to vote with the opposition. This would have been enough to carry the motion, and so to give Playford the most embarrassing moment of his political career.

"I ask the House to oppose the motion," said the Premier. "Knowing what the Leader has in mind, I can assure him and the House that steps already taken will ensure that there is a thorough enquiry into all aspects of the case he desires to ventilate before any sentence is carried out. Action already taken has provided for a suspension of the sentence on Stuart for a month, and for the appointment of a Royal Commission of three Supreme Court Judges to go into the whole matter." A respite until August 31 was granted to Stuart by Mr. Justice Reed, this time on application from the Crown.

The government which would have had Stuart hanged on July 7, in the utterly earnest conviction that his guilt was beyond doubt, had now conceded that evidence gathered privately was impressive enough to be investigated. The decision was welcomed by Stuart's solicitors, by Dixon, and by the secretary of the Police Association. It appeared to have taken the Stuart question out of the arena of public dispute and placed it in the cooler atmosphere of formal enquiry.

Three hours later the war of words was resumed, this time to become far more violent.

7

AN UNDERTAKING TO PARLIAMENT

PARLIAMENT HAD RISEN for the weekend when Sir Thomas Playford, late in the afternoon of Thursday, July 30, announced the names of the Royal Commissioners and their terms of reference. The Chairman was to be the Chief Justice, Sir Mellis Napier, who presided when the Full Court heard Stuart's appeal. The other Commissioners were Mr. Justice Reed, who was the trial judge, and Mr. Justice Ross. The three men were directed to report to the Executive Council on the following matters:

> "1. The facts purporting to be disclosed in certain statutory declarations purporting to be made by Norman George Gieseman, Edna Gieseman, and Betty Hopes all of Burpengarry in the state of Queensland, relative to the movements, actions and intentions of Rupert Max Stuart now a prisoner in Her Majesty's Gaol at Adelaide.
>
> 2. The movements of the said Rupert Max Stuart during Saturday, the 20th of December, 1958.
>
> 3. The reasons why the said statements were not made or furnished to the Supreme Court of South Australia or to an appropriate authority before the dates when they were respectively made and furnished.
>
> 4. The circumstances in which the said declarations were obtained and made."

The terms of reference were criticised at once by Stuart's solicitors. Miss Helen Devaney said to the press on the evening of July 30: "We are far from satisfied with the terms of reference for the Royal Commission. The terms are too restricting." When O'Sullivan heard the news he went further, criticising the choice of Commissioners as well as their terms. According to a reporter in London he said that the thing was a farce, "obviously designed as a sop to public opinion . . . It is completely unfair to Stuart and to the three judges to ask two of them who have made public decisions adverse to Stuart to again review the case . . . This nonsense will satisfy nobody." The Commissioners, he said, should be appointed from outside South Australia, and the terms should include all aspects of the case. Another immediate comment came from the one lawyer on the Opposition benches in the House of Assembly, Mr. D. A. Dunstan, who told the

Sydney *Morning Herald* that the Premier's solemn undertaking to have all aspects of the case investigated had satisfied the Opposition because it meant not only that the new evidence would be examined but that other questions, which had caused grave public disquiet, could be canvassed. "The Premier's subsequent announcement of restricted terms for the Royal Commission," said Dunstan, "is a gross breach of his undertakings to the House."

When Miss Devaney criticised the terms of reference she suggested also a rather different method of enquiry; her client, she said, would invoke section 369 (a) of the state's Criminal Law Consolidation Act. This section provided that "the Chief Secretary on the consideration of any petition for the exercise of Her Majesty's mercy having reference to the conviction of a person on information or to the sentence (other than sentence of death) passed on a person so convicted may, if he thinks fit, . . . refer the whole case to the Full Court and the case shall then be heard and determined by that court as in the case of an appeal by a person convicted . . ." The proposal was supported at once by Professor Norval Morris, who said that a reference to the Full Court would achieve all that the Royal Commission could, with this difference: that the decision of the court could be tested. A government pleased itself whether to act on a report from a Royal Commission; but the decision of a state's Full Court could be challenged by appeal to the High Court. Morris believed that if the government referred Stuart's case now to the Full Court, "the discretion would then be where it should be—in a court, not in a government."

Nobody had publicly mentioned this form of investigation before the Royal Commission was announced. Many lawyers were uncertain, in fact, whether a new trial was possible; more than one solicitor who looked up the Act assumed that the words "other than sentence of death" ruled out a reference to the Full Court in this case, not knowing that by a ruling of the High Court on the identical words in a Victorian statute, the words were deemed to apply only to the sentence of death and not to the verdict of guilty. The Leader of the Opposition, O'Halloran, observed to a *News* reporter on the morning of July 30 that in South Australia, if a man convicted of a capital crime had exhausted his rights of appeal and fresh evidence appeared, no new reference to the court could be made to investigate the evidence. This misunderstanding was not confined to Adelaide; on the same morning "A Legal Correspondent" in the *Sydney Morning Herald*, discussing the moves now open to Stuart, did not mention section 369 (a) of the South Australian Act.

O'Sullivan and Miss Devaney conferred by telephone overnight. On Friday morning, July 31, they announced that they might take no part in the Commission unless its composition were altered and its terms widened. Miss Devaney drew up a petition for a Full Court hearing, read it to Stuart in gaol, and got his signature. The *News* ran a front-page editorial for the second time in three days, headed: "THERE'S STILL A LONG WAY TO GO." "Yesterday," it began, "public opinion won a notable victory. . . . But the naming of the Royal Commissioners and their terms of reference . . . arouse the gravest doubts and fears among all who know something of the inside history of the case . . . No one doubts the integrity or knowledge of the law of Justices Napier, Reed, and Ross . . . But . . . there is Australian precedent for the view that no local judge should sit on this commission—least of all the judge who heard the original trial and his two close colleagues and associates on the S.A. Supreme Court, one of whom sat on the Court of Criminal Appeal in this very case." Either the case should be referred to the Full Court or the terms should be widened appreciably, to include:

> "The scope and limitation of inquiries at Thevenard, Ceduna, and Whyalla into the murder of Mary Olive Hattam.
>
> The action or inaction of all those officers of this State concerned with the law and its prosecution in this matter.
>
> The procedure available to enable an illiterate accused to place his story before the court.
>
> The assistance available to an accused pauper to enable him to collect his evidence.
>
> The reasons why the High Court of Australia indicated it was disturbed at some aspects of the case.
>
> The reason why the relevant testimony obtained this week by a priest and a newspaperman in Northern Queensland was not sought and brought to light in court in the first instance.
>
> The reason why the hair allegedly discovered in the hand of the violated and murdered child was not produced in court so that all should know if it were or were not the hair of the accused, Rupert Max Stuart.[1]
>
> When these and various other matters of the deepest community impact are explored to their depths; when the whole system of law investigation, enforcement and trial in this state have been probed; when the real murderer of Mary Olive Hattam has been brought to book, and sentence duly passed and executed, then and only then will all South Australian men and women go contented on their way."

Alongside the editorial appeared a cartoon by Mitchell which is reproduced opposite.

Even in Sydney, which had harboured some tough newspapermen, this page would have looked strong stuff. In South Australia it was

[1] This was a mistake. Hairs found in the child's hands were put in at the trial after they had been sent by the police to the Institute of Medical and Veterinary Science. There was no attempt to argue either that the hairs could be proved to be Stuart's or that they could not.

probably unique. When the *News* subjected to scrutiny the state's penal system, or the administration of native welfare, its editorial writers had to remember the mental climate in which their criticism would be read. If sales were the test, the *Advertiser* was half as popular again with South Australians; and unless the *News* was prepared to lose money it could not afford to appear a mere organ for discontented minorities. Even the campaign against gerrymandered electorates was not pushed to a point where readers were urged unequivocally to vote out the Playford government. There was some truth in the wry remark by Labor men that the *News* supported their party except at elections. In this case, however, a prudent respect for circulation and advertising was not the only possible explanation. As a body the Labor politicians of South Australia neither displayed nor evoked much enthusiasm. The *News* did not look implacably enough at Sir Thomas Playford to satisfy his political opponents; but they themselves, over the years, gave him no more trouble than the *News*. When the paper published a cartoon suggesting that the Chief

PUBLIC: "Blimey! Tom's not calling in the same docs again, is he?"

—*News*, Adelaide, July 31, 1959

Justice and Sir Geoffrey Reed should not have been invited to examine Stuart's conviction and should not have accepted the invitation, and when an editorial declared that *"the whole system of law investigation, enforcement and trial in this state"* needed examining, it was throwing out to the government and, by implication, the bench, an unusually serious challenge. It remained to be seen how closely, and for how long, the parliamentary Opposition would follow the paper's lead.

Disapproving remarks about the Commission were expressed by individuals and groups over the weekend. In New South Wales the Aboriginal-Australian Fellowship, which had been campaigning a few days earlier to have the death sentence postponed, now drew up a fresh petition asking that the case be referred to the Full Court. Dr. Charles Duguid said in Adelaide that nation-wide disquiet would be heightened by the narrow terms of reference. Forty seamen on a coastal vessel sent telegrams to Playford and the Governor-General saying: "The crew of S.S. *Cycle* demand terms of Stuart inquiry be widened to include full investigation of conduct of case and activities of police." The state committee of the Communist Party said that while it was undesirable to have judges who had already participated in the case sitting on the Commission, the main need was wider terms; after expressing liberal-minded qualms about the admissibility of confessions, the Communists said: "We call upon the working class and progressive organisations to demand a real investigation into the Stuart case and to demand legislation protecting the rights of citizens against arbitrary police action."

On the day this resolution was composed there appeared also a statement from within the Australian Association for Cultural Freedom—a body which had recently been described as "so reliably anti-Communist that there can be no possible suggestion that their resolutions or protests are mere leftist tub-thumping". Its president, who chose the self-perpetuating executive and kept in close touch with every activity of the Association, was Sir John Latham, an old-fashioned rationalist on religious questions, a former deputy Prime Minister in an anti-Labor federal government, and Chief Justice of the High Court from 1935 until 1952. The Sydney *Observer* said of Latham and his colleagues: "They are the sort of people whose views no government can ignore or dismiss . . . They do not want to create controversy for its own sake . . . What they *do* want is to make statements on those rare occasions when liberty is seriously threatened, and make them in such a way that they will be listened to and will have some real and specific influence." They recommended changes in the administration of censorship when the Customs Department declared *Catcher in the Rye* a prohibited import; the changes, very cautious ones, were made. In the case of Professor Orr, the Association was divided. An investigation on its behalf by two Sydney lawyers, Mr. John Kerr and Mr. J. H. Wootten, led to a declaration that Orr and his supporters had foisted "a mass of misstatements, misconceptions and misrepresentations . . . on a public opinion which has no access to the information necessary to check and test it". When the Association intervened in the Stuart case, it was likely to gain an audience not so easily attracted by groups more habitually associated with the criticism of established institutions.

The statement Playford received from Sir John Latham on July 30 urging examination of the new evidence was made by him as president of the Association. It began with an explanation that, although there had been no time to summon a meeting of the full executive, some of its members had considered the case. As soon as Playford announced the Commission, and before the names and terms of reference were known, Sir John Latham had said that his Association was satisfied. By that time Mr. J. H. Wootten, a member of the executive, had flown from Sydney to Adelaide to investigate the case. Wootten conferred with Morris and other university lawyers, with Miss Devaney, and with Strehlow. He then flew to Melbourne to discuss with Latham whether the Association should make another statement. On Saturday, August 1, he was back in Sydney and had written a review of the affair which appeared in due course in the bulletin of the Association, *The Free Spirit*. A summary appeared in the Sydney *Sunday Telegraph* on August 2 and the Adelaide *News* on August 3. In each case the author was called "a Sydney lawyer who is a member of the Executive of the Australian Association for Cultural Freedom", which hardly concealed his identity but which presumably conformed with the New South Wales Bar Council's rules against professional advertising.

Wootten made the first published remarks about the relation between O'Sullivan and Stuart as solicitor and client:

> "Mr. O'Sullivan was, of course, a strange white man who did not speak Arunta and who had no special knowledge of natives. Stuart answered his questions but volunteered nothing. In his questioning of Stuart Mr. O'Sullivan was subject to a restraint familiar to every criminal lawyer. For all he knew Stuart might be guilty and it was no part of his counsel's task to probe to the point where he was forced to an unwilling confession. Nevertheless Mr. O'Sullivan obtained Stuart's statement that he had been forced by physical violence on the part of the police to agree to his confession and to sign it."

Wootten carried the story from the trial, through Dixon's meetings with Stuart, to the discovery of the Giesemans. He turned to the present situation, and reported

> "great dissatisfaction with the terms of reference of the Royal Commission and with its personnel. The way the terms of reference are framed has led one observer to remark that it looks like a Royal

Commission into Father Dixon. However that may be, no enquiry confined to the new declarations can do away with the grave doubts about the Stuart case . . . The information about Stuart's linguistic and cultural background which creates doubts about the authenticity of Stuart's confession was not available either to the trial court or to the counsel defending him. This information alone requires a thorough examination to see whether it would not have materially affected the likelihood of a verdict of guilty.

"But it may be unfair to the South Australian Government to assume that it intended to exclude any relevant matter. The second term of reference is quite general—'the movements of Stuart during Saturday, December 20, 1958'. Stuart's confession is most material evidence as to his movements, and its correctness would have to be gone into under the second term. If the government intends a full enquiry into all matters relevant to Stuart's guilt or innocence, it could have plainly so provided and should now do so. Public anxiety really arises from the contrast between the Premier's blunt undertaking in Parliament and the actual terms of reference.

"The criticism of the membership of the Commission is based on the fact that one member was trial judge and another presided on the Court of Appeal. However, the conduct of neither is really in question and there can be no assumption that the judgment of either might be affected. Nevertheless feeling has undoubtedly run high in South Australia in recent weeks, largely because the integrity of the police is in question. In these circumstances it would be a reassuring and statesmanlike gesture for the Playford Government to put on the Commission (either by addition or substitution) someone who has no immediate connection with the local scene. A more important aspect is the desirability of having on the Commission someone experienced in dealing with partly civilised aborigines . . .

"This is not merely a matter of justice to Stuart. Australia's good name is involved. World opinion is always ready to examine critically our treatment of the aborigines, and the Privy Council appeal has brought Stuart's case to international attention. As it happens there is a distinguished South Australian who combines the qualifications of having no connexion with recent events, and of being a judge experienced in dealing with the very type of aborigine that Stuart is. He is Mr. Justice Kriewaldt, of the Supreme Court of the Northern Territory. If he were put on the Commission, either by addition or substitution, public opinion both here and overseas would be greatly reassured."

From a man who saw no cause for a new enquiry in the Orr case, this was strong comment. The solution he proposed was intended to be conciliatory, but drew no comment from the South Australian government.

In the *Sunday Telegraph,* Wootten's remarks were preceded by a report headed "Expert Claims Confession Impossible", in which extracts were given from Strehlow's letter to the Attorney-General. Other Sydney Sunday papers had sent men to Adelaide to cover the controversy. The *Sun-Herald* reporter predicted "dramatic moves . . . in the S.A. parliament on Tuesday afternoon to block the Stuart Royal Commission going on in its present form". The paper's political commentator, "Onlooker", wrote: "Though the restricted terms of reference make the government's action appear more grudging than it need have been, it is fair to assume that, with a man's life at stake, the judges—two of whom were concerned in the trial and appeal proceedings—will conduct their investigation thoroughly and unsparingly." In the *Sunday Mirror*, an affiliate of *Truth*, Mr. Frank O'Neill announced from Adelaide, after getting on the telephone to Ceduna, that "bitterness and resentment" were sweeping the town at the appointment of the Commission. "Residents of the murder town of Ceduna," he wrote, "claim they can upset vital statements made this week in support of aboriginal Rupert Max Stuart." The one informant he named was Mr. P. S. Morrison, organiser of Ceduna's petition against Stuart four weeks earlier. O'Neill's story, which filled the front page, was headed: "The Sunday Mirror is there: Hang Stuart Cries Angry Town." The *Sunday Mail* in Adelaide had as its main heading: "Punish Only Guilty Man, Says Father." A reporter who went to Ceduna had been told by Mr. Glen Hattam: "If Stuart is not the man who murdered my daughter then I don't want to see him hanged."

* * *

On Monday Miss Devaney received a letter from Playford, who wrote as acting Attorney-General to say that cabinet had deferred consideration of Stuart's petition for a reference to the Full Court until after the Commission reported. He assured her that the terms of reference were designed to give the enquiry the fullest possible scope. "I have personally checked the position with the Honourable the Chief Justice, and he assures me that the terms of reference will enable the Commission thoroughly to investigate the new material submitted, and indeed to investigate all relevant matters in a manner which allows greater freedom of investigation and consideration than those given in terms of section 369." If, in the Commissioners' view, some unforeseen matter arose which justified an addition to the terms of reference, he would bring the matter at once before Executive Council. Miss Devaney said of this letter: "It carries the matter a little further, but we are not completely satisfied that the thorough enquiry into all aspects of the case which the Premier promised in the House of Assembly last Thursday can possibly be carried out under the terms of reference . . ."

When the Labor caucus met on Tuesday morning to discuss tactics for the day there was disagreement about whether or not to press the government hard. Some members were satisfied with the assurance given by Playford to Miss Devaney. Some were afraid that the campaign led by the *News* was not popular enough in the community to be supported with safety. Other members argued vigorously that the Premier's letter altered nothing; one called it a mere subterfuge. A message which reached the meeting from Evatt encouraged those members who wanted vigorous words. It was decided that the leader, O'Halloran, would ask a strong question in the House of Assembly, and that if Playford's answer was unsatisfactory a motion would follow attacking the government for failing to act on its promise of a full enquiry.

As soon as the speaker had read prayers, O'Halloran rose and said: "Last Thursday the Premier, in the House, undertook to appoint a Royal Commission to go into all aspects of the case of Rupert Max Stuart. I am advised by senior counsel that neither the terms of reference subsequently announced nor the Premier's further statement yesterday carry out that undertaking. Can the Premier say whether the government will forthwith widen the terms of reference to include all matters relevant to the guilt or innocence of Rupert Max Stuart?" Playford began by saying bluntly that he had given *no* undertaking to the House in the previous week. He repeated what he had written to Miss Devaney, insisted that the government was most anxious to have a thorough investigation, and said: "I assure the Leader of the Opposition that the government will see that every matter connected with this case is sifted to the ground." "That is an undertaking?" asked a Labor voice. "That is an undertaking," said Playford. For the first time he mentioned Stuart's confession. "The Chief Justice categorically informed me that the terms of reference would enable him, if he considered it desirable, to deal with the confession . . . I would say the terms of reference cover the movements of the accused on the day and the reasons why this information has not been available before, which obviously brings in the confession. If the police have sat on a confession and have not looked for information, that would immediately become obvious under the terms of reference."

As Playford well knew, people who wanted the confession investigated had in mind a possibility far more disturbing than that the police had "sat on" it; while he spoke, some members had in front of them copies of that afternoon's *News* containing passages from Strehlow's letter to the Attorney-General under the heading: "NATIVE LANGUAGE EXPERT CLAIMS: STUART'S 'CONFESSION' FALLS DOWN." Mr. D. A. Dunstan, who had been the keenest of all in his party to insist that the enquiry should be thorough, now pressed Playford to be more specific about the confession. To a reporter from Sydney, Dunstan appeared "a young sallow-faced lawyer, bespectacled and finicky of speech and dress . . ." He was the only lawyer on his side of the house, and the only Labor member to have been educated at St. Peter's College, where many "old families" sent their sons. In 1953 he had unseated an anti-Labor member from a socially complex suburban electorate, and since then he had been the most disconcerting of the Premier's opponents. Dunstan now asked whether the government would extend the terms of reference if counsel for Stuart raised any question about the confession which the Commissioners found themselves unable to consider. Playford asked for the question to be put on notice, after saying: "If Miss Devaney or Mr. O'Sullivan finds there is some matter they desire to place before the Commission that is relevant to the innocence of Stuart, undoubtedly I shall receive an application for an extension of the terms to enable counsel to put such a matter before the Commission." On a strict reading this reply might well have been regarded as promising nothing; and Playford's considered answer the next day did little if anything to clarify it. But since it followed a promise that everything would be sifted to the ground, the Opposition was satisfied.

So far Labor had been more cautious than either the *News* or Wootten in expressing misgivings about the Commission; concern had been voiced about its scope, but not its membership. Later in the afternoon, in a debate on the address-in-reply, one Labor speaker, Mr. S. J. Lawn, supported the proposal to appoint Mr. Justice Kriewaldt and said that the two judges with previous participation in the case should not sit as Commissioners. But this was a short, late passage, in a long speech by Labor's champion rhetorician, and made between an attack on the dictatorship of the Metropolitan Tramways Trust and a denunciation of General Motors. No member on either side took up Lawn's remark.

Several people who saw Playford in this and in later, acrimonious discussions of the Stuart case in parliament, remarked that he seemed unusually ill at ease. His hands came in and out of his pockets, his smile at Labor thrusts came on and off quickly, and his sentences, never crisp at any time, grew very tangled indeed; not even the running repairs done to his prose by the tactful Hansard staff could conceal that. The case was becoming by far the most bothering issue in Playford's twenty-one years of office. It was in a part of the political arena, moreover, where Playford cannot have felt thoroughly at home. He had little formal education and little faith in it. He liked politics to be kept as simple, and as free from serious, sustained disagreement, as possible.

The task of governing South Australia was normally as placid as his own personality. The anti-Labor parties, Liberal and Country, had united in that state earlier and more securely than elsewhere; the Liberal and Country League made sure that the metropolitan districts housing most Labor voters had only one-third of the seats in the House of Assembly, while a restricted franchise and a weighting of seats greatly in favour of the country districts kept the Legislative Council as safely conservative as the House of Lords. Playford's first and last concern was to "develop" the state—by which he meant, above all, to encourage the growth of secondary industry. To this end, in 1946, he took over the Adelaide Electric Supply Company, after two of his own supporters had voted against the measure in the House of Assembly, the Labor opposition had voted for it, the Legislative Council had rejected it for a time, and the Company's board, crying "Socialism!", had prayed King George VI to refuse his assent. Actions like that, together with his retention of price controls and his occasional attacks on restrictive trade associations, led some people to say that Tom Playford was the best Labor Premier in the country. In fact Playford was no more likely to go in for socialism than to betray his Baptist ancestors, by taking to alcohol or tobacco. A government's job, he believed, was to increase wealth, not to re-distribute it.

Playford was famous for his financial integrity, like the grandfather who was Premier before him and who was called "Honest Tom". The earlier Thomas Playford, a radical liberal, went into federal politics and became leader in the Senate on behalf of Alfred Deakin (whose own grandson, Mr. Rohan Rivett, was now pressing the younger Playford so hard). The grandfather never became "Sir" Thomas; at least four times he refused a knighthood on traditional radical grounds. The grandson also declined a knighthood for years. One after another the men around him succumbed to the royal sword while plain Mr. Thomas Playford remained upright. Then, in the federal New Year honours for 1957, he became a Knight Grand Cross of the Order of St. Michael and St. George—a title more elevated than those of knights in charge of his state's pastoral and mercantile resources. The directors of such institutions as the Adelaide Steamship Company, the Bank of Adelaide and the *Advertiser* were often men with a private education (usually at St. Peter's College) who inherited a lot of money, made a good deal more, and gave away some of it to help educate and cultivate the citizenry. The Elder Conservatorium, the Barr Smith Library, and the Bonython Hall were a few of these families' monuments. The Playfords represented a different sort of "old family", usually of Nonconformist stock, who neither ran sheep nor sold goods made by others, who worked their own farms and never became really rich by it. They wanted their sons to learn about grafting and pruning and manure, not algebra or Latin, and they took them away from school as soon as they were big enough to work on the farm. They were strong, plain-spoken men, with simple manners and rough voices. When they voted it was more often than not for an Independent. There were more of them in South Australia than elsewhere, and the Independent member of parliament survived longest in that state. When Playford became Premier in 1938 there were fourteen Independents out of 39 members of the House of Assembly, most of them farmers who had been scratching through years of depression to make a bare living. They could trust a man like Tom

Playford. A Hansard reporter who remembers his first speech in parliament says that it "started off without preliminaries, it ended up without grace notes, and it contained no frills anywhere, only hard contention." He came to office as a cheerful ally of men who belonged to the Adelaide Club, but he himself did not join it.

Playford had never sat in opposition. In September 1959, at the age of sixty-three, he was to break Sir Robert Walpole's record for longevity as Premier. Among colleagues his authority was quite unchallenged. According to Mr. A. P. Rowe, when the Minister of Health was once asked to receive a deputation to discuss the administration of a teaching hospital, his secretary replied that the Premier would deal with it, "as this is a matter of policy". When Rowe came to Adelaide as vice-chancellor of the university, he found that the usual answer from any minister to a question about university matters was: "You had better ask Tom." The usual processes of government, Rowe concluded, did not operate in this society. Few people knew whether the crucial decisions about Stuart were Playford's own, and how far members of the judiciary and Crown Law officers may have contributed to them.

Not alone in his state, Playford had a touchy provincial patriotism. When somebody suggested in 1959 that South Australian time be advanced half an hour to conform with eastern practice, he retorted that if there were to be any change it was the easterners who could put their clocks back. He would travel halfway round the world in the hope of coaxing a new industry to Adelaide rather than to Melbourne. His ability to get more for the state than Canberra intended in negotiations at the Premiers' Conference and Loan Council was legendary. Mr. A. P. Rowe found that although Playford had little sympathy with what the university stood for, "the royal road to the treasury chest" was open once the Premier was convinced that standards were falling behind those of universities in other states. "He stands not for any party or particular group," said one of his most fervent admirers in parliament, "but for the people of South Australia." He exhibited, Rowe thought, "a state-consciousness almost frightening in one of the leaders of a small nation on the borders of Asia . . ." People who warned Playford that his handling of the Stuart case would antagonise Asian opinion might as well have saved their breath.

As leader of parliament he was normally untroubled. Once, to force out a rebellious colleague, he dissolved the ministry and formed a new one next day without the rebel. The battle over electricity was lively, but nobody doubted that he would win. Mr. Kingsley Martin of the *New Statesman* thought him "the most complacent politician I ever met". With a majority as certain as next season's crop of cherries on the farm, he could afford to be serene. But he was seldom serene when the House discussed Stuart. It became a nasty, complicated business for the man who liked to portray himself as a simple farmer, and for the other seven men—all but one of them farmers—who made up his cabinet. On August 4, however, the controversy was quietened for the time being by Playford's answers in parliament. Next day Miss Devaney said that Stuart's solicitors were satisfied by the promise of a thorough investigation.

* * *

Stuart received his first communion on August 10. For some time before his flight to Queensland the priest had been instructing Stuart in the Catholic faith and reading to him from the only book ever written in Aranda—a bible translated by Strehlow's father and corrected by Strehlow himself. Stuart had been baptised on July 17—which as things then stood was eighteen days before he was due to die. A warder was his godfather. Dixon administered both the baptism and the first communion.

The *News* was still throwing large resources into the case. Day after day some aspect of it was treated as the main news. On Wednesday, August 5, the *News* published some of the letters which it had received about its stand, with an introduction saying that more than two-thirds had "contained generous, even embarrassingly kind, expressions of admiration and gratitude for what the *News* has done in the matter of Rupert Max Stuart".

Two days later the paper reprinted an account of the case which had been written in that morning's London *News Chronicle* by James Cameron, whose despatches appeared from time to time in the *News*. That Stuart was still alive, Cameron wrote, "is in great measure due to Rohan Rivett, Editor-in-chief of the Adelaide *News*. Rohan Rivett turned himself into the Zola of South Australia. Such a role is neither familiar nor altogether appreciated in the sedative air of Adelaide . . . Hundreds of uneasy Australians over all the nation, stirred and challenged by the Adelaide *News*, are now keenly watching the cause of a pauper black man who could so easily have gone into limbo unnoticed." Cameron's article was reproduced again in the *News* a few days later, with a note from its London man that no Australian newspaper had ever had such a tribute; and it appeared again as part of an advertisement for the *News* in the *Sunday Mail*.

A reporter from the *News*, Mr. Frank Shaw, was now in Ceduna, sending news of a quest for new evidence against Stuart by senior detectives from the Criminal Investigation Branch in Adelaide. The police roundsman, Mr. Jack Clark, was off to north Queensland for the second time in a fortnight, accompanied this time by his editor. In Collinsville, Rivett gained a further statutory declaration from Allan Moir and one from Billy McNeish, who had not been questioned by Dixon and who told Rivett that he too had seen Stuart working on the darts between two and four o'clock. Both statements were submitted later to the Commission.

The *Advertiser* was reporting prominently formal moves in parliament and the negotiations between the government and Stuart's solicitors. On informal aspects of the case it was less keen than the *News*, or the interstate press, or the weekly *Truth*, which on August 8 wrote of a "mystery witness"—a man found by the police in Adelaide, who knew Stuart, who had never been to Ceduna, and who "made sensational claims" which could influence Stuart's fate. The *Southern Cross*, weekly paper of the Catholic diocese of Adelaide, wrote at this time: "Both Fr. Dixon and those who materially assisted him, especially the *News*, have merited the gratitude of the whole community . . ." Early in August, that did not seem a very controversial sentiment.

Playford had also announced that he had appointed counsel from outside the Crown Solicitor's office, Mr. J. F. Brazel, Q.C., with Mr. C. J. Legoe as junior, to assist the Commission. The government would pay to bring witnesses to Adelaide and to accommodate them. There was no suggestion from the government, however, that it would make any contribution towards the cost of representation for Stuart. Nevertheless his solicitors engaged the man who was usually acknowledged to be Australia's most successful criminal barrister, Mr. J. W. Shand, Q.C. When Miss Devaney rang him in Sydney on Wednesday, August 5, Shand agreed at once to come.

The appearance of a barrister from outside South Australia was soon to appear symbolically important. Apart from the solicitors engaged to defend Stuart, the people most active in the effort to have his case re-examined were immigrants to Adelaide—Duguid and Thorp from Britain, Dixon, Rivett, Borland and Morris from the east, and Strehlow from a German mission in the Aranda country. Before this new enquiry was over, it was to seem that South Australian institutions were themselves on trial.

8

THE COMMISSION SITS

ON THE WINTRY MORNING of August 10, many people queued outside the Supreme Court buildings where the Royal Commission was to sit. A number had to be turned away. The others were ushered in, not to the solemn Victorian court where Stuart had been tried, convicted and sentenced, but to the plainer and lighter room, designed for both civil and criminal proceedings, where his appeal had been heard. At eleven o'clock the occupants of the public gallery, the lawyers at the bar table, the court officers and policemen, and the pressmen who filled the jury stalls, all stood as the Commissioners mounted the steps to the bench.

For two of the judges it was no new experience to be a Royal Commissioner. Sir Mellis Napier was chairman of a federal Commission on banking in 1935-7 (part of Australia's inquest on the depression) and Sir Geoffrey Reed was appointed in 1947 to enquire into charges of bribery and corruption against the Premier of Tasmania. The third Commissioner, Mr. Justice Ross, was the same age as Mr. Justice Reed (67), but was some years his junior on the bench, having been appointed in 1953.

The judges wore neither wigs nor robes, for they were not engaged in a judicial capacity; their task was to inform the executive. They were not bound by the rules of evidence which they would have had to apply if sitting as a court; in general, however, the Commissioners did adhere to the rules. The atmosphere of the enquiry was not to differ much from that of a judicial one. A court official was on hand to call for each new witness. If anybody in the public benches drooped on an elbow or fidgeted, a policeman reprimanded him. Lawyers coming and going bowed to the bench. The chairman himself was as likely to say "this Court" as "this Commission".

No witnesses were to be called on this first day, and senior counsel for both the Crown and Stuart, Chamberlain and Shand, were absent. The point of this sitting was to settle questions of procedure. The Attorney-General was represented by Mr. J. R. Kearnan, Crown Prosecutor, who spoke only to seek leave on behalf of himself and Mr. E. B. Scarfe to appear. At the other end of the table were Miss Devaney and Mr. C. Villeneuve Smith, who sought leave to appear for Stuart. Smith, an Adelaide practitioner, had been invited by O'Sullivan and Devaney to be Shand's junior counsel. Between Stuart's lawyers and the Crown's sat counsel assisting the Commission, Mr. J. F. Brazel, Q.C., and his junior, Mr. C. J. Legoe. The Commissioners were free to decide for themselves how to conduct the enquiry, and it was normal practice throughout Australia to let assisting counsel work out an appropriate procedure.

Brazel was 53. He had recent experience of a Royal Commission very different in character from this one, when he appeared as a witness at a tribunal appointed by the government of Victoria into betting. He was a committeeman of the South Australian Jockey Club, a prominent Catholic layman, and a partner in one of Adelaide's best known legal firms. As a barrister he was more inclined to employ the gentlemanly manner of the old world than the man-to-man approach characteristic of most Australian lawyers. He enjoyed speaking with patrician wit, and his rhetoric leaned towards formality. At this Commission he was to be the only counsel to quote, in Latin, a tag from the *Aeneid.* It was his task to do most of the talking now.

The first question discussed was whether Shand would be allowed to appear at all. When Smith said that the general conduct of Stuart's case would be in the hands of Shand, Sir Mellis Napier observed that the Commissioners were not quite clear whether they could admit counsel who was not registered to practise in South Australia. Brazel suggested that Shand had no *right* to appear, but that the Commission might have some discretion. The Chairman said: "So long as Mr. Shand is prepared to assist this Commission in an enquiry into the truth, then we shall be grateful for any assistance he can give."

Brazel gave a summary of events from the murder of Mary Hattam to the present sitting. It seemed to him that the logical starting point was to examine the people who had offered new evidence. Mr. Justice Ross said that the declarations of these people made the time of death very important, and asked whether the doctor would be called. (Dr. Kathleen Thompson had just been married in Melbourne, and according to press reports she was due to leave for Canada within a fortnight.) Brazel said, and the Chairman agreed, that if she could add nothing to her evidence given already in the courts, there was nothing to be gained by calling her.

Smith here interposed a remark which led directly to the first argument about the proper task of the Commission. It was desirable, he suggested, for the doctor to attend, "to deal with a matter which was never put to her before in the case, namely, the question of hair". "There was ample opportunity at the trial," said the Chairman, "to pursue that investigation." Smith contested this point, and explained that Stuart's solicitors wanted to know whether the doctor saw the hairs that were now alleged to have been found in the girl's hands. Sir Mellis Napier suggested that the Commissioners ought to confine their attention to questions within the terms of reference; "to open the matter as though it were a completely new trial and to allow points to be taken that are neither connected with this new evidence nor raised by any of the proceedings before the three Courts of Appeal . . . that is an entirely different question . . ." Smith rejoined that Stuart's representatives might have to apply for an extension of the terms. During this exchange the Chairman expressed the hope that the proceedings would take no longer than necessary; "after all, you have the whole of our available court at the moment, and sooner or later we must get back to the business of the court." Smith said he appreciated the dilemma; but the Premier had promised "the fullest investigation". Yes, replied the Chairman, but not a complete re-trial. If the credibility of the police were to be attacked, Smith went on, the confession was clearly relevant, and so was what the doctor saw or did not see. The Chairman said that no decision would be made on the point at present, "but we do ask you to confine our attention to those things that really matter."

One thing that really mattered, in the Chairman's view, was that the Commission (which had statutory power to compel the production of any document) should see the written statement of Stuart's which was discussed at the trial. "The learned trial judge," he said, "was unable to permit that to be read by anybody but the accused in person, but he offered to allow the accused to be questioned by his counsel in order to disclose what his version of the facts might be. The offer was rejected, and when the learned trial judge proposed to ask the accused whether there was anything he wished to say about a particular topic, he was requested by counsel appearing for the accused to, shall I say, mind his own business . . . Now the document was flourished in the face of the jury and we think it should be before us." "In the absence of Mr. O'Sullivan," observed Smith, "I cannot say anything about the judge being told to mind his own business and whether it was flourished in the face of the jury." "You can accept my assurance that both those things happened," Mr. Justice Reed interposed; but Smith declined to do so. Mr. Justice Reed felt that the word "flourishing" was a little strong, but that O'Sullivan had "in a sense" waved the document about. "I am certain," said Smith, "that Mr. O'Sullivan would never be guilty of telling you to mind your own business." "That is a metaphorical saying," observed the Chairman. "What happened according to the transcript was that my learned brother put the question to the accused, and Mr. O'Sullivan is reported as saying: 'With all respect, I would prefer that you did not ask any question'." Smith said that the document in question would be handed in to the Commission as soon as O'Sullivan returned from London.

The Commissioners wanted O'Sullivan himself to give evidence. When Smith said that it was not proposed to call him as a witness, the Chairman remarked: "Nobody but he can identify that document. Nobody but he can tell us why it was that this defence or alibi was not presented to the court below." Brazel agreed; the third term of reference, he said (why the statements of the Giesemans and Miss Hopes were not made earlier), really made it compulsory for O'Sullivan to testify; "his presence is vital." "We all think it is," said the Chairman.

Would Stuart himself attend? Brazel said that it would not be reasonable at this stage to ask whether the prisoner would be a witness, but that the right of representation at a Royal Commission was reserved to a person giving evidence. Sooner or later, said the Chairman, Stuart should be asked to do what he had not yet done—"to disclose what he says were his movements". "Subject to Mr. Shand's overall conduct of the case," said Smith, "my instructions are to intimate that Stuart desires to give evidence through an interpreter." He mentioned the name of Strehlow.

After sitting for just under an hour, the Commission adjourned for a week, until Monday, August 17.

* * *

Two days after the Commission adjourned, on August 12, a bill to abolish capital punishment was introduced in the House of Assembly by Mr. D. A. Dunstan, the Labor M.P. and lawyer who had been active in demands for a new and full enquiry into Stuart's conviction. He had given notice of the bill on July 22, the first report of his intention appearing in the *News* on the same page as its earliest reference to Father Thomas Dixon. Outside the House on July 23, Dunstan said the overwhelming argument against capital punishment was "that no court of law is so good an instrument of justice that a man's life should depend on its decisions." The annual procession of university students through Adelaide on August 7 would have included two floats bearing comment on the death penalty, if a police inspector had not ordered them off the road. One, labelled "What price capital punishment?" carried effigies of Frederick McDermott, Timothy Evans, and Stuart. The other bore a hangman's noose, a chair, and a sign which read "Making a statement". In Sydney the fortnightly *Observer* came out on August 8 with an article announced in bold type on its front cover: "SOUTH AUSTRALIA: THE HANGING STATE. BACKGROUND TO THE STUART CASE." The author, "an Adelaide correspondent", wrote: "South Australia *is* an executioner's heaven!" The proportion of murderers executed in the state—42 per cent—was the highest in Australia. "It is unquestionable that there is far more governmental enthusiasm for a hanging in South Australia than anywhere else in the nation." There was very little doubt that "the predilection for hanging is connected with South Australia's political gerrymander." For nearly all men in the cabinet represented country electorates; all recent murders had been in country districts; and, whether rightly or wrongly, it was firmly held that country people were fierce believers in capital punishment. Moreover, "South Australia is middle-class, insular, and self-contained, and inclined to dig its heels in when confronted with comment from outside." Nearly all of the *Observer's* despatch was reprinted in the *News*, and it was mentioned bitterly several times during the debate on Dunstan's bill. Playford himself was said to have been profoundly offended by this portrait of his government and his state.

In Victoria, where capital punishment was still on the statute book, a number of people were making Stuart the occasion for attacks on it. The Methodist weekly *Spectator* cited Stuart to support its argument that "we have had enough of legalised murder as a punishment for crimes which in almost every case are committed by those who have been grievously sinned against as well as grievously sinning." The anti-Labor Premier of Victoria, Mr. Henry Bolte, thought rather that Stuart's situation strengthened the case for hanging. Bolte, whose own cabinet had commuted every capital sentence during four years of office, declared that if Stuart had been sentenced merely to life imprisonment it was unlikely that any further interest would have been taken in him. In the Melbourne *Herald*, a correspondent suggested that the logical conclusion of Bolte's argument was to have *all* crimes punishable by death. No comment was reported from McDermott, who might well have been hanged if an anti-Labor government had won the election held in New South Wales soon after his conviction in 1947.

All Labor members in the South Australian parliament were committed to support Dunstan's motion, for abolition was party policy. As it was a private member's measure its passage would imply no censure on the government, and Liberal and Country League members could in principle vote as they pleased. For some weeks after Dunstan formally moved the first reading on August 12, it was predicted on both sides that the House would give the bill a majority. If this happened, it was a moral certainty that the Legislative Council would reject the measure, as in Britain the House of Lords had rejected Mr. Sidney Silverman's motion to suspend capital punishment in 1948; but the opponents of hanging would have gained considerable ground, perhaps enough to persuade the government to commute more often or even to introduce its own legislation limiting the death penalty to certain sorts of murder.

Wednesday was traditionally private members' day in the House of Assembly. For many weeks, speakers for and against Dunstan's bill contributed obliquely but clearly to the controversy over Stuart.

* * *

The first witnesses were due to be heard before the Commission on August 17. At the sitting on August 10 the Chairman and Brazel had asked anybody who felt able to help the Commission ascertain the truth to come forward. A man rang the office of O'Sullivan and Devaney to say that on the day of the murder he had seen mothers on the beach at Ceduna warning off a youth who was making a nuisance of himself with young girls in the water. The caller rang off, leaving no name. Stuart's solicitors appealed to him through the press to get in touch with the Commission; but no more was heard of him.

Gieseman and his wife and Miss Hopes flew in late on Saturday, August 15, to be greeted by Dixon. Miss Devaney and the press. Allan Moir, travelling separately, was met by the police at each airport on the way down from Queensland. At Brisbane, on Saturday evening, detectives stayed with him between flights and gave him £5 for expenses on behalf of the South Australian government. At Sydney he stayed the night in accommodation arranged by the police and bought a boomerang. On Sunday he went to Adelaide, where Stuart's solicitors had booked him a room. Gieseman, Mrs. Gieseman and Dixon were waiting at the airport. When the plane landed, two men walked across the tarmac, where the public were not permitted, and escorted Moir not to the passenger terminal but directly to a car. Dixon and the Giesemans approached the car, but were told that the boy was being taken away under orders from the Royal Commission. According to a reporter from the Melbourne *Sun*, a cameraman trying to photograph Moir was ordered off by one of Moir's escorts, who pushed him aside and trod heavily on his foot. Neither Stuart's lawyers nor Moir's elder brother, who had flown from Western Australia to see him, could reach the boy on Sunday. The police denied any knowledge of his reception. Next morning—the day on which the Commission was to start hearing evidence—the *Advertiser's* account of the incident was headed: "BOY WITNESS PRECAUTIONS." The first edition of the *News* interpreted it differently. The main headline ran: "Action over Allan Moir called 'denial of rights'. GOVT. SEIZURE OF STUART WITNESS DENOUNCED." "Legal and political men," said the *News*, "and his friends and relatives, are puzzled and angered by the whisking away of Stuart Royal Commission witness Allan Moir after only a hurried greeting on his arrival yesterday." An unnamed "eminent legal authority" was quoted as saying that the refusal to allow Stuart's counsel access to Moir was a denial of rights.

By the time the *News* reached the streets, Moir's arrival had been discussed at the Commission itself. Shand said that Moir was a witness obtained in the interests of Stuart, and asked that he be allowed to see him. Brazel explained that the responsibility for what had happened was his. He had thought it wrong to allow a young boy, a stranger in Adelaide, to wander at large without protection and guidance from a responsible adult; and it had seemed to him that Moir should testify "without any attempts to be interviewed, shall I use that expression——"

"—— I hope you don't mean anything else," snapped Shand. "That is the expression I am using," Brazel said. Moir had not been interviewed by *any* counsel, he went on. Was there any reason, asked Sir Mellis Napier, why Shand should not see Moir before he gave evidence? "Only this, sir," replied Brazel, "that I was proposing to call him almost immediately." Nevertheless, the Chairman took the view that Stuart's counsel should be allowed to see the boy first.

That was not the end of the matter. There were questions about it from Dunstan and another Labor member when parliament resumed for the week on Tuesday. Playford replied that the Commission, not the government, had taken action. Dunstan asked whether the Royal Commissions Act gave any power to take anybody into custody and refuse persons the right to interview him. Playford said he would answer the question in due course, but insisted that the lad was not taken into custody and was not denied access to friends. Next day the *News* said in an editorial that Playford's reply had aroused considerable disquiet in the public mind. "If the instruction was given by Mr. Brazel, was his action endorsed by a minister? If so, under what law of the land was this action taken?" And under what law and by whose authority was Moir's brother kept from him on Sunday, despite repeated representations? In parliament, on Wednesday, Dunstan read out these questions when asking whether Playford now had a reply to his own. The Premier denied that Moir had been detained unlawfully. Brazel had made the arrangements. As far as he himself knew, Moir's brother did not apply to the Commission to know where the boy was, "nor did he disclose his reason for wanting to see him". Members knew quite well that the responsible authorities were under an obligation . . . Who were the authorities, asked a Labor voice—the government? Twenty-four hours earlier Playford had said: "No action was taken by the government in this matter . . ." Now he said: "I am quite happy to accept the word 'government'." A lecturer in political science at the University of Adelaide, Mr. R. L. Reid, commented in the *Australian Journal of Politics and History* that throughout this discussion the Premier "displayed a remarkable ignorance of the canons of ministerial responsibility . . ."

This scuffle over Allan Moir showed how heavily the air of Adelaide was charged with apprehension and suspicion. An uneasy relationship had been established at once between counsel for Stuart and counsel assisting the Commission. Hostility between Playford and his parliamentary opponents had been quickly restored. The *News* was again adopting a tense and vigilant posture towards the Commission and the government. On the day the first witnesses were called, the *News* printed on its front page a cartoon which showed people all over the world looking towards Adelaide, and which carried the words: "And justice must be done."

* * *

The queue was longer on August 17 than on the first day, and fewer people were admitted; only fifteen citizens (including Mr. Eliott Thorp of the Howard League) were allowed to share the public gallery with policemen and witnesses. Two rows of seats reserved by custom for legal practitioners were full. For most South Australian lawyers this was the first sight of Mr. J. W. Shand, Q.C.

In nearly four decades at the Sydney bar, Shand's professional skill, tenacity and daring had made his name known more widely among laymen than that of any other barrister. It was a name familiar already when he began to practise in 1921, for like many successful lawyers he was the son of a leading practitioner. His reputation was built on an unusually wide range of cases, on successes for the Crown and against it, and on performances both in courts and at tribunals of enquiry; in the twenty years before coming to Adelaide he had appeared in a series of Royal Commissions, including the one appointed to investigate the conviction of McDermott. There were spectacular successes before juries, and victories also in cases where the legal issues were more complex and a knowledge of how to play on the humanity of a jury less crucial. For one of his most skilful essays in cross-examination—on behalf of McDermott in 1951—the audience was not a jury but a Commissioner. A reporter who watched Shand on this occasion in merciless pursuit of crucial witnesses said that he made a detective-inspector weep in the box. McDermott was freed and given £500. Shand received no fee. Nor was he guaranteed any payment when he agreed to represent Stuart.

As his audience in Adelaide was to discover, Shand in court was brisk to the point of rudeness, irritable towards other counsel, and not very deferential towards the bench. He was a short man, with hair now thin and white and hearing no longer perfect—an impediment which he seemed to exploit at times, by asking witnesses to repeat answers which pleased him. He asked leave now to appear with Smith "for a witness to be called, Stuart". Chamberlain, back from London, asked leave to appear, with Kearnan and Scarfe, for the Attorney-General. Shand and Chamberlain and Brazel, though none of them could know it for certain, were all making the last appearance of their lives at the bar.

Dr. J. J. Bray, Q.C., sought leave to appear with Mr. C. H. Bright for O'Sullivan, "who is, I understand," Bray added, "an intended witness". The Chairman said that the application was premature. When O'Sullivan was called, or when evidence was given that might reflect upon him, Bray could apply again.

At Brazel's suggestion intended witnesses were ordered to leave the court-room. A declaration from the doctor was tendered by Brazel, in which she said that she could add nothing to evidence given already, and that she had seen Detective-Sergeant Paul Turner remove two or three hairs from a finger-nail of the deceased child, but had not examined them.

Brazel said that the written statement intended to be made on Stuart's behalf at the trial had still not been handed to the Commission. Shand passed up an unsigned copy of it, saying that the Crown had held a signed version of the statement since Dixon left it with the Attorney-General (on July 1). Chamberlain handed up the document Shand described—a carbon copy, bearing Stuart's signature. The original document, Shand said, had been mislaid (by O'Sullivan) somewhere between Adelaide and London. Nobody suggested that there was any doubt about the authenticity of the signed copy now in the Commissioners' possession.

Shand submitted that the Commissioners should examine not only the new evidence, but the alleged confession, the footprints on the beach and the hairs. He argued that a full investigation, as promised by the Premier, was not possible unless these things were considered. The Chairman said that the Commission was required to report on Stuart's movements, and for that purpose it would be necessary to consider whether the confession was a voluntary statement. The relevance of the other matters was perhaps doubtful, but if necessary the Commission would consider Shand's request later. Shand still pressed for a formal extension of the terms; and in doing so he said something which was headlined by every afternoon paper in the country. "With regard to this question of the confession, it has come to our knowledge that on Friday three independent witnesses gave a statement to the solicitor instructing my learned friend assisting the Commission that one of the police concerned uttered these words in their presence: 'We bashed it out of the black bastard.'" Stuart's lawyers, he said, would like to have copies of the statements, which he understood were handed to the Commission on Friday from a Mr. and Mrs. Wardrop and their daughter. Moreover, Shand declared, he would be able to show "quite severe injury with regard to Stuart following on his interview with the police . . ."

Shand asked that in one respect the enquiry be narrowed. The third term—why the statements were not furnished earlier—should in his submission be deleted. If the statements were true, did it matter to the Commission why or why not they were made? "Stuart and apparently his counsel are intended to be cross-examined, going into this sacred ground of professional conduct and privilege." Such an investigation was "unnecessary to the real issue we are concerned with here, and that is whether a man should die or whether he should not". This remark led to Shand's first brush with Sir Mellis Napier, who observed: "We are fully aware of the nature of the enquiry and it does not help us to be continually reminded of it."

"I have a duty to perform to my client," said Shand.

"No doubt," replied the Chairman, "and so do we."

"If it does not help Your Honours I am sorry," said Shand, "but I appear for a client who is in grave danger and I make submissions which Your Honours may disregard, but I make them."

The Chairman said that as he understood it, the object of the enquiry into why the new evidence was not called earlier was to discover why, if Stuart had a complete alibi, that was not mentioned at his trial. Shand suggested that in a Law Society case the accused depended on the police, who did in fact interview Gieseman long before the trial. "I put it that under reference three the very appropriate persons to be called are the police." "No doubt," said the Chairman, "and we shall expect to hear what they have to say."

While the Commission was considering Shand's request for an interview with Moir, Sir Mellis Napier spoke about the press. "In the very nature of things we do sometimes read the newspapers," he remarked, "and it would be easier for us if we were allowed to go about our business without being told what witnesses are going to say before they are called." This remark could have been interpreted as a rebuke to all those papers—from the *News* in Adelaide to the *Times* in London—which had reported what was in the statements of the Giesemans, Miss Hopes and Moir. He went on: "It has not been helpful to us that we should be told where truth and justice lie without being allowed to discover that for ourselves." Among the daily press this rebuke could apply only to the *News*, since no other paper had published editorial comment; but it could have been taken to have a wider reference, to those people—from the Communists to Sir John Latham—who had been offering advice about the composition and scope of the Commission.

9

ALIBI

"Call Norman George Gieseman," cried a court official, and the first witness, a tall and sun-browned man in a two-toned cardigan, loped his way to the box. The Chairman administered the oath and Gieseman sat down. For the next ninety minutes he gave answers, not always grammatical, to each of the lawyers in turn. For Brazel, Gieseman described the composition and itinerary of his show, its arrival in Ceduna eight months earlier, and the movements of his companions there. All except Stuart ate lunch together on the Saturday. Stuart and Moir had left the show at half past nine on Saturday morning. Moir was back about half past eleven. Stuart walked in, half-drunk, about a quarter to two or two o'clock. "You fix that time by reason of the fact that you were preparing to start the show?" asked Brazel. "Yes, for two o'clock." He told Stuart that he could have lunch. At two o'clock, with Stuart in view, he looked at his watch and said: "It's time to start." Stuart went to work on the darts stall. Several times between then and four o'clock he could see Stuart; once he noticed him holding a woman's child while she had a shot. Just after four, when the customers were thinning, Stuart handed over the takings to Mrs. Gieseman and left the parklands with Allan Moir. He next saw Moir at midnight, very drunk. Stuart returned about nine on Sunday morning, saying that he had been locked up all night. He blew Stuart up for getting Moir drunk. Stuart replied that he would not be wanting to travel further, as he had got himself a job on Saturday morning at the Wheat Board. The two men shook hands, and parted on the best of terms before the show left for Whyalla. There he first heard that a child had been murdered in Ceduna. When Detective Phin asked him whether any of the lads left the show during Saturday, he said that only Allan and Max had done so. The detective then talked to Allan, and to nobody else.

Brazel next put a series of questions which were intended to discover why the jury had not heard what Gieseman was now saying. Where was Gieseman during the preliminary hearing, in January? At Moonta Bay. Did he read about the hearing in newspapers? No; he did not read newspapers much when he was moving. He did not read anything about either the preliminary hearing or the trial.

"Did you enquire of anyone, at any time, as to what had happened to this man who had been travelling with you for three months?"

"No. All they said was that he was guilty and all I said was: 'If he says he done it, that is all there is to it'."

"Where was this said?"

"In Queensland or New South Wales."

"Was this said about the time he was to be tried?"

"About the date when he was to be hung, or something." These last two words suggested a vagueness about the stages of the legal process which was to appear even more strongly in other witnesses.

Brazel then turned to the meeting between Gieseman and Dixon in Queensland. "I was asked by Father Dixon," said Gieseman, "to give a description of Mr. Stuart's movements and times from nine o'clock the night before until nine o'clock the next Sunday morning . . ."

Shand's questioning was brief. How far was Stuart from Betty Hopes when he was on the darts? A couple of feet; and he himself had been thirty feet from them both for some time. When Moir and Stuart left, after four o'clock, Betty Hopes "sung out to Allan to bring her back a chocolate". In Whyalla, Shand asked, had Phin asked where Stuart was at any time on the Saturday? No.

To Chamberlain's opening questions, Gieseman said he did not know what his wife told Dixon, though he knew she said she told him the truth.

"You do not think she might have forgotten the time . . . ?"

"No way in the world. She would not forget, nor would I."

"Was that because you looked at your watch at the same time?"

"For a known fact at any entertainment or carnival or picture show, the known time is from two to four. Apart from looking at your watch."

Stuart's language was the next subject of cross-examination.

"What does he say?" asked Chamberlain. "Give us a sort of reproduction of the type of conversation that would go on with Stuart."

"He would just say 'Are you going to have a shot?' and give them the four darts and take the two bob," said Gieseman. "He mostly worked among his own people and didn't sing out much."

"He still held conversations with them?"

"I dare say, yes."

"What language do you speak, Mr. Gieseman?"

"Australian."

". . . What language used you to speak to Stuart?"

"Just the same."

"Did he speak all right?"

"He was a bit hard, but you got used to him. If you are with him for six months you get used to him."

Gieseman said he had never heard the question of Stuart's English discussed.

"Does he talk pidgin?" asked Chamberlain.

"It is broken."

"Has anybody suggested that word to you: 'broken'?" "No."

"Would he say, 'Which way you go along that fella' or that sort of thing?"

" 'Him go fella', and things like that."

"Anyway, you never had any trouble in getting on with him?" "No."

"He could tell you what he wanted to do and make himself understood?" "Yes."

"You could make yourself understood by him?" "Yes."

Chamberlain now pressed Gieseman on what passed between him and Stuart on the Sunday morning.

"In no sense would it be true to say that you had sacked him?"

". . . No, he had himself a job, he said."

It appeared that according to Detective-Sergeant Phin's written recollection of the conversation in Whyalla, Gieseman had given them a different account of this exchange.

"Did you tell Phin that because of Stuart's uselessness and drunken habits you had fired him at Ceduna on the Sunday morning?"

"No."

Chamberlain read out a number of passages from Phin's report attributing statements to Gieseman which Gieseman now denied having made.

"Did you tell Phin that you noticed that Stuart was wearing his circus overalls on the Sunday morning?"

"No."

"He was, wasn't he?" "No."

"Did you tell Phin that you said to him, 'Get those bloody overalls off and get out. You're finished'?"

"No."

"You say that is not true?" asked the Chairman.

"Definitely not."

". . . Did you say," asked Chamberlain, " 'I don't like Stuart, but I don't think any of my employees would know anything about it'?"

"No. . . . He says to me, 'Do you believe any of your lads would have done it?' and I said 'No, definitely not.' He said, 'Was your lads away from the place?' I said, 'The only lads away from the place that day were Allan and Maxie.' He said, 'Could I speak to Allan and Maxie?' And that was the finish."

"Did he ask you not to discuss it with anybody for the time being?"

"No."

"Did he ask you to tell the lad that he would like to have a chat with him?"

"He did say that, yes."

That was the last to be heard of Phin until Allan Moir gave evidence.

When Gieseman left the box Dr. J. J. Bray, Q.C., who had remained in the court-room after his application to appear for O'Sullivan was rejected, rose to say that at some stage he might wish to question Gieseman.

"What questions could you be interested to ask?" said the Chairman.

"As to his movements and availability between December and the present time," said Bray.

"I cannot see that affects you," said Sir Mellis Napier. "Later on we will take it into consideration."

Edna Gieseman was then called and sworn. A lady reporter in the jury stalls described her as "plump and purposeful, with blue eyes, two soft little chins and a mouth like a bruised purple pansy". Her skin was light enough for the aboriginal part of her ancestry to be almost invisible. She was less articulate than her husband, and spoke very quietly; some of her remarks remained inaudible even to the court reporter six feet away. She was examined first by Brazel's junior, Mr. C. J. Legoe. Her account of the midday meal on Saturday was more detailed than her husband's. Stuart, she said, "came home just after we had our dinner . . . I said, 'Maxie, you know you should be on time for your meals.' And he had been drinking anyhow." He asked her to buy liquor for him, and she refused. "I gave him a piece of bread and butter with vegetables on it." Legoe reminded the witness that in her statutory declaration she had said that she told Miss Hopes to give Stuart the food. Stuart, she went on, walked out of the food tent—close on two o'clock, she supposed. Why did she "suppose"? "Well, he came home around a quarter to one—quarter to two I mean." She knew that by having glanced at a wall clock. Another woman in the party, Betty Gadd, agreed to go to the pub for Stuart and returned about a quarter to three with wine and beer. Stuart left the stall, wanting a drink; but Mrs. Gieseman put the liquor in the caravan and sent him back to the darts. At three o'clock she and Betty Gadd opened the Girl in the Goldfish Bowl, the only part of the show which had not started at two. She had seen Stuart go to the darts stall five minutes after his return; and she saw him and Moir leave the showground later, after he had given her £4 takings at about a quarter past four. She had no record of the £4 taken by Stuart. "I did not think it necessary to put down the takings of Ceduna because there wasn't very much and what money we did get was spent on expenses to get to the next place and tucker and rent for Whyalla."

On Saturday evening, Mrs. Gieseman said, she looked around the streets of Ceduna for Stuart and Moir. At the picture show the girl on the door agreed to put an advertisement for them on the screen ("she said that it might be a little hard to see . . . I think there was a technicolor show on that night"). Legoe showed Mrs. Gieseman that in her statutory declaration she had said: "I went along to the pictures and put an advert on the screen, but this did not bring them." She agreed that she had not actually seen it appear on the screen. On Sunday morning, when Stuart returned about eight o'clock, her husband told him he was finished. Stuart threw his overalls down, and said he had a job in Ceduna.

Mrs. Gieseman appeared to grow confused as Legoe asked what she had heard about the case after leaving Ceduna. At Whyalla, she said, she saw Stuart's picture in the paper. At Moonta she read a little bit about the Police Court hearing. "I read a little in some of the papers we bought. We don't buy papers every day." When had she first heard of Stuart's conviction by a jury? At Whyalla, she replied. Legoe encouraged her to see that this was plainly wrong. "I don't understand much about courts or anything like that," she said. Later, when Chamberlain pursued a similar line of enquiry, she said: "I don't understand arrested, charged or sentenced. I don't understand all them big words."

Her account of Dixon's arrival at Atherton was more vivid than Gieseman's. "My husband and myself was in the caravan and Father Dixon came to us and asked us did we know of Maxie Stuart's movements on Saturday afternoon and that is all Father asked us. I told Father that he was there between quarter to two and half past four, and when I told Father that, he nearly dropped." Since giving Dixon the declaration, she said, she had not discussed its contents with her husband. "I never worry about talking to Dad much."

Chamberlain asked about Stuart's English. "He was not that bad . . . I could understand a little bit." Did he talk blackfellow lingo? Yes, to his native friends. And how did he talk to her? In English.

"What sort of English?"

"It was not as good as my talk anyhow."

"Did you have any trouble in understanding him?"

"Sometimes."

"Did he have any trouble in understanding you?"

"No."

At Chamberlain's request Mrs. Gieseman reproduced the conversation with Dixon in Queensland. "He asked us," she said, "did we know the movements of Maxie Stuart between 2 p.m. and 4 p.m. on that Saturday. . . . We told Father that he was at home that afternoon."[1]

When she went on to report Dixon's approach to Miss Hopes, she did not attribute to him any specific reference to times. "I heard Father ask: 'Do you remember the times that Maxie was there that Saturday afternoon at Ceduna?' " Had she known what was going to be done with the statutory declaration she dictated? "I knew it was coming down here to save someone's life." But not until she was in Brisbane on the way to give evidence, Mrs. Gieseman said, did she

[1] This recollection differed from her husband's, from what Dixon himself was later to say in evidence, and from her own earlier answer to Legoe; according to these other accounts it was not the priest who first mentioned times.

hear at what time the little girl was murdered. Stuart had come home on the Saturday, she told Chamberlain, at about a quarter to two, and left at half past four. She looked at a clock when he arrived and at her wrist-watch when he left. When he came in late for what Chamberlain called lunch and she called dinner, his condition was "not real bad". Chamberlain said: "You would not like a drunk aboriginal attending to the sideshow, would you? It might give you a bad name. Or would you not mind?" "Oh," replied Mrs. Gieseman, "they all get on the drink around Ceduna."

On Sunday morning, asked Chamberlain, was Stuart kicked out?

"Not actually."

"Well, . . . was he dismissed? I am trying to use terms I think you will follow. Did your husband tell him . . . to go?"

"He told him he was finished with him because of his drinking but he did not say it in a nasty way or anything."

"Well, you see, that is rather a different story," said Chamberlain.

"I object to that," said Shand.

"Do not argue with the witness," said the Chairman.

"I am trying to make myself clear to the witness," said Chamberlain.

"Which is right, Mrs. Gieseman? Did you part on good terms?"

"Yes."

"Whose idea was it that Max went?"

Before Stuart had a chance to say he had a job, Mrs. Gieseman replied, her husband told him he could not stay with the show while he was drinking and would not help.

Miss Hopes began her evidence just before the Commission adjourned for the day. On Tuesday morning she returned to the box, for a shorter examination than either of her employers. The lady reporter saw her as "a thickset woman of indeterminate and unstated age, an expression of resignation on her lined, sun-burned face. She wore a black dress and a faded red topcoat which did not quite meet across her middle." She told Brazel that on the Friday evening in Ceduna Stuart worked beside her on the darts stall from seven until ten.[2] On the Saturday morning, she said, Stuart worked on the darts from about ten until eleven.[3] Miss Hopes said Stuart was late for dinner, which was eaten about one o'clock; but she also said that he arrived about one. He helped himself to bread and butter and vegetables and took about five minutes to eat them. He then went with her to the darts stall. It was now about two o'clock. Brazel pointed out that these times left fifty-five minutes unaccounted for, but questioning did not lead her to amend or add anything. She was sure that Stuart worked beside her from two until four, by which time few people were about and the stall was closed down. Stuart went into

[2] On every other account he left for the pictures some time before ten.
[3] On every other account he left for Ceduna earlier than that.

Ceduna with Moir, whom she asked to buy some chocolate for her. She supposed that on Sunday morning, when Stuart returned, she was busy clearing up; at any rate, she did not hear him and Gieseman conversing.

When Shand took up the problem of the missing minutes between one and two, Miss Hopes said that lunch was at one and that Stuart came in after the others had eaten. She now said that when she saw him it was "around about one, going on for two". Chamberlain asked how she had fixed the times mentioned to Brazel. "I always look at the clock," Miss Hopes replied.

The name of Allan Moir was called. Nearly five minutes later, he appeared at the door with the probation officer who had been his chaperon, and entered the court: a short, slim youth with a faint smile. Every eye in the public gallery was inspecting him hard; the examination of Gieseman had made it clear that it was Moir's conversation with Phin in Whyalla that led the police to apprehend Stuart. Moir told Brazel that he and Maxie Stuart got to the pictures on Friday night before half time. Maxie, he thought, spoke to a couple of dark girls there. On Saturday morning, he and Maxie left the show about nine, and on the beach were given wine ("dark, I think") by a man named Lennie. About ten he walked back to the show, alone. He left for Ceduna about a quarter past one to buy some boot polish, and saw Maxie there. The two of them got a taxi back to the show.

"You and Maxie went into the carnival together?"

"Yes, I think so."

"Are you sure?" "No."

He went on, however, to say that they both walked to the tent for a meal. Stuart then began to work on the darts, about ten past two, and stayed there, within Moir's sight, until about four. Had Moir always thought that Stuart was at the darts stall between these times? Yes. Brazel then produced a statement which Moir had made in the presence of Rivett at Collinsville on August 7. Moir identified his signature. He said that he could not read, that he remembered signing the document, and that it was read over to him before he signed. He agreed that he had said there: "I thought I saw Maxie working on the dart stall but I cannot be sure," and "I definitely saw him from about three o'clock". Was he sure, asked Brazel, that Stuart did not go off to Thevenard in the taxi?[4] "He could have done," replied Moir.

At what time did he himself leave the carnival in the afternoon? "Some time after four o'clock . . . later than five o'clock . . . about half past five I think." Maxie went with him.[5]

"That means, does it, that at a quarter past five or thereabouts he was working the darts . . . ?"

[4] The evidence that Stuart did so was overwhelming.

[5] In the statement he had signed at Whyalla on December 23, Moir said that Stuart worked on the darts between 6 p.m. and 8 p.m., and that the two of them went up the street at about 8 p.m.

"Yes."

When they set off for the town the sun was "still a bit in the sky". At the beach, ten minutes later, the sun was low down on the horizon. With Maxie and two other aborigines, he drank a flagon of wine on the beach. They climbed some steps from the beach, and Moir passed out; but before this happened, at the top of the steps, Stuart said: "Is there any blood on my chest?" Moir said he looked at Maxie's chest and could see no blood.

"Did he tell you why he was asking you . . . ?"

"He said he had knocked off Lennie[6] or somebody I think it was and dumped it in the sea."

"Did Stuart say that he *had* dumped it, or that he was going to?"

"He said he had."

"He was rather a nasty person in liquor, wasn't he?"

"He always wanted to fight."

"When he was in liquor?" "Yes."

"Was he in a quarrelsome mood that night?" "Not with me."

"What about with the others?"

"When we came off the beach—the others were sparring down on the beach."

Why had Moir not asked him about the person he had knocked over?

"I don't know. I just didn't ask him."

This conversation occurred about half past nine, Moir supposed. Then he passed out, and came to on a tank stand at the back of the picture hall with Maxie. They were told that their names had been on the screen. He returned to the carnival and did not see Maxie until next morning, when Gieseman told Stuart he was through and Stuart said he had a job on the Wheat Board.

"Were they friendly towards one another as far as you could see?"

"Yes."

Moir agreed that in Collinsville on July 30 (in the statement taken by Farrell of the *Sydney Morning Herald*) he had said that on the Saturday morning he came back to the show about a quarter past ten and started work, and that he did not know when Maxie came back. He said this, Moir added, before he remembered about the taxi. He also said on this occasion that it might have been anything from three to six o'clock when Maxie came back.

Shand took over, and for the first time in Adelaide began—in his slow, deliberate, lisping voice—to cross-examine a witness. Did Moir remember saying to a reporter: "What happens if Stuart gets off, do they look for another bloke?" Yes. Did he tell Sergeant Phin at Whyalla that for the whole of Saturday afternoon and evening he was in Stuart's company? Yes. Was that the truth? Yes.

[6] There appears to have been no effort by anybody at the Commission to discover Lennie's surname or to have him called as a witness.

Shand asked Moir about his apparently conflicting accounts of the time he left the show on Saturday afternoon. Had he mentioned half past five? Yes. And ten minutes later, when he was on the beach, the sun went down? Yes. Was he aware that the sun went down later than half past seven that day? No, he thought it went down about six o'clock. Work stopped at the show about four, Moir agreed, and he spent about half an hour at the show after that.

"What did you do in the other hour?" "I don't know."

"You agree you actually left not shortly before six but somewhere about half past four?"

"Could have been from half past four till six o'clock."

To further questioning he both affirmed and denied that it was about four o'clock. "I can't get right," he said. He told Mr. Justice Ross that he had no watch, that he could tell the time, and that the times he had been giving were estimates.

Shand turned to Moir's interview with the detective at Whyalla. After he signed a statement there on the Tuesday, Moir said, the police told him that Stuart had confessed, and gave him a cigar and ten shillings.

"Did they tell you why they gave you the ten shillings?"

"For helping, I suppose."

Moir said that he also gave the police a pair of white overalls belonging to Maxie, and told them that he had left in Stuart's coat some blades belonging to a leather knife.

"Did Phin say that the murdered child had been cut on the face?" "Yes."

Shand questioned Moir closely about his evidence that Stuart had spoken of knocking off Lennie. He took it to mean, Moir agreed, that Stuart had killed Lennie.

"When did you tell the police?"

"I didn't tell them."

"Why didn't you tell them?"

"I just forgot about it."

Shand's voice rose. "You forgot that someone had been murdered?"

Moir said he had it on his mind for a while, until they reached Whyalla.

"Did you remember it when you were talking to Sgt. Phin?" "Yes."

"Did you tell Sergeant Phin?" "No."

Did he think that the man who murdered Lennie might murder the girl? Moir answered: "I don't know." The question was repeated, and he said: "When the girl was murdered I thought he might have murdered the girl."

"Because he had murdered Lennie?"

"Instead of Lennie."

"And so you thought then that what he might have meant was that he murdered the girl?"

"Yes."

"Did you tell the police that?" "No."

"Were you trying to help them?" "Oh yes, a bit."

"How much?"

Smith, Shand's junior, suggested: "Ten shillings worth." Moir smiled. Why did he find that funny, asked Shand. "The rest of the bar did," said Chamberlain. "The way he said it," replied Moir.

Had he ever told the police, or Father Dixon, or anyone else, until today, that he thought Stuart might have killed the girl? No.

Had Phin asked whether he had been in trouble? No. Moir had, he agreed, been in trouble; before his expulsion from a Catholic school for touching a girl's breasts, he had drilled holes in the classroom chairs and sworn at the sisters. He had been in trouble with the police for drinking, and for stealing biscuits and rope, and he had been found guilty by a magistrate of breaking up lavatories in the high school at Norseman.

Chamberlain began by asking Moir whether he had become a little mixed up by a lot of people putting a lot of questions. Moir said he had. Did he tell a man on the telephone from Collinsville that Stuart came back to the show about five or six on Saturday afternoon?[7] No, said Moir, he did not say that. He did tell the man that he was not too sure of the time Stuart came back.

In the taxi on the way to the show, asked Chamberlain, was there some talk between Stuart and himself about girls? No.

Was it not the case that Stuart left Moir at the show and went away in the taxi? "Could have done."

"You didn't see anything more of him till a good bit later in the afternoon?"

"I know he was at the carnival for a while."

Did Moir know what time the taxi reached the sideshow? Yes, about a quarter to two.

"Could it have been as late as five or half past five when you saw Max next?"

"No, earlier than that."

"How much earlier?"

"I don't know."

Chamberlain took Moir through the statements he made in Whyalla. Did he tell Phin that at the pictures on Friday, Stuart "created some trouble by indecently interfering with some half-caste woman"?

"No. There was no trouble with a half-caste woman or any woman."

Did he tell Phin that on Saturday he was in town drinking with Stuart and another fellow, and that he flaked out once or twice during the evening? Yes.

Did he tell Phin that on Saturday evening he saw Maxie with a handful of notes?

[7] This was in the statement secured by the Brisbane *Courier-Mail* on July 29 and printed in the *Advertiser* and elsewhere.

"No, he never had any money," Moir said, but added a moment later: "Yes, he did have some money Saturday night."

"Did he say: 'I have just done a fellow over'?"

No, said Moir; and he himself had not told Phin that.

"After talking about the blood on his chest, did he ask you: 'Do you know where I can get the loan of a dinghy'?" "No."

"Did you tell Phin that he asked you that?" "No."

Did Stuart say that he had done someone in, and that he wanted to dump the body in the sea during the night? No, he was quite sure that Stuart said nothing like that; he said that he *had* dumped something already. Moir agreed with Chamberlain that when drunk Maxie was not a good man to argue with; but he denied that this was why he had told nobody of Stuart's remark about having dumped a body. When Mr. Justice Ross asked Moir how sober he himself was at this time, the boy replied: "I could see where I was going."

To further questions from Chamberlain, Moir said he told Phin about Maxie's reference to blood, and to dumping something, after he learned that the girl had been murdered but before he knew that Stuart had been charged.

Did Phin say what would happen to Maxie?

Yes, he said he could be hanged.

"Did you say: 'I did not know, so I am sorry I have told you anything'?"

"No, I did not say that."

"Were you sorry when you were told that Maxie might be hanged?"

"No."

Chamberlain also asked Moir about Stuart's English. Stuart used bad grammar, Moir said, but could make himself understood.

Released from the box, Moir was shown to the seats reserved for witnesses who had given evidence. Official protection was no longer given to him, and that afternoon he left the court in friendly conversation with the Giesemans and Miss Hopes.

10

A RATHER STARTLING REMARK

MOIR WAS THE LAST of the witnesses whose names were public knowledge. Geoffrey Dowman Spry was now called, and the Commissioners began to hear evidence from people who had been brought by the Crown from Ceduna. Spry, the only full-blood white among them, had lived in the town for some forty years and kept a shop in the main street. His testimony was short and simple. On Saturday, December 20, at approximately a quarter to two, a native who said his name was Stuart, and whom he now recognised from a photograph to be Rupert Max Stuart, entered the shop and asked him to ring for a taxi. He rang the Blackhams, whose car arrived in about a quarter of an hour. Stuart spoke English quite well. Cross-examined by Shand, Spry said that he was first asked about this incident a fortnight ago, by police officers. His employees normally went home for lunch between half past twelve and half past one, and it was at least a quarter of an hour after they came back from lunch this day that Stuart arrived. Stuart wanted to go to Thevenard. This was the first evidence at the Commission to conflict directly with what Gieseman and his wife and Miss Hopes had said. If Stuart went to Thevenard by taxi about two o'clock, he could not have been at the show at the time they swore to having seen him there. Spry appeared no less certain than Gieseman under cross-examination that his memory was accurate.

The next witness, Roy Wells, was black. He was the first of five young aboriginal men to give evidence. A Sydney reporter who visited Ceduna wrote of the west coast aborigines: "They are the people, perhaps, who feel about this murder most fiercely of all." If any of these witnesses felt fiercely towards Stuart, however, they did not betray it.

Wells told Brazel that he had been to school in Western Australia until he was fourteen; he could read English a little bit, and usually spoke it. Early on the morning of Saturday, December 20, he and his friend Clem Chester were driven to Ceduna from a place sixteen miles away where they had jobs on a farm. They reached the town at half past six. He and Chester went to the fun-fair. They saw a stranger, whom they learned later that day to be Max Stuart, sleeping in the knock-em tent. Wells saw also a fellow about sixteen who, he discovered, came from Norseman, near his own home town of Kalgoorlie.

About nine o'clock in the morning he and Chester saw Stuart in Ceduna with the boy from Norseman. About one o'clock, after spending more time at the show, he went back to Ceduna. About five past two, in Spry's shop, he saw and heard Stuart ask for a taxi. Dennis Blackham arrived in the car about half past two. Stuart and the boy drove off towards Thevenard, after Stuart told a group of people that he was going there. Wells walked to the showgrounds, alone, about a quarter to three. Just after he got there—"about three o'clock, quarter past three"—Blackham's taxi drove up, and the Norseman fellow and Stuart got out. Stuart picked up a case, returned to the taxi, and drove off towards Ceduna. About four o'clock he saw Stuart again, walking towards the showground. Wells said that he did not carry a watch, and that he was guessing the times. A Mrs. Betts, seeing Stuart, asked Wells who he was; he told her. About five o'clock he saw Stuart on the darts stall. Later, Wells said that the stalls were all open continuously from the afternoon until half past seven.[1]

Stuart was asked whether he had had a woman. Stuart replied: "No, I had a maiden down the beach." In town that evening, about nine o'clock, he saw Sergeant Walker speak to Stuart, and he heard Stuart say, out of the policeman's hearing: "I kill you like I kill the others." Stuart spoke in English; Wells understood him, and he appeared to understand Wells.

"Have you had some trouble with the police?" asked Shand. "Yes."

"What kind of trouble?" "For being drunk."

"How many times?" "I can't keep up to it."

Shand asked for a list of convictions, which was supplied next day while Wells was still in the box. Did he remember, Shand then asked, that he had been convicted for stealing? After a pause, Wells said that he remembered.

"This year the police have been in contact with you?" "Yes."

"On two occasions anyway you were fined?" "Yes."

"Are you going to ask him what for?" Brazel interposed.

"I made it quite clear," said Shand, "it is 'aboriginal drink liquor'. The fact that he had contact with the police is the only thing that interests me."

Wells said he gave three statements about Stuart to the police, at their request. When Shand asked about times, Wells repeated that he had left the showground for Ceduna at one o'clock.

"Did you go straight from the showground to Spry's shop?" "Yes."

"And as soon as you got to Spry's shop, did you see Stuart?"

"Yes." Stuart came back to the show in a taxi[2]—with the Kelly boys, he thought—about five o'clock.

He agreed that on his account there were three reasons why, on

[1] According to the show people themselves, the stalls were closed from about four until the evening.

[2] On every other account Stuart returned on foot.

Sunday, December 21, he thought Stuart had killed the girl: he was absent from the show; he had spoken of a maiden on the beach; and he had come back about four or quarter past four from the direction where the murder had happened. Why then, asked Shand, did he not tell the police about these things at the time? Wells replied that he did not take much interest. He told nobody what he heard Stuart say about a "maiden", until the police approached him recently.

The next witness was Clem Chester, who lived at Koonibba mission and was not quite as dark as his friend Wells. He told Brazel that on Saturday morning, December 20, he and Wells reached Ceduna about eight or half past.[3] He did not have a watch. At the fun-fair, early in the morning, he conversed with a man whom he now believed to be Stuart, and with a lad. Could he see the lad in court now? "My eyesight is very weak," replied Chester. He and Stuart spoke in English, and Stuart appeared to have no trouble understanding. Later in the day, after lunch at a friend's place, he went again to the show and stayed there for about two hours from two o'clock. He saw Roy Wells. Stuart was not present. He saw nobody running the darts, and he did not see Stuart again.

Shand's first questions were about Chester's eyesight. He could see a pressman in the jury stalls, he said, but not clearly. He could see the court reporter, closer to him, clearly.

"Would you recognise him?"

"I suppose I would—I would not say I would."

Could he see the clock on the wall? Chester pointed to it, but said he could not tell the time by clocks.

Had he seen the darts stall at the show? Yes.

"People going to it?"

"There was a few."

Did he see Stuart in the afternoon? No.

"You say you don't remember seeing him, is that what you say?"

"Yes."

Chester told Shand that he heard—apparently on Saturday—that Stuart had been sacked from the show.

Colin Ware, an aborigine whom Chester had mentioned as a companion and who also lived at Koonibba, now gave evidence. He told Legoe that he was harvesting on a farm last December, and came to Ceduna on Saturday, December 20 by a bus from Streaky Bay which arrived about a quarter to one. From the bus stop he crossed the street to Spry's shop, where he talked with two men under the veranda. A dark stranger, whom he now identified from a photograph as Stuart, walked around the corner. About a quarter of an hour later he saw Stuart and a young lad get into a taxi. He himself took a taxi to his uncle's place about a mile and a half out of Ceduna.

"What time was that, do you know?" asked Legoe.

[3] Wells had said half past six.

"I don't know; about a quarter to two I think."

At his uncle's place nobody was home, so he took the taxi back to town. On the way he picked up Clem Chester and another man. All three decided to visit the sideshows. The taxi dropped them there about two, and he stayed at the show about two hours. He did not see Stuart.

Ware agreed with Shand that he had seen photographs of Stuart in the newspapers; and the police, he said, showed him a photograph. He had made two statements to the police since the Royal Commission was established.

Did the police tell him why they wanted the *second* statement? "Yes," replied Ware, "the times was wrong." At first he had said that he was at Spry's shop at twelve o'clock. A policeman told him that this could not be right, as the bus from Streaky Bay did not arrive that day until a quarter to one. "As you see," Chester added, "we have not got watches . . ."

From the first of Ware's statements, Shand read a passage saying that when he reached Spry's shop, Blackham's taxi was waiting outside. Was that right? No, said Chester, that was wrong. Did he see the taxi leave with Stuart and Moir in it? No, he did not. Had he ever said: "The taxi went off with Stuart and the lad in it"? "No sir."

Shand read from a written statement by Chester the words he had just denied having used. At the sideshow in the afternoon, asked Shand, did he see the darts? "I never seen any." Did he see all the sideshows? Yes.

"Didn't you see any darts there at all?"

"I never saw them at all."

The next witness, Brenda Kent, was a quietly spoken girl of fifteen with a skin so light that nobody would have seen her as an aborigine had she not lived among aborigines. Last December, she said to Brazel, she was working as a domestic at the Thevenard Hotel with another girl, Veda Miller. On the evening of Friday, December 19, she went alone to the sideshows at Ceduna and saw a dark man in overalls. Not until she saw his photograph in the paper did she learn that his name was Stuart. From the showground she went to the pictures, where she sat with a girl named Olive Betts. Stuart and some other boys sat behind her, and when Stuart kicked the seat she and Olive told him not to. He asked Brenda her name, and gave Olive a box of chocolates. He and Olive spoke to each other, but Brenda could not remember what they said. After the pictures Stuart followed them along the street. At the post office the girls rang for a taxi to Thevenard.

Next day at the hotel she and Veda Miller helped to serve dinner, which started at half past twelve. She worked until about half past one or a quarter to two, and went to the room she shared with Veda. About half past two (she was guessing the time, she said), Veda came in and said something about someone else. Brenda went to the front veranda, where Stuart was sitting. She went inside without speaking, and cleaned her room. She and Olive Betts had a bath. The cleaning, bathing and dressing took about an hour and a quarter. She left the hotel, noticing that the clock showed about a quarter to four. Stuart was sitting outside. He asked where the other girls were. She said they were in the hotel. She did not see him again. They spoke in English. She understood Stuart easily, and he appeared to understand her.

Shand asked Brenda Kent what time she usually had her own lunch on Saturday. About half past one, she said. She agreed that it depended upon what time the people in the dining room finished, and she could not remember how many people were there that day. While she was in her room after lunch, where was Olive Betts? "In the room," replied Miss Kent.

Did Olive leave the room after lunch? "I do not know."

"Was she in that room on the Saturday?" asked the Chairman.

"No, it was her day off, Saturday."

To Shand, however, Miss Kent said that Olive *was* in the room.

"Why did you say it was her day off," said Shand, "when I asked you if she was in your room?"

"Because it was her day off."

"But she was still in the room, wasn't she?" "Yes."

"I suppose when you say it was her day off, she could go out any time she wanted to?" "Yes."

"And you know that she was the girl that Stuart was asking about, wasn't she?" "Yes."

She agreed that Olive was the girl to whom Stuart had given chocolates at the pictures.

"Now, when you came back from lunch, was she in the room then?"

"I can't remember." She did not know whether Olive went down to see Stuart.

"Do you know that Olive got money from boys for going out with them?" "No, I do not know."

"You knew she used to go out with boys, didn't you?"

"I didn't know she used to go out with boys."

Olive Betts had not been brought to Adelaide. Veda Miller, who had, was the next witness. She was a little older than her friend, and a little darker. Her account of events at the pictures was similar, except that she told Brazel she saw nothing passed to Olive. Saturday dinner at the hotel began at twelve,[4] she said. To successive questions from Brazel about what time she finished work that day, the witness replied: "about half past one" and "half past two". Then, she said, she left the hotel to visit a friend and saw the man whom she knew to be Stuart sitting outside. He came across to her. "I can't remember the exact words he said to me but he asked whether I had a boy

[4] Brenda Kent said half past twelve.

friend and I told him yes I had a boy friend." He asked where the other girls were, and she replied that they were inside. She told Brenda the man was sitting outside. She went off to her friend's place, and never saw Stuart again.

"You knew it was Olive he wanted to see?" asked Shand.

"Yes." Olive had told her that it was Stuart who gave her chocolates at the pictures.

"When you saw him outside the hotel, was that how you knew it was Olive he wanted to see?" "Yes."

"I suppose you went up and told Olive, didn't you?"

"No, I didn't tell her."

"Olive was in the room, wasn't she?" "Yes."

"And in front of Olive you said that this man was there, you went into the room and said that?"

"Yes, but she didn't come out. Brenda came out."

A few minutes later, however, when Shand asked whether Olive was in the room that afternoon, the witness said: "No."

"You are quite sure that Olive was not in the bedroom any time after you came up from lunch . . . ?"

"Yes." A moment later she returned to her original assertion that Olive *was* in the room that afternoon.

"Why did you say she was not?"

"I don't know. I just forgot."

Brazel wished to clear up one point. To himself the witness had said that at the pictures she did not see Stuart give anything to Olive; and to Shand she said that later she learned Stuart had given the girl a box of chocolates. She now said that it was Saturday night when she learned from Olive of Stuart's present the night before.[5]

The mother of Olive Betts now gave evidence: a large, grey-haired dark woman who appeared to have no teeth. On the day of the murder, she said to Legoe, she came into Ceduna about one o'clock. Around four—she was guessing the times—while standing outside the baker's shop, "I seen a chap coming from the direction of Thevenard . . ." He was a native, and he was walking towards the sideshows. Roy Wells told her this was the chap from the sideshows. She had since seen a photograph of the man in the paper. When Legoe gave her a stack of photographs, she was unable to identify Stuart among them. She usually wore glasses, she said, but had left them at home.

Who told her, asked Shand, that this man was Stuart? Roy Wells told her.

"Did anyone speak to you about it except Roy until the police saw you?" "No."

A policeman had asked her if she was in the street that day, and she said she was. That was all she could remember telling the police.

[5] To Shand, however, she had said that *on Saturday afternoon* she knew Stuart wanted to see Olive because he had given her chocolates.

With help from the Chairman, Shand tried without great success to fix the events of Mrs. Betts' day by reference to her meal times. "We do not have dinner," she said; "we just buy what we can get in the shop."

"Where do you eat it?"

"In the street where we are." She was in the street from two until nearly five. "If it's hot, we stop there, see."

The last evidence heard on the third day came from Donald Kelly, a labourer who lived at Koonibba mission. The barristers called him, as they called all the aboriginal men, by his first name. He said to Brazel that on the day of the murder he came from Koonibba with his brother, their wives and another man in a taxi driven by Mrs. Blackham, after dinner at the mission. Dinner was at twelve o'clock. They left the mission at half past three or later. He had not been carrying a watch, and the time was a guess. The trip, of twenty-five miles, took "about half an hour or more". The car reached Ceduna "a bit after four o'clock". They made for the baker's shop, and he saw from there a native walking from the sea towards the fun-fair. Kelly whistled to the man, and waved when he looked around. The man said that his name was Max Stuart and that he came from the fun-fair. "He was half-shot," said Kelly. Stuart said that he had just come out of gaol and that he had had a fight with a New Australian at the Thevenard Hotel. The right side of his right fist, Kelly saw, was swollen. They gave Stuart thirty shillings when he said he could get them grog, but they never received either the liquor or the money. Kelly and his brother and the third man walked to the fun-fair with Stuart, arriving about a quarter past four. They saw Roy Wells there, and stayed about an hour. Stuart went away with "the other joker, Allan" before they themselves left. Kelly saw Stuart working on the darts for about three quarters of an hour, next to a white lady. On Saturday evening, at half time at the pictures, he saw Stuart again, "pretty full"—worse than he had been in the afternoon. Kelly had no trouble understanding Stuart's English, and Stuart appeared to have no trouble understanding him.

"Did he speak good English?" asked the Chairman.

"Broken down English," said the witness. ". . . I have a better English than him."

Shand asked Kelly about his knowledge of the murder. By Sunday he had heard about it, he said.

"And you read, I suppose, she had been left alone on the beach in the afternoon, is that right?"

"I don't know."

"When do you think she was killed?"

"I don't know." She might have been killed on Thursday or Friday, for all he knew.

* * *

Brazel rose to say that in view of Moir's evidence, it seemed to him, Detective Phin should be called. At the request of Stuart's counsel, Blackham, the taxi-driver, was to be brought over from Ceduna; and in view of today's cross-examination of Ware, a bus driver would be brought to testify as to the time when the bus actually arrived at Ceduna. The drivers of the taxi and bus could not reach Adelaide before Friday afternoon. Before then, Brazel said, he hoped that the other witnesses would have completed their testimony. "We will then reach the stage at which it will be most convenient for Stuart to testify, if he desires to give evidence." Shand said that Stuart would give evidence, but asked that he should be heard after police witnesses.

"In the ordinary course of events he would be," said Sir Mellis Napier, "but for the reasons indicated you will realise that you must necessarily be in the position of accuser so far as the police evidence is concerned, and it should——"

Shand tried to interrupt. "With great respect, I am of course in your hands, but I would say——"

"I am only pointing out," said the Chairman, "that it is you who asked to be allowed to satisfy us that the verdict was not one that should have been returned as it was, or rather . . . to raise in our minds what we regard as a doubt that any reasonable jury must entertain or might entertain. . . . You are now in the position of the accuser and it is the police who should be allowed to answer the evidence . . ."

"I do not accept that position," said Shand, "but I will have to if you say so."

"I am afraid you will have to," said the Chairman. If this were an appeal, he went on, Shand would be out of court. Shand agreed. So it was for Shand, the Chairman said, to disturb the satisfaction which the court must feel with the verdict.

"That, with respect, I submit, is not the position . . ." said Shand. He agreed that all the processes of the law had been fulfilled; "but an exceptional state of affairs has, in the opinion of the government, arisen."

"Not so exceptional," said the Chairman; "it is something that might occur at any time."

"I accept that, Your Honour."

Sir Mellis Napier now made a remark which the *Advertiser* thought so newsworthy as to make the Commission's proceedings, for the first time in the week, its main item of the day. "There has been a campaign of misrepresentation and of abuse that has aroused such a state of uncertainty and distrust in the community that we are on the point of distrusting the verdict of the jury before any evidence has been produced to justify any distrust. In these circumstances the Executive Government has seen fit to direct a further enquiry, but in that enquiry it is not the police who are the prosecutors but it is the accused who is called upon to disturb the verdict that has been arrived at."

Shand submitted that Stuart had to satisfy a court only that in the light of new evidence the case might not have been proved against him beyond reasonable doubt. Stuart was not an accused person, the Chairman observed, but a convicted person; "and while we entirely accept your suggestion that it would be sufficient for you to disclose good reasons for doubt as to the propriety of the verdict, and if we accept that as the onus upon you, it is still the onus upon you . . . It is no longer upon the Crown to adduce the evidence that justifies the verdict . . . We will endeavour, as I think we have endeavoured, to give you every opportunity to present your case as fully and as favourably as you can, but at the same time we have to realise that it is you who are accusing the police, and accusing them of a very, very serious crime . . . They are being charged with perjury, to put it bluntly."

Shand asked that the Commissioners should report whether, in view of the evidence and anything that might eventuate, it would be safe to accept the verdict of the jury which had not the additional material.

"As I understand you," said the Chairman, "I think I should agree with you."

"I understand what has fallen from Your Honour in the same way," said Shand.

In this spirit of tentative harmony the Commission adjourned for the day, after the Chairman had agreed that Strehlow could precede Stuart in the box to give evidence about language. It might help, added the Chairman, if O'Sullivan were heard before Stuart. Nobody commented on the suggestion. Sir Mellis Napier said that the Commissioners would think over Brazel's suggestion about when Stuart should be called, and rule on the matter next day.

* * *

On Thursday morning Donald Kelly returned for further questioning by Shand.

Was he pretty clear what time he got into Ceduna on Saturday?

"No, not quite sure. . . . A bit after four, it was four o'clock or more." Kelly himself played darts, and saw Stuart looking after them. All the other sideshows were going when he left, about a quarter past five.

The last aboriginal witness was Dennis Kelly, who told Brazel much the same story as his brother, but added something new. At the fun-fair he heard Allan Moir ask Stuart if he had had a —, and Stuart replied: "I had a tight one." Asked about Stuart's language, the witness said that he spoke "half and half" English and a native language, and that his English was "a bit on the broken side".

"Could you understand him?" asked Brazel.

"A little."

When Stuart said: "I had a tight one," Shand asked the witness, was his brother Donald Kelly there? Yes, and so was Roy Wells.[6]

When he heard next day about the murder, did he think that Stuart had done it? No.

"Did you think that when he said he had 'a tight one' that meant the little girl?" "Yes."

Did his brother think so too?

"I don't know. . . . I didn't say anything to him about it."

Had he thought, Shand asked again, that Stuart had murdered the child?

This time the witness said, "Yes."

"Did you tell the police about that?"

"No." Today was the first time he had ever told anyone.

Brazel re-examined the four witnesses from the fun-fair on one point—whether the clocks and watches in the party were advanced to Central Australian time (an hour and a half ahead of Western time) when the show reached Ceduna, its first pitch in South Australia. The questioning appeared to show beyond doubt that this had been done.

Shand took the opportunity to ask Gieseman more about events on the Saturday afternoon. "Everything opened at two o'clock?"

"Yes. I started the music . . . At four o'clock I said: 'It is dying off now, stop the music.' We stopped the music and they gradually drifted away." Canvas was draped in front of one or two sideshows. At the laughing clowns, Johnny Woods sat until five o'clock in case there was an odd customer.

Did he remember anything further about Stuart's actions during the afternoon?

"He did slip in a couple of times and change the record."

A short, rugged, sun-burned young man in a yellow open-necked shirt now entered the box. This was William McNeish, who ran the section of the show with which Moir was travelling through Queensland, and who had signed a statement in Collinsville for the editor and police roundsman of the *News*, Rivett and Clark. To Brazel he said that he saw Stuart come home late for dinner on the Saturday; "about one or half past", he guessed. Stuart then went to start work on the darts, possibly at two o'clock. From where he himself worked, on the horse-o-plane, Stuart was in full view. He was quite sure that Stuart did not leave the showgrounds between two and four. About four, they had a cup of tea together.[7] Stuart and Allan Moir then left, at about a quarter or half past four. Stuart's English was "not very good".

"You could understand him?" "Yes."

[6] Neither of them mentioned the remark when giving evidence.

[7] In his statutory declaration, however, McNeish had said: "We had tea as usual, some time after four and before dark while we were getting ready for the show which begins between half past six and seven. Max had tea with us there in the tent."

On Sunday morning, said McNeish, Stuart came to the fun-fair about seven o'clock.[8]

"Did Mr. Gieseman say anything to Max like 'Get off those overalls and get out' . . . ?" "No."

"Did Gieseman and Stuart part good friends or otherwise?"

"Not very good friends."

Had he seen anything in the newspapers later about Stuart being charged with murder?

"I don't read much about the papers."

"Did you read anything about Stuart's case?" "No."

". . . Have you at any time learned from anyone at what time it was said this little child had been attacked?"

"I don't think so."

Who spoke to him about his declaration in Collinsville before he signed it?

"Two blokes." They gave their names, but he could not remember them.

"This was only thirteen days ago," said Brazel; "what is your memory like?"

"Not very good."

"Did they tell you why they wished to get this information about Stuart?" "No."

He had told the two men that Stuart made a nuisance of himself when drunk, and that he was on the liquor in Ceduna.

"Did they ask you if Stuart was at the fun-fair between two and four?"

"Yes."

"What did you say to that, Bill?"

"I just told them he was."

". . . Did they tell you if he was at the fun-fair between two and four he couldn't have committed the murder . . . ?"

"No, they didn't say that."

The Chairman asked: "What did you think this was all about? Why did these people come to you? What did you understand they were doing?"

"They were asking me about Stuart's case."

"But what for?" asked Mr. Justice Reed. "Why?"

"What business was it of yours, as far as you know?" the Chairman added.

"I can't say," McNeish replied. He said that before the two men approached him, he had read in the Queensland newspapers that the Giesemans had said Stuart was at the show from two to four. He did not know that Moir had made a declaration; he and Moir did not talk about the Stuart case.

Shand asked about the tea which McNeish said he had with

[8] Gieseman had said nine o'clock, and Mrs. Gieseman eight o'clock.

Stuart at about four o'clock. Who else had it with them? Johnny Woods and, he thought, Allan Moir. He himself made the tea. At this time the rest of the stalls were closed down.

Did McNeish know, asked Chamberlain, whether his evidence would help Stuart, whether it would save him from hanging or might even help to put the noose around his neck?

"No," said the witness, and repeated the answer when the Chairman questioned him similarly.

"As far as you know," Chamberlain continued, "those gentlemen who were seeing you in Queensland might have been looking for evidence for the police?"

"They could have been."

Had he ever asked Allan Moir what he knew about Stuart's doings on the day of the murder? No.

"Are you on friendly terms with Stuart?" "Yes."

"Here is a friend who has been charged with murder and who has been in your company on the day in question and in the company of another friend . . . And the murder was never mentioned between you. Is that right?" "Yes."

Shand asked: "Did you have any idea at what time in the day or in the night this little girl had been killed?"

"No," said McNeish.

Before the next witness was called, the Chairman gave the Commissioners' ruling on Brazel's inquiry about when Stuart should give evidence. Stuart, as accuser, would have to appear before those whom he was accusing. Strehlow could be called before Stuart, if counsel wished.

* * *

Alexander Adam Phin was a solidly built man of sixty, with the permanent mild frown of one who is slightly deaf. He had retired from the police force, but in December last, as he now told Legoe, he was a detective-sergeant stationed at Whyalla. Phin was not mentioned by name at the trial; but as Mr. Justice Reed said in his summing up, the defence case was that the police "got some information from Whyalla—whatever that was we do not know", which led them to arrest Stuart.

In the first minutes of Sunday, December 21, Phin said, he learned of the murder at Ceduna. On Monday evening he went along the main street of Whyalla to look at a circus which had just arrived, and made himself known to the proprietor, Gieseman. From Gieseman, who struck him as "a good type of man", he learned that one Maxie Stuart had joined the show in Western Australia. "He told me that Stuart had gone off on a drinking bout shortly after arriving in Ceduna . . . on the Friday, and that he did not see much more of him or did not get any service from him . . . and that he had sacked him because he was of no use to him."

"Did he tell you the words he had used to Stuart when he sacked him?" asked Legoe.

"Yes, 'Get those bloody overalls off and get out. You are finished.' "

According to Gieseman, Stuart then adopted a hostile attitude, but took off his overalls, got his belongings, and left. Gieseman said something about the wheat stacks, but Phin could not remember what. Phin was referred by Gieseman to Allan Moir, who, he said, would probably know more about Stuart.

The Chairman then asked: "Did you put any questions to him [Gieseman] as to whether he knew where his people had been on that Saturday afternoon?"

"No, not as far as I can remember . . . I did not try to pin-point any time because at that time . . . I had not been informed when the murder had taken place."

Phin described his conversation with Moir as follows: "I am a police officer. Now don't alarm yourself, Allan, there is nothing wrong as far as you are concerned. I am seeking your assistance in a little matter . . . Do you know a man named Maxie Stuart?"

"Yes."

". . . Could you tell me anything about Maxie?"

Moir said that he was a good fellow sober but nasty when drinking. On Friday evening, Moir said, Maxie left the circus and went into the town, drinking. According to Phin's recollection, "Moir said Stuart went to the pictures, and I think Allan said he did too, and Stuart molested, interfered with some half-caste woman in an advanced state of pregnancy, and there was some trouble about it . . ." On Saturday, Moir told him, he and Stuart drank wine, somewhere about lunch-time, in a cave near the jetty in Ceduna, with a half-caste named Lennie. Maxie was sparring with someone. He and Stuart went back to the circus. Allan did some work there, but he did not know what happened to Stuart. Moir next saw Stuart late in the afternoon or early in the evening in Ceduna, drunk, and carrying a handful of notes. Stuart said: "I just done a fellow over." Moir said he was surprised and asked what Stuart meant. Maxie replied: "Oh, I have knocked them over before," or words to that effect.

When Phin asked who Stuart did over, Moir said: "I do not know, unless it was the big half-caste named Lennie . . ." Moir said Stuart asked: "Is there blood on my chest?" Moir thought he was joking. Stuart then said: "Do you know where I can get a boat, a dinghy? . . . I have just done someone in, and I want to take a body out to sea after dark and dump it." Phin told the Commission that Moir thought Stuart was joking until he looked at his face. "He frightened me," Moir said, "because he looked serious."

Moir returned to the circus. On Sunday morning, Moir told him, Stuart appeared to be under the influence of liquor[9] and Gieseman

[9] Nobody else suggested that this was so after Stuart's night in the cell.

said: "Get those bloody overalls off, get your stuff and get out," or words to that effect. Moir thought Stuart would have a go at the boss, but he went off in a taxi. A half-caste had said something about getting a job for Stuart at the wheat stacks, and Moir thought he could be found there. Moir gave Phin a pair of white overalls which, he said, had been Maxie's.

Close to nine o'clock on Monday evening, Phin said, he told his inspector what he had heard. The inspector rang Ceduna. Phin spoke with both Sergeant Walker and Detective-Sergeant Turner. The inspector himself went round with him for another talk with Moir.

Did Moir say anything to the inspector, in Phin's presence, about a saddler's knife and blades? Yes, he thought Moir mentioned that he had the handle and Stuart had the nineteen blades. Phin had taken possession of the handle, which he now produced in court. Later on Monday night Phin heard that Stuart had admitted killing the child and had been charged with murder. Next morning, Tuesday, he took a written statement from Moir. It was now tendered to the Commission and read out. He told Moir, Phin said, that Stuart had admitted the murder. Moir did not seem alarmed, but asked: "What will happen to him?" Phin replied: "I don't know, but they could hang him for an offence like that." Moir put his hands over his face and his head forward (Phin demonstrated) and said: "Maxie, Maxie. I am sorry now I told you so much."

"You thought that was a genuine kind of remark?" Shand began. "Yes."

"Did you ask him to add it to the statement?" "No."

"Have you made any notes of your conversation with him?" "No."

Did Phin have information, before he spoke with Moir, that a little girl had been murdered on Saturday afternoon?

"My information was that she disappeared at about sundown . . ."

In the written statement, Shand pointed out, Moir said: "Phin mentioned the murder of a female child at Ceduna on Saturday afternoon."

He might have mentioned that, Phin said.

Wasn't it a lesson the police learned, asked Shand, that they should test anyone before accepting him?

An exchange between Shand and one of the Commissioners followed, which a reporter from the Melbourne *Herald* cited as an example of "an undercurrent of feeling . . . evident between the Sydney man and some of the South Australians".

"Perhaps," said Mr. Justice Reed, "you could indicate which police force you are talking about."

"I exclude the Soviet," replied Shand. "Any English-speaking police force."

"That is narrowing it down a little," said the judge. "Perhaps you will bring it to the South Australian police force."

Both men, according to the *Herald* reporter, wore rather tight smiles.

Shand asked Phin if he was taught in the South Australian police force that before he trusted a person he should have reason to trust him. "That is common sense, isn't it?"

"Yes."

"You knew very little about this young man, did you?"

"Very little indeed."

". . . Did you tell him that he had nothing to fear?"

"I believe I did assure him that he had nothing to worry about."

". . . For all you knew he might have been one of the guilty persons?"

"Possibly so." He would then, Phin agreed, have had something to fear.

Shand asked if Moir said that he had "flaked out" during the afternoon as well as in the evening.

"I understood that was before lunch," Phin replied.

"And after lunch too?"

"No, I don't remember him saying he flaked out the second time."

Shand read from a written statement by Phin in which he said that Moir told him: "I . . . flaked out once or twice during the afternoon and evening."

If that was in the statement, said Phin, it would be right.

He agreed that the statement had been written only a few days ago. Shand invited him to compare certain passages in this written account of the conversation on the Monday evening, with the statement taken from the boy in writing next day. The first document, said Shand, reported Moir as saying that Stuart was under the influence of liquor on *Friday* evening; yet in the second document, Moir said that they had nothing to drink on Friday evening. Was there not diametrical opposition here? Phin said he thought not, but when pressed he agreed that there had been "evidently an omission" on his part when taking Moir's statement.

According to Phin's report, Moir said that in the pictures on Friday evening Stuart interfered indecently with a half-caste woman in an advanced state of pregnancy.

"Did you notice," asked Shand, "that when you took Moir's statement on the Tuesday morning there was nothing at all appearing about that in respect of Friday night?"

"I have remembered it since; it was a point I overlooked."

Phin had no doubt that according to Moir this incident happened on the Friday night, and that the words "advanced state of pregnancy" and "indecently interfering" were used by Moir himself.

Shand pointed out that in the later statement, Moir said that *on Saturday* he was sitting outside the picture theatre "next to a half-caste woman who was pregnant". Did Phin remember Moir saying that?

"No, he did not tell me that."

Shand asked him to look at Moir's statement. Phin did so, and agreed both that it contained such a passage and that there was no reference in it to any indecency to a half-caste woman *on Friday*.

"It is possible," said Phin after a number of questions, "that I might have confused the two."

"That is the explanation?" "Yes."

"They are nothing alike, are they?"

Phin agreed, but said: "This interview happened seven months ago."

Shand suggested that Phin had given, at different stages, three different explanations of the discrepancy. What happened in the next few minutes of proceedings was to be discussed more widely, and analysed more closely, than perhaps anything ever said within these walls.

"I am asking you," said Shand, "why you did not ask some questions of Moir and you have given three possibilities."

"I have previously explained that I might have overlooked that," said Phin.

According to the official transcript, the following words were now spoken:

MR. SHAND: Is that the one you say is the real explanation?

NAPIER, C.J.: He is not obliged to explain anything.

MR. SHAND: If he says he can't explain it . . .

NAPIER, C.J.: It is for him to say whether he wishes to go any further or whether he wishes to leave his evidence where it is.

MR. SHAND: If you want to stop me cross-examining I will stop.

NAPIER, C.J.: I have not the slightest intention of stopping you but as far as I am concerned I have heard enough of this.

MR. SHAND: If you are going to take that attitude when cross-examination is going on I think in this case cross-examination must be essentially severe.

NAPIER, C.J.: If you feel it is helping you to convince us well and good.

MR. SHAND: I feel it is impossible to convince Your Honour on this because Your Honour says you don't want to hear any more of it.

REED, J.: That is a rather startling remark to make.

MR. SHAND: It may be but I make it and maintain it.

NAPIER, C.J.: You are at liberty to maintain it and it is for you to say how you are exercising your discretion but you have a court or you have a tribunal that is in the habit of hearing evidence and of assessing the value of a witness and the value of an oath. Everybody makes mistakes at times.

MR. SHAND: If Your Honour regards it as a mistake before I complete my cross-examination it is useless to cross-examine further and I sit down.

Napier, C.J.: It is for you to say what you wish to do but you are perfectly at liberty to continue and you can stay here as long as it suits you.

Mr. Shand: I will ask you three more questions although I have a number of other questions.

Shand asked the questions quickly and sat down. Phin left the box.

* * *

Normally the Commission adjourned at half past four. It was now just after half past three. Brazel reported that there were no more witnesses within call. He went on to say that he now had copies of statements for which Shand had asked. "I draw attention," said Brazel, "to the fact that there are two glaring inaccuracies uttered with great publicity contained in Mr. Shand's statement last Monday morning . . ." On the previous Friday, Shand had said, three witnesses named Wardrop gave a statement to the solicitor instructing Brazel that a policeman had admitted bashing the confession out of Stuart. These statements, Brazel said, were not in existence on Friday; moreover, "none of the persons claims to have heard the words alleged to have been uttered by Mr. Shand last Monday."

Brazel handed out copies of the statements. Shand looked quickly through them and said (according to the transcript): "The statements are a little stronger than I indicated and I admit it."

"Do you wish the witnesses brought?" asked Brazel.

They would be wanted, replied Shand, who also said: "I would like Your Honours to give me an adjournment to consider my own position as to what I intend to do."

The adjournment was granted.

Next morning Shand withdrew from the Commission.

11

EXIT MR. SHAND

WHILE THE LAWYERS, the judges and the witnesses were talking about Stuart, so were thousands of people elsewhere. In most of the Australian press and in radio bulletins, the Royal Commission competed with the tour of Princess Alexandra as the biggest news of the day. Every poster and every front-page headline in the *News* was about the Commission; on the day the first witnesses were heard, the paper devoted to it four hundred column-inches spread over eight pages. The *Advertiser* next morning carried more than two hundred and fifty column-inches. Most papers outside South Australia depended for their stories on the services of the *News* and *Advertiser*. Keeping up with the proceedings was no easy job for newspapermen. Some witnesses mumbled, and so did Shand; and over in the jury stalls, the most sharp-eared reporter could not hear every word. Sub-editors had to decide quickly where to make cuts in very long reports and how to head them. There were a number of mistakes: in London even *The Times* nodded, turning Brazel into Bazell. The *News* had Shand ask Phin whether he gave Moir a *scarf* (the word was *cigar*); a *News* caption confused Brazel with Mr. Justice Reed. The *Advertiser* report of Shand's request for an adjournment led readers into a serious misunderstanding. Shand's collision with Sir Mellis Napier happened too late for the afternoon papers to display. Next morning the *Advertiser* made it appear that Shand had sought an adjournment on account of what Brazel said about statements by the Wardrops. "Mr. Shand admitted," the report went on, "that the statements were 'not quite as strong' as he had indicated." Some, though not all, morning papers in other states reproduced this version.

When the Commissioners entered on Friday morning, Shand and his colleagues Miss Devaney and Smith sat in their places, but the table in front of them—covered the previous day with an untidy pile of papers and books—was bare, except for a copy of the *Advertiser* and a single typewritten sheet of paper. Shand rose and said: "I would like to call attention to something that appeared in this morning's paper. It is there suggested that I asked for an adjournment to consider my position on account of the mention of certain statements. Of course I did not do that. It was a question of my cross-examination that came up; that was why I asked for the adjournment. It is further said that I admitted the statements were not quite as strong as I had indicated. That is not what I said. I said: 'The statements are a little stronger', and that is what the transcript said." Mr. Justice Reed said that his own recollection agreed with Shand's.[1] The Wardrops' statements, Shand said, were apparently made verbally, not in writing, on the Friday, and were not transcribed until the Monday.

Shand turned to what he called "the position that arose yesterday", and read this statement: "My instructing solicitors and myself consider after yesterday that we are not being given, nor will be given, a thorough investigation in this matter. We consider that our continued association with this Commission will in no way help Stuart and will in fact handicap him. We think the particulars[2] have established that this Commission is unable properly to consider the problems before it and we therefore withdraw."

Sir Mellis Napier said: "Mr. Shand, may I say that you perhaps do not realise that while we are engaged on this enquiry, the whole business of the court is virtually at a standstill. We have, therefore, relied upon counsel to give us the assistance that we are entitled to by seeking to arrive at the truth, and by omitting to waste our time on irrelevant matters." No destruction of Phin's credit, said the Chairman, could have altered the fact that Moir made a written statement in December. "So far as Phin's testimony went to conversations with the lad and Mr. Gieseman, you had already made your point that Phin was speaking from his recollection of events that had happened more than six months before he was asked to recall his statement . . . In these circumstances, it was obvious that the Commission could hardly use Phin's recollection of these conversations as contradicting the sworn testimony of any credible witness."

"I am not concerned to argue with Your Honour," replied Shand, "beyond saying this, that cross-examination has more in it than is involved in Your Honour's statement. Time and time again it happens, what might be considered severe cross-examination brings out the truth in other respects, and, personally—in the cross-examination which no one suggests was unfair and which had some object—I have never in my career been stopped before." Shand and his two colleagues walked out of the court-room.

Before they reached the door Brazel began to speak, without a glance in their direction. He said that one of the three witnesses whom Shand had mentioned was seen briefly on Friday; the other two "were not seen, as Mr. Shand still continues to allege in defiance of truth, until a later date". Brazel asked the Commissioners if he might

[1] The *Advertiser* wrote next day: "We accept Mr. Shand's statement. In the difficult surroundings, our reporter mis-heard what Mr. Shand said. We regret the error." The paper reported Shand's other criticism prominently, without comment.

[2] Where the official transcript had "particulars", some newspapers had "past days". The court reporter responsible for this passage admitted later that he may have mis-read his shorthand note.

approach the Law Society to see whether legal representation could be made available for Stuart. "It does seem to me," he said, "that in the turn this Commission has taken this morning, justice could not be done to someone who has been momentarily overlooked, namely Stuart, without adequate representation for him." The Commissioners agreed with Brazel that Stuart should be represented. "It appears to us," said the Chairman, "as it appears to you, that the interests of Mr. Shand's client have been entirely overlooked, and those interests must be considered and protected." The enquiry would have to adjourn, he said, until Brazel secured adequate representation.

The *News* reported Shand's withdrawal with posters and headlines which were themselves to become the subject of prosecution. A poster on the streets before noon said:

SHAND QUITS
"YOU WON'T GIVE STUART
FAIR GO"

A later poster said:

COMMISSION BREAKS UP
SHAND BLASTS NAPIER

The front-page headline on all editions was:

Mr. Shand, Q.C., indicts Sir Mellis Napier
"THESE COMMISSIONERS CANNOT DO THE JOB"

In later editions the Commission occupied the whole front page. There was a report of the morning's events, a picture of Shand and Miss Devaney leaving the Supreme Court, a statement about the *Advertiser* headed "LAWYERS CRITICISE NEWSPAPER: WRONG REPORT", and a photograph with the heading "Chairman under Fire" and this caption: "Sir Mellis Napier, Chairman of the Royal Commission, who interrupted Mr. Shand's cross-examining of a vital witness yesterday with the statements, 'He is not obliged to explain anything, Mr. Shand . . . As far as I am concerned, I have heard enough.' *Sir Mellis Napier will be 77 in October. He has sat in the Supreme Court for 35 years. He was knighted sixteen years ago.*" Inside, under the title "NATION WATCHES STUART COMMISSION", were reproduced a number of headlines from interstate newspapers. A caption said: "How is justice done in South Australia? Following many articles in newspapers in the other capitals in recent weeks, including charges that S.A. is Australia's 'Hanging State', interest in Adelaide's Royal Commission is nationwide."

That interest now became more intense than ever. Other evening newspapers put Shand's withdrawal in bold type on their front pages. "SHAND Q.C. WALKS OUT. STUART ENQUIRY SENSATION. 'Not thorough probe,' he says," wrote the Melbourne *Herald*. In Sydney the *Sun* said: "SHAND Q.C. PULLS OUT! 'Can't get full probe on Stuart,'" and the *Mirror*: "'USELESS!' SHAND QUITS STUART PROBE."

The papers were anxious to get a statement from "the headline Q.C.", as one of them now called him. Shand said nothing to the press before he flew out of Adelaide on Friday afternoon. In Melbourne he said only: "I'm not going back." At Sydney airport, when asked to elaborate his reasons for walking out, he told reporters: "I repeat what I said in my statement. I said I needed unfettered cross-examination, but I was impeded as soon as I tried to cross-examine the first police witness. That is why I withdrew." Did he consider the tribunal was prejudiced? "I withdrew, isn't that the answer?" Why had he said that his continued association with the case might hamper Stuart's cause? "I was virtually stopped in cross-examination. If I had further persisted, it would not have helped my client."

As soon as Shand left Adelaide there were rumours that his departure, and indeed his whole appearance, was part of a plot involving the *News*. "Mr. Shand's walkout . . ." said a Sydney newspaper, "has begun some vicious gossip." One charge whispered widely was that the *News* was responsible for Shand's coming, and that his withdrawal had been deliberately planned in collusion with the controllers of the *News*. Although the allegations never reached print, their character could be inferred, in part at least, from a statement by Rivett which appeared on the front page of the *News* the day after Shand withdrew. It was absolutely untrue, he wrote, that the *News* had anything to do with persuading Shand to appear; the *News* had offered no inducement to Shand or to anyone else.[3]

Alongside this statement was reprinted the first of a number of editorials now being written in newspapers everywhere. One of these was from the Melbourne *Sun*, which said that the quest to find out whether Stuart was guilty beyond all doubt should be pursued, even if "the dignity of the judges, or the Privy Council, or the Parliament, or counsel were all assailed". The paper did not allot blame for the interruption to the enquiry, and made no specific recommendation. In that afternoon's issue of the *Sun's* sister, the *Herald*, the columnist Mr. E. W. Tipping wrote: "Some top criminal lawyers tell us that Mr. Shand, Q.C., did the only thing possible in the Stuart case yesterday by walking out."

Strong editorial words came from the *Sunday Telegraph* in Sydney, which said on its front page that the Stuart case was causing grave disquiet. The presence on the Commission of two judges who had sat on Stuart's trial and appeal was undesirable. "They are known to be men of high integrity. But one of the oldest legal axioms is this: that not only must justice be done, but it must *appear* to be done." The paper's main story was headed: "Q.C's CONDEMN STUART ENQUIRY." A group of Sydney barristers, including two Queen's Counsel, were

[3] Mr. Rupert Murdoch has since told the present writer that the *News* did not pay Shand any money.

said to be angry at Sir Mellis Napier's remark that Shand, in withdrawing, had overlooked Stuart's interests. "Mr. Shand," they said, "has taken the only possible course." The statement went on to criticise both the choice of Sir Mellis Napier and Sir Geoffrey Reed as Commissioners, and their references on the first day to exchanges at Stuart's trial, "which showed that their consideration of the matter was affected by previous events . . . They even went so far as to say that Stuart was now the accuser, and must give evidence before the police who obtained his alleged confession." After other critical comments the statement went on: "No one can have confidence in the findings of the Commission as at present constituted." The closing words were even more hostile. "In dramatically drawing attention to the position, Mr. Shand has acted in the highest traditions of the bar. The bar has a duty never to acquiesce in tyranny and unfairness however exalted the bench." An editorial note explained that because the Bar Council of New South Wales allowed no publicity for barristers, the authors of the statement could not be named. They intended to ask the Bar Council to consider what had happened in Adelaide.

The Bar Council met for this purpose on Sunday afternoon. The meeting adjourned until Monday while members studied the transcript. In Brisbane on Sunday night the president of the Queensland Bar Association said that several of his members were gravely disturbed over the Commission. The *Sydney Morning Herald* on Monday printed a statement from the Minister for Health and former Attorney-General in the New South Wales Labor government, Mr. W. F. Sheahan, Q.C. "Speaking as a barrister," said Sheahan, "I would say that the stand taken by Mr. Shand was correct. It was courageous and in accordance with the best traditions of the legal profession." The Sydney *Daily Telegraph* the same day reprinted a number of comments explicitly or implicitly critical of the Commission, including one by an unnamed "high Commonwealth legal authority" who suggested that the government of South Australia might ask for the loan of a High Court judge. A front-page editorial in Monday's *Telegraph*, headed "More than a life at stake," said: "It should not be forgotten that the millions in the newly-independent Asian countries are particularly sensitive to the civil rights of black minorities" and urged Playford to take seriously the idea that a federal judge conduct the enquiry. The Melbourne *Herald* advised the South Australian government to "consider the whole turbulent atmosphere of this case and particularly the form and composition of the tribunal itself". On Tuesday a leader in the *Sydney Morning Herald* was headed: "PRESTIGE OF AUSTRALIAN JUSTICE AT STAKE." The tone was similar to that of the Melbourne *Herald*, but the Sydney paper set out more plainly the view that the present Commissioners should be replaced.

It was unusual for the Sydney and Melbourne press to be devoting so much editorial attention to a single matter outside party politics. Since all the papers were solidly anti-Labor in policy, their common criticism of the Commission could not easily be explained in terms of any general desire to embarrass the Playford government. The only government which Mr. Angus Maude, editor of the *Sydney Morning Herald*, had ever seriously embarrassed was that of Sir Anthony Eden, when Mr. Maude resigned from the Conservative Party as a protest against his "capitulation to Nasser". Nor was the opinion of interstate papers likely to have been the fruit of collusion. The men in charge of the *Sydney Morning Herald* and the *Telegraph* were not the closest of friends, and neither journal was connected with any daily paper elsewhere. The comments of the Melbourne *Herald* and *Sun* were in one respect the most remarkable of all. Advertiser Newspapers Ltd. was the largest shareholder in the company which operated both Melbourne papers (and the company responsible for them was also the largest shareholder in Advertiser Newspapers Ltd.); but the *Herald* and *Sun* were now closer to the *News* than to the *Advertiser* in their approach to Stuart. The solidarity of interstate comment, now and later, may have owed something to an unholy satisfaction that all this was happening in the holy city of Adelaide.

The *Advertiser* on Monday reported none of the critical remarks made over the weekend by newspapers, lawyers, politicians or clergymen; Adelaide's only morning paper was giving less space than any morning paper in Melbourne or Sydney to an affair in its own city. The *News* on Monday reproduced most of the interstate comment, but had no editorial of its own on the case. At no time between the day Shand left and the day the Commission resumed did the *News* offer an editorial opinion on the controversy.

* * *

In the moments after Shand walked out, Brazel had spoken of approaching the Law Society to find new counsel for Stuart. Next day, Saturday, Sir Thomas Playford announced that the government would pay such counsel. But nobody could engage a lawyer without the consent of the client.

Stuart's solicitors had withdrawn with Shand from the Commission, but as far as anybody knew they remained his solicitors. On Saturday, Brazel was told by Mr. J. L. Travers, Q.C., president of the Law Society, that it was not known whether O'Sullivan and Miss Devaney regarded themselves as still acting for Stuart. Brazel rang O'Sullivan to find out. O'Sullivan said he could not answer, but added: "We stand behind what Shand said." Stuart, O'Sullivan told Brazel, had been visited on Saturday morning by Miss Devaney, who tried with Dixon's help to explain what had happened. In a memorandum to the Premier Brazel wrote: "I gather Stuart said: 'I leave it to you,' signifying, according to Mr. O'Sullivan's impression, his desire for their continued advice. I tried to make it clear to Mr. O'Sullivan that, if he was acting for Stuart, it was his duty to inform his client of the government's offer and let someone know as quickly as possible what counsel should be briefed." O'Sullivan promised to do so by Monday night.

The Council of the Law Society passed a resolution late on Monday afternoon that, as Stuart was still represented by his solicitors, it could not ask or assign counsel to represent Stuart at the enquiry. The statement referred to the possibility that the Commission would undertake "a public enquiry into the manner in which counsel for Stuart conducted his case at the original trial", and said that this would be "incompatible with his duty to his client. This Council adds that it has no reason to think that the practitioners concerned have acted in any way other than in the interests of their client." As O'Sullivan and Miss Devaney had associated themselves with Shand's withdrawal, this last sentence could perhaps be interpreted as a substantial gesture of support, coming as it did from the governing body of the profession, only three days after Sir Mellis Napier said that Shand *was entirely overlooking* the interests of his client. It was later suggested in parliament by Mr. J. J. Jennings (Labor) that one member of the Council of the Law Society had put forward a motion expressing faith in the impartiality of the Royal Commission, and that he had resigned when the motion was not adopted.

If O'Sullivan and Miss Devaney remained Stuart's solicitors, then, and chose not to brief counsel, their client would not be represented at the Commission. The solicitors said nothing in public about their intentions when parliament met on Tuesday, August 25, for the first time since the Commission adjourned. Labor politicians and union leaders in other states were making vigorous protests about the Commission; but when the South Australian House of Assembly met on Tuesday, the Leader of the Opposition, O'Halloran, asked only for information. Could the Premier say whether the government had considered the difficulties encountered by the Commission, and had he any statement to make? Playford's reply was followed by no further question and no attempt to debate the issue. One reason for this reticence may have been the sudden bereavement of the Chief Justice; Lady Napier died on Monday night, having been taken to hospital on the previous Wednesday. What Playford said in parliament on Tuesday nevertheless led to a new controversy—between himself, Brazel, and the president of the Law Society.

Playford said he had received a suggestion from the Law Society, through Brazel, that if the government would drop the third term of reference (why the new evidence was not supplied earlier), "there would be no difficulty then in speedily providing counsel for the Commission to proceed with its hearing." The government, however, believed the third term of reference "very material".

Next day in parliament O'Halloran rose immediately after prayers and asked whether the government would refer the case to the Full Court. Playford replied that the government chose a Royal Commission as the means to a wider investigation than would have been possible by a reference to the Full Court. He went on to read a letter from the president of the Law Society, who alleged that the Premier's statement about the attitude of the Society was inaccurate, misleading, and a breach of confidence. Travers' letter, and a communication from the Law Society which Playford read to parliament next day, showed that there were strong misgivings within the legal profession about the conduct of both the Commission and the government. According to Travers, in discussion with Brazel he had distinguished two issues: the fate of Stuart and O'Sullivan's conduct of his case. Unless it transpired that Miss Devaney was no longer acting for Stuart, he had said, the Society could do nothing. He had expressed the personal view that the Society would take no part "in an enquiry which may be designed in some way to pillory one of its members after he had done a few thousand pounds' worth of free work for the Government". He had mentioned that Dr. J. J. Bray, Q.C., and Mr. C. H. Bright were already attending the enquiry on behalf of O'Sullivan. He had pointed out that if counsel was to be assigned to Stuart and if these two practitioners were available, they would obviously be suitable; but they could not act for both Stuart and O'Sullivan, since O'Sullivan could say nothing which might involve a breach of the professional privilege which he owed to his client. If the Commission was considering only Stuart and not O'Sullivan, then (he had told Brazel) he believed that Bray and Bright would be willing to act. He had made it clear that he had no power to bind the Society, but wanted to clarify the issues to put before a meeting at which he would preside. Playford's statement implying that the Society was trying to drive a bargain with the government and was prepared to override all other matters of principle was incorrect. Furthermore, his conversation with Brazel had been confidential, and should not have been repeated in parliament.

Travers had spoken bluntly about the intervention of the Police Association early in July. Now he had entered the Stuart controversy a second time as president of the Law Society; and later still he was to be involved as a barrister. At 59, Travers was generally acknowledged to be the ablest barrister in criminal practice in Adelaide. Playford knew him well, for in 1953 Travers was elected as a Liberal and Country League member of the House of Assembly—a rare achievement for a Catholic. He might have become Attorney-General, in which event it would have been his responsibility to handle the Stuart case. In 1956, however, Travers had the unusual misfortune, for a sitting member, of being defeated in a plebiscite to choose the party's candidate for his seat. But for this accident, Playford might have drawn comfort by seeing alongside him on the front bench this man with a tough, square face and broad shoulders, and hearing the performance of the government defended in his calm, forceful voice. Instead, Playford had to read out hostile words composed by Travers in quite another capacity.

Playford put down Travers' letter without comment, and read out a report on these negotiations which Brazel had given him two days previously. At the time, said the Premier, it was emphasised that the conversation between Brazel and Travers was confidential, but he had now cleared this report and Travers' letter with both authors. Brazel's account of the conversations did not differ in substance from Travers'. It expressed even more plainly the resentment that had built up among lawyers at the Commissioners' intention to call O'Sullivan. According to Brazel's report, Travers told him that there had been for some time "a growing concern in the profession over the burdens imposed upon lawyers under the Poor Persons' Legal Assistance Scheme. This feeling had now reached a climax, because it was felt by many that Mr. O'Sullivan, who had given a great deal of time to the defence of Stuart, was now to receive as his reward a public cross-examination upon the propriety of his conduct of the defence and the skill (or lack of it) with which he presented it."

It was clear that Brazel had not led Playford to believe that Travers was speaking officially on behalf of the Law Society, or that a broad, overall bargain between the government and the Society had been suggested; Brazel was careful to explain the particular position of Bray and Bright. Playford's only direct comment on what he had read from the pens of Travers and Brazel was this: "In the correspondence I have read it has been assumed that there may be, in connection with the term of reference Number Three, a desire on the part of the government for a heresy hunt into the conduct of the original case . . . The Commission, to get to the truth of the case, may have to call certain witnesses, but it is not in the nature of a heresy hunt in any way." Since nobody imagined that O'Sullivan was to be interrogated to discover whether his opinions were orthodox, "heresy" was not here an apt word; as Travers observed to Brazel, it was the propriety and competence of what O'Sullivan had done that the Commissioners appeared determined to investigate.

Late on Wednesday, O'Sullivan and Miss Devaney sent a letter to Brazel. "We wish to advise," they wrote, "that we have taken the opinion of Mr. J. W. Shand, Q.C. His advice is that it would not be in Stuart's interests to be further represented by any counsel before the Commission. We therefore wish to inform you after consultation with Stuart, with the assistance of Mr. Strehlow as interpreter, that Stuart does not wish to be further represented by counsel before the Commission. We will continue to act as Stuart's solicitors generally."

At question time on Thursday afternoon a Labor member asked "whether the government will see that a further respite is granted to Stuart, who otherwise would be hanged on Monday." Playford said he presumed that Stuart's solicitors would take action next day; and if so, the Crown would not oppose the respite. (A respite—Stuart's sixth—until September 30 was granted next day by Mr. Justice Reed.) The next questioner was Mr. D. A. Dunstan, who asked the Premier whether he would explain firstly, how he came to attribute to the Law

Society a suggestion—the bargain over the third term of reference—which was not justified by either Brazel's minute or Travers' letter; and secondly, why Brazel should have agreed publicly to reveal a confidential enquiry from the president of the Law Society without obtaining the author's consent.

"Does the Premier wish to reply?" asked the Speaker.

"Yes, I always like to oblige my young friend," said Playford, who nevertheless looked and sounded as if he was not liking it at all. He had made the statement, he said, because Brazel authorised him to do so. The Law Society had written to him this morning. "I think members would require a little legal advice to understand what it means, but I shall read it and they can make the best they can of it. Perhaps the honourable member at some stage in his career might advise me." Playford read the letter, which was no more prolix or technical than the communications from Brazel or Travers. The Council of the Law Society, it said, had at no time suggested that the third term of reference be eliminated, or that its elimination was in any way interdependent with the provision of counsel for Stuart. The Society was always ready and willing to help, but it could not assign counsel for Stuart while solicitors still acted for him. It seemed possible that some confusion had arisen between a particular question concerning counsel—Bray and Bright—and some questions in general terms relating to the provision of counsel to the third term of reference.

"Frankly," said Playford, after reading the letter, "I do not know what that means; but I do know what this means." "This" was a copy of a stiff letter from Brazel to Travers denying any breach of confidence. Playford pointed out that, although Travers had suggested to Brazel that the government be asked to eliminate the third term of reference, the Law Society in its official letter made no such request.

Dunstan rose again, to observe that the Premier had still offered no evidence for his initial statement: that the Law Society had offered a bargain. Travers had specifically denied that any such deal was proposed. Was the Premier saying that Mr. Travers had stated an untruth?

"I am always anxious to help my friend," said the Premier. He had outlined the varying accounts of Brazel and Travers, he said; "and I think the House can decide which account is correct." Apart from Dunstan, no member seemed anxious to decide between them; at any rate, there was no murmur when a government supporter rose and at this point asked the Minister of Agriculture a question about the movement of South Australian eggs to New South Wales. Except for Dunstan's efforts, parliament had not really been the arena for this part of the controversy, but merely the means by which it became public. It was an unusual debate: the Law Society was accusing the government of misrepresenting its position on a matter of high importance. The president of this body was not only charging a fellow silk with a breach of confidence committed in his capacity as counsel assisting the Royal Commission; he was also saying that the Commissioners, who happened to be the Chief Justice and two other judges of the Supreme Court, were engaged in an enquiry which might be designed to "pillory" a practitioner.

On the central issue raised by Mr. Shand's withdrawal, the Opposition now decided to attempt action. A meeting of Labor parliamentarians on Thursday morning discussed the deadlock between the Commission and Stuart's lawyers and agreed on a proposal which was announced in the House by O'Halloran during the afternoon. He gave notice that on Tuesday next he would move for the suspension of standing orders to consider a motion that "in view of the public disquiet aroused concerning the present position of the Stuart enquiry, in the opinion of this House the Royal Commission should be reconstituted with other Commissioners, both for the protection of persons involved in the terms of reference and for the protection of the judiciary of this State." After this motion was drafted but before it was read out in parliament, it was announced that the Commission would resume next Monday. Shand, in a telephone interview with the *News*, said: "It is completely unknown in British constitutional history for a Royal Commission on a condemnation of murder to proceed without counsel representing the condemned man."

* * *

While charge and counter-charge were fired in Adelaide during the week after Shand went home, outside opinions flowed in, most of them expressing or implying criticism of the Commission. On Monday, the Bar Council of New South Wales declined to take the stand requested by those of its members who had said that Shand took the only possible course. The Council resolved that comment on the Commission was not within its province, and that it was "not to be associated with the statement attributed to a group of Sydney barristers . . ." Apart from the Minister for Health, Sheahan (who commented both in parliament and outside), two individual Q.C's in Sydney spoke publicly about the Commission. Mr. V. H. Treatt, Q.C., a Liberal member of the state parliament (and former Leader of the Opposition) said that a judge involved in an earlier hearing should not sit on such a tribunal. Mr. Richard Windeyer, Q.C., made a similar observation, and said: "In all my years of legal experience"—he was 91—"I have never heard of such a thing happening. It is incomprehensible." For different reasons each of these lawyers presumably decided that he was not infringing the Bar Council's rule that no barrister should use his name in public professional comment; Treatt spoke in parliament and Windeyer from retirement. A month later, the Sydney press said that the Bar Council was asking Sheahan—who had not practised for many years—and another "eminent Q.C." and possibly other barristers, to explain why they had made public statements about the Commission. None of the reports said whether the second Q.C. was or was not Shand, who had publicly criticised the Commission after leaving it, and who was now lying in a Sydney hospital.

The *Sydney Morning Herald* said that members of all parties were describing the action against Sheahan as "an impudent attempt to prevent a parliamentarian from speaking his mind". The Labor caucus unanimously supported Sheahan's use of a parliamentary position "to discuss all public matters as he thinks fit". The Bar Council denied that it had sought to interfere with the privileges of a minister or member of parliament, but asserted that there were rules which obliged a member of the bar. "A number of comments appearing in the press," said the Council, "have obviously been made in complete ignorance of these matters." In the *Telegraph* a cartoon by Tanner showed a figure representing the Bar Council on a step-ladder beside the traditional figure of Justice as a blindfolded woman holding scales; the Bar Council was saying, to Shand: "Ahem. We think the blindfold can be put to better use as a gag!" Among ministers of religion, the habit of public comment frowned upon among lawyers was commonly regarded as a professional obligation. Several prominent clergymen in Sydney expressed concern and criticism of the Commission in the days after Shand withdrew.

Overseas comments were heard. On Wednesday, August 26, Australian Associated Press quoted critical remarks by the president of the All-India Civil Liberties Council and the president of the Madras Bar Association. Next day, from England, the *News* reported a number of English opinions. On the front page appeared a report from the paper's London office, presumably written by Mr. Douglas Brass, which began: "Some of the most eminent legal and public men in England commented today on the composition and difficulties of the Stuart Royal Commission." Lord Attlee, speaking from his home, said it was "unusual—to say the least—to appoint two judges who had previously been concerned with the case. I should have thought you would need fresh minds on it." Lord Birkett, a former Lord Justice of Appeal, spoke similarly, and so did Sir David Hughes Parry, Professor of English Law at the University of London. Mr. Jo Grimond, the Liberal Party leader, said: "In this country it would be most unusual to place on a Commission the judges who had already heard a case. It would require some very special reason." A representative of the Law Society, unidentified, said: "The composition of the court was read with some surprise. But, doubtless, those responsible for the appointments must have had extremely good reasons. In view of the criticism they will no doubt seek the earliest opportunity of making their reasons known to the public, who would seem to be entitled to the fullest explanation without delay."

In Melbourne the *Herald* reproduced some of these comments and had in the same issue an editorial headed "Make sure of justice." The statement that Stuart would not be represented, said the *Herald*, appeared to deepen the confusion surrounding the Commission; it was hard to understand how Stuart could have made a sound decision on a matter which bewildered most laymen with a claim to higher intelligence. "The point may now have been reached where the South Australian government should consider whether a complete reconstitution of this enquiry is needed . . . It has become a matter of national, and even international, concern that the thorough fairness of the Stuart enquiry should be put beyond all doubt."

On the evening this editorial appeared, the Stuart case was the subject of a news commentary by Professor Julius Stone, Professor of Jurisprudence in the University of Sydney, broadcast in all states by the Australian Broadcasting Commission. Stone described without comment Shand's withdrawal and the Law Society's objection to calling O'Sullivan. He did offer an opinion on what seemed to him two "final issues". "First," said Stone, "is the inadequacy of legal aid to persons accused of grave crimes, if such aid is limited to free services of lawyers. For this overlooks other costs, such as that of searching out and sifting evidence on behalf of the accused . . . Second, and even more important, can a trial be said to be 'fair' when the accused is so ill-equipped in the language used, and so accustomed (as Stuart and other Aruntas apparently are) to acquiesce in white men's statements which they do not understand?"

The *Anglican*, an unofficial Church of England weekly published in Sydney and circulating in all states, now urged that a new trial was the only just course. The same alternative was recommended in *Nation*. In the Sydney *Sun-Herald*, the columnist "Onlooker" said that Playford "must be wondering where his government, long unaccustomed to challenge, went wrong . . . So far wrong as to bring under critical nationwide scrutiny the administration of justice in South Australia, a state which prides itself on the integrity of its legal and political systems . . . The more determined the Playford government appeared that Stuart should die if his guilt was established beyond question, the more scrupulous it should have been to leave no ground for complaint to those in whom genuine doubts had arisen. This was where it went astray." As "Onlooker" saw it, the hanging of Stuart had now become a political impossibility. The reprieve which he confidently predicted was urged by Mrs. Phyllis Duguid in a letter which the *Advertiser* printed on Saturday, August 29, when it admitted correspondence on the case for the first time in four weeks; the delays and uncertainties, she said, had led to a "cat and mouse" situation which everyone would deplore, irrespective of views on capital punishment. Letters from two other people appeared in the same issue. One writer, Mr. Ian McLachlan, said that British judges were always impartial and warned "those few who for selfish purposes" had made "scurrilous jibes and innuendoes" to the contrary that "they injure the state as they expose their own true value". The other writer was "A Parent", who asked whether the public had been allowed to forget a terrible crime "in order that political interests may be served by propaganda". A similar message was telegraphed to the *News* by a man in Alice Springs, and appeared on Saturday's front page: "Out of the wild jungle of law, politics, journalism, and religion, let us hear the almost inaudible cry of Mary Olive Hattam."

The *Sunday Mail*, published in Adelaide on Saturday evening, carried statements by two groups of people urging that the Commission should not proceed on Monday. One was signed by three professors and fifteen other teachers at the University of Adelaide. The authors of the other included the Rev. Frank Borland, Dr. Charles Duguid, Mr. J. Eliott Thorp and the present writer. Playford was sent a petition from twenty-nine South Australian trade union officials, declaring that justice in the state was in danger of being brought into serious disrepute and urging him to re-constitute the Commission. From Sydney the secretary of the Aboriginal-Australian Fellowship wrote asking Mr. Hammarskjold to intervene.

There had been no comment from within the Australian Association for Cultural Freedom since Mr. J. H. Wootten's article four weeks earlier, during the first controversy over the Commission's membership and terms of reference. Sir John Latham now spoke again, in a letter to Playford, dated August 28 from Melbourne, of which part was released to the press next day. The former Chief Justice of the High Court suggested that the Commission be told to report whether, in view of new evidence, Stuart should be given a new trial by judge and jury. "It appears obvious to me that the Commission would report on this matter under the present terms of reference—but it is not obvious to the public. It would at least dispose of the idea that the Commission is itself trying Stuart without any jury." The secretary of the Australian Association for Cultural Freedom, Mr. Richard Krygier, said that the president wrote as a private individual. "I don't know how other members will feel about the letter," Krygier told the *Sun-Herald*, "—some may wish to go further. Certainly the Stuart matter does not seem satisfactory to me as it stands at present."

Playford wrote back to Latham on Sunday after seeing extracts from the letter in the press but before receiving the original. "I am advised," he replied, "that a Commission has a much wider scope for investigation than could be provided at a re-trial. The standing of the Commission, three judges of the Supreme Court, is of the highest possible order. . . . I point out to you that the government cannot, in fact, order a re-trial. It can only submit such a matter for the court's consideration if established facts justify it. The Commission is at the present time investigating these matters." Latham said on Sunday night that Playford had apparently misread press reports of his letter. He had not suggested a re-trial; he had recommended that the Commission be directed to report whether the new evidence justified a re-trial. Stuart's solicitors, Latham added, were incurring a heavy responsibility if they did not allow him to be represented at the Commission. The executive of the Australian Association for Cultural Freedom was to discuss Stuart when it met on September 12; but he hoped, Latham said, that a sensible conclusion would have been reached before then.

Latham's suggestion was seized on by a number of people as offering a solution which might be acceptable to all parties. On August 31, when the Commission was due to resume, the Melbourne *Sun* (which normally carried no editorial) published a front-page leader headed "A Way Out", saying that Latham's letter "comes right to the heart of the problem that has led to such an uneasy national conscience". The *Sun's* partner the *Herald* expressed a similar view that day, and so did the front-page columnist of the Melbourne *Age*, Mr. John Hetherington (a former editor of the Adelaide *News*). In London, *The Times*, which had been following the Commission fairly closely, reported Latham's proposal on August 31, and mentioned it in a leading article. "Disquiet continues in Australia over the conviction of Rupert Stuart," the editorial began. "The disquiet," it concluded, "extends beyond Australia." A less restrained comment was made in London over the weekend in the *New Statesman* by Mr. Kingsley Martin, who had visited Adelaide in 1958. Writing as "Critic", Martin paid a tribute to Rivett and described the appointment of Sir Geoffrey Reed and Sir Mellis Napier to the Commission as "disgraceful". Martin's remarks were reproduced in more than one Australian paper. The *New Statesman* found itself uncommonly close in judgment to Mr. Angus Maude, whose *Sydney Morning Herald* expressed on August 31 the hope that "the Commission will not today resume the course so abruptly interrupted by Mr. Shand's withdrawal."

The Commission resumed that morning.

12

A MOTION OF CENSURE

DARK POLISHED CHAIRS and white squares of blotting paper were waiting for Stuart's counsel, but nobody came to use them. The Commission sat for less than an hour and then adjourned to await a decision by parliament on its future.

O'Sullivan had been asked to attend. At a word from the Chairman he stood—at the table, not in the witness box. Sir Mellis Napier referred to the letter in which O'Sullivan and his partner said they were following Shand's advice that Stuart should not be represented by counsel.

"Now we have your assurance, have we," said the Chairman, "that you have taken your instructions from Stuart?"

"Yes, Your Honour."

"Are we to understand that Stuart does not desire that we should hear him or hear any further evidence?"

"That is so, Your Honour."

"Then, Mr. O'Sullivan, there is one question that we must ask."

The question was about the original of the statement signed by Stuart which O'Sullivan had sought to have read at the trial. The original was mislaid, O'Sullivan replied, but the copy given to the Attorney-General "some months ago"[1] was a signed, carbon copy of the original.

On subsequent occasions O'Sullivan attended briefly at the Commission, but nothing more was heard of the view, expressed so forcefully on the opening day by both Sir Mellis Napier and Brazel, that he was essential as a witness. It was a common opinion among lawyers in Adelaide that protests from the Law Society had persuaded the Commissioners not to press the matter. If this interpretation was correct, it had been a remarkably successful demonstration of professional solidarity. The Commission kept, however, its third term of reference; and its report was to contain a good deal about why no alibi was offered for Stuart at the trial.

After O'Sullivan retired, Brazel tendered the copy of Stuart's statement formally identified by O'Sullivan. It was read out by the secre-

[1] It had actually been passed in less than *two* months previously; but the period could easily have felt much longer than that to O'Sullivan, who had been to London in the meantime, and perhaps to other intimate participants in the affair.

tary, and at last, four months after the trial, the version of events at Ceduna which Stuart gave to his solicitors became public knowledge.

"The statement of Rupert Max Stuart.
I am an aboriginal. I cannot read or write.
I was up at Ceduna the day the girl was killed. I did not kill her. I did not ever see her.
I went in a taxi to Thevenard to get a drink. I did not want a girl. I did not tell anyone I did.
I had some wine there. I was not drunk.
I walked back to Ceduna in the afternoon. I walked on the road first and then on the beach.
I did not walk near the place where the girl was found. I walked in my boots all day. I did not walk barefoot.
I did not take my clothes off and wash myself in the water.
I did not see the little girl or the little boys.
When I got back I worked at the show for a while. At teatime I went down to the hotel to get a drink.
There were two dark fellows on the beach near the hotel. They gave me a drink of wine.
I went up to the street later with Herby. He was my friend from the show. The policeman came and took me to the police station. That was before the pictures started. The policeman let me out next morning.
I got the sack from the show. I got a job with the Wheat Board.
On Monday night I was in bed. I went to have a —.
When I came back the police were there. I was not hiding.
When I came back they were looking at my swag.
Mr. Turner said, 'What is your name?'
I said, 'Max Stuart.'
He said, 'You are the fellow we are looking for for murdering the girl.'
I said, 'I did not do it.'
He said I was hiding.
I said, 'I was not hiding.'
Turner said, 'You didn't go to the lavatory.'
I said, 'I did.'
I showed them where I had walked in the sand. I cannot track. I did not tell anyone I could. It was easy to see my tracks there. Any fellow could see them.
They looked at my clothes. They said they were looking for blood. They did not look at my knees. They took me to the police station.
Mr. Turner said, 'Come on, you know that you killed the girl.'
I said, 'No.'
He said that a few times. Mr. Jones said, 'Take your clothes off.'
I took them off. They looked at me. One policeman behind me said, 'There are some marks.'

I could not see what they were looking at. Mr. Jones said, 'How did you get them?'

I said, 'I don't know.'

They pointed to a mark under my right arm on my ribs. I said, 'That has been there for years.'

Mr. Turner pulled some hairs out of my head and some from my legs. He didn't ask me if he could.

They told me to get dressed. I got dressed. They told me to sit down. I did that.

Mr. Jones said, 'Come on, we know you did it.'

I said, 'No.'

He said, 'Yes, come on, tell me the truth.'

I said, 'I didn't do it.'

Mr. Jones punched me over the eye. I nearly fell off the chair. When I stood up he hit me again on the side of the throat and on the ribs.

He tried to punch me again. I stopped it with my elbow.

Then Sergeant Walker grabbed me round the throat with two hands. He kept pushing his thumbs into my throat. I could not breathe. I thought I was going to die.

The other policemen were all around me. The sergeant said, 'You had better tell us the bloody truth now you know.'

The sergeant let me go. The policeman with the typewriter said, 'You killed the little girl.'

I was frightened. My head and my throat were hurting. I could hardly breathe.

They were all saying things to me. I can't remember it all.

I kept saying, 'I didn't do it.'

One said, 'We have found the dead girl. You must have done it.'

I said, 'Perhaps it was a white man.'

When they searched me they found a blade from a razor in a coat pocket. It was lying on the desk.

One of the policemen picked it up. He said, 'If you don't tell us I will skin you, or kill you,' or something like that. I thought they would kill me if I didn't say what they wanted.

Then I said 'Yes' all the time.

They told me the trackers would say they were my tracks. I can't remember all the things they said.

They asked if a white man made me do it. I said, 'Yes.'

One of them said, 'It is all — about a white man doing it. We were only saying that. We knew it was a black man.'

One of them said, 'She was hard to —, wasn't she?'

I said, 'Yes.'

The man with the typewriter was using it while they were talking to me.

They kept asking me questions all the time until he finished.

One man read it.

He said, 'That is true, isn't it?'
I said, 'Yes.'
He told me to write my name. I wrote my name because I knew they would hit me again if I didn't.
I did not kill the little girl. I never saw her and never touched her."

Was this story consistent with the evidence offered on Stuart's behalf by Gieseman? Did it make the alleged confession more, or less, cogent? There was to be much discussion at the Commission, and some elsewhere, of the questions raised by Stuart's statement.

* * *

"With Your Honours' leave," said Brazel, "I would like to say something about the events that have occurred since we last met." "I think it is time that the truth was published," said the Chairman. In the ten days since Shand and his colleagues withdrew, Brazel said, "strenuous efforts have been made to confuse the public mind. In justice to this Commission and so that the reasoning members of the community can see actually what happened on last Thursday week in its true perspective, it is necessary to remind ourselves what did occur." The witness Phin, said Brazel, could say only what Moir had told him or what Moir signed. Moir could not be on oath when giving his statements to Phin. If anything Phin claimed to have been said by Moir conflicted with Moir's sworn testimony, it would have to be discarded when Moir's evidence came to be assessed.

In reviewing the exchange between bar and bench after the Chairman said that Phin was not obliged to explain anything, Brazel paused at the Chairman's remark to Shand: "As far as I am concerned I have heard enough of this." That could only mean to any rational listener, said Brazel, that the Chairman had heard sufficient on that topic to give it its proper weight; it was also clear that the Chairman was speaking for himself and not for the other Commissioners. However, since what happened had been distorted in various places into a suggestion that the cross-examiner was prevented from carrying out his duty, it was proper to mention that the Chief Justice had said to Shand: "If you feel it is helping you to convince us, well and good," and later, "You are perfectly at liberty to continue and you can stay here as long as it suits you." His own recollection, Brazel added, was that the Chief Justice said: "We will stay here as long as it suits you." Sir Mellis Napier corrected Brazel; he had said: "*You can go on*, we will sit here as long as it suits you." Brazel, Chamberlain, and the other two Commissioners agreed with the Chairman's recollection.[2] These words conveyed, Brazel said, "as clear an invitation as can be given to any cross-examiner to proceed as long as and as far as he

[2] The *Advertiser* and *News* reports of the Chairman's words on August 20 both had: "We will stay here as long as it suits you." Neither paper had the words: "You can go on." Nor, it will be noticed, did Brazel include these words in the correction he himself volunteered.

likes". Then, on "this flimsy pretext", Shand made a statement next day which was "capable of no construction other than an accusation by Mr. Shand that this Commission had been and would continue to be guilty of a grave dereliction of duty. There was not a vestige of justification for this mischievous suggestion . . . Every right-thinking person in this community resents this imputation against the members of the Commission . . ."

A "section of the press", Brazel added, had "seen fit to make these issues an excuse for vituperative and indecent attacks upon members of this Commission". Those at the bar table had been stimulated by countless messages from people in all walks of life expressing disgust at this behaviour; "as one of Her Majesty's counsel speaking, I feel sure, with the support of the bar in this state, I say how much we deplore these calumnies knowing as only we do how unfair, how unkind, and how undeserved they are." What the calumnies were, and who uttered them, he did not specify. Chamberlain said: "I desire to associate myself with every word that Mr. Brazel has just uttered."

Sir Mellis Napier spoke—calmly, deliberately, and with emotion. He thanked Brazel "for saying some things that will come more fittingly from the bar than from me". What happened last Thursday week, he said, "had every appearance of an act of deliberate sabotage of this enquiry, and I desire to say that as the criticism has been mainly directed at me personally, it is more than thirty-five years since I came to this bench, coming as I believe with the approbation not merely of the profession of the law but of the public of South Australia. After eighteen years in the office of puisne judge a vacancy occurred in the office of Chief Justice, and then when the profession and the public had every opportunity to detect any failings or imperfections in my work and must surely have been in a position to judge my qualifications for this office, I was appointed, again as I believe with the approbation and goodwill of the profession and of the public of South Australia, to this office. I have filled it for seventeen years and I have been heartened by the goodwill and respect which has been shown to me from every side. It is a rude awakening to me to find that the reputation and the credit built up over so long should be no more than as a pack of cards to be toppled, to be shattered at a touch by a man of whom I know no more than he presumably knows of me." The Chairman spoke, as Brazel had done, of the press, without naming any paper or any particular offence. "I find it difficult to believe that what has been published in a section of the press represents the real opinion of the public of this state, but so far as I am concerned I would welcome the opportunity of obtaining relief from the obligation of continuing in a matter in which it has been charged against me that I am unfit for the office that I hold."

The judges holding this enquiry, Sir Mellis Napier observed, were those who must have constituted the Full Court on the reference of a petition under the Criminal Law Consolidation Act. The subject of the enquiry was "whether it is reasonable to suppose that Stuart would or might have been acquitted by the jury if the jury had had before them evidence or information that was not forthcoming at the trial . . ." This view and this practice, Sir Mellis Napier said, were by no means peculiar to South Australia. He cited a case in England and one in New South Wales ("the state from which Mr. Shand comes") to support what he was saying.[3] In the same way, "there would be no difficulty in finding precedent for a judge sitting more or less as I am sitting upon a second appeal.[4] . . . It is difficult to pinpoint the fact but I have not the slightest doubt that the same thing must have happened repeatedly in England."[5]

The Chairman concluded with what was, in effect, a reply to all who had urged the Commission not to proceed: "If His Excellency the Governor-in-Council should see fit to request me to go no further with this enquiry I should welcome his instruction, but until that instruction is received I consider it my duty—and I expect that my colleagues will do likewise—I consider it my duty to go on in the path which I regard as that of duty." Mr. Justice Reed expressed agreement. So did Mr. Justice Ross, who added—"for myself, and not after consultation with the other members"—that each member of the Commission, when appointed a judge, swore to do right to all men in accordance with the laws of the state without leave or favour, ill-will or affection. "I am only a fairly recent member of this court and I say nothing about my record, but my colleagues for very many years have impartially administered justice to the entire satisfaction of the public in accordance with that oath, and I am shocked and grieved to know that so many people seem to have accepted the suggestion made by a section of the press that the members of this Commission in disregard of this oath are denying or about to deny justice to Rupert Max Stuart."

The Commission adjourned to await the outcome of Labor's foreshadowed motion.

* * *

To the account of Shand's departure offered by himself and accepted by some people, there had now been opposed another; Shand, on this other account, had not been hampered in cross-examination, and knew that he had not been. This judgment appeared to be implied in Brazel's reference to a "flimsy pretext" and in the Chairman's word "sabotage". He had attributed to the Commissioners, in Brazel's

[3] The cases were *R. v. Wright* (1910) 4 Cr. App. R. 284,291, and *Craig v. R.* (1933) 49 C.L.R. 429,431.

[4] The Chief Justice referred to cases in Victoria and N.S.W. *Davies v. R.* (1937) 57 C.L.R. 170, and *R. v. Gunn* (1943) 43 S.R. (N.S.W.) 27.

[5] The Chief Justice cited the cases of *R. v. Caborn-Waterfield* [1956] 2 Q.B. 379, and *R. v. McGrath* [1949] 2 All E.R. 495.

phrase, "a grave dereliction of duty"; in the Chairman's words a man, presumably Shand, had shattered his reputation at a touch. Brazel and two of the judges had spoken disapprovingly about "a section of the press", and the Chairman had indicated that he meant within South Australia. Clearly, this was the *News*. As the paper had published no editorial opinion on events at the Commission, the alleged offence must have been either that it printed the critical comments of others or that it misrepresented facts. Far from its being improper, as had been widely asserted, for Sir Mellis Napier and Sir Geoffrey Reed to sit as Commissioners, there were ample precedents for their so doing.

The conflict of interpretation was bewildering to many laymen. How, for example, was the interested citizen to judge between the argument of the Chief Justice that prior participation in a case such as Stuart's should not prevent a judge sitting on an enquiry into new evidence, and the view of other experienced jurists (who could be presumed to know that no complaint had been made about the conduct of the trial judge) that such a course was not desirable? Some wild rumours made it harder for anybody trying to unravel the tangled facts. To some people, especially in distant eastern cities, the Stuart case appeared to have become a contest between an "Establishment"—the fashionable phrase was on many lips—in which Freemasons were prominent and an opposition composed largely or entirely of Catholics. The foundation for this view was, presumably, that Playford and the judges were all Freemasons and that Catholics were prominent both among those who had pressed for a new hearing and those dissatisfied with the form it was taking.

The precise connexion, however, between membership of a lodge or church and a particular set of opinions on Stuart's situation was never made clear. It was true that no member of the bench or the cabinet was a Catholic, and that some Catholics had worked keenly for a new and full enquiry. A Catholic priest initiated and conducted the search for new evidence, and later baptised Stuart into his faith. Mrs. Gieseman was a Catholic, though her husband was not. Stuart's solicitors were both Catholics, and so was Mr. J. L. Travers, Q.C. Beyond that point, however, the Catholic players (as one of them, hearing the rumours, remarked) seemed to have their teams mixed. Brazel was a Catholic. So was Mr. J. R. Kearnan, the Crown Prosecutor, who was appearing with Chamberlain at the Commission. Strehlow—Dixon's earliest ally—was a Lutheran. Among the most earnest campaigners during July for a new enquiry, Borland and Duguid were Presbyterians and Thorp was a Quaker. On September 1 a letter appeared in both the *Advertiser* and the *News* from two Methodist ministers, a Presbyterian minister, a Congregational minister and a Congregational layman, urging an end to the Commission and a new trial; the signatories included the president of the South Australian Methodist Conference and the president of the South Australian Congregational Union, though neither signed in his official capacity. A

Presbyterian minister wrote later to the *Advertiser* saying that most ministers of religion had felt "embarrassed and compromised" by this letter. There was no way of telling whether this was an accurate estimate; but it is a safe conclusion that conflicts of opinion over the case were not following denominational lines.

The critics of institutions tend, almost by definition, to be more outspoken than the satisfied. There were undoubtedly people who deplored the pleas for an end to the Commission, and some who disapproved of the earlier demand for a new enquiry, without saying so to anybody but their friends. Among, say, the 60,000 people who purchased the *Advertiser* and not the *News*, it is probable that many had seen the effort during July to save Stuart's life as a less than wholly ingenuous sally in a general campaign against the death penalty. (One of the few correspondents in either paper hostile to the pleas for commutation had said that the campaigners "would be more logical to sign an honest petition recommending the abolition of capital punishment, and to treat Stuart's case on its merits as a capital offence".) Especially to South Australians of conservative temperament, criticism of the Commission after Shand left could well seem unjustified; a united front of Labor politicians, naïve humanitarians, intellectuals, outsiders and malcontents appeared to be exploiting popular prejudices against holders of office and in favour of under-privileged minorities, and to be engaging in a mischievous, undiscriminating and perhaps dangerous attack on one of the most cherished institutions in society. Perhaps dangerous, because if citizens supposed to be responsible were to undermine confidence in the judicial system, anarchy was not far off.

This danger was mentioned in a radio commentary by Mr. Stewart Cockburn, a senior journalist on the *Advertiser* (and a former press secretary to the Prime Minister, Mr. R. G. Menzies), who had reported for his paper each day's sitting of the Commission. In a broadcast over the *Advertiser* station, 5AD, on July 29, Cockburn had reviewed the case in a manner which pointed tentatively towards commutation as a solution. Now he said: "It is the business of defence counsel to create doubt in his client's favour. It is the business of judges to assess the extent and weight of those doubts. We must also remember that if we doubt the ability of our judges to do that, if we doubt their integrity, we are on the way to doubting the very basis of our community's law and order." In another broadcast Cockburn said: "The government, and even the Commissioners, have been bitterly accused of prejudging this case. Has no one on the defence side prejudged it? In particular, has no one at that unconventional court of justice, the University of Adelaide, prejudged it?" In public discussion Cockburn's was a lonely voice; in private conversation, many people in Adelaide agreed with him.

Outside South Australia it was hard to detect any serious conflict of public opinion. Every newspaper and almost every individual who spoke on the matter expressed misgivings about the Commission, misgivings which were doubtless offered with more enthusiasm by Playford's political opponents than by his friends. There was a remarkable moment on August 31 at the biennial congress of the Australian Council of Trade Unions in Melbourne, when 470 delegates, representing one and a quarter million members, interrupted their business to consider a request for discussion on the Stuart case, offered jointly by a union on the far left and one on the equally distant right. The federal president of the Australian Labor Party, Mr. F. E. Chamberlain, put a motion demanding "on behalf of the organised workers of Australia and in the interests of justice . . . the withdrawal of the present judges and their replacement by persons whose impartiality cannot be questioned". The motion was carried without dissent. An officer of the Police Association of South Australia said that his Association might withdraw from the South Australian Trades and Labor Council on account of this resolution: "the first time the Association needs the union's support," he said, "we are let down." Mr. Stewart Cockburn, speaking over 5AD on September 1, wondered how many of the people expressing doubts in other states and countries had seen the transcript of evidence, "and how many were relying on incomplete, inaccurate and unofficial reports circulated to them for motives which are partisan and suspect". In the particular case of Sir John Latham, Cockburn said: "If he knew the whole truth, I believe he would not have entered the discussion publicly as he has, from a distance of several hundred miles."

Within South Australia, differences followed party lines. Some supporters of Playford—including more than one member of the Liberal and Country League state executive—were expressing private criticism of the government and of the Commission, and there was even rumour of dissension in the party room at this time; but in public the ranks held firm. On Tuesday, September 1, the Labor Party tried to put its motion for new Commissioners. The opportunity for debate was welcomed by the Melbourne *Age*, Australia's most cautious daily paper, which said: "Today the South Australian government has the chance to set at rest increasing public disquiet . . . The debate in Parliament should provide the government with the occasion to revise the present proceedings, which cannot now reach any decision which would be sufficiently respected . . ."

Before the Opposition could put its motion, the House had to agree to suspend standing orders and practices. Whether a debate occurred would depend, in effect, on Playford; as one of the two Independents in the House of Assembly, Mr. T. C. Stott, was away from Adelaide, and one Labor member was at the A.C.T.U. congress in Melbourne, the government could expect a majority of at least two if the Premier decided not to have a debate.

More than a hundred people, including Mr. J. D. O'Sullivan and Detective-Sergeant Paul Turner, crowded the usually deserted galleries. After question time the Labor leader, O'Halloran, moved the procedural motion. He was allowed ten minutes, and a minister would have ten minutes to reply. Neither, according to the rules, was supposed to refer at this stage to the conduct of the Royal Commission. O'Halloran did little more than report disquiet expressed by others—the English lawyers, quoted in the *News*, Latham and other Australian lawyers, the A.C.T.U. congress. His own experience, O'Halloran added, was that in South Australia "people in all walks of life are gravely concerned . . ." Labor believed that Stuart should be proved guilty beyond doubt or have his innocence accepted. "We desire that some of the aspersions that are unfortunately being cast at the judiciary should be eliminated . . . Parliament should discuss the matter with a view to advising the Executive . . ."

Playford replied. The government, he said, was prepared to take complete responsibility. "There is some public disquiet, but is that not to be expected when we had a campaign raging for about a month during which the vilest crimes have been charged against the judges, the police and every one of our institutions?[6] Is it not to be expected when we endeavour to introduce mob rule rather than rule by parliament and rule by the courts?" As the Premier did not name any of the mobsters, there was no way of knowing whether they included Sir John Latham or Lord Attlee. "My government," he said, "stands for the maintenance of law by the courts and not by a newspaper." The House divided noisily, a Labor member calling: "The Master has spoken." The one Independent present, Mr. P. H. Quirke, voted with the Opposition. "I have always supported the principle that a member be heard," he explained later, "but whether you agree with what he is saying or not is another thing." The motion to suspend standing orders was lost by seventeen votes to nineteen.

At once O'Halloran asked for time next day to discuss a motion of no-confidence—a very rare event in this parliament. Playford agreed, but said that he would object to the courts being brought into a censure motion. Dunstan collided with the Speaker in attempting to argue that anything at all, including matters before a Royal Commission, could be discussed on a motion of censure. Dunstan and another Labor member marched out of the House, followed soon by others. In the tradition of subtle Australian parliamentary wit, a government voice called after Dunstan: "Goodbye, Mr. Shand."[7]

[6] Though Hansard did not record it, according to the *Advertiser* Mr. H. H. Shannon, (Liberal and Country League), here cried "Calumnies!"

[7] Next evening in Canberra, during a debate on the federal budget, there was further repartee over the Stuart case. When Senator Aylett (Labor, Tasmania) referred to the Commission critically, Senator Pearson (Liberal, South Australia) said: "You leave that alone." Senator Aylett said of Stuart: "He has about as much chance as the man in the moon. I have never seen a judge in my life who could change his decision." Senator Mattner (Liberal, South Australia) observed: "You are as low as a snake's tail."

Playford's refusal to allow a debate on Tuesday did not make himself and the Commission any more popular with the newspapers. On Wednesday the Melbourne *Herald*, in a leading article headed "Justice or Confusion?" said it was puzzled by Playford's reference to a raging campaign and allegations of vile crimes, and by Sir Mellis Napier's remark that he had been charged with unfitness for office. Sir John Latham, said the *Herald*, had put the issue temperately. "The general run of people who have suggested re-examination are certainly not engaged in any plot against the South Australian government or the state's judiciary." The proceedings in parliament provoked a writer in the London *Daily Herald* on Wednesday morning to review the controversy and to criticise Playford. As in most overseas comments, Stuart's race was prominent in this account.

The *News* on Wednesday published its first editorial on the case since Shand's withdrawal. In substance it was close to the Melbourne *Herald* editorial of the same day. Noting the Premier's declaration that his government stood for the maintenance of law by parliament and the courts and not by a newspaper, the *News* said: "This reference to the rule of parliament was made in the course of preventing parliament from discussing the Commission."

* * *

Both Independents were in their places on Wednesday, and the Labor member who was absent on Tuesday flew back from Melbourne in time for the censure debate. As soon as the House assembled at two o'clock, O'Halloran moved: "That the Standing Orders be suspended to enable me to move the following motion without notice: 'That in view of public disquiet concerning the Royal Commission and the flagrant denial by the government yesterday of the rights of parliament to discuss the issue, the government does not possess the confidence of this House.'" The procedural motion was carried. O'Halloran's flatly delivered speech on the substantive motion was virtually a repetition of what he had said the previous day with a protest added at the government's refusal to allow a debate.

The next speech, by Dunstan, was very different in character; it was, in effect, a hostile reply to Sir Mellis Napier's defence of the appointment of himself and Sir Geoffrey Reed as Commissioners. The three judges had been in his experience, said Dunstan, completely fair, sound and courteous, and were held in high regard and in warm affection. Nevertheless, "it is most undesirable that any Commissioner should go to an enquiry having expressed an opinion already about matters upon which he is to enquire."

It was, he agreed, perfectly proper for a judge who sat on a case to be asked whether new evidence could have disturbed the verdict of the jury; "but where the judges are appointed to a Commission of Enquiry and asked to pass upon matters which are not mere matters of new evidence but matters upon which they have already sat, it is a completely different matter. No precedent can be shown where that has happened." It was true that a trial judge did not decide matters of fact. "It is also the case, that the trial judge may invite the jury, quite properly and fairly, to consider certain views and he may properly express his views on the weight of the evidence to the jury. To a certain extent, though perfectly properly and fairly, that is what Mr. Justice Reed did in the trial in the first instance. With great respect to him, I do not think it fair to him to have been asked to sit on the Commission to pass on matters on which he had already sat as the trial judge, and I think, again with great respect to him, that it was unwise of him to accept."

Dunstan now referred to "a matter of which I was ignorant when the Commission was appointed". From the transcript of argument in the Court of Criminal Appeal, he read a passage[8] in which O'Sullivan suggested that Stuart's confession was compiled with the aid of assault, and the Chief Justice said: "That is utter rubbish." Dunstan commented: "The Premier, after consultation with the Chief Justice, assured the House that the matter of the confession would be dealt with by the Commission, but His Honour has already, when he was acting as a judge, not as a Commissioner, passed an opinion on this matter so forcefully that you could not have gone further, and he is now being asked to review that opinion . . ." The Chief Justice also offered the opinion as appeal judge, said Dunstan, that any discrepancies in the police evidence were merely matters of mistake and not of intention. "That, again, is something that he is being asked to pass upon as a Commissioner. With great respect to His Honour, I do not think he ought to be asked to do it and I do not think he ought to accept the duty of doing it."

Dunstan made no attempt to discuss Shand's withdrawal (which he plainly had in mind when he spoke of "the final matter that has caused public disquiet"), beyond saying that he believed parliament should be able to discuss it, and that having looked at the transcript he was "extremely distressed at what took place". He did refer directly to one thing said at the Commission when it resumed on the Monday of this week. "I do not know," said Dunstan, "what right Mr. Brazel claims to speak for the Bar of South Australia . . . I do not claim that right, but I do know that very many members of the legal profession have approached me and have expressed disquiet similar to that which I have expressed before this House today." He believed that the Commission should not continue and that the government should permit a full discussion of it in parliament.

Three more Labor members spoke before anybody rose from the other side. Mr. S. J. Lawn suggested, as he often did, that Playford was "not worried much about trying to justify the actions of this Government, because he is sitting pretty on a gerrymandered electorate

[8] Quoted on p. 38 above.

. . ." He also said that hanging was not severe enough a punishment for whoever committed the crime at Ceduna—a remark which opponents of Dunstan's bill to abolish the death sentence noted with relish. Lawn challenged the Premier's statement that newspapers had brought about all the disquiet. "Why, the press of South Australia is as much in the corner of the Playford government as of the Liberal Party in every other state of the Commonwealth!" ("More so, I would think," added the Leader of the Opposition.) Mr. Frank Walsh spoke more briefly and less vividly, concluding: "We want to retain in the judiciary that confidence that has been in it over many years. It should not be subjected to criticism because of something the executive has done. That is why we wanted to place the matter before the executive yesterday, but we were denied the opportunity." Mr. J. J. Jennings, who followed, insisted that the Opposition was criticising the government, not the Commissioners. "We . . . sympathise with them in the awkward and embarrassing situation in which the Government has placed them." The Premier, he said, was far more worried than he admitted about the well-informed protests from all over the world. "It is only the accumulated arrogance of twenty years' dictatorship . . . that has prevented him from gracefully giving in."

The object of these remarks rose. He spoke of the trial, the appeals, the outbreak of public controversy. "I say with feeling that it is not pleasant for any Executive Council to have to make a decision on a matter concerning capital punishment . . . I am certain there is no predilection by anybody associated with the administration of justice to hound a person down, particularly when it is claimed he is innocent. I do not think any member would assume that any member of our police force, judiciary or executive would desire that. However, these were the claims that were being made in the public press."[9]

The police, said Playford, were accused "in the press" of forcing a confession by violence from an innocent man. "I do not believe that any member who knows our police force, and who respects our police force for what it is, would seriously consider a charge of that kind. . . . That was one of the questions publicly stated as being at issue; that a man had been forced to confess: that he had had a confession bashed out of him. No honourable member would accept that." It was to be alleged on Stuart's behalf that these words were improper.

Playford defended both the appointment of a Royal Commission rather than a reference to the Full Court, and the choice of its members. If anyone could bring forward evidence on Stuart's behalf, Playford said, he knew it would receive the fullest consideration.

"You cannot speak for the Commission," interjected Lawn.

Playford pounced on the remark. "Honourable members opposite have said they have confidence in the Commission, but how can a

[9] The *Observer* article on "The Hanging State" (see p. 99 above) had included the phrase "predilection for hanging".

person have confidence in the Commission on the one hand, and have no confidence in the judgment of the Commission on the other hand? It is a remarkable trick of the mind."

The Premier touched again on matters before the Commission when he referred to the statement of Stuart's which had been read at the Commission on Monday. "His whole statement and his confession that one honourable member says should have been read in court was that he did go to Thevenard in the afternoon. That was Stuart's statement."[10] The Speaker stopped Playford from going further.

A few moments later the Speaker intervened again. "I have some documents here——" Playford said. The Speaker said that he should not refer to them. They should be exhibited, said the Premier, "because a very important lesson could be learned from them. However, I accept your ruling, sir." Before doing so, however, he removed any remaining doubt about which newspaper he was accusing of libel, by showing clearly to every member, visitor and reporter present, a poster of the *News* of August 21, reading:

COMMISSION BREAKS UP
SHAND BLASTS NAPIER

"I will quote from a newspaper," Playford went on, "because I think that is within Standing Orders." From the same day's *News* he read a headline:

Mr. Shand, Q.C., indicts Sir Mellis Napier
"THESE COMMISSIONERS CANNOT DO THE JOB"

"These words were never spoken," said Playford, "yet they are put in inverted commas, and that is the sort of thing that has been used to try and drag our judges down. These words, or anything like them, were never spoken. They are the gravest libel ever made against any judge in this state."

"Why wasn't a libel action taken against them?" asked a Labor member, Mr. Fred Walsh.

"The government will consider action at the appropriate time to protect our judges, make no mistake about that," replied Playford. ". . . If the government took action today it would immediately be held as an attempt to try and stifle public opinion . . . I believe that the Commission, considering the gross insults and attacks levelled at it, has been very forbearing, and I believe this House should carry a resolution of commendation to Sir Mellis Napier, who, in one of the most tragic times of his life,[11] has been subject to the vilest abuse and

[10] It was a curious slip to call this statement professing innocence a "confession". In the statement, moreover, Stuart did not say that he went to Thevenard in the afternoon. The first reference to time was: "I walked back to Ceduna in the afternoon" (see p. 150 above).

[11] It was only nine days since Lady Napier's death.

yet has carried on his duties manfully and, I believe, with great dignity . . . I suggest that the Royal Commission be allowed to complete its work and bring in its recommendations. They would be public recommendations; and then if the Leader of the Opposition or any other person had any comment to make on them I should be happy to hear them before further action was taken. Needless to say, Mr. Speaker, I oppose the motion."

The debate had been going on for two hours, and lasted another two, with speeches from four more Labor members, two Independents, and only two supporters of the government. The Independent who had been absent on Tuesday, Stott, said that certain aspects of the Commission had caused him anxiety. He believed the terms of reference to be too narrow; but he could not vote for the present motion, because to do so would be to say that he had no confidence in the judiciary and suspected the police. The other Independent, Quirke, was less troubled; he had found complete confidence in the Commission among South Australians.

Playford's oldest supporter in the House, Mr. H. H. Shannon, came close to suggesting that the whole affair was instigated by the *News*. "How the new matters arise is something that arouses my curiosity. How came it that certain people through a certain newspaper on North Terrace journeyed to Queensland? Who paid the expenses? Who was the instigator who knew that there was something for them to get? They are all very interesting factors that people are curious about. I do not know whether even the Royal Commission will be able to discover the driving force that sent people to the northern tip of Australia to come back with further evidence. It is a strange thing that a certain employee of this newspaper went so far afield." The other L.C.L. member who spoke, Mr. R. R. Millhouse, accused the Opposition of "a cynical attempt to cash in upon the newspaper campaign that has been waged in this State . . ." Only one Labor member, Mr. J. S. Clark, spoke up for the *News*. "I suggest," he said, "that but for the actions of that newspaper and people associated with it, we possibly would never have come to the stage where a Royal Commission was felt to be necessary at all. The newspapers have normally not been remarkable for their friendliness to my party, but I believe we must be fair on an issue of this nature." Mr. Fred Walsh, the man who flew back from Melbourne for the debate, spoke in a different vein; he denied that the Opposition had been "led by any section of the press that at the next state election will be defending the government . . . If it were true, as the Premier suggested this afternoon, that that section of the press were guilty of libel, I should be pleased to know what action was to be taken against it."

A number of speakers, for and against the motion, pointed out that they were not lawyers. Two Labor members argued that the enquiry should satisfy laymen as well as the professionally instructed. Mr. R. R. Loveday referred to the Chief Justice's statement that the constitution of the Commission could be justified by precedent. "That may be so. I do not know anything about those precedents, nor do I think the man in the street knows or cares anything about them—all he is concerned about is that justice should appear to be done." Mr. Fred Walsh made a similar but more far-reaching point, in what amounted to the most radical words in the whole debate. "If the present Commission continues, even if counsel represents Stuart at that Commission and even though the weight of evidence may be against Stuart and it is determined that he is guilty and the Commission makes no recommendation about a re-trial or anything else it may have the power to recommend, I still think a large section of the people of Australia will believe that he has not been given a fair trial or a fair go."

When the house divided, the support of the two Independents gave the government a majority of four. Next day, Thursday, the annual agricultural show opened in Adelaide and parliament adjourned for its duration. No discussion in that chamber had raised such fundamental questions about the relation between the legislature, the executive and the judiciary since 1867, when a judge of the Supreme Court, who had declared a number of colonial enactments invalid, was removed from office.

* * *

"LET'S GET THE RECORD STRAIGHT," said the *News* on its front page the day after this debate, in an editorial whose authorship and precise meaning were eventually to be discussed before a jury.

> "The Premier, the Royal Commissioners, and others have attacked the *News*, sometimes by implication and inference, sometimes by exaggerated insult, for our behaviour in the celebrated Stuart case. Yesterday Sir Thomas Playford charged that we had engaged in a campaign to discredit the members of the Supreme Court who are sitting on the Royal Commission.
>
> "Worse still, Sir Thomas Playford, under parliamentary privilege, accused the *News* of alleging 'the vilest crimes' by his Government and the judges. The *News* is quite prepared to defend itself at the appropriate time and in the appropriate place, as may be directed.
>
> "But meanwhile, let's set the record straight. The *News* has AT NO TIME alleged any crime by any member of the government, the Supreme Court, or even the South Australian police. However, we conceive it as our duty to report all statements in such an important matter.
>
> "The *News* is fully prepared to concede that it can make a mistake, like anybody else. We refer specifically to the headline which Sir Thomas brandished in parliament yesterday. It said: 'These commissioners cannot do the job.' The Premier, with some emotion, exclaimed that Mr. Shand never said any such thing.

"Well, the Premier is right. And we were wrong. Mr. Shand did not use these words, and the headline should never have been published and we regret that it was.

"Also Mr. Shand did not single out Sir Mellis Napier in his attack, and a poster which read 'Shand blasts Napier' should not have seen the light of day, and again we regret that it did. It should have read 'Shand attacks Commission.'

"But what Mr. Shand did say should be remembered—and we leave it to our readers to judge just how incorrect was our headline."

The statement made by Shand before he withdrew was then quoted. The editorial went on to say that after considerable controversy in eastern states, the *News* sought out Father Dixon, became convinced of his sincerity and paid for his visit to Queensland, where he secured for Stuart a possible alibi.

"Only then—and not before—the *News* stated that the hanging should not go on until this new evidence had been properly tested.

"We have never claimed that Stuart is innocent—merely that he must be shown to be guilty beyond all doubt before being hanged.

"The *News* sees it as its duty to fight always not only for justice to be done, but for justice to appear to be done.

"WE MAINTAIN THIS STAND, AND WILL CONTINUE, WITH PRIDE, TO FIGHT FOR THIS IDEAL."

On the same page the *News* reprinted a leading article from that morning's issue of the *Canberra Times*, an independent daily. The title—"Justice on Trial"—and parts of the text were more severe than anything so far published in an Australian newspaper. The investigation was said to be "assuming the nature of a tragedy of errors . . . the public conscience is utterly and almost hopelessly confused. Now, not only the guilt or innocence of Stuart is obscured, but the integrity of three eminent judges is in question. Unhappily, nothing that has transpired in the South Australian Parliament during the past two days has done anything to assist. On the contrary the issues have been irrevocably—or at least very nearly irrevocably—clouded. . . . One more such 'victory' as the Playford Government achieved in the two debates this week and the reputation of Australian justice will suffer untold harm, not only within Australia but overseas."

From Canberra, where these words were written, the federal political correspondent of the Sydney *Daily Telegraph*, Mr. Alan Reid, had flown to Adelaide earlier in the week; and on this same day, September 3, his first despatch appeared. A colleague once wrote of Reid that he gave the reader "the wicked pleasure of being in the presence of a crisp-minded man who must have tapped more telephones, steamed open more letters and looked through more keyholes" than a security man. Reid now predicted that the Stuart affair would "finish up a Dreyfus-type case, whatever the outcome, with one side passionately believing the verdict was wrong whatever the verdict".

The letters which the *News* and the *Advertiser* were printing certainly supported Reid's story of a divided community. The *News* said it was receiving hundreds, some critical of the paper's stand but the vast majority supporting it. The *Advertiser* did not say how many letters it was getting; but if those printed were a fair sample, most of its correspondents were solidly behind the government and the Commission. The morning paper still made no comment of its own. In Sydney, an editorial opinion favourable to Playford appeared at last. It was in the *Bulletin*, an ex-radical weekly now made up mainly of serious literary criticism, antique cartoons, rural anecdotes and sternly anti-Labor politics. "The Labor moves in the S.A. Parliament to subvert the Stuart Commission," said the *Bulletin*, "failed, as everybody, including the movers, knew they would, and the Opposition came rather badly out of the scrap. Playford is the hardest bit of granite the sob-sister press and politicians have to encounter, and he usually justifies himself." The parliamentary interlude was judged differently by another Sydney journal, *Nation*, which criticised Playford's assertion that no member of parliament would believe that the police would extract a confession by force; this, said the paper, was "almost an open invitation for the establishment of a police state".

* * *

O'Sullivan was asked to attend the Commission again when it resumed on Friday, September 4. Shortly before he arrived Sir Mellis Napier said: "We think we should have an assurance that it is Stuart's express wish not to be here or else require his attendance, one way or the other." O'Sullivan said: "Stuart does not wish to be represented by counsel, or to give evidence, or to have any witnesses called." Did he desire not to be present? asked the Chairman. Or, said Mr. Justice Reed, to have anybody here on his behalf "merely for the purpose of listening and telling him what is happening here"? Only the prisoner and his legal advisers, said Mr. Justice Ross, could explain why an alibi was not set up at the trial, "and they are not giving us that information. There might be two reasons why that is not given: one, which I hope is not being put forward, that we are not giving the prisoner's case a fair hearing, or the second, which might be forced on the Commission, is that there is no reasonable explanation." Mr. Justice Ross added that he had great sympathy with O'Sullivan's personal difficulties and admired the way he had fought for his client; "but these are matters which I think carry a great responsibility to the legal advisers of Stuart."

"I appreciate that," said O'Sullivan.

For a moment the matter of the alibi was discussed in quite

precise terms. Sir Mellis Napier said: "You will perhaps bear in mind that so far Stuart has not himself endeavoured to tell us or anybody . . . where he was at the relevant time." Mr. Justice Reed added: "He hasn't so far said he was working at the darts stall at the fun-fair between two and four that afternoon."

"He said in his statement," replied O'Sullivan, "he was working at the show during the afternoon."

"During the afternoon," observed the Chairman.

"Not during that period," said Mr. Justice Reed.

"He has not excluded it," replied O'Sullivan.

"He hasn't said so yet, even up to this moment," said Mr. Justice Reed.

"I don't know that I can go further into it," said O'Sullivan.

"We are only indicating the difficulties which arise," said Mr. Justice Reed.

The Chairman closed the discussion: "So long as the situation is clearly understood and Stuart is acting, shall I say, with his eyes open, and if he is not prepared to help us with our enquiry, there is nothing we can do about it. Thank you, Mr. O'Sullivan."

O'Sullivan undertook to find out whether Stuart wanted someone to attend the Commission on his behalf.

* * *

Each person who now gave evidence was examined first by counsel assisting the Commission and then by counsel for the Attorney-General. Nobody could believe this a satisfactory means of discovering the truth; a police witness, to take the most obvious example, would be unlikely to receive from anybody except counsel for Stuart a cross-examination searching enough to discover whether he was trying to hide something.

The procedure of British courts, as an Adelaide lawyer, Mr. H. G. Alderman, Q.C., observed when acting as a Royal Commissioner in Queensland, "is based on the attrition between two biassed and contending parties. In that way we believe that we get the best result which could easily be unsatisfactory if one side were neutral while the other interests were partisan or biassed." At Royal Commissions custom had added a third participant unknown in the courts—counsel briefed not to work for a contending party but to "assist". If the witnesses were questioned only by him and by counsel for the Crown, their evidence would be tested in a manner less balanced than envisaged in British judicial theory. That was now the situation at the Royal Commission on Stuart. It pleased nobody. Who was to blame? Shand and his colleagues, for sabotage? The Commissioners, for sitting when they should not have, and for denying Shand a thorough enquiry? There were some spectators of the impasse, including Sir John Latham and a number of newspaper editors, to whom it seemed that, wherever the blame lay, the Commissioners would be unwise to go on taking evidence, on the ground that once uneasiness about the Commission became widespread, any finding other than one wholly for Stuart would leave many people troubled. The Premier could not take this view. The Commissioners and their assisting counsel had declared that Shand's withdrawal was mischievous, and he himself believed that the vile libels of a newspaper had been responsible for public disquiet. To ask the Commission not to go on hearing evidence would have been, as Playford saw it, to capitulate in the face of a wicked campaign.

13

A STATEMENT FROM GAOL

STREHLOW WAS THE FIRST new witness to be called in the absence of counsel for Stuart. In view of his wide experience as a witness in the Northern Territory, it was not surprising that of all the people who gave evidence, he appeared so far the most comfortable in the box.

Brazel asked, among other things, whether he had been helped to form any opinion about the confession by reading the account of the interrogation which, according to the police, preceded it. Strehlow said that as a constable had written this account a day or two later, from memory, he would discount it fairly heavily as a linguistic document.

Before Chamberlain cross-examined, he asked whether there were any claims that conversations in the presence of Strehlow between the prisoner and his solicitor were privileged. The Chairman asked Strehlow if, when he approached the Attorney-General, he was acting on Stuart's instructions.

"I was acting as a private citizen interested in the case," the witness replied.

"You were not betraying any confidence?" "No."

"I think we would like to feel assured about that," said the Chairman. Soon, however, it was to be argued on Stuart's behalf that, in the ensuing examination of Strehlow, Chamberlain did ask improperly about privileged communications between Stuart and his counsel.

Chamberlain opened with questions about aborigines and time. By and large, Strehlow said, aborigines thought in terms of the sun and meals rather than clocks; but an intelligent aborigine who worked among white men in a job where things happened at fixed times would be quite likely to learn to give those times. He had not seen Stuart take an interest in clock times.

"You have not taken the trouble to find out, have you?"

"I have not, no."

Had Strehlow seen himself quoted in the *News* of August 4 as saying that Stuart's confession "fell down"? Did he realise that this was to say, in effect, that it was a fake?

Strehlow said he could not accept it as genuine.

"Let us see if we can use a little plain Australian," said Chamberlain. "I am not a student of linguistics . . . Didn't you mean when you made that statement to the *News*[1] to give it out to the world that the police evidence against Stuart was faked?"

"It meant that there was some doubt."

"Is it possible," asked the Chairman, "to give a direct answer to the question? If you could, it would be quicker."

"Yes or no?" said Chamberlain.

"It did not ring true to me."

Strehlow said he knew that O'Sullivan did not ask for an interpreter at the trial. Had he published his opinion on the inadequacy of Stuart's English without having had any conversation with him in the language?

"No, I had listened to him speaking to others . . ."

"So the only testing of Stuart's English you have done is to sit by while Mr. O'Sullivan asked questions and got answers?"

"If Stuart had come from another part of Australia I would not have been able to form an opinion quickly on the type of English he was speaking, but because he came from the Northern Territory, it was quite easy to pick up certain hall-marks in . . . English that is spoken in the Northern Territory." He had formed this opinion (at the gaol) in about an hour.

Could he remember any of Stuart's words? It was difficult to remember, said Strehlow, after four months.

The statement which O'Sullivan wanted to have read at the trial was now produced by Chamberlain, who put questions about its substance and language. He drew Strehlow's attention to the words: "I went in a taxi to Thevenard to get a drink. I did not want a girl." Strehlow said he remembered that in the police court a taxi-driver gave evidence that Stuart spoke of wanting a girl at Thevenard. It would be quite simple, he agreed, to ask Stuart in English whether he was looking for a girl in Thevenard, and to get an answer.[2]

In what language did Stuart tell him that he had gone looking for a girl, had intercourse with her, and paid her four pounds?

"He told me that in Aranda."

"But it could just as easily have been found out in English, couldn't it?" "That part could have been, yes."

"Did anyone ask Stuart why he had told O'Sullivan that he was not looking for a girl?"

"Not in my presence."

When Strehlow said that Stuart had never mentioned any times in relation to his journey to and from Thevenard, Chamberlain asked: "Didn't you try to find out from him?"

[1] The statement had appeared in the Sydney *Sunday Telegraph* two days before it was published in the *News*, and seemed to have been drawn from a copy of Strehlow's letter to the Attorney-General.

[2] Chamberlain here appeared to have in mind the application for leave to appeal to the High Court, in which it was implied that Stuart first mentioned the girl at Thevenard when he spoke in Aranda with Strehlow.

"No . . . we hoped to check on that from independent witnesses . . ."

Had Strehlow ever heard Stuart's legal advisers ask him when he went to Thevenard and how he went back? No.

Chamberlain returned to the linguistic issue, with questions about the style of three documents—the confession, the police record of the preliminary interrogation, and the statement taken by O'Sullivan. The language of the interrogation seemed natural enough for Stuart, Strehlow said, except that all the past tenses were correct. "He is like the rest of the people in the Northern Territory who are very fond of putting in present tenses and mixing them with past tenses."

"That is another ground upon which you suspect the written confession?"

"Very much so."

But in Stuart's statement, vouched for by his solicitors, were not all the past tenses accurate? Moreover, was it not a complete chronological description of events, containing no great trace of Aranda or northern dialect? Strehlow agreed. Then did he doubt the authenticity of that document? "I was told by Mr. O'Sullivan," he replied, "that he had in fact taken Stuart's replies and put them into, shall I say, slightly more correct English." Some passages, he agreed, appeared to be in Stuart's own words.

"And you do not blame Mr. O'Sullivan for producing a document like that . . . ?"

"He explained to me that was his setting out of information which he got from Stuart, and I agreed with that; I should be prepared to accept it as that."

Chamberlain suggested that an honest transcriber of either the reported interrogation or the confession might still lose a little of the flavour of the language. "That applies to the small references," said Strehlow, "it does not apply to words like 'unconscious', 'awoke', or 'stated', and things like that. I do not think you could mis-hear that as anything else."

Strehlow was questioned about his knowledge of a court case at Alice Springs in 1956, in which Stuart was charged with supplying liquor to an aborigine. He agreed that, according to O'Sullivan at the High Court, Stuart gave no evidence but somebody handed in a document on his behalf. He had also heard another version, that Stuart did speak for himself after a friend had coached him. Strehlow was shown a transcript of the evidence in the case. He said that it reproduced Stuart's bad rambling style excellently; it was full of repetition and irrelevance. He did not dispute Chamberlain's suggestion that Stuart could have given that evidence unassisted by anybody. Was he surprised to see Stuart, in this document, mentioning "about one o'clock", and "two o'clock", and "half past five"? No: Stuart would think of one o'clock as the time the shops closed, two o'clock as the time they opened, and half past five as the time they closed again.

Chamberlain referred next to Strehlow's opinion, expressed in the letter to the Attorney-General and later in print, that the murder was not a black man's crime. Was the rape and murder of small girls a common *white* man's crime?

"You hear about rape and murder connected with white man's society," said Strehlow. He agreed that one way to test the theory would be to examine Stuart's own history. Chamberlain was about to introduce evidence which he had not tried to offer at the trial and which would presumably not have been admitted had he done so. Counsel for Stuart, had one been present, would possibly have objected when Chamberlain said:

"You know that in 1957 he was convicted of aggravated assault in Cloncurry?" "That is correct," said Strehlow.

"Did you know . . . that he had approached a ten-year-old child, a girl, in bed, put his hand under her clothes, tried to put his hand on her private parts and put the other hand over her mouth to stop her from crying out?"

Strehlow said he had heard rather that Stuart "had gone to the room to thieve something and made his way out by touch, feeling with his hands along the way as he was coming out; that is what I was told."

"Who reported that to you?"

"I think it was Father Dixon," Strehlow said. He had not heard of Stuart's admission to the police that when he had drink he was unable to control himself with women; nor had he heard that in 1955 he was gaoled for fifteen months after knocking a nurse unconscious in a lavatory at a dance in Alice Springs.

"Would they be important items of history, do you think, showing Stuart's attitude towards women and the effect of drink on it?"

"They would be of interest."

"Do you think 'interest' is the right expression?" asked Sir Mellis Napier.

There was a difference, Strehlow said, between touching and knocking somebody, and actually committing rape and murder.

"In both these cases," said Chamberlain, "I am suggesting to you that Stuart was interrupted before he got as far as he might have wanted to go."

"That is hypothetical, of course," said Strehlow.

"That sort of thing would show a tendency?"

It was the combination of rape and murder, Strehlow said, that he thought uncharacteristic of people who had grown up in an aboriginal environment.

Finally Chamberlain took Strehlow through the confession. The witness repeated his view that the narrative had a conciseness and relevance not possible for somebody who had never been taught how to construct English prose. After discussion about the irony of certain passages in Strehlow's letter to the Attorney-General, Chamberlain asked about his remark there that the author of the confession could distinguish "she" from "he" and "her" from "him" whereas pidgin used " 'im" for all four pronouns. Strehlow added now that even in Northern Territory English it was common for people to use "he" and "him" of females. Stuart, he said, generally used "he" when speaking of either a man or a woman. Chamberlain pointed out that in his short statement from the dock Stuart said: "They say I killed her." Strehlow suggested that Stuart's English would have improved in gaol during the four months before his trial, though even now he still often used "he" and " 'im" inappropriately.

The Commissioners tried to offer a substitute for the normal re-examination of a witness by friendly counsel. Both the Chairman and Mr. Justice Reed asked whether Strehlow wished to explain or extend what he had said. The Chairman asked if he ever had from Stuart an account of what he did that afternoon. Did he indicate what time he had gone to Thevenard? "From the way he was talking," said Strehlow, "it seems he had gone there in the forenoon . . ."

* * *

The next witness, Dr. D. M. Williamson, was in the box for only a minute. He told Brazel that within the last week he had examined a girl whom he now identified in court: he had found her hymen unruptured; in layman's language, she was a virgin. The girl, Olive Betts, was sworn. She remembered going to the pictures at Ceduna on the night before Mary Hattam was killed. She saw there a dark stranger, whom she identified now from a photograph as Stuart; but she did not speak to him nor he to her; nor did he give her anything.[3] She went home to the Thevenard Hotel, where she was working. Next day, some time after breakfast and before midday dinner, she left the hotel for her sister's place, where she stayed until the evening.[4] After tea she went to Ceduna.

"To the pictures again?" asked Brazel.

"No, down to the sideshow."

On Saturday morning she saw the dark stranger in the street at Ceduna, but he did not speak to her nor she to him. She saw him again in the pictures on Saturday night,[5] and again no words were

[3] Brenda Kent and Veda Miller, with whom Olive Betts shared a room, said that Stuart gave her a box of chocolates (see pp. 120, 122 above).

[4] Brenda Kent said that she and Olive Betts had a bath at the hotel after the midday meal. Veda Miller said twice that Olive was in the hotel room on Saturday afternoon, and once that she was not (see pp. 121-2 above).

[5] On all other accounts, Stuart was not at the pictures on Saturday night. He was outside the hall where the pictures were shown, but Miss Betts was saying more than that. She told Brazel plainly that she herself went to the pictures on Saturday night, and to his question whether she saw Stuart "in there", answered "Yes." Miss Betts said that she went to the pictures on both the Friday and Saturday evenings; according to the *West Coast Sentinel* the same films were showing on each night.

exchanged. To a question from the Chairman, the witness said that nobody gave her any chocolates at the pictures on Friday night and that she had not told Veda Miller that somebody gave her chocolates.

* * *

The Commissioners now heard the three people whose statements had been the subject of warm words between Shand and Brazel—Mr. and Mrs. Allan Wardrop and their seventeen-year-old daughter Christine. Wardrop, an expansive middle-aged man, had been until early in 1959 the proprietor of a café in Port Lincoln, the town from which Detective Frank Whitrod rushed to join the search for Mary Hattam's murderer. He told Brazel that he knew Whitrod well. On the Friday night after the murder, in the rooms of the Returned Servicemen's League at Port Lincoln and in the presence of the branch secretary, Mr. Horrie Baker, Whitrod said that Stuart had "got his corner". Baker said: "You gave it to him Frank." Wardrop himself said: "Well, it serves the bastard right." Another night, possibly the next night, Whitrod came to the café late for something to eat. When Mrs. Wardrop asked what sort of Christmas he had, Whitrod replied that it was not a good one, because of the murder at Ceduna. In the kitchen, Whitrod said that when Stuart confessed, "the police did their block and really belted him". Wardrop said: "You are sure he did it, Frank?" Whitrod said: "Well, he has confessed." Whitrod then described how Sonny Jim, the black tracker, said when Stuart walked across some sand: "Him do it, him do it." It was then, according to Wardrop, that Whitrod said the policemen "did their blocks and gave him a belting".

Chamberlain asked if Wardrop had ever told anybody that Whitrod said: "We bashed it out of the black bastard."

"Never," said Wardrop.

"You saw that headline in the *News*, did you, attributed to you?"

"Yes."

". . . I suppose you were horrified, really, to see it?"

"Was I ever!"

Wardrop agreed that he had a brother-in-law working on the *News*. He had not got in touch with this man.

"Well, weren't you highly indignant with the *News*?" "Very."

"Did you have any theory as to how you had become misconstrued?"

"I know exactly how I was misconstrued. Could I say something?"

"You will be able to in due course. I will not stop you from giving your explanation, but I want you to answer my questions in my way first . . ."

Had he communicated with anybody about this report between the Monday, (August 17) when it appeared, and the Thursday? No; his brother-in-law rang him on Thursday and said: "What is this about the bashing?" Wardrop said he replied: "You printed them, brother, you get out of it as best you can." It was, Wardrop told Chamberlain, a "misunderstanding, a betrayal of confidence, an indiscretion on my part, call it what you will".

How would Shand have known on the Monday morning that the Commission had a statement from him? His brother-in-law, Wardrop replied, knew that he had been to the Commission, though not what he had said. On the Friday he signed a brief statement in the presence of Mr. N. C. Ligertwood, solicitor assisting the Commission. He signed a fuller statement on the Monday night.

"After the *News* had spread the story?" "Yes."

In the statement taken by Ligertwood, Chamberlain pointed out, Wardrop had not attributed to Whitrod the words "got his corner", but had said: "I could come to no other conclusion but that Stuart had been subjected to physical violence."

Wardrop said that there was not really any difference; "to me it is just a legal technicality . . . physical violence, getting his corner, give him the one two three, what's the difference, it is all the same."

Wardrop agreed that he had once been arrested by Whitrod for illegal sale of liquor and fined about sixty pounds. He had told Whitrod he was in strife in the Middle East during World War II.

"You came home," said Chamberlain, "for disobeying a lawful command in the field?"

"No, refusing to go on parade. We didn't shoot any officers or anything like that."

"You got eighteen months for what you did?"

"Yes, but I still wear this [R.S.L.] badge." He bore Whitrod no malice for arresting him on the charge of sly grogging, Wardrop said; "It was a matter of pay up and shut up . . . I was as friendly with Frank as anyone in Port Lincoln when I left there."

When did Wardrop first speak to anyone about Whitrod's admission at the café? "I first spoke about it to my wife on the evening of the 23rd of April, the day Stuart was sentenced to death."[6] Until he read the judge's summing up, he took no interest in the trial.

Wardrop's wife told Brazel that she remembered Whitrod coming into the kitchen of the café about midnight one Saturday after Christmas and asking for a meal. She, her husband and her daughter were present. She asked Whitrod what sort of Christmas he had. The detective replied that it was spoiled by the murder at Ceduna. He described details of the murder and the identification of the footprints by the black tracker. Whitrod then said: "When he confessed we really belted him."

She knew four months ago that her husband was concerned about the case, when the judge (so he told her) stated that the only evidence was the confession.

Stuart had been due to hang several times, Chamberlain remarked.

[6] Stuart was sentenced on April 24.

"You were not that much concerned about it that you thought you had better intervene before he did hang?"

"I wasn't very interested myself."

"When were you?"

"When my husband got up at night worried about it, I could see he was concerned."

". . . Did you have the idea Whitrod's story was that they got the confession out of Stuart by violence . . . ?"

". . . I knew that if they hit him afterwards it left doubts about whether they belted him to get the confession."

Had she told Ligertwood that she could not remember whether her daughter was present while Whitrod was speaking?

Yes, but after talking with her husband and her daughter about it, she was now sure that the girl could not have been there.

Had her husband followed the progress of Stuart's trial?

"Yes, he always read everything . . . Yes, he was interested."[7]

Had she seen in the paper a suggestion by O'Sullivan that the police had beaten Stuart?

Her husband had mentioned it. He had shown her the headline and said: "Can you remember what Frank said to us on that night?" She had replied that she remembered.

". . . When did you first try and find out about what Christine knew?"

"We never discussed it as a family until after my husband made the statement. We sat up one morning until about four o'clock talking about the whole thing."

Legoe examined Miss Christine Wardrop, who said that she remembered Whitrod coming in for a meal late one evening after Christmas. She heard him speak about the murder, but she did not hear any reference to an assault. She was not in the kitchen all the time.

"You heard the whole story from Whitrod about the crime, didn't you?" asked Chamberlain. "Yes."

"The black trackers and so on?"

"I did not hear anything about black trackers . . . I think my mother said she remembered something about it." She remembered the family sitting up until four o'clock one night soon afterwards talking about it.

What were they talking about?

"We were all saying we did not really want to go. We were worried. We went through the whole of the case from the beginning."

The Commission adjourned for the weekend.

None of the Commissioners invited the Wardrops, as they had Strehlow, to add anything after examination by counsel was com-

[7] This was not consistent with the evidence of Wardrop himself.

pleted. Wardrop thus had no opportunity to return to what Chamberlain had prevented him from explaining in cross-examination: how, in his view, Shand came to assert that all three Wardrops would say they heard a policeman use the words: "We bashed it out of the black bastard." According to Mrs. Wardrop, what she heard led her to suspect that Stuart was assaulted before he confessed as well as after; but neither she nor her husband nor her daughter claimed to have heard this admitted. It was now hard to see how Shand could have thought the Wardrops' statements "a little stronger" than he had indicated. Shand had inspected the statements for only a minute or two when he spoke, and if he had read no more than the first part of Wardrop's statement perhaps he thought it quite as strong as he had said: for in his account of the conversation at the R.S.L. rooms, Wardrop did not specify whether Whitrod's remark about physical violence referred to a time before Stuart confessed or after. But in Wardrop's account of the later conversation in the café, the only assault said to have been mentioned by Whitrod occurred after the confession. The *Advertiser* report, in which Shand was said to have admitted that the statements were "not quite as strong" as he had indicated, was certainly inaccurate—the court reporter, Mr. Justice Reed and others sitting close to Shand agreed about that; but it was prophetic.

* * *

A reporter from the Sydney *Mirror* tried to pursue the investigation privately over the weekend, by setting off for the gaol "to discover by independent enquiry whether or not Stuart can speak English" and to discuss with the prisoner whether he wanted to appear or be represented before the Commission—a point which, as the reporter wrote, had taken up a good deal of time at the Commission. "But South Australian officialdom closed the gates in our face. We could not get at the truth." The Chief Secretary, Sir Lyell McEwin, said to him: "The press has raised the colour question all over the world over this case. I am not taking any side, but I am sick of all the talk over this matter."

Stuart's colour was discussed also in the *Observer*, which said: "It is absurd for those who think Stuart should not hang to push their campaign to the extent of raising the question of colour prejudice. Last week someone even pulled Earl Attlee from the retirement of Cherry Cottage to pronounce on South Australia's treatment of Stuart as an example of bad relations between the races . . .[8] Whether Stuart should or should not hang depends not on the colour of his skin but on whether he committed the act of murder, and whether that crime is a hanging matter . . . The colour of his skin has probably helped him,

[8] This appears to have been inaccurate; as reported in the Australian press, Attlee spoke only of the composition of the Commission and not of Stuart at all.

but it must not be allowed to cloud the issue, which is: can we be sure that justice has been done when a man hadn't the wits to stand up for himself? The doubt that this can ever be so is enough in itself to suggest that hanging be abolished."

In the Sydney *Sun-Herald* on Sunday, "Onlooker" wrote his sternest review of the affair. "In that tightly-knit and slightly smug community," he said of Adelaide, "where the best families have held sway since the earliest days, the Establishment is more of a reality than anywhere else in Australia. Its headquarters is the Adelaide Club . . . Journalistically, its voice is the sedate morning *Advertiser*, a firm supporter of the Playford regime; and a thorn in its ample flesh is the brash evening *News*—the 'section of the press' whose un-Adelaideish campaigning in the Stuart affair has earned heavy rebuke from bench, bar and government. How ironical that the Establishment, so long entrenched politically, so serene judicially, should be rocked to its foundations by . . . a wandering degraded blackfellow . . ." After referring to "revealing expostulations" by Playford in parliament, the columnist said: "Sir Thomas' language is extravagant. It verges on the dictatorial. It is that of a man not only unused to having his will crossed but unable to admit the possibility that he may be mistaken in any course he takes."

On Monday the *News* reproduced this comment (noting that the *Sun-Herald* was "Australia's biggest circulation newspaper") and added a denial, by the editor, that its own actions were "un-Adelaideish". "We believe," wrote Rivett, "that the Australia-wide sense of justice which demands that the guilt of a man should be established beyond even the most slender of doubts is as deeply embedded in this city and this state as it is anywhere in Australia."

* * *

O'Sullivan appeared before the Commission on Monday morning, September 7. Certain advice received from Shand, he said, had been communicated to Stuart through Dixon and Strehlow. A statement had been prepared on that advice and signed by Stuart giving his answers to questions from Their Honours. The secretary read out the statement, in which Stuart declined to have anything to do with the Commission and gave his reasons.

The first reason was that in parliament the Premier had publicly declared that the police would not have bashed a confession out of Stuart. "The Commissioners," said Stuart,

> "are thus now confronted with the embarrassing alternative of either making a finding which accords with the government's predetermined views against me, or of reporting to the Executive which appointed them that the Premier's statement in the House in the midst of their deliberations was incorrect and unfounded."

Second: "In the Court of Criminal Appeal, the chairman, Sir

Mellis Napier, strongly criticised my counsel's attack on the police. In the Commission where the credibility of police evidence relative to my alleged confession is a crucial issue, he intervened and stopped the cross-examination of Phin, the first of seven police witnesses to be called. This fact, taken with the Premier's declared attitude in the House of Assembly, leads me to believe that this vital issue has already been unconsciously decided against me."

Third: "The Commissioners have said that as I am accusing the police of violence towards me, the onus is on me to establish my innocence. There is nothing in the terms of reference which requires this and it is contrary to British justice because it deprives me of the benefit of the doubt which is a long standing right belonging to every accused person."

Fourth: "The Commissioners have permitted and participated in cross-examination of a witness[9] concerning privileged communications between me and my then counsel, Mr. J. D. O'Sullivan. I am advised that this, too, is contrary to the principles of British justice, and I am further advised that it now appears that the Commissioners are obliged to violate recognised principles of law . . ."

Fifth: "The Chairman of the Commission and Mr. J. F. Brazel, Q.C., publicly made serious allegations against Mr. Shand, Q.C., and his juniors, by saying that they withdrew from the Commission in order to 'sabotage' it. The Commissioners refused to allow to be read before them statements by my counsel in answer to these grave accusations."

Sixth: "A variety of irrelevancies" had intruded on the enquiry, including capital punishment and the treatment of coloured minorities. "Without in any way inferring the slightest criticism of the personal integrity of the Commissioners, I feel that an atmosphere now exists which renders it impossible for them dispassionately to pass on the matters before them." If a re-trial were ordered at this stage it would be "extremely difficult to empanel a jury which could approach the matter with an open mind". The Commissioners were asked to recommend a respite of a further three to six months, followed by the appointment of a single commissioner drawn from another state or New Zealand.

The statement ended: "This has been read over to me and this is my statement." Under the signature, "Rupert Max Stuart", appeared the signature of Strehlow and the words: "This document was read and explained by me in Aranda to Rupert Max Stuart who has informed me that he wishes to accept the advice of his counsel."

[9] Presumably Strehlow was meant. In the Sydney *Telegraph* Mr. Alan Reid wrote of "a tremendous row . . . blowing up in legal circles" in Adelaide after Strehlow had been "questioned—without anyone protesting —on what took place while he was acting as interpreter for O'Sullivan in Stuart's cell".

"I am concerned," said Sir Mellis Napier, "at the inaccuracies and the absurdities contained in this extraordinary document. But we can, I think, accept the assurance that Stuart does not wish to be present, does not wish to give evidence." Addressing O'Sullivan, the Chairman said: "at the present time there is before us nothing that was not before the Privy Council when they told you that on the material before them there was no justification for any attack upon the police". The Chairman also said that "the obstacle to Stuart being supplied with legal representation is that you claim the right to represent him and prevent anybody else representing him".

The account of Shand's withdrawal given in the statement signed by Stuart was criticised by Mr. Justice Ross. "Mr. Shand was not stopped by the Chairman," he said. "He was invited to go on. If he was stopped he made no appeal to the other two Commissioners." If the Commissioners had entirely disbelieved Phin, that would not have helped Stuart's case, for what Moir and Gieseman told him was pure hearsay. Although the Commissioners did not stop Shand, they could properly have done so on the ground of irrelevancy; "the stopping of counsel from cross-examining is something that happens every day in the courts." Under the Royal Commissions Act, the Commissioners were not bound by the laws of evidence or procedure, but could inform their minds in any fit way they chose. "I think the experience of three experienced judges should carry more weight than the opinion of the no doubt disgruntled counsel concerned."

"I wish to say, if I may," said O'Sullivan, "that Mr. Shand is advising Stuart." He himself had sought advice from the Law Society and had done nothing contrary to it. "I appreciate the position as you have put it but I do say on my own behalf that I have done what I conceive to be my duty in this matter."

"We do not doubt," said the Chairman, "that you have done what you believe to be your duty, and it may be that in a tortuous sort of way you are considering the interests of a man who could not assist his case if he were to come and to help us by telling us the facts, but that may or may not be so. What other justification there can be for his not appearing to urge his case I personally fail to see . . . For the present I maintain an open mind. I simply point out to you what any ordinary person would think if a man chooses to say nothing when he is given the opportunity of clearing himself." The only inference that ordinary people would draw, said Sir Mellis Napier, was that Stuart well knew that to tell the truth would not advance his case. "No doubt all this will be published and used for the purpose of vituperation . . ." A memorandum from Shand was not published in the Commission, the Chairman explained, because "we feel that those who publish things of this sort should do so without the privilege that applies to a report of our proceedings".

Later in the week Brazel described the statement from Stuart as "the polysyllabic document which was presented here above his signature

. . ." The Melbourne *Herald*, in a perplexed leader, said: "It is hard to believe that the barely literate Stuart . . . could speak with real awareness of his position." Dixon and Strehlow were said to have explained the situation to the prisoner at various times and to have asked him, on behalf of the lawyers, whether he wished to be represented at the Commission, or to engage new solicitors. This explanation must have been a difficult feat. In English or Aranda, it was hard to imagine Stuart's following some parts of the statement signed by him on September 7. "Who," asked Mr. Stewart Cockburn on 5AD, "translated such words as 'constitution' and 'establishment' into Aranda . . . ?" He was not, of course, the first client in legal history to have an incomplete understanding of what a lawyer was saying on his behalf. But in advising the condemned man to boycott the Royal Commission on the ground that it would not give him a thorough enquiry, his lawyers were incurring a heavy responsibility, which became even heavier when the Chairman said that Stuart's refusal to give evidence must be interpreted by "ordinary people" as evidence of guilt, and that if Stuart stayed away he did so "with his eyes open". Unless a further respite was granted, those eyes would close on September 30.

14

A CLOUD OF WITNESSES

THE TAKING OF EVIDENCE resumed when O'Sullivan withdrew. Mr. Horace Baker who, Wardrop said, had heard an admission by Detective Whitrod, was called. He was branch manager in Port Lincoln of a firm selling motor spare parts, and for nearly three years he had been secretary of the R.S.L. there. Baker said that he could remember no occasion on which he, Whitrod and Wardrop were together at the R.S.L. rooms. The statement that he and Wardrop heard Whitrod say Stuart "got his corner" was fantastic.

Detective Frank Whitrod entered the box. Had he used any expression at the R.S.L. club, asked Chamberlain, indicating that Stuart received violence at the hands of the police? "I have never used those words or said that Stuart was subject to violence at any time or anywhere." He knew the expression "got his corner", but he had never used it. Baker, Wardrop and himself had never discussed the Stuart case. It was possible that at some time he described events at Ceduna to the Wardrops, but he never said that violence had been used. On one occasion he had arrested Wardrop, who would not be the sort of man he would confide in.

Brazel also asked about "got his corner". It was a gambler's term, said Whitrod, meaning, as far as he could make out, "his share in the proceedings".[1] He had never heard it used in any other sense. He might have been in the Wardrops' kitchen at the time mentioned by them, and the crime might have been discussed; but he had said nothing to suggest that Stuart was assaulted.

"We would like to hear the witness's account of how that confession came to be obtained," said the Chairman. ". . . It is curious, because never at any stage, either in the presence of the jury or since, has anyone, the accused or anyone else, suggested that any violence was used to force him, except insofar as Stuart says that in the unsworn statement which was not read to the jury."

"I think there was some reference made by Stuart from the dock," said Brazel.

Whitrod described in detail the apprehension and interrogation of

[1] In a list of underworld argot published in the *Australian Police Journal*, April 1950, a C.I.B. man in Sydney defined "corner" as "a share, especially a share of plunder". See S. J. Baker, *Australia Speaks*, 1953, p. 126.

Stuart, as narrated already by himself and his colleagues at the trial. He himself took no part in the interrogation other than to type the confession at Stuart's dictation. Apart from the opening words and references to dates, the confession contained Stuart's actual words. Stuart's English, he said, "was the language of an uneducated white man . . ." He did not think that O'Sullivan, at the trial, asked him any questions about Stuart's English.

The next witness, Mrs. Dorothy Newham, was also asked about Stuart's language. At the Alice Springs Police Court in 1956, she said, she was the depositions clerk when Stuart came before the magistrate for supplying liquor to an aborigine. He wanted to submit a statement written for him by someone else; but the magistrate explained that if he wanted to give evidence he must do so himself. Without assistance, Stuart then gave evidence, questioned witnesses, and seemed to have no trouble in understanding what was going on. He told his own story clearly and well, and she typed it exactly as he spoke. This statement, now produced and read out, was the document which the prosecution had sent to the High Court—improperly, the federal judges said—after the hearing of Stuart's application for leave to appeal. It was to be regarded by the Commissioners as important evidence.

A plain-clothes constable from Cloncurry, Mr. Alfred James Corbett, was the next witness. The Chairman asked why he had been produced; it appeared, he said, that Stuart was being kept in the background and rumours were serving in place of evidence. Chamberlain said that the constable would give evidence on Stuart's ability in English. In putting questions to Strehlow about Stuart's sexual history, however, Chamberlain had indicated another reason for hearing about events at Cloncurry. Corbett read a statement, taken in 1957 at Cloncurry, in which Stuart admitted having touched a sleeping nine-year-old girl between the legs and put his hand over her mouth when she woke. According to Corbett, Stuart said that he knew this was wrong; but he did not know any big women, and when he had liquor he could not control himself. Stuart did not put forward the excuse that he had gone in the room to thieve and had felt his way out; that was in another case. His capacity to understand English was good.

• • •

Father Thomas Dixon, who more than anybody else was responsible for this Commission, was called under the fourth term of reference—the circumstances in which statements from Gieseman, Mrs. Gieseman and Miss Hopes were obtained. A tall, heavily built, balding man entered the box and took the oath on his own Bible.

The absence of counsel for Stuart was now most apparent. The priest appeared to find some of Brazel's questions awkward in form, and was inclined to include in his replies information Brazel had not sought, as if lacking confidence that the story would be told fully otherwise. Brazel, for his part, insisted with icy politeness that the witness stick to the point. ("I am sorry; I will repeat the question, and ask you to answer it specifically, if you can. Be so kind as to tell me whether . . .") For Brazel the examination was made more difficult by the fact that the priest had declined to submit a written statement on which he could be examined.

Dixon explained that he first visited Stuart when the Catholic chaplain to the gaol said he had difficulty communicating with the prisoner in English. "I spoke his broken type of English," Dixon said, ". . . and where I found it hard in English I tried to put it into Arunta and, combining both, we got on." He described the approach to Stuart's solicitors, the visit to the Attorney-General, the journey to Queensland.

"It is clear from your recollection of the conversation," said Brazel, "that the hours two to four were introduced into the conversation for the first time by Mr. Gieseman: is that correct?"

"That is correct." He had asked Gieseman to describe Stuart's movements from nine o'clock on Friday night until nine o'clock on Sunday morning.

He knew, Dixon agreed, that in the statement prepared for the trial, Stuart said that he went to Thevenard and returned to Ceduna partly by road and partly along the beach.

"At any time," asked Brazel, "did Mr. Gieseman say that he supports that . . . ?"

"I cannot remember that," said Dixon; it was a vital matter of fact, he agreed, but he could not recall whether he had asked the Giesemans about it.

When Brazel asked about Miss Hopes' declaration, he referred to her evidence at the Commission that Stuart came home to the show not at two o'clock but at one. Had she told Dixon that?

"I do not think so."

"That comes as a surprise to you now?"

"The time element is a surprise, but the statement does not come as any surprise."

"Is that an oblique way of saying that Miss Hopes is not very reliable?"

"I think she is very nervous."

Had he asked Moir, at Collinsville, specifically whether he could speak of Stuart's movements between two o'clock and four?

"I don't remember that. I don't think I did."

"The newspaper headlines," Chamberlain began, "report you as being very triumphant when you got in touch with the Giesemans. Is that correct?"

"I don't think so."

". . . You didn't express jubilation?"

". . . I was glad and happy I had not been made a fool of in the eyes of the world."

". . . Did you think you had piled up an alibi that would save Stuart?"

"I hoped so, but I was not so sure. Everyone is not so sure even yet."

Before asking about the priest's relationship with Stuart, Chamberlain said: "I want you to understand that I have got every respect for the dictates of your faith, and if there is anything I ask you and you do not want to tell me, please let me know."

"There is no privilege between me and Stuart," said Dixon.

When had he decided to look for the Giesemans?

"I made the decision after I asked the advice of Miss Devaney and after senior counsel had been consulted."

"Who was senior counsel?"

"Mr. Brazel."

"Someone has told you that Mr. Brazel has been advising the Stuart interest?"

"Yes, that is what I have been advised."[2]

Chamberlain produced a copy of the pamphlet *Why not hang Rupert Stuart?* Dixon said he remembered this passage: "Stuart has never been tried at Darwin. Once, at Alice Springs, he recited a statement in court after all-night briefing by a half-caste from Adelaide, who also wrote out a statement for him to sign. He did not 'conduct his own defence fluently'." He had provided this information, Dixon said; that was what Stuart had told him. At Chamberlain's request he read a letter from O'Sullivan and Miss Devaney to the High Court in June, in which it was said that in the case at Alice Springs, Stuart had put in a typed document.

"That is the story that was given the High Court," said Chamberlain. "You see that? Stuart had not given the evidence but had produced a document which was acted upon . . . You see there are two different stories: (1) that he gave evidence himself after being taught; and (2) that he did not give evidence at all, but produced a document which someone else had written out . . . You do not see anything inconsistent with what Stuart told you and what was in the letter?"

"Yes."

From the same pamphlet Chamberlain cited a passage about Stuart's conviction for aggravated assault against a child in Queensland. "Stuart's story to you about that," said Chamberlain, "was that he was quite innocent of any indecent intention?"

"Yes."

[2] The official transcript recorded no comment here by Brazel. According to the *News* he said: "That is the first I know of it," and according to the Sydney *Telegraph*: "That's news to me." In the latter paper, Mr. Alan Reid reported that Brazel's disavowal led to a "furious 'behind-the-scenes' dispute with Stuart's solicitors".

"You believed him?"

"Well, I made some enquiries in Queensland when I was there . . ."

"When he told you that story did you believe him?"

"I did not know what to believe."

"At what stage in your dealings with Stuart did he give you that version of his conduct?"

"When it came out in the newspapers brought up by the police."[3]

". . . He had been protesting all along his innocence in connexion with the murder?"

"He never protested once . . . I had to ask him every time . . ."

"Was there any difference in his demeanour talking about the murder of Mary Hattam and talking about the aggravated assault on the little girl in Cloncurry?"

"He just gave the impression he was not guilty of them and that was that."

Did the witness think Stuart sincere when he denied any indecent intention in Cloncurry?

"Yes, but I didn't exactly believe him straight away, as I never do. I keep my eyes and wits about me and try to get at the truth eventually."

When Chamberlain asked if he had heard the prisoner's version of an incident in Alice Springs when a nurse was knocked out, Dixon said that according to Stuart he was recovering some liquor planted in a lavatory when a girl came in; he grabbed her and pushed her aside and went out.

At Sir Mellis Napier's invitation, Dixon gave what he understood to be Stuart's account of the Saturday in Ceduna. Several times, the priest said, he asked Stuart at what time he got in the taxi for Thevenard. Stuart said, pointing overhead: "The sun up there." (Later, the priest added that Stuart also said: "one o'clock".) At Thevenard, Stuart said, he spoke to a girl who came out of the hotel and who said she had seen him at the pictures. With another girl whom he noticed standing at the side of the hotel he had intercourse, for which he gave her four pounds. A white man gave him a bottle of wine and declined payment. He drank the wine on the way home, returning fast along the beach. Back at the show two dark men gave him twenty-five shillings to get some wine. He asked Mrs. Gieseman to buy it, and when she refused he asked "young Betty" instead. He worked on the darts for a couple of hours, until about sundown.

"It was sundown when he went up to the town again?" asked Mr. Justice Reed.

"I have asked him several times on the point since," Dixon said, "and he points to the sun being 'up there'. I said: 'Really dark?' He said: 'No, when the sun up there, when it starts to go down.'"

[3] The Police Association's statement referring to this case was published on July 3 (see pp. 58-9 above).

Could Stuart tell the time, asked Chamberlain. "No."

"Are you sure of that?" "Positive."

"He would not know it was a quarter to four if he was in here now?"

"I don't think so."

"Are you sure about that? Would you be surprised if only a morning or so ago I asked the gaoler at the Adelaide Gaol to go and talk to him and ask what time it was, and he looked at his watch and said 'five to nine'?"

"Very much."

In re-examination Brazel asked about the girl at Thevenard. Dixon agreed that in the statement which was to have come from the dock, Stuart said he did not want a girl. Had he pursued the apparent inconsistency in Stuart's stories?

"No . . . I was not upon any detective work."

Did he get from Stuart the name of the woman at Thevenard?

"I tried to; he did not know the name."

Brazel asked, in "fairness to a little girl", whether Dixon had noticed Shand's imputation that it was Olive Betts with whom Stuart had intercourse. "Do you accept my suggestion that Mr. Shand by his suggestions was imputing that?"

"I am afraid I cannot, only for the reason that I do not know."

According to Stuart, he said, the person involved had short hair, white wedge shoes and short white socks, was about twenty-three and had had experience of this kind before; he had seen her outside the pictures on Friday. Stuart did not say that according to his belief she worked at the hotel.

At the end of the day, three more witnesses called by the Crown spoke about Stuart's English. Colonel W. C. N. Waite, visiting magistrate to the Adelaide Gaol, said that he had interviewed Stuart for five, six or seven minutes every fortnight over some months. His English was "quite good . . . the average or even above the average of aboriginals" he had dealt with. Brigadier C. F. Stevenson of the Salvation Army said that he had spoken several times with Stuart before the trial. "What is your opinion of his capacity to speak and understand English," asked Brazel, "having in mind he is an aboriginal native?"

"He speaks good English."

Mr. G. E. Smith, a welfare officer of the Aborigines Department in Adelaide, said that he had spoken with Stuart on June 3 for about ten minutes. Stuart spoke quite freely, in English. "He speaks as an ordinary white person would speak." He gave a connected narrative without prompting.

• • •

In his first minutes at the Commission Shand had announced his intention to show that Stuart had a serious injury after his interview with the police. No more was heard of this allegation until September

4, when in the Sydney *Telegraph* Mr. Alan Reid reported from Adelaide that, according to Shand, a police photograph taken soon after Stuart confessed showed, under strong magnification, a fresh wound over one eye. On the morning of September 8, three witnesses were called to refute this charge. The first was Dr. G. C. H. Nicol, surgeon at Adelaide Gaol, who had examined Stuart within three days of his arrival. Stuart mentioned no injury, and the doctor saw no mark of violence on him.

"Is it expected," asked Sir Mellis Napier, "that Mr. Shand will give evidence?"

Chamberlain said that the only ground for thinking so was "a newspaper paragraph purporting to be sent by the correspondent of an interstate newspaper . . . I conceive it my duty to be at some pains to clear this matter up. I am grateful for the suggestion that the official photograph should be published . . . I have an offer to get it in the Sydney press if it is done straight away, and I think Sydney might be a place which would be interested in it." The gaol doctor, asked to examine photographs through a magnifying glass, said that on one of them he could see a mark on the right of the forehead which he took to be a small, old scar.

Mr. D. C. Aebi, in charge of the photograph and fingerprint section of the Police Department, said he had examined police photographs of Stuart with a magnifying glass, and found below the right eye a mark which was apparently an old scar. On the right of the forehead he could see a little whitish mark which might be either a blemish in the photograph or an old scar. A constable who was at the police studio when Stuart was photographed said that he saw no sign of injury on Stuart. With the consent of the Commissioners, Chamberlain released the photographs to the press. Most papers printed them. "WAS HE BASHED?" the Sydney *Mirror* asked readers, over reproductions which lost so much clarity in radio transmission that the outlines of Stuart's head had to be heavily re-touched.

From Mataranka, in the Northern Territory, came Constable Dennis Conaghan to give evidence from memory about Stuart's conviction for common assault against a woman in 1951. Stuart had said that he was in a cubicle in the ladies' lavatory at the Soldiers' Club when the woman walked in. He pleaded guilty and was sentenced to six months. Stuart did not suggest, and the constable had never heard it suggested, that he was in the lavatory because he had left some liquor there; it would not have been possible for Stuart to leave liquor there during the day. Although Chamberlain asked whether the witness had any difficulty communicating with Stuart in English (he said he did not), this was plainly not the only reason for hearing him. In reviewing the evidence later, Chamberlain was to refer to this incident and the case at Cloncurry as indicating "trends" in Stuart's sexual history.

The three C.I.B. men who flew from Adelaide to investigate the murder now gave evidence. Their leader, Detective-Sergeant Paul Turner, appeared first. At the trial, asked Chamberlain, did any question to him from O'Sullivan suggest that Stuart did not understand English?

"No, none at all."

Was it true that any violence was applied to Stuart?

"No, none at all. On the contrary, he was given a number of cigarettes at various stages."

"Did you notice among his possessions at any time," asked Brazel, "a razor blade of any description?"[4]

"Yes. . . . I think there were nineteen blades in a little container. They were blades of a leather knife about the size of a razor blade." Early in the interrogation they were taken from a pocket in Stuart's jacket and placed on the office table. Turner himself examined them. He did not recall whether Stuart was asked about them. "I may have asked him what they were, or something of that nature." They were not handled while Stuart was naked, nor was there any threat made to skin or otherwise injure Stuart with them. On the face of the dead girl there was nothing even remotely resembling a cut with a sharp instrument.

Stuart's English, said Turner, compared equally with that of any part-aboriginal he had interviewed. On the language of the confession Turner said, with the same exceptions noted by Whitrod: "They were the exact words . . ."

Constable Richard Jones, when asked similar questions, gave similar answers. The last of the C.I.B. men to be called was Sergeant William Low, the fingerprint man and photographer of the party, who said that he saw no violence or threat of violence to Stuart, and no mark of recent injury on him.

* * *

An interlude followed in which Chamberlain called a witness, but suggested before he entered that his evidence would not be acceptable, and indicated in general terms what it would be about. The witness was a police officer, Detective G. C. Modra, who accompanied Stuart from the aeroplane to the gaol in December and initiated a conversation—"without, of course, any caution". The evidence, Chamberlain said, "would probably be successfully objected to on the trial in a criminal case . . ." Why then was he offering the witness? Because it seemed to him "inconsistent with the allegation which has been made that Stuart had been forced to make the confession by violence". Also waiting outside the court-room were three warders from the Adelaide Gaol, who could give evidence, Chamberlain said, about conversa-

[4] This question presumably arose from the version of the interrogation given in Stuart's statement prepared by O'Sullivan for the trial and read to the Commission on August 31.

tions with Stuart immediately after his conviction. He could see no legal objection to the evidence; "but the fundamental objection which I have always thought there is to putting warders in the box, is that there is a sort of camaraderie between a prisoner on a capital charge and a warder who is possibly his only confidant and friend . . ." Why then was he offering the witnesses? "My own feeling is, and I feel this fairly strongly myself, I am here, amongst other things, to represent the public authorities involved in this enquiry, including the police, and there have been some very very serious allegations indeed made against them." It was therefore his duty to put forward evidence which was "quite inconsistent with the allegations which have now been made about the police and their conduct".

"Despite what some people may think," said Sir Mellis Napier in the ensuing discussion, "we are trying to do what is the fair thing."

"That is exactly why I took the opportunity of mentioning this thing to Your Honours," said Chamberlain, "because what has been said by terribly ill-informed people . . ."

"We need not go into that," said the Chairman.

Brazel was given copies of statements by Detective Modra and the warders. The detective's evidence, Brazel thought, would not be admitted by a judge. To the warders in charge of him just after the sentence was pronounced, Brazel said, Stuart appeared to have made a remark "the probative value of which, in my view, is substantial, and it does not appear to have been induced by any observation made by either of the warders." Perhaps there was a sense of dependence by Stuart upon them which induced him to make a possibly unguarded remark. Brazel said that in the case of a third warder on Chamberlain's list, to whom Stuart was said to have spoken at the gaol, "there was something in the nature of greater dependence." That would not make what was said to him inadmissible in a court, but Their Honours might think that the remark was made in circumstances "which would render it perhaps a little, not unfair, but unnecessary, to be used."

At a re-trial, observed the Chairman, the judge would be likely to recommend that the evidence of the detective should not be led. The Commissioners withdrew to discuss the warders. Three minutes later the Chairman announced that they would not be heard.

Chamberlain called two of the warders to speak about other matters. The first said that Stuart could tell the time accurately from a watch and that his English "would be on a par with an uneducated white man". The second, who was from Yorkshire, said that in various conversations he and Stuart had no difficulty whatsoever in understanding each other.

That was the end of the evidence. In the four days when Shand was present the Commissioners had heard fifteen people. In the three days when no counsel examined on Stuart's behalf, twenty-three new witnesses had appeared.

As the Commission was on the point of adjourning until the next day, when counsel were to sum up, Dr. J. J. Bray, Q.C., asked whether he might renew his application to appear for O'Sullivan.

"If he is not a witness," asked Sir Mellis Napier, "where do you come in?"

"He was led to understand originally his evidence would be required, but he has not in fact been called."

"I do not know that he was told that his evidence would be required," said the Chairman, "but that information would be required from him, and he has given it to us.[5] He is not a witness, and that is the end of it."

"Does Mr. O'Sullivan," asked Mr. Justice Reed, "wish to put any further information before us?"

"Only this," replied Bray, "that he is quite willing to give any explanations as to why no attempt was made to secure witnesses at the trial."

"The conclusion is fairly obvious, is it not?" said the Chairman: "that his client did not tell him. If there is any other explanation, it is for him to say whether he will give it or won't . . . If you wish to call him to give evidence, and you inform Mr. Brazel what it is about, no doubt he will be called, but unless we have some indication of the directions in which he can help the Commission, we do not propose to call him."

The Commission adjourned until the morning of Wednesday, September 9, which was generally expected to be its last day.

[5] If the Chairman was implying that O'Sullivan had been wanted only to identify Stuart's statement from the trial, he was not quite correct. On the first day (see pp. 98-9 above), he and Brazel both said that it was essential to have O'Sullivan give evidence about why the alibi was not offered at the trial.

15

ENTER AND EXIT MR. TRAVERS

On Tuesday evening Bray rang Brazel to say that Shand now thought Stuart should give evidence, without being represented by counsel. O'Sullivan would convey this advice to the condemned man next morning; and if it were accepted he would terminate his retainer. On Wednesday morning, ten minutes before the Commission was due to sit, Brazel learned that the position had changed again. Stuart had been advised to appoint a new solicitor in place of O'Sullivan and Miss Devaney, so that the services of senior counsel could be made available to him by an anonymous benefactor. The first edition of the *News* reported that at half past ten, when the Commission was to have resumed, its members were conferring in chambers with Brazel, Chamberlain, O'Sullivan and his legal representatives (Bray and Bright), and Mr. J. L. Travers, Q.C. It was now an open secret that Travers was the senior counsel who might appear for Stuart. It remained a closer secret that the anonymous benefactor intending to pay him was News Ltd.

The Commissioners entered the court after eleven o'clock, and sat for only fifteen minutes. Brazel reported what had happened overnight and said that it appeared that Shand had now reversed his advice "completely and without any reason whatever being furnished". If new counsel were appointed for Stuart, he said, the proceedings would now take a course of considerable perplexity. He suggested the Commission adjourn until Friday. Chamberlain agreed reluctantly; but he added a protest, and a warning, that "what has been done is in the nature of one more attempt to frustrate this enquiry". Shand's advice that Stuart should give evidence unrepresented, said the Crown Solicitor, was designed to put those associated with the enquiry on the horns of a dilemma. They would have either to refuse to cross-examine an unrepresented man, or to cross-examine and be open to the charge that "star chamber" tactics were being used. If the Commission granted new counsel an adjournment of perhaps three weeks—"no counsel could absorb all the material . . . under two or three weeks"—there could well be yet another change of front. The stage might come when the government would say they must desist.

"One of the virtues of any judge," said the Chairman, "is patience and the faith in the greatness of truth that in the long run it will prevail. It seems to me that we can meet some of these troubles, these things, when they arise, Mr. Chamberlain." The Commission adjourned until Friday morning.

The only attempt at a public explanation of the lawyers' change of policy was made by Reid in the Sydney *Telegraph*. Shand and O'Sullivan, he wrote, "parted company" after a telephone conversation late on Tuesday night; when Shand offered his new advice, O'Sullivan replied that this would be "tying the hangman's knot". Reid said he understood that Shand was persuaded to change his advice by the Chairman's comment, on Monday, that if Stuart chose to stay away "ordinary people" must conclude that to tell the truth would not advance his case. It was known, according to Reid, that O'Sullivan was "worked up" at the prospect of Stuart's facing a hostile bar table unaided. To another reporter O'Sullivan denied much of Reid's story, but he confirmed that unlike Shand he thought that Stuart should give evidence only if represented by counsel. In Sydney, Shand denied that he and O'Sullivan had disagreed.

"Deeper into Confusion" was the title of an editorial in the Melbourne *Herald* on Thursday. Anxious comments appeared in two religious newspapers. In Melbourne the *Tribune*, a Catholic diocesan weekly, said that although it would not enter into the fierce disputes which had arisen over the Commission, "a fresh start with new personnel was clearly desirable . . . Nothing like this must occur again, both for the sake of justice and for that of our Commonwealth's good name." In the *Anglican*, a long editorial review of the case said that it had been confused throughout by "small bungles, little messes". The paper predicted that Stuart would not be hanged, "whether he deserved it or not", and expressed the hope that the report of the Commission would enable the executive to refer all the conflicting evidence to a jury. When the *News* later reprinted most of this editorial it wrongly described the *Anglican* as "the official journal of the Church of England in Australia"; and a Labor member of parliament, misreading the *News*, called it "the Anglican paper for Adelaide". Sir Thomas Playford said that the *News* had "dealt only with a portion and that other aspects had been omitted". The introductory passage omitted by the *News* did include a reference to Playford as "sagacious"; but the portions reprinted gave a quite accurate account of the *Anglican's* views.

On Thursday morning, according to the Melbourne *Sun* and *Age*, Playford called on the Commissioners. The press could learn nothing about the reasons for his visit; its very occurrence was nevertheless a reminder that the judges were sitting not as a court but to report on facts at the request of the government.

Mr. C. Villeneuve Smith stood at the bar table on Friday morning for the first time since he walked out with Shand, to apply on behalf of Travers for leave to appear for Stuart. Travers, he said, was briefed to appear in another case next week, and "for reasons which are not easily ascertainable or intelligible . . . the acting Attorney-General, Sir Thomas Playford, through the Crown Solicitor, Mr. Chamberlain, has said that no adjournment of the case . . . will be considered". It would therefore be impossible for Travers to appear at the Commission until the other case was over. "I understand that it is common ground that it would take at least three weeks for any counsel to absorb these matters." The Chairman said that two weeks should be ample. Smith remarked that Chamberlain had said three weeks would be needed. Chamberlain, who had estimated that it would take new counsel two or three weeks to absorb the material, now said that "on reflection" he thought ten days would be enough.

"Are you in a position to tell us," asked Mr. Justice Reed, "whether or not Stuart is going to give evidence?"

"My instructions don't go to that," said Smith. ". . . Perhaps I should not say this, but I would guess . . ."

"Don't guess," said Brazel.

". . . that Mr. Travers will be anxious to assist the Commission in every way. I can say no more than that."

It might be, said Mr. Justice Reed, that after an interval of three to five weeks, Stuart would not give evidence.

A little later Smith said to Mr. Justice Reed: "Of course, Your Honour has the advantage of having sat throughout the Commission. I have not."

"That was an advantage you denied yourself, didn't you?" said the judge.

". . . I did my duty as a junior," replied Smith, "and would do so again."

"Yes, Mr. Smith," said the Chairman. "I think you had better say no more on that subject."

Mr. Justice Ross asked whether no other counsel than Travers was available. Smith said: "Clearly the case calls for a counsel of eminence, and one suited to this type of work, especially as it involves questions going to police credibility, a matter on which Mr. Travers is eminently suited to assist Your Honours."

Chamberlain said that when Shand withdrew from the case, the government immediately offered to pay for any new counsel whom Stuart's solicitors saw fit to engage. "That happened, so it seems to me, a very long time ago. We have been told time and again since then that Stuart does not want to engage counsel at all. Now we are told that he suddenly conceived the ambition to have Mr. Travers." Why did this not occur to Stuart earlier? "There is such a thing as other counsel. Mr. Villeneuve Smith claims that there is not any one of Mr. Travers' capacity, particularly to attack the police."

"I did not say attack them," Smith objected.

"Test their credit, then . . . But there are other counsel as well.

There is other business in the country . . . the business of the Criminal Court ought to go on."

"It must go on," said the Chairman.

Brazel suggested that he could perhaps adopt a more impersonal attitude in the matter. "Stuart is to be executed on September 30 . . . The basis of the application is that the sittings of the Commission should be suspended until the convenience of certain counsel is met." Which was to prevail—the work of the Commission or the engagement of counsel? Stuart's advisers, moreover, should be able to say whether he would give evidence if an adjournment were now granted. "To keep him in suspense for another five weeks as to his ultimate destiny would, it may turn out, be fruitless and a needless waste of time."

Sir Mellis Napier remarked that Stuart himself had never said that he was on the beach between two and four, and that if he could assist in the enquiry he should testify on that subject. Until somebody came forward with evidence that the confession was obtained by a threat or violence, asked the Chairman, what was there to consider? It would appear that "the result of this enquiry is more or less a foregone conclusion unless and until there is placed before us something that would justify us in saying that the verdict of the jury would, or might, have been different if they had been informed as we are now informed." Of all the words spoken this day, these were reported most prominently. They seemed to imply that if, as Sir John Latham suggested, the Commissioners had been directed at that point to report whether, in view of the evidence then available, steps should be taken to give Stuart a new trial, Sir Mellis Napier's answer would have been: No.

"Under the circumstances," said the Chairman, "it seems that the evidence of the party principally concerned is essential to a full enquiry, but whether we should compel him to come forward without assistance is, of course, another question . . . We think that the only course open to us is to adjourn this enquiry until one day next week and to then enquire whether we have any assurance that Stuart will be called . . ." The other Commissioners said that they agreed entirely with the Chairman's views. Mr. Justice Ross added that Shand's withdrawal left open in his mind "the inference that he did not desire to have his client called . . . and that he wanted to enlist the sympathy of the public and press . . ."

Smith said he was happy to tell Mr. Justice Ross that this assumption was quite incorrect.

"It seems to me," said Sir Mellis Napier, "that it has got beyond the stage when tactics[1] and manoeuvring should prevail any longer . . . If your suggestion, Mr. Smith, is that the reason behind the shilly-

[1] The reporter from the Sydney *Mirror* heard this as "antics"—a word which his sub-editors understandably raised to the headline.

shallying is distrust of the impartiality of this tribunal, I would only say how obvious it is that 'evil communications corrupt good manners'."[2]

"No such suggestion was made," said Smith. "The integrity of Your Honour the Chief Justice or your learned colleagues has never been questioned by myself, Mr. Shand or Miss Devaney, or any person in the conduct of Stuart's interests . . ."

"All I can say," said the Chairman, "is that I am glad to have your assurance, and I accept it, but I do regret that the English language should be used in such a way as it has been used to convey the impression when they are not the actual feelings of the people using the language."

"Not by me, sir," said Smith, in the boldest of all sallies during this exchange. "I have never accused Your Honour of 'tactics and manoeuvrings'."

"That may be," said the Chairman, "we have heard enough. We shall adjourn until 10.30 a.m. on Wednesday next."

* * *

Next day the *Sydney Morning Herald* said that the questions now occupying the Commission—whether Stuart would give evidence and whether he would be represented by counsel—were "irrelevant to the main issue". Since Shand withdrew, the paper observed, Stuart had had no counsel to test the evidence given. "There has not therefore *appeared* to have been the 'fullest investigation' which public opinion required . . . Can the Commission now, in the light of all that has happened . . . return any finding that can possibly satisfy public opinion? . . . The case for ending the present investigation now, before Stuart gives evidence, and for appointing a second Commission from outside South Australia seems unanswerable." The same morning, in Manchester, the *Guardian* said that public disquiet in Australia and elsewhere was unlikely to be assuaged by anything less than a fresh start to the enquiry. "Sufficient doubts about Stuart's guilt now exist to permit the South Australian government properly to reprieve Stuart unconditionally. Once that is done, the present Royal Commission or a newly appointed one can do its job unhampered by the emotional appeal from the public that a man's life is at stake."

The Australian Association for Cultural Freedom took up the issue again over this weekend. On Saturday the executive met in Sydney with Sir John Latham in the chair, and on Sunday the secretary informed Playford in a letter that the executive unanimously endorsed the proposal about a re-trial made by Latham at the end of August, and made two further suggestions: that counsel for the Crown should support any application for a reasonable adjournment on Stuart's behalf, and that Stuart should have the same right as an accused person

[2] I CORINTHIANS, xv, 33.

in court not to give evidence. "This rule should not be infringed directly or indirectly."

The papers on Monday displayed this letter prominently. In the Melbourne *Age* two days later, Mr. John Hetherington wrote: "Considering the Association's membership, the letter should silence suggestions that critics of the Stuart proceedings are sentimental ratbags,[3] political trouble-makers, or members of the underworld." In a letter to Playford released to the press on Tuesday, September 15, the advice of the Association was applauded by a man who had not so far made any public comment on the case. Sir Edward Hallstrom, described in *Who's Who in Australia* as "philanthropist and public benefactor", was known especially for his gifts to medical research and hospital care, and for his promotion of Australian zoology. After referring to the suggestions from Latham and the Association, Hallstrom said that appropriate action by the government of South Australia would gain the complete approval of "the vast majority of Australian citizens as well as citizens in other countries in proceedings which have reached world publicity".

In less respectful language the *Observer* also supported Latham. "Why Mr. Playford should resist the re-trial suggestion is hard to work out . . . He has really put on a surprising performance. If one wants society to order its affairs in a traditional way, one should follow the rules oneself." In Melbourne, the Catholic weekly *Advocate* criticised Chamberlain's remark that the proposal to brief Travers was an attempt to frustrate the enquiry. The paper said that Latham ("one of the greatest jurists in this country's history") had "made the pointed criticism that there is a feeling that the Commission is actually trying Stuart again without benefit of a jury . . ." The *Catholic Worker*, an independent monthly also published in Melbourne, expressed more hostility to the Commission and the government than any other journal, saying bluntly:

> "We are on the side of Mr. Shand . . . Surely it was asking heroic humility of these gentlemen to conduct an enquiry which might lead to the conclusions that one had presided over a trial at which justice had not been done, that what the other regarded as rubbish was the unadulterated truth. To have a Royal Commission at all meant an abandonment of the sensible principle that judges should not be the arbiters of fact in criminal matters . . . The role of the state in this sorry affair is unprecedented in the history of criminal law. The terms of reference of the Commission were deliberately framed to constrict the enquiry. The state appeared through two sets of counsel—one ostensibly to assist the enquiry; the other to defend the prosecution. The Premier demonstrated his disinterestedness by telling parliament that no South Australian

[3] Overseas readers may be helped by a phrase of Mr. R. G. Menzies: "the lunatic fringe, or, to use the Australian expression, the ratbags".

should give credence to the allegations against the police. We now read that the principle that an accused shall not be forced to give evidence is about to be jettisoned."

When parliament resumed on Tuesday, September 15, Mr. J. J. Jennings (Labor) asked whether the government was averse to Travers' appearing.

"No," said Playford. "The government has always been most anxious that Stuart have counsel, and indeed it has offered to pay for counsel . . . Whether Mr. Travers can represent Stuart depends upon commitments he has to other clients." To a further question from Dunstan, Playford replied that he had instructed Chamberlain not to oppose an adjournment of Travers' other case if the Commissioners desired to facilitate his appearance; "but I understand that the Commission itself felt that, unless it had some assurance that some material evidence would be produced, it would have some doubts about granting a long adjournment."

"How could any counsel give any assurance before going into his instructions?" asked Dunstan. "It would be impossible for anyone to do that."

Playford did not answer that question, but repeated that the Crown Solicitor was advised not to oppose an adjournment of Travers' case if the Commission desired it and if the trial judge would grant it. "I understand that no application was made for an adjournment and that the case is proceeding."

The criticism implied in Jennings' and Dunstan's questions was spelled out plainly in that afternoon's *News*. "The government must realise," said an editorial, "that it runs the risk of being accused of a clumsy tactical manoeuvre to prevent Mr. Travers from appearing. This raises the question whether an attempt is being made by the Playford government, ignoring the chairman's expressed belief in the value of patience in eliciting the truth, to force proceedings to a conclusion."

That evening Travers sent a statement to the Commission, which the *News* printed fully in all editions next day. "I can come to no other conclusion," he wrote, "than that for some reason which has not been disclosed to me, my presence at the Commission is not at all welcome." On September 10, he said, Brazel refused to put before the Commissioners a letter setting out the conditions on which he could appear; and on the same day Chamberlain made it clear that so long as he was in control of the Crown's affairs Travers' case would not be adjourned. In addressing the Commission on September 11, Chamberlain "seemed firmly of the opinion that a Royal Commission charged with the duty of testing the truth of police evidence was no fit place for any counsel who would—to use his expression—'attack the police'." Sir Mellis Napier had used expressions—"tactics and manoeuvrings, and shilly-shallyings"—which Travers strongly resented. The Chairman also wanted an immediate undertaking as to whether Stuart would be called as a witness. To give an assurance one way or the other at that stage would plainly have been "a gross breach of the professional duty of counsel to his client. I must say respectfully, but plainly, I can in no circumstances be a party to such a breach." For these reasons, Travers withdrew his application for leave to appear. He wrote, of course, as an individual lawyer and not as president of the Law Society; but his protest, and in particular the charge that he was being asked to behave in a manner which seemed to him improper, was all the more striking when it came from the elected leader of the profession. He was here supported, moreover, by the Australian Association for Cultural Freedom.

Travers asked that his statement be read to the Commission on Wednesday. It was not read, but the Chairman observed that nothing said at the Commission had been intended to reflect on Travers, "whose assistance we should have been very glad to receive if he had been available and prepared to accept the brief and appear before us within a reasonable period". These words were spoken after a short conference between Travers and the Commissioners. At twenty-five minutes past ten Mr. Justice Abbott had adjourned the case in which Travers was involved, after receiving a message that the Commissioners wanted to see Travers in chambers. Ten minutes later Travers was back in his place and the case continued.[4] In another ten minutes the Commission itself resumed. None of the parties to the discussion in chambers divulged publicly what it was about; but the Chairman's remark about "a reasonable period" appeared to imply that Travers' other engagement remained an obstacle. Later in the day, however, Playford was to give parliament an account of the conference quite incompatible with this one.

A figure unknown in the courts of South Australia now stood before the Commission. Mr. John Starke, Q.C., a member of the Victorian Bar, sought leave, with Smith, to represent Stuart. He was not ready yet to go ahead with the case. After Mr. Travers was unhappily unable to accept, he said, he was called out of court on Tuesday and asked if he would come over at once. He had not yet seen Stuart. The Chairman said that the Commission had admitted one interstate counsel already, and added: "I would like to have an assurance that this time it is for keeps." Starke assured the Chairman that once he was prepared, he would proceed "with as much expedition as lies within my power, consistent with my duty to my client".

Starke was granted leave to appear and given an adjournment of nineteen days, with the understanding that he could ask for a little longer if necessary. The Chairman raised the question of Stuart's giving evidence, but Starke was not pressed to give any assurance on

[4] It ran thirteen days, until October 5, when Travers' client was found not guilty of perjury.

the matter—despite the recent insistence of all three Commissioners and Brazel that such an assurance was essential at this stage. It was hard to see any cause for this change of front other than Travers' indignant statement. As with the demand that O'Sullivan give evidence, it seems probable that the Commission took silent note of a protest from the profession, expressed in each case by Travers. Chamberlain, who had thought ten days a long enough adjournment when Travers was seeking longer, now said that on behalf of the government he entirely consented to the arrangements for Starke. "I think it is right that I should say that, because there are some suggestions . . . that the government is in some way desirous of obstructing this enquiry."

Suggestions of this character were made again as soon as parliament met that afternoon. Dunstan said that both Travers and O'Sullivan disputed the account given by Playford of the Crown's attitude to his appearance. When his case opened yesterday morning, said Dunstan, Travers had not applied for an adjournment because counsel for the Crown told him that his instructions, from Chamberlain, were to oppose it. Playford replied merely that Chamberlain agreed with the account he had himself given the house. "I understand," he went on, "that this morning the judges on the Royal Commission saw Mr. Travers in chambers and that they made an arrangement . . . suitable to him, but . . . only a few minutes later the Commission was informed that Mr. Starke, Q.C., from Melbourne, had been briefed by Stuart . . . so that the arrangement for Mr. Travers to appear had been cancelled. I am now speaking from hearsay, but I will verify the position." If he did verify it, parliament was never told. "I believe that this morning the Commission made it clear to Mr. Travers publicly that it would have facilitated his going on with the case." This again, presumably, was hearsay; for the Commissioners had not said that they were prepared to accept the list of conditions on which Travers, in his statement, told them he would appear. The statement itself, and Travers' action in releasing it to the *News* before the Commission met on Wednesday, appeared to express an irrevocable intention to withdraw his application to represent Stuart. After the conference in chambers, moreover, the Chairman still referred to the other case as an impediment.

So ended a curious, confused stage of the affair, in which the central issues often disappeared from sight. The proposal to have Travers appear had led to new turmoil, and in particular to unusual public criticism, by a senior legal practitioner, of the Crown Solicitor, of counsel assisting the Commission, and of the Chairman himself. Would Starke's appearance enable the Commission at last to satisfy all parties and public opinion? Cautious relief was expressed by the Melbourne *Herald*. Now that Starke had been admitted, the paper said, the Commission might be heading away from the delays and tangles of its earlier course. A spokesman of the Labor Party writing in the same paper was less hopeful: when a leader among South Australian lawyers said what Travers had said about the Commission, he thought, "there will be very few who'll believe that justice is being done."

A good deal of the disquiet about Stuart rested on an apprehension that he was in some sense a victim of racial prejudice. This view was rejected in a review of the case offered to English readers by an Australian correspondent of *The Economist* just after Starke took over. The writer said that Stuart "would probably be dead today if he had not been seven-eighths black". It was "because of his colour that there is such concern to see that justice is done; and this is as true of the government and judiciary of South Australia as of those who have given money, time and millions of words in the fight for his life." The correspondent seemed to agree with critics who thought that the wrong judges had been appointed to the Commission. "Nor have the proceedings of the Commission reassured the public about its ability to do any sifting to the ground . . ." Of Stuart's refusal to give evidence, the writer asked: "Did Stuart's lawyers think that they could best serve him by discrediting the enquiry, and best discredit the enquiry by leaving him silent in his cell and unrepresented before the Commission? Did they play for delay, believing that time was on his side? Did they think that his appearance would do his case more harm than good?" After saying that it was reasonable for the Commission to refuse as long an adjournment as Travers sought, the writer concluded: "The issue is broader than the life or death of this aborigine. The Stuart case lends support to those who, like *The Economist*, are opposed to capital punishment. Whether or not the new evidence overthrows the original verdict, it shows up the disastrous finality of the death sentence. As it happens, the doubts have arisen while Stuart is still alive. They might well have done so after his execution."

That event was now postponed yet again, from September 30 to November 9.

16

LIFE FOR STUART

"MR. STARKE," said Sir Mellis Napier when the barrister from Melbourne sought leave to appear, "your name is not unknown to us and it carries with it a feeling of respect." It was a compliment both to the man in front of the Commission and to his late father, Sir Hayden Starke, who had sat on the High Court for thirty years. Starke had not much professional experience before 1945 except as advocate for soldiers at courts martial in the Middle East. By 1959, at the age of forty-five, he was well on the way to enjoying a stature at the Melbourne bar comparable with Shand's in Sydney. His cross-examination, plainly spoken but subtly constructed, impressed juries; and so did his blunt, vernacular style. In superficial ways Starke and Shand were dissimilar. Starke was as far above average height as Shand was below it; he appeared to work at lower emotional temperatures; and his demeanour was more clubbish. But like Shand he could adopt, if a client's interest seemed to him to require it, a determined stance towards the bench. In the course of his appearance for Stuart some hard words were to pass along the bar table, and some from bar to bench.

Starke finished a case in Melbourne and settled down to read the documents relating to his new client—which now included close to 200,000 words of proceedings at the Commission. He flew to Sydney and talked with Shand. On September 27 he was back in Adelaide, and he visited Stuart with Miss Devaney two days later. The South Australian government had agreed to pay his fees, which were probably as high as those of any Australian barrister.

• • •

The business of justice moved slowly in South Australia. Even in normal circumstances it might take eighteen months or two years for a civil matter to come before the Supreme Court. When three judges were occupied for weeks as Commissioners and a fourth, Mr. Justice Piper, was absent from the bench on account of illness, the queue of cases had been growing. (The largest single category of people affected by the delays were men and women seeking divorces.) By releasing the Commissioners for other work, the adjournment shortened the queue slightly.

The High Court sat in Adelaide during the recess. Since it was not impossible that Stuart's case would come before them again on appeal, it may be presumed that the federal judges were careful to avoid any discussion of the subject that was uppermost in every legal mind. They attended on September 23 the annual dinner of the Law Society, and heard there some vehement remarks on the Stuart controversy by a senior practitioner, Mr. J. N. McEwin, in a speech proposing a toast to the bench and the legal profession. "It is a matter of deep concern," he said, "that certain of our judges have in recent weeks become involved in a campaign of irresponsible misrepresentation that must be unique in a British community . . . It has for long been the prerogative of the press to criticise our sportsmen, our politicians, our company directors and everyone else in the public eye. Maybe this is fair enough in a democratic community. But when those who administer justice, and the very administration of justice itself, are publicly assailed, a serious and intolerable public mischief is created. It is an attempt to substitute trial by newspaper for trial according to the law. Journalism has, I suggest, fallen to a very low level, indeed, when it aligns itself with the rabble who line the pickets and hoot the umpire." Two days before these words were spoken the death had occurred of Mr. Eliott Thorp, chairman of the Howard League, who had been at the centre of the campaign here deplored. He had presented to the authorities the petition for a reprieve circulated by his League, and at the end of August he signed a public statement supporting Shand and urging the Commission not to proceed. Until a few days before he died, at seventy-two, Thorp regularly queued for a place in the public gallery.

On September 27 the death of Mr. Justice Piper removed from the bench the only judge who had not been involved in any proceedings about Stuart. Apart from the Commissioners there now remained only two judges of the Supreme Court, Mr. Justice Mayo and Mr. Justice Abbott, of whom the latter was due to retire at the end of October.

* * *

When the Commission met on October 5, Starke asked for an adjournment until October 13 and for the right to "full and unfettered" cross-examination of a number of witnesses. He asked that these witnesses should be called before he had to decide whether Stuart himself would give evidence, and he resisted the ruling that Stuart was the accuser and the police were the accused. "The criminal law to the point of illogicality favours a person in jeopardy . . . Nowhere in the terms of reference can it be remotely suggested that the executive places the onus on the shoulders of Stuart. That being so the normal tenor and tendency of the criminal law should be applied." Starke disagreed with the Chairman's view that the Commission had nothing before it that was not before the Privy Council when the English judges said that there was no justification for an attack on the police. A statement by Stuart accusing the police of violence had been tendered, Starke said. The Wardrops had been called. Strehlow's evidence on language had been heard. The Giesemans and others had given evidence which, if true, must reflect on the confession. All this, Starke submitted, was material which either expressly or by implication accused the police, and which was not before the Privy Council.

Stuart was in the shadow of the gallows, his new counsel observed, and had been within nine hours of execution. "In these circumstances is it not right to listen with sympathy to the argument of counsel?" It was possible, he suggested, that Stuart, innocent though he might be, would be damaged badly in cross-examination because of his deficiency in language and education.

"I understand," said Mr. Justice Reed, "there was a proposal to have an interpreter for him if he goes into the box."

"There may be," replied Starke. "I would sooner let Your Honours hear him talk. He can talk English, make no mistake about that. He doesn't talk pidgin English. To give you one example, the other day I used the word 'generally' to him. I thought he would have understood it but he didn't. He didn't understand words you would expect him to understand. I want Your Honours to hear him talk, for the way he talks, and for the obvious significance it would have in relation to the statement."

Apart from one short interjection, Chamberlain had taken no part in the discussion so far. He now rose, holding a piece of paper, and read slowly from it a statement which contained a startling announcement. Strong attempts had been made, he said, inside and outside the Commission, to frustrate its object: the proper investigation of the allegation that Stuart was wrongly convicted. Time after time the pretext had been advanced for these tactics that Stuart's life was at stake. It was obvious that the material produced so far had gone nowhere near creating any doubt about the propriety of the conviction. It was also obvious, as the Chief Justice had pointed out, that the one person who could now give evidence in support of the allegations was Stuart himself. Twice the Commission had been assured that Stuart would be a witness; and twice, under the same advice, that he would not. The decision whether to call Stuart had still not been made. "In these circumstances the government has reached the conclusion that it would be no longer proper to delay its decision as to the carrying out of the death sentence; and I am therefore instructed by the Honourable the Acting Attorney-General to inform Your Honours that Cabinet has decided to recommend to His Excellency that the sentence should in any event be commuted. Although Stuart's interests appear to have been lost sight of by a great number of the people who have associated themselves with his cause, the government believes that it would no longer be fair to him to continue the uncertainty of temporary respites. It also considers that the Commission should be given the opportunity to continue with and complete its enquiry unembarrassed by any further talk about 'the shadow of the gallows'. This decision is of course in no way designed to prejudice the Commission's enquiry into the propriety of the conviction. On the contrary it is hoped that it will enable Your Honours to proceed without the possibility of further obstruction." There was now no reason, said Chamberlain, why the Commission should not be told promptly whether Stuart would be called.

Stuart was told the news by a warder. The nation learned it from the afternoon papers. It caused relief, perplexity and anger.

Meanwhile Chamberlain replied to Starke's submissions, which he said would involve "an interminable delay"—and cost—to the government. "Without reference to us we were committed to pay fees which I will say nothing about except that they are considerably in excess of those we would be normally called on to pay . . ." This was, perhaps, said Chamberlain before he sat down, "a further reason why there should be no further avoidable delay".[1] Brazel suggested that the commutation supplied a reason why Stuart should testify before recalling witnesses, and might be the ground for a slightly shorter adjournment. Starke said that in no circumstances would he be ready until October 13.

"If there is a new trial," said Mr. Justice Reed to Starke, "then in the ordinary course of events your client would again be placed in jeopardy of another verdict of murder." (A possible implication of this remark—that Stuart could yet hang after all—was not discussed here, but it was later in press and parliament.) Mr. Justice Reed went on to ask whether Chamberlain's announcement would have any effect on Starke's submissions. Starke replied that it would not. "To say that I am not relieved would be an understatement, but . . . from the age of twenty-seven to seventy in gaol is a very very long time, and I would feel my duty to be just as high for all practical purposes as if he were going to hang."

The Commissioners left the bench briefly to consider Starke's requests. They agreed to an adjournment until October 13; but then, said the Chairman, "you should be in a position to tell us whether you are calling Stuart and to call him then if it is desired to call him at all." Starke said that he wished to consult his colleagues, and that he would like an adjournment of thirty minutes "to consider my position"—the words Shand had used before he withdrew.

"What do you mean," asked the Chairman, "by 'consider your position'?"

[1] The expense appears to have been on Playford's mind. A fortnight later, in parliament, he told a questioner that the original estimate of what the Commission would cost was now out of date. "Mr. O'Sullivan has brought counsel from Melbourne at government expense. Also the proceedings were prolonged for three weeks and counsel had to be paid for the whole of the period while the Melbourne counsel acquainted himself with the facts of the case." The South Australian government paid Starke in all £3,119.1.0 for appearing, and his two juniors £682.10.0 each.

"Things that have arisen," said Starke. ". . . I do not want to speak prematurely or in heat."

The half hour was granted.

Starke returned to say that in view of the Commissioners' ruling, and in view of the Chief Justice's observation that it was a foregone conclusion if Stuart did not give evidence, he would call his client. "But in making that announcement I desire to say he will be called as a witness under protest, and the most emphatic, vehement and powerful protest at my command."

The only comment on these words was a question from the Chairman: "Did I say it was a foregone conclusion, Mr. Starke?"[2]

"In my submission," said Starke, "whatever words have been chosen, I have been directed to call Stuart at this stage on pain of an adverse report."

Permission was given for Starke to call Strehlow first, to point out aspects of Stuart's way of speech. Starke was also assured that the relevant witnesses could be recalled later and fully cross-examined on Stuart's behalf.

* * *

"LIFE FOR STUART", said the *News* in the stop press of its first edition. In Sydney, the national centre for prophetic journalism, the oracles had been divided on whether Stuart would hang. "Onlooker" of the *Sun-Herald* had said firmly at the end of August (as he now reminded readers) that the hanging of Stuart was a political impossibility. The *Anglican* had made a similar prediction with equal firmness. Reid in the *Telegraph* had reported a feeling in Adelaide that he would hang. The day before commutation was announced, Mr. Frank O'Neill in the *Sunday Mirror* wrote, from Adelaide, that Stuart "almost certainly will go to the gallows barring a miracle".

The *Advertiser* and the *News* responded to the reprieve as they had to earlier crises of the Commission. Neither expressed an editorial opinion of its own; the *News* reported the comments of journals elsewhere, and the *Advertiser* did not. The *Advertiser* printed two letters, both hostile to the decision. "The government," said one of the writers, "appears to have yielded to pressure of maudlin sentiment." Senior police officers in Adelaide, according to one press report, were disgusted by the decision. Somebody threatened to take the Premier's life for sparing Stuart's. On the evening of the announcement a man rang Playford's house in the hills above Adelaide. "Is it right that Stuart is not going to hang?" asked the caller. When told that this was so, the man said: "Well, the Premier will be killed." Police guarded the house all night and stayed close to Playford next day.

In parliament on October 6 the Premier was told by one of his own

[2] See p. 195 above.

back-benchers, Mr. J. A. Heaslip, that the commutation had aroused "utter confusion in the minds of the public". "Does it mean," he asked, "that this man, who has been proved guilty of murder, will at the end of ten or fifteen years be released and be in a position to murder some other innocent little girl?" There were cries of protest from the Opposition. Playford replied that the general practice was to consider a petition for release after about twelve years, but that it depended on the executive of the day.

The only people to express public approval in South Australia immediately after the commutation were Professor Norval Morris and Father Thomas Dixon, who agreed that the action removed the pressure of time from the search for truth. In Sydney, Dr. H. V. Evatt said that he had himself suggested a reprieve to Playford some time ago, and that the announcement would "lift a heavy weight off the national conscience". In Melbourne Sir John Latham said to a reporter: "The Commission is still going on, and there is nothing I could say which will alleviate the confusion which has arisen all along. 'No comment' is my comment." Among newspaper editorials, the most sympathetic was that of the *Canberra Times*, which said that since commutation had become inevitable, the decision was better taken now; the Commission might be able to complete its enquiry in a less clouded atmosphere.

Unequivocal satisfaction with the decision was expressed nowhere among the daily papers of Melbourne and Sydney. The editors of the Melbourne *Sun* and *Herald* each found the timing of the decision strange; compassion for Stuart, said the *Sun*, could hardly have inspired the decision, since the government had let six months go by without lifting the death penalty. In the *Age*, Mr. John Hetherington said that the reprieve naturally pleased opponents of capital punishment, including himself. "But how the decision can be logically justified, in a state which has hanged several men in recent years for crimes certainly no more savage than the murder Stuart stands convicted of, is not clear." The *Sydney Morning Herald* was severe. "As matters stand now it cannot be assumed that Stuart was properly convicted. That is for the Royal Commission to investigate." If Stuart were to have a new trial and be found guilty, the judge would have to sentence him to death again. "On the other hand, if the Commission declares that justice was done at Stuart's trial, then the operation of the law will have been varied for reasons —however humane—which have nothing to do with the law or its traditional processes. It is difficult to see how respect for the law can fail to be prejudiced." The *Daily Telegraph* printed a statement by Professor A. K. Stout that the decision was not so much ill-timed as irrelevant. "The fight is not to get the sentence commuted, but to decide his innocence or otherwise." In the *Telegraph* there also appeared this comment by the cartoonist Tanner:

"It's either blind justice—or someone saving face."

—Daily Telegraph, Sydney, October 7, 1959

The Sydney *Sun* attributed the decision to "public uneasiness", and said that the government had made, in effect, "a judgment of doubt reinforcing the original doubt which prompted the appointment of the Commission". Sydney's other afternoon paper, the *Mirror*, described the action as extraordinary. "It can only make confusion worse confounded . . . Sir Thomas Playford is usually the most astute of politicians. But in this case he appears to be entangled in a mesh into which he plunges more deeply with every effort to extricate himself."

Two religious journals added their opinions. The *Anglican* said that the decision should be approved unanimously, with the clear understanding that it did not anticipate or prejudge the findings of the Commission. *La Fiamma*, which is controlled by the Capuchin order and enjoys the largest circulation among Australia's foreign-language press, welcomed a humanitarian act but said that it could be considered only as a political expedient made under pressure, and as such would "create prejudice, mistrust, and suspicion in the country . . . What a mess!" In England, the reprieve was reported prominently by the B.B.C. and some newspapers. In the London *News-Chronicle*, James Cameron described it as a major victory for the *News*.

Stuart's escape from the scaffold was not popular in Ceduna and Thevenard. *Truth* found the area "in a ferment" over it, with residents "almost unanimous in condemning the government's decision . . ." Mr. P. S. Morrison, the former chairman of the Murat Bay District Council, said (according to *Truth*) that it "was obviously due to political and religious pressure and the influence of fanatics on the government. Of course Stuart should have been hanged." The wife of the hotel-keeper at Ceduna said: "We all think Stuart should hang . . . What's the use of having a Royal Commission when, before it gives a decision, the government lets Stuart off?" An unnamed housewife said: "There's only one sort of punishment to fit that crime." Mr. G. D. Spry, the storekeeper who had given evidence at the Commission, said: "The people feel they have been let down and that the parents of the dead girl have also been let down by the government. They had a right to expect Stuart to pay the penalty and it is shameful that he is not going to hang if he is guilty." An account similar to *Truth's* of opinion around Ceduna was given in the *West Coast Sentinel*, which reported: "FEELING HIGH OVER CABINET'S DECISION IN STUART CASE. The rape and brutal murder of the little girl was without question the most atrocious crime in the book, and people of this country[3] consider that the death penalty could never be applied again if not in this case. The opinion is strongly favoured that the government, by its indecision, has permitted itself to be hoaxed, used, and abused, and has suffered a big drop in prestige as a result."

In the week this comment appeared, the Murat Bay District Council resolved to open a fund for a headstone and surround for the grave of Mary Hattam, in a corner of the cemetery at Ceduna. The fund was over-subscribed.

* * *

Why had Stuart's sentence been commuted? At the Commission, Chamberlain gave what purported to be a complete explanation: that it would not be fair to Stuart to continue the uncertainty of temporary respites, and that the Commission should be able to carry on "unembarrassed by any further talk about 'the shadow of the gallows' ". The Crown Solicitor was careful to say that the reprieve did not imply any doubt about Stuart's guilt. Yet in parliament more than a week later, Playford said that the decision was made for "a number of reasons which have not been stated publicly . . ." but which he could tell the house "in confidence"—without, however, ordering the press gallery to be cleared. There had been a very strong attack on the state's legal system, he said, and it had to be made clear that the government and the courts "desired to see justice done in its fullest sense. The reason the government commuted the sentence was, firstly, that this man had been under sentence for nearly nine months,[4] and numerous respites had been granted, and secondly, the Commission was in a very difficult position to get the true facts of the case because . . . while it was not a trial it nevertheless would have

[3] i.e., the west coast of the state.

[4] Stuart was sentenced to death on April 24, five months and eleven days before the reprieve.

material bearing upon whether Stuart would hang or not." How this answer made the decision more intelligible was difficult to see; weeks later Mr. J. A. Heaslip asked in parliament whether the Premier would "explain as fully as possible the commutation of the sentence on Stuart . . . so as to allow the public to have a far better understanding than they have regarding the reasons . . ." Playford replied that when the Commission completed its work, he would be prepared "to state the reason". That was the last of his enigmatic remarks on the matter.

The suggestion that compassion for Stuart contributed to the reprieve left some people unconvinced and others indignant. If the effect on the mind and spirit of a man were to be a ground for reprieve, then the government might have announced by now that it would not hang John Whelan Brown, who had been sentenced to death a month before Stuart; the government itself, by contesting the High Court's order for a new trial, was responsible for keeping the noose suspended over Brown longer than over Stuart. But why, if Stuart was guilty, should he be shown any compassion at all? The government, believing in capital punishment, had decided that this was a crime for which the murderer must hang. Should not the character of the crime, rather than the effect on Stuart of postponing the execution, be decisive? That, plainly, was a question in the minds of people in Ceduna and elsewhere. The rest of Playford's account was vague. Just *when* had the sentence of death of Stuart begun to put the Commission "in a very difficult position to get the true facts of the case . . ."? Certainly his refusal to appear at the Commission had this effect; but what, precisely, was the connexion between the death sentence and Stuart's unwillingness to give evidence? And why did the Premier choose a moment during the enquiry to waive the sentence?

An immediate and confident explanation of the reprieve was offered by Mr. Alan Reid of the Sydney *Telegraph* (who was in Canberra when the news came). "It is claimed," he wrote, "Sir Thomas . . . was opposed to commuting Stuart's death sentence until the last moment." But "powerful forces" intervened to persuade him; "when the Commissioners virtually insisted that Stuart had to go into the box if they were not to return an adverse finding the Government's situation became almost untenable. Unless Stuart went into the box there could not be the full enquiry promised by the government . . . But if he went in while under the death penalty it could be said that he was labouring under too great a strain to present his case adequately." Finally convinced of this, Playford agreed with a course which would leave Stuart free to give evidence, "but not under the threat of hanging if he did not appear".

Some support could be given to this account by a remark at the Commission unreported in most of the press. A few minutes after the reprieve was announced, Mr. Justice Reed said: "The Commission has considered that it would be almost not decent to require a man under the sentence of death to get into the witness box." This was plainer speaking than Playford ever offered on the decision. It seems not impossible that the Commissioners let Playford know that if Stuart could give evidence without his life at stake, their enquiry could more easily be—and appear—full and fair.

The private member's bill to abolish capital punishment, moved by Dunstan, was still before parliament when Stuart was reprieved. When Dunstan introduced the measure he argued that no court could be infallible, and spoke of "events that are taking place elsewhere in this state at the moment" as "clear enough evidence . . . that mistakes can occur". Playford hinted, on the other hand, that if he chose to mention Stuart he could "submit an additional argument" for retaining the death penalty; but he gave no clue to its character. The debate was serious and sustained, lasting for eight private members' days spread over three months. It was accompanied by a prolonged correspondence in the *Advertiser*, in which the murder at Thevenard was cited both by supporters of hanging and by opponents.

Other events helped to keep the debate lively and topical. Capital punishment was abolished in New Zealand. The Labor opposition tried in vain to end it in Victoria. It was restored in Ceylon, whose government thereby ignored the findings of a Royal Commission chaired by Professor Norval Morris. In Adelaide, Morris himself urged abolition in an interview on television with *News* journalists. Next night, on the eve of the year's most popular football match (and three days before Stuart's reprieve), somebody painted on the pavement at the Adelaide Oval: "No More Hangings". The Congregational Union of South Australia invited Dunstan to address its assembly, and then sent to the government a resolution that capital punishment should be abolished.

"It is not a party political matter," said Playford in opposing the bill. For several weeks some L.C.L. politicians were agreeing privately with Dunstan that the bill would be passed by the Assembly. But on November 11 every L.C.L. member voted against the motion, the Independents went one each way, and the measure was defeated by two. Dunstan said that Playford had asked his followers not to embarrass the government. Whether this was true or not, a majority against capital punishment would have been disconcerting to a government anxious to justify all its actions towards Stuart.

The bill certainly saved the life of one convicted murderer. A man named Kiker, who admitted having shot a taxi-driver, had his sentence commuted on October 13, on the ground (Playford announced) that the law prescribing capital punishment was under challenge in parliament. This reason was never given by Playford in any account of why Stuart had been reprieved. Whether Dunstan's bill nevertheless contributed to that decision was a subject of some speculation in Adelaide. Did the commutation help avert a vote hostile to capital punishment by allaying qualms within Playford's party? Understandably, those who could have answered such a question with authority made no effort to do so.

It is unlikely that the reprieve would have been granted if Stuart's advisers had pursued their boycott, and if the Commissioners had, as expected, finished hearing evidence early in September. In a sense, then, the divergence of advice between Shand and O'Sullivan, which kept the Commission sitting past that time, may also have removed from their client the threat of death.

In June and July, Dixon and his allies had asked the government merely to exercise the prerogative of mercy. The government had then declined to do so. Once Dixon visited Queensland the central question was not whether the sentence should be reviewed but whether the verdict against Stuart should be set aside. His newest counsel now began to argue that it should.

17

THE PRISONER SPEAKS

In the crowded public gallery on October 13 were several residents of Ceduna who had queued since early morning. Stuart sat between uniformed warders in the dock, wearing possibly for the first time in his life the uniform of urban man: shoes and socks, shirt and tie, and a suit coat that matched his trousers. He looked shorter and slighter than the police photographs suggested, and not quite as dark; since the photographs were taken, in midsummer, he had been away from the sun for more than nine months.

In Sydney that morning a dark-skinned man was speaking to the press about Stuart. Mr. Learie Constantine, the West Indian politician, lawyer, and former test cricketer, who was in Australia for a conference of the Commonwealth Parliamentary Association, said that if the Commission found Stuart guilty he might have something to say about the case, and would "comment about certain differences in some of the evidence". A colleague from Uganda reported that many delegates to the conference had discussed the case since they reached Australia the previous night.

A minute after the Commission resumed the warders took Stuart to a cell. His voice stayed in court, on tape, while the Commissioners pored over phonetic accounts of what they were hearing and Strehlow gave them a lesson on the Aranda language. At Starke's invitation, Strehlow said that on August 19 he and Shand had visited the gaol with a technician and a tape recorder. Strehlow had spoken an Aranda version of the confession, which Stuart translated sentence by sentence into English.

"Do you consider," Starke asked Strehlow, "that the reproduction in English of the Aranda translation of the confession should be as good as the original—assuming it to be genuine—or better, or worse?"

Strehlow said that he would expect the reproduction in English to be better than the original, and that in fact it was worse.

"You made a literal translation?" asked Starke.

"Yes, using the correct tenses, and that is why I say that if anything the rendering he gave ought to be better than the original."

A recording of the exercise was played, after the Commissioners had been supplied with a document setting out, in parallel columns, the original confession, Strehlow's Aranda version of it, and the phonetic account of Stuart's translation back into English. Without doubt

Stuart's English, as heard on tape, was worse than that of the confession. Where the confession had "He offered me a drink," the listeners in court heard Stuart say: "He gibb me a drink."

"Is 'offered'," Starke asked Strehlow, "a word which in your experience this class of man would use?"

"A lot would not understand what it would mean," said Strehlow. "The normal phrase is 'gibb'."

Where the confession had: "Just after coming out of Thevenard town I stood and I finished that bottle," Stuart said: "I went out from Sebenard pub. I's standin. I drank that bottle." Strehlow said of the version in the confession that aborigines without a good education rarely, if ever, used a main clause and a subordinate clause in English.

Where the confession had: "She went unconscious," Stuart, on tape, said: " 'E went out." It was common, explained Strehlow, for people like Stuart to confuse "he", "she", and "it", which in Aranda were not distinguished. Of the word "unconscious", Strehlow said: "He would not know what it means."

"He instructs me at this moment," Starke added, "that he still does not know the meaning of the word 'unconscious'. Do you find that hard or easy to accept?"

"Easy."

Starke asked a similar question about the word "rape" in the confession, and Strehlow gave a similar answer.

After eliciting Strehlow's comments in detail, Starke led him through a summary of the features of Northern Territory English as demonstrated by Stuart's translation. Strehlow listed these features as a confusion about the use of definite and indefinite articles; the use of singular forms of nouns where English uses the plural; the use of "he" or "she" after a noun; the use of the present tense of verbs instead of the past; the wrong use of the present tense; the infrequent use of such connectives as "but", "also", and "however"; a limited vocabulary; and off-centre syntax. As an example of this last feature, Strehlow quoted part of the statement taken from Stuart in the police court at Alice Springs: "When I went back I walked up near the taxi rank couldn't see nobody I stopped on Fogarty's corner, I looked up towards the police station seen nobody there so I walked up to the billiard room, then when I seen Noel Beardsley I never talked to him at all as he was still playing billiards. I stopped in the Stuart Arms veranda then I never go in the hotel at all."

Starke questioned Strehlow on other matters, including time. The witness said that he had seen Shand show Stuart a watch. "He looked at the watch and after a short delay he said: 'Quarter past six'. That was wrong. Mr. Shand said: 'You have another look.' This time he said: 'Oh no, I am wrong, it is a quarter to six.' He realised that the certain interval was a quarter hour. The second time he was right."

"Would you expect him," said Starke, "if he concentrates, to be able to read a clock or a watch?"

"I should say so," said Strehlow. "He should have had a lot more practice since then. On this occasion it took him quite a while to work it out."

Stuart's English, Strehlow said, had become slightly quicker since May; and since his imprisonment in December "a very considerable improvement" must have occurred.

Strehlow was in the box all the morning. After lunch Stuart was brought back into the court. The Commissioners were now, at last, to hear him speak. Mr. Justice Reed administered the oath, having been assured by Starke that Stuart would understand. Starke asked that the shorthand writers should take down the words phonetically. "That will not be easy," said the Chairman. A strictly phonetic rendering would have shown that Stuart, like some of the wheat-lumping and hole-digging aborigines who gave evidence earlier, had in his pronunciation certain characteristics not found in that of white Australians: in his case a rolling "r", an imperfect "th", and, compared with the speech known to its students as broad Australian, an "o" unusually long and an "ee" unusually pure. It was a soft voice: when it dropped too low, Stuart's counsel would repeat a reply more loudly.

"Your name is Rupert Max Stuart," said Starke, "and you are at present at Adelaide Gaol?" "Yes, sir."

"Will you look at the judges, Max, and keep your voice up so every one can hear, especially Their Honours?"

"Yes."

"How are you feeling?"

"Right."

Thus began an examination that went on in all for five hours, spread over three days, interrupted by the normal adjournments, by intervals of legal argument, and by the arrival in Adelaide of Sir William Slim, who was paying his last visit as Governor-General and whose presence required Sir Mellis Napier to act as Lieutenant-Governor. To Starke and most of the time to Chamberlain, he was "Max"; to Brazel "witness", and to the Commissioners "Stuart". As the lawyers and judges questioned him, his hands were behind his back, his head was up, and his weight shifted slightly from foot to foot. Sometimes, before answering, he pushed his broad lips out and looked up. Sometimes he said "What's that?" and sometimes his own counsel asked Chamberlain to simplify a question. The answers were quick and laconic.

After a series of biographical questions the story reached Ceduna. Three girls, said Stuart, were sitting in front of him at the pictures on Friday night.

"You kicked them, kicked the bench or touch them in any way?"

"No."

"Half-time you stay in the theatre or go outside?"

"Went outside."

"You see anyone there?" "Yes."

"Who?" "Girl."

"One of the three who had been in front of you?"

"One who was sitting in the back."

". . . What she say?"

"Asked me where I come from and tell 'im[1] we just got in this morning on the travelling show. Ask if I could sit with her."

"What you say?"

"I said: 'If your father and mother not there I go and sit with you but if your father and mother there won't go and sit with you.'" The girl said her parents were there. She also suggested that he come and see her tomorrow, and pointed "down Thevenard".

At twenty-five minutes to three Starke pointed to the clock on the wall opposite Stuart and said: "What time?" After a slight pause, Stuart said: "Twenty-five to three." On the Saturday morning, he said, he got up at nine o'clock. He now described the morning visit to the beach with Moir, the meeting with a half-caste ("He offered 'im drink"), the drinking out of a flagon. He put the flagon in a sugar bag, he said, walked "up the town", and "left 'im down the lavatory behind picture wall". He went up the street, talked to "few dark fellas", and went into a shop, where "fella in the shop" rang up a taxi. At one o'clock he and Moir "jumped in" a taxi and went "down to fun-fair". "Allan went out, got off the taxi. I got off the taxi." He looked for Gieseman, did not find him, and "went back into taxi".

"What were you looking for Norman Gieseman for?"

"What that?"

Mr. Justice Reed repeated the question.

"If he was there I go my job, if he not there I sneak away."

He took the taxi to the pub at Thevenard and asked the driver to come back, but he did not. He saw a New Australian, then "one girl" who came out of the pub, and who had been sitting in front of him at the pictures. "I ask her about this other girl." She said the other girl was asleep and after a word about Allan Moir she went back into the pub. Then he saw the other girl, to whom he had talked at the pictures. She went with him to the back of the hotel and "had naughty", which took about five minutes.

"You have had naughties before in your life?"

"Oh yes."

"What would you say about this girl: had she done a naughty before or not?"

[1] Some peculiarities of Stuart's speech at this stage of the examination were later attributed by the Chairman to the elliptical form of Starke's questions. That could hardly account, however, for the use of "'im" instead of "her".

"I think she done it before." He supposed she was about twenty. He gave her "four quid".

A white fellow, who was drunk, gave him a drink from a bottle of wine. He said he would buy the rest of the bottle, but when he found that his wallet was empty the man gave him the wine.

"What did you do with that bottle?" "I drank it."

"What did you do with it after that?"

"When I had finished I threw 'im away."

"How did you feel when you throw him away?"

"I feeling light."

"How did you walk when feeling light?"

"I walk fast."

"By what track did you walk down to Ceduna?"

"I went on the road for a while and then I cut down the beach." On the way back he got the flagon left behind the picture hall and drank four inches or so of wine from it. Near the fun-fair, two dark fellows asked if he could get them a flagon and gave him twenty-five shillings. He knew now that one of these men was named Kelly. He did not say to either of them that he had a tight root, or that he had had a maiden on the beach.

"Do you know what a maiden is?"

"No."

". . . From the time you got into the taxi outside the shop in Ceduna and went to the show, down to Thevenard and came back to the show again—how long?"

"Hour."

"When did you get back to the show?"

"Two o'clock."

"How long you there?"

"From two to four."

For the first time, Stuart had testified to the alibi offered for him; but the answer raised in turn a simple, large question: if he could say this now, why had he never said it to anybody before?

In the tent, he said, he had bread and cabbage. Betty Gadd agreed to buy liquor. He gave her some money, and she bought wine and beer, which Mrs. Gieseman put in the caravan. He himself worked from two to four on the darts, and took "four quid", of which Mr. Gieseman gave him "eight bob". After tea in the tent, he and Moir went into the town. On the beach they drank with three dark fellows, one of them Herbie Sumner. Stuart had a friendly spar with one of the fellows.

He did not say to Moir: "I got blood on my chest." He did not speak of knocking somebody off or over. He did not say that he wanted to dump a body, or that he wanted a dinghy. In Ceduna, when Sergeant Walker told him to get out of town, he did not say either within Walker's hearing or later: "I will kill you like I killed the others."

What did Gieseman say next morning? "He said: 'You're finished, take those overalls off, you're finished. Don't want you any more.' . . . I took my overalls off . . ."[2] Then Stuart went away with Herbie Sumner and arranged a job in the Wheat Board. On Monday night, at the premises of the Wheat Board, the policemen came for him.

Detail by detail Starke took Stuart through his account of the interrogation. "Jonesey punched me . . . in my right eye . . . in my ribs . . . side of my throat." The punch on the eye drew blood from a cut in the middle of the right eyebrow. Walker choked him. Turner put on the table some blades from Stuart's pocket and said he was going to skin him alive. Stuart was frightened that he would be killed. He was saying: "I don't know," but by and by he said "Yes" to everything. Because he was frightened he signed a paper typed by one of the men. They read the paper to him after he signed his name.

* * *

On chairs reserved for witnesses sat his champions Dixon and Strehlow and his captors Turner and Jones. Dixon made notes from time to time and passed them to Starke. After reading one of them, Starke said that when Stuart used the word "never" he could mean "not"; this helped to remove a minor inconsistency in the evidence. Turner was not making notes. He knew, and Stuart knew, what really happened that night at the police station; and to the man who was telling the truth it must have seemed an appalling reflection on human credibility that an utterly false account could be taken so seriously.

* * *

In the statement that went unread at his trial Stuart said (as reported by O'Sullivan): "I walked back to Ceduna in the afternoon." Starke now asked: "When is afternoon?"

"After dinner."

"When is dinner?" "Twelve o'clock."

"Afternoon after twelve o'clock?" "Yes."

Next Stuart gave his version of offences at Cloncurry and Alice Springs. In Cloncurry, he said, he sneaked in after some drinking to steal a rifle. A little girl got up. He pushed her on the chest and ran off with the rifle. He pleaded guilty later to stealing the rifle and to touching the little girl. He did not know that he was pleading guilty to touching her between the legs. The assault on the nurse at Alice Springs he described as he had to Dixon: she came into a lavatory while he was recovering a bottle of wine; he threw her on one side and ran away. When he was charged at Alice Springs with

[2] Gieseman and his wife had said that Stuart was not wearing overalls on the Sunday morning, and McNeish had said that he thought not. Moir had said that he was; and according to Phin, both Gieseman and Moir had told him so in Whyalla.

supplying liquor to an aborigine, another prisoner wrote out something on paper for him and also practised with him "nearly half the night . . . to say something in court".

"Why," asked Starke, "if he had written it out for you in advance?"

"In case the magistrate would not read it."

"When you got in, the magistrate would not read it, is that so?"

"Yes."

"What did you do then?"

"I went on talking myself."

"How did you go?"

"I got six months."

Starke smiled, and Mr. Justice Reed helped him to frame the question more precisely. "How did you get on with the talking?"

"All right."

When Starke began to ask about what Stuart told O'Sullivan before the trial, Brazel rose and said: "Before my learned friend puts that question I would enquire whether he concedes by so doing that other counsel at the bar are at liberty then to cross-examine upon what passed between Stuart and his counsel?"

"I am making no concessions whatsoever," said Starke. "I am merely following the bad example set by you, Mr. Brazel, earlier." To the bench, Starke said that Brazel was trying to get him "to concede that everyone is able to cross-examine as to privileged matters. My friend is merely by tactical manoeuvres trying to get me to concede that what he had already done is legitimate."

"It is nothing of the sort," said Brazel.

"My friend can ask the question," said Chamberlain.

"You can go on, Mr. Starke," said the Chairman.

Before the trial, asked Starke, had Stuart told O'Sullivan about the girl at Thevenard?

"No . . . I was frightened to say . . . He might think I was the fella that killed that girl."

"Who did you first tell about that?" "Mr. Strehlow."

"After the trial?" "Yes."

"Were you frightened Mr. Strehlow would think that about you?" "No."

"You had known him since you were a little boy?" "Yes."

Did he see a little girl that Saturday afternoon? No.

Did he have naughties with or rape or kill a little girl? No.

* * *

Chamberlain's manner was as friendly as Starke's. "You remember," he began, "when you were tried . . . ?" "Yes."

"Do you remember you were in the dock over there?" "Yes."

"And some men over the other side?" "Yes."

"Do you know who they were and what they were there for?"

"Yes . . . to find me guilty."

Did he hear the taxi-driver, Blackham, give evidence before the magistrate and at the trial? Yes.

Did he hear Blackham say that he talked about looking for girls? Yes.

"Did Mr. O'Sullivan ask you whether that was right . . . ?"

"Yes, I think, I am not sure."

". . . You told him you were not looking for a girl?" "Yes."

"You told him a lie about that?" "No."

"Well, you were looking for a girl, weren't you?" "Yes."

". . . You did not want him to think you were looking for a girl because they might think you had murdered the little girl on the beach?"

"That is right."

How did he know that he worked at the show from two o'clock that Saturday?

By the sun.

How did he fix four o'clock?

"Four o'clock, we knock off at four o'clock."

"How do you know it was four o'clock?"

"Mr. Gieseman had a watch."

"And you saw Mr. Gieseman's watch, is that right?" "Yes."

The court-room clock showed 3.34 as Chamberlain asked: "What is the time now, Max?"

Stuart paused, then said: "Twenty-five to four."

"Can you tell the time easily, or do you have to think a bit?"

"I think a bit."

"You know the time was two o'clock when you started working by the sun, is that so, did you look at a watch at two o'clock?"

"Yes."

"Whose watch?" "Mrs. Gieseman."

"Max, do you know what part of the day the little girl was supposed to have been murdered?"

"I do not know."[3]

". . . Did you tell Mr. O'Sullivan about working from two o'clock to four o'clock at the show?"

"No."

"You knew those times, didn't you Max?" "Yes."

". . . You did not tell Mr. O'Sullivan any of that?" "No."

"Why not, Max?" "Because he did not ask me."

Chamberlain sought, as Starke had done but by different questions, to get a definition of afternoon.

"What time does afternoon start?"

"Straight after dinner."

[3] Here and elsewhere the court reporter was making Stuart's replies seem more formal than they sounded. In this case the *Advertiser* reporter gave the answer as "No." The answer "Dunno" was frequently given.

"Did you have any dinner on that Saturday?" "Yes."

"Where did you have it?" "In the tent."

"Was that after you had come back from Thevenard?" "Yes."

"That is when the afternoon started?" "Yes."

". . . Up to the time you had dinner, what part of the day do you call that?"

"One o'clock."

"What part of the day do you call it, that is before dinner?"

"Afternoon."

"What part of the day do you call it up to the time you have dinner?"

"Twelve o'clock."

"What is it, morning, afternoon, evening, or what?"

"Middle day."

By Mrs. Gieseman's watch, Stuart said, it was a little after one when he had dinner. He had not told O'Sullivan about the time, and O'Sullivan had not asked him.

* * *

At Chamberlain's request three men entered the court. Stuart said he knew them. The three men, warders from the gaol, withdrew, and Chamberlain asked whether Stuart remembered, after the trial, waiting downstairs while the jury were out talking. Starke objected that Their Honours had rejected this evidence once and should do so again. The Chairman said that the situation had changed; on the first occasion, Stuart was not giving evidence and was not represented. "And something that has happened since . . ." added Mr. Justice Reed. Starke said: "At the time he was under sentence of death and now he is not; that would be irrelevant." To the Chairman, Starke replied: "Your Honours were not going to let it in without representation for Stuart and you should not let it in with representation. It is either fair or not fair." Chamberlain submitted that on the first occasion Stuart had not given evidence attacking the good faith of the police.[4] Brazel said that if Their Honours intended to apply the Evidence Act, "then . . . he can be cross-examined as to statements he made elsewhere inconsistent with testimony given here today."

The Commission adjourned for ten minutes to consider the matter. Stuart was escorted out of the court-room and brought back a little before the resumption. A warder poured him a glass of water. He sat in the witness box, hands clasped, index fingers moving, and looked up at the slowly turning fan, at the ceiling, at the royal crest over the bench with its legend, which he could not read, let alone understand: "DIEU ET MON DROIT".

[4] See, however, p. 190 above. On the earlier occasion Chamberlain gave as his reason for offering the three warders as witnesses the need to refute "the allegations which have now been made about the police and their conduct".

The Chairman said that the Commission would defer a decision about the warders. Chamberlain resumed his cross-examination. Who was the first person to whom Stuart said that he was working from two till four? Starke intervened. "I would find it surprising that I have to object to the Crown Solicitor cross-examining privileged communications between my client and his legal adviser after the stage of the trial. I agree I have opened it up to the stage of the trial, but after that I should not even have to object . . ." Chamberlain left the subject and turned to the offence at Cloncurry. Stuart denied having made a number of remarks attributed to him by the local policeman, Corbett; in particular, he denied having said that he touched the little girl between the legs, or that he felt like having a girl.

"The magistrate who gave you six months," said Chamberlain—"did anyone tell him that you had put your hand between the little girl's legs?"

"No."

". . . What did the sergeant tell the magistrate you had done?"

"Oh, I just forgot what he said now."

"You know what an accident is, do you Max, something that is not your fault?"

"Yeah."

"Did you tell Mr. Corbett that you never meant to do anything rude to the little girl, just an accident?"

"I think I must have told him like that, I forgot."

"You never told him you did anything rude or bad to the little girl?"

"No."

The vice-regal visit of Sir William Slim kept Stuart in gaol all next morning. In the afternoon Chamberlain took him through the statement prepared for his trial, asking of each sentence whether he understood it and whether it was true. The words: "I did not want a girl," said Stuart, were not true. Nor were the words: "At tea-time I went down to the hotel to get a drink." He went not to the hotel, he said, but to the beach. The words: "They did not look at my knees" (referring to the questioning by policemen at the wheat stacks on Monday evening) were not true. The rest of the statement was true, including the description of the assault on him at the police station. The blow that Jones gave him over the eye nearly knocked him off the chair; for a while he could not see through the blood. The cut took a couple of weeks to heal.

Stuart agreed that he had travelled to Queensland with a boxing show, but said that when fighting he had never been struck over the right eye. Had he fought elsewhere as well as in the boxing show? Yes; he had been in fights with New Australians in Mount Isa when he worked in the mines there; he did not like New Australians.

Chamberlain asked for a close account of the interrogation. Was it true that Stuart said (as asserted in the statement written out by O'Sullivan): "Perhaps it was a white man"?

"No, it was not true."

"You never said that?"

"What's that?"

"You didn't say: 'Perhaps it was a white man'?"

"Yeah."[5]

"You did say it to the police?"

"Yeah."

"What did they say to that?"

"They said: 'That's a lie about the white man.' "

"Who was it that talked about the white man first, you or the police?"

"They was talking about it first."

A few questions later, however, Stuart said that it was he who introduced the white man, after a policeman hit him.

From Stuart's own statement Chamberlain moved to Constable Richard Jones' account of the interrogation. Stuart contested much of it, but not all. He accepted as substantially accurate the report of Turner's questions and his own answers about his movements until he set off from Thevenard on Saturday afternoon.

Did Turner say: "Can you track?"

"He didn't ask me if I could track . . . He didn't say nothing about tracks."

"Did he say: 'The person who raped and murdered this little girl left tracks in his bare feet'?"

"Yes."

"Did he say: 'We have had these tracks examined by two black trackers . . .'?"

"Yes."

". . . Did you tell Mr. Turner that black trackers would know the tracks? You thought they would?"

"Yes, I thought——"

"Did you say that?"

"I don't know whether I say it or not . . . I didn't say nothing."

"Did Turner say: 'We are going to let them have a look at some of your tracks'?"

". . . No."

"Did he ask you what you thought they'd say if they saw your tracks?"

"Yes."

"What did you say to that?"

"I never said a word."

[5] This was one of several stages of the cross-examination when discussion became confused. "Sometimes," wrote the reporter from the Melbourne *Herald* and *Sun*, "he gave directly contradictory replies to the same question when it was repeated. This led the Crown Solicitor . . . to exclaim . . . 'I give up'."

". . . Did you say this: 'I will tell you the truth. I was there and saw the little girl murdered but I didn't do it'?"

"I didn't say that."

". . . Did you say: 'I saw a white bloke kill a girl on the beach'?"

". . . No."

". . . Did you say this to Mr. Turner, talking about a white bloke: 'He pulled out a gun, made me pick up the little girl on the beach, carry her into the cave'?"

"Yes."

Chamberlain gave Stuart an opportunity to withdraw this answer if it rested on a misapprehension. "I do not think you understood me. Did you say to Turner a white bloke pulled out a gun and made you carry the little girl into the cave?"

"Yes," Stuart said again, and added: "that was a lie."

". . . Why did you say that, Max?"

"Because I was frightened." Before this, he said, the police had punched and choked him.

". . . Did you tell them that the white man said he would kill you if you ever told anybody what you had done?"

"Yes."

". . . Did you say: 'The bloke drove off in his car and I walked back along the beach and went back to Ceduna . . .'?"

"Yes."

"Did they say: 'Your story is not true, the little girl was raped and murdered in the cave'?"

"Yep."

". . . The blood in the cave showed that the girl had been murdered in the cave, they told you that?"

"Yes."

"Did you say: 'I must have done it but I do not remember doing it'?"

"Nuh."

". . . Did Turner say: 'You have remembered everything else clearly enough, I think you can remember what you did'? Did Turner say that to you?"

"Yes."

"Did you say: 'I might as well tell you what I did; I did do it. I was pretty full or I would not have done it'? Did you say that?"

"No, I did not say that."

Stuart said that after the police had beaten and frightened him, he told them things to please them.

"Did they ask you if you called the little girl to come and see the little birdies?"

"They asked me."

"They were the ones who mentioned the birdies?" "Yes."

"What did you say when they said that?" "I said: 'I dunno.' "

". . . Did they ask you how she was dressed?" "Yes."

"What did you say when they said that?" "I said: 'I dunno.' "

"Did you say anything about a white coat and red bathers?" "No."

"Did they ask you if she had a white coat or red bathers?"

"No—yes, they did."

"What did you say?" "I said: 'I dunno.' "

". . . At any time when they asked you if you killed her, did you say: 'Yes'?"

"Yes, a few times I made a mistake."

On the Tuesday morning in the cell at Ceduna, he agreed, Jones or Turner came with a bit of rock and some bathers.

"Did Turner say: 'Is this the stone you killed the girl with?' "

"Yeah."

"What did you say?"

"I said: 'I don't know.' "

Did Turner ask also about the bathers? "Yeah."

"And what did you say?" "I said: 'I don't know.' "[6]

"Did you say: 'They are the same colour, they look like it'?"

"No, I don't say that."

Chamberlain asked Stuart to tell the Commissioners what happened when he was convicted of assaulting the nurse at Alice Springs. Stuart told the story in these words, which were to be discussed keenly as evidence about his facility in English.

> "This other fella was drinking and me and him had a bit of an argument and he went up the street and I followed him and I seen him again up the town, and we got more grog and went down to the Todd River and finished the two bottles and went up the street of the town and I told him to watch them policemen and I went in the pub, the Mountain Arms, and got a flagon of wine and then we went up behind Anzac Hill and had a drink up there and he went up Middle Park, up to the reserve and I came down to town and I got some more grog in town there, and went down to Todd River, the same place we were drinking that morning, and when I finished that bottle I was on my own then and I went to this lavatory to get this bottle and when I got inside I heard a mob of women coming and I could not get out, so one of them came in and I grabbed her and throw her to one side and I run away."

The cross-examination moved back to Thevenard. Did he see there one of the girls he had seen at the pictures? Yes.

"Did you talk to her?" "Yeah."

"What did you say?"

[6] Next day Strehlow said, in answer to Starke, that "I dunno" was often a rendering of an Aranda word better translated as "Know nothing about it."

". . . I said: 'Where dat[7] other girl . . . one who was talking to me Friday night?' "

Chamberlain gave Stuart some photographs, and asked whether the girl with whom he had this conversation was among them.

"Yes, this one here," said Stuart, holding up a photograph of Brenda Kent.

"Did a girl come out of the hotel?" Chamberlain went on.

"Yeah. No, no, no, not from the hotel."

"Did you see where she came from?"

"When I seen her she was standing." She might or might not have come out of the hotel.

"Is the girl you had intercourse with amongst these?" asked Chamberlain, indicating the remaining photographs.

"Yeah," said Stuart. He pointed to a photograph of Olive Betts, the girl who said that she had not seen Stuart at Thevenard that day, and whom a medical practitioner had certified as, in layman's language, a virgin.

"You had a good one?" "Yeah."

He had paid her four pounds borrowed from a half-caste, whom he intended to repay by borrowing from Gieseman. He did not find out her name.

Again Chamberlain led Stuart's memory to Alice Springs, this time to the conviction for supplying liquor. In the Northern Territory, Stuart agreed, he was at the time given all the privileges of a white man.

"You were up late the night before, practising what you were going to say, weren't you?" "Yeah."

". . . Did you tell Father Dixon," asked Chamberlain, "that . . . you had a paper written out by . . . your friend, and you showed it to the magistrate and it was copied down?"

"Yeah," said Stuart; but he agreed that in fact he himself gave evidence unaided.[8]

When Chamberlain put a long question on this subject, and asked: "Do you understand me?" Stuart said that he did not. Chamberlain went on:

"Did you tell Father Dixon that you didn't stand up and give evidence but you had a piece of paper which you handed to the magistrate which was copied out?" "Yeah."

Was that true, Chamberlain asked.

The answer consistent with his previous replies was "No." But Stuart said: "Yeah."

* * *

[7] This was one of the few places in which a court reporter tried to reproduce peculiarities of pronunciation.

[8] In his first petition for commutation (see pp. 56-7 above) Stuart had given a different account of this episode.

On the morning of October 15, his third day in the box, Stuart sat for forty minutes while the lawyers argued about whether the warders should be heard. Chamberlain, as before, said that they should. Starke, after being shown their statements, said that they should not. Brazel said that it might be quite valuable to hear whether what Stuart said to the warder was consistent with his own evidence here.

After an adjournment of five minutes the Chairman said that the Commissioners were not entirely in agreement. "None of us has any clear view one way or the other, but we feel that in case of doubt we should lean against the admission of the evidence . . ."

"I find myself," said Chamberlain, "in the unfortunate position of having a strong view about the matter in the public interest . . ."

Before Brazel began to question Stuart, Starke asked "whether it is in the interests of justice that there should be two cross-examinations?"

"I take it," said the Chairman, "Mr. Brazel will not be cross-examining in the ordinary sense."

"That is so," said Brazel. "I am concerned with term three . . . why the said statements were not made or furnished to the Supreme Court . . ."

"We rely on you not to cross-examine in any hostile sense," said the Chairman, "but simply to clear up the evidence."

Brazel asked Stuart whether, at the preliminary hearing, he heard the little boy Peter Jacobsen say that he went down to the beach with the little girl after lunch, that he and another boy left the beach, and that when they came back the girl was not there.

Stuart said "Yeah" at intervals. He remembered also the fisherman, Jacobsen, saying that he came in about a quarter to four and saw nobody on the beach. He said that after the preliminary hearing he had no idea what time the little girl was killed, or what time she was missing.

"Did you listen to the evidence in this court when you were being tried for murder?"

"Yeah."

"Did you hear all that was said?"

"Some." He remembered Peter Hattam saying that when he and the other boy returned to the beach about three or half past three, the girl was not there.

"Did you hear the judge at your trial talking to the jury?"

"Yeah."

"Did you hear what he said to the jury?"

"Yeah, I can't understand it."

Did he hear O'Sullivan say that he went to Thevenard in a taxi *about two o'clock*?

"Yeah."

"Did you ever tell Mr. O'Sullivan that that was not right?"

"Yeah."

"When?"

"I didn't tell him."

"Did you hear the judge say the little girl was attacked . . . Do you know what 'attack' means?"

"No."

"Do you know what 'rape' means?" "No."

"*Hurt* about three fifteen?" "Yeah."

"Where were you at three fifteen that day?" "In the fun-fair."

"Did any people see you there at that time?" "Yeah."

"Did you ever tell Mr. O'Sullivan you were at the fun-fair at three fifteen?"

"I don't remember."

Brazel sat down. At Starke's request Stuart turned to the judges and pointed to a mark over his right eye.

"Is that where some of the hair has gone?" asked Mr. Justice Reed.

"Yes," said Starke.

Stuart left the witness box, and the court-room, and the world of free men and women, to wait for someone to tell if he was to go free, to begin a life sentence, or to appear yet again in court for a new trial. Later in the month he was moved from the Adelaide Gaol to Yatala Prison Farm on the northern outskirts of the city.

Strehlow, who had heard all Stuart's evidence, was recalled for linguistic comment on it. Starke asked him to compare his account of the assault at Alice Springs with the narrative in his confession. He had noticed, Strehlow said, that in giving the account to Starke, Stuart left out entirely the relevant fact that he put a bottle in the lavatory. Chamberlain remarked, and the Chairman agreed, that this was a matter for judgment and not for expert evidence. Mr. Justice Reed said he would be interested to know whether Strehlow would describe Stuart's account of events at Alice Springs as "a rambling statement". Strehlow said: "A very fluent rambling statement."

"Why 'rambling'?"

"Perhaps I should say 'irrelevant'."

Would Strehlow say that Stuart was talking in pidgin English, asked Sir Mellis Napier. "No, it is what I would describe as Northern Territory English."

"Was it anything but perfectly good English?"

"I think if you took it down phonetically you would still find some of these things."

"If any of us were taken down phonetically," observed the Chairman, "we would be surprised at the result . . . Do you mean to tell me you regard that man as inadequate in the way of English?"

"I would say he has not got full fluency of expression," replied Strehlow. All white men, educated or not, would know a word like "accident"—used the day previously by somebody; but Stuart did not; ". . . if your vocabulary is so limited that you do not know common words every uneducated white man knows you must limit the way you express yourself to talking in a certain way."

To Chamberlain, Strehlow said that he heard few subordinate clauses in Stuart's evidence. Nor, he agreed, did he hear many displaced personal pronouns.

"You think his English has improved a lot in the last nine months?" asked Chamberlain.

"It would be a reflection on the warders if it had not improved."

The Chairman remarked that Strehlow had not seen Stuart between a time many years ago and last May. A few minutes later, the Chairman said: "We have heard Stuart for ourselves, and if anyone says Stuart speaks pidgin English, well, we know what to think of them."

". . . I have never understood it to be said anywhere," replied Starke, "that he speaks pidgin English as distinct from what is called Northern Territory English."[9]

The Crown called another witness to speak about Stuart's English—Mr. Milton Liddle, a wood merchant and taxi-driver from Alice Springs who knew Stuart and who had been brought as interpreter in case one was needed. He had always spoken with Stuart in English, he told Chamberlain, and had no trouble in doing so. It was some time last year, he thought, when he last saw the prisoner.

"Has his English improved much since you last saw him?" asked Chamberlain.

"I do not think so."

Starke, now facing his first hostile witness, made the most of this question and answer.

"That means he has improved a little?"

"May have."

"Why did you say: 'I don't think he has improved much'?"

"I didn't know the way to put the words, I suppose."

"You picked the wrong words?" "Yes."

The witness stood down, having given Stuart's counsel a little light exercise before his long tussle with the policemen.

* * *

Shand died of cancer on Monday, October 19, having entered hospital for an operation after his return from Adelaide. Many tributes were now spoken. "I had the honour to be his friend for very many years . . . ," said Dr. H. V. Evatt. "His assumption of very heavy responsibility in the Stuart enquiry when his health was rapidly failing was an example of his devotion to duty." Among the tributes, one was quoted in a parliamentary question to Playford by one of his supporters. A former Registrar in Divorce in New South Wales, Mr. J. Doughan, said that Shand was a fearless advocate for those he felt were dealt with unjustly, and that this had been illustrated when he

[9] Strehlow had however used the word "pidgin" in his affidavit to the High Court (see p. 46 above), and O'Sullivan had described Stuart's speech as "very broken pidgin English" (see p. 46 above). Dixon had spoken of "conversational pidgin or Territorian English" (p. 65 above).

took up the cudgels for an unfortunate—Stuart—in another state. Mr. J. A. Heaslip, the author of questions implying disapproval of Stuart's reprieve, read out this statement from a report in the *News* and asked: "Can the Premier say how this unfortunate, or so-called unfortunate, has been dealt with unjustly in South Australia, and whether the publication of this statement to the general public of South Australia is justified?" Playford said that he knew of no injustice; the man was convicted and his conviction upheld, but as it was claimed that additional evidence was available a Royal Commission was appointed "at considerable expense to the state". At the Royal Commission Starke spoke briefly of Shand's death. A columnist in the Sydney *Sunday Telegraph*, who said that Starke told him the story, wrote later: "There was a pause while he waited for his sentiments to be echoed by the members of the tribunal or by the counsel assisting them. But no word came. So Mr. Starke went on with his job."

18

POLICEMEN IN THE BOX

DETECTIVE-SERGEANT PAUL TURNER entered the box before lunch on Thursday, October 15, and stayed there for the afternoon and part of the next morning. Starke asked first about the identification of Stuart's footprints. Supposing the trackers had been eye-witnesses, asked to identify Stuart from his face, would it have been fair to bring him out of the station obviously in custody?

"He wasn't obviously in custody," Turner said; but he agreed that this would not have been fair.

"If it wasn't fair as a facial identification, do you claim it was fair as a footprint identification?"

"Yes."

Starke said he understood that the tracks found on the beach had not been photographed.

"They weren't clear enough to be photographed," said Turner.

"Was any attempt made for them to be photographed?"

"We examined them with that purpose in view." None of these tracks was sharp and clearly defined.

At the police station, Turner said, he had not measured Stuart's foot. "I could see it was approximately the same as the footprint on the beach."

Turner agreed that, like any decent person, he was revolted by this crime, and that he had a particular dislike of crimes involving sex. He remembered that, in a previous case involving sex, it had been alleged that he and another officer had assaulted a man named Martin. He agreed that a doctor, called for the defence, gave evidence about a bruised eye. He recalled that the man was acquitted. He did not recall that the judge adjourned the case without hearing counsels' addresses; though if Starke said so, that was probably right. He had not hit the man.

He objected to a number of allegations made in newspapers. "For one thing, that the hair found in the child's hand was never produced in court.[1] Another thing, that Stuart was not able to speak English properly. And there were other matters." As president of the Police Association, he agreed, he had made statements to the press.

"You suggested to the press that Stuart had been locked up on the Saturday night for offensive behaviour, did you not?"

[1] For a reference to this mistake by the *News*, see p. 84 above.

"Yes . . . I know now that it was a mistake." He had not, however, made a statement directed against Stuart.

"Who was it directed against?"

"It was directed towards the protection of officers who were being accused"—here Turner's voice almost broke—"of attempted murder."

"Who was being accused of attempted murder?"

"I was."

"That is what it would have amounted to," said the Chairman. "Suppose this man had been hung on perjured evidence: that would have been murder."

He agreed that he had referred to a prosecution at Darwin which was in fact at Alice Springs. "It was told to me that it was Darwin, and I had no way of checking up." He could have found out through the Northern Territory police, but it was not an official matter.

Turner said he knew it was wrong to make public statements about pending proceedings. He did not, however, agree that he had been wrong to make a public statement after Stuart applied to the Privy Council. "Not only did you make a statement, as I said," Starke went on, "but you caused to be published the affidavits to be used by the Crown, didn't you?" When Turner denied having done so, Starke read a report from the Melbourne *Herald* of July 23 quoting Turner.[2] The report, said Turner, was false.

"Not only because it quoted you, but as far as you know no officer of the Association had been authorised to make that statement?"

"Definitely not, and also the facts were wrong in that report."[3]

He had seen a hair in each hand of the dead child, which could have been, he agreed, a vital clue.

"You thought that it was a possible lead—sufficiently so to take a hair from Stuart . . . ?"

"A tuft of hair."

How, then, had he come to leave out of the official report of his investigation all reference to the hairs? Turner said that it was not

[2] See p. 66 above.

[3] Three days later, this denial was repeated on Turner's behalf in the Full Court when Miss Helen Devaney sought leave to withdraw a writ of attachment for contempt of court against him. She had sought leave to issue this writ just before the Privy Council hearing. After the Privy Council rejected Stuart's application, Turner's solicitors were informed by O'Sullivan and Devaney that no further action would be taken. The application was formally dismissed on October 19. His counsel said that Turner denied ever having made the statements published. But see the further statement by the *Herald* in its issue of October 21: "The facts are that a senior reporter telephoned Turner at 9.27 a.m. on July 23, and spoke to him for six minutes. He telephoned him again at 9.59 a.m. to check and clarify several points. Post Office records give the times, and show that they were person-to-person calls. What was published in the *Herald* was an accurate report of what Turner said in answer to questions and of statements he volunteered."

his report; he typed it, but at the dictation of Jones. He agreed, however, that he would have drawn Jones' attention to any mistake or important omission. When Starke put it that taking the hair from Stuart was a "minor sort of torture, part of the general bullying", Turner said the suggestion was ridiculous.

"Especially ridiculous," retorted Starke, "because not one word of taking any hair off his body is in any part of the police brief?"

"What is that question meant to be?" asked Chamberlain.

"Arising from the word the witness used," replied Starke. "It may be strong and severe cross-examination, but it is proper cross-examination."

At the trial and in earlier evidence to the Commission, Turner had been asked how far Stuart's confession came into existence by question and answer, and how far it was unprompted narrative. Starke raised this issue again.

"You . . . would ask him, for instance, 'When did you arrive at Ceduna?' "

"No, that was not asked during the typed statement."

Starke then read from Turner's evidence at the trial the words: "Some questions were asked—for a start, I said: 'When did you arrive in Ceduna?' "

At first Turner did not agree that there was any conflict. Then he said that his memory would have been better at the trial.

"Do you now admit you were wrong?" "Obviously."

"Were the words: 'I killed her because I did not want her to tell what I done' in answer to a question?"

"It could have been," replied Turner. ". . . I do not remember clearly. . . . I think it probably was in answer to a question. . . . I cannot be certain."

Starke said that in earlier evidence to the Commission, Turner had told the Chairman "in clear and positive terms" that this information was given in answer to a question. "You were positive when His Honour asked you three or four weeks ago?"

"I was not positive. I am not positive."

How much of the information in the confession had been elicited in the prior oral questioning? "During the interrogation, didn't one of you suggest that he took off his clothes?"

"No, we allowed him to tell the story of the murder, and that is how he told it to us." Turner said he was positive on the point.

Starke called for the notes dictated by Jones and typed by Turner, and asked the witness to read from them. Turner read: "I said: 'Did you take your trousers off before you raped the child?' " He agreed with Starke that he had been wrong.

Starke asked a number of questions about these notes, which purported to reproduce the interrogation of Stuart. The interrogation lasted about half an hour, Turner said, and the report of it was written some eighteen or nineteen hours later.

"What special facilities do you think you have for reproducing verbatim a conversation some eighteen hours later . . . ?"

"Memory gets training through practice."

When the Chairman agreed with this observation, Starke said: "My whole challenge is that this . . . purports to present a verbatim account which in my submission is impossible and therefore is a dishonest document. If it was written in substance one could accept it but in quotes one cannot accept it."

"I think that is a matter for argument," said the Chairman.

Mr. Justice Reed asked Turner whether the words in quotation marks "were literally the very words which Stuart and you used".

"Yes, to the best of my recollection."

"Not to the best of your recollection," said Mr. Justice Reed, "but the very words used?"

It was an endeavour to reproduce the conversation verbatim, said Turner; but "in an odd case or two they probably would not be".

"If you cannot really remember the very words," said Starke, "don't you think as a matter of fairness you should not use quotes but simply use the method of substance?"

"No, I don't agree. It is an honest account, and it is the truth."

When Starke asked why notes were not taken at the time—"as is the practice elsewhere in Australia"—Turner said: "the production of a notebook and the taking of a note dries up the source of information in many cases."

Was it not unfortunate, said Starke, that the police did not question Blackham, the taxi-driver, until three weeks after the murder?

"I don't see that it made any difference," said Turner.

"Surely you will agree that time does affect the human recollection?"

"Yes."

Why were the Giesemans not interviewed?

"A verbal statement was obtained from them. . . . All they could say was that Stuart was absent from the show on the Saturday afternoon and he got the sack for being absent." The Giesemans told Phin, Turner said, that Stuart arrived back on Saturday somewhere about six o'clock.

Would Turner swear Phin said that?

"Not definitely six o'clock."

"Well, what did he tell you, then?"

"Somewhere around six o'clock, and he worked at the show to somewhere around eight o'clock."

". . . Can you swear he mentioned either time?"

"Yes, he mentioned somewhere around six o'clock . . . He might have said when the hotel closed. He said six o'clock or something connected with six o'clock."

Some blades found in Stuart's pocket, Turner agreed, were on the table from an early stage in the interrogation.

"Those blades could be called lethal weapons?"

"Could be." But he was quite sure that nobody picked them up.

"Quite sure they did not?"

"They might have picked them up, but not to threaten him with them."

"Did you pick them up?" "Yes."

"What for?"

". . . I picked them up to examine them and find out from him why he was carrying them."

"While interrogating him about the murder which a knife had nothing to do with?"

"Yes."

Turner agreed that when Stuart was interrogated, the police had discovered the basic facts of the murder; they knew what the child was wearing, that she had been criminally assaulted, and hit on the head with, they believed, a stone. They also believed, because of the blood around the cave, that she had been killed there. "And therefore," said Starke, "if you had wished you could have put all those matters to Stuart by way of leading questions?"

"Yes."

Starke reminded the witness that he had agreed, after first denying it, that he was the first to mention, by way of a question, the removal of Stuart's trousers. "Can you recall if any other suggestion was made by way of a question to any vital matter?"

"I cannot recall any . . . I am sure there was nothing else referring to the actions of the murderer."

"The actions of the murderer?"

"Movements of the murderer, I should say."

Starke read from Jones' notes these words: "Turner said: 'Did you take her bathers off?' He said: 'Yes, I pulled them off.' "

"That has nothing to do with his movements," said Turner.

". . . Is that a serious answer?" asked Starke.

"It certainly is. I do not mean moving his arms, but moving about on the beach."

When Turner left the court, Chamberlain asked whether the witness could be released, as he was waiting to go to Melbourne on duty.

"I should be loth," said Starke, "to prevent any Adelaide citizen from going to Melbourne."

* * *

Most of Starke's questions to Constable Richard Jones related to the interrogation at Ceduna. Was it true or false that Turner picked up blades from the table? It was false. Was it true or false that Turner asked some questions about blades? False.

"Would it shake your recollection at all to hear that Turner has sworn that after the blades were put on the table he picked them up and asked Stuart some questions about them during the interrogation?"

"No, because in my memory it is false."

Jones said later that when he searched Stuart, he found no blades.

Why were six police officers present during the interrogation?

"They were all interested in the case."

"You were all tired, you had had a long day, up since five o'clock?"

"It is not usual for a police officer to shirk his duties."

". . . You played league football in two states?"

"Yes."

"The others are all pretty big police officers of various sizes?"

"Yes."

"Did it ever occur to you this might strike terror into this aboriginal's heart?" "No."

From the record of proceedings against Stuart in the police court, Starke led Jones through his evidence about how the confession was composed. Jones said he remembered having said that Stuart "dictated every word".

"Of course it isn't true, Mr. Jones, is it?" said Starke.

"Yes."

Starke suggested that there was a difference between taking down a statement word for word and composing a narrative by question and answer. When he asked Jones again if it was false to say that Stuart dictated every word, the detective replied: "Under the circumstances you put, then that is false."

Jones said that for a number of lines after the formal opening, the confession was elicited by question and answer. To the best of his memory, however, it was Stuart himself who used the word "awoke".

"In other words," said Starke, "after the dictation starts you say that most of the rest is dictated by him, save . . . two dates plus the last formal words?"

"Yes, just like he gave the account of the Alice Springs events . . ."

"Just answer the question," said the Chairman.

The phrase: "I cannot read English", Jones said, was volunteered by Stuart and was not (as Starke suggested must be "clear as crystal to a child") evoked by a question. Nor did he agree with Turner's evidence that the words: "I killed her because I did not want her to tell what I done" were the result of a question.

Why, asked Starke, had his written report included no reference to the hairs cut from Stuart's head? "Because Turner told me at Ceduna that the hairs were no value at all . . . We argued the point on this, as a matter of fact. I said they were of value and Turner said they were not."

"Do you know that Turner has told this court he considered they might be of value . . . ?"

"I do not know that, but I know he was of opinion in Ceduna that they would be no good."

Later Starke said: "You yourself, of course, have been accused of violence before this, haven't you?"

"I cannot recollect any person accusing me of violence before."

"Mr. Jones, would you like a further opportunity?"

"I suppose I have been in some cases, but I cannot recollect the cases . . . It would be unusual if a police officer wasn't accused of something like that."

A source in Ceduna, Jones said, gave against Stuart information "practically the same as we got from Whyalla—that Stuart was a person who when in drink was likely to do a murder like this one."

When Starke asked who gave this information, the Chairman ruled that Jones should not answer; "it is a matter of public policy that sources of information should not be disclosed." Starke was allowed to ask whether the source was a policeman. Jones said it was not.

Starke suggested that Stuart knew nobody in Ceduna, and asked whether the informant was a resident of the town. Chamberlain objected, and the Chairman asked Starke not to go any further. To the Chairman, Jones said that the information came to the police about six o'clock on Monday night, from only one person. Starke submitted that "if some person in Ceduna was saying things about Stuart which are a mere invention, it may be very relevant to find out who the poisoned mind is."

* * *

Jones was followed into the box by Detective Frank Whitrod. Again Starke asked about blades. He himself saw none, Whitrod said.

"Did Turner pick them up?"

"I did not see him."

"Stuart says he did. Is that true or false?"

"Quite false."

"Does it shock your recollection that not only Stuart says it, but Turner himself says it?"

"That does not shock my recollection at all." But if Turner said the blades were there, Whitrod added later, then they were there.

Starke's questions moved from Ceduna to Port Lincoln. He had been, Whitrod agreed, a member of the committee of the R.S.L. club in Port Lincoln, which had no liquor licence; he had drunk beer there on Friday nights, and as a committee member he had approved of the illegal sale of liquor after six o'clock.

"You, the man who, to put it colloquially, knocked off Mr. Wardrop for illegally selling liquor?"

"That is so."

During the discussion on whether Whitrod had taken the law into his own hands, the Chairman said to Starke: "I am not interfering with your cross-examination, but there are some things that excite one's sympathy."

Starke said that he would be the last man not to sympathise with R.S.L. activities; "but I am not a member of the police force, and here is a man who, as the evidence shows, raided and convicted a witness here and is doing exactly the same thing himself."

Whitrod agreed that he had visited the Wardrops' premises for a few meals since the proprietor's prosecution on a charge involving liquor. There was no apparent hostility. He denied that he had drunk wine at Wardrop's café after hours, that he had taken bottles away, and that he had consumed food and wine there without payment. There might have been a conversation with the Wardrops late one night in their kitchen, and he might have answered some questions from them about the case. He could have told the Wardrops that Sonny Jim said: "Him do it," and that Stuart had confessed. But he denied having said that the police belted Stuart. On the Friday evening after the murder, he and Baker and Wardrop could have been drinking at the bar of the R.S.L. club.

Starke reminded the witness that according to Wardrop he had said Stuart "got his corner". Whitrod said that he knew the phrase implied a man getting the proceeds of something. Starke suggested that a man who served on the lower deck in the wartime Navy, as Whitrod had done, must have heard the phrase used to mean "got a belting".

"No," said Whitrod. "I don't know that at all."

When Starke asked about the composition of Stuart's confession, Whitrod, unlike Jones, said that the words: "I killed her because I did not want her to tell what I done" and: "I cannot read English" were the result of question and answer.

There now occurred a passage of cross-examination in which the answers surprised many people who had followed the case.

"Do you say," asked Starke, "there was an officer of the Department of Native Affairs[4] present during the interrogation?"

"He wasn't present during the interrogation, I don't think. . . . I know there was a native welfare officer outside the room during some time, and whether he came inside at any stage I do not know . . . I think I would have seen him if he had come in the room."

Did Whitrod remember having said recently, in Port Lincoln: "How could we have bashed him; there was an officer of the Welfare Department present?"

Whitrod said that he did not remember saying this, but he would not deny it; "I may have said something like that."

When Dr. Charles Duguid and others had deplored the absence of a welfare officer during the interrogation, no reply came from the Aborigines Department. If the welfare officer of the Aborigines Department based on Ceduna, Mr. A. R. A. Kleinig, had been present at the interrogation, as Whitrod now implied was not impossible, why had the Crown not produced him? If, as Whitrod thought more likely, he was at the station but not present at the interrogation, why had he not been invited in to observe it? Why had no other policeman

[4] The correct title is Aborigines Department.

mentioned the welfare officer? Why had the Aborigines Department itself been so reticent? Later evidence was to throw some light on the problem, but not to solve it.

Starke changed the subject. Did Whitrod know a young lawyer named Cameron Stewart, and did he remember the case of a man called Kranz three or four years ago? To both questions Whitrod answered negatively.

Did he remember saying at the time of this case, in the presence of Cameron Stewart, that he did not like examining women, because in the presence of a woman police officer "you cannot hit them over the head with a rubber hose"?

"I would deny saying anything like that."

"Do you remember Cameron Stewart saying he did not believe such things ever happened, and your saying: 'Listen, lad, if you don't treat them like that, you would not get anywhere'?"

"No, this conversation is entirely incorrect. I would say it is a lie."

"Well, you cannot even remember Cameron Stewart?"

"I certainly cannot."

"So you cannot know why Cameron Stewart should have any feeling against you, can you?"

"No."[5]

* * *

Sergeant William Low, the C.I.B. photographer who went to Ceduna, entered the box again. No attempt had been made, he said, to photograph footprints near the cave. It would not have been difficult to photograph them or to make plaster casts, but he had not considered either of these things worth doing; so far as he could recall, the possibility of taking photographs or plaster casts was not discussed.[6] During the interrogation of Stuart, Low agreed, it was said that he had scratches on his back. It would have been possible to photograph scratches found on Stuart's back, but that was not done.[7]

Low was invited to inspect a police photograph of Stuart through a magnifying glass. Starke suggested that over Stuart's right eye, Low

[5] On the day after this cross-examination occurred, a Mr. Cameron Stewart, formerly of Adelaide, appeared in court at Alice Springs on behalf of a part-aboriginal drover who pleaded not guilty to a charge of drunkenness and alleged that he had been assaulted by two uniformed native trackers while white policemen watched. "Australians today," said the Melbourne *Herald* in an editorial on the case, "are increasingly sensitive to any suspicion of police discrimination against coloured people." The trackers were dismissed from the Northern Territory Police Force, charged with common assault, and convicted. A white sergeant was reduced in rank and a constable fined.

[6] Low was here differing from Turner (see p. 231 above).

[7] At the trial (see p. 28 above), Low said that the scratches were not a suitable subject for photography.

would see a white mark, which had nothing to do with this case, and another mark as of a recent cut. Low said that he could see only a white mark.

No welfare officer of the Aborigines Department, Low said positively, was present during any part of the interrogation. He believed that a blade was taken from Stuart's pocket, but he did not see Turner pick it up.

"Stuart has sworn that Turner picked this blade up . . . Are you prepared to contradict Stuart's oath on that point?"

"As far as I can, yes."

"Stuart has sworn that he was threatened with it. Are you prepared to deny that?"

"He definitely wasn't threatened with it." He had seen a suggestion in the papers that Turner picked it up; and if Turner said so, he believed him.

Starke said that it was totally contradictory of Low to deny Stuart's assertion that Turner picked up a blade, but to accept the assertion when it came from Turner. At first Low did not allow that there was a contradiction, but after a time he agreed that there was.

Low knew that according to Sonny Jim, someone said, when bringing Stuart from the police station to have his footprints taken, that this was the man who killed the little girl.

"And is that true or false?"

After a pause which Starke suggested was fifteen seconds and which Low agreed was "very, very appreciable", he said: "Well, I do not know. I did not hear it said."

Why, asked Starke, had he paused so long?

"I was thinking whether I had heard it or not."

Low agreed that it would have struck him at once as an unfair thing to do.

"But because of its impropriety," said Starke, "you could not have forgotten such a thing?"

"It is possible I could forget it."

"You were struggling with your conscience then. You heard it, didn't you?"

"I did not hear it said at all."

". . . Are you sure, or is it just that you cannot remember, that you saw no violence at all that night?"

"I saw no violence at all."

"But you are not sure that there was no violence in that room that night?"

"Yes, I was there all the time."

"If you did see violence, would your loyalty allow you to say so?"

"Yes, I am certain of it."

"You have been worried during the last few weeks, haven't you?"

"Not unduly."

The last of the C.I.B. men from Adelaide left the box for the last time.

* * *

Constable Howard Herde, who was stationed at Thevenard at the time of the murder and who gave evidence at the preliminary hearing and the trial, was called at Starke's request. With Constable Green, he said, he had arrested Stuart on the Saturday night; he saw no blood on Stuart's white overalls, and no sign that they had been washed recently; Stuart was not drunk and shcwed no alarm. He denied Sonny Jim's testimony that the police described Stuart as the murderer before his footprints were taken.

"I suppose up to that point you thought highly of Sonny Jim, didn't you?"

"He is another native."

"A black tracker, and he told lies about the police?"

"He is another native."

The activity of the welfare officer, Kleinig, became a little clearer during cross-examination of Herde. On the Monday night, the witness said, Kleinig came to the police station just before Stuart was brought out from the room where he was interrogated.

Herde did not agree with a suggestion by Starke that around Thevenard there were half-caste girls of slack morals, whom it was known a native could get.

* * *

Constable John Fairweather was brought from Port Lincoln. On the night of the interrogation, he told Starke, he saw no blades. No blade had been picked up, nor had Turner asked Stuart any question about blades. Fairweather agreed that a few days before giving evidence he had been drinking in Port Lincoln with Mr. Horace Baker (whose testimony had conflicted with Wardrop's). They did not, however, discuss aspects of what they would say. "The main thing we were wondering was what Mr. O'Sullivan was doing in Port Lincoln."

"Did Baker remark that you cannot get into trouble if you say 'Yes' or 'No' in the witness box?"

"I cannot remember him saying that."

To a number of questions about events at Ceduna, Fairweather replied that his recollection was not clear.

Sergeant N. L. Walker, now at Burra and formerly in charge at Ceduna, was questioned by Starke about the arrest of Stuart on Saturday and the interrogation on Monday. Was it not horrifying for the police to think they could arrest and release a man without charging him? "Do you regard it under any circumstances a proper action on your part to deprive a man of his liberty without charging him?"

"Not under normal circumstances," said Walker, "but on that occasion it could not be helped." No written record was made of

Stuart's first arrest and release. "I can only plead that . . . I had a very busy time trying to search for the body of the girl, then knowing that the body of the girl had been found, and then preparing for the C.I.B. men when they came around the next morning, and I didn't write my journal in for, I think, two days."

Walker was still giving evidence when the Commission adjourned for the day. Next morning, October 20, Starke asked him what information had come from Phin in Whyalla on the Monday evening.

"Must I answer that?" the witness asked the Commissioners.

"Yes," said the Chairman.

"Phin phoned," said Walker, "and said that he had spoken to some of the circus personnel at Whyalla, and that one of the former employees, a man named Stuart, had been dismissed or sacked—he used that word—on the Saturday afternoon. He also said that Stuart was a man inclined to violence when he was in drink. . . . That is all he said . . ."

"What was it in the information you got from Phin," asked Starke, "that materially added to the information you already had so as to put him [Stuart] in the category of a definite suspect?"

"Only that Sonny Jim said the footprints were of an educated native."

". . . The real thing, I suppose, coming from Phin, was that he was violent towards women, the sort of man who might commit this crime. I suppose that was the first thing that struck you in the eye?"

"Yes."

Starke showed Walker that his written account, in the station journal, of Phin's report contained no suggestion at all that Stuart was violent towards women when in drink. Nor was there in the journal any reference to Sonny Jim having said that the prints on the beach were those of an educated native. It attributed to Phin only the information that "Stuart had received the sack for drinking on Sunday morning." Walker himself had written: "The information . . . tied up with pair of showman's dark trousers with red braid attached found on the beach near the scene of the murder. Stuart now definite suspect." Starke quoted Turner's evidence that as soon as he saw these trousers he realised that they had nothing to do with the murder and had obviously been there for weeks. Walker said he had agreed with Turner.

"Why did you associate the information passed on by Detective-Sergeant Phin with the trousers which you now swear you knew had nothing to do with the murder?"

"It was just a hunch . . ."

"It was a hunch contrary to what you believed?"

"I thought it could be a possibility . . ."

Walker said, unlike every other policeman so far except Turner, that he saw blades on the table while Stuart was being interrogated. He did not see them in Turner's hands, he did not know what happened to them later, and he could not account for the absence of any reference to them in the property book.

Walker said he did not catch Stuart by the throat or choke him. He saw no violence done. To Brazel, before withdrawing, he said that when he brought Stuart from the cell to be charged on Tuesday morning, there was no sign of any cut in his right eyebrow.

* * *

Dr. G. C. H. Nicol, medical officer at the gaol, was recalled and cross-examined on two things: Stuart's appearance when he examined him on arrival, and the medical evidence for virginity. He agreed with Starke that Stuart had thick, bushy eyebrows; he had seen no healing cut in one of the eyebrows, but he would not say that it was not there. He found it very difficult to believe that a woman who had been a prostitute for three months, as mentioned in a textbook of forensic medicine quoted by Starke, could have an unruptured hymen; but he would not deny it. He himself had seen an unruptured hymen in a pregnant woman.

Brazel questioned him further. "How many cases, in your experience, if any, have you had of an unruptured hymen following coitus?"

"Only one that I remember."

"Out of thousands of cases?"

"I wouldn't say thousands."

"Speaking as a medical practitioner of wide experience, what would you say as to the probabilities if you found an unruptured hymen in a girl fourteen to fifteen: that she had or had not had sexual experience?"

"I would say that she had not."

Mr. D. C. Aebi, the head of police photography, returned to discuss photographs of Stuart which, he now said, he had examined with a glass a little more powerful than Starke's and with a microscope. Starke suggested that the witness could see in one photograph a cut like an open mouth over the right eye.

"No, I can't see a mouth," said Aebi.

Starke and Aebi both looked at a negative of the same picture, which, Starke said, showed the cut much more clearly. Aebi said he could see nothing. If he looked more carefully, Starke said, Aebi would see "a little black mark . . ." "I see a little black mark on the negative, possibly about the same consistency as the darkness of the skin fairly close to it." In his view, Aebi told Chamberlain, the mark was an old scar. Each of the Commissioners peered at the negative in turn through Starke's glass, without comment.

Mr. Allan Wardrop was wearing his R.S.L. badge when he entered the box for the second time. Starke explained that he would give evidence on several matters which he had been unable to tell Their Honours about when he appeared earlier. He told Starke that on July 10 (four days after the respite granted for an approach to the

Privy Council), he went to see his brother-in-law, Mr. Jack Fahey, a sub-editor on the *News*, and told him: "I know Stuart got a hiding." Fahey thumped the table and said: "I say hang the boong." Then and later, Fahey urged him to stay out of the affair. On the Wednesday after the Commission first met (that is, on August 12), Fahey rang. He seemed to think now that what Wardrop had said was of some importance, and suggested that he see Miss Devaney. Wardrop replied that he would go not to Stuart's representatives but to "the proper authorities". When he gave evidence at the Commission, he had not seen any of Stuart's lawyers.

At Starke's invitation Wardrop spoke about his relations with Whitrod. It was three or four years, he said, since Whitrod initiated a charge against him under the liquor laws. He regarded Whitrod as having done his duty; since then he had persuaded Whitrod to stand for the committee of the R.S.L.

Starke, himself an advocate in courts martial in the Middle East, asked Wardrop about his conviction there during the war.

"How many of you were charged?"

"Fifty-seven." They were charged with mutiny for refusing to go on parade. He was sentenced to imprisonment for thirteen months. The officer concerned in the incident was later court-martialled and imprisoned for five years. Wardrop and his fellows were unconditionally pardoned and given an honourable discharge.

Chamberlain asked Wardrop whether he had informed Stuart's solicitors about "the liquor activities of the R.S.L. at Port Lincoln".

"No, Mr. Starke asked me what the position was . . . and I told him."

". . . You know that there is a sort of gentleman's understanding about this question?"

"I have always known that."

"But you always tell the truth in any circumstances?"

"Yes."

Chamberlain asked how he came to be involved in the mutiny.

"For accepting a captain's invitation to go aboard his ship and come back to Australia," Wardrop replied.

Had he been prosecuted for desertion?

"They called it desertion, but I was not enjoying the flesh pots of Egypt, but was in the wilds of New Guinea. When I explained it, they said they would charge me with being A.W.L." He was in custody on this charge at the time of the mutiny. After being discharged from prison he did no more service; "I was a mental and physical wreck."

Brazel asked if Wardrop had learned how Shand attributed to him the assertion that a policeman said: "We bashed it out of the black bastard." Wardrop told this story: "My brother-in-law rang me on the Wednesday morning and said: 'Why don't you see Miss Devaney?' I said: 'Not on your life. I will go to the proper authorities.' He said:

'I have told Rivett and Rivett told me to bring you over from Port Lincoln.' . . . I said: 'I do not want anything. I am going to the Commission.' I did." Then on the Monday morning his brother-in-law, Fahey, rang. After being assured that the *News* would not print anything about it ("We can only put in the paper what is said in court," Fahey said), Wardrop said he had been to the Commission. Apparently Fahey told somebody at the *News*, and the *News* told Shand.

"You said something to your brother-in-law," asked Brazel, "which he has interpreted as the version Mr. Shand used?"

"That is my explanation."

Wardrop left the court-room while Baker, secretary of the R.S.L. at Port Lincoln, was questioned about a telephone conversation between himself and Wardrop on August 12, the day Fahey urged Wardrop to approach Miss Devaney.

At this time, Baker agreed, he and Wardrop were mates. Early in the telephone conversation they discussed matters relating to a sub-branch of the R.S.L. He denied that Wardrop said: "Horrie, do you remember one night when we were down at the R.S.L. and Whitrod came in and . . . told us that Stuart had got a hiding?" According to him the conversation went as follows: "He said: 'I am worried about this murder case.' I said: 'What connexion is that with you?' He said: 'You remember Frank Whitrod saying they bashed this chap?' I said: 'Allan, I have never heard that. You are romancing.' That was the end, the time signal came and we finished . . . The whole conversation would not be much more than a three-minute call."

Starke produced a receipt which showed that the call lasted nine minutes. Baker suggested that some of the time might have been taken up finding him. "I don't sit on the phone all day."

Baker agreed that he had been a friend of Wardrop's for years, and that he was "on quite a friendly basis" with Whitrod. If Wardrop was telling a downright lie, said Starke, "there was no particular reason to pick on you to associate you in such a thing?"

"No."

When Starke suggested that Wardrop had never struck him as a stupid man, Baker replied that he had, often; "he has had a motion of censure passed against him, and he is the only one in the sub-branch who has had a time-limit put on him . . ."

"He talks too much?"

"Yes, and too much rot."

"You are extremely hostile to him?"

"Not now, always . . . More so at the moment."

". . . You had a go at him outside the court yesterday, didn't you?"

"I spoke to him after he spoke to me first. It was something I tried to avoid."

Was it Baker's view that Wardrop, having got a flat denial from him that the conversation with Whitrod took place, was so silly as to go to the solicitor and make statements involving Baker up to the hilt?

Yes, that was his view; "that is what amazed me."

Wardrop now gave his version of the telephone conversation. "Did you have to wait to get on?" asked Starke. "No, I got through practically immediately . . . I asked Horrie if he remembered that night when we were in the R.S.L. and Whitrod came in and he told us that Stuart had got a hiding, and he said: 'Eh', and paused. He said: 'I have got a faint recollection, yes, that is right, what about it?' I said: 'Well, Horrie, I have worried and worried and worried about it, I think I had better go and tell the Commission.' He said: 'You don't want to do that, all this new evidence that has come up . . . it looks as if Stuart is going to get out of it, it looks to me as if this young lad Allan Moir did it.' I said: 'Be that as it may, I am still going to go along to the Commission.' He said: 'Well, you have always been in trouble, you may as well be in some more.' I said: 'Well, I am going, anyway.' "

To Brazel, Wardrop said he thought that about three minutes of the conversation was devoted to the Royal Commission and the rest to other matters.

* * *

After an adjournment for lunch, Phin was recalled. Starke asked him to recapitulate what he had heard from Gieseman in Whyalla, and said: "You did not bother to check up on what time or times Gieseman had seen Stuart during the weekend, did you?"

"No, sir."[8]

"And you did not discuss any hotel closing time with Gieseman, did you?"

"No, sir."

Phin then repeated what he said Moir had told him on the Monday evening.

"Did he say to you that Maxie returned to the circus on the Saturday?"

"Yes, sir, I think he did."

"Did you pass this information on to anyone that evening?"

"Yes."

The most important matters spoken about by Moir were, he thought, the blood on the chest and Stuart's reference to having "done someone over". When Starke read out from the station journal a report of information from Whyalla, Phin said that the note did not cover all that the police at Ceduna had been told. He himself had told them of Stuart's question to Moir about blood on the chest.

The last two witnesses to be called at Starke's request, the taxi-driver Blackham and Constable Green, were flying from Ceduna and could not appear until the next day. The Chairman suggested to Brazel another possible witness; "we are a little puzzled about this

[8] Turner's evidence (see p. 234 above) differed here.

welfare officer Kleinig; where is he, and can we hear what he was doing on the Monday night?" Brazel said that he was in Ceduna, and that a statement had been taken from him which would be tendered tomorrow; he did not think Kleinig could assist the Commission. "I suspected at one stage that he was present at the police station in the interests of Stuart to see he received counsel or protection. But it is plain that that was not the purpose of his being brought there at all." In an affidavit tendered next morning and signed on July 31, Kleinig said that on Monday evening Sergeant Walker asked him to come to the police station, and there requested him to follow up a remark by Stuart about a man named Lennie and a leather-cutting knife. Kleinig went out to Koonibba mission, and returned to the police station about 1.30 a.m.[9] He waited outside the open doorway of the office. He saw Stuart seated and Whitrod typing; he also saw Turner and Jones. He heard no loud voices. As he stood outside the door with Constables Herde and Green, one of them said that Stuart had confessed. He never spoke to Stuart.

Chamberlain suggested that when addresses by counsel began, Starke should go first. Since he himself was defending "the status quo and the police force and the institutions of government" he should hear what was to be said against them before he addressed them.

Starke submitted that he should follow Chamberlain, because he had two opponents. "Mr. Brazel has not been the friendliest of friends, indeed he has taken the Crown case pretty well under his wing, although not with the same vehemence as Mr. Chamberlain."

"His position has been that of Judge Advocate," said the Chairman.[10]

The tenor of Brazel's conduct, said Starke, had been hostile to Stuart. There was no reason why it should not have been; but it seemed hard that he should be replied to twice.

The Chairman ruled that Chamberlain should address first, then Starke, then Brazel.

• • •

On the morning of Wednesday, October 21, the last day on which the Commission heard evidence, there was a bewildering episode. Starke proffered a witness. Brazel looked at a note of what the witness

[9] Brazel said that this must have been a mistake, as P.M.G. records showed that Turner called C.I.B. headquarters, reporting that Stuart had signed a confession, at 11.45 p.m.

[10] A Judge Advocate appears at a court martial "to superintend the proceedings, . . . to advise the court on points of law, of custom, and of form, and so far to assist the prisoner as to elicit a full statement of the facts material to the defence" (Earl Jowitt: *The Dictionary of English Law*). A correspondent of the *Observer* thought that Brazel seemed rather to represent "a third party, the South Australian way of life, against the various wise men from the East".

intended to say, and reported that his evidence "casts doubt upon the validity of the confession by direct reference to the circumstances in which it was said to be obtained". The man's name was McGuffie. "I first saw him at ten this morning," said Starke. ". . . He was a member of the Criminal Investigation Branch. He is now a taxi-driver." He alleged, said Starke, that he had conversed with Constable Jones some two or three weeks after the murder, in the Gresham Hotel at Adelaide, and that Jones there made "a most material admission". He had regarded the conversation as in confidence, "and it did not concern him much because he was informed that Stuart was guilty all right. By chance last night he met my instructing solicitor in a cab . . . They had a conversation which, I understand now, caused him to doubt Stuart's guilt, and as soon as that doubt reached his mind he informed my instructing solicitor of this conversation, wrote it in a letter which was received this morning, and repeated it to me this morning."

The Chairman and Brazel each pointed out that it was many weeks since members of the public who felt that they could assist had been invited to come forward. "He has come before the evidence has ceased," said Starke; "what does it matter whether it was the first day or the twentieth day?"

The Commissioners adjourned to consider whether they would hear McGuffie, and decided to do so. In that case, said Brazel, Their Honours might consider whether Stuart should be examined further about conversations (the alleged admissions to warders) which, a few days ago, it had been decided to exclude. "I put that most earnestly," said Brazel, "because it does seem to me that to permit . . . the testimony of the police to be assailed upon this crucial point and not . . . to permit . . . statements of a similar nature to be extracted in relation to Stuart . . . is a little one-sided." The Chairman said that they were carrying tenderness to Stuart to extremes; he was troubled by the considerations Brazel had urged.

Starke said that evidence similar to McGuffie's against one of the police officers had been given already by Wardrop when the Commissioners decided not to hear about Stuart's alleged admissions. Wardrop, the Chairman observed, had come forward as people had been invited to do. "This has the appearance of a partisan witness . . . He comes as a witness for one side, not as a witness to assist the Commission by telling the truth."

"There is no particular vice," said Starke, "in a witness coming before the court on one side or another."

"But one must realise in the case of Wardrop he did come to the Commission," said the Chairman.

"Surely this is a matter of argument as to weight," said Starke.

"It may be," said the Chairman.

Starke suggested that the evidence of the warders had been ruled out "because of the special nature of the relationship and the circumstances of the alleged admission" and it would not be a fair thing to re-open the ruling just because more evidence of a certain type came along. "I do not propose to tender this witness if I am still at risk of Your Honours reconsidering the decision which I understood had been made and which I believed was final . . ."

"I don't know whether you think it would be a good bargain," the Chairman said to Starke, "to tender this witness with the risk of that being re-opened. We have had a look at the witness"—McGuffie was present during most of this discussion, but had now left the room at Chamberlain's suggestion—"and may I say that so far as I am concerned, I doubt whether you will be well advised."

"I seem to be looking right down the muzzle of a gun," said Starke.

"I am afraid you are," said the Chairman.

Starke withdrew his application, saying: "it should not be taken that in any way I am now doubting the instructions we received . . . In view of Your Honour's intimation, in view of the fact that Your Honours would not be very impressed with the witness, I feel his evidence would not be of very great value to me . . ."

No more was heard of McGuffie. Why, in fact, had he not come forward sooner? Starke's answer was that only on the previous evening had the man come to doubt Stuart's guilt; but if—as would seem likely—he was following the proceedings with some interest, what crucial information or argument could have come fresh to him so late? What did the Chairman mean when he said that, having looked at the witness, he doubted whether Starke would be advised to call him? One thing was clear: once the Chairman indicated that whatever it was he alleged against Jones would carry little or no weight, Stuart's case could not be helped by having both his evidence and the evidence of the warders admitted.

* * *

Chamberlain recalled Dr. D. M. Williamson, who had examined Olive Betts, and whom he now asked to comment on the passages from a work on forensic medicine which Starke had put to another practitioner. An unruptured hymen after coitus, Williamson said, was pretty rare, and in this case he did not think that the condition of the hymen was consistent with her being one of those rare examples.

Dennis Blackham, the youth who drove Stuart to Thevenard, had arrived from Ceduna. He told Brazel that on the Saturday he worked from nine o'clock in the morning until he had lunch about half past one. Approximately half an hour later he was called by telephone to Spry's shop, where about a quarter past two he picked up Stuart and a younger companion. As at the preliminary hearing and at the trial, Blackham said that the boy got out at the fun-fair and that Stuart went on to Thevenard where, Stuart said, he wanted to find a girl. It was, he thought, about half past two when he dropped Stuart at Thevenard. The boy paid him at the fun-fair; and Stuart paid him at Thevenard.

To Starke, the witness said that he had no written record at Ceduna to help him remember dates, times or other facts. He had conferred that morning with the solicitor instructing Brazel, who read over "a bit" of his evidence at the trial.

"The bit relating to times?" "Yes."

Starke showed Blackham that at the preliminary hearing, he had said that Stuart paid him not at Thevenard but at the fun-fair. Blackham agreed that "one's recollection of events does get blurred by time . . .", and that such things as the paying of money were "easier to remember than clock times". He agreed, too, that his dinner might have been finished on that day by one o'clock.

"The police came to you about three weeks after the murder?" "Yes."

". . . It wasn't until then that you first realised that the man you had driven to Thevenard must have been the man who committed the murder?"

"Yes."

". . . Do you agree that time is the most difficult of all things to remember, even after twenty-four hours?"

"Yes."

"You had no particular reason for remembering Stuart, did you?"

"No."

"It may be with the number of trips you took to Thevenard that quite honestly you are mistaken about the time you picked him up? That may be so?"

"Yes."

"And if I put it to you that it might have been one o'clock when you picked him up, that might be true, mightn't it?"

"Yes."

On sexual opportunities at Thevenard Blackham gave different evidence from that of Herde, the policeman who had been stationed there. From what he heard in the taxi, Blackham agreed, he believed that there were young girls in the vicinity of the Thevenard Hotel whom coloured people used to visit for immoral purposes. He had given similar evidence at the trial.

Constable Leonard Green, of Ceduna, was the last of forty-five witnesses. Chamberlain examined him first.

Had he seen any knives or blades around the station?

Yes, he had seen some blades on the sergeant's table when he cleared the office on the morning after Stuart's arrest. He did not know what had happened to them.

The witness told Starke that he and Herde were waiting with the trackers in the yard of the police station when the interrogating officers came out with Stuart. At that time he did not hear any policeman say, as the trackers testified, that Stuart was the murderer.

"Was Mr. Kleinig with you while you were waiting outside?"

". . . No, I did not see Mr. Kleinig at all that night."

From Kleinig's affidavit, Starke read a passage stating that he was standing with Constables Green and Herde, and that one of the constables told him Stuart had confessed.

"I cannot remember Kleinig standing out there," said Green. ". . . I did not see him there." He did not say that Stuart had confessed. Until Stuart was brought out, he did not know that Stuart had confessed.[11]

A series of questions from Starke about the blades elicited no more relevant information than Green had given to Chamberlain; he found them in the office on Tuesday morning, and he had no idea what had happened to them. Nobody had asked him about them until yesterday.

* * *

"As far as I know," said Brazel, "unless my friend pulls another rabbit out of the hat before tomorrow, that concludes the evidence which Your Honours will be asked to consider."

Addresses by counsel began on the afternoon of the next day, October 22.

[11] There appears to be a conflict here with Kleinig's affidavit (see p. 247 above).

19

LAST WORDS FROM COUNSEL

Chamberlain argued that the new material reinforced a case against Stuart that was already overwhelming at the trial; and the trial, he observed, had been three times examined in courts of appeal without being questioned. The information subsequently put forward about the alibi, the prisoner's command of English, and the conduct of the police, would not have been regarded by courts of appeal as new evidence. Nevertheless, "the government did take steps to have it examined in case it might have some substance and in the expectation or the hope perhaps that the outburst of ill-informed criticism which by then had blown up, might be satisfied . . ." The Commission had proceeded with almost miraculous patience, until at last Stuart was really represented by counsel who made a straight issue of all the possible evidence. "In my submission, it has fallen short—in view of the fuss which has been made about it, ludicrously short—of establishing anything which throws any real doubt on the conviction. Indeed, as the enquiry proceeded, so far from any doubt being cast on the jury's finding, more and more circumstances emerged which fitted in with it and confirmed it."

The evidence of Moir was an example. He must have figured in certain minds as a possible substitute murderer. "I can't think of any other special reason why Mr. Rivett should have taken the trouble to have a special interview with him and drag out of him all the discreditable material which was put in a declaration given to us by the courtesy of Mr. Shand." However poor Moir was as a witness, "there is something in his not very bright intelligence, something that is a little hard to get around, in his talk about Stuart's conversation about the disposition of the dead body. Something went on that put that idea into Moir's mind." The evidence of the aboriginal witnesses established that Stuart caught a taxi from Spry's shop as Spry and Blackham deposed, that he was not at the sideshow but at Thevenard in the early or middle afternoon, that he came up from the direction of the beach late in the afternoon, and that he spoke to his friend about having had a virgin on the beach. Shand had asked why these people, knowing what they knew, did not go to the police. The answer was that to them the police were more or less natural enemies.

Strehlow had said this was not a black man's crime. Like so much of his evidence, this was "a wild and baseless assumption". It was the crime of a savage, whatever the colour of his skin might be. Stuart was a man whom alcohol stimulated to strong and uncontrollable impulses towards women, irrespective of their condition and age, and a man cunning enough to produce appropriate lies. Moreover, there were trends running through Stuart's other cases, in Cloncurry and Alice Springs, to the confession in this case.[1]

There was no new evidence against the police except that of the Wardrops. What could O'Sullivan have done with Wardrop's statement if it had been in his hands at the time of the trial? It could have been used only to attack Whitrod's credit, not to attack the credit of any other policeman; and by no stretch of imagination could a statement about violence after a confession have been described as relevant to the issue. In any case, Wardrop was completely irresponsible. Baker, a very sound and sensible man, said that Wardrop talked too much: would Whitrod be so silly as to put himself in the power of this man? It had taken Wardrop a long time to decide that his conscience prompted him to come forward. To the solicitor and the Commission he gave differing versions of what Whitrod had said, and he could not appreciate what the difference was. "I hesitate to think that the whole thing was a concoction. I prefer to think there was a conversation with Wardrop when Whitrod came back . . ."

"How could it have got on to the subject of violence?" asked Mr. Justice Reed.

"I can see how it could get on," said Sir Mellis Napier.

Chamberlain said Wardrop had a chip on his shoulder because of his career in the army and his dealings with the police. The most charitable explanation was that he had a distorted recollection of an innocent conversation, in which someone might have said to Whitrod: "You might have done him over, Frank," and Whitrod could have replied: "Would not have done him any harm if we did."

"Or: 'he deserved it'," said Mr. Justice Reed.

Chamberlain agreed, and added: "I would not like to speculate or try and estimate what goes on in a mind like Mr. Wardrop's."

The next thing which had not been before the court was Strehlow's evidence that Stuart could not have composed the confession. If one thing rather than another was the source of all the troubles in this case, it was the remark of the High Court that it caused them some anxiety. "It was based on two things—on Mr. O'Sullivan's protestations to them that he only got this statement from Stuart in broken pidgin English and with the greatest difficulty, and . . ." Here Starke interrupted to say that Chamberlain should not speculate about why the High Court judges made their observation.

"I should find some difficulty in attributing it to anything else," said the Chairman.

[1] Starke was to allege that Chamberlain had made improper use of material admitted as evidence of Stuart's linguistic ability.

Chamberlain said that it could not have been anything other than O'Sullivan's protestations and Strehlow's affidavit. It was unfortunate that the affidavit was there, and that it was not answered by the ample evidence which had since been produced. As Strehlow said, the best transcriber would inevitably give a little flavour of his own style to what he was taking down. "For instance, a word like 'awoke', now I do not suppose Stuart said that word." But apart from things of that sort, Strehlow condemned the confession on a number of grounds. At the head of the list was that the times were given, white man's times, which aborigines did not know. Yet Stuart calmly looked at the clock and told the time, and said in support of the alibi that he looked at watches during the afternoon. Strehlow said that an aborigine could not have given correct personal pronouns as in the confession. When Stuart was giving the pantomime performance with the tape-recorder he played up to that reasonably well; "but when he came to give his evidence in the box, and perhaps forgetting himself a little, his personal pronouns were not so bad." Stuart's performance in the box, when he told the story about assaulting a nurse in Alice Springs, completely belied Strehlow's view that the man could not give a connected narrative. Strehlow told the Commission that he explained to Stuart the document about violation of professional privilege and ministerial ineptitude. ("I was wondering how one puts that into Aranda," said the Chairman.) If Strehlow liked to assure the Commission that Stuart could understand that, it was a pretty good indication of his impression of Stuart's intelligence.

If a couple of police officers had it in mind to assault a man, they would not be silly enough to bring in the local sergeant—"one who is more like an administrative officer in a country town than a police officer," the local junior hard out of training college, and another junior from Port Lincoln, and the fingerprint man, without troubling to coach any of them up as to what they should say. "If this was a conspiracy to fake the evidence, it was mightily strangely executed."

In the verbal interrogation as reported by the police, Stuart was driven into a number of changes of ground, "until the mention of tracks, to a man like Stuart who knew all about tracks and who had had experience with tracker witnesses, forced him into a lying attempt to try to explain the tracks away by a story of a white man forcing him to carry the body into the cave. That is exploded by the condition of the cave. He then turns to the story that he must have done it but does not remember, and then he says he remembered but would not have done it but for the drink, and then he gave details which he could not really have known unless he committed the crime . . ."

It was difficult to work the suggested allegations of violence into this picture. Were lies tortured out of Stuart one by one? "One could understand the allegation of a number of policemen threatening him and berating him until he says: 'All right, I did it' . . . but it is a little difficult to fit in to the way the police gave that evidence anything other than the theory that it is either true or it is a cold-blooded and murderous invention." In cross-examination Stuart made the vital admission that he told the police the lie about the white man forcing him to carry the body into the cave. "It was a surprise probably to Your Honours, it was to me, and I stopped and made it perfectly plain, he repeated it two or three times to make it perfectly plain, that he meant to concede that he had told the police that lie."

If the police had beaten Stuart into submission they would be unlikely to spoil it all next morning by asking him, as Turner had: "Is this the stone with which you killed the little girl and are these her bathers?" and having him protest that he had made no such admissions. Blows of the sort Stuart alleged must, moreover, have left traces. Yet nobody who saw him soon afterwards noticed any sign of violence. The photographs taken when he reached Adelaide showed no sign of it. The mark alleged by Starke "does not exist except in the imagination of people who want to see it". There remained nothing but Stuart's word for the allegations of violence, against the testimony of all the police officers, who were subjected to a cross-examination of the greatest skill. Starke had all the arts of a cross-examiner, "including the dominating finger, the rather raised voice down to the dreamy voice, the confidential chat as between good friends . . ." It was the last of these arts that young Blackham fell for.

Chamberlain had been speaking for two hours when the Commission adjourned until Friday, October 23. He carried on for some forty-five minutes on that day.

The police might be open to criticism, he said, on aspects of their investigation; but the question still remained whether they were telling the truth. There was undoubtedly a conflict between Phin and Turner about what Phin said over the telephone from Whyalla. Where Phin thought he mentioned the body and the dinghy, Turner said nothing about it. One or other must be mistaken, but neither had any reason to lie about it. There was no doubt that the information from Phin was sufficient to combine with what the police knew already to make Stuart a definite suspect. Nor was there anything sinister in the evidence of the police about blades. Turner admitted picking up one of the blades and asking Stuart about it; other officers, except Walker and Green, had no recollection of them. This very conflict of evidence might help to show that the blades had not been used improperly; for if they had, and if there had been a conspiracy to conceal the fact, the policemen would not have risked telling different stories.

Chamberlain turned to "the so-called alibi . . . the real reason for the setting up of this Commission". Dixon was without doubt sincere, but he was no Father Brown. Examined beside Stuart's own story, the alibi was a complete fiasco. "The sideshow evidence . . . broke down by reason of its own absurdities and contradictions, but it broke down for the even better reason that all along it was flatly in conflict with Stuart's own story." Stuart and O'Sullivan both knew at the preliminary hearing that, according to Blackham, it was about two o'clock when he picked up Stuart. They also knew that the child had disappeared in mid-afternoon. There were three months before the trial in which to investigate carefully Stuart's movements over this period. Yet in the statement Stuart planned to give to the jury there was no hint that Blackham's time was wrong. O'Sullivan, in cross-examining the doctor at the trial, was trying to put the murder as late in the day as possible. By processes not quite clear—"because Father Dixon was not apparently first on the scene with the Giesemans"—the priest turned up with an alibi which Stuart had himself repudiated. Stuart now purported to have been clear all along that he worked at the show from two to four; but he had never said so to Dixon in twenty or thirty interviews. When the Giesemans turned up with their alibi, an heroic but not very good attempt was made to fit Stuart's story into it.

Stuart was telling a patent untruth when he said, having been asked why he never told O'Sullivan that he had worked from two to four: "Mr. O'Sullivan never asked me." "If the jury's verdict is to be questioned on material produced in those circumstances, of all those changes of ground and all those deficiencies, then what becomes of the principle that a case ought to be judged according to the way it is conducted, and what becomes of the practice of the conduct of the case by counsel?" Beyond all that, there was unimpeachable evidence that it was after two o'clock when Stuart started for Thevenard. Blackham was bewildered into agreeing with Starke that it could have been an hour earlier; but at the trial and at the preliminary hearing and to Brazel, he had said that it was about two. Spry's evidence was a vital piece of confirmation, and the two girls at the Thevenard Hotel, Brenda Kent and Veda Miller, said that it was well after two o'clock when they saw Stuart.

The evidence with regard to the third girl from the hotel, Olive Betts, positively confirmed Stuart's guilt. He told a lie about finding a girl at Thevenard because he knew that if it was believed this would be a point in his favour. The story of the whole incident was fantastic. He identified Olive Betts as the girl, and there was no doubt that she was an untouched virgin, despite Starke's heroic efforts to suggest that she was not. The story served to condemn the whole of Stuart's evidence.

In his submission, Chamberlain concluded, the justice of the jury's verdict, and the justice of the decision of the courts of appeal, stood confirmed. "The lesson to be learned from the Commission is that attempted trial by newspaper is a dangerous and a malignant thing which can involve the dragging down of institutions upon which our way of life depends. If the time and effort which have been so lavishly spent have served to demonstrate the wisdom of adhering to the tried processes of law, they will not have been wasted."

* * *

Starke said that he did not understand the comment about trial by newspaper. The government of the state, not a newspaper, had set up the Commission. He was surprised to hear Chamberlain make no reference to the transcript of evidence; in important ways he had mis-stated the effect of the evidence.

Three issues of fact were before the Commission: the alibi, Stuart's language, and the question whether violence was offered to him by the police. It was not, however, for the Commissioners to decide what the facts were. They should rather decide a quite different question: what a reasonable jury might do.

Why was Stuart's alibi not offered earlier? Their Honours might regard this as an important issue, and he would satisfy them that it was not a mere afterthought. Stuart's statement prepared for the trial was not in conflict with the alibi. In the statement he said: "I walked back to Ceduna in the afternoon," and in evidence here Stuart said that afternoon was after dinner. Why was the alibi not raised at the trial? At the preliminary hearing in January, there had been no evidence about the most likely time of the murder, except the doctor's suggestion that it was most likely to have happened at half past six. At that stage, nobody could have conceived that the hours from two to four were important. At the trial the doctor amended her evidence in a way that made the relevant period from half past four to half past eight. Only when the boy Peter Hattam got into the box at the trial, and said that there was no sign of his sister on the beach about half past three, could any reasonable counsel have recognised the overwhelming importance of two to four. Even then, what was O'Sullivan to do if it did occur to him that he must get an alibi for this period? Was he to apply for an adjournment? In any case, what did he know about the Giesemans? He did not know where they were at the time of the trial. He had been told that Gieseman had sacked Stuart, and if he did catch up with the fun-fair Gieseman might say that Stuart was away all the afternoon, or that he knew nothing about him. It had been suggested somewhere that O'Sullivan could have asked the police to help him track down Gieseman and get a statement. In such circumstances, said Starke, when the defence was a hard attack on the police, they would be the last people he himself would ask to work for him.

Why did O'Sullivan not ask Stuart? Because until the Hattams were called, there could have appeared to be no point in asking Stuart where he was from two to four. By the time this period could have come into O'Sullivan's mind, "it was impossible for him to do anything except go on a wild goose chase after a person whose name he did not rightly know, whose location he did not know and whose answers to his questions he could only conclude might be unfavourable." Why then did not Gieseman and the others in his party come forward with the alibi, if they were public-spirited people? It was clear from the evidence both that they all knew Stuart had confessed, and that they did not know what the vital period of time was. It would never occur to them that their knowledge that Stuart was at work from two to four could have any significance. Chamberlain had offered no criticism at all of the Giesemans' evidence. The only way he attacked them was to try to excuse Blackham and extol Spry. Their Honours had heard how the evidence for the alibi came into being. The evidence from Ceduna, brought to dispose of the alibi, came into being very differently; police officers turned Ceduna upside down for evidence to support the police, and very little they came by.

Gieseman, he had been told, was a particularly impressive witness. "There is only one thing about his evidence," said the Chairman, "which does suggest some question of doubt, and that is that he strenuously denied that he ever sacked the man."

Starke agreed that Gieseman may have overlooked this incident; but in the eyes of a jury, properly instructed, would that destroy his credit altogether? At all events, that would not destroy the credit of Mrs. Gieseman, Miss Hopes and McNeish; they told a story substantially the same, which constituted a solid block of evidence. "Your Honours have heard how it came into being, and my friend did not suggest that Father Dixon was dishonest, and nobody questions his sincerity or honesty." He was not a shyster who sidled up to the witness and said: "Come on, whatever you say, say two to four." Of Moir, Starke said he agreed with Chamberlain that his evidence and affidavits conflicted on almost every conceivable subject.

Without having seen Spry, he was prepared to concede that he was a most impressive witness. But he had not been asked for his recollection until July. The Giesemans, it was true, were asked not much earlier; but they had very good reason to know whether Stuart was with them or not. "The Giesemans know he is there after lunch, as he has to work for them. Spry has no particular reason to remember whether it is before or after lunch." This was "Johnny come lately" evidence. "Who do they come up with? Spry, and a handful of aborigines whom Mr. Chamberlain did not mention." It was Spry against Gieseman and the others. "If ever there was a true jury issue, this was it."

Blackham, according to Chamberlain, had made an admission about times because the cross-examiner had been nice to him. Yet Blackham had admitted not only that his memory now was vague, but also that even immediately after the event he could not be clear at what time he drove Stuart.

The aborigines were in all but one case guessing about times. According to the first of them—Wells—Stuart and Moir left Spry's shop in a taxi at half past two; he saw them arrive at the showgrounds in the taxi at three to a quarter past, the taxi having taken, on this account, three-quarters of an hour to travel a few hundred yards, and Wells having got there before it on foot. Then, in cross-examination, Wells said that he saw Stuart at Spry's shop at one o'clock,[2] and that it was from three to a quarter past when Stuart and Moir drove away. This was remarkable evidence. The next aborigine, Chester, admitted that he could not tell the time. The evidence of Ware really supported Stuart's case, for it rather suggested, though without precision, that he saw Stuart at one o'clock at Spry's. Ware made one statement that he reached Ceduna by bus before twelve, and a second statement after police told him that the bus did not get in until a quarter to one. "That is improper police work. When they are up there knowing full well there is a fierce dispute as to times and trying to influence a witness who has given a statement to make a statement about another time is improper . . ." Brazel had said that the bus driver would be brought to testify as to the time when the bus actually arrived, but he had not appeared. Why not?

"There is a good explanation which I will give," said Brazel.

"You will not," said Starke. "The evidence is closed."

"I will if I wish to."

"No you won't, not at any time."

"It would be for us to say," said Sir Mellis Napier; "we have not yet asked for it."

Starke continued his assessment of the aboriginal witnesses.

Mrs. Olga Betts, who gave evidence that she saw Stuart at four o'clock in Ceduna, said she was guessing. So did Donald Kelly, who said that after four he saw Stuart in the town, and Dennis Kelly, who said that he arrived in Ceduna after four and saw Stuart walking towards the fun-fair and that at five he saw Moir and Stuart leave it. Veda Miller said that she too was guessing when she fixed half past two as the time she saw Stuart on the veranda of the hotel at Thevenard. Brenda Kent said on one occasion that she was guessing, but she also said that when Stuart was on the veranda, a clock showed about a quarter to four. She was the only aboriginal witness who was not basing all evidence about time on guesses. Leaving out the confession, it would be impossible for Their Honours to say that a jury considering the evidence for and against the alibi might not find a verdict favourable to Stuart.

The next question was the girl at Thevenard. There was an outside possibility that the hymen was not ruptured. It was possible, too, that in the circumstances Stuart could have got sexual gratification

[2] This was not exactly what Wells said. Wells told Brazel that he saw Stuart at Spry's about five past two. To Shand, he said he left the showground at one, went straight to Spry's and at once saw Stuart. Starke was thus overstating the discrepancy between Wells' two accounts by the time taken for this walk. But since this time cannot have been more than a few minutes, the discrepancy was still close to an hour.

short of full intercourse. A third possibility was that the girl was not Olive Betts. Stuart had been handed photographs. When he was asked which was the girl who came out of the hotel, he pointed to Brenda Kent—who was nothing in his life—without hesitation. When he was asked which girl he had intercourse with, "there was a considerable pause, he went up and down, and said: 'This one'." It was not a ready identification. He might well have assumed that the photograph of the girl was there, and have chosen the only familiar face—that of Olive Betts, whom he had seen at the pictures. If Stuart was lying, as Chamberlain argued, when he said that he had a girl, surely the best thing would have been to choose *none* of the photographs? He was only putting his head in the noose if he chose one. "Unless he is genuine, why should he identify anyone? And yet he did."

Stuart had never been presented to the Commission as a man who could not talk English. "My opponents have definitely caused that impression to grow so that they could meet it . . . Let us concede, as we have always conceded, that he can speak English." He was nevertheless a man of low intellect, and of ignorant and uneducated speech. He had been an amazing witness. "He was asked what he did and where he went, but there is not one piece of contradiction in all his evidence. He has not varied in his accounts and about the assault. They were consistent, except with the unread statement, where he told lies." Nevertheless, murder gave the greatest motive for telling lies. "That is why I was very loth to make any decision about calling him until I had to, because I thought there was very little for Stuart in it if he were put in the box; because of his lack of intelligence he might do himself a great deal of harm. Now it is there, and I have to submit that Your Honours will not believe him except where corroborated, or for other reasons."

Starke took up a comment by the Chairman that although he had conceded that Stuart could speak English, Shand "said differently". The suggestion that Stuart would give evidence through an interpreter, Starke said, was made not by Shand but by Smith before Shand came to Adelaide. "And I had not seen Stuart," Smith added.

Chamberlain had spoken of Stuart's admission that he told a lie to the police about a white man. At one time in his long cross-examination, he might have lost concentration and said "Yes" or "No" almost at random, but apart from that, Stuart had given a very reasonable explanation. He had started telling the truth and he was not getting anywhere; then he tried a lie, a silly lie—after the assault had commenced, according to Stuart's statement.

The incident at Cloncurry and the case of the nurse at Alice Springs were, he assumed, let in as evidence on the issue of language. If they were not, they should be rejected altogether. At a trial, a jury would have to be warned that these acts could not be used as evidence for the probability that Stuart committed this crime. Chamberlain, he submitted, made improper use of these incidents.

Stuart's alleged confession contained inherent improbabilities. It had him taking off clothes before the attack, crossing the beach for a wash after killing the girl, and returning naked to the cave for his clothes. There were two implausible things here. First, on a fine Saturday afternoon in December, a murderer exposes himself naked on the beach to wash himself clean of blood. Second, and more important, an uneducated aborigine with drink in him, and with his lust up, acts as a cold, calculating, civilised human being as he stops to take off his clothes. Why was this in the statement? Because the police had a man with no blood on his clothes. Turner first put it to him in interrogation that he had taken his trousers off.

Stuart's conduct after the murder should be considered. Instead of leaving town he took a job near the scene of the crime. When picked up for drinking on Saturday night he showed no worry, but actually gave cheek.

Strehlow was a scholar of distinction, but also a man who had lived with aborigines and worked among them as an administrator. Why had the Crown called no other aboriginal expert to contradict him? The police had chased aborigines up and down the Nullarbor to bring them to the Commission; Their Honours might well think they had chased expert linguists too, and none had been brought. The Chairman here observed that although Strehlow had told the High Court of having conversed with Stuart "in Arunta and pidgin English", yet in evidence he admitted that Stuart did *not* speak pidgin.

"It is northern English," said Starke.

"It is not Northern Territory English as he described it," said the Chairman; Starke, he added, had spoken to Stuart sometimes in almost pidgin English, and "on the rare occasions that he slips it is often in response to your questions".

Starke said that he was not confident of changing Their Honours' approach to such matters as tenses and participles, but there were other things. The word "unconscious" in the confession was beyond belief. Sir Mellis Napier said it might well be that more of the confession than the police admitted came into existence by question and answer. Once you conceded that a good deal of it arose in this way, said Starke, "then you concede that all the police are perjurers. All of them." For the police said that with a few well-defined exceptions, the confession was taken down as dictated. Jones, at the preliminary hearing, said that every word in the statement was dictated.

The problem of Stuart's English was not a simple one. The chaplain at Adelaide Gaol, on Dixon's evidence, said that Stuart did not seem to understand him. Chamberlain argued that Stuart's story in the box about the day he assaulted the nurse was a good account. Yet although his ramblings during that day were designed mainly to plant a bottle which he went back to recover, he did not mention the bottle until he finally referred to visiting the lavatory before the assault. The test of Stuart's English reproduced on a tape-recorder had been described by Chamberlain as childish. "Again, he makes out Stuart to be a man of remarkable histrionic ability. This uneducated man is supposed to have the power to produce a second-rate performance for a recording." There was no doubt that the test was genuine; it was beyond Stuart's power to make it otherwise.

Their Honours would agree that some police in some circumstances would assault prisoners; and these were just the circumstances in which such a thing might happen. "You have a very terrible and horrible crime; you have the police believing in the guilt of their culprit, and perhaps some of them—I do not know—have young daughters." Chamberlain had said that a policeman would never attack a prisoner in front of others; but the history of the Police Disciplinary Board in Victoria showed that this was a fallacy.

"The difficulty you have here," said the Chairman, "is that you have such a miscellaneous collection. . . . Do you say they would conspire together?"

Possibly they did, possibly not, said Starke. A comment like the Chairman's, but stronger, had been made by the acting Attorney-General. "Of course you will take no notice of that, but it is calculated to embarrass you."[3]

"We must face that possibility," said the Chairman, "and I can assure you that we shall do our best."

No policeman, said Starke, had ever admitted an assault on an accused person. Yet some detectives thought that they were helping the community by using force to expose criminals who otherwise would not be caught. In this case, the evidence of the police was "shifty, evasive, untruthful, and riddled with prevarications".

Stuart's charges against the police were corroborated in three ways. First, by Wardrop. Second, by the photographic evidence of a recent cut across Stuart's eyebrow. "I do beg Your Honours to use the most scientific means at your disposal, and . . . you will see it on both the negative and the positive." Third, by the evidence that threats were made with a blade.

Wardrop had given an impressive display of impartiality in going to the Commission and not to Stuart's solicitors. Shand attributed to him something inconsistent with his own testimony, but Wardrop could not be blamed for that.

"It could be," said the Chairman, "that he gave someone else a more exaggerated account than he subsequently gave the solicitor. If one has to find an explanation for what happened that, I think, is the most likely explanation."

"Well, with respect," said Starke, "I cannot understand that. Why then would he make two statements with the same breath that are opposed?"

[3] The *Advertiser* next morning headlined its report of the day's proceedings: "STUART'S COUNSEL CRITICISES PREMIER."

The Chairman said that Wardrop's original statement was probably not in accordance with the statement made later to the solicitor.

Mr. Justice Ross remarked that, according to Wardrop, Whitrod referred to an assault *after* the confession.

"Yes," said Starke, "but once you accept Whitrod said it, you might take it that he was trying to make it a little better for himself." Chamberlain had attacked Wardrop but had not mentioned his wife, whose evidence looked attractive; and if Wardrop was making mistakes then so was she. Baker, whose evidence conflicted with Wardrop's, was angry with him, and was a man prepared to say what suited him best. His evidence, moreover, had to be rejected as improbable. Why on earth would Wardrop mention Baker's name to the solicitor if he knew that as soon as it was checked Baker would say: "This is a lie"? It was true that Wardrop had a conviction in the army; but he was pardoned, and was now a member of the R.S.L. He had been prosecuted by Whitrod for sly grogging; but the two men were friendly after that.

The first of the police witnesses, Turner, tried "to square his conscience by going as near to the truth as he safely can . . ." Turner gave evidence about the tracks on the beach which conflicted with that of Low and Herde; he and at least one other policeman gave "almost farcical answers" about the measurement of these tracks. It was an example of the "extremely slack police work" in the case. Turner admitted having made "incorrect statements to the press". Further, "he admits that at least one of those statements was made while judicial proceedings were pending, and although he knows that he is wrong, he refuses to admit he has done anything wrong." According to Turner, he thought at Ceduna that hairs might provide a possible clue; but Jones swore that Turner had told him the hairs were of no value at all. Both Turner and Jones said that the record of the interrogation was dictated by Jones, with Turner acting only as a typist. They said this because if both admitted a hand in it, they would get into grave difficulties in cross-examination. Their evidence could not be true. "It is a very remarkable thing when you get two detectives, one of senior rank, denying a thing of this nature."

After speaking for most of Friday, Starke continued for about two hours when the Commission sat, for the last time, on Monday, October 26.

Their Honours would remember his argument that the part of Stuart's confession which described the removal of his clothes was implausible. In cross-examination, Turner firmly denied that the police had suggested to Stuart that he took off his clothes. When Jones' evidence from the trial was produced, stating that Stuart was asked whether he took his trousers off, Turner eventually admitted that he was wrong. Turner and Jones both swore that the report of the interrogation, made next day, reproduced the conversation verbatim, although this was humanly impossible; in the end, it was admitted that this was not true. There has been "a classic example of prevarication" when Turner swore that, according to Phin, Gieseman spoke of six o'clock, or when the hotel closed, as the time Stuart returned to the show on Saturday. From Phin it was learned that no such thing had been said.

The blades had been first mentioned by Turner not in cross-examination but when nobody was appearing for Stuart. The detective deserved no marks for that, however, since Phin had said already that the blades were probably in Stuart's possession. Turner told "a downright lie" about the blades. To Brazel, when he first gave evidence, he said that they were not handled after being placed on the office table. Later, to Starke, he repeated this denial, but went on to say that someone "might have picked them up, but not to threaten him with them". Turner agreed that he knew the body had not been cut; so for what other purpose than to threaten Stuart would he have picked up the blades? Here, Turner "let the cat out of the bag". All the other policemen involved in the interrogation, except Walker, had an extraordinary lack of memory of the blades.

Jones was swearing to the impossible when he said that nearly all of Stuart's confession was dictated without interrogation. Whitrod denied that the blades had been picked up, and admitted only after prolonged questioning that in drinking at the R.S.L. he was breaking the law. He denied nothing in the conversations testified to by Wardrop and Mrs. Wardrop except the vital portions. Low, less a policeman than the others and more a backroom boy, was clearly showing signs of distress in the box—as when he took at least fifteen seconds to answer the question whether, as Sonny Jim swore, the tracker was told before the footprint test that Stuart was guilty. Herde and Walker were prepared to deprive people of their liberty without trial.

The last matter involving the police was the journal written up by Walker the day after the interrogation. Although on Phin's evidence the men at Ceduna were told what Stuart (according to Moir) said about blood, a body and a dinghy, there was not a word of it in the journal. "What is wrong is very hard to say, but it does display something very rotten in the state of Denmark."

If the Commissioners conceded that the police had been untruthful about how the confession was composed, and about the blades, they could turn with comfort to Stuart's own evidence and to the corroboration of it. "Of course, Your Honours have not to make a finding on this . . ."

Was Starke suggesting, asked Mr. Justice Reed, that they should make *no* findings of fact?

Starke said that they should "not make findings of facts as to . . . violence and so on, but merely consider whether there is evidence which would or might raise a reasonable doubt in a jury".

When the Chairman remarked that a re-trial was "never an entirely satisfactory solution", Starke said that through nobody's fault the case had had extraordinary publicity, which might make it impossible for justice to be done by a re-trial. If Their Honours thought that except for this publicity a re-trial might be a very wise thing, then their recommendation should be to release Stuart.

The Chairman said that when a re-trial was impossible, "you think pretty seriously before you say the doubt is such as to justify his being released."

"In my submission," Starke replied, "Your Honours ought to leave that to the Executive . . . it would be wrong to Stuart, because the newspapers have made it difficult for him or the Crown to have a re-trial, that he should get a less just solution than otherwise."

For some purposes, said Mr. Justice Ross, "we have to consider the quality of the evidence, haven't we?"

"Yes, Your Honour, but when you reach a stage like the Giesemans and Spry, that is such a typical jury question that it would be wrong, with respect, for Your Honours to make up your minds on it."

Starke gave a general summary of the police evidence. They knew all the vital things in the confession, such as the bathers and their colour, and the stone, and they could therefore ask leading questions. "In view of the slipshod police methods one cannot blame Your Honours or the public for having exceeding disquiet . . ." Having measured a footprint, they neither noted the measurement nor checked it against anything; although they could have made photographs or plaster casts, they did not. Blackham was not approached for three weeks, and Spry for much longer. The test in front of the trackers was unfair. "That was most unsatisfactory," said the Chairman, who also said: "To be just, you have to remember what sort of places Ceduna and Thevenard are, and how they lie, and remember that here is a station where there are about two men and a murder is committed and Christmas is approaching, and it makes it more understandable than excusable."

Starke offered a different reason for the shortcomings: if you have doubts about the guilt of a man from whom you have a confession, he suggested, you may not go on detecting in case you find you have hooked the wrong fish.

The Commissioners should recommend a re-trial. In the face of all this evidence, a reasonable jury, properly instructed, might or would acquit Stuart. "And not to say so, in my submission, would display an arrogance of mind which could not have any part of the judiciary . . . Your Honours, let right be done."

* * *

Brazel's address was the shortest; and, as Starke had expected, it was wholly unfavourable to Stuart. Despite the vicissitudes of the Commission, he said, it was gratifying to know that Stuart had found at last in Starke, "an advocate, shall I say, worthy of this very difficult task". He differed from Starke about the Commissioners' responsibility: "The report would lack a great deal of value unless Your Honours reached a positive finding as to what were the facts . . ." Their paramount task, he suggested, was to say whether there was any substantial reason to doubt the propriety of the verdict against Stuart.

The first question to consider was the credibility of Stuart's evidence. Was his story in the witness box consistent with his conduct during and after the trial? Mr. Justice Reed had said at the trial: "The defendant, as his counsel admits, went to Thevenard about 2 p.m. or a little afterwards . . ." Stuart's testimony now was that although he knew from watches that he had been at the fun-fair from two to four, and although he heard the judge say that the child was attacked probably about half past three,[4] he told nobody, until he saw Shand in August, that he had been at the fun-fair at that time. He had seen Dixon, Strehlow and O'Sullivan, "and yet he concealed from them apparently that he had proof of his innocence available. Your Honours will ask yourselves if that is consistent with a creditable witness." After Shand withdrew, Stuart said that he wished to take no part in the proceedings. ("On Mr. Shand's advice," interjected Starke.) Was this, asked Brazel, the behaviour of a man who knew in his heart that he had an alibi?

The alteration in Stuart's story about why he went to Thevenard could be of considerable significance. Why should he change it in such a vital particular? It was difficult to accept Stuart's explanation—that to admit wanting a girl could suggest to O'Sullivan that he was implicated in the murder. The story "could have, indeed, a sinister construction".

To Dixon, the man who befriended him, Stuart said that he worked on the darts for a couple of hours before sundown. This was quite inconsistent with the story he now told the Commission. Dixon, moreover, had expressed certainty that Stuart could not tell the time. Since he *could* tell the time, this was a strange deception of the priest.

The matter of Olive Betts was "a phase of the enquiry which may possess a most sinister aspect", since the view was well open that she had been introduced as, "shall I put it, a sexual alibi . . ." At the preliminary hearing and at the trial, Blackham's evidence that Stuart mentioned a girl was challenged by Stuart's counsel. At the Commission, in cross-examination of Brenda Kent, Shand "made the accusation in plain terms that she was a harlot—this little almost child we saw here later on". This must have been the result of a calculated instruction from Stuart; and the calumny was repeated by Stuart in the box.

Starke interjected: "There is not the slightest bit of evidence he ever knew Olive Betts' name."

[4] The time Brazel had put to him was actually 3.15 (see p. 228 above). This did not affect the point.

"I am addressing Their Honours," said Brazel.

When asked to select the girl with whom he had intercourse, Stuart chose unhesitatingly the photograph of Olive Betts. "Would not an intelligent jury ask why she had been introduced into this matter?" If, of course, Their Honours' view of Stuart's testimony was such as to render doubtful the voluntariness of the confession, that was the end of the matter.

The Commissioners had also to consider the credit of the police witnesses, each of whom had been cross-examined at considerable length and with considerable skill. Starke's method was to induce a witness to commit himself to certain voluntary propositions, of whose ultimate outcome the witness was not aware, and then to confront the witness later with what appeared to be an inconsistency. The cross-examination thus became an academic discussion, and the witness was put in the position of having to justify what he had said in another court. "That is a very expert and excellent method of cross-examination. It might explain to some extent why the witnesses were inclined to argue with my learned friend and give what he calls an unresponsive answer—a practice not to be commended among witnesses." Inconsistencies in the police evidence had been, properly, detailed by Starke. Their Honours would know what weight they felt should be given to this evidence, "having heard it submitted in reply to this searching cross-examination". On the matter of the blades, one should try to get back into the atmosphere on that night in that little police station. The energies and interrogation of these police officers were directed to getting an admission from Stuart. It was not suggested that the blades played any part in the murder. One could well understand a policeman in such a group completely forgetting the presence of, say, a tram ticket which had nothing to do with the crime.

Starke had said that Whitrod, like Wardrop, had been sly-grogging. But there was a big distinction between what the two men had done. If anyone made a profit out of the sale of liquor at the R.S.L. club, it was not Whitrod but the club; in Wardrop's shop, it was Wardrop.

On the confession, Their Honours might well take the view that it was largely the transcriber's rendering into conventional English of what he understood Stuart to say. The main question was whether its effect was or was not to support the oral confession. Similarly, in the case of the police witnesses, were their departures from fact, if any, mistakes, or complete fabrications?

One passage in Wardrop's evidence which had not been discussed might throw some light on his behaviour. It was a fair inference that by August 12 he had committed himself to his brother-in-law on the *News*, and had either to go voluntarily to the Commission or have pressure on him from a newspaper to do that or have his statement published. "He had put himself—if I may put it this way—in the hands of a newspaper, and it is significant that it was on that day . . . that he rang Baker . . ." Starke had argued that, if Wardrop was going to fabricate something, you would not expect him to communicate with Baker. Their Honours might consider the other possibility, "that having embroiled or involved himself by his statement to the newspaper, whatever it was, he was seeking support from Baker: support which, if you believe Baker, he did not get.

". . . I have been exercising my imagination, such as it is, to know what way this could have arisen with both parties [the Wardrops on the one hand, Whitrod and Baker on the other] being honestly and perfectly conscientious." Suppose Wardrop had said: "You must have felt like belting him after he confessed," and Whitrod said: "Yes, we did." The ambiguity might carry to Wardrop something that Whitrod was not intending. "That is something that occurs to me on the spur of the moment." Brazel made no specific comment on the evidence of Mrs. Wardrop.

He did not want to make any criticism of the Giesemans; but they were being asked in July about a commonplace incident some seven months before. He could not understand Dixon's evidence that when he met Gieseman and said he had come from Stuart, Gieseman said: "I am afraid I cannot help you." "I regard that," said Brazel, "as a curious statement in the circumstances." If, as Gieseman said, he did not interest himself in the newspapers during the preliminary hearing "which is curious in view of his association with Stuart"—and if he had not followed the trial, why would he make that remark to the priest? It might be either that Stuart's movements were difficult to define, or that Gieseman really did not remember.[5]

Spry, if his evidence was accepted, and Stuart, if what his counsel said at the trial was accepted, completely disposed of the alibi. Of the aboriginal witnesses, Starke quite properly said that Chamberlain put no stress on them. Starke was not present when these witnesses appeared; he himself was, and found them "an impressive group of witnesses". The evidence of the Kelly brothers, about seeing Stuart and buying liquor and so on, was strikingly corroborated by that of Stuart. It was true that they did not speak by the clock; that, of course, did not make what they said about times unreliable.

It was a curious fact that Strehlow never conversed in English with the prisoner. True, he said that he heard him speak with his counsel, but Strehlow himself spoke always in Aranda. Starke spoke to Stuart in pidgin—"or, shall I say, brief sentences", and was answered in like manner; but when Chamberlain cross-examined in a different strain, Stuart "gave examples of his capacity to indulge in connected speech", and to express several ideas in one sentence: for example: " 'He hit me on the ribs and on the side of the throat

[5] Gieseman's remark appears to have been made after a reporter had told him Dixon was coming (see p. 70 above). Chamberlain, who chose not to make anything of this remark in his own address, mentioned that "Father Dixon was not apparently first on the scene with the Giesemans" (see p. 256 above).

and on the eye and he tried to punch me on the side of the head, but I blocked that.' "

The bus driver from Ceduna had not been called, "because it was not possible—"

For the second time Starke protested against Brazel giving evidence on the matter. "This is a thing that I have never in my experience heard attempted before, and I very strenuously object to my learned friend endeavouring to do what he must know is a breach of privilege."

"We can form our own minds upon it," said the Chairman, "but I think you had better leave it, Mr. Brazel."

"Well, the position was . . ." said Brazel; but Starke objected again, pointing out that Their Honours had ruled. Brazel abandoned the explanation.

When Mr. Justice Reed asked Brazel to comment on the suggestion that the significance of the period from two o'clock to four did not appear until fairly late, Brazel said he was sure that one of O'Sullivan's first steps would have been to get an account from Stuart of his movements on the day; at the latest, the significance of the period emerged to Stuart when Mr. Justice Reed summed up.

"A bit late for the purpose of this trial," said the Chairman. Brazel observed that Stuart had come to the Commission and said: "I have known this for nine months, that I was there from two to four, but I did not speak about it until Mr. Shand came along."

Starke's suggestion of a re-trial, Brazel concluded, was completely unreal. On the ground merely of the widespread publicity given to the matter, it would be impossible to gather a jury none of whom had formed some judgment. The report would deal with all the matters relevant to a re-trial. How then could there be a real re-trial after the public had been given the Commission's views on the case? "A re-trial is out of the question."

There was a little discussion by Starke and Chamberlain about just when the period from two to four first appeared crucial. Sir Mellis Napier said he thought Starke was justified in saying that the times did not emerge as clearly at the preliminary hearing as at the trial. The Chairman thanked counsel for their assistance, and the Commission adjourned for the last time, seventy-seven days after its first sitting.

20

A VERDICT CONFIRMED

As the Commissioners finished hearing evidence, the proprietors of the *News* offered to buy the *Advertiser*. For the capital of Advertiser Newspapers Ltd. they offered either shares and cash to the value of £14 million, or £12.6 million in cash. It was said to be the largest takeover bid in Australian history. The editorial content of the *Advertiser*, it was suggested, would be controlled by a trust having on it "such public figures as . . . the Chief Justice". The offer was smartly rejected. "We believe," said the *Advertiser's* chairman of directors, Sir Lloyd Dumas, "that our shareholders—and the South Australian community generally—have a real pride in the *Advertiser* and would never agree to its being modelled on the *News*." Sir Mellis Napier, it appeared, would not after all be invited to join a trust set up by the company which, in the Premier's view, had libelled him.

The proposal was described in parliament by Mr. H. H. Shannon as effrontery. "We have had quite ample experience," he said, "of their lack of responsibility in the field of providing the public with the news of the day, but despite that, they decided they would like to take over the only paper that can be trusted to give, at least, a fair account . . ." Shannon spoke again about the *News* a few days later, when he asked: "Has cabinet decided whether or not to justify the government and the Supreme Court bench of South Australia by taking the steps that the Premier indicated previously might be taken against the publishers and editor of the *News*?" The question was a candid expression of the view that a prosecution of the *News* could "justify" politicians as well as judges. Playford said that it would be appropriate to await the report of the Royal Commission before making a decision.

The press was discussed by Mr. Justice Abbott on October 30, his last day as a judge. At a crowded sitting of the Full Court on the occasion of his retirement, Mr. Justice Abbott (who had been Playford's Attorney-General before appointment to the bench) attacked critics of the Royal Commission and especially the press. "Despite the horrifying attacks and quite unjustifiable criticism which some members have been called upon to endure in recent months," he said, "I am sure that the calm and outwardly unruffled manner in which they have proceeded on the even tenor of their way has redounded not only to their own credit but has added to the stature of the South Australian bench. The widespread confidence among all sections of the public in the integrity and capacity of the judges of this state, despite what amounted to a sustained campaign of irresponsible invective, has never been more apparent. My friend the Rt. Hon. Lord Merriman,[1] a very eminent and highly respected member of the judiciary in Britain, wrote to me when the muddy tide was in full flood: 'Your press seems to have a good deal more licence in criticising judges than is customary here.' I hope and am happy in believing that exuberance of irresponsible journalistic licence is past and that not again, in the lifetime of any of us, will it recur."

A fortnight after these remarks were spoken, "an Adelaide correspondent" wrote in the Sydney *Observer*: "In big cities crusading newspapers are part of everyday life. They may be a misguided, annoying, or inconvenient element; they may have to be fought and countered; but they do not call forth wrath and indignation. The fury that descended upon Rohan Rivett in South Australia was remarkable. The parliament was full of extreme epithets about 'mob rule' and 'trial by newspaper'; the Commissioners let their feelings be known; the Crown and the Q.C. assisting the Commission expressed uncontrolled antipathy towards the *News*. It was all an orgy of naked anger, and Adelaide's Establishment made no secret of the fact that it intends to 'sweat off' on Rohan Rivett."

The retirement of Mr. Justice Abbott and the earlier death of Mr. Justice Piper left only four men on the bench of the Supreme Court. On November 16 the *News* predicted that Chamberlain and Brazel would be the two new judges. Their appointment was announced officially later that day. The *News* devoted nearly twelve column-inches to the careers of the two men without mentioning the Royal Commission or the name of Stuart. The *Advertiser* reported Brazel's appearance at the Commission, but not Chamberlain's. Interstate papers were less inhibited; the *Sydney Morning Herald* headed its report: "STUART LAWYERS MADE S.A. JUDGES." If Stuart were to have a re-trial it would now have to be conducted either by a judge who was involved in the Commission or by Mr. Justice Mayo, who sat on the appeal.

* * *

Twice, during November, members of parliament asked when the Royal Commissioners were likely to report and ministers replied that they did not know. As late as December 2—a day before the parliamentary session was due to end—Playford told a questioner that the government had no control over the matter, and that if it was concluded in time the report would be presented to parliament. It was presented late on the afternoon of December 3. A typewritten copy was tabled in each House. About midnight, when the last business

[1] A former Conservative M.P. who became President of the Probate, Divorce and Admiralty Division of the High Court.

for the year had been done and only the farewell speeches remained, Mr. D. A. Dunstan was given permission by the House of Assembly to ask a question. In view of the Premier's undertaking that the government would allow a debate on the report, would the government recall parliament for this purpose as soon as possible? It was of course impossible, Dunstan said, for members to debate or even study the report in the dying hours of the present session; and it was undesirable that it should be some time in the middle of 1960 before the report was debated. "I did not state that I would provide a time for debate in the House," replied Playford. "What I said was that I should be happy to hear any comment any honourable member desired to make . . ." The government would not call parliament together to debate the report. He himself had only scanned its contents briefly. "Another good reason why this matter should not be debated at this stage is that I have been reliably informed that certain legal action is pending in connexion with it . . ." A member asked if the legal action involved public money. "It very easily could," replied Playford. He and the Leader of the Opposition and the Speaker wished everybody a happy Christmas and a prosperous new year, and at 12.34 a.m. the House sang "God Save the Queen".

Newspaper readers learned on the morning of December 4 that the Commissioners had found the verdict against Stuart wholly justified. There was, they reported, no truth in the suggestions that his knowledge and understanding of the English language was inadequate, for the purpose either of enabling him to follow the evidence and instruct his counsel, or of giving his version of the facts to the jury. "His vocabulary is, no doubt, limited, but when he wishes he can speak English, not pidgin or what Mr. Strehlow has described to us as 'N.T. English', but reasonably good English, that is to say, that he speaks English as it is commonly spoken by people who have had some but not a great deal of education." There was therefore no reason why he should not have told O'Sullivan and the jury where he was on the afternoon in question. In the unsworn statement he said: "I walked back to Ceduna in the afternoon." The Commissioners were unable to believe that O'Sullivan would have prepared the document in those terms without asking Stuart what time he returned. The obvious inference was that if Stuart had in fact returned before two, he himself was not aware of it.

"Anxious consideration" had been given to the evidence for and against the alibi. "In the result we are clearly of the opinion that, so far from proving that the petitioner was working in the show, when the little girl was attacked and murdered, the new evidence proved quite conclusively that the petitioner did, as the confession relates, walk back from Thevenard to Ceduna along the beach, in the vicinity of the cave, in which the body was subsequently discovered . . . within the period during which the child must have been raped and murdered."

Stuart's evidence in support of his allegation that the confession was extorted from him could not be accepted. Having considered the criticism to which the evidence of police witnesses was—quite properly—subjected, the Commissioners had no doubt that their testimony was given honestly.

The Commissioners would have no hesitation in coming to the conclusion to which the jury came at the trial. "Taking the evidence we have heard, in conjunction with the evidence that was taken at the trial (and not canvassed before us) we think that the conclusion is one to which any reasonable jury would come after a proper direction on this evidence."

The morning press on December 4 displayed these findings prominently and quoted also from the body of the report; but no paper could reproduce anything like the whole of the document. When printed, some weeks later, it ran to forty foolscap pages. Until the printed version appeared, nobody could read a complete copy of the report without visiting Parliament House.

The *Advertiser* devoted more space than any other newspaper to the report, and in the same issue published its first editorial comment on the Stuart case. Since doubts about the verdict against Stuart had been created among a section of the public, the paper said, the government was clearly justified in appointing a Royal Commission. "During the ensuing enquiry, it was plain even to people with little knowledge of such investigations that the Commission was bent on sifting the additional evidence with extreme care . . . Stuart's own counsel were at no disadvantage in this most searching enquiry. Indeed, they were allowed a measure of freedom which in itself testified to the Commission's resolve to give them every opportunity of submitting a case favourable to Stuart. Despite emotions raised in some quarters by the investigation, and some discreditable incidents associated with it, the Commission did not waver from this course.

"The same calm, deliberate and penetrating search for the truth is manifest in the report which this Commission has now submitted. . . . There is no equivocation in the findings.

"The assurance, given after so exhaustive and searching an enquiry, that the Commission sees 'no valid reason for apprehending any miscarriage of justice' will be welcomed by responsible people, not only in this state, but in other places where the remarkable nature of the case had attracted attention. Our courts have justified the confidence traditionally placed in them. No less reassuring to South Australians will be the Commission's rejection of allegations that members of the police force used threats and violence to extort a confession from Stuart. Some of their evidence was subject to keen criticism during the enquiry, and was perhaps not faultless, but the Commission is satisfied that their testimony was given honestly."

The *News* said in its editorial column on December 4: "The full text of the report has not yet been made available outside Parliament

House. It is therefore impossible to comment in detail at this stage. The full hearing and report of the Commission has been in accord with the democratic principle that every aspect of a case involving life and death should be thoroughly aired. Whether, or not, there is agreement with all the conclusions, it is a matter of great satisfaction that the issues raised have been fully investigated." Neither Adelaide paper printed, this day or later, any comments by individuals on the report; nor did the *News* ever "comment in detail". No letter supporting or criticising the findings was printed in Adelaide. Both the *News* and the *Advertiser* declined to print a letter from two university lecturers pointing out that passages critical of the police were omitted from their summaries of the report. The writers then sent a letter to the *Age* (Melbourne) and the *Sydney Morning Herald*, but in vain.

The *Sydney Morning Herald* quoted Father Thomas Dixon's comment that he was surprised and sad at the Commissioners' decision, and that he still believed Stuart innocent. In the Sydney *Sun* he was further quoted as saying: "I really feel it has not been a thorough investigation. A lot of aboriginal psychology has been either overlooked or not taken into account." These words were reported under a heading "STUART FINDING 'FAIR'. EXPERT OPINION." The expert was Professor A. K. Stout, the Sydney philosopher, who said: "The Commission appears to have conducted a fair enquiry. It seems to me that one ought to be satisfied that it has been a pretty thorough investigation, which the trial was not."

Every daily paper in Melbourne and Sydney had offered editorial opinion on the Commission during its course; but none commented, favourably or unfavourably, on the findings. In Sydney the weekly *Bulletin*, which earlier had supported Playford's handling of the affair, now said that the findings "should satisfy those whose minds have been agitated by the matter". Apart from an article by the present writer in *Nation*, no other analysis of the report seems to have been published by the end of the year.

The response of the press in Adelaide was not surprising. The *Advertiser* had never shown any misgivings about the attitude of either the government or the Commissioners towards Stuart. Having expressed satisfaction with the report on behalf of "responsible people", the makers of the *Advertiser's* policy could well have thought that the community should be allowed to forget an unfortunate affair. The threat of prosecution may well have inhibited the *News*: it is hard to see any other reason why the paper which had been so active in provoking the enquiry should have published no correspondence on the report and invited no comment on it from anybody.

Why did newspapers elsewhere express no editorial opinion on the report? If every editor was utterly convinced, it was puzzling that none of them published a word of satisfaction that justice had not, after all, miscarried. If an editor did feel less than wholly happy about the findings, there was a technical reason why he might decide not to pursue his qualms: it would have been rash of him to publish an analysis in any degree critical which was based only on those extracts compiled by newspaper reporters in Adelaide. An editor seriously determined to pursue the matter could no doubt have arranged for somebody to transcribe the whole report; but even then, whoever assessed it would need to know his way through the 1,359 pages of its proceedings. This could have been done, but not quickly. It may be that interstate papers were waiting for a lead from the *News* (or from Stuart's lawyers) which they did not get. Editors may have decided, moreover, that they were in danger of boring readers if they wrote more about Stuart. His situation had provoked large headlines day after day from July to October—a rare thing for any peacetime story. Had his life still hung on the findings of the Commission, interstate papers might have shown a keener interest in the report. Whatever their reasons, most editors summarised the report in their news columns and left it at that.

On the last day of the year the *Truth* weeklies in Melbourne and Adelaide and the affiliated *Daily Mirror* in Sydney printed what one of them described as "the greatest untold story of 1959". The story was unsigned in the weeklies and signed in the *Mirror* by Mr. Lawson Glassop[2] of the South Australian *Truth*. "While Rupert Max Stuart was in the shadow of the gallows," he wrote, "he confessed to three Adelaide Gaol warders that he had murdered a little girl. He told them: 'I wouldn't have killed her, only I was drunk.' And Stuart said to Det. G. Modra: 'I wouldn't have killed her, only I was full of plonk.'

"This was the evidence which the warders and Det. Modra waited to give before the Stuart Royal Commission. But they waited in vain. After hearing legal argument, the Commission refused to allow the evidence to be given. . . . But the Stuart case is over, so no reason exists for not publishing the vital information . . . Some people still think Stuart is innocent. I checked back on the facts to establish *beyond doubt* that Stuart is guilty."[3]

Glassop made fairly clear from what source he had gained his information. "As far back as August,"[4] he wrote, "I learned that police had interviewed one of the warders to whom Stuart talked." In a report from Adelaide in the same day's issue of the Sydney *Sun*, the policeman whose name was linked most closely with Stuart's was himself quoted as releasing the evidence which the Commissioners declined to hear. "Rupert Max Stuart confessed to the

[2] Author of the highly praised war novel *We Were the Rats*.

[3] The *Daily Mirror* version is here quoted. The *Truth* version omitted the last two sentences and had: "If any lingering doubt remains about Stuart's guilt this disclosure of his admission should remove it and brand Stuart for what he is—a man who outraged and murdered a little girl and then lied about it in the witness box."

[4] See p. 95 above.

Ceduna murder minutes after being sentenced to death, a senior detective revealed today. He told two warders leading him from the court, 'I only killed her because I was drunk.' In a cell several hours later, Stuart repeated his statement to another warder. The detective is Det.-Sgt. Paul Turner, of Adelaide C.I.B., who led the investigation into the murder . . . Det.-Sgt. Turner explained today that the confessions by Stuart to the warders was the evidence which the Royal Commissioners had refused to hear. 'But the case is closed now, so I think it is not wrong to release this evidence,' he said." The *Sun* report made no reference to Detective Modra, and had Stuart using to the warders slightly different words from those quoted by Glassop.

Several versions of what Stuart really said after his conviction had been circulating in Adelaide for months. On one report he said: "I gave them a good run for their money," and in one version of this report he added that the verdict against him was correct. Another report had him telling a Protestant minister that *if* he killed the child, it must have been when he was drunk. It was unlikely now that the accuracy or inaccuracy of these reports would ever be the subject of any judicial enquiry.

Neither the *News* nor the *Advertiser* printed a word about these revelations. In the Sydney *Sun-Herald* "Onlooker" wrote: "His guilt having been firmly established, why have Adelaide police taken it upon themselves to release incriminating statements which the judges, exercising their discretion in Stuart's favour, deliberately excluded from the enquiry? . . . True, nothing now revealed or alleged can affect Stuart. He committed a foul crime and is lucky to have escaped being hanged. But this gratuitous disclosure is more likely to renew than to allay criticism of the police made during the hearings of the case." In another Sydney journal, the *Catholic Weekly*, the editorial columnist "Criticus" was no less reproving. "No wonder," he wrote, "the police concerned with the Ceduna murder came in for a lot of criticism over their handling of the case . . . Surely the judge and not the arresting police must decide what will and what will not be made public . . . how otherwise can the public be expected to have confidence in either its police or its courts?" Turner was still president of the Police Association, having just been re-elected unanimously for his fifth term. As quoted in the press, he did not say how he came to think that the case was closed. The government, not the Commissioners, had to decide Stuart's fate, and it could take as much or as little notice of their report as it pleased. Since the cabinet, as far as anybody knew, had not considered the report, Turner appeared to be acting on his own prediction of what the government would decide.

Professor Norval Morris was less certain than Turner that the case was over. Questions about Stuart were put to him in Melbourne on January 3, in a television interview by reporters from the *Herald* and *Sun*. Mr. E. W. Tipping, who had been one of the first reporters to pursue the story in July, and who had spoken with Dixon before the priest flew to Queensland, asked whether the Royal Commission had satisfied those people working for a re-trial. Morris said: "I'm not so sure that one can confidently say that it is all over. Also I'm not so sure that we can say we are satisfied with a report that we have not yet read." It seemed fortuitous, Morris said, that the report had been tabled in parliament only a few hours before a long recess. Press reports of the findings had included a suggestion, Morris said, that Dixon had gone to Queensland looking for an alibi to cover Stuart from two o'clock to four o'clock. "I know and you know," he said—addressing Tipping—"that that was not true. He did not know what he was looking for. He went to try to find all the information he could, to fill out a story which was vague and not helpful."

"In your opinion," Tipping asked, "is Stuart guilty or not guilty?"

"That's a hard one," replied Morris. "He seems a strong candidate for guilt, but I am still troubled with lack of evidence . . . a startling lack of scientific evidence."

This interview was reported prominently in the Melbourne *Sun*, and not at all in Adelaide.

A hostile comment on the Commission was made in February at an annual conference on Aboriginal Advancement in Sydney, which was attended by Dr. Charles Duguid and Mr. D. A. Dunstan on behalf of the Aborigines' Advancement League of South Australia. A resolution deplored "the extraordinary constitution" of the Commission, and "the inconsistencies and double standards" evident in its report. The conference asked the Federal Council for Aboriginal Advancement to refer the matter for investigation by the International Commission of Jurists, a body whose Australian section, founded in 1958, had as president Sir Owen Dixon, Chief Justice of the High Court. In the *Sun-Herald*, "Onlooker" said that the conference could have interested itself in the case only on the supposition that Stuart, being an aboriginal, did not get a fair deal. "Rubbish! If he had been a white man he would almost certainly have been hanged without much ado . . . The composition of the Royal Commission . . . would have been equally open to question whether Stuart's skin was black or white." In the same note, "Onlooker" remarked that on March 1, Mr. J. D. O'Sullivan and Miss Helen Devaney were admitted to practice in Victoria. Stuart's lawyers, he wrote, "evidently felt there was no legal future for them in S.A." By way of contrast, he reported, two other lawyers prominent in the case had been elevated to the bench. "No comment," he added—an odd conclusion for a column headed "Candid Comment".

In Adelaide, *Truth* had already reported that not only O'Sullivan and Miss Devaney but also Mr. C. Villeneuve Smith, who appeared as junior to both Shand and Starke, had applied for admission to the Victorian Bar. "All three declined to make any statement . . ." wrote *Truth*, "but it is believed that they feel there are better opportunities in Victoria." Starke moved the admission of O'Sullivan and Miss Devaney in March, and of Smith in April.

There appears to have been no direct comment in parliament on the report of the Royal Commission until October, when Mr. D. A. Dunstan referred to it in a speech on the Estimates which was not reported in any newspaper. Dunstan described as "extraordinary" the Commissioners' view that O'Sullivan could easily have secured the Giesemans as witnesses at the trial. He was "distressed that it should have been suggested that Mr. O'Sullivan did something less than his duty". The Commissioners should have recommended "that some independent assistance should be available to counsel to make enquiries" when assigned a case by the Law Society. Dunstan expressed "uneasiness" about the report, and found it "strange that the Commission seems to have adopted one attitude towards one witness's credibility and a completely different attitude towards another witness's credibility when, in fact, the complaints that could have been made about each witness were identical". He was unable to dismiss the evidence of the Giesemans "as cavalierly as the Commission has seen fit to dismiss it". After reading the transcript of evidence and the report, he considered that Stuart was a liar, a most unsatisfactory character, and could understand English. But the Commissioners, it seemed to him, went "a bit far" when they said that no jury would have had any doubt.

21

AN EDITOR ON TRIAL

THE CHARGES AGAINST Rivett and News Ltd. were laid on January 19, 1960, some seven weeks after the report was tabled. They were graver than was generally expected. Serious offences, it was alleged, were committed by the publication of the headline which Playford had quoted in parliament: "*Mr. Shand, Q.C., indicts Sir Mellis Napier* 'THESE COMMISSIONERS CANNOT DO THE JOB' "; the poster: "COMMISSION BREAKS UP SHAND BLASTS NAPIER" and the poster: "SHAND QUITS 'YOU WON'T GIVE STUART FAIR GO.' " The meaning of this last poster, according to the summons, was "that the Chief Justice and the judges were biased and unfair in carrying out their duties as Royal Commissioners . . . and that they were unfitted for judicial office."[1] Similar meanings were found in other phrases. In issuing each of the statements, the defendants were said to have published a seditious libel; and a defamatory libel, knowing it to be false; and a defamatory libel. There were in all, then, nine charges against the company and nine against Rivett.

Seditious libel is a common law offence, and as an English judge observed in 1910, "it is a weapon that is not often taken down from the armoury in which it hangs . . ." According to Stephen's *Digest of the Criminal Law*, a seditious libel is one published with seditious intention—that is to say, "an intention to bring into hatred or contempt, or to excite disaffection against"—among other things—"the administration of justice . . ." It may be punished by a fine, or imprisonment; the sum or the term is decided by the judge. The remaining charges were laid under a South Australian statute. For maliciously publishing a defamatory libel knowing it to be false, a person could be sent to prison for two years or fined £1,000, or both; and for maliciously publishing a defamatory libel (without knowledge of falsity) the penalty was one year and/or £500.

Rivett was ordered to appear before a magistrate in the Adelaide Police Court on January 25. If the magistrate found a case to answer, the charges would be heard before a judge and jury in the Supreme Court. The judge would presumably be Mr. Justice Mayo, since of all

[1] When the Commission met after Shand's departure, Sir Mellis Napier said it had been charged that he was "unfit for the office" that he held. These words were at the end of a sentence in which "a section of the press" in South Australia had been mentioned, and appeared to refer to the *News*.

the bench only he had not been involved in the Commission. Of the other judges, three were subjects of the alleged libels; a fourth, Mr. Justice Chamberlain, appeared at the Commission for the Attorney-General and closed his address with a denunciation of "attempted trial by newspaper"; and the fifth, Mr. Justice Brazel, had said in a speech as counsel assisting the Commission: "a section of the press has seen fit to make these issues an excuse for vituperative and indecent attacks upon members of the Commission."

Mr. J. L. Travers, Q.C., appeared for the Crown, to prosecute the company which, a few months earlier, had agreed to pay his fees if he represented Stuart at the Commission.[2] At the preliminary hearing both News Ltd. and Rivett were represented by Mr. H. G. Alderman, Q.C., who had been Brazel's partner until the latter's elevation to the bench.

When he opened the Crown case before the magistrate, Travers said that the *News* on August 21 knowingly distorted Shand's withdrawal. Quoting from the official transcript of proceedings, Travers argued that on August 20 the Chairman did not stop Shand from cross-examining Phin; on the contrary, his words—"as far as I am concerned, I have heard enough of this"—meant that the point, a minor one, had been settled in favour of Stuart's counsel. Next morning Shand had made a statement in which there was no hint of dishonesty or unfairness on the part of the judges. Shand here complained only that the terms of the enquiry were too narrow; nowhere did he suggest anything stronger. The defendants had seized on this incident as an opportunity to wield the poison pen, to strike a savage blow at one of the most cherished institutions of a civilised country, the Supreme Court, and more particularly at three of its judges.

In the face of information from its reporters, the *News* produced a poster, in red letters five inches high—a terrific thing, with a terrific libel, plainly suggesting dishonesty of the vilest kind on the part of the judges. "Fair go" was a common Australian expression, and nothing could be more serious than the charge of absence of it in a judge. Neither Shand nor anyone else had made such a charge. On the same day the defendants published another placard, as red and as large as the first one, alleging that the Commission had broken up—which meant that it was disbanded or wrecked. In fact the Commission had adjourned for the humane purpose of letting the accused person be represented. The further suggestion that Shand was blast-

[2] In the *Sunday Mail* (jointly produced by the *Advertiser* and the *News*) a staff writer said on February 6: "Are Queen's Counsel obliged to accept a brief from the Crown? It's been a talking point in Adelaide this week. A legal man tells me that at present Queen's Counsel regard themselves as being under an obligation to make themselves available to the Crown on request." According to the ethics of the legal profession an advocate, like a taxi-driver, is bound in normal circumstances to work for any client who requests his services and who can pay for them.

ing anyone was false. To write thus of the Chief Justice, who was also the Governor's deputy, was proof of malice and contempt and hatred. On the front page, a photograph of Sir Mellis Napier was headed: "Chairman under fire." Could anyone think that an apt expression? Under the picture it was said that the Chairman "interrupted" Shand's cross-examination of Phin. Was this an apt word? In an editorial on September 3 the *News* issued a further attack, masquerading as an apology.

The paper had printed the vilest libels. It had attempted to stir up mass distrust and hysteria. The easiest way to undermine stability in any country was to shake confidence in the judiciary. The offence of seditious libel had been clearly established; there was a seditious intention to bring hatred or contempt of the administration of justice. Either of the other two charges of criminal libel, whichever was found to be appropriate, would be cumulative with the charges of seditious libel.

Travers had said that the Crown would call certain executives of the *News* to admit that they knew perfectly well that the libels were false. Mr. Murray James, the paper's chief of staff, was called as the first Crown witness and examined by the Crown Solicitor, Mr. J. R. Kearnan, who was appearing with Travers. To a number of questions about his duties and his colleagues and other matters, James said: "I decline to answer on the grounds that it might tend to incriminate me." At Travers' request, the magistrate (Mr. R. J. Coombe, S.M.) explained that the court must know whether there were real grounds for this apprehension, and directed James to answer the question: "What is your position at the *News*?" James would not answer, even when the magistrate insisted. He was therefore committed to custody. The next witness, Mr. K. S. May, personal assistant to Murdoch, gave his occupation as journalist but declined to answer any other questions even when directed by the magistrate. He too was on the point of being held in custody, when Alderman, counsel for the defendants, suggested an adjournment of five minutes. When the court resumed, May answered questions freely about the editorial hierarchy of the *News*, and the purpose and composition of posters. James was brought back into court later, and in answer to the magistrate said he was assistant editor and chief of staff.

In the next four days the Crown called three directors of News Ltd. and a number of its employees, including the men who reported proceedings at the Commission and the typists who took down their stories. Each of the directors and some of the journalists declined to answer certain questions. On the third day the news editor, Mr. Norman Sewell, declined to answer questions about the composition of posters and headlines on August 21. Next day Sewell was recalled, and again refused to answer. Travers drew a document from his pocket and handed it to the witness. It was a pardon, issued by the Executive Council, guaranteeing him immunity from prosecution—

"a procedure," wrote the *Advertiser*, "said to be unique in Australian legal history . . ." After a short conference with Alderman, Sewell said that the poster "SHAND QUITS 'YOU WON'T GIVE STUART FAIR GO'" and the headline were drafted by Rivett. He himself had drafted a poster which read: "*Stuart Shock* SHAND Q.C. WALKS OUT OF ENQUIRY." This Rivett rejected. The Crown also called court reporters to give evidence about the relation between what Shand said, their shorthand notes, and the typewritten transcript of the Commission. On the fifth and last day of the hearing the Crown called Mr. Rupert Murdoch, managing director of News Ltd., who declined to answer a long series of questions from Travers, including whether he himself wrote the editorial, published on September 3, headed "LET'S GET THE RECORD STRAIGHT."

When the case for the Crown closed, Rivett, prompted by Alderman, said from the dock: "I reserve my defence." It was a year to the very day since Stuart, prompted by O'Sullivan, had spoken the same words in the Police Court. The magistrate found that there was a case to answer. Rivett was committed for trial and granted £100 bail.

* * *

As the matter was now *sub judice*, direct public discussion of the issues involved in the trial of Rivett was impossible. In private conversations, which were widespread, opinion ranged from unqualified support of Rivett's stand to an equally unqualified hope that he would be sent to prison for a long time.

The trial began on March 7, before Mr. Justice Mayo and a jury of twelve men, reduced by sickness to eleven from the third day. Flowers, banners and pennants decorated the city, and at night many buildings were floodlit; for the trial coincided with the Adelaide Festival of Arts, an array of music, drama, exhibitions and spectacles. In the public gallery at the Supreme Court from time to time sat writers from other cities who were in Adelaide for discussions and poetry readings. An anthology of South Australian writing which included an extract from Rivett's book *Behind Bamboo* was published as a contribution to the Festival. Rivett himself was chairman of a committee in charge of outdoor activities.

On the day the case opened the Governor of South Australia, Sir Robert George, finished his term and sailed home to Britain. After Sir Mellis Napier had stood at the head of the farewelling line at Outer Harbour, it became his responsibility as Lieutenant-Governor to preside at meetings of the Executive Council as well as to be leader of the judiciary. The bench in general and the Chief Justice in particular were vindicated, just after the trial of Rivett began, by the Judicial Committee of the Privy Council. A memorandum from Sir Mellis Napier had led the government to appeal to London against an order of the High Court for a re-trial of John Whelan Brown for murder. The South Australian Attorney-General was granted leave to appeal to London on the day when Stuart was refused it. The appeal was heard in January, and on March 9 the Judicial Committee gave its judgment, setting aside the order of the High Court and restoring the original verdict. The Full Court in Adelaide, dismissing Brown's appeal, had given a strong hint to the executive to commute Brown's death sentence, and the decision to do so was made at the end of March. In Stuart's case the terrible effect of prolonged uncertainty was given as a reason for reprieve. Yet Brown had been left in doubt for a full year.

At the trial Mr. J. L. Travers, Q.C., appeared again for the Crown, with Mr. J. R. Kearnan and Mr. K. P. Lynch. Mr. H. G. Alderman, Q.C., appeared again for News Ltd., with Mr. N. C. Ligertwood. Rivett now had separate counsel—Dr. J. J. Bray, Q.C., who had applied without success to represent O'Sullivan at the Commission. Mr. C. L. Hermes appeared with Bray. The company and Rivett pleaded not guilty on all counts. Travers' opening covered much the same ground as his introductory remarks in the Police Court, with the added information, drawn from Sewell by the pardon, that Rivett himself wrote one of the posters after rejecting a suggested draft. This, Travers said, was the product of a mind either unbalanced or seething with malice. The posters were part of a rabble-rousing process. Turning from the posters to the headlines, Travers said: "They're crook at first, and now they're incompetent." He drew attention to the photograph of the Chief Justice on the front page, and to the comment, which he said was curious: "Sir Mellis Napier will be 77 in October. He has sat in the Supreme Court for 35 years. He was knighted 16 years ago." There had been no biographical particulars of the other Commissioners. The information about the Chairman was apparently printed to give weight to the statement that the Commissioners could not do the job.

Again the Crown called witnesses employed by News Ltd. In the Police Court, Alderman had not cross-examined any of them. On the second day of the trial he did so for the first time, asking Mr. K. S. May, personal assistant to the managing director, whether it was the practice of newspapers to use quotation marks to enclose the gist or summary of what followed. It was a frequent policy, said May; there was an example on the front page of the *Advertiser* this morning, in the headline: "MRS. CALWELL 'HOME LOVER'."[3] Cross-examined by Bray, he said that he had never known Rivett to have an unbalanced mind, or to be seething with malice. The chief of staff, Mr. Murray James, told Bray that he found such epithets "incredible". When Kearnan asked if he had found Rivett somewhat excitable and

[3] Mr. A. A. Calwell had just been elected leader of the federal Opposition to succeed Evatt, who had become Chief Justice of New South Wales. The report attributed to Mrs. Calwell such remarks as: "I am completely absorbed in the home", but not the actual words "home lover".

mercurial, James replied that he was a man with terrific drive, not excitable but intensely enthusiastic.

"To the point of being fanatical?"

"No, I would not say that."

James said that the word "blast" was a favourite of newspapers, signifying an attack or criticism. One of the journalists who had reported the Commission told Alderman that when Shand left the court after reading out his statement on August 21, "he was most upset." Another reporter said that as Shand spoke on that morning, "he appeared to be taut and under strain," and that in the exchange with Sir Mellis Napier over Phin's evidence he sounded agitated. A court reporter, called by the Crown to give evidence about Shand's actual words, agreed that on the morning he withdrew he appeared to be under some emotional stress.

Mr. James Wilson, assistant editor, gave evidence on the fourth day that the editorial of September 3, "LET'S GET THE RECORD STRAIGHT", was drafted by the managing director, Murdoch. He agreed with Travers that Murdoch wrote editorials most infrequently. To Bray, he said that there was nothing unusual about an editor-in-chief scrapping a poster submitted by the news editor and doing one of his own. Sewell, the news editor, repeated his evidence that this had happened on August 21. It was unusual, he told Travers, for Rivett to draw a poster for the first edition.

Three directors were called on the fifth and sixth days. Mr. Reginald Wiltshire, a chartered accountant, told Kearnan that he had known Sir Mellis Napier, Sir Geoffrey Reed and Mr. Justice Ross personally for years, and always regarded them as men of the highest integrity. He took "blast" to be a synonym for "harshly criticised". He had expressed regret to the chairman of directors, Sir Stanley Murray, about the poster containing this word, but he took no action to dissociate himself from it publicly. Cross-examined by Alderman, he said that he was annoyed by the headline, which he thought undignified. To Bray, Wiltshire said he told Rivett that he disagreed with the method of reporting Shand's withdrawal, but no formal censure had been passed on Rivett by the directors. A second director, Mr. Ewen Waterman, company director and grazier, told Kearnan that he was disturbed at the crude wording of the poster he saw on August 21. Alderman asked whether he would have resigned from the board if he believed that the *News* was making a personal attack on Sir Mellis Napier. "I think I would have," Waterman replied. The chairman of directors, Sir Stanley Murray, pastoralist, solicitor, and director of several companies, said in answer to Kearnan that the words: "These commissioners cannot do the job" conveyed to him the substance of what Shand had said. He told Bray that he had never set in motion any process which could lead to a censure of Rivett, and that he would describe Rivett as a conscientious and responsible editor.

Evidence for the Crown ended on the eighth day. During a legal argument conducted in the absence of the jury and lasting several hours, Alderman and Bray submitted to Mr. Justice Mayo that there was no case to answer on three counts of seditious libel. They persuaded him. When the jury returned, the judge instructed them accordingly. Rivett and News Ltd. had not, in the view of the judge, been seditious; it remained for the jury to decide whether they had indulged in defamation.

If the defendant in a criminal case calls witnesses (apart from character witnesses), or tenders any documents, his counsel loses the right of last address to the jury. In this case the defence chose to call no witnesses except two as to character, and to tender no documents. When Travers tendered a part of the transcript of the Royal Commission containing Phin's evidence, Bray argued unsuccessfully that if the Crown wished to put in a portion of the record it should put in all. In later argument it became clear that the defence wished the jury to know what Brazel had said at the Commission about Shand's statements. An attempt by defence counsel to question a journalist about remarks by Brazel was forestalled by the judge. On another occasion, when the jury was out of court, Alderman said that a remark at the Commission by the Chief Justice himself negatived any suggestion of seditious intent. Once, in front of the jury, a director of the company said that he knew, from something the Chairman said after Shand's withdrawal, that His Honour was "disturbed". To anybody familiar with what was said when the Commission resumed on August 31, these references were clear enough. Although the prosecution was now arguing that Shand had not attributed impropriety to the Commissioners, Sir Mellis Napier and Brazel plainly believed that he had.[4] The Crown hoped to persuade the jury that Shand's protest was far less strong than the Chairman and assisting counsel had apparently taken it to be. But their comments did not reach the jury.

Rivett made an unsworn statement from the dock, as Stuart had done. After referring to his career and his imprisonment by the Japanese, he said:

> "When the *News* had obtained Father Dixon's story of evidence of an alibi for Stuart I formed no definite opinion except that it should be investigated. The community would be shocked if there remained any doubt about the conviction of a man who was to be hanged within a few days. With the approval and active co-operation of Mr. Murdoch I went to Queensland from the fifth to the ninth of August in connexion with the story. We felt it was the duty of a responsible newspaper to urge that every aspect of the case be sifted so that all should be satisfied that justice had been done and appeared to be done.
>
> "When the Commission started we gave it a good coverage. In order to be fair and because of the great interest, we published

[4] For Shand's own comments after leaving Adelaide, see p. 137.

in some detail not only what had happened that day but what had happened on the previous day since our corresponding edition. This is unusual but we did this so that our readers would have a complete picture of the Commission proceedings.

"Reading carefully what had happened on Thursday afternoon, August 21, it was quite clear that the reason why Mr. Shand wanted time to consider his position in the case was because he thought he was not getting and would not get a fair go. His protest, 'I feel it is impossible to convince Your Honour on this because Your Honour says you don't want to hear any more of it,' led Mr. Justice Reed to say: 'That is rather a startling remark to make.' . . . The reason Mr. Justice Reed found the remark startling seemed clearly because this was a direct attack on the chairman. Reading Mr. Shand's statement in the morning it never occurred to me, and I still believe it is not true, that he was referring only to the terms of the Commission or that the Commission was unduly restricting its terms. . . .

"To me the morning of August 21 was ordinary, but there was keen interest in developments. I understood from the reporters there was a good deal of tension at the Commission. I need not describe the host of decisions coming up to me as the morning wore on . . . I certainly had no time for the subtleties which I think have been attributed to me here and I was certainly never angry nor malicious. Why should I be?

"When I read what came through on the telephone I coupled it with the statements of the previous afternoon . . . I could come to no other conclusion—nor do I think that anyone could—but that Shand was saying the behaviour of the Commission and particularly that of the Chairman was and would be unfair and that the hostility to Shand and his juniors was such that it was better to leave Stuart without any counsel at all rather than to have them there. This was the only way I could interpret Shand's words, emphasised, as they were, by his withdrawal. If such an accusation by a Q.C. to a Royal Commission is not a blast or severe criticism (which is common usage), I do not know what is. I thought then, I think now, that Shand's words and behaviour in such a situation did cause the Commission to break up or adjourn indefinitely until other representation could be found for Stuart—an event which might never have happened at all.

"I agree that Shand's statements were aimed in particular at Sir Mellis Napier. This is both because of the interchange between them on the previous day and because of Shand's reiterated complaint on the Friday of being stopped in cross-examination. So I had no doubt that it was a fair summary to say that Shand did indict or charge Sir Mellis Napier. I am convinced from following the Commission proceedings that my interpretation was shared by counsel assisting the Commission and by Sir Mellis himself.

"I believe that the sixty words of Shand's statement, particularly the words: 'This commission is unable properly to consider the problems before it' were fairly and accurately summarised in the heading: 'These commissioners cannot do the job.' I believe that the words: 'You won't give Stuart fair go' fairly and accurately summarised Shand's words as reported in the state edition of the *News*, read in the light of the previous day's events, especially: 'We consider we have not yet been given nor will we be given a thorough investigation into this matter.' We used the quotes in accordance with the almost invariable practice in headlines to make it clear that the statement was not ours. The words in quotes, again in accord with practice, contained what we considered a fair and accurate summary of what Shand said. Considerations of space often make it impossible to reproduce in a heading or poster the very words used . . .

"There was certainly no intention of casting any reflection—either on my own part or that of the newspaper—on the Commission. On July 31 I had said as editor and never ceased to hold it now that no one doubts the integrity or knowledge of the law of Justices Napier, Reed and Ross."

Of the caption under Sir Mellis Napier's photograph, Rivett said:

"His age, judicial experience, and honor from the throne were all of interest and fairly given, I believe, to show the public the stature of the man attacked . . .

"I was in constant touch with Mr. Rupert Murdoch, the managing director. It is with his authority and indeed, at his request, that I state what follows . . .

"Mr. Murdoch knew of the first poster before it went out. He suggested the headline: 'These commissioners cannot do the job.' Later, because on further consideration he thought the first poster too long, he gave me the wording for the second poster: 'Commission breaks up. Shand blasts Napier.' He offered no other criticism of the first poster. Nonetheless, I accept responsibility as an editor should. I am mentioning my conversations with Mr. Murdoch only to indicate that no individual feelings of mine were involved . . . I was not censured or rebuked or even mildly criticised at any meeting of the board or even in private conversations . . .

"I was not in Adelaide on September 3. I had nothing to do with the editorial of that date.

"When the report of the Royal Commission came out we loyally accepted it, and gave it a good coverage, although, from our point of view, it was then stale news, having already been published in the morning paper.

"I am a loyal citizen of South Australia and I respect the administration of justice in this state. I had no intention of defaming anyone. I did not knowingly publish anything false, and I don't think anything I published was false . . . Your Honour and gentlemen of the jury, I am not guilty of the charges laid against me."

Two character witnesses were called by Bray on Rivett's behalf. A Methodist minister said that as a prisoner of war he had formed a high opinion of his courage and unselfish conduct; their friendship had continued since, and Rivett's general character and reputation was that of a man of complete sincerity and honesty, with high ideals and a deep love of his country. A bank officer who had known Rivett since 1942 said that he regarded him as a man of high integrity, sound judgment, and excellent reputation.

Kearnan, not Travers, addressed the jury for the prosecution. Rivett, he said, had magnanimously offered in his unsworn statement to take the responsibility; but the law saddled him as an editor with the responsibility if he published a libel. Rivett had rejected an innocuous headline and poster and composed libellous ones himself. Journalists claimed the licence to summarise statements within quotation marks in headings; they might do that if they wished, but if they quoted falsely they did it at their own risk. The *News* had deliberately distorted Shand's words. The headline said that the Commissioners could not do the job, and the posters implied that this was because they were corrupt, dishonest and unfair. If Murdoch, as Rivett claimed, had suggested the headline and one of the posters, it would have been of great interest to hear him say so as a witness for the defence. If Murdoch was their author, then in the editorial of September 3 he seemed not only ashamed, but frightened for himself, when he said this his own brainchild should never have seen the light of day. The fact that Murdoch and Rivett put their heads together to contrive libels did not exclude the editor from his responsibility.

Bray told the jury that the *News* had given a faithful picture, in essence though not in actual words, of what Shand had said. The jury was not asked to decide whether the paper had used crude or coarse language. A poster or a heading was like the title of a book; you had to read the contents to find what it was all about. He himself agreed that the words: "Shand blasts Napier" were in bad taste; but they were not defamatory. The transcript of the Commission showed that Shand was criticising the Commission, and the Chairman in particular. On the eve of his withdrawal he had used a threatening tone and rude words to the Chairman. The statement next morning, that his presence would handicap Stuart, was an insult to the Commission.

The jury was given a clear invitation by Bray to see the prosecution as politically inspired. It had been conducted, he said, with immoderation. It was the result of a fit of pique on the part of the government. The Premier had said that the *News* accused the judges of the vilest crimes. This gross exaggeration showed a mind carried away by wounded pride. Why were there *nine* counts? The fact that charges of sedition, since withdrawn, were ever included, suggested the hysteria of those behind the prosecution. Twentieth-century journalism was on trial here. Was the jury going to say that the press could not summarise lengthy statements in layman's language in headlines and posters? Did the words used broadly summarise Shand's words and actions? The press of South Australia was at liberty to use the techniques of our age and the language of our people.

Alderman said that when judges came down from the pedestal to the level of Commissioners, there was apt to be confusion. If there were an appeal in this case, the situation would be curious; for of the five judges available, three were members of the Commission and the other two appeared at it. This was the sort of thing that happened when judges sat as Commissioners. (After an interjection from Kearnan, Alderman said that the Full Court would almost certainly dismiss an appeal at once so that the defence could go on to the High Court.) According to the standards of South Australia, the lawyer from Sydney did get a fair go; but Shand himself had said, in effect, that he did not. Like Bray, Alderman suggested that there were political motives behind the trial. It was a most unusual action for the Crown to brief Travers, the acknowledged leader of the criminal bar. Kearnan had said that he himself had no special interest in the case. Well, *someone* was interested in the case.

Mr. Justice Mayo, summing up, told the jury that the case was an important one. It involved questions concerning the position of the press and the latitude that might be used in putting before the public the events occurring at a Royal Commission. No inference was to be drawn for or against the prosecution or the defence because neither side called Murdoch as a witness. If Murdoch had been called by News Ltd., Alderman would have lost his right of reply. This right was presumed by counsel to be of more importance than any evidence Murdoch could have given. Rivett had read an unsworn statement, not subject to cross-examination. This might be regarded as subtracting from the value of what he said, but he had exercised a legal right, and his conduct in doing so was not to be regarded as evidence of guilt. The jury was entitled to take into consideration evidence that those who knew Rivett regarded him as a man of high character; and they would realise that men of high character did give way at times to impulses not in keeping with their usual character. This was a matter for the jury.

Rivett had said that he intended only to give a fair and accurate report of the proceedings; if the jury agreed, that would negative malice on his part. Sewell had drafted a poster for which Rivett had substituted another, described as more cogent. Did the jury think that the wording of the posters and headline went beyond mere report? If so, and if the words were regarded by the jury as fair and accurate comment in the public interest, they should not be treated as defamatory. The jury would not overlook the views of directors of News Ltd. who had been critical at least of the two posters; and the editorial of September 3 was an indication that persons directly interested were somewhat concerned at the effect the words might have had.

The eleven jurymen retired after ten days, having been advised by Mr. Justice Mayo to consider the problems calmly and dispassionately. In South Australia a jury is allowed out for four hours, and its verdict, in other than capital cases, must be that of at least ten members. They were granted an extension of time. Fifty minutes later they reported that the defendants were found not guilty on eight counts, and that on the ninth the jury could not agree. Their disagreement concerned the poster: "SHAND QUITS 'YOU WON'T GIVE STUART FAIR GO.'" As directed by the judge, the jury found that it was not a seditious libel. They themselves found that it was not a defamatory libel published with knowledge of falsity. They disagreed about whether it was a defamatory libel.

The jury had decided that in publishing the headline which Playford described as "the gravest libel ever made against any judge in this state", the *News* had not committed the offences alleged.

The matter was still *sub judice*, and no direct comment on the result appears to have been published in Australia. In the London *Observer* on March 27 the case was reviewed by its Australian correspondent, Mr. William Fitter. Tremors from the sorry story of Stuart, he wrote, would "continue to disturb and influence Australian thought for some time". In the trial of Rivett the "angry reaction of South Australia's behind-the-scenes ruling clique" showed through blatantly. In the view of experienced newspapermen, the *News* did overstep the bounds of propriety in some headlines and posters. But instead of the Commission citing the company and its editor for contempt of court, an obviously piqued government "threw the book" at them. "What is significant about the *News*-Rivett trial is that it is the first time the public as represented by a jury has had the chance to give a decision rather than express its opinion on the wider issues of the case."

During April and May the Crown neither proceeded with the ninth charge nor withdrew it. Playford, when asked in parliament whether the government intended to press it, gave no clue. Early in May, during a debate in the federal House of Representatives, a South Australian member (Mr. P. Galvin) expressed the hope that the Playford government had been taught a lesson by the jury; the people of the state, he said, had been horrified when "the dictator" attempted to stand over, victimise, intimidate and almost blackmail an editor who had the audacity to criticise the government. The prosecution was an attempt, Galvin asserted, to stop the paper from campaigning against Playford in future.

For ten weeks after the trial Rivett was on bail. The outstanding charge was withdrawn on June 6. Two days later the *News* said in a leading article that it had "wished for a long time to express its confidence in the judges of this state", but had been deterred up to now "by rumours of possible legal action and a prosecution". The paper regretted certain misunderstandings. "Never at any time did we intend to identify ourselves with any of Mr. Shand's statements regarding the conduct of the Commission." Nor had it intended "to suggest that any member of that Commission was in any way unfitted to adjudicate properly on the issues before it. It is common practice in our courts that a judge who has heard a case will not sit on appeal. That is all we intended to convey. We realise that when the number of judges is limited, as it is in this state, this practice of necessity must be departed from at times." The *News* regretted its own part in these misunderstandings; "but we do not regret having supported the request for a further enquiry into the Stuart case." Many people "must feel easier in their minds that the fresh evidence has been fairly tested and weighed by the Royal Commission and that Stuart is now paying the penalty imposed by the law as a result of a report which we accepted without question. It is with satisfaction now that, after the dust of conflict has settled, we can re-affirm what we have always believed, that the members of the Supreme Court of this state are men in whom we and the public do and can have the utmost confidence."

In certain respects this article represented a revision of editorial judgment rather than a re-affirmation. The *News* had not exactly "accepted" the report "without question"; it had applauded the thoroughness of the enquiry but made no comment on the conclusions. Moreover, the view that a trial judge must at times sit on an appeal was relevant only if the paper had abandoned its own argument that there were two clear alternatives to having Sir Mellis Napier and Sir Geoffrey Reed sit as Commissioners (to appoint a judge from outside the state, and to have the judges sit as a Full Court).

Would this expression of confidence in judges have been published but for the prosecution? The paper itself declared that the only effect of the charges was to *delay* such a statement. How it had this effect was not explained. Mr. Rupert Murdoch had, after all, written an editorial defence of the paper's position on September 3, when Playford first threatened action, and had referred then to the judges ("The *News* has AT NO TIME alleged any crime by any member of . . . the Supreme Court . . ."). A less negative tribute could surely have been offered on that occasion, had the managing director wished to make it. It is difficult to rule out the possibility that, although the prosecution of the *News* failed in the courts, it altered the tone in which the paper discussed the Stuart case.

Five weeks after the last charge against him and the company was withdrawn, Rivett was replaced as editor-in-chief; an "acting managing editor" was appointed from a weekly paper in Perth also controlled by Murdoch. Although some people thought that the change must have been connected with the Stuart case, neither Murdoch nor Rivett gave any support to this interpretation. It is safe to conclude, however, that the announcement pleased those who deplored the paper's part in the affair and dismayed those who admired it. In May 1961 Rivett was appointed director of the International Press Institute, a body which has its headquarters in Zürich and which is concerned principally to resist threats by governments to freedom of the press.

Late in 1960 five police officers alleged that they had been libelled in a number of issues of the *News* between July 29 and September 4, 1959. They cited a number of reports and headlines, a letter and an editorial. The authors of the writ were Mr. Paul Turner, who was now an Inspector, and four of the other officers who were at the police station at Ceduna with Stuart. (The remaining officer, Mr. Richard Jones, had resigned from the force.) The matter had not come to court when this book was completed.

22

GUILTY OR NOT GUILTY?

Readers of the full report of the Royal Commission, when it was printed as a parliamentary paper, discovered an important passage omitted from newspaper summaries. In effect the Commissioners pass a severe judgment on the police and the Crown law authorities for letting the controversy occur: "We feel obliged to point out that the need for this enquiry could hardly have arisen, if the evidence which we have taken had been made available to the court of trial." Ceduna was no doubt difficult of access and Christmas was close; "but the plain fact is that the prosecution was content to rest its case upon the confession, without seeking for the testimony by which it has now been fortified." There are other criticisms of the police. The "so-called identification" of footprints after Stuart confessed was "plainly valueless". It was "irregular" for Sergeant Walker to enter no charge against Stuart and his companion Sumner on the Saturday night, and the men should not have been released without appearing before a justice or giving bail. The Commissioners do not think that these things, or any "shortcomings" in Walker's notes about messages from Whyalla, justify any doubt of the policemen's integrity.

In discussing the evidence of Constable Richard Jones (a passage which was also left out of the newspapers) the Commissioners offer criticism closer to the central issue. They are not quite happy about his notes of Stuart's interrogation having been written up so long afterwards; and they do not accept either his claim that this report was word perfect or his repeated testimony that the body of Stuart's confession was dictated verbatim. "In saying this, we have no doubt that the witness was speaking incautiously, and with less than the care that is expected of a police witness in a case of this kind . . . We have no doubt that the petitioner had more help with the wording of the written confession than Jones was prepared to admit." The words "*the show was situated at Ceduna Oval*" were "no doubt" elicited by question and answer, and "it is not unlikely that the word '*unconscious*' was the result of a question intended to clarify an expression which was regarded as ambiguous."

In an appendix annotating the confession, the Commissioners say that the word "*awoke*" may also have been the result of a question; in that event, they say, no significance would attach to the word, though "as a matter of interest" Stuart had elsewhere used the phrase

"I lay awake". The Commissioners do not explain why it should be a matter of interest to point out, in a note on an archaic verb, a colloquial use of the adjective; and if the word was in fact a policeman's and not Stuart's, this was surely of some significance since police witnesses had denied it.

Starke had submitted that, if a good deal of the confession was composed by question and answer, then all the police were perjurers. The Commissioners, though deciding that question and answer yielded rather more of the confession than the police admitted, find that they gave their evidence in good faith. Their main purpose in annotating the confession is to refute most of Strehlow's criticisms of the document by showing that words and idioms which he challenged had been used by Stuart himself either in evidence to the Commission, or in court at Alice Springs in 1956, or to the constable at Cloncurry in 1957.

Some of the annotations might be disputed. Alongside *"the picture show wall"*, which to Strehlow seemed an educated usage, the Commissioners set, from Alice Springs, *"the Stuart Arms veranda"*. But these two phrases are less similar than the Commissioners suggest; the former is a row of three separate nouns, while in the latter *"Stuart Arms"* is a single name; in evidence, Stuart himself said "picture wall". The words *"I jumped in a taxi"*, the Commissioners note, not only appear in the confession but were used by Stuart in Alice Springs and in evidence. Strehlow did not dispute this expression. The Commissioners draw attention to it as "somewhat unconventional", and say that this and the phrase *"I got off there"* (also used in evidence) "have an evidentiary value which approximates to that of a fingerprint". This comment suggests an imperfect familiarity with popular speech, for the first of these two phrases is quite common in Australia.

The Commissioners neither accept nor reject the criticism of *"raped"*; there was, they say, no means of testing whether, as claimed, Stuart did not understand the word. "In his evidence here he said that he did not know the meaning of *'private parts'*, although he had no difficulty in understanding it when questioned in Cloncurry in 1957." In the witness box Strehlow said that although any white man would know a word like *"accident"*, Stuart did not. This reference, say the Commissioners, was "perhaps unfortunate". The following passage of cross-examination by Chamberlain is then reproduced:

> "You know what an accident is, do you, Max, something that is not your fault?" "Yeah."
>
> "Did you tell Mr. Corbett that you never meant to do anything rude to the little girl, just an accident?"
>
> "I think I must have told him like that, I forget."[1]

Since the cross-examiner included a definition in his question, and since Stuart's second answer was so vague, there could be argument

[1] The transcript actually has *"forgot"*.

about whether this exchange demonstrated that Stuart really knew the word.

A number of the annotations are quite cogent. Of "*lavatory*" the Commissioners note that Strehlow was sceptical but that Stuart used it freely in evidence. Although Strehlow disputed "*the three of us*", Stuart at Alice Springs said "*the four of us*". Strehlow pointed out that the writer of the confession knew that the preterite of "*put*" and "*hit*" showed no change of form, but Stuart used "*put*" in this way at Alice Springs and "*hit*" in the recorded translation test. The word "*offered*", which Strehlow said Stuart would not use, was spoken by him both in evidence and at Alice Springs. Strehlow said that "*seen*" was more common than "*saw*" in Northern Territory English; that appeared to be so with Stuart, but he did say "*saw*" once in evidence. Strehlow argued that the sentence: "*I went back to near the cave where I had taken my clothes off and put them on*" was opposed to all the stylistic and grammatical features of Northern Territory English; but in cross-examination Stuart said: "*Where did she come from in the first place?*"—a construction similarly untypical of Northern Territory English as Strehlow described it, in that the prepositions "*where*", "*from*" and "*in*" are used correctly, "*she*" is used rather than "*he*" or "*'im*", "*did*" is used properly, "*the*" is not omitted, and the idiom "*in the first place*" owes nothing to Aranda or to pidgin.

Even allowing for both an improvement in Stuart's English in gaol and a tendency on the part of transcribers to ignore differences between Stuart's speech and normal usage, the Commissioners establish that Stuart was more nearly capable of dictating the confession than Strehlow believed.

The report is scathing about assertions after the trial that Stuart's English was inadequate. Until late in the enquiry, the Commissioners say, they were left to understand that he would give evidence through an interpreter. They find Strehlow's affidavit to the High Court and subsequent letter to the Attorney-General "misleading"; it conveyed the impression that Stuart spoke "pidgin" as that expression is generally understood, though in evidence he said that Stuart's English was not pidgin. The affidavit was further misleading in suggesting that Strehlow had gained considerably more information from Stuart than O'Sullivan had been able to obtain, "probably because of language difficulties". The only information mentioned, say the Commissioners, was about the girl at Thevenard; and Strehlow admitted that Stuart could easily have told that to O'Sullivan. They refer to the petition for commutation signed by Stuart on July 1, in which the ground urged was inability to speak English; in an attempt to explain away the deposition from Alice Springs in 1956, the Commissioners rightly observe, this petition gave an account of the document which was disproved in the course of their enquiry.[2]

[2] See pp. 56-7, 226 above.

The essay in translating the confession to and from Aranda did not impress the Commissioners, who note that on Strehlow's evidence English and Aranda do not lend themselves to straightforward translation; and in any case, Stuart, however fluent he might be in either language, was not in the habit of turning one into the other and found it difficult to transpose the Aranda form and idiom into the English convention. "He was obviously bi-lingual in the sense that he was not only speaking, but was actually thinking, in the English language and idiom." The force of the Commissioners' judgment here must be fairly clear to the reader of Stuart's evidence; it was quite plain to anybody who heard him give it.

There was, in the Commissioners' view, "an element of exaggeration and extravagance, even of misrepresentation", about Stuart's capacity for English in the presentation of appeals to the High Court and Privy Council. In the Privy Council, O'Sullivan said that he had been unable to find an interpreter for the trial; in that case it was his duty to inform the court, which would not have entered upon the trial until an interpreter was provided. At the trial there was no hint that Stuart had an alibi, or that he could not follow the evidence or instruct his counsel, or that he was incapable of dictating the confession.[3]

Since Stuart was quite capable of giving evidence in English, and had had previous experience of criminal proceedings, it seemed to the Commissioners that the attitude of the defence in rejecting the offer of the trial judge to let counsel assist and prompt Stuart through his statement from the dock was "designed to play upon the sympathy of the jury . . ." It was "difficult to resist the conclusion . . . that the trial judge was discouraged from asking questions, lest the true measure of the petitioner's understanding and command of the English language should be disclosed to the jury".

Some statements on Stuart's behalf certainly led to under-estimates of his fluency in English, and not only in minds disposed already to imagine that any aborigine in trouble with the European newcomer is a defenceless Stone Age man. When Professor Julius Stone asked whether the trial of such a man could be fair without better facilities for interpreting, he was taking a mistaken view of Stuart's linguistic equipment. Strehlow, who first described Stuart's English as pidgin, contributed to this view; so did O'Sullivan, especially when he said that in the event of a new trial Stuart would give evidence in Aranda.

[3] O'Sullivan did ask Jones at the trial whether the words "rape" ,"native", and "lavatory" were used by "the aboriginal defendant", and put it that the document contained nothing superfluous and omitted nothing important. So far as one can tell from the depositions, this was the only reference at the trial to Stuart's capacity for English. There was considerable cross-examination at the preliminary hearing and at the trial which implied that the wording of the confession was more *literate* than Stuart could have managed. In the Court of Criminal Appeal, before he met Dixon or Strehlow, O'Sullivan said that Stuart "could not make a coherent statement".

When Dixon spoke to the *Sydney Morning Herald* in July he said nothing about Stuart's ability to give evidence; he asserted only that knowing Stuart's "simple conversational pidgin or Territorian English . . . his own peculiar style of English", he was convinced that the confession "could not have been dictated by him in the form it was presented". The Commissioners properly object to "pidgin".[4] They are not very happy about "Territorian"; but in discussing the evidence of Jones they imply agreement with the general proposition of Dixon, and Strehlow, that there were certain words in the confession which the police swore were dictated by Stuart unprompted, and which could not have been.

In retrospect it is apparent that Stuart could have told his story adequately to the jury in the manner suggested by the trial judge. It does not follow that O'Sullivan believed so at the time. According to Dixon, the regular chaplain could get little out of Stuart; and according to O'Sullivan at the Privy Council, it had been difficult to elicit Stuart's version of events before the trial.

Mr. J. H. Wootten, reviewing the case for the Australian Association for Cultural Freedom, observed that O'Sullivan faced a problem familiar to criminal lawyers; for all he knew the client might be guilty, and it was not his job to push the man into admitting it. It was not quite true, however, as Wootten believed, that Stuart "answered questions but volunteered nothing" to his counsel; O'Sullivan told the English judges that Stuart had made "long irrelevant unintelligible statements . . ."; and the lawyer did obtain from Stuart (as Wootten pointed out) a statement protesting innocence and alleging assault. The Commissioners find it "difficult to resist the conclusion" that O'Sullivan knew his client's English was adequate but chose not to disclose the fact to the jury. If their inference is regarded as less than certain, and if it is true that Stuart was more articulate in Aranda than to O'Sullivan or the chaplain in English, then one can understand that the provision of an interpreter could have been considered seriously. In the early proceedings the Crown appears to have changed its mind over the aboriginal tracker Sonny Jim. A police witness said that for a native Sonny Jim spoke English well. He nevertheless gave evidence at first through an interpreter, and later carried on in English.

The Commissioners do not mention that witnesses differed substantially about Stuart's English. A number of people found him as

[4] This word is of course used variously. R. A. Hall, professor of linguistics at Cornell University, observes that it "is almost always taken to mean some kind of broken, imperfect, jargon-like speech". He thinks this usage wrong, and writes: "Pidgin English is any one of several kinds of reduced language, based on but differing from English, used in different parts of the world as a *lingua franca* among speakers of different languages but native to none of them" (*Hands off Pidgin English*, Sydney 1955). Obviously Stuart did not speak "pidgin" thus defined: on the other hand, though certainly imperfect and perhaps broken, his speech was not "jargon-like".

intelligible as an ordinary white person. But one aborigine from Ceduna said that he spoke "broken down English . . . I have a better English than him." A second aborigine said that Stuart's English was "a bit on the broken side", and when asked: "Could you understand him?" replied, "A little." Gieseman said: "He was a bit hard, but . . . if you are with him for six months you get used to him." Mrs. Gieseman said: "He used to talk all sorts of lingo," and his English was "not as good as my talk"; sometimes she had trouble understanding him. The comparison with the deposition from Alice Springs, as mentioned above, showed Stuart's familiarity with features of English speech which Strehlow found suspicious when they appeared in the confession; but this record of Stuart's speech diverges further from normal English usage than does the confession: the deposition contains nine errors of tense, while the confession (about half as long) contains none. The reader can see for himself that in evidence at the Commission Stuart, though readily intelligible, departed often from normal usage. The Commissioners suggest that the departures may have been deliberate, that Stuart "can and does speak good or reasonably good English when he wants to"; that he "began by speaking good English" but "as he gained confidence he tended to follow the lead of his counsel". It was not only when Starke was questioning, however, that Stuart's speech diverged from "reasonably good English". To say that he spoke better or worse English by choice is to attribute to him a sophistication for which there is no other evidence.

Much in the confession, as the Commissioners observe, reported undisputed facts which the police could have learned only from Stuart; in his unsworn statement and in evidence, he confirmed the substantial accuracy of those parts of the confession not relating to the crime. In one respect, they note, the confession was more reliable than the unsworn statement. Stuart said in evidence that late on the Saturday he went to the jetty (as in the confession), not to the hotel (as in the unsworn statement). The only dispute, according to the Commissioners, was with respect to the timing of the various events in Stuart's day. According to the confession, after returning from Thevenard Stuart worked "for about two hours". Stuart contended that the hours were from two to four, whereas the contention on the other side was that he worked from *after* four o'clock for about two hours, and left, as the confession had it, "about sundown". This conflict "might easily be avoided by imagining a gap between the end of the two hours, during which the petitioner was working, and sundown, when he went down to the jetty with Moir. But the evidence definitely excludes that possibility." Four witnesses from the show said that Stuart had lunch before two, worked the darts until about four, and left with Moir then or shortly afterwards.

At this point the report contains two surprisingly tendentious sentences: "It may be that this was not altogether a matter of choice. Before the hunt for the Giesemans started the petitioner had given his story of the afternoon to Mr. Strehlow and Father Dixon, and that story—as he had given it to them—left no room for any gap." The implication seems to be that Dixon induced the Giesemans to oblige with a story that fitted the one Stuart had given him. In plainer words, the alibi was concocted. Yet the Commissioners do not reject, elsewhere in the report, the evidence of Gieseman and Dixon that when they met in Queensland the priest gave no hint about what information he sought. The Commissioners may be attributing to Dixon, however, an intention more precise than he himself acknowledged. They write that according to his account of conversations at the gaol, "it was impossible to rely upon the petitioner's ability to fix the time of day and, in particular, the time when he had returned from Thevenard to Ceduna, and it seemed to the witness that the members of the Gieseman troupe might have been able to give evidence upon that subject." If this means that Dixon had in mind to ask the Giesemans when Stuart returned from Thevenard, then it is an inaccurate account of the priest's evidence.

The Commissioners cite a part of Allan Moir's evidence about when he and Stuart left the showground on Saturday afternoon. "He and his evidence were utterly demolished, but it was apparent that his belief—for what his belief might be worth—was that the sun was on the point of going down when he and Stuart reached the beach." The layman may think that if someone's evidence is utterly demolished—if, as the Commissioners also write, "it was impossible to rely upon anything that he had said"—then his belief is worth nothing. Nevertheless "there are occasions," say the Commissioners, "when a cross-examination which tears a witness to shreds seems to get down to bedrock, and to leave an impression of reality beneath the debris." Why this particle of Moir's evidence rather than any other seems to be bedrock is not argued. The report does not refer to Chamberlain's suggestion that Moir must have figured in certain minds as a possible substitute murderer. After Shand's severe cross-examination of the boy he had been mentioned rarely in the proceedings; Starke spoke of him only to dismiss his evidence as worthless.

The circumstantial evidence which supported the confession seemed to the Commissioners "clear and coherent"; a number of cross-bearings, as it were, all pointed to the same conclusion about Stuart's movements. Each of the seven or eight witnesses concerned must be allowed some margin for error about times; "but the suggestion that they could all be as much as two hours astray is really incredible". According to the confession, they write, Stuart had set out from Thevenard to walk to Ceduna at one o'clock, and according to the record of the oral interrogation it was one o'clock when he got the taxi to Thevenard. Moir said that it was after one when he saw Stuart outside Spry's shop. At the trial, Blackham said that it was after two when the taxi left Spry's. At the Commission he agreed that it might rather have been one o'clock, but the Commissioners think this unlikely. He normally had lunch at one, and he remembered on this day that lunch was late and that he was finishing it when the call came. It was true that he made a number of trips to Thevenard, but this was his last for the day. Spry, who said that it was at least two when the taxi left, was "quite unshaken in cross-examination". Certainly he had not been approached to make a statement for some months, but it was apparent that he had realised very shortly after the event that the man for whom he called the taxi was the Stuart who was being charged with the crime.

Veda Miller, one of the girls at the Thevenard Hotel, spoke to Stuart at half past two, according to herself and Brenda Kent. They were guessing the time, but it was "very difficult to believe that they could be wrong by more than, say, half an hour . . ." and there was no reason to doubt Brenda Kent's evidence that Stuart was outside the hotel for some time after that. Roy Wells and Mrs. Betts, who said that they saw Stuart in the street at Ceduna, had no means of fixing the time; but it passed belief that what they honestly thought to be about four o'clock was in fact about half past one. The evidence of the Kelly brothers was even more intractable. They had dinner at Koonibba at twelve and were driven twenty-five miles to Ceduna. They said that they left the mission about half past three; this was no doubt an estimate, but it was plainly impossible that they could have been at Ceduna before two. It was admitted that they gave Stuart money. It would be difficult to believe that they invented their account of accompanying him to the showgrounds; and if they did accompany him, that disposed of the Giesemans' evidence that Stuart came in before two. Stuart's evidence was that when he did come in, Moir was working on the knock-em. This was consistent with the Kellys' evidence, but not with Gieseman's testimony that it was after Stuart had come back and had his lunch when he (Gieseman), seeing it was two o'clock, said: "It is time to start."

Another summary than the Commissioners' could have made the evidence against the alibi appear rather less "clear and coherent". Wells, for example, said that Stuart returned to the show in a taxi, whereas on every other account he was on foot. There were other oddities in the evidence of this witness, as Starke pointed out. Ware appeared to differ from other witnesses about when the taxi left Spry's shop. Moreover, if it passed belief that the aboriginal witnesses could be two hours astray, why did it not pass belief that the Giesemans and their employees could be two hours astray in their estimate of when Stuart returned from Thevenard? If they were telling lies, that would be a simple explanation of the discrepancy; but the Commissioners do not attribute to them "any deliberate intention to falsify their evidence . . ." It could be argued that Gieseman, Mrs. Gieseman, Miss Hopes and McNeish were not each giving an independent recollection (as for example Spry and Brenda Kent and Roy Wells were doing), but that the last three were merely echoing the boss. Starke suggested that the evidence from Ceduna might not be that of independent witnesses, since all had been collected by a party from the C.I.B. which set off as soon as the Giesemans offered an alibi, "turning the town upside down for evidence to support the police . . ." It hardly seems plausible to suggest that senior C.I.B. men would put times into the mouths of witnesses. Yet that is exactly the sort of conduct which the report apparently attributes to a priest.

The Commissioners find the evidence of the Gieseman party not only refuted by that of other witnesses, but unconvincing in itself. First, it was "somewhat difficult to believe" that, when a statement had been taken from Moir in Whyalla, the other members of the troupe would make no attempt to follow the course of proceedings against Stuart. Second, the Giesemans and Miss Hopes were "not entirely candid" in their accounts of what happened when Stuart returned on Sunday morning. Gieseman told Phin that Stuart was sacked, but at the Commission he denied it. Mrs. Gieseman remembered her husband abusing Stuart, but she was prepared to say—and the Commissioners found it difficult to accept—that Stuart then came into the tent and told her about his job at the Wheat Board. "We cannot believe that Mrs. Gieseman was altogether happy under cross-examination upon this subject . . ." Miss Hopes, the Commissioners point out, was plainly mistaken about Stuart's work on the Friday night and Saturday morning.[5] McNeish was "at least . . . prepared to admit" that Stuart was dismissed on the Sunday in circumstances not entirely friendly; but he was recollecting matters in which he had, apparently, very little interest. In evidence he said that about four o'clock he gave Stuart a cup of tea, not the evening meal; but in the statutory declaration he said: "We had tea as usual, some time after four and before dark . . . Max had tea with us there in the tent." The latter seemed to the Commissioners the more likely.

Is it incredible (or to use the exact words of the report "somewhat difficult to believe") that in their nomadic world the show people did not follow reports of the trial? That Gieseman was not in the habit of reading papers much, and that he thought: "If he said he done it, that is all there is to it"? Is it, moreover, as the Commissioners remark about Stuart's visit to the show on Sunday, "sufficient to say that, if the witnesses are mistaken in their recollection of this—an out-of-the-way—occurrence, they may well be mistaken as to the time when the petitioner came back on the Saturday"? The Commissioners hint that the differing testimony about this incident is somehow suspicious; but they do not suggest, and it is hard to conceive, what motive any of the witnesses had for concealing the truth about it.

When the evidence of the Gieseman party "is considered in the light of facts which are not in dispute", the Commissioners find it "far from convincing". But on what criteria does one take marks off one

[5] See p. 111 above.

witness for inconsistencies, or conflicts with known facts, and not from another? Jones testifies wrongly about details of the confession and is merely described as "incautious". Turner gives differing answers about the handling of blades during Stuart's interrogation, which the Commissioners do not find sinister. Turner differs from Jones about the hairs taken from Stuart, from Low about the photographing of tracks and from Phin about Gieseman's oral statement in Whyalla; but none of these conflicts trouble the Commissioners. Nor do they comment on the disagreements between Olive Betts and the other girls at the Thevenard Hotel about whether Stuart gave her chocolates on Friday and whether she was at the hotel after lunch on Saturday. On crucial matters the evidence of all these witnesses is broadly accepted. When Gieseman's remark about his lack of interest in the case, and his account of the last meeting with Stuart, are taken as evidence that he may be unreliable on other matters, is he not being judged by harsher standards?

The Commissioners offer no comment on what some people thought the most impressive aspect of Gieseman's evidence. When Chamberlain pressed him on his memory, he replied: "at any entertainment or carnival or picture show the known time is from two to four." He and his companions could not be persuaded to express any doubt about their recollection that Stuart worked during this period. It should be noted, however, that not only the Gieseman party but some of the people whose evidence conflicted with theirs had some reason to know the time. The aborigines wandering around Ceduna did not; but Spry and the two girls from the Thevenard Hotel were all working to a routine.

In the evidence of Stuart himself the Commissioners point to serious inconsistencies and to conflicts between his evidence and that of his supporters. As Chamberlain and Brazel had argued, Stuart refuted the assertions of Strehlow and Dixon that he could not tell the time by a clock. To nobody did Stuart name two to four as the time when he was working; but in the witness box he said that when he returned to the fun-fair from Thevenard he saw two o'clock on Mrs. Gieseman's watch and when he knocked off work he saw four o'clock on Gieseman's. If this were true, it is inconceivable that he should have kept it to himself for so long, especially as (on his own account) he had understood at the trial what was said about times. Either he knew all along that he had not been at the showgrounds between two and four, or he had no idea what time he was there but was prepared to agree with the Giesemans' estimate once they came forward with it. In either case he must have been lying about the watches. The confession had him leaving Thevenard as early as one o'clock. Stuart said at the Commission that it was one o'clock when he went to Thevenard in the taxi. Turner, cross-examined by Starke, said that in oral interrogation Stuart was not asked the time he got back to Ceduna, but on his story seemed to have returned about two o'clock. In the unsworn statement there was not the vaguest reference to time other than: "I walked back to Ceduna in the afternoon." All of this conflicted with Blackham's evidence, unchallenged at the trial, that it was two o'clock or a little later when he picked up Stuart and Moir; but none of it conflicted with the recollection of the Gieseman party.

Whether or not he was guilty, he harmed his case gravely by saying that he had seen watches at two and at four. If Stuart had told the Commission that he had no precise knowledge of what time he came and went on Saturday afternoon, that might have explained why he had never anticipated the Giesemans' evidence, and in particular why he did not tell O'Sullivan during either the preliminary hearing or the trial that an alibi should be available. Starke argued that at the preliminary hearing the time of death was somewhat indefinite. The Commissioners agree, but think that "the evidence of the fisherman, Jorgensen,[6] made it fairly clear that the child had disappeared before four p.m." Starke argued that, although Jacobsen mentioned a time at the preliminary hearing, he was called not for that purpose but to identify the body, and if an identifying witness happened to mention a time it would hardly impinge on the mind of defence counsel. Starke was quite justified, remarked the Chairman, "in saying that the times did not emerge as clearly as they did at the trial". On reflection, however, the Commissioners seem to have decided that the defence could reasonably have been expected, before evidence was heard at the trial, to see that the crucial time was before four o'clock. It is possible on this point to agree with either Starke or the Commissioners; but it is surely not possible to believe that a man who knew he had begun to work at two and stopped at four should have failed to tell his counsel so even after hearing the whole of the trial.

Other lies had been admitted by Stuart in cross-examination. Was he also lying when he said that he had sexual intercourse with a girl at Thevenard? The Commissioners declare that Shand left no doubt in cross-examining Veda Miller and Brenda Kent that the girl whom Stuart had expected to see at Thevenard was the third girl from the hotel, who had been sitting in the pictures with the other two. According to Strehlow, Stuart said that the girl was "slightly short and stumpy", that she worked at the Thevenard Hotel, and that another girl went into the hotel and got her. Olive Betts, who could be described as "slightly short and stumpy", deposed that the day in question was, as the other girls had testified, her day off, and that while Stuart was outside the hotel she was spending the day with her sister. To clinch the matter, a doctor testified that she was a virgin. When Stuart gave his evidence he said that the girl with whom he had intercourse was not one of the three from the hotel who sat in

[6] The name was Jacobsen.

front of him at the pictures, but another girl sitting at the back to whom he talked at interval. He said that at Thevenard he accosted a girl who came out of the hotel and who was one of the three in front of him at the pictures. After she went back inside he saw the other girl standing on the footpath. He could not say where she had come from. They had intercourse at the back of the hotel. From photographs he identified Brenda Kent as the girl who came out of the hotel and Olive Betts as the girl with whom he had intercourse.

The story sounded to the Commissioners like a fairy tale. Was the girl, they ask, supposed to be Olive Betts or was she not? "If she is supposed to be someone else the whole story is fantastic." There was, they add, an obvious similarity between this excursion into fantasy and the conduct which the police attributed to the petitioner during his questioning; in each case he altered the story to admit what he thought was already known, but tried to take the sting out of it by adding a false ending.

Although Olive Betts' testimony had puzzling aspects, the medical evidence put it beyond reasonable doubt that Stuart did not have intercourse with her. Was there or was there not somebody else with whom he confused Olive Betts when shown photographs in the witness box? The Commissioners find Stuart "intelligent and quick-witted"; yet if the story of intercourse was an invention, it was not very shrewd of him to pick Olive Betts as the girl; to identify any particular person was to invite contradiction by her.

It does not follow from Stuart's lies that he is a murderer. Innocent people may lie in court if they believe it will help prove their innocence. They may also lie if they believe, however wrongly, that judicial machinery exists to convict those who happen to be caught in it. (A possible explanation of the discrepancy between the evidence of Olive Betts and that of her friends is that although she had very little to do with Stuart, a generalised fear of the law made her unwilling to admit any relationship at all.) But one would certainly want strong independent evidence before concluding either that Stuart was handing out darts from two to four or that he was assaulted by policemen.

The Commissioners reject in detail his allegations of assault. They note that at the time of the trial, as indicated in his unsworn statement, Stuart appeared uncertain which officer picked up a blade. At the Commission, after Turner had said that he examined the blades and might have asked what they were, Stuart was certain that it was Turner who picked them up and threatened to skin him. There was, however, nothing improbable in Turner's evidence, the Commissioners argue, and nothing sinister in the fact that all but one of the policemen had no recollection of the blades; it was nine months later when they were asked, and no stress had been laid upon the blades at the trial. In other respects Stuart's evidence appeared to the Commissioners untrustworthy. Although he said in the unsworn statement and in answers to Starke that the assault on him began quite early in the interrogation, he conceded under cross-examination that the police report of the early stages of questioning was substantially correct. It was obvious from his evidence that at least up to the point where he spoke of leaving Thevenard, he knew what he was saying and was in no way agitated.

Other circumstances suggested to the Commissioners that his evidence was untrue or much exaggerated. One blow from Jones, he said, caused a cut over his eye which took a couple of weeks to heal. A police photographer could see no healing wound on a photograph taken two days later; "and on our own inspection of the photograph, we are unable to express any opinion one way or the other." The injury was unnoticed by anybody at the time. At the trial it was not mentioned. The affidavit by Kleinig, the welfare officer, stated that he stood outside the open doorway of the office while the confession was being dictated, saw Stuart and three of the policemen, and heard that all the voices were subdued. The hair which Stuart alleged was pulled out by the roots appeared to the Commissioners, under a magnifying glass, to have been cut. Finally, Stuart's signature on the confession showed, when compared with six other specimens, no sign of agitation or nervousness.

The Commissioners were not impressed with the Wardrops' evidence about alleged admissions by Detective Frank Whitrod. They note that wide publicity was given to a wrong account of what the Wardrops would say. Stuart, they point out, never alleged that Whitrod used violence. An admission by Whitrod could affect only his own credit, not that of any other witness. Wardrop, moreover, suggested that Whitrod spoke of violence *after* Stuart confessed, not before. Wardrop did not seem to the Commissioners a reliable witness. There were discrepancies between what he told the solicitor and what he said in evidence. Although he said that he had read no reports of the trial until the last day, Mrs. Wardrop gave evidence that he followed its course in the papers. He denied having asked his daughter whether she heard Whitrod's admissions; but his wife and daughter said that after Shand's statement was published the family conferred for four hours, freely discussing the conversation with Whitrod. In Mrs. Wardrop's evidence, it was "really impossible to distinguish between recollection and reconstruction".

Whitrod, on the other hand, came through a very searching cross-examination "unshaken", and Baker, who also disputed the Wardrops' story, seemed "an honest and reliable witness". It was in any case improbable that Whitrod would talk in this way to Wardrop who, on Baker's evidence, had a reputation for being too talkative; "on our own observation of the witnesses, we think that it is unlikely that Whitrod would have chosen Wardrop as a confidant." The alleged admission was of something that never happened according to Stuart, and could not have happened according to all the evidence heard. "On this point the affidavit of Mr. Kleinig is really conclusive." It was not suggested that the Wardrops "deliberately concocted or invented" a conversation; perhaps it was put to Whitrod that the police *must have felt* like assaulting Stuart after he confessed, and Whitrod said something which was taken as assent.

This speculation by the Commissioners might be plausible if only one conversation were involved; but Wardrop was testifying about *two* incidents; and it is most unlikely that a misunderstanding of that character could survive a second discussion. Both to the solicitor and in evidence, Wardrop claimed that at his café, some time after the conversation at the R.S.L. club, Whitrod said that when Stuart confessed the police did their blocks and belted him. Surely this must be either the truth, or a fantasy, or a concoction? In the second conversation, moreover, not only Wardrop but his wife was said to have taken part. At the club, say the Commissioners, there may have been some conversation between Baker and Whitrod and Wardrop; "but we think that, if Whitrod had made any suggestion of violence being used by the police, Baker would have remembered it . . ." But could he have forgotten altogether a conversation in which the murder was even discussed? Yet Baker said in evidence that he could remember *no* occasion soon after the crime when the three men were together at the club.

The analysis of Wardrop's evidence is silent on one matter that Starke put to the Commissioners. According to Wardrop, Baker agreed, in a telephone conversation on August 12, that he had a faint recollection of Whitrod's admission. Baker denied this on oath. If Baker was here telling the truth, why should Wardrop have repeated to the solicitor two days later a story which he knew would be refuted? To be loquacious and careless is one thing; but behaviour such as Baker here attributed to Wardrop is self-destructive.[7] Why, finally, should the Commissioners think the affidavit of Kleinig, the welfare officer, conclusive evidence that Stuart was not assaulted, since he did not reach the police station until the confession was being typed and appears to have left again as soon as he heard that Stuart had confessed?

It is true that Stuart did not allege any assault after his confession. According to Mrs. Wardrop, what Whitrod did say made her think that Stuart may have been assaulted earlier. Starke suggested, without making much of it, that Whitrod might have been "trying to make it a little better for himself". Starke agreed that any admission by Whitrod could not properly be used to impair the credit of other police witnesses.

* * *

[7] Brazel made a comment on this matter, without, however, explaining why Wardrop should have approached Baker unless fairly sure that he would support the story (see p. 268 above).

Three other points are made briefly in the report. First, Strehlow's assertion that this was not a black man's crime is dismissed on grounds similar to Chamberlain's; this was neither a black man's crime nor one to which white men were addicted, but one committed when the self-control and decency which normally restrain men were released or overcome. A possible explanation for such conduct was strong drink, and the petitioner had been drinking fairly heavily. Secondly, the Commissioners reject Starke's argument as to the improbability of Stuart's behaving as described in the confession—stripping before the crime, running later to wash on the open beach. There could be no doubt that this was what the murderer did—"i.e. the man whose footprints ran down to the pool and back again"—whether or not this was Stuart;[8] and it was a risk a man like Stuart might take when he had been drinking. Third, the tracks themselves. The new evidence proved that Stuart must have passed along the beach at or about the time the thing happened. If the footprints were not his, whose could they be? Before they saw Stuart, "the black trackers, . . . said that the prints were those of a man answering his description."[9] It was significant that the bare footprints came to an end at or about where Stuart left the beach. All in all, the Commissioners are satisfied both that the confession was genuine and that even without recourse to it there was ample evidence to support the verdict of the jury. They print in an appendix evidence about Stuart's conviction at Cloncurry, which was introduced by the Crown on the ground that it related to his capacity for English and subsequently cited as indicating a trend in his sexual history. The Commissioners refer to this evidence only on linguistic matters and offer no comment on Chamberlain's other argument.

The Commissioners say that the Executive "conceded something which the practice of the courts would not allow in the ordinary course of things" when it allowed Stuart to re-open his case by setting up an alibi which he had not attempted to set up at the trial and by giving the testimony he elected not to give to the jury. "The reason for granting that concession is, of course, the suggestion that the petitioner is an illiterate aboriginal native", incapable of following the evidence, addressing the jury adequately, or indicating or assenting to the confession he signed. All these suggestions, however, were before the Executive on July 6 when it decided not to commute the death sentence. At the end of July it was widely believed

[8] If the man was not Stuart, however, the Commissioners could not know for certain that he was naked when he went to the pool.

[9] The Commissioners err in attributing this statement to *both* trackers. Sonny Jim said at the trial that he told a policeman the tracks were by an Aranda man. Harry Scott said that he was told before seeing the tracks both that Stuart was an Aranda man and that the tracks were those of an Aranda man.

that the statutory declarations from Gieseman's fun-fair gave sufficient grounds in themselves for investigation. Are the Commissioners implying here that if fresh evidence of the sort offered by the Giesemans had been offered on behalf of someone who did *not* purport to have unusual disabilities, he would have been hanged without further investigation? It is not a comforting thought.

Whether or not Stuart was guilty, his own evidence at the Commission, taken together with the practice of the courts, makes it difficult to argue that he suffered a miscarriage of justice.[10] If an accused person is convicted after deliberately choosing not to call evidence which is available to him, he cannot plead that a miscarriage has occurred simply because that evidence might have affected the verdict. On Stuart's own story to the Commission, he knew all along that the alibi was likely to be available. It is hard to believe, but that is what he said.

In the present writer's opinion, Stuart was probably guilty. He was certainly capable of dictating something broadly like the confession which he signed. The Wardrops' evidence and Starke's cross-examination of the police raise a suspicion that Stuart may have been assaulted or threatened; but the course of his own evidence raises a far stronger suspicion that the account of the interrogation in his unsworn statement was not true. The evidence against the alibi is on balance more persuasive than the evidence for it. It seems improbable that the police, as Starke hinted, should have put times into the mouths of nine different witnesses without this emerging in Shand's cross-examination of them. It is unfortunate that more evidence was not offered on the timing of events during Saturday afternoon. The Kelly brothers' story that they arrived from Koonibba well after two o'clock (they said half-past three) could in principle have been checked: they said that Mrs. Blackham drove them, and Dennis Blackham said that his mother took over the car which he was driving when he picked up Stuart and Moir. If Mrs. Blackham had been called and agreed with both her passengers and her son, that would have been more conclusive evidence than any other that Stuart was not back at the show by two o'clock; for he admitted having seen the Kellys on his way there. Again, it should have been possible to come closer to settling whether the show shut about four o'clock, as Gieseman and others said, or remained open continuously from afternoon to evening, as one of the aborigines (Wells) said. The Commissioners prefer the evidence that the stalls were open at least until six o'clock or so. Since this was disputed by everybody who worked at the show, would it not have been useful to hear some of the thirty or forty people said to have visited it, in addition to the

[10] In an appendix the Commissioners print remarks by Sir John Latham and other judges about the practice of the courts in relation to fresh evidence.

aborigines who testified in passing on the subject but who were called primarily for other reasons?

It has been suggested above that the evidence at some points is more tangled than the Commissioners indicate, that the Wardrops' testimony is dismissed a little lightly, and that the members of the Gieseman party are judged more harshly than other witnesses. The most unsatisfactory passage in the report is the one which insinuates that Dixon let the Giesemans know what times he wanted them to name. To the present writer, the evidence of witnesses from the fun-fair, and especially of Gieseman himself, is hard to dismiss with certainty as mistaken or dishonest.

What is to be said of Stuart's demeanour towards Dixon in gaol, and in particular of his remarks, when expecting to die within hours: "Some bloke lucky . . . Bloke who done this"? In the priest's mind these words, spoken in that situation and only in response to questions, tended to confirm Stuart's innocence. There would seem to be two other alternatives. Either Stuart, though actually a murderer, believed now that he was not; or he was guilty, knew it, and was displaying an almost superhuman self-control.

Might Stuart have been acquitted if his companions had given evidence at the trial? Gieseman said in his statutory declaration that he had told Phin in Whyalla that Stuart was back for lunch and left with Moir at four. The Commissioners appear to think that statements taken from Gieseman and his party soon after the event would have been rather different from those secured by Dixon in July; but nobody can now be sure. If they had said then what they said later at the Commission, the Wardrops might have come forward in time for the trial. The evidence about a child at Cloncurry would have been inadmissible so long as Stuart stayed out of the witness box. If he had entered the box, alleged violence against the police and thus exposed himself to cross-examination about his character, he could have been asked about the child at Cloncurry. If he had denied having committed an offence against her, the conviction could have been proved; but any subsequent reference to the details of the offence would have been rigorously excluded. Can one be sure that in such circumstances, twelve reasonable men would have had no reasonable doubt?

23

LESSONS FROM STUART

To THE MIND of the Crown Solicitor there was one lesson: "that attempted trial by newspaper is a dangerous and a malignant thing . . ." The view is shared widely in British communities that the press should not be permitted to usurp any function of the courts. Did the *News* try to do so?

One member of parliament suggested that it was somehow sinister of the paper to involve itself in the search for fresh evidence; but Playford never carried his denunciation to that length. Once, on July 29, the paper said that Dixon had offered "physical and psychological evidence" which "pointed strongly to Stuart's innocence". But these words were part of an editorial which urged the Crown itself to undertake a new investigation, and which did not reject the possibility that such an enquiry would confirm the original verdict. If the authorities had thought that the *News* was here setting up as a court, they would presumably have prosecuted. On no other occasion did the paper express an opinion about Stuart's guilt or innocence. On July 31 it insisted that the Commission investigate whether there were defects in Stuart's trial and that the whole legal system be "probed"; but nobody said publicly that it was improper to express these opinions and no prosecution was launched in respect of them.

In the traditional debate about the place of the press in a free society, the central question has been how far a newspaper may express with impunity its opinions about individuals and institutions. This question was not raised directly in the trial of Rivett. If the Crown had prosecuted the *News* in respect of its demand on July 29 for a new enquiry, or its disapproval two days later of the terms and membership of the Commission, or its re-publication of the *Observer's* article on "the hanging state", the defence would presumably have been that the paper had a right to publish these things. The Crown case was rather that the *News* had attributed to a man, Shand, opinions which he himself never uttered or implied; and the defence was that this had not been done.

The Rivett case was nevertheless a serious encounter between a newspaper and a particular government. It was not, as with a typical prosecution for contempt of court, a case in which the minister responsible for administering justice lent nominal authority to a charge which was virtually inevitable given the state of the law. The government back-bencher who believed that a verdict of guilty would "justify the government and the Supreme Court bench" was not alone; counsel for both editor and company urged the jury to treat the prosecution as an essay in politics, and long before the summonses were served Playford warned that they were coming in a speech defending his government. "If the government were to take action now," he told parliament on September 2, "it would be accused of trying to stifle public debate." But was he not trying to stifle debate by threatening, at a moment when controversy was at its most violent, that the *News* would later be brought to court? His personal threat hung over the paper for eighteen weeks before the charges were laid, and may have affected its reception of the Royal Commission report. Playford was acting Attorney-General when he accused the *News* of trying "to drag our judges down". Even before a jury failed to agree with him, it could be argued that the Premier was seriously confusing his political situation with his responsibility for the criminal prosecution.[1]

The performance of the *News* was far from perfect. If Wardrop was right in his account of how a brother-in-law on the *News* extracted from him a summary of his evidence, and if the man was acting on orders, then somebody in a high place on the paper was interfering imprudently with the conduct of the Commission; and in the course of communicating the story to Shand, it was possibly someone from the *News* who distorted it seriously. At one point in the hostile comment on the *Advertiser* published on August 21, it was implied that Shand was rebuking the morning paper when in fact he was criticising Brazel. The managing director himself wrote an editorial saying that a headline should not have appeared. It was unfortunate that the paper which had been so active in getting the Royal Commission appointed should have published no analysis, favourable or otherwise, of its findings. But in making possible Dixon's search for the Giesemans, the *News* performed a service which earns a sort of tribute from the Commissioners themselves, when they remark that by the end of July "there was, certainly, a case calling for an investigation . . ."

* * *

The popular press, writes Francis Williams in *Dangerous Estate*, exists "to shout, protest, expose and play hell. Naturally the process is hardly agreeable to those conscious of more solemn obligations. The administrators of society always find it difficult to understand the resentments of the administered, especially when they are conscious

[1] On the day after Rivett's acquittal the government displayed a further confusion about the proper limits of its responsibility for law and order, when South Australia became the only place in the world where Mr. Tom Lehrer was prohibited from singing publicly some of his essays in grisly satire.

that they mean so well by them." The "administrators" in Adelaide certainly found the *News'* stance over Stuart disagreeable, though in one respect they flattered the paper unduly. Playford and others spoke as if all disquiet about the Commission was a crop planted by the *News*. Certainly the paper was the earliest to express regret that Sir Mellis Napier and Sir Geoffrey Reed were sitting as Commissioners; but is it conceivable that editors and lawyers in other states and abroad would let themselves be used as mere amplifiers of a mischievous journalist in Adelaide? Sir Mellis Napier quoted with care other cases in which judges had sat on an appeal after presiding at the trial; but there were readers of *The Times* as well as of the *News* who continued to think that it was not wise for himself and Mr. Justice Reed to accept appointment. Every lawyer knew cases of the sort mentioned by the Chief Justice. Some nevertheless thought the practice unwise; and in a case with the peculiar features of this one it should not have been hard for either a judge or a politician to foresee that comments like Lord Attlee's were likely.

The Chief Justice said that the Commissioners were those judges who would have had to constitute the Full Court had the matter been referred there. In that case, one lesson from Stuart may be that the South Australian bench needs more occupants. But neither he nor Playford said why a single judge could not have sat, as Mr. Justice Kinsella sat on the McDermott Royal Commission in Sydney. Mr. Justice Ross, the one available judge who had taken part in no proceedings about Stuart, would have been an obvious choice. Outside the state there was, as some suggested, Mr. Justice Kriewaldt of the Northern Territory Supreme Court. If, moreover, the three judges had been sitting as the Full Court and not as a Commission, the possibility of an appeal to the High Court would have settled some misgivings.

A large part of the controversy during August and September arose out of the special nature of the tribunal. Shand could have hoped to gain no tactical advantage (to take the lowest judgment of his motives) from walking out of the Full Court; if he had grounds for complaint they could be put later to the High Court, and if he had not, there would be no point in trying to bluff the High Court that he had. Lawyers would have been unlikely to object to the terms of the enquiry if they were laid down by statute and judicial tradition rather than by *ad hoc* decision of the executive. The peculiar, half-judicial and half-political character of a Royal Commission virtually invites counsel to appeal to a tribunal—public opinion—in which the rules of evidence are loose, each member is judge and jury, and verdicts are inclined to be hasty and passionate.

Some Australian judges and lawyers were convinced long before 1959 that judges should not accept Royal Commissions, or should do so only in narrowly defined circumstances. When the Chief Justice of Victoria, Sir William Irvine, rejected in 1923 a request that a judge of the Supreme Court should act as a Royal Commissioner, he wrote to the Attorney-General:

> "Parliament, supported by a wise public opinion, has jealously guarded the bench from the danger of being drawn into the region of political controversy. Nor is this salutary tradition confined to matters of an actual or direct political character, but it extends to informal enquiries, which, though presenting on their face some features of a judicial character, result in no enforceable judgment, but only in findings of fact which are not conclusive and expressions of opinion which are likely to become the subject of political debate."

The proposed subject of this particular investigation was very different in character from the Stuart case. Irvine, moreover, was discussing whether the Royal Commissioner should be a judge or somebody else, not whether the Commission itself was an appropriate instrument. But his general point was that to risk putting a judge's findings of fact into the arena of political debate was to endanger the high confidence which judges enjoy. In Adelaide, a Royal Commission composed of three judges became the centre of a parliamentary and public controversy unique in Australian history.

Victorian judges expressed themselves in 1954 even more strongly than Irvine, when they declined to make one of their members available to the federal government for its Royal Commission on Espionage following the defection of Vladimir Petrov. They declared that there was no obligation on any judge to undertake the duties of a Royal Commissioner, and that except in national emergency no judge should do so. The Victorian Bar Council supported this stand, saying:

> "Like all executive action, the proceedings and findings of Royal Commissions may properly be, and frequently are, the subject of political controversy. Judges are not exempt from criticism, but it is most undesirable that they should intrude into areas where their conduct, not as judges, but as persons performing an administrative function, may give rise to reflections upon them. It is not easy for the public to remember that such reflections are not upon them in their judicial capacity, and the reputation of the courts must inevitably suffer."

Not all lawyers in Victoria agreed with this view; nor did judges in other states. In the event, the Commonwealth secured judges from New South Wales (Mr. Justice Owen, who was chairman), Queensland (Mr. Justice Philp), and South Australia (Mr. Justice Ligertwood) to form its Commission. The appearance of Dr. H. V. Evatt, Q.C., as counsel for certain witnesses while he was Leader of the Opposition, his hostile encounters with Mr. Justice Owen and his subsequent expulsion from the Commission, made the Victorian judges and barristers appear rich in foresight. This aspect of the Petrov Commission was recalled during another political-judicial controversy, on the eve of Evatt's appointment over Mr. Justice Owen, early in 1960, as Chief Justice of New South Wales. On this occasion, *Nation* said of the Petrov enquiry: "This was a Royal Commission, an intensely political one. It was not a court of law, and justices who step into that kind of arena must take the rough with the smooth."

Like Irvine before them, the Victorian judges and lawyers in 1954 were thinking of a Royal Commission whose political character was more obvious than in the case of the Stuart Commission. But Stuart had been the centre of vigorous public dispute for a month before the Commission was appointed, and in parliament his name had been mentioned by the Opposition. "We are sitting here," Mr. Justice Ross said one day, "not as a court but as a Royal Commission. We could just as easily have been three laymen or one layman . . ." In the debate on Labor's censure motion, Dunstan was speaking in terms very like those of the Victorians when he said that, as judges, members of the judiciary would not be subject to public criticism, "but as Commissioners they would be . . . and they ought not to be in that position." The view was not confined to the Labor Party. "To have turned judges into fact-finders," said the *Observer*, "as Mr. Playford has done, can merely end up discrediting the functioning of the judiciary." Professor Geoffrey Sawer, professor of law in the Australian National University, wrote in *Nation*: "Perhaps this case shows you should never have a Royal Commission on a judicial proceeding; it certainly shows that the Royal Commissioners should not come from the court whose activities may be in question." One lesson of the Stuart case may be that the judges of the High Court have set a wise example to their brothers in the states by refusing all requests (and there have been many during sixty years of the federation) to sit as Royal Commissioners.

There is a further unhappy aspect of a Royal Commission on a judicial matter. In his closing address Brazel urged that "a real re-trial" could not be expected after the public had been given the Commissioners' views on the case. If, in other words, Royal Commissioners choose to report fully on the issues before them (as Brazel said should be done in this case), the outcome of their enquiry can be only to upset the verdict or uphold it. There are disturbing implications here. The Chairman said in discussion with Starke that "when you reach the point at which a re-trial is impossible you think pretty seriously before you say the doubt is such as to justify his being released". If, as Brazel argued, the mere publication of the report would rule out a re-trial, must a man in Stuart's position raise not only enough doubt in the mind of the tribunal to warrant a new trial, but a larger doubt that would justify his release?

To rule out a re-trial was of course to prevent the matter ever coming again before a jury. To those who believe that in criminal matters the jury should always have the last word, this alone might well make a Royal Commission the wrong body to consider new evidence. The appearance that Stuart was being tried by judges bothered a number of people, including Sir John Latham and the Labor M.P. who said that even if the weight of evidence was against Stuart, "a large section of the people of Australia" would believe that he had not been given a fair go. It is a maxim of jurists that a jury may think differently from a judge.

* * *

In South Australia and elsewhere, there was a good deal of indignation when the president and secretary of the Police Association took part in controversy about Stuart's conviction, and in particular when they referred to matters which were not mentioned at the trial. Even if the president had not been the officer in charge of the investigation, and even if further judicial proceedings had not been possible, this would have been the kind of action which could imperil public confidence in the police force as a fair and dispassionate instrument of the law. In all the circumstances of this case the intervention was—to use Travers' word—"appalling". If, as the jury and the Commission found, Stuart's confession was offered freely, one can readily sympathise with Turner and his colleagues for feeling anger and pain at the doubts that were being expressed in the papers early in July. One would nevertheless expect Turner to be told, after the first outburst, not to give way again to his feelings. No such instruction seems to have been given, for he made further statements in July, expressed no regret about them at the Commission and, at the end of the year (according to the Sydney *Sun*), talked to the press about evidence that the Commissioners had decided not to hear. It was unfortunate enough that the policeman himself saw nothing improper or even imprudent about this last essay in public relations; but it was alarming that his superiors let him make it.

* * *

While the Royal Commission sat, a good deal of concern was expressed about the admission of confessions as evidence. In Sydney a delegate to the annual state convention of the Liberal Party spoke of "a case in another state" when moving that statements by accused persons be rejected as evidence unless made in the presence of a solicitor. The resolution was carried. In Malaya, a newspaper reviewing the affair after Stuart's reprieve said it was certain that, from now on, there would be "a more searching examination in the preliminary stages of any future confession tendered by police against an alleged murderer, white or coloured, in Australia". Stuart will be mentioned for some time in the continuing debate on when, if at all, confessions should be admitted. Those who doubt Stuart's guilt are likely to think that his story strengthens the case against admitting confessions. Those who do not share such a doubt may nevertheless be troubled at the evidence of police witnesses about how Stuart's confession was composed. The Commissioners' own remarks have been quoted already. This recent observation by an English judge, Sir Patrick Devlin, is a reminder that not only in South Australia do policemen speak of confessions "incautiously":

> "Rather than become engaged in a discussion about whether a question was or was not necessary to remove an ambiguity, some police witnesses seem to have preferred stoutly to deny that they asked any questions at all and even to maintain that they hardly opened their mouths. Consequently, statements have sometimes been put in evidence which have been said to be the prisoner's own unaided work as taken down by the police officer and in which the prisoner has recounted in the stately language of the police station (where, for example, people never eat but partake of refreshment and never quarrel but indulge in altercations) the tale of his misdeeds. The fact that it took two hours or so to fill a page of foolscap could presumably only be explained on the basis that the prisoner was carefully picking his words."[2]

Lord Justice Devlin goes on to suggest that the fault to be looked for when the police are obtaining confessions "is not the frame-up but the tendency to press interrogation too hard against a man believed to be guilty". The danger of that tendency has been summed up by another English writer, Glanville Williams, who says in *The Proof of Guilt* that a confession "may even, it seems, be made for no better reason than to put an end to police questioning".

Some Australian lawmakers have thought that aborigines may be more prone than other people to confess too readily. In Queensland no confession by an aborigine is admitted in court unless the judge is satisfied after questioning the defendant in chambers that he understood its meaning and made it voluntarily. In the Northern Territory, the Welfare Ordinance of 1953 provides that no confession from a "ward" (nearly all full-blood aborigines are wards) is admissible unless it was made in the presence of his counsel or of a welfare officer. Stuart was not a "ward" in the Northern Territory, but as soon as he entered South Australia he became in law an aborigine. The Aborigines Act of that State specifies nothing about judicial

[2] In the preface to his book *The Criminal Prosecution in England,* where the above passage appears, the author says that as he holds judicial office he would not think it right to express a personal opinion on matters involving praise or criticism of the police. One reviewer remarked that if this is judicially abstaining from criticism, the police ought to be worrying about the book he will write when he leaves the bench.

proceedings. It says in broad terms that it is the duty of the Aborigines' Protection Board "to exercise a general supervision and care over all matters affecting the welfare of the aborigines, and to protect them against injustice, imposition, and fraud".

There may or may not be a case for giving aboriginal defendants special safeguard; and if there is, it may or may not be a good idea to define as aborigines, for this purpose, people as familiar as Stuart with the world of white Australia. But since Stuart was in fact defined as an aborigine by South Australian law, and since that law did offer aborigines "protection", the absence of the welfare officer, Kleinig, from the interrogation at Ceduna was unfortunate. At the request of the police he searched for a man who might help to test Stuart's story, and then he waited outside the room until Stuart signed his confession. It appears never to have struck him or the police that he might have been inside. It was a fault of policy, not personality. There is no evidence to suggest that Kleinig was advised to be present in such circumstances.

How to define an aborigine and whether to write special provisions for him into the law are (like every other problem relating to such a small minority) not questions of pressing practical importance in Australia. They will, however, become a little more pressing as time goes on, for the social and geographical mobility of aborigines throughout Australia is steadily increasing. Whatever principles are settled on should be applied uniformly. Either by mutual agreement or by handing the matter to the federal government, the states should put an end to a situation in which a man like Stuart is an aborigine in some places and not in others.

In the Northern Territory an aboriginal defendant is allowed to have somebody else read out in court a statement prepared on his behalf. In South Australia he is not. It is surely unjust that an illiterate, whether dark or white, should be less easily able than other people to tell his story to the jury. Either no defendant should be allowed to read a statement prepared by his lawyer, or the illiterate man should be allowed to have a proxy read it. At the Privy Council hearing on Stuart, Lord Tucker suggested that as a result of this case the first alternative might be chosen. If the authorities are unwilling to take this hint they should change the law to make the second alternative possible.

* * *

Was Stuart harmed by an inadequate system of legal aid for poor people? "Could the evidence," asked a Labor M.P., "that has been accumulated since the original trial have been made available had money been forthcoming to prosecute an enquiry?" The Commissioners said that in a case of this sort the obligation was on the Crown to provide the witnesses and to see that they were available. Playford assured parliament "that there is no difficulty about the attendance of witnesses, the search for information, or the production of information if it is desired by the counsel". Starke said that a lawyer whose case involved a direct attack on the police would be unlikely to enlist their aid in his search for evidence. If O'Sullivan had been wondering whether to have, say, the Giesemans, called, and wanted to speak with them first himself, the cost of approaching them would have been his own; there was no provision for expenses of this sort under the Law Society's scheme. There is no evidence, however, that O'Sullivan ever thought of approaching the Giesemans. It might be argued that if a lawyer knew that he would not have to foot the bill himself his preparation of a Law Society case could be more thorough. Certainly a system whereby the state recompenses lawyers for representing poor people, by paying fees or at least out-of-pocket expenses, is desirable both to give the poor client a more nearly equal chance with the rich one in the kind of case which may require, for example, considerable travelling, and to protect the practitioner himself from financial hardship involved when a case is unusually long or for some other reason costly.

Without evidence that O'Sullivan wanted to interview the Giesemans, then, it cannot be said that Stuart's defence was handicapped by lack of money. But as the Commissioners say, it would have been "prudent" for the police to take statements from members of the troupe other than Moir.

* * *

On several occasions the name of Stuart was compared with that of Alfred Dreyfus. Was there any parallel between the aborigine convicted in Adelaide of murder and the Alsatian Jew sent to Devil's Island in 1895 for having betrayed the French Republic?

If Stuart was an innocent man picked up because of the colour of his skin and convicted on untrustworthy evidence, and if, when doubts were raised about his guilt, the authorities for a long time refused to exercise clemency or to order a fresh investigation because they believed that to do so might endanger the established order, then the cases would indeed be similar. But there is no clear resemblance between the position of Jews in nineteenth-century France and that of aborigines in twentieth-century Australia. In places like Ceduna, the expectation that they will behave violently, especially when drunk, may be livelier than the facts warrant; but even if one believes that Stuart was framed it is impossible to argue that an aborigine in South Australia represented any threat, real or imagined, to the holders of power. Nothing except a complacent but genuine certainty of Stuart's guilt prevented the politicians from sparing his life early in July.

In the phase of the affair that began when Shand left the Commission, there were elements that made it not absurd (though it was perhaps melodramatic) to compare Stuart with Dreyfus. The issue now became far wider than the guilt or innocence of one man; the community was bitterly divided, and when the Crown Solicitor addressed the Royal Commission he declared that he was defending not only the police force but "the status quo . . . and the institutions of the government".

One large difference between the two cases may be worth emphasising. A sympathy with Jews as such played no part in having the conviction of Dreyfus investigated. For Stuart, a sympathy with aborigines was crucial. The people most responsible for having his case re-opened became interested in Stuart because he was dark. Stuart's racial origin was never, of course, the only thing at issue. It was mentioned rarely in the South Australian parliament and not at all by Sir John Latham. A guilty concern towards aborigines, and a sensitivity to opinion in the non-European world, nevertheless helped to dramatise Stuart's plight and therefore to save his life.

His survival depended on a series of events any of which could easily not have happened. If the gaol chaplain had not called on Dixon; if Strehlow had been away from Adelaide in May; if O'Sullivan had not applied to London; if a newspaperman had not elicited a statement from the priest; if Rivett had not been impressed with the story: if these and a number of other things had not happened, Stuart would have been hanged.

While the Commission was still hearing evidence, but after the commutation, Playford said to parliament: "If we had proceeded with the execution and subsequently it was found that an injustice had been done, the state's reputation would have suffered." Had he forgotten already that he and his colleagues did their utmost to have Stuart executed on July 7? If Dixon had taken a week more than he did to find the Giesemans, it is morally certain that Stuart would have been hanged on August 4, and the "case calling for an investigation", recognised as such by the Commissioners, would have been of rather academic interest. Stuart's lawyers might not have bothered to press for that investigation when their client was dead. The criticism which Playford faced during August and September was mild compared with what would have broken on him in those circumstances; and it was only an accident of timing, not any decision by the government, that prevented such an outcome.

It was difficult, the Commissioners write, "to see why any heat or excitement should have been injected into the agitation for further enquiry or re-hearing". This is an astonishing remark. Having been rebuffed by the government, people who had genuine doubts about Stuart's guilt were forced by the impending execution to move quickly. In the campaign to keep Stuart's case open there was some recklessness and more sentimentality; there were, for example, mistakes of fact in the pamphlet produced by Dixon and his allies late in July. It would no doubt startle Sir Thomas Playford to be blamed for any of these things, but it was he and his ministers who turned the exploration of misgivings into a race with the hangman. Had the Stuart case occurred in a state where convicted people are not put to death, Strehlow and Dixon and others could have afforded to express themselves in language as temperate as that of the Commissioners. The simplest lesson from this story is that it strengthens the case against capital punishment.

* * *

Some of the disagreements described in this book may never be resolved among those who remember the case. This is true in particular of judgments about motive. Were Stuart's legal representatives disingenuous in what they put before the High Court and the Privy Council? Did the government resort to a Royal Commission rather than a formal judicial enquiry in order to avoid an appeal? Did Shand walk out because he genuinely believed that the Chairman was protecting a police witness, or was this merely a pretext for an action planned in advance? There is no sure way of settling disputes about such questions.

In the view of the present writer, most of the responsibility for letting the effort to identify a murderer grow into a violent and general controversy does not lie with Stuart's defenders, however darkly one may interpret their motives, or with those who campaigned for a reprieve and then for a new enquiry, however deluded one may think them. If Stuart had been reprieved early in July, if a policeman had not been allowed to engage in public defence of the conviction, and if judges involved in previous decisions against Stuart had not been appointed as Royal Commissioners, very little passion would have been aroused by Stuart's plight. The formal responsibility for decisions in each of these matters was shared by Sir Thomas Playford and his ministers. In each case they and whoever they consulted were apparently unaware or unconcerned that their decision would provoke intense hostility among a far wider range of opinion than normally engages in public controversy. It was the response of men who were convinced that the affairs of the society were in good hands, and that only the naïve and the mischievous would either doubt this general truth or challenge any particular application of it.

Only within a society with some claim to be called free can a case like this one arise. Strehlow, for example, could imply that the police had extorted a confession out of an accused man, and editors could publish his views, without fear that he or they would be arrested. Only in a country happier than most could the issue become so nationally absorbing; to worry about the fate of one obscure man convicted for murder may appear, to people living through the history of Hungary or South Africa, an enviable luxury. The line from Australia to a police state is long. It is nevertheless continuous. When Playford explained the protection of the witness Moir in terms that led a political scientist to declare him ignorant of the canons of ministerial responsibility, when he asserted that the police would never extort a confession out of an innocent man, and when Rivett was accused of seditious libel, one was reminded that the free society is a precarious achievement, depending as much on the absence of seriously divisive issues as on allegiance to liberal principles among holders of office. On a map of the world the threats to freedom in South Australia which arose during the Stuart case were doubtless small; but they are worth taking seriously.

* * *

Stuart himself must have known vaguely that principles were being invoked in his name, but he can hardly have been aware what they were. Guilty or innocent, he troubled the white man's world more deeply than he knew. His case exposed the political and judicial system to a scrutiny which was unpleasant but which, if the lessons are learned, may in the long run be invigorating. This can, of course, be no comfort to the parents of Mary Hattam.

EPILOGUE

1959–2002

24

ADELAIDE

The Stuart case came into my life because my wife Judy, an anthropologist, was studying South Australian Aborigines and I was Adelaide correspondent of *Nation*, a fortnightly journal published in Sydney. Judy was invited to the meeting at the home of Dr Charles Duguid on 27 June 1959 (reported on pp. 51–2 of this book) at which Father Tom Dixon and Mr T.G.H. Strehlow first aired their worries about Rupert Max Stuart's conviction for murder. Judy took full notes, gave them to me, and I began to keep a file of the increasing number of items that appeared on the subject in the *Advertiser*. I sent off a piece for the 18 July issue of *Nation*, dwelling on the doubts and on the statement from the Police Association designed to quell them.

I was in the history department at the University of Adelaide and moonlighted for the paper—literally so, for my pieces were usually written in the evenings and posted by express airmail to reach Sydney next morning. Tom Farrell, a senior reporter on the *Sydney Morning Herald*, read my piece on 18 July and flew to Adelaide next day. (pp. 64–5) I had mentioned the case of Frederick McDermott, convicted in New South Wales for murder and released when evidence in his favour turned up long afterwards. I now learned that Farrell had been McDermott's saviour: his investigation as a reporter on Sydney's *Daily Telegraph* provoked a Royal Commission which found in 1952, sixteen years after McDermott's conviction, that he could not have committed the crime. That precedent disposed Farrell to look into the Stuart case. I learned recently of another reason for his interest: he had been at school in the South Australian town of Tailem Bend with Glen Hattam, father of the murdered child.

Stuart's execution had first been set for 22 May 1959. The date was moved to 19 June to allow for his appeal to the High Court, then to 7 July when the federal judges deliberated longer than expected, then to 20 July when Stuart's lawyers resorted to the judicial committee of the Privy Council, then to 4 August when that body decided to hear the petition on 28 July. Stuart would almost certainly have been hanged on 4 August had Farrell not gone to Adelaide, for it was he who persuaded Father Dixon to express his doubts publicly in the *Herald* on Tuesday 21 July; and that decision led directly to the involvement of Rohan Rivett's *News* and thence to the Royal Commission.

During the next few turbulent months I could send on a Tuesday a story of any length which I knew would be published intact on Saturday (except for a few deletions on legal advice, mainly relating to the law of contempt). Over those months *Nation* was a principal source of information and opinion about the case for interested people outside Adelaide, mined by interstate papers with and without acknowledgement. As well as my own pieces, the editor Tom Fitzgerald and his deputy editor George Munster assembled cover stories on the case, among them Strehlow's analysis of the confession and profiles of Sir Thomas Playford and Stuart's defenders Shand and Starke.

When the Royal Commission was announced I decided to write a book on the case, whatever its outcome. The inquiry began in the university's second term vacation, and a long queue formed out in Victoria Square for each day's hearing. Stuart's lawyers could not afford to have a clerk in the courtroom collating the transcript of evidence as it came in batches from the stencilling machine. To avoid the queue I volunteered to do that job.

As a consequence I had a ringside seat, or rather a seat inside the ring, at the bar table, opposite Stuart's instructing solicitor Helen Devaney and his barristers Jack Shand Q.C., from Sydney, and Cairns Villeneuve Smith, of Adelaide, as they faced the bench and the witness box. (David O'Sullivan was not there as instructing solicitor because the commissioners had said that they might want him to appear as a witness.) I had the world's best view of a powerful and merciless cross-examiner at work, the glare from Shand's cold blue eyes passing just over my head on its way to the box. When Shand and Villeneuve Smith and Devaney walked out of the commission on the morning of Friday, 21 August 1959, I walked out after them, my presence evidently unnoticed, or my identity unknown, by anybody in the press gallery.

That suited me, for I wanted to tell the story, not to be part of it. In this book I appear as "the present writer" only where it seemed relevant to note my participation, such as my role in drafting the leaflet *Why not Hang Rupert Max Stuart?* (pp. 77–8) In 1960 the writers of current history I most admired contrived to make the author both omnipresent and invisible. That mode flourished in long *New Yorker* pieces which became books, such as Lillian Ross's *Picture,* a fly-on-the-wall account of the making and (in her view) unmaking of John Huston's film *The Red Badge of Courage.* Her book was technically a model for mine, though only up to a point. Ross managed to be a fly on *every* wall, an unseen presence in the company of all the contending parties. I had much better access to Stuart's defenders and sympathisers than to his prosecutors and their masters and allies. I was a member of the university staff club, and had lunch there with Dixon and Rivett at their first meeting (p. 69), but the Adelaide Club, on the other side of North Terrace, was *terra incognita*. Wanting the book to be not only even-handed in consideration of evidence but also even-textured in portrayal of the actors, I left out scenes from one side because I couldn't match them with scenes from the other. Some stuck in my memory. During a break in commission proceedings David O'Sullivan, having a smoke on the neo-classical balcony of the Supreme Court, looks out on Victoria Square and muses that this isn't too bad when you reflect that it's all about the fate of one Aborigine. At a dinner party put on by Rohan and Nan Rivett in honour of John Starke Q.C., there's an empty place at the table for Rupert Max Stuart. One evening Helen Devaney, suspecting phone-taps, asks me to deliver a note to Rupert Murdoch at his home in North Adelaide, where I find the owner of the *News* lounging in front of the television, watching the station he owns. He chuckles as he quotes the pithy and teasing headline he has just composed for the cover of his magazine *TV Week*: "Graham and Panda do it again". (Graham Kennedy and Panda Lisner win Logie awards for *In Melbourne Tonight.*) He speaks of Rohan Rivett with affection and condescension. (I think, though I can't be sure, that he used the word "headstrong", as he does in later recollection.) I make a note after this visit that while the father who bequeathed him the *News* was an editor who became a proprietor, young Rupert—not yet thirty —seemed a proprietor who wanted to prove himself as editor. He appears cool; though later, in the foyer of the Supreme Court awaiting the verdict on charges of criminality and sedition against his paper and its editor, he makes a nervous joke about not having brought pyjamas and toothbrush.

Some people believed that Rupert Murdoch must have paid for J.W. Shand Q.C. to represent Stuart. At the time Murdoch denied to me that News Ltd had paid Shand any money, but I still wondered whether he might have dipped into his own wallet for the fee. I was wrong. Tom Farrell told me this year that while in Adelaide he had urged Helen Devaney to engage a top outsider and recommended Shand, with whom he had worked at the McDermott Royal Commission. Devaney responded, Farrell thought, with the diffidence of a small-town lawyer; but she agreed to let him ring Shand on her behalf and ask him to take her call, warning the great man that he would be getting no fee. Contacted on 5 August 1959, Shand at once accepted the brief. He probably knew then that he had the cancer that would kill him, after surgery, on 19 October 1959. "On his deathbed", wrote Evan Whitton sixteen years later (in the *National Times* on 20 August 1975), "he is reported to have said: 'Before God, I believe Stuart is innocent.'" We'll never know whether that belief would have survived Stuart's cross-examination, which began six days before Shand died.

In the *Australian Dictionary of Biography*, P.A. Howell gives an account of the commission's chairman, Mellis Napier, on the day of Shand's walk-out: "on the morning his wife had collapsed from a stroke which proved fatal, he lost patience with Stuart's counsel for relentlessly cross-examining a witness. Napier immediately corrected himself, but he was hounded for the lapse." I don't agree that Sir Mellis "corrected himself" (pp. 132–3), but Howell may be right in attributing the intervention to his distressed state of mind. I learn also from Howell's entry that as chancellor of the university and therefore chairman of its council, Napier behaved at this time with impeccable liberalism towards me, hurt though he was by some of what I was writing in *Nation.* To Hugh Stretton, professor of history, who advised him that a recommendation for my promotion from senior lecturer to reader would come up at council's next meeting, he replied, "If you say that this is an honest scholar doing his job in an honest way then I will support you," and support he did, despite "attempts by the council's conservatives" to block my promotion.

T.G.H. Strehlow's diary (provided to me by Barry Hill) records his thoughts and feelings before, during and after his appearance at the commission. (pp. 169–73) At first, Strehlow writes, he does not want to be drawn into the case. "I owed so much to Stuart's grandfather, who had been my trusted companion on thousands of miles of journeyings on camel back in the 1930s. I had been afraid that Stuart, if I went to see him, would confess that he *had* committed this horrible double crime. I had finally gone to the death cell with a very heavy heart, and had been glad to find out that he seemed to be innocent after all." The grandfather was a man named Tom Ljonga who had revealed much to Strehlow about the songs, ceremonies and sacred objects of the centre. Strehlow dreads discovering that the grandson of this dear friend and precious informant is a murderer.

Strehlow has two heritages, Arrernte and German, and when he hears that a Royal Commission is to inquire into Stuart's conviction he celebrates by listening to a record of Rudolf Kempe conducting the third act of Wagner's *Die Meistersinger*, bought for his birthday in June but not played since "that first dreadful day when news came that the High Court of Australia had rejected Stuart's petition for leave to appeal … But now that it seems as though the corner has been turned at long last, I can enjoy 'die Meistersinger' again". His jubilation is cut short by the announcement that two of the three commissioners are Mr Justice Reed and Sir Mellis Napier —in the diary, "Sir Malice". Strehlow's distress at the pathetic death in Alice Springs hospital of the painter Albert Namatjira on 8 August, just before the commission sits, is connected with his feelings about Stuart, for both were Arrernte men caught, in a phrase coined by a Lutheran pastor close to Namatjira, "between two worlds".

When Strehlow goes into the witness box on 4 September the diary shows him vividly aware of the disadvantage he suffers by being called while Stuart's lawyers are still boycotting the inquiry, so that he has no friendly counsel to lead him. He draws no comfort from the presence of J.F. Brazel Q.C. as "counsel assisting" the commissioners, for Brazel has already told him that he will be cross-examined "like any other witness".

Facing interrogation by Roderic Chamberlain Q.C., senior counsel for the crown, Strehlow sees "a bald-headed man, with slitted eyes … thin lips distorted into a perpetual evil grin", who is "obviously a favourite with the judges". Strehlow's wife Bertha tells him afterwards that though she was "squirming with anxiety" for him, he looked "cool and completely at ease." I too thought he looked comfortable. (p. 169) "Of course, I wasn't", he tells the diary. "My mind was completely taut, and I watched every question like a poisoned dart, and tried to look forward several questions ahead. Providence itself must have been on my side—how I avoided some of those traps, I still don't know! There must be a God of Justice about even in S.A." Bertha tells him that Chamberlain must have been irritated by his composure. That was a loyal spousely misreading. Chamberlain was confident that on the crucial issue of Stuart's competence in English he had damaged Strehlow's credibility, which would collapse altogether when Stuart himself spoke from the witness box. (pp. 213–28) The diary shows Strehlow unaware of any damage, but falling into a depression about the condition of South Australia. He yearns to get out and "breathe the air of a free Australia—a land beyond reach of Playford and the members of the Adelaide Club." At home on 12 September, with Stuart at the commission and still under sentence of death, Strehlow writes, "I am beginning to wonder whether it was not a mistake on my part, after all, when I listened to Father Dixon on 16th May in this very room, and decided that I would go down and see Rupert Stuart. Since that time the whole State of South Australia, the whole of Australia, and many men and women in many parts of the world have been aroused and made uneasy about Rupert. And yet, we are all powerless even to stay his execution or to commute his sentence. Sir Mellis Napier and Sir Thomas Playford between them can snub the pleas for justice and fair play of hundreds of thousands of honest men and women; and because of South Australian State Rights no power on earth apparently can halt them. The people of S.A. could, if they rose in protest. But is it possible to find anywhere in an English-speaking country a more docile and slave-minded people than the church-going South Australians? And are not the Lutheran country people among the most docile and slave-minded elements of this population? If Rupert is to live, only God can help him now."

In the event Sir Thomas Playford decided that he would live, and the people of South Australia did not rise in protest at the royal commissioners' confirmation of the verdict against him. Strehlow couldn't bear to go and hear them deliver their findings. "All that effort came to nothing", he writes. Then, in a sentence which Barry Hill sets in astonished italics: "*Perhaps it is a consolation that Stuart's life has been saved.*" To Hill, this "perhaps" reveals that Strehlow had been more interested in "the Stuart case" than in Stuart, and Hill observes that once the case was over Strehlow retreated "into his own cave of dark thoughts about the tendency of Adelaide to close ranks against the outsider."

On events outside the courtroom, in the political arena, new light has been cast in two biographies of Sir Thomas Playford and in the recollections of Don Dunstan. Among Labor members of parliament, as I report, young Dunstan was the keenest to insist that the inquiry into Stuart's conviction must be thorough. (p. 90) His book of political memoirs, *Felicia* (1981), has a chapter entitled "The Establishment Bares Its Teeth" in which he recalls his difficulty in persuading the Labor caucus to take a strong line: "the older die-hards were reluctant to have us involved in the case, which they did not think was popular." The most he could get them to agree to was that the leader of the opposition, Mick O'Halloran, would ask Playford a "strong question" in parliament on 4 August about the commission's terms of reference. Dunstan makes it clear, at this moment and later, that Labor's opposition to Playford's conduct of the affair would have been faint without his own strenuous advocacy.

Stewart Cockburn's *Playford: Benevolent Despot,* published in 1991 ten years after its subject's death, confirms judgments that the Stuart case troubled him more than any other episode in his 26 years as premier. "He would telephone me every night", Chamberlain told Cockburn in 1985, "and want to know what had happened in the Royal Commission that day." The premier received several death threats (I report one on p. 206), which appeared not to scare a man who had served country and empire in the AIF: "if I find anyone wandering around my property looking for me", he assured the police commissioner, "I'll deal with him myself. I'll fill his arse with buckshot."

But Cockburn shows that his discomfiture had two more sources than I knew. First, his own daughter, a medical practitioner, had "a blazing row" with Playford in which she called him a murderer. Second, though he defended doggedly in and out of parliament the appointment of Sir Mellis Napier and Mr Justice Reed as commissioners, he later told a confidant that this was the rare occasion on which he did not sleep well after a difficult decision. Few people, I said, knew how far members of the judiciary and crown law officers may have contributed to crucial decisions about Stuart. (p. 93) Now we know that Playford followed advice from the chief justice about whom to put on the commission, and that he came to believe he had been wrong to ask for it. Cockburn, a sympathetic biographer, observes that Playford's choice of Napier and Reed was a sign that during the long months of this affair his "capacity to judge his fellow men soundly and his intuition about public opinion" had "diminished if, indeed, they had not entirely deserted him."

Cockburn is also illuminating on why Playford decided in the end that Stuart would live. The decision was announced on 5 October. He gave no reason at all when securing the consent of cabinet: first he rang the attorney-general saying he presumed his concurrence, then another minister saying he and the attorney-general agreed, and so on. "It was an interesting revelation", as Cockburn remarks drily, "of the Playford style in Cabinet decision-making during a crisis." Nor did Playford offer any explanation to Chamberlain, who would have to break the news to the commission. "Joe, we've got to commute the sentence on Stuart," he said, using Chamberlain's nickname. As the crown solicitor recalled the moment in an interview with Cockburn in 1985, he asked the boss what he was to say to the commission. "Tell them what you bloody well like!" he snapped. When I reported (p. 209) what seemed to me Chamberlain's unconvincing account of the decision, I was of course unaware that he had been left to make it up.

So what *was* the reason? Chamberlain's guess at the time, which in 1973 he said had later been confirmed, was that Playford had succumbed to pressure from the Commonwealth government, "disturbed by the way in which the newspaper campaign was smearing Australia's image in the eyes of Asian people, by portraying us as pursuing a racist campaign against a probably innocent black man."

Another biographer of Playford, Sir Walter Crocker, writing in 1983, was surprised at this account, even though Playford had told him of "a secret letter from Canberra", signed, if he remembered rightly, by Menzies' minister for external affairs, asking the premier "to consider the effects on Australia's reputation overseas if Stuart was hanged". As an experienced diplomat, who in 1959 was Australian high commissioner to India, Crocker had never heard the Stuart case mentioned by makers of Asian opinion. (It may be, however, that his own memory of the matter was defective after all those years: he has Sir Garfield Barwick as the minister in 1959, when in fact the portfolio was held by R.G. Casey.) Crocker thought it more likely that Playford had been responding to "the violently overt reactions inside Australia itself, not least inside South Australia." That had been close to the view of the Sydney *Daily Telegraph*'s Alan Reid, whom I quote (p. 210) as observing that unless Stuart went into the witness box the case would not be getting the full inquiry promised by the government, and that if he did so while under the death penalty Playford's critics could say that the condemned man was labouring under too great a strain to present his case adequately. Chamberlain finds this comment the most sensible made by any newspaper writer on why Playford had yielded.

Reid, flying in from time to time, told me in a letter written while my book was in the press that he hoped I was dealing with "the newspaper side". "It is a long time", he wrote, "since I have seen an issue divide newspapermen the way this one did." Old friendships had been destroyed. At the centre of journalistic conflict were Rohan Rivett, editor-in-chief of the *News*, and Stuart Cockburn, a senior reporter for the *Advertiser*, who had enjoyed years of mutual respect and were now, suddenly, enemies. Journalists tried in vain to persuade the hard-bitten veteran from Sydney to one side or the other. "I'm afraid that I shocked some people by announcing that I was not in Adelaide to be converted but to report and that I didn't give a continental whether they hanged Stuart or did not hang him as it was still a good story either way." Reid had found the conflict in Adelaide "a wonderful study … ranging from Rohan, firmly astride a white horse with a Crusader's glint in his eye, and Rupert, the young proprietor, delighted at the trouble he had stirred up and yet intermittently fearful as to what might be the outcome, down to Stewart Cockburn, starry-eyed, mixed up, finally believing that Rohan had betrayed the press".

Sir Thomas Playford believed that Rohan Rivett and his young master had betrayed more than the press. Cockburn reports "an apocryphal story … that Playford personally sifted through law statutes to identify appropriate charges which could be brought against Rivett. When he came to the section of the Act dealing with seditious libel he is said to have jabbed his finger at it and exclaimed: 'That's it. We'll have a go at him on this. The penalty's death.'" I had no doubt that in laying those astonishing charges Playford was impelled by personal animus. The more blame he could heap on Rohan Rivett, it seemed to me, the more easily might he put out of mind the troubling fact that his conduct had variously disturbed, outraged and bewildered so many other people within and beyond his own state and country, from the unworldly priest Father Thomas Dixon to the former chief justice Sir John Latham to Lord Attlee. The only substantial statement lawyers would not let me include in my book was that Playford hoped Rivett would go to gaol for a long time. I learned this from somebody who heard him say so. I couldn't use it, experts on the law of defamation advised, unless my informant was prepared if necessary to say in court that he had heard Playford make that remark. Apologetically and graciously, he was not. ("Dear Ken, the pleasure of hearing from you is reduced only slightly by the embarrassing nature of your request." It could have cost him his job.) I ended up reporting the hope but not attributing it to Playford. (p. 282) I read with wonder in Stewart Cockburn's biography of Sir Thomas Playford that I found the prosecution "disgraceful—the peevish revenge of an 'Establishment' for having been disturbed and made to look ridiculous in the eyes of the world." As I never wrote those words or any like them, I guess Cockburn must somehow have got his notes mixed.

Though the court action against Rivett and the paper failed, and though the policemen who alleged that the *News* had libelled them (p. 292) withdrew their suit, Playford had the satisfaction of seeing Rivett removed from the editor's chair only a few weeks later. The last charge hanging over Rivett was withdrawn on 6 June 1960. On 8 June the *News* published a leading article which I saw as evidence that the prosecution of the paper and its editor may have altered the tone of editorial comment on the case. (p. 291) Two weeks earlier Rupert Murdoch had moved from Adelaide to Sydney, where he had just bought the *Daily Mirror.* On 12 July the *News* published a short statement by Murdoch announcing that Rivett was no longer editor.

Writing for the 30 July issue of *Nation,* and remarking that Rivett's dismissal had gone almost entirely unreported in papers that had given headlines to his trial, I said that it was impossible to tell from Murdoch's brief statement whether Rivett's departure had any connection, direct or indirect, with the Stuart case. "But the announcement", I wrote, "must please those who deplored the paper's part in the affair, just as it must dismay those who admired it." Rupert Murdoch in Sydney assured Tom Fitzgerald and others that his removal of Rivett had nothing to do with the Stuart case.

Perhaps more persuasively, so did Rohan Rivett, who rang me after reading *Nation* to suggest that we talk over a beer in a city hotel. I was drawing on that conversation when I added the event to the manuscript of my book, which was already with the publisher. (p. 292) Rivett would never edit another paper, and never overcame his sense of loss at having to leave the *News*; but when we met over the years between 1960 and his death in 1977 I don't recall his ever mentioning the dismissal, and as far as I know he never gave anybody else an account attributing it to the Stuart case. Forty years on, after talking with his widow Nan and reading through the extensive collection of his papers in the National Library of Australia, this is what I wrote in the entry on Rohan Rivett for the *Australian Dictionary of Biography*: "Murdoch was certainly unhappy with some editorial decisions taken after he had left for Sydney. He said privately that he needed to be on the spot in order to give a steadying hand. 'Headstrong' was his word for Rivett. Even friends and admirers could describe Rivett as over-enthusiastic, or as courageous but unstable; he himself owned up to a 'fairly volcanic' nature, and said later that he had not expected the relationship with Murdoch to last forever." Murdoch, I say, "offered Rivett more generous terms than contractually required. He would later do the same to others in his long line of dismissed editors, but he appears to have remained singularly uncomfortable about the first."

This episode has attracted other writers about South Australia and authors of books about Rupert Murdoch, who became numerous during his ascent from owning a single provincial Australian paper to becoming one of the world's two or three largest media proprietors. No two authors tell it quite the same way. Among South Australian interpreters, Don Dunstan in 1981 implicates the Stuart case and Stewart Cockburn ten years later does not. "While the immediate cause", writes Dunstan, "appears to have been the editor's failure to follow the formula of sensational but shallow reporting, there seems little doubt that Rupert Murdoch was deeply disturbed by the position into which the *News* had got *vis-à-vis* the authorities in the Stuart case." Cockburn sees the rupture as caused entirely by "Murdoch's perception of his Editor-in-Chief's emotionalism and instability".

George Munster's 1985 study of Murdoch, *A Paper Prince*, dwells on the *News*'s edition of 7 July reporting the death of the left-wing British Labour politician Aneurin Bevan, in which Rivett "wrote a front-page editorial saying that this rebel would be greeted by his peers in heaven, and gave over two feature pages to Bevan's career." This was hardly, Munster observes, a topic to hold Adelaide's readers, and he sees in this issue of the paper "a coded message: it told his supporters that he was not giving up. Murdoch would not take it and sent a letter south, which Rivett found on his desk the next morning: he was to leave that day." Munster had good access to Murdoch's thoughts at this time as close colleague and friend of *Nation*'s editor Tom Fitzgerald, who was being pressed by Murdoch to become editor of the *Daily Mirror*. (I happened to be in Sydney, and in *Nation*'s office, when Murdoch bought the paper. Murdoch sprinted up the creaking stairs and burst into the tiny office saying: "I've got it!" He began at once urging Fitzgerald to join him as editor, and when Fitzgerald said, "But what about *Nation*?" Murdoch, noticing me, replied that I could run it. Not even for a moment did I imagine this new life, for I knew how highly Tom Fitzgerald valued his journal and his independence.)

In Munster's account a breach which might have happened anyway is precipitated by Rivett's continuing, at least subtextually, to harass the Playford government in the aftermath of the Stuart case when Murdoch wanted the paper to lay off. Murdoch himself gave a more explicit version of this explanation when speaking to William Shawcross for his 1992 book *Rupert Murdoch: Ringmaster of the Information Circus*. "We'd won the Stuart case", Murdoch told Shawcross, "so I wanted to cool it for a while. Rohan agreed with me absolutely. Then a couple of weeks later he had a front page [on the case] denouncing [the government] more angrily than before. It became clear that what would be a reasonable partnership if I was there, was not going to work in my absence." If Shawcross had checked in files of the *News* he would not have found any such denunciation, only the tribute to Bevan, which Murdoch's memory over thirty years had evidently transformed into a polemic better justifying his action. "I liked Rohan", he told Shawcross. "He was strange and egocentric, but a good, well-intentioned man." From imperial heights he could now look down benevolently on his dead friend and mentor.

Shawcross also interviewed Rivett's widow, Nan, who said that although she thought a break was inevitable, "Rohan couldn't believe that Rupert had sacked him. He was very upset about the Stuart case; he had borne almost all of it. After going through prison camp all this was too much. He hated losing the paper. The progress of Rohan's idealism and enthusiasm under Keith [Murdoch] to his disillusion under Rupert was very sad." Nan Rivett was not exactly attributing her husband's dismissal to the Stuart case, but lamenting that Murdoch had not stood by Rivett as he tried to recover from it.

Ten years after Rivett's sacking, the chairman of the Herald and Weekly Times group, Sir Philip Jones, gave me an account of it different from any other I've heard or read. Murdoch, so Jones told me, had dismissed Rivett for libelling judges during a murder case. When I demurred, he insisted with all the certainty of a man long used to getting his way. He had been sitting next to Murdoch in an aeroplane when Rupert decided to sack Rohan. Rupert, he went on, wanted to get into the Adelaide Club and was told that he wouldn't unless he got rid of Rivett. I didn't and don't know what to make of this story, except that it appears to be the version that had gone into the upper reach of the firm's collective memory. Like the larger saga of the Stuart case, the Rivett case itself resists composition into a single narrative.

Reviewers of my book tended to dwell more on its conclusion that Stuart was probably guilty than on my asking whether a jury might have had a reasonable doubt if the Giesemans had given evidence at his trial. (p. 309) Fairly new to authorship, I was surprised to discover that even an appreciative reviewer might not be a thorough reader. *Nation* gave the book to Geoffrey Sawer, professor of law at the Australian National University, who thought well of it but told readers that I had not considered whether capital punishment should be abolished. Had a paragraph dropped out? No; on p. 320 I found these words: "The simplest lesson from this story is that it strengthens the case against capital punishment." The sentence I found most gratifying in Sawer's review was this one: "Mr Inglis concludes that Stuart was probably guilty, but he is not dogmatic about it, and the reader may develop some alternative suggestions." The Manchester *Guardian*'s reviewer, however, said that I had found Stuart, without qualification, guilty. My letter on the point to the editor of this admired organ of liberal opinion was not published. I received instead an airletter from the reviewer himself, Geoffrey Moorhouse, replying as acting literary editor, finding his double role "a bit embarrassing", and telling me that "the weight attaching to the word 'probably' in a court of law is clearly considerable; it is rather less in a book review." I could only send up an appeal to the spirit of the late C.P. Scott, creator of the paper, who had done his best to inspire in its writers a reverence for facts.

Don Dunstan concluded both that Stuart was probably guilty and that a better informed jury might have acquitted him. Of people convinced that Stuart was innocent, Ted Strehlow had lost interest in the case and Father Tom Dixon had not. Dixon congratulated me generously on the book. "I think I have disposed of nearly 20 copies", he wrote to me on 9 April 1962, adding optimistically, "I am sure the urge is growing fast to read it. The more intelligent are quite interested & are very satisfied when read, though they don't all seem to reach your conclusion." As to that, "I have asked myself several times whether it had been good for you to state your 'probably guilty' verdict, & each time I get a different answer … I think we agree to differ on the 'time 2–4' assertions by Stuart, though I must admit them damaging to the cause. I think we agree to differ on Strehlow also." Though we remained good friends, I don't think Dixon was ever able to understand how someone whom he respected, and who had studied the evidence closely, could have read it so wrongly.

Father Dixon was writing to me from a parish in suburban Sydney, St Brigid's, Coogee, where the provincial superior of his order had sent him. Two of Stuart's lawyers, David O'Sullivan and Cairns Villeneuve Smith, had also left Adelaide, fearful that their standing in the courts of that city had been damaged by the vigour of their defence. They had been encouraged to work at the bar in Melbourne by Stuart's last counsel, John Starke Q.C. Their adversary Chamberlain had been appointed to a vacancy on the Supreme Court before 1959 was out, and so had "counsel assisting" at the Royal Commission, J.F. Brazel. Sir Mellis Napier remained chief justice until 1967, when he chose to retire, after 43 years, at the age of 84.

A committee raising money for O'Sullivan and Helen Devaney (p. 64) had encountered some reluctance. Responding to an inquiry from the Melbourne-based Council for Aboriginal Rights on 30 August 1959, I wrote: "Maybe, as some say, the lawyers will in the long run be richer and more famous for having taken the case; but as things stand now, they have sacrificed more than anybody else on Stuart's behalf—and they are going on with it." In the event it could be said that O'Sullivan and Villeneuve Smith gained from the case, the one briefly and the other for longer, and that Devaney did not. O'Sullivan, whom Starke admired as a "fighting Irish type of barrister", quickly built up a flourishing practice at the Victorian bar. One night in February 1963, driving back from a case in the western Victorian town of Warrnambool, O'Sullivan was killed when his car collided with an unlit hay carrier. Cairns Villeneuve Smith became a Q.C. in 1975 and a county court judge in 1983. When he died in 2000, an obituary in the *Age* said that his fight against the death sentence for an Aboriginal in Adelaide "led to Victoria gaining a legal star." Helen Devaney, as I mention (p. 277), also secured admission to the Melbourne bar but decided to stay in Adelaide and practised there for the rest of her working life, convinced that she had been denied a magistracy by her part in the Stuart case. Two years before her death in 1975 Devaney was reported in the *Advertiser* of 15 August 1973 as saying that she believed Stuart did not commit the murder, and in next day's *Australian* that if he did it while drunk the crime was not as bad as painted. She might have sued Stewart Cockburn had she lived to see him attribute to her a telegram sent in 1965 by somebody named Devaney in Melbourne when Sir Thomas Playford was at last defeated. "Mills of God grind slowly. How O'Sullivan must be laughing and others still alive exulting. Stop. Evil brings its own recompense."

Did the Stuart case contribute to the end of Sir Thomas Playford's 26-year reign? His government had always enjoyed the protection of an electoral system—South Australia's own gerrymander, the "Playmander"—which gave only one-third of seats in the House of Assembly to the metropolitan districts occupied by 60 per cent of the population, including most Labor voters. Only a huge swing could threaten his tenure, and that happened in 1962, when Playford hung on with the help of two "Independents", and again in 1965, when he lost. There is no way of assessing the contribution of the Stuart case to that outcome short of asking old voters who had changed their allegiance and new voters who had opted for Labor candidates why they had done so.

Playford's inheritor Don Dunstan was nevertheless certain that the Stuart case had "seriously tarnished" Playford's government; he saw it as "the beginning of the end." Stewart Cockburn, a more detached observer, believed that it was "one of the principal catalysts" precipitating Playford's downfall, giving Dunstan an opportunity to sense and catch the tides of change. In Sir Walter Crocker's view the case focused discontents against the Playford regime and shook it. Two political scientists, Neal Blewett and Dean Jaensch, surveying in 1971 *Playford to Dunstan: The Politics of Transition,* judged Playford's response to the case as exhibiting his "authoritarian style, his parochial complacency and his insensitivity to public opinion." They perceived in all this "the inevitable hubris of men too long in power."

Sir Thomas Playford lived on his cherry farm in the Adelaide hills until he died in 1981 after seeing the start of a second ten-year Labor administration (Dunstan and Labor gained power in 1970). The Stuart case was the one matter on which he was reluctant to talk. He would only say that if the police had been allowed to use all they knew about Stuart's previous convictions—which is what I presume he tried to table in parliament on 26 August 1959 (p. 162)—the public would have shared his own certainty that Stuart had committed that terrible murder. Unlike Sir Robert Menzies, who gave hundreds of boxes of papers to the National Library on his retirement, the only substantial documents Sir Thomas Playford lodged in the South Australian Archives were two manila folders containing letters and petitions he had received on the Stuart case.

Did the case contribute to the abolition of capital punishment? Concurrent with the case, Don Dunstan introduced a bill to remove the death sentence from the statute book. The ensuing debate demonstrated that in South Australia, as elsewhere, the abolitionists had the better of the argument. They could show from evidence around the world that the end of capital punishment was not followed by an increase in murder and other crimes of violence. Playford resisted this data with his usual scepticism towards book learning. But the Stuart case made it difficult for him and his colleagues to refute another powerful argument, that people convicted of murder should be allowed to stay alive because evidence occasionally turned up (as it had for Shand's client McDermott) that a court had erred. Sir Thomas Playford contributed, however inadvertently, to this aspect of the case against capital punishment, and so did Sir Mellis Napier and his fellow commissioners. Stuart would have been hanged on 22 May 1959 had O'Sullivan and Devaney not appealed on his behalf to the state's full court, on 19 June had they not gone to the High Court, on 7 July had the High Court not taken longer than expected to hand down its judgment, on 20 July had the lawyers not petitioned the Privy Council, on 4 August had Father Dixon not found the Giesemans, on 31 August had the Royal Commission confirmed the verdict by that date, on 30 September had it done so by then, and on 9 November had Playford not decided that, after all, he would live. Stuart's execution had been deferred seven times. The fourth stay, on 4 August, was granted because Playford accepted the need for "a thorough enquiry" (p. 81) into newly discovered evidence; and when the commissioners had completed their enquiry they acknowledged that this evidence constituted a "case calling for an investigation". (p. 319) Yet they found it difficult, they declared, "to see why any heat or excitement should have been injected into the agitation for further enquiry or re-hearing." This seemed to me an astonishing remark. (p. 319) Only if the noose had not been hanging over Stuart could the campaigners have afforded to be calm. The commissioners' inability to recognise that plain fact displayed the judicial obtuseness of men cocooned in an environment of bench, chambers and club.

Playford's remaining years in power yielded one case that tested his belief in capital punishment and revealed that the Stuart case had left it intact. The hangman who would have executed Rupert Max Stuart put a man named Glen Sabre Valance to death in Adelaide Gaol on 24 November 1964. The crime—the killing of a woman—was horrible, the convicted man's guilt was not in doubt, and there was no constituency for reprieve other than dedicated anti-hangers. The execution of Valance was a terminal rejection of abolitionist arguments and sentiments on the part of Playford's doomed regime.

Labor's ascent to government made commutation of any death sentence certain; and in 1976, to deprive his successors of the power to hang, Dunstan put through parliament the prohibition he had first attempted as a private member in 1959. Queensland had abolished capital punishment in 1922, New South Wales in 1955, Tasmania in 1968, the Northern and Australian Capital Territories in 1973, Victoria in 1975; and Western Australia—where two men were hanged in 1964—would follow in 1984.

The last person executed in twentieth century Australia was Ronald Joseph Ryan, hanged in 1967 for shooting a warder while escaping from Melbourne's Pentridge gaol. Robert Peter Tait and Rupert Max Stuart had been saved from the gallows by liberal opinion. Ronald Ryan and Glen Valance were not. Sir Henry Bolte, having been forced to spare Tait, was grimly resolved to get Ryan. John Starke, Stuart's counsel and Tait's saviour, was by 1967 on the bench of Victoria's Supreme Court, and conducted the trial at which a jury found Ryan guilty of murder. As the law required, Starke pronounced the death sentence, though he sympathised with protesters who were clamouring for commutation both on principle and because of doubts about Ryan's responsibility for the killing. "For the rest of his life", writes Mike Richards in *The Hanged Man. The Life & Death of Ronald Ryan* (2002), "Starke would worry terribly about his role in sentencing Ryan and agonise about whether he could have done more to save him from the gallows."

One way and another the cases of Stuart, Tait and Ryan hastened the end of capital punishment in Australia by provoking such divisive controversy about the policy. The case of Valance suggests that had Sir Thomas Playford remained in office his government might well have gone on executing murderers; but the case of Stuart had helped to end his regime. It did not end Playford's attachment to capital punishment. Ruminating in retirement, he told Sir Walter Crocker he was inclined to think that as crimes of violence increased, "the man in the street" would one day secure the return of the death penalty.

At the end of my book I proposed several other "lessons from Stuart" in the last chapter. In summary:

1) There are perils in appointing judges as royal commissioners into judicial matters.
2) Confidence in the police is jeopardised when they become partisans in public controversy over their own behaviour.
3) The extraction and admission of confessions require more safeguards.
4) The arrangements for taking evidence from Aboriginal witnesses may need to be improved and should not depend on the accident of which state or territory they happened to be in when charged.
5) The state should recompense lawyers who represent poor clients.

I suspect that policy on the use and composition of royal commissions since 1959 has continued to depend on the politics of particular times and places. I doubt whether one episode of imprudent intervention by policemen in one state has had any generally deterrent effect. A widespread concern around and beyond Australia about how confessions are gathered and used may have been heightened a little by this case. Stuart's situation is certainly cited in discussions about the disadvantages faced by Aboriginal witnesses having to follow rules and rituals they may not fully understand. Uniformity of laws affecting Aborigines was made possible by a national referendum in 1967, and the judgment of a Northern Territory court in 1976 (Anunga's case) ensured that no confession would ever again be extracted from an Aboriginal person anywhere in Australia as

Stuart's had been in the police station at Ceduna. Legal aid services in South Australia were improved in the Dunstan years, when the Commonwealth and the state together financed a legal services commission supplying means-tested advice and representation; it co-existed with the old voluntary scheme administered by the Law Society which had delivered O'Sullivan and Devaney to the defence of Stuart. The Stuart case contributed to this and other law reforms by helping to dislodge a regime that would have opposed or at least delayed their implementation.

The case had a broader effect on the state's legal system, discerned by Alex Castles, professor of law at the University of Adelaide, when he looked back from 1987 at *Lawmakers and Wayward Whigs: Government and Law in South Australia*. In 1959 Castles had been the first university lecturer to take an active interest in the case after hearing Dixon at Dr Duguid's place and being disturbed by his testimony. "The Stuart case was more than a passing event", Castles wrote. As controversy widened, the custodians of the law demonstrated their conviction that the system of laws they had serenely inherited "was both unchallengeable and omnipotent." This state of mind was epitomised for Castles in the man at the pinnacle of the system, Sir Mellis Napier. "The notion that he or his colleagues might have the regrettable but human capacity to err seemed to many involved hardly to impinge on the chief justice's thinking, even as he chaired the royal commission on the matter." He had never wanted that inquiry, possibly foreseeing that its most durable outcome would be to heighten what Castles describes as "the pressure of changing community attitudes" demanding new directions in the workings of the law and more generally "helping to ensure that the law and its instruments remain subject to the ultimately necessary sanction of public examination." Dunstan's choice of judges and his agenda for law reform were intended to serve that quiet but momentous shift in the making and administration of the law which Rupert Max Stuart had helped unwittingly to initiate.

25

YATALA

HE HAD BEEN LOCKED UP in Adelaide Gaol since 23 December 1958, leaving only for visits to court and commission. Late in October 1959, when the commission's hearings were over, he was driven out to the Yatala Labour Prison, on the city's northern outskirts. Yatala's forbidding Victorian architecture and its site next to a quarry together expressed a commitment to severe discipline and hard labour. Here Rupert Max Stuart would live continuously for fifteen years, and for several spells after that.

As the prisoner later recalled his occupations, he spent three years making buckets for mops, then learned to use a machine in the boot shop, and later worked as a butcher in the kitchen, where he ate so much that he got a double chin and a stomach "like Ayers Rock". His father, down from Alice Springs with his mother on a visit, did not recognise him. "I said, 'I'm Max Stuart.' He said, 'No, no. He was a little skinny bloke.' I said, 'That's me!'" He also went to the prison's school, up to grade five. Learning English, he would say, was the one useful thing he did in gaol. He corresponded with Father Dixon from the beginning, at first with the help of warders and from 1966 in his own hand. "This is the best gaol I have ever been in", he wrote in 1968, not needing to tell the priest that he was qualified to compare amenities in Queensland and the Northern Territory. "I wish I can give you back what I owe you," he wrote in 1972. "I think I owe you my life."

Dixon had visited Stuart twice in 1960; but the prison authorities thought his presence unsettling and he did not go to Yatala again until 1973, the third year of Dunstan's premiership. By that time he was no longer Father Dixon, having (in words he used of another priest in a letter to me) "quietly slipped off the collar and donned the marriage suit." "I had come to an end", he explained when he left the priesthood in 1969. "I had done my bit. I went in when I was twelve and gave it the best years of my life. I was not terribly happy with the system." He and Joan, whom he married in 1970, remained loyal to their church. Knowing no other vocation, he looked for work as a teacher and in 1973 began to teach French at St Ignatius—'Riverview', the Jesuit college in Sydney.

In 1974 Dixon wrote to me: "I am anxious to get down to my own story on the Stuart case." Could I help him "to recall with some accurate details some of those days when you and I were together"? "I don't want to overlap your own book. I feel there is quite a lot absent from that supervolume to warrant a book that would be fresh and personal." I replied from Port Moresby that although after almost 25 years I wouldn't trust my memory of things not mentioned in the book, I did recall clearly, from the lunch at which he and Rivett first met (pp. 69–70), "the volatile, passionate Rohan being impressed that someone apparently as unvolatile and calm as yourself was saying the things you were saying." Over the next few years we talked two or three times.

During the May vacation of 1973 Dixon made one of several return journeys to South Australia with his book in mind. Access to prisoners was now more liberal than it had been before the Dunstan years, and he was allowed to talk with Stuart in Yatala. "He was very sensible and balanced", Dixon wrote to me.

Ted Strehlow also visited Yatala in 1972 and 1973. Stuart, he found, had taken up watercolour painting. Strehlow was allowed to give him palette, paper and paints, and to make small payments (which he kept in an account awaiting the prisoner's release) for paintings which he hung on the walls of his office at the University of Adelaide. He was now Professor Strehlow, appointed in 1970 to a personal chair—no common honour for a researcher. His *Songs of Central Australia,* a tribute to Aranda culture and a gift to Australian literature, was published in 1971. People who wondered why it took Strehlow ten years to visit Stuart may or may not have known of his strengthening conviction that he was surrounded by persecutors, including imagined enemies in Adelaide and even in its university, who had never forgiven him for his commitment to Stuart. Moreover, in 1968 he had left his wife after 33 years to begin living with his 36-year-old secretary and research assistant Kathleen Stuart, whom he married in 1972. That surname happened to be her first husband's. For the rest of Ted Strehlow's life and beyond, Kathleen Stuart Strehlow became a significant person in the life of the other Stuart. She and their baby now accompanied Ted when he visited Yatala.

In Dunstan's time Stuart could even, if he agreed, be interviewed by journalists. To a survivor of the old regime, Sir Roderic Chamberlain, this was a horrifying innovation. Over half a century of legal practice, he told one of the reporters allowed to meet Stuart in a visitors' room, he had never heard of anybody interviewing a convicted murderer. "WE TALK TO RUPERT MAX STUART", announced the *Advertiser* on 2 September 1972. Stewart Cockburn's story began with his recollection of being in court as reporter for the paper and hearing the late Mr Justice Reed sentence Stuart to be hanged by the neck until he was dead. Thirteen years later, sitting with Stuart and an *Advertiser* photographer in an unguarded visitors' room, he found the forty-year-old prisoner "powerfully built, running to some early middle-age fat"—thanks to that stint in the kitchen—"a fleck of grey now in his black, wavy hair". They talked for an hour. The reporter was allowed to give him two cigarettes, but not a packet. On prison pay of 35 cents a day, Cockburn reflected, he could afford only twenty a week.

Stuart wrote some words for the photographer who accompanied Cockburn—"I can write very good now R.M. Stuart"—and read aloud some of the written questions the reporter had prepared.

"Did it make life more bearable in prison to be able to read?

'Oh yes, when you can read and write it changes your life, you know.'" He had also learned to play chess. "Had he heard of Fischer and Spassky? 'Yair, I think Fischer's got one point to go, ain't he?'" He was better informed about world champion chess than about Australian politics, for he believed the prime minister was a chap named McMillan, not McMahon, and he could not think of Gough Whitlam's name. He did know that a federal election was coming, and he hoped Labor would win: his own treatment at Yatala, "real hard" early in his sentence, had been "a bit better" under Labor. But he appeared not to think well of the newly liberal approach to Aboriginal affairs now affecting both federal and state policies. "He thought white people were 'spoiling' the Aboriginal people nowadays. He didn't think Black Power would help the Aborigines. Things were better as they were before."

A reader might wonder whether Stuart meant all that, or whether he was giving answers that would help to shorten his time in gaol. Knowing that Stuart had made an application for parole which was turned down in February 1972, Cockburn asked why he thought it had not succeeded. He had no idea.

Cockburn had been briefed by his keepers, who told him that Stuart had recently king-hit one prisoner and threatened to kill another. Hadn't he been in quite a few fights with other inmates and with prison officers? "Yair, quite a few." Why? The question may have released memories of his days boxing in Jimmy Sharman's travelling troupe. (p. 9) In early days at Yatala, "fellers would look at me over there in the other corner, you know, and I'd knock 'em straight over—bang! During the last four or five years, I've changed a lot." How come? He had started "waking up" to himself. Going to meetings in gaol of Alcoholics Anonymous had helped, "just to practise for when I get released". And whenever that was, he would go to Queensland or the Northern Territory and keep right away from pubs.

When Cockburn reached the subject at the centre of any visitor's curiosity, Stuart's demeanour changed (so the interviewer thought) from friendly to wary, and some of his answers were as difficult for the interviewer to interpret as they had been to friend and foe at the Royal Commission. (pp. 223–8)

"Max, do you ever think about the little girl, Mary Hattam?"

"Nuh."

"Do you regret what happened to her?"

"Nuh."

Then (tendentiously):

"Do you think you would have done it if you hadn't been full?"

"Nuh."

After several more questions:

"Nuh. I didn't kill her. To this day I just can't remember."

"You mean you don't know whether you killed her or not?"

"Nuh. Every time I think of her I feel real bad, you know."

"You do feel real bad? At the thought you might have done something like this?"

"Yair. Nuh."

After several more questions,

"Nuh, I didn't kill her. To this day I just can't remember."

"You mean you don't know whether you killed her or not?"

"Nuh. Every time I think of her I feel real bad, you know."

"You do feel real bad? At the thought you might have done something like this?"

"Yair. In the night ... when I pray ... I pray for her." (The dots are Cockburn's, presumably signalling pauses.)

"Every night?"

"Every night, yair."

Cockburn was close to saying, with Chamberlain at the Royal Commission: "I give up." "I felt his answers went whichever way my questions led him. The answers conflicted. Perhaps he didn't understand the questions. Perhaps he didn't try to." Amid all that confusion and contradiction the sub-editor of the paper headlined one sentence: "I PRAY FOR HER". On the evening of the interview, Stewart Cockburn rang Ted Strehlow to tell him that Stuart had confessed. As Strehlow later reported the conversation to Tom Dixon, he replied: "That is strange. I have also seen him and he has not mentioned it to me." Later in the exchange, according to Strehlow, Cockburn said: "Of course, he denied it immediately afterwards."

Dixon, reading Cockburn's story in Sydney, wrote a letter to the editor of the *Advertiser* disputing interpretations of Stuart's words and protesting about a final sentence reflecting "how even those who'd fought so hard to prove his innocence never wrote or called." The letter was not published but was given to Cockburn for reply. "The impression I gained during the interview", he told Dixon, "was that he was a liar and I would not care to place any faith in the truth of what he said. I acknowledge that I must therefore regard his confession [at Ceduna] with suspicion and that his guilt or otherwise must rest on an assessment of the circumstantial evidence available." Dixon was able to read that as a large concession, since the crown's case had centred on the confession; but Cockburn clearly believed that other evidence amply established Stuart's guilt.

Cockburn had been billed as the first *South Australian* journalist to speak to Stuart in all those years. His visit to Yatala had actually been prompted by the publication a few days earlier, on 26 August 1972, of an interview with a journalist from Sydney who wrote as Nola McMahon. Her story was the most substantial item in the first issue of a short-lived fortnightly journal, the *Digger*, which happened to be launched just a month after Tom Fitzgerald had run out of money to sustain *Nation* and closed the paper down. The *Digger*'s title alluded to Rupert Murdoch, who had descended on London and bought the Sunday *News of the World* and the daily *Sun*, and was increasing their circulation by devices which provoked the satirical *Private Eye* to name this rough Australian intruder "the dirty Digger". This first number of the *Digger* gave a lot of critical attention to

Murdoch, and if the editor had been able to tell readers how he came to be publishing "Nola McMahon's" interview with Stuart, that too would have been part of the Murdoch story.

Her real name was Noela Whitton. With her husband, Evan, who had been working for Murdoch's Melbourne weekly *Truth,* she came in 1971 to Sydney, where he had joined the staff of the new *Sunday Australian.* Evan Whitton was an energetic practitioner of what was coming to be called investigative journalism, especially on legal matters, and would win Walkley awards for his work. Having read my book, Whitton asked his editor if he could go to Adelaide and do a story on what seemed to him a miscarriage of justice. (He had read the book with all the more interest because Father Tom Dixon had taught him English at Downlands, a school run by the order of the Sacred Heart in Toowoomba.) The editor, Bruce Rothwell, wasn't keen. Whitton took leave in January 1972 and drove with Noela to Adelaide at their own expense, having told Rothwell that the paper could have first refusal of anything that emerged from the journey. At the office of the state's comptroller of prisons, Lloyd Gard, he asked permission to talk with the prisoner. Gard refused, on the ground that whatever he wrote after interviewing Stuart might be held to prejudice the fair hearing of any application for parole.

Whitton persisted, pointing out that a book on the Stuart case was about to be published by his principal prosecutor, Sir Roderic Chamberlain. Chamberlain had retired from the Supreme Court in 1971, although he was still chairman of the board which recommended for and against parole. Chamberlain's board had lately paroled two men convicted of murders around the same time as Stuart while rejecting his own application.

Evan Whitton had interviewed Chamberlain with some delicacy while waiting to see Stuart. "He asked me a number of discreet questions about the case and about the methods of the Parole Board," Chamberlain recalled in 1973, "but without associating the two subjects." He was certainly planning to associate the two subjects when he filed a story having at its centre an interview in Yatala. Though Gard went on refusing to allow that, he was overruled by Dunstan's chief secretary after Whitton lobbied the minister for education, Hugh Hudson. So Evan and Noela Whitton became the first journalists to interview Rupert Max Stuart. Among other participants in his story Evan Whitton spoke by telephone with Sir Thomas Playford, who asked him to pass on a message in Sydney to Ken May, whom Murdoch had called over from Adelaide and who was now his chairman in Sydney: would May please ring Sir Thomas?

The Whittons returned with a rich record of their visit to Adelaide. But after an initial show of interest Rothwell rejected the story—on instructions, so he told Evan, from higher up. When Whitton tried out his old editor at *Truth,* he too said that he had been told not to accept anything from him on Stuart.

Why not? On paper such an instruction would have come from Tom Fitzgerald, lately become "editorial director" of Murdoch's Australian papers. In fact Fitzgerald found himself by-passed on matters of policy and personnel—a situation which he soon found intolerable, resigning from Murdoch's employ after less than two years. Real authority was exercised on Murdoch's behalf by Ken May. Whitton's explanation for the otherwise mysterious decision not to publish his Stuart interview is that Playford had intervened to remind May of a deal done in 1960: the Premier would drop the last charge against Rivett, and Murdoch would drop the Stuart case. If Whitton is right, it is further evidence of the pain suffered by Playford over the case that in his seventh year of retirement he would want to suppress any renewed public interest.

Evan Whitton's first instinct was to resign, and before long he would do so. For the time being, though, the Whittons agreed that the story would be Noela's. The *Sydney Morning Herald* did not want it; nor did the *Reader's Digest.* The founder of the *Digger,* Bruce Hanford, a friend from *Truth* days, welcomed it as a strong item for his inaugural issue. So Noela Whitton became Nola McMahon, and her husband's presence at the interview was made invisible.

Her story gave a more vivid account than Cockburn's of the little world in which Stuart was confined. "This is a vicious, violent man", she was told by the comptroller of prisons, who had tried to prevent the interview. "I couldn't allow him near a woman." She (and Evan) had to talk with Stuart through a thick glass wall in the visitors' room of the highest security block, where prisoners were locked into individual cells which they left only to drill in a huge cage. Stuart knew it well, having served sentences of a month there after fighting. Cockburn would interview him in the more open block where he had spent most of his time, sleeping in a dormitory, eating in a cafeteria-style mess, allowed into a courtyard where outdoor games were played, and able to sit at a table with visitors.

"Can you hear me?" Noela Whitton asked. "He leaned over near the glass and said 'I think it's all right.' I stood up and put my face close to his. In this curious position we talked for just over an hour, our voices going to each other through the grill above our heads."

He spoke of two women, one with whom he was exchanging letters and one who came to see him. The correspondent, whom he described as a girlfriend, was Edna Gieseman, the part-Aboriginal woman he had known at the Funland Carnival, (pp. 9–10, 109) who had now separated from her husband Norman and was working as a school cleaner in Townsville, where she had a job waiting for him, if and when he was paroled, at the meat works. The visitor was a music teacher, an Englishwoman named Isabel Penny, in the habit of visiting lonely prisoners. It was at the suggestion of this good kind lady, he said, that he had joined Alcoholics Anonymous. "She made him believe in himself", Noela Whitton would later say of Miss Penny, "and gave him hope that he might get out."

The Whittons, having heard of her visits, had already talked with Isabel Penny and discovered that she was the person who (before any visit by Strehlow) had encouraged Stuart to paint. She showed them a watercolour of the Simpson desert done in 1971. They marvelled at it. "A Namatjira in all its painstaking details", wrote Noela, "but signed by Rupert Max Stuart."

Like Albert Namatjira himself, the young Stuart had been introduced to the white man's art by a teacher from the south. For Namatjira it had been the Melbourne artist Rex Battarbee, and Stuart would recall seeing the two of them painting together. He himself at the age of ten was among children at Jay Creek to whom the anthropologist Charles Mountford, up from Adelaide in 1942, had given crayons and paper, carrying home sketches signed "Max" depicting items from the complex culture of the centre: a kangaroo, a date palm planted by some Afghan cameleer, a white-feller tent.

Namatjira's mentors and their critics agreed that the art they were teaching him to create was in the European tradition, especially as represented in Australia by the German-born Adelaide painter Hans Heysen, who had formed an Australian generation's perception of the gum tree. The ghost gums of Hermannsburg in Namatjira's paintings were Heysen-like; but the colours were his own, as Mountford observed in 1943, "showing better than those of any European artist I have seen the brilliant colour of Central Australia—the rich reds, the deep violet-blues, the golden-yellows—colours that Southerners find difficult to believe until they have seen them with their own eyes." Twelve years in Yatala had not erased the colours of his country from Stuart's mind. He told Noela Whitton that the painting Isabel Penny showed her had been copied from a black and white print to which he added colour. "And he put his fingers lightly to his temple and said 'The colour … it's still in here … I remember the colour.'"

He played the guitar and the squeezebox, he said, and he cherished a new transistor bought from his earnings at prison tasks. At the news that Father Dixon was no longer a priest and was married, he laughed heartily and said, "Good luck to him."

And had he killed Mary Hattam?

"Nuh", he replied. "But I think I've got a rough idea who did." (Thirty years later Noela Whitton doesn't recall whether she asked him who that was.)

"Why did you sign the confession if you didn't kill the child?"

"I was scared. They told me they would cut my head off if I didn't. They bashed me. I was scared."

"Did you ever tell Mr O'Sullivan that you knew who did it?"

"I didn't tell O'Sullivan. I was stupid. I was more or less charged then and he didn't ask me. I couldn't do anything."

"Did you ever tell anyone that you did kill Mary Hattam?"

"No."

"I heard a story that you told some warders in Adelaide gaol."(p. 275)

"I never told any warders in Adelaide. I never told anyone."

After all those years, she asked him at the end, "what do you think about the whole thing?"

"Them black trackers was a bodgie."

Of all the evidence assembled against him in 1959, what stuck most in his mind now was the testimony—false testimony, he said, and would go on saying in and out of gaol—of the trackers known as Sonny Jim and

Harry Scott that the footprints he made at the police station in Ceduna were identical with those found near the cave in which Mary Olive Hattam was murdered. (pp. 3, 14) Noela Whitton's Stuart was a more coherent and consistent witness than Stewart Cockburn's. "Should this man be in gaol?" the headline over Whitton's story asked Readers of the *Digger* were more likely than readers of the *Advertiser* to answer No.

That was certainly the Whittons' view. Back in Sydney Noela told Tom Dixon she had been deeply impressed by the man's "capacity to survive, unmarked by prison life, his sense of joy and interior balance." Recalling this impression over coffee in Glebe thirty years later, she says he seemed somehow outside, even above, Yatala; and to Evan's mind comes William Wordsworth's phrase (first encountered in Tom Dixon's English class at Downlands?), in tribute to the imprisoned Haitian revolutionary leader Toussaint L'Ouverture, about "man's unconquerable mind". She sent Stuart $25, half of her small payment from the *Digger*; and when she went out to Yatala again, briefly, on a later visit, he showed her a medallion inscribed "Max" on one face and "Noela" on the other.

In Adelaide Noela Whitton had tried to persuade Isabel Penny to press for Stuart's parole, but his kindly visitor was too diffident for that: as she wrote to Tom Dixon, she feared that if she approached unsympathetic officials they might stop her seeing him. Helen Devaney was unresponsive to Dixon's approach on the issue, apparently not wanting to be involved after all these years in the fate of her old client. Noela Whitton was determined to make and publicise a case for parole. Though the *Digger* was virtually unknown and sold few copies, she saw to it that on the day of publication one reached the desk of every media chief of staff. That evening she was on the ABC's *This Day Tonight,* she and the interviewer Peter Manning in Sydney talking with Sir Roderic Chamberlain and Don Dunstan in Adelaide about the possibility of parole. Chamberlain, it seemed to Noela Whitton, wallowed in the horror of the crime. Tom Dixon, watching in Sydney, wrote down and annotated Chamberlain's description of the murder as "'an animal performance to entice a little girl into a cave, force her open with a stone (a new piece of evidence!), rape her, kill her with a stone and leave her there and go off and do more drinking.' This is more of an emotional outburst than a judicial summary", Dixon wrote. Peter Manning asked Chamberlain and Dunstan whether the man who had conducted the crown case against Stuart and who was now chairman of the Parole Board had a conflict of interest. Certainly not, replied Chamberlain. Yes, replied Don Dunstan, and said so again in parliament; Sir Roderic should disqualify himself from any further application by Stuart.

Chamberlain at once issued a vigorous rejoinder, observing that all five members of the board had voted against parole. They included not only the comptroller of prisons, Lloyd Gard, but also a psychiatrist and nominees of the Chamber of Manufactures and the Trades and Labor Council. Moreover, said Chamberlain, the government could at any time overrule the board by exercising the prerogative of mercy. Dunstan said nothing about that. The *Advertiser* published an article by A.B.C. Wilson, chairman of the SA Prisoners' Aid Association who had lately used a Churchill Fellowship to investigate penal methods in many countries. "I would be surprised", he wrote, "if any parole authority in the UK or north America would permit a person who had been connected with the prosecution of an inmate to sit in judgment on that person's parole application."

The board considered a fresh application from Stuart in April 1973. This time Chamberlain did disqualify himself, reluctantly and with embarrassment, after publication of a remark he had made a few months earlier.

The Whittons and Stewart Cockburn had not been the only reporters allowed to interview Stuart in 1972. Cadets on Melbourne newspapers were reading my book in course work for a Diploma of Journalism at the Royal Melbourne Institute of Technology. Four of them, Stephen Foley and Ben Ainsworth of the *Sun News-Pictorial* and Pam Graham and Jenni Brown of the *Herald,* decided to do some investigating of their own and set off in two pairs for Adelaide during the September vacation. They did not expect to publish any account of their experiences, but as keen apprentices they took full notes. Foley, known by 2002 as Steve, and now a senior editorial executive at the *Age,* has generously allowed me to draw on an account he wrote up at the time. He and Ainsworth called first on the premier. Dunstan picked up the phone. and authorised a visit to Yatala, where the superintendent, R.G. Taylor, allowed them fifteen minutes with the prisoner. Like Cockburn and unlike the Whittons, they sat, unguarded, at a table in the low security block.

"His lined face was full of character", Foley wrote. His teeth were stained yellow with nicotine, and two were missing after a fight in prison. He set a tin of tobacco in front of him and accepted the offer of a cigarette, taking long drags. He said he didn't miss the drink, and was confident he could stay off it when he got out. He was writing for the prison's Alcoholics Anonymous magazine. He was also studying German and painting landscapes from memory. "It's beautiful country out there. The first thing I'm gonna do when I get out is go bush for a long walkabout." He had been reading, among other books, Douglas Lockwood's *I The Aborigine.* Professor Strehlow had come to see him last week. Two girls (Graham and Brown) had been there this morning. "You can't talk to them like fellas", he told the young men. (Noela Whitton, by contrast, had felt that he was confiding in her as a woman—about, for example, his resolve not to marry in haste as he thought too many ex-prisoners did.) He had no real complaints about Yatala. Taylor, the superintendent, had told the reporters to stay off the case, and Foley thought he talked more freely once it was clear that they would. From the beginning, though, the reporters noticed "no sign of nervousness or shyness—he was completely at ease." Time ran out. "We all stood and shook hands. Max thanked us for coming, saying he enjoyed the chat."

From the visitors' room Foley and Ainsworth went to the superintendent's office, "There is a lot of sympathy for Stuart outside this gaol", Taylor said, "but I have none." He had king-hit one bloke and tried to kill another. "Every little while he goes through a phase. Won't wash or clean up his cell. You've just got to stand over him." They may have noticed, said the superintendent, that he had a simple intelligence. "On the contrary", wrote Foley, "we found Max quite coherent, reasonably sharp and not what you would call a simpleton."

Could they send Stuart a copy of *The Stuart Case*? He had said to them, "I haven't read Inglis' book, but I would like to. It was in the library but someone took it out." To Cockburn he had said that maybe it was in the library but he had never asked for it. To Whitton he said that he had never read it, and she could not confirm a report that it had been removed from the library. Taylor responded to the reporters' request after a long pause. "I would have to say no to that. He has been interviewed a lot over the past few days and could possibly see this building up to his release. Besides, he could not understand it—the book would only confuse him." When I met Evan and Noela Whitton for coffee in May 2002 they had brought along a copy of the book—to please an old author, I supposed, by showing how well thumbed it was. They had another reason, as I found, when at their suggestion I opened it and read on the flyleaf the signature of Rupert Max Stuart. Noela had taken it to Yatala on her second visit. It must have been the first time he had seen in the book. Then she had to take it away. I don't know whether he ever read it when at liberty.

"He will never get out", the superintendent told the young men. "He will come up for parole again, but he will never be released." Sir Roderic Chamberlain gave them a similar view when they interviewed him in the comfortable front room of his home on the other side of the city, at Glenelg. Stuart's application for parole was refused, he said, because he had been violent. He was not fit for release. On the matter of his intelligence, which had come to interest the reporters, Chamberlain allowed that he "had a certain simple intelligence and a very keen native cunning." Certainly he had pulled the wool over Father Dixon's eyes. Sir Roderic said that his forthcoming book would expose "the completely misguided campaign" on Stuart's behalf, and he appeared disappointed that this interview was not for publication, as he wanted publicity for the book. He was a cordial host. "He assumed a pose", Foley observed, "feet outstretched, body upright with one arm draped across the top of the chair. His hair was thin and snow white; he had a warm face that smiled at you constantly."

That description would have surprised their next interviewee, Professor T.G.H. Strehlow. The small and cluttered university office to which he admitted them had the blinds drawn, the windows barely open and a radiator on, as if to simulate the climate of central Australia. They were meeting a man more and more suspicious of the world around him, who, as he told them the story of his involvement in Stuart's case, "spoke in a hushed voice as if he feared being overheard, sometimes dropping almost to a whisper".

The two pairs of reporters were engaged in a friendly race, seeing who could get first to whom. Neither team managed to see Sir Thomas Playford, now aged 76, though he did answer the telephone. "Sir Thomas clearly had unpleasant memories of the case," Foley wrote after a short conversation, "to the point of denying he was directly involved with it." "I'm retired", he said, "and don't want anything to do with politics now. Good day."

The second pair of journalism students, Pam Graham and Jenni Brown, met in Yatala "a meek, quiet, broken-spirited man", they thought. They did ask him about the case; and like Cockburn and unlike the Whittons they elicited apparently conflicting answers about the murder. He had not killed the little girl; he had never seen her. Then: "Was it because you were drunk that you don't remember if you killed the child?" "Yeah, probably", he replied, but later in the interview he denied having said that.

Seven months later, on 17 April 1973, the Melbourne *Herald* made use of Pam Graham and Jenni Brown's notes. The Parole Board was considering a fresh request from Stuart, and Sir Roderic Chamberlain had insisted on occupying the chair. The young women had the rare experience, for cadets, of seeing their names in the story at the top of page one, not for anything Stuart had said but for a remark by Chamberlain, who had told them, they reported: "Stuart should have hanged. I would have pulled the lever myself. He is nothing but an animal." "DON'T SET THIS MAN FREE", said the headline, and above it, over the masthead, quotations from Chamberlain, who had spoken to the paper that day by telephone from Adelaide ("I would never let Stuart out of prison"), and from Stuart ("He's the only reason I can't get parole"). Chamberlain conceded that he might have made those remarks; they were "intended to be informal", and in a "light-hearted manner … in an off-the-record chat". That was at odds with his evident hope that Foley and Ainsworth, who called on him a day later than Graham and Brown, would give his book publicity. In a late addition to that book he mentioned talking with the "two girls and two young men", but not what the "girls" had quoted him as saying.

Chamberlain responded at once to this revelation by announcing that he would not sit on the Parole Board's hearing of Stuart's application. Don Dunstan, declining to comment on Chamberlain's reported remarks, said that Sir Roderic's decision was quite proper. In Chamberlain's absence, nobody at the board's meetings was a former or present employee of the state (the comptroller of prisons having been replaced by an academic in the field of social administration). In May the four board members deferred Stuart's application, and on 14 August 1973 they decided to let him out.

The fate of Rupert Max Stuart was still big news within and beyond South Australia—it was the main story next morning not only in the *Advertiser* but in Melbourne's *Sun News-Pictorial.* Stuart was shaken awake by another Yatala inmate who had heard the radio news at 6 a.m., then he read the details in the *Advertiser,* accompanied by a photograph taken on Cockburn's visit. He saw that the decision had been greeted cordially not only by the premier but by the leader of the opposition, Dr Bruce Eastick, who had referred to him as "Mr Stuart", said that he had completed his debt to society and hoped that he would be given "every opportunity to accept a satisfactory role in the community."

A senior prison officer said that Stuart had been too excited to eat much breakfast and had asked him to write out a telegram to someone in Queensland because his hands were shaking. The officer would not tell the *Advertiser* who the addressee was, but Stewart Cockburn reasonably guessed that she was Edna Gieseman. Another prison officer said that he had lately added welding to his other jobs, making steel reinforcing rods faster than anybody else in the prison's concrete products shop, and could certainly get a job in that trade. He would be released, said the acting chairman of the Parole Board, when suitable arrangements were made for his accommodation and employment.

To what place, among which people, would the board liberate him, and on what conditions? Queensland, the destination of his telegram? Tom Dixon, asked in Sydney for an opinion, opted for an Aboriginal environment in the north of that state, saying that Stuart had friends there. Adelaide offered a variety of options. A group known as the Evangelical Fellowship of Aboriginal Christians collected offers of fifteen jobs and seven homes in that city. Don Miell, a boat builder, urged the Parole Board to release Stuart into his own home. Miell had known Stuart many years earlier, employing him in 1949 to drive a truck at a yellow ochre mine in the Simpson desert. "A shy, timid lad of seventeen," he recalled, and remembered talking to him under the stars about the blacks' Dreaming and the whites' Bible. He could not believe that Stuart had committed the murder. As a member of Alcoholics Anonymous, Miell enjoyed easy access to Yatala and over the years made regular visits which Stuart appears never to have mentioned to Dixon or Strehlow or any interviewer. Miell assured the board that if Stuart lived at his place he would employ him as a welder. Strehlow thought he should go north to live among his own people. Speaking by telephone to the Melbourne *Sun News-Pictorial's* Stephen Foley, who had interviewed him a year earlier, he said that he had last seen Stuart in Yatala three weeks ago. "He regards me as the man who saved him from execution", he told the reporter. Strehlow had found him cheerful, fit and keen to return to the centre.

Might he go to Hermannsburg, the Lutheran mission in his father's country to the west of Alice Springs, where Strehlow had been born and where Stuart had spent some time as a child? He would be welcome there, said a nephew, Helmut Pareroultja, who had just spoken to him by phone. "Us people", he was quoted as telling a reporter, "think he didn't do it—kill that little girl. Uncle Rupert said that he did not know what went on in the High Court. He didn't understand all the hard language. But now he does. He went to school in gaol and he has learned English. He has told me that he will come back here to help his people."

Whatever the facts, Herman Pareroultja declared that his uncle's conviction in a South Australian court meant nothing under tribal law. "He won't be punished when he comes back here." "Under tribal law", the reporter wrote, "if Stuart's people were convinced that he had wrongly committed murder, they would spear him in the thigh." When the reporter tried to pursue the story of a wife named Mary, said to be mother of

Stuart's child, some people at Hermannsburg would say nothing and Herman Parereoultja said only "she has gone—finished."

In the event he and the Parole Board both preferred another destination in the centre. He would go to Santa Teresa, the Catholic mission one hundred kilometres south-east of Alice Springs where Father Dixon had been the first priest-in-charge. Stuart in youth had lived for a while at Santa Teresa. These days his mother spent some time at the mission and some in Alice Springs. (His father had died in 1966.) He had other relatives there, and from Yatala he had been corresponding warmly with a young woman at Santa Teresa named Catherine Young.

The prospect of Stuart's release was bound to provoke controversy. "There will be many in the community, perhaps even a majority", said the *Advertiser* in an editorial, "who will disagree with the decision to release Stuart. They have no right, however, to contest the decision of those best placed to make it." The opponents included two opposition members of parliament, one of them representing an electorate that included Ceduna, who disagreed vehemently with their leader. Joyce Hattam, mother of the murdered child, could not sleep on the night she heard the news, and believed that fourteen years was too light a sentence for so terrible a crime. To a police sergeant in Ceduna, however, it seemed that nobody in the town begrudged Stuart his freedom. There were comments from outside South Australia. Evan Whitton, now writing for the Fairfax weekly the *National Times*, described Stuart as "a great survivor", thought he would probably be unwise to stay in South Australia, and reported Sir Roderic Chamberlain as still hoping that he would not be released at all. In the weekly *Nation Review*, which had inherited *Nation*'s name and some of its character, Bruce Muirden rehearsed the events of 1959, dwelling with admiration on the intervention of Rohan Rivett's *News*, for which he had worked at the time. "Oddly", he observed, "the same newspaper failed to mention its crusade in a recent historical supplement celebrating its fiftieth birthday."

Though I was living in Port Moresby at this time, I was well informed on what the papers were saying and not saying. I had assigned royalties from my book to the John Howard Society, a name which in those days meant not a conservative Australian Liberal politician but an eighteenth century English penal reformer who had inspired people throughout the empire to work for more humane and rational modes of punishment. The South Australian branch had been active in the 1959 campaign to review Stuart's conviction, had welcomed the new arrangements for parole in 1970, wanted the *de facto* abolition of capital punishment to be made statutory, and was pressing the Dunstan government to conduct a promised review of the state's prisons, of which one outcome, the society believed, should be the demolition of Yatala.

The secretary of the society was a consulting psychologist, Dr Eric Price. For some thirty years from 1960, wherever I was, he sent me every item in the *Advertiser* and the *News*, and any he happened to notice from elsewhere, usually with an attached note. With a 1972 batch: "I see that

Max is working in the brick yard. This is a barbed-wire enclosed compound just outside the walls, and there isn't the same feeling of being shut in by the walls there." And now: "It was a bad mistake to allow the press to interview Stuart some time ago, or to publicise parole board decisions. Nothing could be worse for his integration into the community." The event was cancelled by order of the premier, "following advice from people close to Stuart that the publicity would prejudice his chances of rehabilitation." I bless the memory of Eric Price as I draw on his cuttings and comments.

The prisoner at last left Yatala on 18 October 1973, in an operation so ineffectually planned to avoid publicity that the *Advertiser* could splash across its front page next day Stewart Cockburn's story that the prisoner had been "SMUGGLED OUT OF ADELAIDE IN POLICE PLANE". He was heading for Santa Teresa—in a Piper Cherokee, the paper reported, flying via the northern South Australian town of Oodnadatta, where Stuart was reported as giving the name Max Brady when he and his escorts booked into a hotel for the night. Wearing a neat dark suit and open-neck shirt, having a receding hairline, moustache and dark glasses, Max Brady was instantly recognised as Max Stuart by a shop assistant from whom he bought a towel, shaving cream, safety razor, blades and a toilet bag, explaining that he had left his shaving gear behind in Adelaide. And when the plane landed at Santa Teresa mission, having bypassed Alice Springs, Stuart was met by not only a dozen or so relatives and friends but also a reporter and a photographer. A Catholic priest in Alice Springs, asked about reporters' access, said that Stuart should be allowed to have his privacy.

He had grinned when Yatala's superintendent shook his hand and wished him luck, and said that he had no complaints about his treatment in gaol. Twenty years later Stuart vividly recalled his exit from Yatala:

"I was down at the garden. Ten o'clock, the Superintendent put out a search for me. There I was scrubbing at the milking machines.

He said, 'What are you doing there?'

I said, 'I'm working'.

'You're supposed to be on the plane. Eleven o'clock you're going.'

'Bullshit' I said. Anyway I went. …

There were two police, my parole officer and the pilot. We're travelling—down to Oodnadatta. We booked in the bar there in the pub, straight across from where I could see people, you know, on a hot day, having a schooner … And I'd forgotten about what beer looked like …

I said, 'Oh well, if they're going to drink, I'll just go back to my room.' I was drinking pumpkin wine, and I was singing my head off—I had my guitar. I said to the Parole Officer, 'You can have your bar, I'm getting happy going home.'

I came to Santa Teresa, and I couldn't still believe it, how everybody welcomed me, you know. All my relations—uncles and aunties—they had a party that night, a big dance they put on for me."

The reception was as cordial as the one his nephew Helmut had promised at Hermannsburg

Stuart woke up believing that he was still in Yatala. "That next morning, I'm laying down for the bell to ring … and old Father Clancy came up.

'Mate!'

'Yeah?'

'Breakfast's on!'"

When he began to clean up his room and make up the bed, Father Clancy said: "'Hey, you've got to forget about this! You're free now.' I still didn't believe it. I used to walk a hundred yards from the church, standing there looking up the road, wondering when the police were going to come to pick me up. I didn't feel that I'd escaped, and I had a guilty conscience, thinking 'People hate me' and all of that. 'They don't love me.'"

The terms of Stuart's release showed why the Parole Board preferred Santa Teresa to any more open environment. He was to reside at the mission, accept employment and undertake studies as directed by his parole officer, not change accommodation or employment without that officer's written approval, abstain from alcohol and illicit drugs, and not be alone with any female under the age of sixteen. "Stuart is free to roam about the mission", said William Baker as acting chairman of the board, "but he can't leave it." Sir Roderic Chamberlain, about to resume the chairmanship, declared his continuing disapproval of the decision to let Stuart out. As South Australia had no power to extradite him for any breach of conditions imposed in that state, he said, the man had virtually been given a free pardon.

Chamberlain's book *The Stuart Affair*, long awaited, was published just before Stuart's release. Its conclusion is that the affair "demonstrated once more the truth of the proposition that there is no tribunal in which truth is so likely to prevail, whether of guilt or innocence, as a British court", and every piece of evidence from the case is marshalled to arrive at that imperially patriotic conclusion. The book contains, as I mention above, new information on why Stuart was not hanged. Chamberlain also gives a complete list, not published until now, of Stuart's previous convictions, and quotes the admission he was said to have made to warders at the end of the trial.

Chamberlain was not alone among prosecutors when he chafed at the rule in British law that prevents the crown from mentioning the criminal record of a defendant who chooses (as Stuart did: pp. 29–30) not to give evidence on oath. He lists in the book 25 offences committed by Stuart over ten years: in Chamberlain's summary "eight of drinking liquor and four of supplying alcohol to Aborigines (those being in the days when Aborigines were not allowed to drink intoxicants); two of being in a prohibited area; two of being unlawfully on premises; four of stealing; two of common assault of which one was on a female adult; two of aggravated assault of which one was on a female child; and one of making a false declaration." Most of these offences were trivial. The two the prosecutor would most like to have cited in court were the assault on a female adult and the aggravated assault on a female child. (Any assault by a male on a female or a child was "aggravated".) The female adult was a nurse in Alice

Springs, the female child was a nine- or ten-year-old at Cloncurry. Both episodes are described in my book, for Chamberlain had been able to get them on the record of the Royal Commission in his cross-examination of Strehlow and in a statement from a policeman called to give evidence of Stuart's capacity in English. (pp. 172, 183) Chamberlain also publishes the testimony of warders that as Stuart was being escorted from the dock after hearing the sentence of death, he had said: "That's what the bloody plonk does for you. I'd had nearly a flagon of wine or I wouldn't have grabbed her." John Starke had successfully opposed the admission of the warders' evidence, but only after the commissioners had read copies of what they intended to say. (pp. 189–90, 221) Sir Thomas Playford presumably had the record of convictions in mind, and possibly also the words allegedly heard by the warders, when he said that nobody who knew all that the police knew could doubt Stuart's guilt. (When asked by Noela Whitton, we saw, Stuart denied having made any admission to the warders.)

As well as these additions to the story, Chamberlain's book has one remarkable omission. His summary of the royal commissioners' findings makes it appear that they offered no criticism of the police, leaving out entirely the passage in which they reject a policeman's evidence that Stuart's confession was taken down verbatim. (p. 292) The prosecution of Rivett and the *News* for seditious and criminal libel gets only three paragraphs, hostile to the defendants. Rivett, like Stuart, exercised his right not to give evidence on oath. At his trial, as at Stuart's, Chamberlain was not allowed to make anything of that choice. But as he now observes, "there is no such restriction after it is all over", and he comments with relish on that decision by this "modern Zola". Perhaps the author had both Stuart and Rivett in mind when he selected as epigraph a verse from the Book of Proverbs: "He that keepeth his mouth keepeth his life: but he that openeth wide his lips shall have destruction."

"The Stuart campaign", Chamberlain writes, "can be seen in retrospect as an early instance of the phenomenon which has become so familiar in more recent times: the revolt against authority." For Tom Dixon that was possibly the most startling statement in the book. In order to sustain the theme, Chamberlain diminishes Dixon's role and magnifies Rivett's. "He hints solemnly at my part", Dixon wrote to me soon after the book was published, "but forgets about me when he gets to the newspapers." But the principal villains are "university intellectuals, who knew very little about the methods of the detection of crime, and still less about the facts of the Stuart case". My book is not mentioned in Chamberlain's; but I spot myself, unnamed, in a passage near the end, as "one of the intellectuals" attempting to cast doubt on the commissioners' findings in a manner "both ill-informed and mischievous."

The *Advertiser* carried a long review by Stewart Cockburn on the day of publication, most of it quotation and paraphrase, ending with the judgement that the book is "meticulously reasoned … a damning indictment of Stuart and a persuasive vindication of the SA police and judicial systems, and also, of course, a piece of advocacy". If only K.S. Inglis' book were still in print, "the two versions could be read side by side and each of us could make a personal judgment." In vain had Melbourne University Press sent the *Advertiser* a copy of my book as part of an effort to move stocks of it in a "re-issue" at the time of the controversy over parole. When *The Stuart Case* first appeared Cockburn had written me a cordial note, saying, "nowhere can I fault your dispassionate account of the whole case." It was evidently no part of his present brief to compare the two books.

In the *Canberra Times* Geoffrey Sawer wrote, "that while the academic's book was notably judicious and judicial, the judge's book is less so." He found Chamberlain's partisanship self-defeating. Another professor of law, Alex Castles of Adelaide, reviewed the book in the *Adelaide Law Review*. "Sir Roderic writes with the flair of an experienced journalist", Castles considered, "combined with the wiles of a leading prosecution counsel, to present what can only be regarded, in the last analysis, as his own *personal* view of the Stuart case and its ramifications." Though adding little to my account, and neglecting issues I had explored and documented, Castles thought that Chamberlain book had "helped immeasurably to recapture more than Inglis the feelings which permeated at least some sections of the State during the Stuart case." Castles considered that Chamberlain showed "little understanding of the traditional role of the press in a democratic society" and failed to give due credit to such people as Father Dixon and Mr Strehlow who had come forward to perform what they believed to be "a public service to probe for the truth in a matter in which a convicted murderer might still die on the gallows."

Just after *The Stuart Affair* appeared, another book was rumoured. When Stuart's release was announced in mid-August the editor of *Nation Review* invited Rohan Rivett to contribute a personal reminiscence of the case. "He declined", the paper reported, "saying that to tell the whole story would involve both us and him in rather more defamation actions than either we or he could entertain at this time. To tell half the story, he argued, would be worse than telling no story at all." In November the *National Times* reported that Rivett's story was to be published, "and there are claims that the book will shake Adelaide's establishment." These days Rohan Rivett was a freelance journalist, broadcaster, public speaker and author. He published several books, though not one on the Stuart case, before dying suddenly of a heart attack in 1977. Among Rivett's papers in the National Library of Australia is the manuscript of a novel about an evening paper named the *Chronicle*, whose publisher Armand Russell and editor Donald Dare are lightly fictionalised versions of Rupert Murdoch and Rohan Rivett. The Stuart case appears as the Derby case. Sir Roderic Chamberlain is Sharkface. "Despite desperate attempts by Sharkface to prevent his release", the author writes in an epilogue, "Derby has now been a free man for some time. Some of his defenders, like Donald Dare, are still not dogmatic as to his guilt or innocence."

26

ALICE SPRINGS

Rupert Max Stuart had been locked away in 1959 from the Australia of Sir Thomas Playford and Sir Robert Menzies, when the watchwords for Aboriginal policy were protection and assimilation. He was released in 1973 into the Australia of Don Dunstan and Gough Whitlam, where people spoke a new language of self-determination and land rights. Midway through his incarceration, voters in 1967 had given overwhelming support to a referendum empowering the federal parliament to make laws for Aborigines throughout the Commonwealth. By 1973 the winds of change were blowing in every state and territory. In the Northern Territory, Santa Teresa, Stuart's new home, and Hermannsburg, where he might have gone, were among places where missions were being transformed, not altogether comfortably, into autonomous communities. "The old idea of a mission where the poor Aborigines are treated by kindly missionaries in a gentle and fatherly way", wrote Father John Clancy of Santa Teresa in 1972, "is giving way to a concept of a community of people interested in taking an active part in the conduct of their own affairs." Clancy was "priest-in-charge", as Father Tom Dixon had been from 1954 to 1956; his successors would be "community advisers". As missionary authority declined, so did both religious observance and civil order: the mission now reported offences unknown in Dixon's time: "stealing, destruction of property, abuse of alcohol leading to fights, bad temper, stand-over tactics, neglect of children ..." Access to motor vehicles made the one hundred kilometre journey up the dusty road to Alice Springs easier now than in Dixon's day, and that could cause more trouble. Stuart alone among the men of Santa Teresa was not allowed to make that journey. This was not the ideal environment for the parole of a man with a history of fighting and drinking.

The parole officer who had travelled with him from Adelaide, Fred Gould, stayed a few days and arranged to keep in touch with Father Clancy. "He is finding life new and strange here", Clancy wrote to Tom Dixon two weeks after his arrival, but he was "making a real effort not to put a foot wrong." Three weeks later, "he is finding things pretty difficult settling down in the quiet of a Mission." Stuart later recalled that for the first few mornings he had sat in his room waiting for someone to open the door. His feelings were disturbingly mixed, as he imagined fearfully that he was back in gaol but also wished that he was still there. "When I'm walkin' out I look over my shoulder. Whose lookin', you know. I wanted to get back in … I was a bit homesick to come back to Yatala." A plan to have him use the English he had learned in Yatala to teach children in the nuns' primary school lasted for only a month: "kids being kids", Fred Gould reported, "they played up and gave the teacher hell." He was put on to making cement bricks for the houses and other public amenities which were complementing the stone buildings constructed twenty years earlier by Dixon and men of the mission.

In March 1974, his fifth month out, Dixon had a reassuring letter from Stuart. "I am amazed at Stuart's calm & serenity, especially his balanced tones", Dixon wrote from Sydney to me in Canberra on 18 March 1974. "His mother is living at Santa Teresa & he has a girl friend who wouldn't be much over 30 & whom I know very well." Male companionship, however, before long had him in trouble. In November Rupert Max Stuart was back in the news for breaching the conditions of his parole which required him to stay on the mission and off alcohol. In court at Alice Springs he was charged with disorderly behaviour at the outpatients' department of the town hospital, and next day, while out on bail, with disorderly behaviour in one of the main streets. The magistrate proposed to detain him in custody until the charges could be heard, but was persuaded by a lawyer from the Aboriginal Legal Service—a Whitlam-age resource unknown for court appearances by the younger Stuart—to let him return on $50 bail to Santa Teresa. His parole officer, coming up from Adelaide, would talk with him there. In court on 4 December Stuart was found guilty on one charge, acquitted on the other and fined $5—a lenient penalty, showing sympathy with the plight of a man just out of gaol and learning to live in a new and hazardous world. "We think he realises", the Strehlows wrote to Dixon, "he has tried the patience of the saints themselves." Back he went, under the patronage of Saint Teresa, to resume his re-education.

Reports that it was not going well troubled authorities in Adelaide. The Parole Board was now chaired by Justice Roma Mitchell, whom Dunstan as attorney-general had made the first woman in Australia to be appointed a queen's counsel and then the first to sit on a superior court. She had made penal reform one of her many good causes. Nobody could have been more kindly disposed to Stuart. The board nevertheless revoked his parole on 21 July 1975. Despite Sir Roderic Chamberlain's prediction that once the parolee was out of South Australian jurisdiction he could never be brought back, the magistrate who had heard the charges against Stuart late in 1974 readily agreed to release him into the custody of two policemen up from Adelaide. As they escorted him on the flight to Adelaide, the premier said only that his behaviour had deteriorated and Justice Mitchell said nothing. He had been returned to his two old homes in the city, first Adelaide Gaol and then Yatala. The *Advertiser*, in an editorial headed "The Stuart enigma", was both compassionate and puzzled. "Did the former murderer ever really have a chance to rediscover freedom and rehabilitate himself? What were the pressures on him? There are so many questions, and so few answers. As matters stand, some citizens will now feel chagrined at an experiment which failed; and others will be pleased and will say 'We told you so!'"

Citizens in both camps could well be surprised when after only a week Stuart was released from Yatala and taken back to Alice Springs, as the newspapers added yet another photograph to the files showing Stuart, policemen and an aeroplane. Last time he had been dressed in the dark suit of urban man; now he wore flared blue jeans, a blue and white check shirt and what the captions described as a brown cowboy hat: stockman's gear which policemen had bought for him in Alice to wear on the journey down. When he first saw Adelaide airport at the end of 1958 he had been unable to read or write. This time he bought at the bookstall Alexander Solzhenitsyn's *August 1914*. A woman who happened to be seeing off an English friend noticed the reporters and photographers clustered around Stuart and wrote reproachfully to the *Advertiser* in the voice of an old and not wholly benign paternalism or maternalism. "When I told this friend who this 'hero' was and what lenient treatment he was receiving from the law of our land, she was horrified … Anyone who has worked among the Aborigines, as I have, knows how they love to have their photographs taken. It's the next best thing to drinking hard liquor! So you can imagine how proudly Stuart will show your paper's photographs to his mates." Sir Roderic Chamberlain, inevitably asked for his opinion, replied that the decision amazed him. "If it was worth calling him up", he said, "it was worth leaving him in custody."

Justice Roma Mitchell and her colleagues had considered two petitions on Stuart's behalf, one from a customary source and the other from a significant new voice in Aboriginal affairs. Father John Clancy had flown from Santa Teresa to tell the board that in June he had been celebrant at Stuart's marriage (in the church that was a monument to Father Dixon). His bride was the girlfriend Tom Dixon had told me about in March, Catherine Young, a nursing assistant at the mission's hospital who had lived all her life at Santa Teresa. She and Stuart had been corresponding during his later Yatala years. Dixon believed that the prospect of marrying her may have tipped the balance in favour of Santa Teresa and against Hermannsburg, and that while still in gaol Stuart had probably negotiated with the Young family to have their daughter "according to the customary and tribal law". So the marriage was both traditional and Christian. Father Clancy told reporters that it had been a major factor in the Parole Board's decision. "She's a very great person and well respected", he said. "We've got great hopes." The priest had so far been reticent on the matter of Stuart's conduct. Now he said that it was when he went to Alice Springs and got into the company of certain people that the trouble started.

Credit for the prisoner's release was also claimed by Charles Perkins, an Aborigine whose name was as familiar as Stuart's to other Australians. Perkins had been the country's most senior indigenous public servant, chief adviser to the minister in charge of the Whitlam government's new Department of Aboriginal Affairs until he was suspended recently on a year's leave without pay. He and a close Aboriginal friend, Gordon Briscoe, who worked in the federal Department of Health, happened to be travelling on the same flight south from Alice as Stuart and his police escort.

Like Stuart, Perkins and Briscoe were children of the centre, and they recognised him as kinsman. "You wrote a book about my uncle!" said Briscoe when we first met, at the Australian National University in the 1980s. Stuart counted Perkins as a son of his mother's cousin and had known him when he was a child. Perkins and Briscoe were younger and lighter-skinned, and those facts of life had turned them towards destinies different from his. In 1945, when Perkins was nine and Briscoe was seven, they had been taken from Alice Springs with their mothers' consent to Adelaide, where they lived in an Anglican home for boys of mixed ancestry. By 1952, when the unschooled Stuart was on horseback outback, Perkins was apprenticed as a turner and fitter. When Mary Olive Hattam was killed, he was playing professional soccer in England (as later would Briscoe). Next year Perkins was back in Adelaide, playing for Croatia and working (with Don Dunstan's encouragement and counsel) to amend or abolish laws which imposed "protection" on Aborigines. For a time he saw Dr Charles Duguid's Aborigines Advancement League, the first organisation to take up Stuart's case, as an ally; but then he was among young Aboriginal activists who either tried to take over such bodies or bypassed them, speaking up for themselves rather than remaining clients of liberal-minded whites, preferring politics to philanthropy. He moved to Sydney, and while Stuart was learning to read and write in Yatala Perkins was studying anthropology and sociology on the way to becoming in 1964, at the age of 26, Australia's first Aboriginal university graduate. In 1965 he was the most conspicuous participant in a "freedom ride" through towns of northern New South Wales, investigating and protesting at discrimination against Aborigines. As the winds of change blew hard under Whitlam, Perkins' career soared and crashed. His superiors would not tolerate forever his determination to combine the conflicting roles of public servant and public critic. Was he breaching the tradition of bureaucratic impartiality when he called Australia "a rotten stinking hole"? "Bugger tradition!" Finally Gough Whitlam himself said, "I have had Charlie Perkins."

Exiled from Canberra, he bought a caravan and headed for Alice Springs with his wife Eileen, of German Lutheran descent, and their children Hettie, Adam and Rachel. Perkins now began to re-discover his ancestral Aboriginal heritage. As the only Aboriginal living in or around Alice Springs who was familiar with the workings of the distant federal government, he gave people expert advice on how to get money for their own health and legal services. He organised and chaired an Interim Central Australian Land Council in anticipation of a Whitlam bill to establish such bodies. In September 1975, as Stuart began his second spell at Santa Teresa, Charles Perkins was elected as the first chairman of the Central Land Council. The council was to have great significance for Aboriginal lives, and would profoundly affect Stuart's, though neither he nor anybody else knew that in 1975.

On the day Stuart was being returned to Adelaide, Perkins was just back from longer flights, richly reported, to denounce his country's racial policy and practice in the USA, where he invited Muhammed Ali to come and see for himself, and England, where he distributed outside Ten Downing Street a leaflet headed "Australia is a racist country". The sight of Stuart sitting in the cabin between two policemen moved Perkins to affirm not exactly Black Power (a movement he believed not applicable to Australia) but certainly black solidarity, and in particular Arrernte solidarity, in the face of official white oppression. "It is understood", reported the *Advertiser,* "Mr Perkins told Stuart during the flight not to speak to the police." He did indeed. Gordon Briscoe remembers that he startled other passengers by calling out, "Don't you talk to the coppers. They can't just go around picking up blackfellers whenever they like. We'll look after you."

Soon after touching down in Adelaide, Perkins went into action on several fronts. He urged the Aboriginal Legal Service to be advocate for Stuart's immediate release. He reproached the police for being too severe, the premier for speaking without full knowledge, the Parole Board for bringing Stuart back. "I think they have realised what stupid people they have been", he said; and interpreted the whole episode as "an opportunity for those people to degrade Aborigines." On another tack he criticised Father Clancy and the mission for not being "a bit stronger" with Stuart, and counselled Stuart to act "with a bit more decorum".

Whether or not the board would have released Stuart without Charles Perkins' intervention, he was off again to Santa Teresa. Perkins' parting advice was that he should go not to the mission but to some cattle station near Alice Springs. Stuart did not think much of the idea. "That would be like putting my head in an oven", he said, perhaps meaning that the grog would be too easy to come by out there. In later recollection he mentioned other reasons. After not riding a horse for all those years, "you'd get really saddle sore, and you're alone from your loved one".

On landing in Alice Springs as at takeoff from Adelaide, and again on arrival at Santa Teresa, Stuart was interrogated by reporters. "I'm going to settle down and try to keep out of trouble", he told them. "I'm sick of reading about myself and hearing about myself on the radio. I just want to live a normal life." He would not give them a photograph of his wife but spoke a little of her. "She's a good girl. She doesn't smoke or drink. I think she'll look after me all right."

The formal conditions for keeping out of trouble were now changed a little. He could visit Alice Springs for approved purposes, such as going to the hospital, he did not have to abstain totally from alcohol, and he would report for the first time to a parole officer on the spot, appointed by arrangement with the board in Adelaide. There were plenty of labouring jobs he could do, Father Clancy said.

Six weeks later Stuart was back in Yatala. When police in Alice Springs on the evening of 2 September stopped a car with only one headlamp, they found Stuart at the wheel and charged him on five counts as well as the missing headlamp: driving while unlicensed, without due care and with a prohibited amount of alcohol in his blood, giving a false name and—a separate charge, somehow—offering information calculated to deceive. They had booked him well and truly.

A solicitor for the Aboriginal Legal Service told Dixon that the police in Alice were hostile to the town's most famous offender; but when he recalled these days in old age Stuart would say stoically that he had been doing the wrong thing and the cops were just doing their job. In court on 3 September his lawyer put it to the magistrate that his client had travelled from Santa Teresa to see the parole officer and a dentist, in a car driven by another man who appeared so drunk by the time they reached Alice that the passenger had taken over. The magistrate fined him $140 on four of the charges, the crown withdrew the count of deception, and the one for driving without due care was adjourned for 28 days, never to be heard.

An application for extradition to South Australia was once again granted without argument, and two policemen up from Adelaide again escorted him on a southbound flight. "I am sorry that I do not have better news of Max Stuart", wrote Eric Price in a note accompanying a thick batch of clippings. "One wishes that if it was considered necessary to revoke his parole he could have been held in Alice Springs Gaol, where he'd be closer to his wife & in his own environment. No doubt Max will be granted parole again later." He was, but this time after a longer spell in Yatala, from September 1975 to July 1976, when he was released without any publicity: "It is understood he will work as a laborer on the mission", reported the *Advertiser*; and that was just about all the paper could find out from either civil or ecclesiastical sources.

Tom and Joan Dixon visited Santa Teresa later that year. Dixon had not seen the mission for twenty years. Its material progress amazed him: a new health centre (where Stuart's wife Catherine worked), a bakery, a community hall with canteen, cement brick housing for a population now approaching 600, hundreds more than in his day, among whom able-bodied men such as Stuart were paid between eighty and a hundred dollars a week compared with three dollars in the 1950s. Some of his old friends said they regretted the cement bricks, preferring the old stone homes of his day, and some were apprehensive about that canteen: though so far it did not stock liquor, they feared that a vote allowing it to do so would be carried. Anyway, people brought in grog, as never in the old days, a change both reflecting and advancing a disregard for tradition. Dixon had read in Sydney about spiritual and moral decline at his old posting, and now he saw and heard the evidence of it. "The young people are not interested in the old ways", one old-timer told the Dixons. "Sometimes they drink and they fight. It is very hard for us." In two families he had known, men had been killed fighting with their brothers.

The Dixons were relieved to find Stuart looking strong and well. But Father Clancy had recently gone, and he was not getting on with his successor, Father Brian Healy, "community adviser". He had been showing "uppishness", the priest told the visitors. Stuart himself spoke severely about men who were "nuisances and trouble-makers", and said of the women that although they were still non-drinkers at the mission, "in the Alice, while the church bells are ringing the women are going to the nearest wine shop." One of his own recent trips into town, he confessed, had been provoked by breaking his hand in a fight. From the hospital, where he was allowed to go, he ran away to Amoonguna, south of Alice, and was back in town without approved cause when a policeman picked him up and sent him off in a taxi to Santa Teresa.

That was one cop who was not out to get him. Sooner or later, though, some policeman would take out the book; and, on 23 October 1976, after fourteen months of precarious freedom, Stuart was back in court: driving a mission vehicle without permission into Alice Springs, not reporting there to his parole officer, drinking and fighting. The officer in charge of the town's Criminal Investigation Branch told the court that tribal elders had been unhappy with Stuart's behaviour. He was becoming a frequent flyer between Alice and Adelaide.

This next stretch in Yatala was to be the longest so far since his first release two years earlier. Soon after this return Ted Strehlow wrote to Tom Dixon exasperated by Stuart's frailty but as certain as ever that he had been wrongly convicted. "I stuck up for him 1959, not because I believed he was virtuous but simply because I remained certain that he had NOT murdered Mary Hattam. I still believe in his innocence, despite his alcoholism and his social uselessness."

The object of Strehlow's judgment believed that it was only half-right: the grog was his undoing, but he could still beat it. "I'm going to give up drinking," he wrote to Dixon from Yatala, "not for my wife, or my family, or my friends and my black people, I'm going to give it up for me and myself. I can do lots of good things in life, without drinks and go drinking to get drunk. I know drink did me no good in the past and still is doing me no good … I can do good things without drinking and can't be happy with drinking. I can make people happy. I can make friends if I'm not drunk … I have a good wife, she been good to me, always write to me as you know, she comes from a good family and I really want to make her happy by doing the right thing, keep the married life happy."

It was a long letter—in very good English, Dixon remarked and as the writer reflected when he read it over. "I hope you can read my writting", he added. "I couldn't do this twenty-four years ago and I can only thank Her Majesty's prison at Yatala for this." Writing came so easily now that he imagined using the pen for more than correspondence. "May be one day I'll write a book on my own life story", he concluded. That would make four, alongside mine, Chamberlain's and the one he knew Dixon was writing. In another letter from Yatala he gave Dixon permission for that project, though without enthusiasm, thinking only of the notoriety the book could bring him. "I know I'll be getting nothing out of it. I'll only be getting very, very bad name."

When Dixon visited Stuart at this time they spoke of Strehlow's 1969 book *Journey to Horseshoe Bend,* an account of accompanying his dying father Carl south from Hermansburg in 1922, when Ted was fourteen, recording his anguish, his love of the landscape, and his unforgiving conviction that the Lutheran authorities in Adelaide were to blame for Carl Strehlow's death. Stuart said he had read it three times and enjoyed it. He had also read Chamberlain's *The Stuart Affair*, and judged it a lot of bullshit. Dixon always talked to the prisoner in English, for the benefit of any eavesdropping warders: he still remembered the rebuke he had suffered in 1960 for supposedly unsettling Stuart. Strehlow spoke with him in Arrernte so that those listeners would not understand a word.

Strehlow, now nearly seventy years old, was an alien in the new world of Aboriginal affairs. "Land rights" struck his ears as a slogan wielded by misguided whites and trouble-making, untraditional blacks. The Central Land Council seemed to him a device for the likes of Charlie Perkins to get control of Aboriginal land and pocket the profits from mining royalties. With Pastor Paul Albrecht, his father's successor at Hermannsburg and now over eighty, Strehlow encouraged the staff of the mission in mid-1976 to hold meetings around the their territory which would expose the council as an unrepresentative minority. Their campaign had the opposite effect when a meeting convened by the mission in November became a rally of support for the cause of land rights.

In the next two years Strehlow suffered further estrangement from Arrernte kinsmen. When the University of Adelaide would not give his new wife Kathleen the academic status he demanded for her, he and she carried his collection of ethnographic treasures off to their suburban Adelaide home, which became the site of a Strehlow Research Foundation. Strehlow declared his intention to bequeath everything to Kathleen and their infant son Charles, including a collection of sacred artefacts, *tjuringa,* about which, so donors believed, he had given undertakings he no longer appeared to recognise.

Stuart never forgot what he owed to Strehlow. Early in 1978, when he read in Yatala that his benefactor had been censured by the second chairman of the Central Land Council, Wenten Rubuntja, he sent him a letter of comfort. He may or may not have known that when Rubuntja criticized Strehlow he was responding to an onslaught which had begun with a letter in the Alice Springs *Centralian Advocate* headlined "'Leader' a fraud—Strehlow". He assured Strehlow that he "didn't like that Rubuntja when he said in the papers about the sacred things ... He's no older than me, he should never say things like that." He disputed Rubuntja's claim to know the old songs which gave an Arrernte man authority. He recalled the songs he himself had learned from his grandfather Tom Ljonga, the cameleer who was so valuable a source for Strehlow's own access to traditional knowledge. "Rubuntja has no songs that I know of ... I'm only a little lad in that line but I can put it over Rubuntja, any time, any place, anywhere."

Once, as he told Tom Dixon, Stuart had actually contested Rubuntja's knowledge of the songs during an encounter in the community hall at Santa Teresa in 1976. As Dixon paraphrased Stuart's account. which he plainly accepted as true: "A certain young man named Rubuntja was claiming a certain land ownership. Stuart asked the chairman to clear the hall of the women. When this was done, he challenged Rubuntja to sing his song to show his connection with that land. He couldn't."

Dixon depended on Stuart for his judgment of Wenten Rubuntja, and so probably did Strehlow. It was a mixture of fact and fiction. In putting down Rubuntja, Stuart put down in particular his age: Wenten Rubuntja was actually several years the older, in a culture where age mattered. Moreover, Rubuntja knew far more of the songs, and the law they embodied, the whole story of what anthropologists had named the Dreaming, than Stuart was admitting to his mentors. Rubuntja came to be recognised as custodian of the Yeperenye Dreaming, the story of the giant caterpillar perceived by Arrente people as the ancient creator of their landscape. Born north of Alice Springs in 1924, succeeding Charles Perkins as chairman of the Central Land Council in 1976 and re-elected in 1978, Wenten Rubuntja was on the way to becoming a prominent campaigner for land rights. In 1976, when the Fraser government weakened the Aboriginal Land (Northern Territory) bill which had been pending at the time of Whitlam's dismissal, it was Rubuntja—carrying a *tjuringa*—who led a delegation to lobby the prime minister in Canberra. He happened also, like Stuart, to be a painter: Albert Namatjira was his father's cousin, and he would acquire an independent reputation for his work wherever Aboriginal art was exhibited. The lives of Stuart and Rubuntja would intertwine as neither foresaw when the former disparaged the latter to Strehlow.

Nowhere else in Stuart's correspondence with Strehlow and Dixon, as far as I know, does he speak of his own proficiency as bearer of Arrernte tradition. Yet the man who could dare to joust with Rubuntja (whatever actually happened in that encounter) had evidently kept in his head through all the Yatala years the songs he had learned from the old men as a young initiate. Literature on prisons is rich in evidence of people who keep up their spirits, even retain sanity, by drawing on remembered stories, liturgy, poetry. Arrernte songs were all of those things. Tom Dixon had found Stuart "very sensible and balanced" in 1972 after spending twelve years, most of his adult life, in gaol (sometimes in solitary). Nola Whitton had been impressed a year later by the prisoner's "sense of joy and interior balance", and her husband had been moved to think of Wordsworth on "man's unconquerable mind". In Stuart's testimony about Wenten Rubuntja we glimpse a mind furnished with Arrernte knowledge which helped to sustain him in Yatala.

Tom Dixon thought Stuart's letter to Strehlow was "a wonderful demonstration of loyalty". That loyalty was further tested later in 1978 when the weekly magazine *People* featured photographs of secret ceremonies which Strehlow had sold to the German magazine *Stern*. Strehlow was innocently appalled that the photographs had been republished in Australia. *People* apologised to Strehlow; but this episode, writes Philip Jones in the *Australian Dictionary of Biography*, "incensed his critics and alienated old

Arrernte friends". Conflicts with elders of both the Arrernte and academic tribes probably helped to bring on his death. Strehlow suffered heart attacks in 1975 and 1976, and died suddenly of a third one in his university office on 3 October 1978. "It was very upsetting to hear about old Ted", Stuart wrote to Dixon from Yatala. "I'll miss him more than a lot. He was my friend, not only my friend, but my family's too. If it wasn't for him and you I wouldn't be writing this letter today … Old Ted is finished now but he's still in my mind and prayers."

For the whole of this period Stuart was in Yatala's minimum security division, working as a gardener. He looked a bit overweight, Dixon thought, but still strong and healthy. On 8 December 1978, after just over two years, Stuart was let out on parole for the fourth time. Press photographers at the now customary airport press conference caught for readers a grey-haired 45-year-old man. Reporters noted a cowboy hat in one hand and a cassette radio in the other. "I feel good", he told them. "I am going to make a fist of it this time. I won't be coming back." Sir Roderic Chamberlain, interviewed as usual, said as usual it was a scandal that Stuart should be at large. Eric Price attached to the cuttings a note saying: "I just hope he can leave the grog alone."

Journalists now addressed readers new to the story. "There is a generation to whom Stuart's name means nothing," wrote Stephen Foley, one of his 1972 interviewers, in Melbourne's *Sun News-Pictorial*, "and another, perhaps, who would sooner leave it that way." He had in mind people in Adelaide who did not want to go on being reminded that "no other case in South Australia's history, and, arguably, Australia's memory, ever provoked the storm this did."

Back at Santa Teresa the man who had been at the centre of that storm was yet again unable to make a fist of his freedom. "That Mission was good when there were no drunks out the Mission", he said in a letter to Tom Dixon. "That's when you were there but now it's no good." He wrote these words not from Santa Teresa but from Adelaide, where he was yet again in gaol, this time after less than five months out. Under the familiar headline "RUPERT MAX STUART BACK BEHIND BARS ", the *Advertiser* of 28 April 1979 had hardly to change any words from accounts of his earlier returns, other than to note that this was the fourth. When Tom Dixon went out to Yatala soon after his return he learned that somebody from an Aboriginal educational service—another innovation of the 1970s—had been out to see the prisoner, and that he had enrolled for a course in mechanics. Kathleen Strehlow visited Stuart a few days later, counting him among the responsibilities willed to her by her dead husband.

His latest term in Yatala lasted just over a year. "STUART ON FIFTH PAROLE", reported the *Advertiser* on 1 August 1980. This time he was not given a media send-off at the airport, the authorities hoping that the quieter his return to the centre, the better his chance of staying there. Exactly two years later, at the end of July 1982, he was arrested out at Hermannsburg, where he was not supposed to be. "STUART IN YATALA", reported the *Advertiser* on 2 August. "At least he managed two years this time!" wrote Eric Price. In Alice Springs the lawyer from the Aboriginal Legal Aid Service assigned to represent Stuart admitted to the magistrate that she could say little on his behalf.

Her client might not have told her what he later told Dixon in Yatala about the circumstances of his arrest. Max and Catherine Stuart were staying with Helmut Pareroultja, the nephew who had urged him to choose Hermannsburg in 1974. Possibly he was there on secret ceremonial business, which he was obliged by kinship to undertake. The police, as Dixon recorded Stuart's version of the event, had "hauled Rupert out of the camp in front of his stricken wife and carted him off to the 'slammer', no reasons, no excuses."

Dixon attributed this "latest incarceration" to an over-zealous parole officer, looking to his own position. Kathleen Strehlow had a darker explanation. Sharing her late husband's conviction that he was surrounded by enemies, she convinced herself that the parole officer had been acting on their behalf, punishing Stuart for siding with the Strehlows in the conflict over possession of sacred items which had begun in Ted's lifetime and outlived him. She marshalled forces to thwart the enemies, bringing Stuart's mother down from the centre, asking the superintendent of Yatala to let the prisoner come to the Strehlow house for a day, appealing to the responsible minister and even to the premier. She asked that she herself be heard by the Parole Board, accompanied by Don Miell, who had employed the young Stuart and visited him in prison. On Kathleen Strehlow's reading of events, Stuart's allegiance to a white man and his memory was the cause of his return to gaol.

This sixth term lasted two years, of which the final months were at the Cadell Training Centre, a minimum security prison on the Murray River where he worked as a farm labourer. Later he told Dixon that another Aboriginal inmate of Cadell had talked with him about someone who might have been Mary Olive Hattam's killer. His account, though unspecific, was of great interest to Dixon as he worked on the book in which he hoped to establish Stuart's innocence. "I might write to you again when I see that Black Fellow from South Australia. I have been look for the people like that and thinking on it."

Stuart was released without publicity on 3 July 1984 for his sixth period of parole. He was nearly 52. "Is it time he was given an unconditional release", asked an *Advertiser* journalist, Chris Milne, "this convicted murderer who is described by one acquaintance as 'a courteous, well-mannered old man' now, and is considered a model prisoner?" The question would "arouse sympathy in some and hostility in others. For the Stuart case has been the most divisive, legally, socially and politically, in recent SA history."

Three months out, Stuart wrote to Dixon in terms suggesting that his tributes over the years to the regime at Yatala had been composed with an eye on their first readers, the warders. "I am sorry that I didn't write to you when I was in that Rat Box. I didn't want write any letters to all of my friends when the people look over my shoulder but I still think of you and

Mother Joan as my Mum and Dad. I am over here at Hermannsburg now for a little time, then I'm going back to Santa Teresa Mission." Apparently he was allowed to be in Hermannsburg under the new conditions of parole (which were not made public). If he did not breach them, the authorities told him, he would discharge his parole entirely by 1987. He was now looking forward to Tom Dixon's book, as he said in a letter which ended by repeating a thought he had expressed when authorising the project in 1978. "Seen that I can read and write now I might as well write a book about it. So why not?"

The Wizard of Alice: Father Dixon and the Stuart Case, by Thomas Sidney Dixon, was published in July 1987. He had been working on it since 1972. In 1975, he told me, "Joan and I motored over via Pt Augusta to Ceduna. It was with no little trepidation that we drove into the town, she at the wheel & I talking on to a tape. I walked from Thevenard to Ceduna, following Stuart's movements as closely as possible, had a good look at the so-called cave, interviewed the C of E Minister about certain personalities and even went into Spry's shop & saw him in situ." (On Spry, see p. 117) In Adelaide he had interviewed another Church of England minister, the one who had been at Ceduna and was said to have refused to sign the petition that went around town for Stuart to be executed. He now gave Dixon some idea of local feeling at the time. "I even went & had a cup of coffee with Inspector Paul Turner, who was still trying to blow down my ear about the smartness of the trackers. I asked him why he didn't get the hairs examined by today's technology & all he said was 'What would be the use?' Our meeting, at my request, was amiable." He found Helen Devaney terribly ill after radical surgery for cancer and "very guarded and unwilling to acknowledge any of the hearsay she used to pass on to me in those days." He talked with Jack Clark, the police reporter Rohan Rivett had assigned to accompany him on his search for the Giesemans. He spent days in the state library reading files of the *News* and of the *West Coast Sentinel.* He tried to get information about tides on the west coast for 1958–9.

Reporters in 1959 had compared this priest pursuing evidence about a murder with the fictional Father Brown, hero of G.K. Chesterton's detective stories. For ex-Father Dixon, sleuthing now in South Australia, the one encounter that turned up new material was with Allan Wardrop, the former café-proprietor from Port Lincoln whose testimony the royal commissioners had dismissed. Wardrop and his wife and daughter all swore they had heard Detective Frank Whitrod admit that policemen had bashed Stuart. (pp. 174–7, 243–6, 305–6) When Dixon questioned Mrs Wardrop soon after the commission reported, on 4 January 1960, she had told him Whitrod had said: "We kept cuffing him along. He wouldn't confess, we belted it out of him." In 1974 Dixon easily found his way to Wardrop, who had enrolled for a degree in law after having his curiosity about it aroused by the case. For at time he had practised as a solicitor in Adelaide with Helen Devaney, and now he worked on his own. The commissioners had preferred the word of another witness from Port Lincoln, Horrie Baker, secretary of the local RSL, who put Wardrop down as a big talker and disputed much of his evidence. Wardrop now told Dixon that he had once confronted Baker about his performance at the commission. He recalled saying, "You told some pork pies against me", and Baker replying, "What else could I do? I had to live at Port Lincoln." The Dixons drove to Port Lincoln and learned that Horrie Baker had died of a stroke the previous year, at the age of 54, after the death of a son in Vietnam.

Dixon explains his title—*The Wizard of Alice*—in a foreword. "Twenty-seven years ago I met Rupert Maxwell Stuart. Looking back over those years I can only wonder at my persistence in maintaining my earliest impressions of his innocence. I have had to ask myself whether this persistence was because of poor judgment on my part or a wizard deceit on his part."

The book's central conclusion is that six policemen at Ceduna on the night of 22 December 1958 made up a confession for Rupert Max Stuart and assaulted him until he put his name to it. The author recalls the moment when he became unalterably certain of this fact. It was on 29 July 1959, at Atherton, when the Giesemans told him that Stuart was working within their sight from two to four o'clock. "I had made a great discovery on the anniversary of my Ordination. I had found out the truth."

The publisher sent me a copy inscribed by the author, "with gratitude for the great days during 1959 and the years since". He had "wanted to write a book different from yours and Chamberlain's, in the sense that I didn't want to tackle something 'legal', since that side of the case is finished, i.e. a dead issue … I haven't heard from any of the 'heavies' yet. Those around me who have bought the tome are finding it interesting to the point of 'engrossing'." Late in August he told me that Edna Gieseman had just rung from Townsville to say that *The Wizard* had arrived.

Some of the heavies to whom Dixon sent copies responded, some didn't. From Sir John Starke of the Victorian Supreme Court, counsel for Stuart at the Royal Commission, came a gratifying response. "I read your book in the week-end and congratulate you on a literary achievement." As history, moreover, he much preferred the book to Chamberlain's: "Most of your conclusions I agree with."

Starke was caustic about the account in what purported to be Stuart's confession of his stripping before the rape and going down to the beach later to wash himself. "For an ignorant aborigine with his lust up to have the foresight to anticipate that if he raped the girl he might get blood on his clothes and so get caught beggars belief. To go further and say that on a hot Saturday afternoon after the event he walked down the beach in full view to wash himself is strictly from Alice in Wonderland … The clothes he was wearing at the time were the subject of minute inspection by the police and no blood was found on them. The whole cave, roof and walls, was spattered with blood. If Stuart had his clothes on when he raped the girl they must have been covered with blood. Confronted with this dilemma I have no doubt the police concocted this part of the statement. Having arrived at this conclusion the whole of the police evidence must be tainted and flawed."

Starke nevertheless remained worried about Stuart's lies. "I cannot myself dismiss the guilty inference as entirely untenable"—as he could, he said, in the case of Lindy Chamberlain, the baby and the dingo.

I reviewed the book for *Quadrant* in December 1987. I set out the argument of the book and indicated the points at which it did not convince me. Stuart in the witness box had shown himself more at home in English, I thought, and more familiar with clocks, than Dixon allowed. Telling the commission that he had been working at the show from two o'clock to four, Dixon wrote, was to be Stuart's "undoing". He meant that once Stuart had given those times, he could not explain cogently why he had never mentioned them earlier. Dixon shared my own belief, I said, that Stuart's legal advisers put those times into his mouth. (We may have both been wrong, as I was to learn in 2002). Whatever the explanation, this one answer wiped out any possible claim—I should have said any *legal* claim—on Stuart's behalf to have suffered a miscarriage of justice, given the invariable judgment of our courts that if accused persons are convicted after choosing not to call evidence available to them, they are not allowed to plead that a miscarriage has occurred simply because that evidence might have affected the verdict.

Nor did I think Dixon took seriously enough what had seemed to me (and, as I now know, to Starke) damaging inconsistencies in Stuart's account of his movements on the day of the murder. The author did persuade me, I said, that the evidence of Aboriginal witnesses contained more confusions than I had noticed, and more than Stuart's counsel picked up, but not that they had collaborated in a concoction, or that the white shopkeeper Spry made up his evidence in order to help establish Stuart's guilt. "I think he is rightly severe on the Commissioners", I added, "for dismissing without good reason the contrary evidence of the Giesemans, which still makes me wonder what verdict the now imaginary jury might have brought in."

I ended by hoping that the book would find many readers, who might well be impressed by details I had not mentioned. I had in mind the evidence he had gathered from Allan Wardrop and the doubts he had aired about identification of footprints and of hairs found in the murdered child's hands. The tracks in the sand, he suggested, were the wrong size to have been made by Stuart's boots, and the hairs were the wrong colour to have come from his head. I had difficulties on each of these points which Dixon might well have dismissed as legalistic. The man who was said to have confirmed Wardrop's testimony, Horrie Baker, was dead. The scepticism about tracks and hairs depended on what people in Adelaide were said to have said to the two young women from the Melbourne *Herald* in 1972. The colour of the hairs, however, could be established if they were still in the keeping of Adelaide's Institute of Medical and Veterinary Science, where they had been lodged in 1959. (p. 84) Nobody, myself included, appears to have thought of asking whether they were still there.

The Wizard of Alice had been out for almost a year before the Adelaide *Advertiser* ran a piece on it. "KILLER OR VICTIM?" asked the headline introducing two pages by Mike McEwen at the front of the Saturday magazine section. This was the first time, over nearly forty years, that the *Advertiser* had used a question mark about Stuart's guilt. Across two pages, readers were given a history of the case, profiles of Dixon and Stuart and a respectful review. In at least three critical areas, McEwen concluded, Dixon had sown doubts about the verdict of courts and commission: the strands of hair, the confession and the timing of events on the day of the murder, especially between two and four in the afternoon. "His whole book", wrote the reporter, in a judgment contradicting all that the *Advertiser* had said at the time, "must be read as a serious indictment of the justice system as it was then, and in particular of the procedures used to convict Stuart and then to affirm his guilt." McEwen had talked with Dixon, and ended the piece with this statement by him: "From the point of view of any legal recourse, the case is defunct. I can only hope the Government might review the case and consider granting Stuart a pardon."

Dixon was heartened by the article. By contrast, Stewart Cockburn, now retired and living in Adelaide, was moved to write a letter for publication in his old paper repeating his longstanding conviction that Stuart had suffered no injustice.

Straight after his story appeared, McEwen flew to Alice Springs, hoping to meet Stuart there. He happened to be away in Katherine, but spoke to the reporter by telephone. "NEW EVIDENCE COULD CLEAR ME, SAYS STUART" was the next day's headline above McEwen's account of their conversation, accompanied by a recent photograph of Stuart in front of a waterhole near Alice Springs: cowboy hat, long white hair, moustache and beard, hands on hips, hem of checked shirt hanging out of jeans. Dixon had said that Stuart "always seems a bit embarrassed that people might know who he is and that he has been convicted." McEwen's interview confirmed that impression. "Inside me I still feel guilt", Stuart was reported as saying. "People still point at me and that's something I have to live with." "After 29 years of living with the stigma of being a convicted murderer and rapist", McEwen wrote, he was looking forward to a review of that verdict; "but I haven't got the money."

He was living on the dole, he told the reporter, and working part-time for the Central Land Council.

Four months later, in October 1987, having weathered the last three years of parole, Rupert Max Stuart became in the white man's law an unconditionally free man.

27

A NEW MAN?

On a visit to Darwin in 1989 I happened to meet a lawyer from Melbourne who was up to do some work in the Northern Territory for Aboriginal legal services. While taking a case in Alice Springs he had talked with Rupert Max Stuart, both in town and out in the bush. Stuart seemed to be off the grog, though he spoke of times when he had been on it, drinking rum by the bottle. The lawyer had heard that Stuart might be seeking a pardon, but wondered whether he would bother when he appeared to have such a secure place among his own people. Practitioners of white man's law were now alert as never before to what Aborigines themselves meant by "the law", a word defined by Jay Arthur in her book *Aboriginal English* (1996) as meaning the body of religious and cultural knowledge that informs and directs Aboriginal society. Rupert Max Stuart, this lawyer had found, was highly respected as an older man who knew the law—in Aboriginal English, a lawman. This sounded like a different person from the drinking, fighting, parole-breaching Stuart of the years between 1973 and 1984, the dates of his first and last release from Yatala. What had transformed him, I learned later, was working for the Central Land Council.

The first time the lawyer from Melbourne met Stuart was at the council's headquarters in Alice Springs, and the next time when he was out on the job as a field officer.

After his release in July 1984 Stuart had spent some time at Hermannsburg and some at Santa Teresa. In both places he was back on the grog. On the advice of the priest in charge at Santa Teresa, Stuart and his wife travelled north to Bathurst Island where the fathers of the Sacred Heart had another mission and where temptations were fewer. Some time in 1985 they returned to Santa Teresa, and from there he applied for an advertised part-time job with the Central Land Council. The appointment would be made by Pat Dodson, an Aboriginal man lately appointed to the new position of director. In 1975 Dodson had been ordained as a Catholic priest, having joined, like Tom Dixon, the order of the Sacred Heart. He had been born at Broome in 1947, spent childhood years in Darwin, and after the death of his parents in 1960 gone with his brother Mick to a boarding school in rural Victoria. He had left the priesthood in 1981 and come to the Central Land Council, where he was manager of training and information until appointed director. He had happy memories of Stuart. As a boy of nine or ten he had liked to hang around fun-fairs, and met

Stuart at one—possibly the Giesemans'—working the country between Alice Springs and Darwin. In Katherine, Stuart got the boy to mind the merry-go-round while he took a break. When the show reached Darwin, Stuart stayed briefly with the Dodson family. Over the years Pat Dodson read a lot of bad news about Rupert Max Stuart, but they never met between that time in Darwin and the day of his interview for the job. Dodson took him on. For the rest of his parole period he was a part-time field officer (also on unemployment benefit), then from 1978 full-time.

When Charles Perkins became the first chairman of the Central Land Council in 1975 it had only an informal authority, conferred by an Aboriginal Land Rights (Northern Territory) Bill which had not quite got to parliament when the governor-general dismissed Gough Whitlam. As enacted under the Fraser government next year the measure was diluted, but retained the provision for Central and Northern Land Councils as statutory bodies, which they became in 1977. Their principal purposes were to identify and consult traditional owners to administer land held by Aboriginal trusts, to settle disputes over land, to protect sacred sites and to negotiate with mining companies and commercial enterprises. The historian Tim Rowse could say that by 1985 the councils had secured an important voice for Aborigines in matters important to them. In that year the Central Land Council was party to the negotiations that returned the site of Ayers Rock to its traditional owners as Uluru, and was prominent in protests against the Hawke government's planned amendments to the *Aboriginal Land Rights Act*. (Kinsmen of Charles Perkins, now head of the Department of Aboriginal Affairs, were among delegates from the Territory who occupied his office demanding, and in the event getting, an audience with the prime minister.) By 1989 the Central Land Council was composed of some 80 councillors representing nearly 60 communities, had an annual budget of more than four million dollars, and had validated traditional owners' entitlements to about half the land in its region.

Field officers had a variety of tasks. Stuart was given charge of a council vehicle, on strict condition that he was sober when driving. He picked up delegates to council meetings and drove staffers out into the country. If a mining company wanted to put a road through certain territory, he might be assigned to talk with people who lived there, asking about sites affected by the proposed development and acting as interpreter for them in discussions with white council staffers and other outsiders. Thanks to the new knowledge he had acquired in Yatala the locals appreciated Stuart as one of their own who could understand the language of claims and rights. Thanks to the old knowledge he had carried into Yatala, retained and supplemented as he travelled the country, he gave his colleagues access to traditions which had to be accommodated in order to help resolve contention between white and black, and within Aboriginal communities, about the proper uses of land. One white lawyer who travelled with Stuart in the field was surprised by the range of his familiarity with old songs and stories as he listened and talked about the life-endowing totems across various desert landscapes: caterpillar, native cat, possum, kangaroo. "The colour … it's still in here", he had said to Noela Whitton about his paintings in 1972. "I've got my book in my head", he would say later to another interviewer. He could well have thanked Her Majesty's prison not only, as he once did in a letter to Tom Dixon, for giving him some education in English, but also for locking him away from a Westernising culture which might have eroded his memory of the law, as it did for so many age-mates and juniors. It might even be said that Yatala kept Rupert Max Stuart sober and alive as people like him became alcoholics and died young, sometimes violently.

During his decade in and out of parole Stuart himself risked such a fate. Only he can know how far his own inner resources and his wife Catherine prevented him from succumbing; but in the public world the Central Land Council was his lifeline. Pat Dodson contributed to Stuart's destiny no less significantly than that other Sacred Heart priest Tom Dixon.

The Central Land Council gave Stuart occupation, income, and respect. In 1994 he could say: "Even now I'm still a branded man, you know. If you're a branded man, you're branded for life." But he could also say, describing his job at the council: "When they find out whose are the royalties, I used to write the cheque! A crim! *The Land Council trusted me.*" He was talking, not writing; the italics are mine, to mark what seems to me the council's profound significance in the transformation of Rupert Max Stuart, convicted murderer, into the Max Stuart who was on his way to political and ceremonial eminence.

The new regard was embodied in the nickname "Yatala", used by Aborigines both around Alice and in the bush. Possibly the word was first employed as a term of intimate reproach by Catherine at the onset of a lapse into bad old ways. "Bloody Yatala!" he remembers her calling out. "You gotta go to church!" On other lips the name could convey indulgence, understanding, even endearment. We know where you've been, the users were saying, and we think no less of you for that. Perhaps even more, if we believe you didn't commit that murder, or if we admire you, whatever the facts, for surviving, for transcending, the agony imposed on you by white society. Some white colleagues believed that "Yatala" was a name to be spoken only behind its object's back; but when Max Stuart was asked in 1996 to approve a public account of his life he assured the author that he was proud of the nickname.

Max Stuart's reputation as a worker for the Central Land Council served him well when he stood for election to its governing body. So did his connections with Santa Teresa. In 1989 he became a delegate and executive member for the region which included the former mission, the community now known also as Ltyentye Apurte. Hermannsburg, meanwhile, had become Ntaria. From now on he was much involved in the council's affairs. In 1991 he was among council leaders who came out against the establishment of the Strehlow Research Centre, a museum set up in Alice Springs after long negotiation between Kathleen Strehlow and the Northern Territory government. This centre was to house most of Strehlow's collection of sacred objects, *tjuringa,* which the government had agreed to buy from his widow. The council, which Strehlow had urged the Arrernte to oppose, argued that the Territory should not be paying for *tjuringa* which belonged by right to its people, and that the collection should not be locked away in a museum. It was a long time—thirteen years—since Stuart had written from Yatala assuring the Strehlows of his support in their dispute with Wenten Rubuntja over the proper destiny of the collection. Now, as a senior Arrernte man, he agreed that it should all be returned to the donors. His deep sense of obligation to Ted Strehlow did not extend to Kathleen, and when he spoke at the centre's opening ceremony he implicitly blamed her for foisting on the Territory an institution which would prolong the wrongful possession of the *tjuringa.* "I don't think Strehlow would have liked this museum", he declared. "We need those things. We need them for ceremony and schooling our younger generation … All Aborigines need them things to be put in our sacred sites and not in a museum." Strehlow, as Stuart surely knew, had believed to the end that the present custodians of sacred sites could not be safely entrusted with the objects their elders had put into his keeping. Evidently he wanted to combine loyalty to "old Ted" with commitment to the council's position. He invoked the memory of his grandfather Tom Ljonga, dwelling on what Strehlow owed him. "My grandfather", he said, "taught him all about objects and ceremonies." And he affirmed the abiding importance in his own life of the traditional knowledge Tom Ljonga had taught him as a child. "When I feel lonely", he told the gathering, "I just start singing my songs that my Grandpa taught me and I'm happy …"

These were the words of a man who had authority to do for others what Tom Ljonga had done for him; and in the same year, 1991, Max Stuart initiated the most famous of all Arrernte, his relative Charles Perkins. No event in either of their lives reveals so eloquently the new complexities of Aboriginal culture as this ceremony at which the man from Yatala endows the man from Canberra with the strength of traditional manhood.

In 1984 the Hawke government had made Perkins head of the Department of Aboriginal Affairs, the highest office yet held by an Aborigine. After working harmoniously with one minister, Clyde Holding, he was dismissed late in 1988 by another, Gerry Hand. His career in the white world having ended in irrevocable disaster, Perkins was ready for a spiritual return to the world of his Arrernte ancestors. He had been elected in Alice to the new Aboriginal and Torres Strait Islander Commission as a commissioner for the Northern Territory. He was active, as was Max Stuart, in the Arrernte Council, a constituent of the Central Land Council. The man nicknamed "Yatala" used to call Perkins "Mr Parliament".

One evening in Alice, as Perkins told his biographer Peter Read, two senior Arrernte men approached him.

"'You've got a big mouth, eh? You're talking about Aboriginal rights all over the place, Aboriginal this and Aboriginal that?'

'Yeah, that's right, I'm doing my best …'

'Well, what do you know about Aboriginal [law]?'

'Oh, well, I know a little bit.'

'You know nothing. You're a little boy… . We'll tell you about Aboriginal law.'"

One of these men was Max Stuart.

Perkins accepted the offer. Stuart and the other man took him out into the bush somewhere between Alice and Hermannsburg for more than a week of instruction about the law.

Some Arrernte purists thought that this procedure fell short of a proper initiation; others allowed that given his age and ill-health—only one kidney worked, and that weakly—it was enough. In the words of his comrade Gordon Briscoe, Charles Perkins had been made human in the Arrernte way. "He was allowed to speak of neither the ritual of 'the rules' nor the physical pain", Peter Read reports, "but he hinted at a profound emotional and intellectual fulfilment. Clearly, he had confronted one of the great mysteries of his life." He had also committed himself to intricate relationships and responsibilities, as he helped people of the centre play by the rules of white authority and bureaucracy while doing his best to observe the old culture's rules about who could be approached, through which intermediaries, for what purposes and when. "After his initiation", his son Adam recalled, "Father was no longer his own man in Alice Springs." The oppression of his new Arrernte status combined with his need for European medical science to make Perkins and his wife take off again for Sydney. He died there in 2000, but his body was returned to Alice. Towards the end he spoke with a grandson about secret Arrernte ceremonies that were to follow the departure of his spirit.

It was also in 1991 that Max Stuart and Tom Dixon met for the last time. Mike Parer, publisher and friend, had given him a journey to the centre by way of celebrating the golden jubilee of his ordination. Dixon and Parer visited Uluru, Alice Springs and Santa Teresa in May 1991. Close to the Rock the old builder of stone houses at Santa Teresa chuckled at occupying a suite in the Sheraton Hotel. In Alice he and Parer bunked and fed themselves at the visitors' quarters of his old missionary order; and they spent three days and nights out at the mission. "How the place had changed even from my last visit in 1976", he wrote to me. "Much better housing was evident with TV, Refrigerators, Radiators on wall (for winter), water laid on, showers etc. and cooking appliances." A council now ran the place with the help of white officers. "But something was missing. They had separated from each other according to local groups. Very few went to Mass. In fact, an elder who had been a work-boy with me in the '50s … complained about the absence of a priest and the teaching of no catechism in the school." He would have found similar secularisation and separation over at Hermannsburg.

Max and Catherine Stuart and their children were living not at Santa Teresa but in Alice Springs, where he and Dixon spotted each other in Woolworths. Stuart was accompanied by a colleague from the Central Land Council whom he introduced to Dixon as "my lawyer". Max was "cheerful and confident", Dixon told me, "and drank only for reasons of thirst". Stuart found his old friend "all right talking, but not strong." Tom Dixon was 75.

His eyesight was too bad for driving, he told me after the journey, and a chest infection had "nearly toppled" him; but the hand in which he wrote of these afflictions was as firm as ever.

In mid-1988 it had appeared likely that Dixon's book would become the basis for a television mini-series. The writer, Sylvia Johnson, invited him to collaborate on a project whose title, "White Man's Crime", signalled Stuart's innocence. Early in 1989 she submitted a treatment to the Australian Film Commission saying that the series would tell "the story of Tom Dixon and his fight to save the life of a young Aboriginal, Maxie Stuart, wrongly convicted of the rape and murder of a nine-year-old girl in the racist, conservative South Australia of 1959". The AFC's assessors were enthusiastic, and so was the Australian Broadcasting Corporation's head of television drama, Sandra Levy; but when she left the ABC other hands filed the proposal for three years and finally abandoned it. Dixon was sorry, though he had thought that the script dwelt too much on his relationship with Stuart and too little on the question of innocence or guilt.

Late in 1991 Dixon gave his blessing to another plan for turning the story into television drama. Rachel Perkins, the youngest and in Peter Read's view the most self-consciously Aboriginal of Charles Perkins's children, had embarked on a career as producer and director of films after serving an apprenticeship at Impartja, the indigenous television station in Alice Springs. She and Max Stuart had known each other since 1975, when she was a schoolgirl and he was on his first parole. Rachel Perkins now suggested to Ned Lander, who had made strong films on Aboriginal subjects, among them *Dirt Cheap* and *The Wrong Side of the Road*, that they produce together a series of documentaries on the Aboriginal experience of Australian history. Perkins and Lander secured investors for the project, including the ABC and the Special Broadcasting Service, where her father had become a member of the board. "I volunteered to allow them access to the 'Wizard' with no cost", Dixon wrote to me early in 1992. "They then went to Alice Springs and interviewed Maxie on tape, getting most of what they wanted the fourth time. Apparently his memory is not good about the early days of the case." Perkins and Lander said they would get back to Dixon later in the year

The prospect of this film softened Dixon's disappointment that *The Wizard* had attracted so little notice. In his last letter to me, written on 27 February 1992, Tom lamented the silence of certain people to whom he had sent copies. "I find it hard to realise", he wrote, "that the book is that much of a failure." He worried about Nan Rivett's judgment that he had not given enough credit to Rohan. He had replied acknowledging her late husband's crucial part. "Without my affidavits there would have been no Royal Commission, & without Rohan's money I wouldn't have gone to N.Q. etc.etc." Rohan, he wrote to me now, "never confided much to me along the way and I never probed him." Tom looked back along that way with both pride and sorrow. "There is always a certain sadness left behind all our endeavours in the case, the sadness of Vergil's 'Lachrimae Rerum', I feel, & that makes the whole business so poignant & unresolved."

Perkins and Lander made their film, but not in time for Tom Dixon to see it. His heart was beginning to fail when he wrote that letter, and he died in August 1992. Joan Dixon sent me a copy of the eulogy at his funeral by a priest who spoke of the connection between the Dixons' love of birds and their attraction to creation theology as "a window through which to view the integration of environmental concerns and a rejoicing in the father who has made us and this beautiful world in which we live." He spoke also of *The Wizard*—"Few who read the book and know its author will fail to be moved"—and of Dixon's sorrow that those readers were so few. "In another time and another climate of thought", the eulogist concluded, "he might have been a hero. He had those qualities. Truly, a remarkable, and remarkably lovable man."

Joan Dixon sent me also a little card showing Jesus at prayer and inscribed to record Tom's religious and secular commitments:

In loving memory of
Father Thomas Dixon, B.A.
Priest, Missionary and Crusader for Justice.
He Sang the Praises of God And All Creation.
Born Into Eternal Life
2ND August, 1992.
Aged 76 years.
MAY HE REST IN PEACE.

Rachel Perkins and Ned Lander inscribed their film "To the memory of Tom Dixon". Lander had asked me in April 1992 if I would let them use *The Stuart Case* and also if I would appear in the film. "We have approached Tom Dixon and Max Stuart", Lander wrote, "and they have agreed to participate." I said yes to the first request and no to the second, having "decided long ago", I wrote, "that television is a medium for me to watch, not to be in." The title for the whole series was *Blood Brothers.* One film would be devoted to Rachel Perkins's father. The film on Stuart, Lander told me, would look at "various aspects of the case, in particular questions relating to language, literacy and the law." The makers called it *Broken English.*

Apart from a little newsreel footage, the events of 1959 were re-created by actors. Sir John Starke, now aged 80, and Don Dunstan, 67, gave recollections and opinions. Max Stuart, aged 60, appeared at the beginning and the end, and his voice was heard from time to time during re-enacted scenes, alternating with the actor Bill Hunter, who spoke a narrative written by Lander. (In an early draft, I heard, the narrator was to be me, played by Barry Otto.) An Aboriginal actor, Lawrence Turner, played the young Max Stuart—convincingly, I thought, though he was so gentle and passive that it was hard to imagine him hurting a fly, let alone breaking his hand in a fight.

People who saw *Broken English* on either SBS in 1993 or the ABC in 1994 told me that it convinced them utterly of Stuart's innocence. I find on the internet this summary of the case from a paper about the film delivered at Los Angeles in 1996: "Rupert Max Stuart, an Arrernte man, now a respected elder … was falsely accused of the rape and murder of a white Australian girl …" As an essay in what was now called docu-drama *Broken English* seemed to me skilful, but vulnerable to the criticism of that genre for blurring the line between fact and fiction. Here the blurring was done less by departures from history, which were few, but by omission of nearly all evidence which could have made a viewer doubt. Television is rarely a medium for complexity, and an account of the Stuart case in one hour, by makers sympathetic to his cause, was bound to leave out a lot. The film's one revelation was the testimony by Sir John Starke, deep in retirement from any position which would have required him to curb his famously powerful tongue, saying to the camera what he had written to Dixon after reading *The Wizard.* He had said it also into a microphone in 1991, telling Jon Faine on ABC radio that he believed Stuart probably innocent and had no doubt that the confession was bashed out of him. The film audience was treated to both the booming voice and the glaring eyes, which together had withered many a victim in court. Starke derided the commissioners' rejection of Allan Wardrop's evidence (pp. 305–6) and their acceptance as genuine of the story signed by Stuart in Ceduna that while very drunk he had carefully taken off his clothes so that they would not be stained by blood, then walked naked across the beach to wash in the sea.

Broken English showed the Max Stuart of 1992 at the wheel of a Toyota four-wheel drive, white-bearded and cowboy-hatted, driving through the red earth of his country, telling his life story, comparing his plight in the face of the law with the professional advice now accessible to Aborigines, affirming his innocence. Tom Dixon would have been pleased to see that the makers judged it necessary to use sub-titles for his English. At the very end Stuart muses, in the global idiom of his second culture, naming the singer who had been all the rage when he went into Yatala: "Yeah, some people think that I'm guilty and some people think I'm not. Some people think Elvis is still alive, but most of us think he's dead and gone."

Though Max Stuart was not writing the book he had imagined in correspondence with Tom Dixon, he was letting other people put him into history. In 1994, the year the ABC showed *Broken English,* he contributed to a series called "Talking History" in *Land Rights News,* a publication of the Central and Northern Land Councils. With the help of an invisible interviewer he crafted a self-portrait appropriate for a man of importance in that body. From his earliest years on the government settlement at Jay Creek he recalled both dependence on the white occupiers and an idyllic pursuit of traditional nourishment. "People in our day would just get tea and sugar, a little bit of flour, a stick of tobacco from the Government … But mostly I think we lived off our land. We were getting the bush tucker: kangaroos, wallabies, whatever, goannas"; also wild figs, wild oranges, wild onions, yams, witchetty grubs. He learned to use weapons old and new: by the age of seven he could make spears and boomerangs, and he and his brother shot dingoes, for food as in the old times and for white men's money: seven shillings and sixpence for a scalp. Moving around the centre with his father who drove a donkey wagon carrying mail, he mounted a big white horse, the first of many he would ride as a drover and a stockman. In 1944 he went into the army: "I was big for twelve. I told them I was eighteen." (The military authorities recruited able-bodied young males to do labouring jobs, unloading trains and trucks, repairing roads, so releasing real soldiers for more warlike activities. Uniformed and paid by the army, they had reason to believe they were in it. As in New Guinea, the war had made some of the natives unexpectedly useful.)

After the war he went droving. His longest journey took him from Elsey Station up on the Roper river (cherished in white Australian memory as the home of Mrs Aeneas Gunn's *We of the Never Never)* down to South Australia for the first time in his life, alongside "a drunken old drover" named Dick Scobie. "Every man had to be like him: drink what he drink and ride rough horse what he'd ride, do the same as him." He worked as a stockman on several stations. "Then I went down South Australia, got 25 years in Yatala Labour Prison." Any reader new to the story of Stuart's life was left wondering what that could have been for.

His wife Catherine—"a good wife"—had died four or five years ago. Before she died he had taken her out west to land which he hoped to live on, "and told her he was going to fight for it." An editorial note explained that Max Stuart "is a senior claimant in the still unresolved Lake Amadeus Land Claim. He plans to return to live on his traditional country at Wiputa, near Watarrka (King's Canyon) National Park, when the claim is resolved." Back there, he said, he would put up a sign: "No drinking". "If my friends are coming to visit me, no grog aboard ... because if they drink one can while they're at my place, that's going to ruin my place and my life. I want that for myself and for my children."

While doing research on other people's country for the Central Land Council, Max Stuart was asserting his own claim to land in the region known as Lake Amadeus, some 250 kilometres south-west of Alice and to the north of Uluru. The *Land Rights (Northern Territory) Act* of 1976 had opened a can of witchetty grubs, as two governments, white pastoral and commercial interests and Aboriginal occupants engaged in labyrinthine contests over entitlement to land. Stuart had grounds for claim running back through his father's line. He and his nephew Helmut Pareroultja were both among parties to a dispute over the Lake Amadeus land heard in 1987 by Mr Justice (Michael) Maurice as Aboriginal land commissioner. Maurice's judgment, favourable to Stuart and rather less so to Pareroultja, contains passages showing that he had been enthralled to hear the stories spun by claimants to prove their territorial attachments. Helmut Pareroultja was "a remarkable man", and the commissioner cites his invocation of various dreamings—kangaroo, euro, fairy owl, possum, native cat—with the relish of someone who has read a gripping novel. At the end of a discursive paragraph on the Stuart case and its aftermath Justice Maurice writes: "There is, perhaps, a touch of irony in noting that one result of this inquiry has been to recognise Rupert as probably the most senior traditional Aboriginal owner for Kings Canyon."

That appeared to settle the matter of Stuart's and other people's entitlements, until the Northern Territory government asked the Federal Court in 1989 to block the granting of Lake Amadeus land to traditional owners. When the Federal Court decided not to intervene, the government in Darwin made a fresh move, persuading four Aboriginal women, at least one of whom was a close relative of Stuart's, to ask the Federal Court to prevent the granting on other grounds. By 1994 the Lake Amadeus claim had reached the High Court. When Stuart's "Talking History" piece appeared in *Land Rights News* he was not long back from a hearing at the High Court in Canberra, where he had accompanied a lawyer from the Central Land Council, David Avery. Both men enjoyed thinking back to 1959, when the name of Rupert Max Stuart had been attached to a petition heard by this court. (Avery: "You've been here before?" Stuart: "Yeah, but they wouldn't let me in last time.")

Marion Frith, a reporter for the *Canberra Times*, visited the flat in Kingston where Stuart was staying and talked with a cold and homesick man. Apart from *Broken English*, which had so far been shown only on SBS, I think this was the first appearance in the media of the two Stuarts, the convicted murderer and the participant in contests over land rights. Frith gave readers a clear account of the Stuart case but could not get the subject to discuss it. "That was all in the past", he said. "Anyway, I'm pretty right with the white people. I'm not one for this black bastard and white bastard stuff." The paper used that remark in the caption to a photograph of a man looking all of his 62 years, dressed for Canberra's autumn but still wearing his cowboy hat.

He was discomfited that the present case pitted black against black. A dirty business, he called it. "We should all be at the one table, sharing our food and that." He could hardly wait to be back to his patch of ground down the creek from King's Canyon. "I like to live like my own grandfather", he told the reporter. "Then you were born with nothing and you went out with nothing on. Better than all this garbage we got here now." His life today was good, and he hoped to keep it that way for himself and his kids, aged ten and nine, by following that grandfather's ways. "If they grow up in town they be listening to the other kids, watching TV, all that Kung Fu stuff." In his romantic post-assimilationist vision the traditions of his people would protect the children from the temptations which had ensnared their father. "I like to see my kids learn … from the land, not inside the school-room. That's the way."

Though Max Stuart remained a winner in the matter of Lake Amadeus, conflict continued over the land between black and black. During one argument, on the football ground at Hermannsburg, Helmut Pareroultja was run down and killed by a motor car. Perhaps to get away from such troubles, Stuart now gave less attention to the arguments over land rights out west and more to claims rights there, and more to the claims for establishing native title in and around Alice Springs, his mother's country.

The High Court's momentous ruling of 1992 in the Mabo case, which put an end to the doctrine of *terra nullius*, followed by the Keating government's *Native Title Act* of 1993, had provoked a spate of litigation over whether and where "native title" had been extinguished and where it was still valid. At Alice Springs Max Stuart would be a vigorous participant in deliberations on the question.

Stuart authorised another public account of his life in 1996, when a selection of art created by children at Hermannsburg and Ernabella missions, assembled by Lucienne Fontannaz, was exhibited in Adelaide's State Library. Among the works were some of the crayon drawings the ten-year-old Max had done for Charles Mountford at Jay Creek. Jenny Tonkin of the State Library composed for the display an accompanying biography of Stuart, which she sent to him for approval and which was used again, revised, for an exhibition of photographs of indigenous people. "While in prison he learned to read and write English", visitors to the library were informed, "and he can now argue with white fellas on their terms as well as his … He has fought long and hard for the return of sacred objects to Central Australia, and is currently Chairman of the Central Land Council".

Max Stuart had been elected to that office in March 1998 after a spell as deputy. The position was always keenly contested, giving the holder prominence, prestige and a salary of $70,000 a year. "I am proud to be Chairman", declared Stuart in his first annual report, for 1998–9. The high moment of that year, as he wrote, was a meeting of all eighty delegates at Kalkaringi, in the north-west of the region. "We talked about recognition of our laws", he wrote (his words tidied up by the council's media office) "our rights to our land, protection of our sacred sites, a fair say in government, and a fair go in education and other government services out bush. We talked about it before we went and at Kalkaringi we put out a statement to the government and everyone saying this is what we believe."

As well as these generalities the meeting had considered the campaign by the Northern Territory's Country—Liberal Party government for the elevation of the Territory to statehood. With individual members of that party Stuart enjoyed a relationship of wary cordiality; but the statement endorsed under his chairmanship at Kalkaringi was severe in its judgment of the party's performance in office. "A lot of people", declared the chairman, "were thinking this government has been in power for twenty years and what have we got here. Not much … because the government opposed just about everything we were fighting for. And statehood would give that same government more power and then we would be even worse off." Among his own activities he mentioned visits to museums in Adelaide, Melbourne and Sydney for negotiations over the return of sacred objects. "Some of those sacred objects were given to people", he wrote, "some of them were stolen. We need them back home so that we can put the young ones through our kindergarten and the older they get, they will learn more in the culture."

On the custody of sacred objects, Stuart in office took a more lenient view of the Strehlow Research Centre than he had expressed at its opening in 1991, saying that at least those treasures were safe in a museum. The *tjuringa* still in the possession of Strehlow's widow and son were another matter. In October 1999, when Carl Strehlow put up for sale in Adelaide a set of materials described in the catalogue as "the Aboriginal crown jewels", Stuart's intervention by telephone from Alice Springs helped to abort the auction.

The main item in the chairman's second report, for 1999–2000, was that "after a lot of hard work by the Central Land Council and the Arrernte people, the Federal Court recognised the Arrernte as the native title holders of Alice Springs." He enlarged on this achievement with a retrospective bitterness now common in the rhetoric of the region's Aboriginal leaders. "It took a long time for us to get that justice and recognition. For the first 60 years of this century we weren't even treated like humans, and I remember it well. Under the Aboriginals Ordinance we were restricted to making daytime visits to Alice Springs, a town that is on our Arrernte country and where our sacred sites are located. We even needed a permit to visit our own people in town … We had to stand by and watch as our people got sicker and poorer and had their families and sacred sites taken from them, while the people who came from all over to Alice Springs got rich and built big houses on our country." These days Max Stuart was sounding like Charles Perkins.

The chairman's report connected the Federal Court's decision with a royal visit for which he had been host. "The Queen came to Alice Springs and met us Arrernte, and I think it was the first time ever that the Arrernte have been acknowledged by the Crown as the first mob and the traditional owners of Alice Springs … It seems the Queen has less trouble acknowledging native title holders than the Northern Territory Government."

Max Stuart could be adroit at giving political significance to the ceremonial events which the job of chairman required him to attend. He had gone to Sydney to be in the great walk for reconciliation in May 2000. "It was a good day", he reported, "and I was pleased that so many people did it, even though the Prime Minister couldn't find the time." He had accompanied Sir William Deane when the governor-general handed back Tempe Downs and Mount Wedge to the traditional owners, happy at the victory but also "sad that these are some of the last bits of country to be returned under the *Land Rights Act* and there are still so many people who will never get their land back."

A ritual occasion could also be an opportunity for affirming amity among his own people. Welcoming the Queen on 30 March 2000, the chairman presented her with a painting which the media handout described as the work of "a senior clan custodian". "I told her", Max Stuart said later, "I got a gift for her to take back to the palace." As insiders knew, the artist was Wenten Rubuntja. The Northern Territory government had invited him to paint for the Queen a picture entitled Yeperenye Dreaming. Other Arrernte recognised him as custodian of this story, which represented the creation of Alice Springs by the giant caterpillar that was its totem. The gallery through whom the work was commissioned hailed it as "recognition of a great artist and statesman."

Wenten Rubuntja, too, had come a long way since Stuart disparaged him to Tom Dixon and Ted Strehlow in the 1970s. His term as chairman of the Central Land Council from 1976 to 1980 was followed by another, from 1985 to 1988. He was active in many Aboriginal organisations, and became a kind of artist laureate: the delegates from all over Australia who met Paul Keating in 1993 to discuss the implications of the High Court's decision on Mabo presented the prime minister with both a plan and a Rubuntja. Now approaching eighty, he was a less vigorous participant than Max Stuart in their people's affairs; but these two Arrernte seniors were now on terms of mutual respect. It was fitting for one of these white-bearded old men to give the Queen a painting by the other.

Rubuntja's style now derived less from Namatjira than in earlier days, influenced by the dot paintings of the people out west at Papunya; but it was Namatjira, the Arrernte painter, who had inspired all the artists of the centre, from the amateur Max Stuart to the esteemed Wenten Rubuntja. "How you going, Max?" the Queen asked him in a version of their meeting he liked to tell later. "Are you part of the Namatijira family?" Yes, he replied, and recalled for her the sight of Albert sitting in a creek bed, painting and drinking. Then he told her that he was organising a corroboree for herself and the Duke. This was one of the proudest days of his life, he would say: an old crim welcoming the Queen to his country.

Some weeks later he halted the Olympic torch on the first leg, from Uluru, of its journey around the continent. At Heavitree Gap, gateway to Alice Springs, a nicely scripted ritual encounter was enacted. "Who are you and what is your business on Arrernte land?" the chairman of the Central Land Council asked a twelve-year-old white boy named Brendan who was carrying the flame. He was speaking in Arrernte, and a translation was supplied to the lad and the media. Brendan remained silent, for "this was men's business", reported Debra Jobson for the *Sydney Morning Herald,* in a place sacred to men, and Brendan was too young to answer. "We seek permission to proceed across sacred lands", said the white adult male in charge of the torch relay. "A hundred Aboriginal schoolgirls gathered on the Ghan railway tracks cheered wildly", Jobson wrote, and told readers that this moment was highly significant to the Arrernte, who had recently won a native title claim proving that they were the traditional owners of the town site in Alice. "Mr Stuart … said it would tell others in the world that asking permission of traditional owners was like getting a passport into another country." The campaign for native title could not have got better publicity. This being an occasion for harmony, the chairman did not tell the world about the days when the Arrernte and all other Aborigines needed a permit to enter the town.

Did anybody tell the Queen that her host at Alice Springs had spent much of his life in one of Her Majesty's prisons, and that he might well have died forty years ago had it not been for the judicial committee of her

Privy Council? Who among the millions who saw their meeting on television or read about it in the papers knew that Max Stuart was Rupert Max Stuart? No media report I saw of the event made the connection. Nor did any account I read of his intercepting the Olympic torch, or receiving Sir William Deane, or participating in any other newsworthy event during his time as chairman.

I wonder why not. When I asked a senior official of the Central Land Council, he said that in his experience journalists were pretty ignorant, even those designated as Aboriginal Affairs correspondents. I remembered from Papua New Guinea the media pack that used to travel with prime ministers and other Australian dignitaries on visits, flying up with them and out with them, touching down only to report what they and their hosts said and did, not pausing to take in any local knowledge. But wouldn't journalists working for the papers in Alice Springs and Darwin know who this man was, or had been? No, said the man at the council; they're just as ignorant. Moreover, as he observed, most of the reporters covering such events had not been alive in 1959.

The council itself gave journalists no help. Back in 1994 its *Land Rights News* had at least mentioned his years in Yatala, though without saying why he was there; but the biographical note in each annual report during his time as chairman jumped straight from the young drover to the council field officer. Conversely, accounts of the Stuart case may omit his life after Yatala, and not always out of ignorance. The author of the entry on that subject in the recent *Wakefield Companion to South Australian History* left out the Max Stuart of the Land Council because she did not want to intrude on his privacy. Among people who remembered the case, moreover, many assumed that Rupert Max Stuart had died—as in collective memory he had. To be sure, the film *Broken English* in 1993 had shown him in old age; and so had the *Canberra Times* in its 1994 story about his visit to the High Court, and later the Adelaide State Library in its exhibition centred on Aboriginal child art. But these were mere glimpses, by small audiences, leaving general ignorance intact.

Even the anthropologist Ruth Latukefu, who had once (as Ruth Fink) studied Aborigines, did not know, when she wrote to the *Australian* in October 2000 giving cordial support to a letter from Max Stuart on behalf of the Central Land Council, that the writer was also Rupert Max. The letter, drafted to his instructions in the council's media office, was sent in vigorous response to a remark by a former governor-general. "Mr Hayden", said the writer, "... reckons that there is plenty of 'goodwill' towards Aboriginal people in Australia but we should just stop whingeing and shut up otherwise there won't be." A lot of people, he went on, wanted to make Aboriginal history disappear. "I am 70 now and this is our history. We weren't treated like humans in the twenties, thirties, forties and fifties." Recalling his own constrained life in and around Alice Springs, he catalogued restrictive and punitive laws under which, he said, half his family were kidnapped. He concluded, "in 1976 we got the *Land Rights Act*, which gave us some of our land back but now the Government is talking in Canberra to make it weaker. They put a bullet in the *Native Title Act*, then another bullet in our heritage protection laws and now our history is getting one too." If John Howard read Max Stuart's letter he may have seen it as another deplorable essay in "black armband" history. To the historically-minded anthropologist it all rang true, as Ruth Latukefu said in her own letter of support. When I asked if she realised who this Max Stuart was, she replied that although she had known about the case of Rupert Max Stuart it had never occurred to her that this was the same person. Her mind, like many others, had simply rejected the possibility. "Is he still alive?" asks one of the journalists who had interviewed him at Yatala thirty years ago.

Rupert Max Stuart went similarly unrecognised by people who watched on television an event which gave him even more cause for pride than his welcome to the Queen. That he had done *ex officio*, as chairman of the council. But his prominence in the Yeperenye Federation Festival was a tribute to his own status as lawman. The festival was held on Saturday 8 and Sunday 9 September 2001 at Blatherskite Park, on the edge of Alice Springs, generally known as the showground. The National Council for the Centenary of Federation, appointed by the Commonwealth government to create and co-ordinate a year of celebratory activities, had commissioned a series of National Centrepiece Events, and the Yeperenye Festival was to be the most imaginative and ambitious of these.

The National Council delegated the project to the Central Australian Aboriginal Media Association, a wholly Aboriginal body formed in 1980 to sponsor enterprises in broadcasting and media production. As one of two artistic directors for the festival, CAAMA chose Rachel Perkins, who since *Broken English* had formed her own production company, Blackfella Films, and in 1998 made her first generally released feature, *Radiance,* a searing story with a script by Louis Nowra. On her initiative, emissaries from CAAMA got in touch with all the peoples of the region through the Central Land Council and engaged its chairman, Max Stuart, as "cultural liaison officer", to travel around with them.

The project was huge. The opening spectacle was planned to be a match for the opening ceremony of the Sydney Olympics, in a place to which tons of gear had to be brought from all around Australia by road, train and air, including a gigantic screen, twelve metres by eight, weighing six and a half tonnes. Homebush had its own water and toilets, but at Blatherskite Park they had to be provided for an estimated 20,000 people. "The Arrernte story of the ancestral Yeperenye caterpillar", said a media release, was to be the backbone of the spectacle. "The theatrical spaces will reflect the metamorphosis from caterpillar to butterfly." As experts on the Yeperenye dreaming the makers consulted Max Stuart and Wenten Rubuntja, whose representation of it may now have been hanging in Buckingham Palace.

The festival was to be both a national event and a local event of complex significance. Max Stuart saw it as an occasion for bonding groups of people separated by history. In the old days, he was quoted as saying, "there was no East Arrernte, West Arrernte, North Arrernte, we all sat in a circle. I want to bring that back, bring it to life." He saw two other purposes in the festival: it would be a demonstration of Arrernte identity to the world, and a display of reconciliation between black and white Australia. "I met the Queen, I walked over the bridge, they were good things but this will be better. Our country was taken away from us, but in the festival, let's forget about that, let's be happy and welcome people from all over the world."

For CAAMA staffers, who were assembling the large local cast, the festival would be not only a display of tradition but an episode in the struggle for land rights, showing the world not only that Arrernte culture, language and dancing were well and truly alive, but that the performers were still fighting for the land of their caterpillar story—land "locked up", said one CAAMA officer, "by pastoral lease, the crown, the town of Alice Springs itself." Another person from CAAMA had a word about peoples of the centre who looked on the Arrernte as town drifters cut off from their past. "If we want to go to Warlpiri country or Pitjantjatjara country, we've got to have a permit. But they can come here and play up and do things we wouldn't dream of doing in their country." He wanted those other groups to know that the Arrernte "have still got law here."

Max Stuart, a senior Arrernte lawman, was commentator on the dancing by young Arrernte men that opened the festival on Saturday afternoon, and they danced to his recorded voice, singing the songs in which the caterpillar story is embedded. They were richly painted all over and they wore cone-shaped head-dresses. A century earlier, similarly outfitted men had danced in front of Professor Baldwin Spencer's cinematograph for the research project which made the Arunta for a time the most famous "savages" in the world, his notion of their "dreamtime" profoundly affecting anthropological and lay understandings of the sacred in traditional societies. Now, possibly for the first time since Baldwin Spencer screened them in lectures, those dances were being performed again for a wider world. In 1902 the dancers had sung as they danced, and Baldwin Spencer recorded them on a phonograph. The performers in 2001 could not sing the songs as their ancestors had done. They needed the voice of Max Stuart. Nor could they do the dances without coaching, and he provided that. "Max knew the dances", Rachel Perkins tells me, "and had to teach the other young men as no one had danced the Yeperenye dreaming for at least fifty years."

Other groups sang and danced their own dreamings. A group from Victoria with access to no traditional paint or dress or songs were applauded for coming to affirm their common identity with brothers and sisters who had retained traditional culture. So did a group from Flinders Island no darker than the two largest guests, Malcolm Fraser and Gough Whitlam, who had achieved a reconciliation of their own. Whitlam was given a part in the show, re-enacting with the son of Vincent Lingiari a ceremony which had now entered history, the handing back of the Gurindji people's land in 1975.

At sunset on Saturday Max Stuart's voice accompanied an animation of the Yeperenye story as a huge and illuminated caterpillar whose legs were those of 2,500 children inside it crawled across the landscape. On Sunday afternoon Max Stuart sat on the stage introducing the event's performers, and he himself, tapping two boomerangs, sang song after song of his own country. At the closing ceremony he announced that it was dedicated to the memory of Charles Perkins. "He also told me", Rachel Perkins recalls, "that he and others saw a fire light type of thing appear out of nowhere at the Arrernte men's camp at the festival grounds, and Max told me that it was my father's spirit."

"Max's role", a Land Council staffer said to me later, "developed into something more than may have been intended originally. He performed it brilliantly". When it was all over he was exultant. "The spirit is still dancing", he said. He was proud that his own memory gave him access to so much Arrernte history. "Even though I spent twenty years in South Australia I never forgot it." An attentive watcher of the event on television could have spotted among the credits, "Men's cultural director: Max Stuart", but apart from that he was never identified in the broadcast even as Max, let alone as Rupert Max.

By the time the festival came off he was no longer in the chair, having been defeated at an election in July 2001 by a brother-in-law, Kunmanara Breaden, who now became chairman for the third time. He had lost narrowly, and was disappointed. He had been a popular chairman, working comfortably with his Aboriginal director David Ross, affable with staff, skilful at running meetings, a colourful speaker when representing the council in public, charming in conversation, amiably dignified in welcoming celebrities. He had vigorously pursued the council's policies. After the defeat, he remained active in council affairs, and enjoyed general regard as a sort of chairman emeritus. When the electors of the Territory voted Labor into office the council invited him to its first meeting with the new minister responsible for Aboriginal affairs.

In that same year the ABC's *7.30 Report* identified him as former chairman in a story about the prime minister having to face demonstrators when he came to turn the first sod for a railway line from Alice Springs to Darwin. "ARRERNTE STAND STRONG, TREATY NOW, SHAME HOWARD SHAME", proclaimed the posters and T-shirts. The ABC's reporter found Stuart's attitude equivocal, at first urging the demonstrators on, then shaking hands with John Howard and saying to camera only: "I don't know nothing about the protests." "The weight of the occasion was enough, apparently", the reporter thought, "to have turned his head." Not a bad bloke, Stuart said later of the prime minister. "Told him I voted Labor".

As usual in the media, this report did not connect the elder statesman of the Land Council with the young man convicted of murder. Soon, however, the medium of film would reveal their identity to a wider audience than ever before. *Black and White,* a feature film based on the Stuart case, would be released late in 2002 in Australia and in 2003 internationally. The film's producer and director, Helen Leake and Craig Lahiff, had both grown up in Adelaide faintly aware that the case had affected the climate of their city. "The story itself", Helen Leake told me, "is not about Max's guilt or innocence, that's a matter of public record, rather is more a 'big picture' look at how the case divided Adelaide and, indeed, wider society." Louis Nowra, who wrote the screenplay, told me that the film would present two versions of what happened, the prosecutor Roderic Chamberlain's and the defender David O'Sullivan's. "The audience will have to make up its own mind." The actors in those two roles had been chosen with an eye on the world market which the film's international backers hoped to reach. Robert Carlyle of *The Full Monty* and *Trainspotting* was O'Sullivan, Charles Dance of *Gosford Park* and *Dark Blue World* was Chamberlain. Max Stuart was played by David Ngoombujarra, who had appeared in *Crocodile Dundee* and *Rabbit-Proof Fence*. "As a young Aboriginal growing up in a white man's world", advance publicity had him saying, "I saw much injustice being done to my people and had many bad experiences myself … So of course I sympathise with Max Stuart; he was forced into a confession he clearly couldn't have made by himself."

Nowra's script includes two of Stuart's actual interrogators at Ceduna, Detective-Sergeant Paul Turner (Roy Billing) and Constable Richard Jones (Gary Waddell). Nowra served history as well as briefing himself on character and incident by interviewing Turner when he was dying of emphysema and not caring how he was to be portrayed. Turner told Nowra that he and his colleagues had laughed the confession out of Stuart. "Jesus, Max", they had said, "we've all got pissed and done dumb things." When Nowra asked what happened next, Turner replied, "The laughter stopped." "It was said in a rather chilling fashion", Nowra recalls, "and then I asked if they gave him a whack or two. 'Yeah, after the laughter stopped', he wheezed." Sir Mellis Napier and Justices Abbott, Mayo and Reed would have been surprised by that testimony. Tom Dixon, Allan Wardrop and Max Stuart would not. The judges would have said, as they did of Wardrop's evidence, that on this account Stuart had already confessed when the policemen bashed him. It's a moot point whether a jury hearing what Turner told Nowra would have voted to convict.

The real Max Stuart would make an appearance at the end. The makers had been up to talk with him, and he approved their project about his young self. Later they decided to use his old self, as captured by Rachel Perkins and Ned Lander in *Broken English*. This film, like that one, would end with the subject at the wheel on the road from Alice, and a hugely enlarged audience would see and hear him say: "Yeah, some people think that I'm guilty and some people think I'm not. Some people think Elvis is still alive, but most of us think he's dead and gone."

At time of writing, I haven't seen the film. Knowing that it leaves out the large character of Jack Shand, reading publicity that enlarges Rupert Murdoch's role, seeing Robert Carlyle assert that David O'Sullivan was an Irish immigrant active in the Labor Party when he was actually born in South Australia and ran for the Senate on behalf of the breakaway anti-communist Democratic Labor Party, anticipating Charles Dance's English accent speaking for the robustly Australian Chamberlain, wondering what lines have been given to two imaginary characters Detective Sergeant Karskens and Mrs Aston, I expect to watch *Black and White* as a very old survivor from early Tudor England might have sat through the first performance of *The Famous History of the Reign of King Henry VIII* at the Globe Theatre and marvelled at the blend of fact and fiction Will Shakespeare had contrived from events in the spectator's own memory.

Max Stuart was flown down on his once-familiar route from Alice Springs to Adelaide for a private preview in May. "Well, that ain't half bad", he said after emerging from the dark. "But it's a bloody long time to go without a cigarette." Later in the year he would be on show alongside public screenings of the film.

Though the makers of *Black and White* had artistic cause for inviting the audience to be its own jury, that approach also expressed a private division of opinion about Stuart's guilt or innocence. The director, Craig Lahiff, believes that on the evidence he should never have been convicted. Louis Nowra thinks that he was probably guilty. So the case continues to divide judgments on it. Sir Thomas Playford, Sir Roderic Chamberlain and the royal commissioners had no doubt that Stuart was guilty. I would have added the *Advertiser's* Stewart Cockburn, who at various times from 1959 until as late as 1996 asked Stuart's defenders, and doubters, to recognise that Stuart had been properly convicted; but at the end of 2001, and after reading the screenplay of *Black and White,* he said to a reporter from his old paper that he had become "terribly impressed by the case put by Father Dixon." That would have pleased Dixon, who had been the first and remained the most dedicated believer in Stuart's innocence. Ted Strehlow was the second. Jack Shand, if reported accurately, agreed. So did Noela Whitton, whose husband Evan had concluded in a review of *The Wizard of Alice* that, as "all the evidence for and against Stuart cancels out exactly ... he should not have spent one minute in prison, let alone getting to within hours of the gallows, then spending the best part of fifteen years behind bars." Rachel Perkins and Ned Lander presented in *Broken English* an eloquent case for the defence.

Other verdicts occupied points on a spectrum between certainties, from Sir John Starke's (probably guilty) through Rohan Rivett's ("not dogmatic as to his guilt or innocence") to Don Dunstan's and mine (probably guilty). My own estimate of probabilities remains pretty much as it was in 1961, and so does my view that a properly informed jury might have had reasonable doubt about Stuart's guilt. I might have signalled those two conclusions more clearly by saying that I thought the case warranted the Scottish verdict "not proven".

New doubters appear. Richard Walsh, Sydney editor and publisher, believes in 2002 that, "as in the O.J. Simpson case, the question remains: did Stuart do it or was he fitted up because he was black?" In London the Australian-born Bruce Page, investigative reporter and former editor of the *New Statesman,* visiting the case in the course of writing a book about

Rupert Murdoch, hopes "to examine criminal records to see if there is any chance of identifying a more likely perpetrator."

Over the years the principal candidate for that role has been Allan Moir, the lad from the fun-fair who was known to have been drinking with Stuart on the morning and evening of the murder. (p. 11) Members of the University of Adelaide's law school had another possibility put into their minds by a man from Ceduna, a white man, who told them in mid-1959 that on the day of the crime he had seen another white man in the dunes but had been scared to tell anyone. Thirty years later Don Miell, the man who had been the young Stuart's employer at the ochre mine, then his gaol visitor and supporter, stumbled across what he believed to be the truth. On 18 May 1989, stuck in Ceduna for a few hours with engine trouble while driving from Adelaide to Perth, he dropped into an Aboriginal welfare office and met two Aborigines who told him in vivid detail, naming names, that an Aboriginal man from the Murray river region had raped and murdered the child and had been killed in his turn by other Aborigines. Miell has been trying ever since to interest people in this story, so far with little success. At the age of 86 he would offer vigorous testimony if any authority were to review Stuart's conviction.

A formal request to the South Australian government for a pardon might set off such a review. In the mid-1990s lawyers advising Stuart were inclined to prefer a "petition for mercy", on the ground that where a pardon would grant formal forgiveness, a successful petition would have the conviction "vacated". "Max is now over 65 years of age", one of the lawyers wrote to me in 1995, "but reasonably fit in central Australian terms. However, I am conscious that there may not be that much time left to see whether the record can be amended." The petition was delayed; there was a concern that if the hairs found in the dead child's hand were still in official keeping they might have been mixed up, accidentally or deliberately, to implicate Stuart. I understand that an approach to the South Australian government is still being considered.

Evan Whitton, whose experience as a searching reporter of crime has made him severely critical of the British judicial system, and in particular the adversary character of court proceedings, argues for a different approach. "In France", he writes, "police in the Stuart case would have been supervised by a *juge d'instruction*; there would have been no intimidation and no fabricated confession. The *juge* would have put into the dossier everything for and against Stuart in case his lawyers can show the truth is elsewhere." Had the *juge* recommended that he stand trial, "Stuart would have been questioned by a judge whose task was 'the manifestation of the truth', not by a Chamberlain determined to win." Some of Whitton's readers believe that he idealises the French and other European systems, and he does not imagine that Australia will abandon the adversary procedure at the drop of a pamphlet. He does hope, however, to see in this country an equivalent of the Criminal Cases Review Commission lately established by the government of the United Kingdom in response to concern about wrongful convictions. This is a body composed of both lawyers and non-lawyers (one, for example, a forensic psychiatrist) who conduct their inquiries unconstrained by the adversary system. It would be open to the government of South Australia to set up an *ad hoc* version of that body if it were pressed to review the conviction of Rupert Max Stuart.

If the statement written down by policemen at Ceduna is to believed, Stuart at first told them that he had seen a white bloke kill the girl, then said that he didn't remember doing it, then that he was pretty full or wouldn't have done it, then made a full confession. (p. 25) (Stuart tried to tell the court, and told the Royal Commission, that the confession was untrue and had been bashed out of him.) If the warders from Adelaide gaol are to be believed, he admitted the crime and blamed the grog. (pp. 189–90, 221) In *The Wizard of Alice* Tom Dixon attributes to Stuart an explanation consistent both with the warders' testimony and with his innocence. "Stuart himself", he writes, "always confided to me that the police, the courts and the warders had convinced him that he must have done it but that he had had too much to drink and couldn't really remember, and, in the end he believed them all." On that view Stuart's admission of guilt demonstrated the supposed readiness of Aborigines to give verbal assent to whatever whites tell them. Reading *The Wizard* again in 2002, I wondered what Max Stuart would say about that.

Over the years I had sometimes thought of trying to talk with Stuart, but I always baulked at the absurdity, even effrontery, of turning up out of the blue to ask a stranger, and an Aboriginal stranger at that, whether he was a murderer. Now that I was tracking his life since 1960 with help from *The Wizard,* Tom Dixon's letters and Eric Price's press cuttings, other questions came to mind. Why, for example, had he chosen Santa Teresa as the place of parole? How, after breaching that parole so often, had he managed at last to stay clear of trouble? James Warden, historian to the Central Land Council, whom I had known when he was a post-graduate student at the ANU, offered to arrange a meeting. In Alice Springs on 13 May 2002 I spent two hours at the headquarters of the Central Land Council with Max Stuart and James Warden and a tape recorder. Our conversation ranged all over his life, and I have drawn on it already at a number of places in this narrative.

"Max Stuart to speak to you", said the council's receptionist on the phone a few days before I flew up from Canberra. (I learned later that in the small and intricate world of Alice, this caller, Dana Bohring counted herself as Max Stuart's grand-daughter, her biological father being an old white friend of his high up in the counsels of the Country—Liberal Party.) Now I heard a voice I had heard twice before, once from the witness box in 1959, once from the wheel of his Toyota in *Broken English.* Yeah, he would talk with me. Not Saturday, when he would be out roo-shootin'; but Monday would be OK. That day in James Warden's office I was relieved to see him turn up, knowing that the producer and director of *Black and White* had been kept waiting three days after the appointed time until he came in from the bush.

As he exchanged jovial pleasantries outside the door with a visiting anthropologist, this white-haired, white-bearded, potbellied old man needed only a red gown and hood to be the Father Christmas who had handed out presents to the children of Santa Teresa. (Not quite your conventional Father Christmas: between Ho Ho Hos he had taken a bottle of rum out of a pocket and after several swigs had told the children to fuck off.) The anthropologist patted his potbelly and asked how he was. Well, thanks. He had given up the grog. (On Sunday Warden had driven me out to Santa Teresa, where a stern notice at the fence warned that alcohol was forbidden, and the roadside for the last few hundred metres was green with Victoria Bitter cans emptied just before the drinkers entered the old mission.) But he couldn't give up smoking, and he wheezed a bit as he said it.

He was wearing a long-sleeved dark blue shirt, brown trousers with cuffs and elastic-sided boots—size nine, as he would have cause to show me. We talked at a table in a small conference room under large photographs of council chairmen, the present one, his brother-in-law Breaden at one end and himself at the other. I thought of those interviews in Yatala thirty years ago with the Whittons, Cockburn and the young journalists. They had been allowed to give him a cigarette or two. I was paying $350—a normal fee, I had been advised, for an interview with someone of this man's standing.

His nephew Gordon Briscoe, briefing me in Canberra, had urged me to begin by saying "Wadi Chilpy, Pulya", his phonetic rendering of the Arrernte for "Greetings, old man". When the moment came, I couldn't bring myself to say it. I began by mentioning my acquaintance with Tom Dixon. "Passed away, poor old thing", he said, and we began a comfortable conversation. Sometimes he answered a question in one sentence, sometimes he expanded and rambled. He talked much of Ted Strehlow, and when he spoke of the relationship between Strehlow's father Carl and his own grandfather Tom Ljonga he gave me a sample of the storytelling I had been told to expect.

"Old Strehlow asked him how many wives did he have. He said: 'I got nine wives.'

And Strehlow's father said, 'You'll have to send eight away and keep one.'

'Any one?'

'Yeah, any one.'

And he scratched his head, hmm, and he said:

'How many donkey you got?'

'And I got, er, twelve donkeys.'

He say, 'Ah, well, you got to send eleven donkeys to Adelaide and stay here.'

'No, I can't do that with my church.'

'Well, I can't do that with my tribal wives. You got your business, I got my business.'"

When he described his efforts to stop the sale of *tjuringa* from the Strehlow collection, he was most critical of Carl, the young son of Ted and

Kathleen, believing that his older half-brother John should have been consulted. "Should be John the eldest son. In the blackfeller way, anyway." He explained his own position during the controversies of the 1970s in terms I couldn't quite understand, saying that he stood beside Strehlow on the whitefeller side but not on the blackfeller side. He spoke with high respect of Strehlow as a senior Arrernte man. If Ted was alive to argue about what should happen to the sacred objects, "he'd tell me to bugger off."

Gordon Briscoe and others had told me that he might or might not talk about his own initiation. He did, sparely, but precisely enough to explain how he had come to know stories over so wide a territory. It happened in 1947, when he was fifteen. "Donkey and camel from Jay Creek to Haast Bluff. Then had to walk down to Ernabella, leaving job. Had to walk with the old people. No planes. They just had to walk. From Ernabella to Helen Springs. Blokes come from Jingili tribe, had corroboree. Kimber Creek. Only blackfellers there."

And did he have any more initiations after the first one? An ignorant question, I was advised later. You are only initiated once; whatever happens after that is consolidation. But he let that pass, and answered, "Many times." And after Yatala? "Yeah, I went back to school again ..." I wondered whether Strehlow, who thought Stuart had acquired only a superficial knowledge of tradition (p. 8), might have been surprised to hear all that.

He filled me in on his life during and after the war. When the army put him into uniform, one of his jobs had been to dig graves in the new Adelaide River War Cemetery for the bodies of people killed in Japanese air raids on Darwin. He started to drink rum at Elsey station when droving with Dick Scobie. After the spell with Jimmy Sharman's boxing troupe he went droving with his own plant. "And I got sick of that and sold it off. And I got in with the hurdy gurdy mob with the Giesemans. That was my bad luck. I should come straight home but I went and wanted to see more country to learn a bit more. But I learned a bit more all right. Right in a bad corner with a rope around my neck."

He was talking with arms and hands as well as words, as I'd been told Arrernte speakers do. No wonder he had seemed so meek in the witness box, hands clasped behind back. After about three-quarters of an hour a packet of cigarettes appeared in one hand and a lighter in the other. Time to go out for a smoke, but not a long one. These days he could afford to throw away a cigarette half-smoked.

Could this good-humoured old man possibly be a murderer? I was finding it hard to see him committing any act of violence until I noticed that one of the hands gesturing so expressively, the right one, had a broken knuckle on the index finger. I remembered that his fists had earned him a living from Jimmy Sharman, that he had often been convicted for assault, that he had fought with prisoners in Yatala and with other men at Santa Teresa and around Alice. But murder and rape? As I absorbed this meeting afterwards I thought of Huddie Ledbetter (Leadbelly) and imagined myself among young Americans of the 1940s adulating this snowy-haired elder statesman of folk music as he sang his theme song "Goodnight Irene", who might not have heard, or might not have believed, that he had a long list of convictions for violent crimes, including murder.

When we were back at the table he took out his wallet and flipped it open to show me a photograph. It was a tiny version of the one in the front of this book, taken for the *Advertiser* when he and his escort of policemen arrived at Adelaide airport on 23 December 1958. Did he carry it around as a reminder of that moment, or simply as an image of his handsome young self? I was too startled to ask; but this seemed the time to try talking about the murder.

Was he still hoping for a pardon? Yes; and he began to talk freely about the Stuart case with little prompting. I had no need to ask him what he thought of Tom Dixon's hypothesis that whites may have persuaded him to admit committing the crime while too drunk to know what he was doing. From the time he was saying his prayers in the condemned cell until today, "as long as I'm alive I'll say I didn't do it." The black trackers had been telling lies. "What size boot you think this one?" he asked me, lifting one leg. "Nine?" "Exactly. That track they followed was size seven … It was a real put up job." The cops had bashed the confession out of him. When I told him that the dying Paul Turner had admitted bashing him after he confessed, he said "That was before. The cops kept banging me. Good riddance to the bastard, anyway."

I asked about the evidence discovered by Father Dixon which, if believed, would have given him an alibi: his whereabouts between two o'clock and four o'clock on the day of the murder. He had told the Royal Commission that he had been working at the fun-fair during that time but had not said so to David O'Sullivan because O'Sullivan never asked him about it. (p. 220) I had found it impossible to believe that if he knew that all along, he had never told his counsel. (p. 303) Had he? At first he replied that he *had* told O'Sullivan, and then that he had been "two-way" (meaning "confused", Gordon Briscoe explained as we transcribed the tape) when O'Sullivan and Devaney asked him questions. When I asked again, he said, "I knew the time but couldn't read or write or say a word in English", and then, "I woulda got out if I could speak like what it is now". And what did he think about the Aboriginal witnesses from Ceduna who swore that they had seen him around town between those hours? "All liars. I think they were all liars."

In the course of talking about witnesses hostile to his cause, Max Stuart told me that one of them had later been killed for his testimony by some Aborigines who had "finished him off in blackfeller way." He named the man. I don't, not wanting responsibility for making public a revelation that could provoke even now an inquiry into an unsolved or unrecognised crime. But if this did happen, Mary Olive Hattam's murder is not the only one in the history of the Stuart case.

I asked about the hairs found in the dead child's hands. Explaining perhaps unnecessarily what a DNA test is, I asked whether he would agree to have one. Yes, he said. I didn't know until next day that his present legal advisers were apprehensive on the matter, fearing that the hairs in official custody may have been mixed up. Nor did I learn until that same day, in a telephone call from a friend in Adelaide who had been making inquiries at the Institute of Veterinary and Medical Science, that the hairs had been thrown out years before the discovery of the DNA molecule. So we will never know the answer to a question some people revisiting the case had seen as crucial.

So who did he think committed the murder? Not Allan Moir, who was too drunk to have done it; and not any other white man. "I might write to you again when I see that Black Fellow from South Australia", he had written to Tom Dixon after a conversation at the Cadell Training Centre in 1984, the last year of his imprisonment. That man from South Australia was now dead, he said, poor bastard; but before he died he had revealed the identity of the killer. He named the man and the place he came from. Both were different from the name and place of the man Don Miell had told me about, and he said firmly that Miell's story was wrong. When I passed that response on to Miell in Adelaide, he said on the telephone that it surprised him. For the first time in many years he had met Max in Adelaide when he flew down to look at *Black and White*. Miell found Stuart at 72 "a bit vague." He had told Max, he said, of his continuing effort to gain attention for his story about the man from the Murray who had killed the child and then had himself been killed. Max had listened, without questioning, and never mentioned the man he had named to me as the killer. This is one of the puzzles I wish I could have explored further with Max Stuart before writing these words.

Our conversation moved to Yatala. "You had to be tough on the inside", he said, "because you trust nobody in there, even your own cell mate. You wake up in the morning with a knife in your back." He recalled one fight which had earned him fourteen days in solitary on bread and water. He spoke with mixed feelings about prison discipline. You could be punished for not keeping your cell so clean that you could just about shave by looking down at your face on the floor. But, "I think that's what shaped me mind up properly too." "I don't want to go back in there again, you know"; but these days he would like to see young fellers who kill people get heavier sentences, and in prisons which were not like farms.

He recalled in detail the joyful day of his first release on parole from Yatala, beginning with the gaoler saying "Mr Stuart"—not Max—"Mr Stuart, are you ready?" Then the warmth of his arrival at Santa Teresa, which he had preferred over other places for parole because so many people he knew lived there. Though he had not taken seriously Edna Gieseman's plan for him to go to Townsville, his memory of her was warm: "She wanted me to go and see her. I might even do that this year, when I go at the Mount Isa rodeo".

He talked proudly of his work for the Central Land Council both as field officer and in the chair. "Helpin' my people." His people had more luck now, though things ought to be better. "We should have more interpreters for station mobs … and houses with bigger backyards, and with native title we might get more. And the government has got to realise who we are and what we are."

Did he still paint? No, his eyesight was not good enough. But he did write poems, I discovered next day, and through a friend he let me have the verses reproduced below in my transcription from Max Stuart's handwriting on a page of an unused 1999 diary:

Yella feller
Max Stuart
Halfcaste

The God-Men say when die go sky
Through pearly gates where rivers flow.
The God-Men say when die we fly.
Just like eagle—hawk and crow.
Might be. Might be. I don't know.

My father told me of the day
When white man arrived with horses and waggons
Loaded with poles and wire.
And my people said there going to build
A big fence all right
The poles were thirty feet high.

There was only one wire—and later two—on top.
Obviously it wasn't straight line as a paddock for cattle.
In any case, the fence kept going in a straight line.
And then one day the wires began to sing,

We were told it was a telegraph line,
But we didn't know what that meant.
Writing along sky they said also talk along sky.
The telephone man showed my father a telephone set
And said it could be used
For talking to invisible men.

My father wouldnt believe him.
So he put the receiver to his ear
And a man's voice said Gooday Jack!
My old man dropped it and ran away.
He thought a spirit had spoken to him.

Yeller feller Half caste

Like the story about Tom Ljonga's wives and the German missionary's donkeys, it is a droll evocation of the encounter between cultures that had created Max Stuart, a man with a whitefeller name, a dark but not quite black skin and a familiarity with the songs of both his Arrernte ancestors and of Elvis Presley.

Did he still think of writing the book he had talked about with Tom Dixon? Yes, he wanted to do that, so that his kids and grandchildren would not grow up thinking the old bastard no good. "If the Indians and Chinamen can write books, so can we." Then, at the end of our time together, with a flash of the charm I had heard about: "*You* write my life story."

In genteel whitefeller fashion I had proposed bringing the $350 later in the day and leaving it with Dana at the desk, but he asked if I could let him have it right away, before he went into town. "I'm that broke," he said. So James Warden drove me to the nearest ATM, where I joined a queue of whites and blacks with credit cards. What had happened, I wondered, to the $200,000 or so Max Stuart had been paid for his three years as chairman? I had my answer a few days later in a newspaper feature about the famous Aboriginal actor David Gulpilil, who lived in the north of the Territory and who also said that he was broke. Wealth in Aboriginal society is communal, the author of the piece explained: "Money tends to permeate through needy relatives and friends." The higher the income of a man in Max Stuart's position, the more expensive his responsibilities.

We were back in a few minutes. He tucked the banknotes into his wallet behind that image of himself when young, gave me a firmer handshake than the one I had received two hours earlier, and said "Safe journey 'ome, mate." Then he set off for town to get on with his life. Next day he appeared at the Alice Springs courthouse, not because he was in any trouble but to hear a judge of the Federal Court hand down a determination which would advance slightly the cause of those people, including himself, who were claiming native title over crown land in the town. When the hearing was over, Justice Olney and Max Stuart stood outside the court together, talking.

My motel, the Territory Inn, was just across the road from the Todd River, dry at this time of the year, where Albert Namatjira, as Max Stuart told the Queen, used to sit and paint and drink. Many black people were sitting on the river bed now. One of them, strolling into the foyer of the Inn, introduced himself as a grandson of the artist whose prints decorated the walls. James Warden picked me up here for my journey home. As we drove across the Todd River bridge he reflected that for Australians in quest of reconciliation the right ending to the story of the Stuart case in 2002 would be a declaration by some appropriate tribunal that he had been wrongly convicted. But in fact, he said, the story might have no ending: like the Todd River in the desert, it just ran out.

After takeoff, as the desert replaced Alice Springs in the landscape below, I felt that I had been in the company of a person who had achieved some kind of redemption. A great survivor, Evan Whitton had called him, and that was in 1973, when what seemed remarkable was that he had come almost unscathed through fourteen years in Yatala. Thirty years on he had been the elected leader of an organisation devoted to helping his people, and was one of the most highly respected Arrerntemen.

Having escaped the noose against the longest of odds in 1959 he has outlived all the agents of the state that condemned and punished him, all his lawyers and all his champions except the other Rupert, who has not quite forgotten him. A recent message from New York to the Central Land Council asked how he was faring. The answer is that, no less than the inquirer himself, he has lived a life virtually unimaginable in the Adelaide of 1959.

I doubt whether Max Stuart will try hard to have his conviction overturned. Among his own people, who now notices his brand? In the wider world, the film *Black and White* leaves guilt or innocence an open question and lets him have the last word. If he is innocent, his story is about a man who was the helpless victim of the legal system and the racist culture which it embodied, who endured a terrible injustice and then transcended the fate to which he had been condemned. If he is guilty, his rehabilitation, his psychic survival as an intact and apparently serene personality, is even more remarkable. Either way, he is fortunate that the process of convicting him was flawed.

Mary Olive Hattam would have been 52 in 2002. When her brother Peter, two years older, was asked what he thought about the making of *Black and White*, he said he would rather the story had been left in the past. "It's safer there." The headstone on his sister's grave in the cemetery at Ceduna, a winged angel, holds this inscription:

IN LOVING MEMORY OF
MARY
ONLY DAUGHTER OF
GLEN AND JOY HATTAM
AND DEAR SISTER OF PETER
PAST AWAY 28TH DECEMBER 1958
AGED 8 YEARS
"IN GOD'S CARE"

The gates bear the initials M H, making the whole cemetery her memorial.

EPILOGUE SOURCES AND ACKNOWLEDGEMENTS

Most of the sources used for the epilogue are indicated in the text. Many letters from Max Stuart and some from other people are published in T.S. Dixon, *The Wizard of Alice: Father Dixon and the Stuart Case,* Alella Books, Morwell, Victoria, 1987. Much information has been taken from David Horton, ed., *The Encyclopaedia of Aboriginal Australia,* Aboriginal Studies Press, Canberra, 1994.

A set of end-notes giving sources for particular passages is available on request from the publisher.

For help of various kinds I am much obliged to Jay Arthur, David Avery, Richard Baker, Gordon Briscoe, Katrina Budrikis, Alex Castles, Pat Dodson, Steve Foley, Bill Gammage, Ian Hancock, Barry Hill, Jane Hodgson, Joan Kerr, Craig Lahiff, Ned Lander, Helen Leake, Don Miell, John Morton, Julia Munster, Kay Nantes, Sybil Nolan, Louis Nowra, Peter Read, Rachel Perkins, Eric Richards, Nan Rivett, David Ross, Tim Rowse, Jenny Tonkin, Bob Wallace, Sue Wallace, Gerry and Marion Ward, Evan and Noela Whitton and Jay Winter.

Silvia Kwon and Chris Feik of Black Inc., whose idea it was, have been a pleasure to work with.

The epilogue would not have been possible without the generosity and insight of James Warden.

As always, I am grateful to Amirah Inglis for inspiration and forbearance.

CHRONOLOGY, 1958–2002

1958

20 December. Mary Olive Hattam murdered.

22 December. Rupert Max Stuart interrogated and signs typed confession.

23 December. Charged with murder.

1959

21–29 January. Preliminary hearing.

20 April. Trial begins.

24 April. Jury brings in verdict of guilty, judge pronounces death sentence to be carried out on 22 May unless condemned man appeals.

4 May. Appeal to Full Court.

6 May. Appeal dismissed.

10 May. Father Dixon visits Adelaide Gaol.

14 May. Dixon visits solicitors O'Sullivan and Devaney.

18 May. T.G.H. Strehlow visits Adelaide Gaol.

20 May. Applies for leave to appeal to High Court.

21 May. Respite granted to 19 June.

2 June. High Court reserves judgment.

17 June. Respite granted to 7 July.

19 June. High Court refuses leave to appeal.

27 June. Dixon and Strehlow address meeting at home of Dr Charles Duguid.

6 July. Executive Council resolves not to commute sentence. Solicitors decide to petition Privy Council. Respite granted to 20 July, later extended to 4 August.

21 July. Statement by Dixon published in *Sydney Morning Herald.*

24 July. Rohan Rivett, editor of *News*, meets Dixon.

25 July. Dixon flies to Queensland, fare paid by *News.*

27 July. Statutory declarations at Atherton, Q., offer possible alibi.

28 July. Judicial Committee of Privy Council dismisses petition but suggests examination of new evidence.

30 July. Sir Thomas Playford announces Royal Commission. Respite granted to 31 August.

10 August. Commission has preliminary session.

17 August. Commission begins to hear evidence.

21 August. J.W. Shand Q.C., counsel for Stuart, withdraws. Commission adjourns. *News* posters and headline on Shand's withdrawal composed by Rivett and Rupert Murdoch, publisher.

28 August. Respite granted to 30 September.

31 August. Commission resumes, adjourns.

3 September. *News* apologises for poster and headline of 21 August, defends general stand.

4 September. Commission resumes without counsel for Stuart.

11 September. J.L. Travers Q.C. seeks leave to appear for Stuart. Commission adjourns.
15 September. Travers withdraws request on grounds that his presence appears unwelcome.
16 September. Commission resumes. John Starke Q.C. seeks leave to appear for Stuart. Commission adjourns.
5 October. Counsel for crown, Roderic Chamberlain Q.C. tells commission death sentence commuted. Commission resumes, adjourns.
13 October. Commission resumes.
13–15 October. Stuart gives evidence.
22–26 October. Starke and Chamberlain address commission.
26 October. Commission adjourns for last time.
3 December. Report of Royal Commission presented to parliament finds verdict of guilt wholly justified. Stuart begins life sentence in Yatala.

1960

19 January. Nine charges of seditious libel and criminal libel laid against Rivett and News Ltd for posters and headline of 21 August.
28 January. Magistrate finds editor and company have a case to answer.
7 March. Trial in Supreme Court begins.
17 March. Jury finds defendants not guilty on eight counts, disagrees on the ninth.
6 June. Last charge withdrawn.
12 July. *News* announces Rivett no longer editor.

1972

Interviews by journalists yield first news of life in Yatala.
February. Parole refused.

1973

18 April. Sir Roderic Chamberlain announces he will not sit on next consideration of parole.
18 October. Paroled to Santa Teresa.
Sir Roderic Chamberlain, *The Stuart Affair.*

1974

4 December. Convicted in Alice Springs for disorderly behaviour.

1975

June. Marries Catherine Young.
21 July. Returns to Yatala after breach of parole.
28 July. Second parole.
3 September. Returns to Yatala after breach of second parole.

1976

July. Third parole.
24 October. Returns to Yatala after breach of third parole.

1978
3 October. T.G.H. Strehlow dies.
8 December. Fourth parole.

1979
28 April. Returns to Yatala after breach of fourth parole.

1980
30 July. Fifth parole.

1982
30 July. Returns to Yatala after breach of fifth parole.

1984
3 July. Sixth parole.

1985
Begins work as field officer Central Land Council.
October. Completes parole.
T.S. Dixon, *The Wizard of Alice.*

1989
Elected delegate and executive member Central Land Council.

1991
Opposes opening of Strehlow Research Centre.
Initiates Charles Perkins.

1992
2 August. Tom Dixon dies.

1993
Docudrama *Broken English* shown on SBS, later ABC.

1994
April. Attends High Court hearing in Canberra of dispute over Lake Amadeus land.

1998
July. Elected chairman Central Land Council.

2000
30 March. Welcomes Queen Elizabeth II to Alice Springs.
8 June. Challenges carrier of Olympic torch before admitting him to Arrernte land.

2001
July. Defeated in election for chairman Central Land Council.
8–9 September. Men's cultural director Yeperenye Federation Festival.

2002
7 June. Feature film *Black and White* opens Sydney Film Festival.